# Military Space-A Air
### Opportunities Around the World

by

**L. Ann Crawford**
**Executive Vice-President, Military Marketing Services, Inc.**
**and Publisher, Military Living Publications**

**William "Roy" Crawford, Sr., Ph.D.**
**Chief Executive Officer, Military Marketing Services, Inc.**
**and Military Living Publications**

**President - R.J. Crawford**

**Vice-President - Editorial - J.J. Caddell**

Editor - Deborah K. Harder

Assistant Editor - Melanie Macchio

Cover Design - Lynn Olinger


Military Living Publications
P.O. Box 2347
Falls Church, Virginia  22042-0347
**TEL:** (703) 237-0203
FAX: (703) 237-2233
E-mail: militaryliving@aol.com
Website: www.militaryliving.com


Printed in Canada

# NOTICE

The information in this directory has been compiled and edited either from the activity/facility listed, its superior headquarters, or from other sources that may or may not be noted. All listed facilities, their locations, hours of operation, and telephone/telefax numbers could change.

Flight schedules, including destinations, routings, frequency, time en route and stopovers of flights, and aircraft (equipment) used, are always subject to change; however, many of the flights listed in this guide have followed the same geographic routes for over 50 years. Major changes in air routes occur largely with the repositioning and redeployment of United States Military Forces around the world. The eligibility of Space-A passengers could and does change from time to time; however, we have published the most up-to-date passenger eligibility and other Space-A information.

The "how to travel Space-A" supporting information in the appendices is subject to change, but the latest changes to these appendices were included at press time. The elementary "how to travel Space-A" supporting information, among other things, is contained in our book, **MILITARY SPACE-A AIR BASIC TRAINING AND READER TRIP REPORTS,** and in our map, **MILITARY SPACE-A AIR OPPORTUNITIES AIR ROUTE MAP.** This book should be used as a guide to Space-A air travel with all of the above in mind. Please forward any corrections, deletions or additions to the publisher at P.O. Box 2347, Falls Church, VA 22042-0347.

This directory/guide is published by Military Marketing Services Inc. and Military Living Publications (T/A), a private firm in no way connected with the U.S. Federal or other governments. The directory is copyrighted by William Roy, Sr. and L. Ann Crawford. Opinions expressed by the publishers and writers herein are not to be considered an official expression by any government agency or official.

The information and statements contained in this directory have been compiled from sources believed to be reliable and to represent the best current opinion on the subject. No warranty, guarantee, or representation is made by Military Marketing Services, Inc., Military Living Publications, the authors and editors as to the absolute correctness or sufficiency of any representation contained in this or other publications and we can assume no responsibility.

# Copyright 2001

**William Roy, Sr. and L. Ann Crawford**
**MILITARY LIVING PUBLICATIONS**
**MILITARY MARKETING SERVICES, INC.**



Library of Congress Cataloging-in-Publication Data

Crawford, Ann Caddell.
  Military living's military space-A air opportunities around the world/ L. Ann Crawford
and William "Roy" Crawford, Sr.
    p.cm.
  Rev. ed. of: Military Living's military space-A air opportunities around the world/
William "Roy" Crawford, Sr., L. Ann Crawford. c1998
  Includes index.
  ISBN 0-914862-95-2
    1. United States--Armed Forces--Transportation--Directories. 2. Air
travel--Directories. 3. United States--Armed Forces--Facilities--Directories. 4. Airlift,
Military--United States--Directories. I. Title: Military space-A opportunities around
the world. II. Crawford, William Roy, 1932- III. Crawford, William Roy, 1932- Military
Living's military space-A air opportunites around the world. IV. Military Living
Publications. V. Title.

UC333 .C73 2001
355.3'4--dc21

                                                          2001032660

**ISBN 0-914862-95-2**

# INTRODUCTION

Military Living's **Military Space-A Air Opportunities Around the World** is a comprehensive guide to military Space-A air opportunities worldwide, which are provided by all of the military departments (U.S. ARMY, U.S. NAVY, U.S. MARINE CORPS, U.S. COAST GUARD, and U.S. AIR FORCE). This edition has been completely revised, and contains more than 325 Space-A departure/arrival stations/locations worldwide. In response to our readers' needs, we have provided information regarding **Space-A air opportunities for active duty, guard/reserve, and retired uniformed services (U.S. ARMY, U.S. NAVY (U.S. MARINE CORPS), U.S. COAST GUARD, U.S. AIR FORCE, USPHS AND NOAA) personnel and their families.** These Space-A air opportunities are provided by the active Army, Navy, Marine Corps, Coast Guard and Air Force, as well as the Army and Air National Guards and Reserves. You can save thousands of $$$ with this directory.

## HOW THIS DIRECTORY IS ORGANIZED

This directory is divided into four major sections: **Section I - Continental United States (CONUS); Section II - Outside the Continental United States (OCONUS); Section III - Foreign Countries; and Section IV - Detailed appendices, containing information essential to Space-A travelers.** This particular organization of the materials has been selected because it matches the CONUS, OCONUS and Foreign Country organization of the Space-A Travel Regulation, Chapter 6, (and selected relative portions of other chapters) DoD 4515.13-R at Appendix A in this book.

Listings within each section of this book are alphabetized by state, territory, foreign country, and/or arrival/departure geographic areas. Some listings in Sections II and III have changing arrival/departure locations and limited Space-A air opportunities. These listings have been placed in **composite (roll-up) listings.** These arrival/departure stations are easily identified in this book's contents.

This directory also provides country and state abbreviations; the three letter station location identifier code assigned by the Federal Aviation Administration (FAA) (i.e. BWI=Baltimore/Washington International Airport, MD) and the four letter International Civil Aviation Organization (ICAO) identification code; (i.e. RJTY=Yokota Air Base, JA) the new Space-A passenger regulations; personnel entrance requirements; a station (arrival/departure) cross-reference index; a brief description of aircraft on which most Space-A air travel occurs; verification of reserve status for travel eligibility form; sample webb sign-up form, Space-A travel request form, remote sign-up form using the small aircraft Operational Support Airlift system (OSA), Julian date calendars, 24 hour clock, standard time conversion table, Passport and Visa information, Space-A questions and answers and travel tips and other Space-A support information. Among other things, several sample listings follow which explain in detail how to use this directory.

## HOW TO USE THIS DIRECTORY

*The following is an explanation of each element in a sample listing.*

Arrival/Departure Location/Station (Official Name of Station) and three letter FAA Location Identifier (LI) /four letter ICAO Location Identifier. Mailing Address of Unit Responsible for Space-A Passenger Activities (Processing)

**ARRIVAL/DEPARTURE LOCATION/STATION MAPS:** As a key part of our ongoing efforts to improve and simplify **Military Space-A Air Opportunities Around The World** we have included detailed maps of over **40 major Air Force, Air Mobility Command (AMC) Stations worldwide. The maps are designed and completed by professional cartographers. The maps show key support facilities; military passenger terminal, base exchange, shoppette, auto service/gas, commissary, temporary military lodging, clubs and messes, medical/dental, chapel, parking and other key support information. Major routes to and from the facility and directions and distance to the nearest major city are given. Future editions are expected to contain maps of additional locations.**

**LOCATION:** Here you'll find specific driving instructions to the arrival/departure location/station from local major cities, interstate/national/state/country highways and routes. More than one routing may be provided. **USMRA:** Coordinates in Military Living's **United States Military Road Atlas** which are given for each CONUS and OCONUS location. **ML-ARM:** Coordinates on Military Living's Military Space-A Air Opportunities Air Route Map for each station/location. **LST:** is the local standard time relative to Greenwich Mean Time (GMT). **NMC:** is the nearest major city. Distance in miles and directions from the arrival/departure station/location to the nearest major city are provided. **NMI:** is the nearest major military installation. Distance in miles and directions from the arrival/departure station/location to the nearest major military installation are provided.

Main installation telephone numbers: **C-commercial.** This is the installation's main or information/operator assistance telephone number accessed via the civilian/commercial telephone system, when dialed from CONUS (North America Dial Area) and **DSN** is the **Defense Switched Network,** which is the DoD worldwide voice telephone system. The number given is, in most cases, for information/operator assistance. When dialing into the following geographic areas using the DSN system, the following area code prefixes must be used:

| | | |
|---|---|---|
| 317 (Alaska) | 312 (Canada) | 313 (Caribbean) |
| 312 (CONUS) | 314 (Europe) | 315 (Pacific) |
| 318 (Southwest Asia) | | |

(CAUTION-these main Commercial and DSN  information numbers are not the passenger information numbers, in most cases.)

The telephone information section of the listings in this book, contains detailed civilian and defense telephone numbers and prefixes for dialing from a civilian telephone to a military telephone (where this capability exists). These numbers as listed, as well as other numbers in each listing, assume that the call is being placed from a commercial or defense telephone respectively in, North America for civilian systems and in the CONUS for DSN. By way of example, the telephone information section for Ramstein Air Base in Germany looks like this: **Main installation numbers: C-011-49-6371-47-1110, D-314-480-1110.** All telephone information sections for Germany and for most installations in other countries with civilian to military dialing capabilities follow this same basic pattern. The main civilian number breaks down as follows: the first set of numbers **(011)** is the international dialing access number for North America; the second set of numbers **(49)** is the country code for Germany; the third set of numbers **(6371)** is local area/city code within Germany; the fourth set of numbers **(47)** is the civilian to military conversion number; and the last set of numbers **(1110)** is the line or extension number. **IMPORTANT: All local area codes in Germany and several other countries in Europe begin with a "0" which is not used when dialing into the country but must be added if dialing within the country.** In Germany, if you are within the boundaries of the local area code, you will not need to dial the local area code **(6371)** when dialing a civilian number or a defense number. Dial the military conversion number **(47)** and the military extension when dialing from a local commercial telephone. The DSN area codes are not used when dialing in the same area code, i.e., the DSN area code of **314 (Europe)** is not used when dialing a DSN number in area code **314 (Europe)** from another telephone with an area code of **314 (Europe).**

Visitors to foreign countries should keep in mind that telephone systems in North America are the best and most reliable in the world. They are also the easiest to use. Don't expect your knowledge of American telephone systems, especially civilian telephone systems, to be of much use to you in foreign countries. Most foreign country telephone systems can be quite baffling when first encountered. For instance, in the United Kingdom, when dialing a particular location, the number you should dial is determined not only by the location you are dialing to, but by the location you are dialing from. When calling someone from within the U.K., we recommend that you consult the local telephone directory for the proper dialing codes or use operator assistance. **The standard 10 digit North America Dialing Plan (Area Code XXX, Switch Code XXX and Line Number XXXX) is found in very few foreign countries.** Most foreign country telephone systems have less than 10 digits and a few have more than 10 digits.

*Editor's Note:* When placing overseas calls, one should dial slowly, particularly pausing where we have placed a hyphen in the telephone number, ie. 011- (pause) 49- (pause) 6371- (pause) 47-(pause) 1110. Also, when dialing a fax number, press your pause button (refer to your manual for instructions) anywhere we have placed a hyphen in the fax number. In spite of the great technological advances in international telephone systems, there remains an echo effect in international calls over very long distances.

**REGISTRATION INFO:** Commercial and defense telephone numbers, recording numbers, (and when the recorded information is updated), and remote sign-up C and D fax numbers. Complete information is given to dial these numbers from the CONUS. We have also included, where available, **E-mail addresses** for Space-A Registration and **Web addresses** for information regarding arrival/departure stations/locations. Terminal and Registration building number and hours of operation are given. Driving directions to the passenger service area and other pertinent information is also provided. **Pax Service Office:** Location, hours, telephone number(s), staffing and other useful information. **Pax Paging:** Location, hours, telephone number(s), how to request paging service.

**PAX LOUNGES:** General information about available lounge facilities. **General:** Locations, hours, telephone number(s), facilities and services. **Family:** Location, hours, telephone number(s), services and restrictions. **Distinguished Visitor/Very Important Person (DV/VIP):** Location, hours, telephone number(s), facilities and services. Grades served. **Protocol Service:** Location, hours, telephone number(s), facilities and services. Grades served.

**FOOD SERVICE: Cafeteria:** Locations, hours, telephone number(s), other pertinent information. **Dining Hall:** Location, hours, telephone number(s). **In-Flight Kitchen:** Location, hours, telephone number(s). **Community Club:** Locations, hours, telephone number(s). **Enlisted Club:** Location, hours, telephone number(s), facilities and services. **O Club:** Location, hours, telephone number(s). Grades served. **Non-Commissioned Officer/Chief Petty Officer (NCO/CPO) Club:** Location, hours, telephone number(s). Grades served. **Restaurants:** Location(s), hours, telephone number(s). **Snack Bar/Fast Food:** Location(s), hours, telephone number(s), other pertinent information. **Vending:** Location(s), hours, telephone number(s), useful information.

**TRANSPORTATION: Air Tickets:** Location(s), hours, telephone number(s). **Bus (Commercial, Shuttle/Government):** Location, hours, telephone number(s). **Car Rental:** Location, hours, telephone number(s), agencies and information. **Limo Service:** Location, hours, telephone number(s), agencies and information. **Taxi (Commercial and Government):** Location, hours, telephone number(s), commercial, shuttle, and/or government. **Trains:** Location, hours, telephone number(s), call for local train info. **Parking:** Location(s), hours, telephone number(s), short & long term information.

**TEMPORARY MILITARY LODGING (TML):** Location, hours, telephone number(s) and fax number(s) when available. All ranks, Navy Lodges and DV/VIP, information is given for each arrival/departure station and at nearby installations when not available at the arrival/departure station.

**TRAVELERS AID: American Red Cross:** Location, hours, telephone number(s), duty and 24-hour telephone numbers. **Chaplain:** Location, hours, telephone number(s), duty and 24-hour emergency telephone number. **Emergency Relief:** Location, hours, telephone number(s), type of relief organization. **Lost/Found:** Location, hours, telephone number(s), agency providing service. **Security Police:** Location, hours, telephone number(s), other pertinent information. **USO:** Location, hours, telephone number(s) may be off base.

**OTHER SERVICES: Exchange:** Location, hours, telephone number(s), other pertinent information. **Bank/Money Exchange:** Location, hours, telephone number(s), information on currency conversion. **Hair Styles:** Location, hours, telephone number(s), barber & beauty shops. **Laundry/Dry Cleaning:** Location, hours, telephone number(s), self-served laundry facility. **Medical:** Location, hours, telephone number(s) (commercial & defense), emergency care for AD and retired. **Postal:** Location, hours, telephone number(s). Commercial Package/Telegraph facilities: Location, hours, telephone number(s).

**ATTRACTIONS:** Key attractions at the station/location or in the nearby area.

**Note: All of the above support facilities may not be listed due to the availability of some services or limited Space-A air opportunities from some stations/locations.**

# SCHEDULED ROUTES/MISSIONS

The Air Mobility Command (AMC), regular scheduled routes/missions have been listed in tables at the originating arrival/departure stations for easy reference and use. These scheduled routes/missions originate largely in the CONUS. A limited number of AMC routes/missions originate in OCONUS and selected Foreign Countries (where AMC aircraft are stationed). **It is important to note that these flight missions travel from their originating or home station on a mission/trip, stopping at few to many stations en route for varied periods of time (from a few hours to overnight to several days or more).** In almost all cases these flights/missions return to the originating or home station. If the originating station is not located on or near a CONUS coast, then the flights tend to "stage"/stop for an overnight crew rest at a coastal base in CONUS before continuing overseas on their missions. The limited number of missions which do not immediately return to their home station, remain overseas at a station for staging to participate in a future mission or for scheduled maintenance and return to service. There may be one to many missions flown over an established AMC Route. The scheduled routes/missions in this edition are greatly improved and have been simplified for your use.

**Snapshot Schedule** These schedules are presented to give you the customer a good idea of Space-Available Air Opportunities at a given air passenger terminal. Also, we have arranged the schedules to show the ENTIRE mission from the originating station, through each en-route station and to the terminating station. Most air terminals/stations only show the next destination, not the entire mission from beginning to end. **ALL SCHEDULES ARE SUBJECT TO CHANGE WITHOUT NOTICE.**

You will need to contact the Air Passenger Service at each terminal/station from which you wish to depart on a Space-A trip, to get the latest schedule for Space-A air opportunity flights .**Note:** All telephone, telefax and E-mail numbers, as available, are at each listing in this book.

**ORIGINATING SCHEDULED ROUTES/FLIGHT:** All of the originating scheduled routes at each station/location are listed under/at that station, i.e., all the Scheduled Routes originating at McGuire AFB, NJ (WRI) are listed under/at McGuire AFB, NJ. Each Route/Flight Schedule is made up of three major components: **First** is the header or title which gives valuable information about each mission and its route. **Second** is a graphic picture which shows, among other things, the originating station of the flight, last CONUS station before traveling overseas, directions flown, all stations en route, the turnaround point, first return route CONUS station and final destination. **Third** is a table which shows the unique three letter Location Identifiers, Airport/Station official names, Country/State abbreviations (two letter), and Days En Route from the beginning of this mission accumulated at each station en route.

An example of the header, taken from CONUS section NJ, is as follows: **MCGUIRE AFB, NJ (WRI); REGION: ATL; OPERATOR: AMC; TYPE: CGO W/PAX; ROUTE: A7R3A; SCHEDULE: 1ST & 3RD MON; EQUIPMENT: C141B.** The explanation of this sample header is as follows: **MCGUIRE AFB, NJ** - This is the originating station name and location for this mission. This is where the aircraft and its crew are stationed (live), i.e. this is the home base for this system of equipment and personnel. **WRI** - WRI is the three-letter FAA Location Identifier (LI) for McGuire AFB, NJ. **KWRI** is the four-letter ICAO (International Civil Aviation Organization) indicator. **REGION: ATL;** - The Air Mobility Command (AMC) worldwide routes are divided into two regions; Atlantic and Pacific. This route is in the Atlantic Region. **OPERATOR: AMC;** The AMC operates military heavy lift aircraft with United States Air Force Crew members. Also, there are Contract Air Carriers that operate heavy lift aircraft with civilian crew members. Only the AMC have regularly scheduled routes which are operated either by AMC or **COM** = Contractors. Commercially contracted flights are now called Patriot Express. **TYPE: CGO W/PAX;** - The type mission flown on this route is cargo with passengers. There are also all passenger **(PAX)** type missions and **MIXED** (cargo and passenger) missions. **Route: A7R3A** - This is the mission route number assigned to this specific mission consisting of the aircraft, its crew, the route flown and the task to be accomplished. These numbers change as the mission elements change, therefore a specific route reference number (RRN) has very little meaning for a Space-A traveler. **SCHEDULE: 1ST & 3RD MON;** This means that this route with the assigned equipment and crews (a mission) originates from MCGUIRE AFB, NJ (WRI) on the 1st & 3rd Monday of each month. **EQUIPMENT: C141B** -The equipment for this mission/route is a **C141B STAR LIFTER.** Further details regarding this aircraft are at **Appendix M. Additional information is sometimes found at the end of a table.** The **Note:** (✚) = MEDEVAC: ADW to ADW. The configuration of the aircraft when traveling from and through these stations is for MEDEVAC service (usually 50% of the aircraft space is configured for litter patients and 50% is normal airline seating facing to rear of aircraft for ambulatory patients and other passengers).

Next we have included an example of the graphic and other key information. The example which matches the header above is as follows:

## ROUTE/MISSION GRAPHICS

{WRI *SW* ➠ ADW (★) *NE* ➠ LGS *NE* ➠ RMS ⇌ RMS *SW* ➠ ADW (★) *NE* ➠ WRI}

Please read across the graphic from left to right. The graphic above shows the routing/mission as follows: {WRI **SW** ➠ **ADW**=McGuire AFB, NJ (WRI), the originating station, Departure southwest to Andrews AFB, MD (ADW), first En Route Station; ( ★) = Last Station in CONUS; **NE** ➠ **LGS** = Departure northeast to Lajes Field AB (Azores), PT (LGS), second En Route Station;**NE** ➠ **RMS**    RMS=Departure northeast to Ramstein AB, DE (RMS), which is the mission/route Turnaround Point Station and third En Route Station; **SW** ➠ **ADW** = Departure southwest to Andrews AFB, MD, fourth En Route Station; (★) = First Station in CONUS on return to CONUS leg of this CONUS to Overseas and return route/mission; **NE** ➠ **WRI**}= Departure northeast to McGuire AFB, NJ, the terminating station.

## ROUTE/MISSION TABLE

Please read across the table from left to right and then read down the table from top to bottom. The heading for each route/mission table is as follows: **LI (Location Identifier)** - This is the Federal Aviation Administration coordinated three letter location identifier code for Stations/Airports in the United States, its possessions and Canada. Foreign Country three letter LI codes have been coordinated by the Department of Defense. The International Civil Aviation Organization **(ICAO)** has established an international identifier which is a four letter (code) used in international aviation and communications. Many military stations in foreign countries have converted to this indicator. For a complete list of both types of indicator, see the **LI/ICAO Cross Reference Index found in the back of this book. AIRPORT/STATION** - This is the official name of the airport or takeoff/landing facility along with the terminal/passenger processing facility. **CTRY/STA** - The two letter U.S. Postal Service abbreviation for the U.S. and Possessions is used. Foreign Country two letter abbreviations are taken from ISO 3166, prepared by the International Organization for Standardization. **Please see Appendix W State, Possession and Country Abbreviations. DAYS EN ROUTE** - This is the number of days or lapse time measured from the departure day from the originating station. In our example **ROUTE: A7R3A** (Route Reference Number), the flight departs WRI at +0 or Mon, departs ADW at +0 or Mon, departs LGS at +1 or Tue, arrives/departs RMS +2 or Wed, departs ADW +3 or Wed and terminates at WRI. **Some missions/trips like CONUS MEDEVAC are accomplished in one day, others take 2 to 7 days to fly their missions and a few may take up to 12 or more days to complete their missions.** There are zero days en route for CONUS MEDEVAC since each mission is completed in one day.

| LI/ICAO | AIRPORT/STATION | CTRY/STA | DAYS EN ROUTE |
|---|---|---|---|
| WRI/KWRI | McGuire AFB | NJ | +0 |
| ADW/KADW | Andrews AFB (✚) | MD | +0 |
| LGS/LPLA | Lajes Field AB (Azores) | PT | +1 |
| RMS/ETAR | Ramstein AB | DE | +2 |
| RMS/ETAR | Ramstein AB | DE | +2 |
| ADW/KADW | Andrews AFB (✚) | MD | +3 |
| WRI/KWRI | McGuire AFB | NJ | |

**Note:** (✚) = MEDEVAC: ADW to ADW

## EN ROUTE ROUTE/MISSION/SCHEDULES

Each route/mission/schedule, in its complete format, showing originating stations, all en route stations, the terminating station and other relative information **is detailed only ONCE in the book. This action is necessary to conserve space and make the book a practical size. No new information would be presented by listing the complete schedule again under each en route and terminating station.** In addition to the tables for **ROUTE/MISSION,** we have included tables which show the **EN ROUTE SCHEDULES** that apply to each originating, en route and  terminating station. There are en route schedules which originate at other stations in the system and transit/stop at the en route and terminating stations. We have listed the originating stations (in this case WRI - McGuire AFB, NJ) and the route reference number (RRN) for each EN ROUTE SCHEDULE. For example route number A7R3A which is shown in the table above originates at WRI - McGuire AFB, NJ and transits ADW - Andrews AFB, MD and other en route stations during this missions. This technique allows us to detail the complete schedule for a mission only once and record/print it at the originating station. **However, this technique does require the reader to refer to (look up) the en route schedules at the originating stations to determine where en route missions are coming from and more importantly where they are going.** For ease in reference we have included the page number where the originating stations begin in the text.

### EN ROUTE ROUTE/MISSION/SCHEDULE

**[Andrews AFB, MD (ADW)]**

| AIRPORT/STATION | LI-MISSION (page #) |
|---|---|
| McGuire AFB, NJ | WRI-A7R1A (51); WRI-A7R3A (51); |

**[Lajes Field AB (Azores), PT (LGS)]**

| AIRPORT/STATION | LI-MISSION (page #) |
|---|---|
| McGuire AFB, NJ | WRI-A7R3A (51); WRI-A7V3A & B (51) |

**[Ramstein AB, DE (RMS)]**

| AIRPORT/STATION | LI-MISSION (page #) |
|---|---|
| McGuire AFB, NJ | WRI-A7F1S (51); WRI-A7R1A (51) |

To continue our example, we see that our RRN, A7R3A, is located on page 51, after page 49, which is the beginning page for the WRI - McGuire AFB, NJ listing. This originating mission code is posted with the WRI starting page under each en route station. In this case, the en route stations are: ADW, LGS, RMS, If a station is visited more than once, we refer to the originating schedule for that mission only once at each en route station.

## UNSCHEDULED ROUTES/MISSIONS

There are UNSCHEDULED ROUTES/MISSIONS, which in most cases, show the destinations from the listing (the flight may or may not originate at the) station, the type of equipment flown, and the frequency of the flights. Calling to confirm unscheduled routes/missions is highly recommended. We have listed below, as an example, the UNSCHEDULED ROUTES/MISSIONS information from the Washington NAF, DC (NSF), located at Andrews AFB, MD (ADW), east side of the base/main runways.

[Washington NAF, DC (NSF)]

### UNSCHEDULED ROUTES/MISSIONS

There are no scheduled flights from the Washington NAF. Most flights are planned 48 hours prior to departure. Call for information. There are unscheduled flights to the following locations: Beaufort MCAS, SC **(NBC)**; Brunswick NAS, ME **(NHZ)**; Fort Worth NAS/JRB, TX **(NFW)**; Cherry Point MCAS, SC **(NKT)**; Jacksonville NAS, FL **(NIP)**; Mid-South NSA, TN **(NQA)**; New Orleans NAS, LA **(NBG)**; New River MCAS, NC **(NCA)**; Norfolk NS, VA **(NGU)**; Oceana NAS, VA **(NTU)**; and Pensacola NAS, FL **(NPA)**. Equipment flown varies with flights and distances. Most aircraft used are C-009A/B, C-12A-J, C-130A-H, P-3C and T-39.

# COMPOSITE ROUTES/MISSIONS LISTINGS

In some cases we have combined the routes/missions of minor departure locations in a central region, in order to conserve space, without diluting the value of the information. We call these roll up or composite listings. See the listing below.

## OTHER UNITED STATES PACIFIC ISLANDS

**BUCHOLZ ARMY AIRFIELD/KMR (KWAJALEIN ATOLL), U.S. Army, KA (KWA) (USA), Republic of the Marshall Islands,** Kwajalein Missile Range, ATTN: CSSD-KA-IS, P.O. Box 26, APO AP 96555-2526. ML-ARM: (167°45'E/8°45'N). NMC: Honolulu, HI. NMI: Hickam AFB, HI. For information contact Hickam AFB at **C-808-449-1515, D-315-449-1515, Rec: C-808-449-1854/6833, D-315-449-1854/6833, Fax: C-808-448-1503, D-315-448-1503.** Available: Open air passenger lounge, DV lounge, snack bar, combined club, limited bus service, transient hotel for official visitors only, nice beaches and excellent scuba diving. U.S. Customs Service Airport. ***Note: Permission/official approval required to visit KWA (see Appendix B).***

### EN ROUTE SCHEDULES

| AIRPORT/STATION | LI-MISSION (page #) |
|---|---|
| March ARB, CA | RIV-5J43B (10) |
| Travis AFB, CA | SUU-ZJ43A (13) |
| Hickam AFB, HI | HIK-8H43A (96) |

**JOHNSTON ATOLL, JO (JON) (USA),** FCDSWA Term Ops JQ/AMC REP, Johnston Atoll, APO AP 96558-5000. ML-ARM: (160°30'W/16°00'N). **C-011-808-621-3044 ext 2252. D-312-441-2252, Fax: C-808-621-3044/2343, D-312-441-2343.** ***Note: Permission/official approval required to visit Johnston Atoll (see Appendix B, Personnel Entrance Requirements).***

### EN ROUTE SCHEDULES

| AIRPORT/STATION | LI-MISSION (page #) |
|---|---|
| Travis AFB, CA | SUU-ZJ43A (13) |
| Memphis IAP, TN | MEM-IDB7B & 7D45A (70) |
| Hickam AFB, HI | HIK-8H45A (96) |

## MEDEVAC ROUTES/MISSIONS

The U.S. Air Force operates an Aeromedical Evacuation (MEDEVAC) system in the CONUS, OCONUS and foreign countries. Below is a sample CONUS MEDEVAC schedule. There are five primary CONUS stations in the system: Andrews AFB, MD (ADW), Keesler AFB, MS (BIX), Kelly AFB, TX (SKF), Scott AFB, IL (BLV) and Travis AFB, CA (SUU). All CONUS missions are flown by C-009A aircraft (see Appendix M for a detailed description of the aircraft) and all of these aircraft are permanently based at the above primary stations. There are four C-009A aircraft stationed at Ramstein AB, DE (RMS) and three C-009A aircraft stationed at Yokota AB, JP (OKO) which are used for inter-theater MEDEVAC missions. The OCONUS and foreign country intra-theater MEDEVAC missions are flown by C-141B and C-17A aircraft configured for MEDEVAC and their schedules are listed in the regular AMC Cargo Schedules.

The MEDEVAC system schedules are weekly schedules, beginning on Sunday. The MEDEVAC missions are based on proforma schedules, the routing of these schedules may change, to meet requirements for patient movement. For example, if there are no requirements to drop off or take on patients, an EN ROUTE STATION may be skipped or overflown. Likewise, if patients' requirements become known at a non-scheduled station, that station will be added en route and the schedule will be changed to meet this new requirement. All CONUS MEDEVAC flights are flown in a 24 hour period. Flights depart and arrive on the same day unless otherwise indicated. Originating flight departures are between 0800 and 0900 hours unless otherwise indicated in the schedule. Show time is two hours before departure.

Like the Regular AMC Mission Schedules, there are CONUS MEDEVAC ORIGINATING and EN ROUTE SCHEDULES. First we explain the

Originating Schedules. In our example, first is the header information: **SCOTT AFB (BLV/KBLV); MISSION 614/MEDEVAC; SCHEDULE: MON; EQUIPMENT: C009A.** Scott AFB, IL is the originating station. The mission number is 614/MEDEVAC. The route is flown each Monday and the equipment is the C009A Nightingale aircraft. Please see Appendix M for complete details regarding this aircraft.

Second, the following graphic shows the originating station of the flight, the path of the flight, en route stations, its changing compass directions, and the terminal station.

{BLV *E* ➡ ADW *S* ➡ NGU *SW* ➡ SKF *NW* ➡ NKX *NW* ➡ SUU}

| LI | AIRPORT/STATION | CTRY/STA |
|---|---|---|
| BLV/KBLV | Scott AFB | IL |
| ADW/KADW | Andrews AFB | MD |
| NGU/KNGU | Norfolk NS | VA |
| SKF/KSKF | Kelly AFB | TX |
| NKX/KNKX | Miramar MCAS | CA |
| SUU/KSUU | Travis AFB | CA |

Reading from left to right we see that the route/mission begins at Scott AFB, IL (BLV) and flies east with en route stops at Andrews AFB, MD (ADW), the flight continues south to Norfolk NS, VA (NGU), southwest to Kelly AFB, TX (SKF), northwest to Miramar MCAS, CA (NKX) and northwest to Travis AFB, CA (SUU) the terminating station.

**[Andrews AFB, MD (ADW)]**

**EN ROUTE/SCHEDULE**

| | |
|---|---|
| Scott AFB | ADW-126/MEDEVAC (30) |

## ★ ★ ★ IMPORTANT NOTE ★ ★ ★

Scheduled Military Services (U.S. ARMY, U.S. NAVY, U.S. MARINE CORPS, U.S. COAST GUARD, U.S. AIR FORCE) flights by Service owned and operated aircraft and contractor furnished and operated aircraft change often with respect to the key elements of destinations, routing, schedules, aircraft equipment, and mission.

**There are frequent, minor (and sometimes not so minor) adjustments made in these key elements with very limited prior notice. These unannounced changes are particularly true of MEDEVAC flight missions which are very sensitive to patient requirements. Many of the CONUS, OCONUS, and foreign country routes have been flown for more than 50 years with constant modification of some or all of these key elements to meet the needs of the Uniformed Services and other supported United States Interest. We have provided a snapshot or profile of typical information one would expect to find concerning these key elements for this edition.**

**We encourage you to keep current on changes in MILITARY SPACE-A AIR OPPORTUNITIES AROUND THE WORLD by subscribing to our worldwide travel newsletter Military Living's R&R TRAVEL NEWS (Please see the central order coupons in the back of this book). Lastly, we encourage you to telephone, fax, e-mail, or visit your intended Space-A departure location prior to registering for Space-A travel in order to obtain the latest information regarding the key elements of Space-A travel.**

## ★ ★ ★ BASE CLOSURES ★ ★ ★

**United States Base Closures in CONUS and OCONUS:** In September 1995 the fourth and final Base Closure and Realignment Act became law. The September 1995 law along with previous directed closures in the Base Closure and Realignment Acts of October 1988, 1991 and September 1993 are so noted at the beginning of each listing affected with the DoD estimated date of closure. Some bases have already closed and consequently have been deleted from this directory. It should also be noted that all final closure dates will be established and may change as the DoD completes the final closure plans and funding becomes available to effect the closures. Also, only the bases with Space-A Passenger service have been addressed in this book. **There are no channel bases (major flight locations) contained in the 1995 base closure law.**

**United States Base Closure in Foreign Countries:** The closure of U.S. bases in foreign countries has ended. The last announcement of base closures under the Secretary of Defense's authority to close bases in foreign countries was made 23 February 1995. This last announcement virtually completed the draw down in foreign countries. The result is a 57 percent reduction in Europe. The overseas site return, reduction and standby operations announcements began on 29 January 1990 and ended with the announcement made 23 February 1995 and included base closure actions in 20 foreign countries. **There are no major flight bases closed with this last announcement of the DoD.** A past closure announcement was made by DoD on 19 February 1997 which diverted the closure of six more bases in Europe, all to occur before the end of 1998. There were no Air Force bases on the list. Recent (1999) announcements to close overseas bases (in foreign countries) are indicated at bases listed in this edition, i.e., Rhein-Main Air Base, DE.

# HOW TO USE THIS DIRECTORY
# TO PLAN A TRIP

Many readers are initially confused about how to route a Space-A trip using this book. We have attempted to make routing your Space-A trip as easy as possible; however the information is not initially easy to comprehend. Very few people are able to just pick up this book and plan a trip if they have not read HOW to use this directory (below). There is simply too much information!

We have put some samplestogether below of how you should go about planning a trip using this book. Please keep in mind that Space-A planning and use is a dynamic venture. Routes and, more importantly, schedules will change over the course of time. Schedule departure days and recurring frequency of departure and routing are the items most likely to change, so verify your itinerary before traveling!

If you carefully read and understand the information below, your ability to plan your trip will be greatly increased, and your task considerably less daunting.

First, answer the following questions:

# Do you have a specific destination to which you wish to travel?

**This is called Backward Planning.** (This will limit the number of places which you can use as your originating station.) In this case, you will work backward by planning your trip from your desired final destination.

**Step 1:** Choose your destination, and look in the table of contents under that state/possession/country in the table of contents, and familiarize yourself with the possible places into which you may fly as your final destination. Look at the en route schedules under the listing of the place you have selected as your final destination on that page to see where originating flights go to/from that location, and then go to step 2.

**Step 2:** Go to the cross reference index (in the Appendices) and locate the three/four letter location identifier for the destination station you have chosen. Please read the introduction at the top of the appendices. This index will reference every page on which that destination appears. You can then look at those pages to see which originating stations (military installation/airport) you may travel from to reach your destination.

**Step 3:** At this point you have two options. You can decide if you wish to travel to the originating station using commercial air, bus, train, car, etc., or if you want to use Space-A to get to that originating destination. (Note: Please remember that military dependents/eligible family members) with a DD-1173 ID card cannot (in most cases except Active Duty dependents traveling with their sponsors on emergency leave or house-hunting) travel point to point by Space-A within the continental United States (CONUS). See Appendix A for further details on eligibility. It is only the service member (Active, Retired or Reservist) who may travel point-to-point within the CONUS).

**Step 4:** If you need to plan another leg to your trip, simply start again with Step 1, using your originating station selected above as your destination. Repeat the above steps as necessary. You will have to use the flight information provided in the schedules (regarding the days of the week on which these flights occur) in order to plan efficiently, and limit your time between flights.

**Editor's Note on Multi-legged trip planning:** For overseas destinations, you may wish to plan several legs to your trip, especially if there is not an originating station to your desired destination near your home/starting point. If you can fly from an originating station near your home to an OCONUS destination, and from that place, fly on to your final desired destination, you will have a lot more options!

# Do you want to travel from a specific originating station (military installation/airport), but are less concerned with where you are going?

**This is called Forward Planning.** (This will decrease the number of places you can select as final destinations, but will also decrease you travel expenses associated with getting to your originating station.)

**Step 1:** In this case, plan your trip by looking in the table of contents for your desired originating station, and go to that page. Examine all of the possibilities for final destinations.

**Step 2:** If you want to add another leg to your trip, after you have done Step 1, then look in the table of contents for the flights originating from your final destination selected in Step 1. Repeat this step as necessary.

**Final notes:**

Don't forget to plan your return trip home! In order to be higher up on the Space-A Roster, be sure to sign up for your return at your destination station before you leave home (provided that you are not remaining at your destination station more than 60 days which is the time limit that you can remain on the Space-A rooster with out a new sign-up).

If you plan a multi-legged trip, be sure to **sign up** on the Space-A roster at **all originating flight locations!**

**Important Warning!** If you have planned a trip with more than one leg, then you will have to sign up again on the Space-A roster after you fly out of a location, as you will have fulfilled your Space-A from that location, and will be removed from the roster! For example, if you have applied for space-a travel from Ramstein AB, DE to CONUS, but while waiting for this transportation you take a flight from Ramstein AB, DE to Aviano AB, IT, then your application for space-A from Ramstein AB, DE to CONUS will be deleted from the computer system when you fly out of Ramstein AB, DE to Aviano AB, IT. To keep your application to CONUS in place at Ramstein AB, DE, fly from Rhein-Main AB, DE to Aviano AB, IT. Many first-time Space-A travelers miss this important point and end up at the bottom of the list on the day they wish to fly. It is no fun to be stuck at a military installation/airport when you thought you would be flying home!

We do provide limited Space-A assistance and counseling (hopefully after you have reviewed the contents of this book). If you have a simple question, send it to us via e-mail at: militaryliving@aol.com, or Fax: 703-237-2233. For longer questions/assistance, call Roy Sr, or Ann at 703-237-0203 between 1530-1730 hours Eastern Standard (daylight) Time. Please no collect calls.

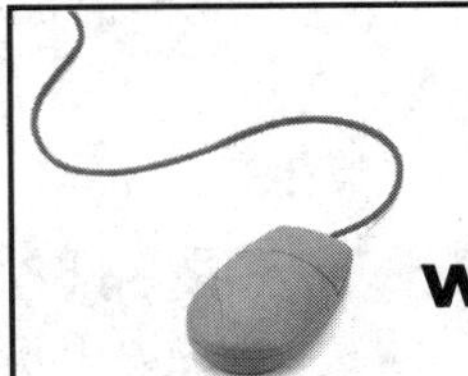

# WANT TO TRAVEL? WANT TO HAVE FUN AND SAVE MONEY?

## We have the Prescription for You.

The following is a reproduction of the R&R Travel News newsletter:



# R&R Travel News™

A worldwide travel newsletter published by  ©2001 Military Living Publications www.militaryliving.com

## New Lodging at Novato USCG Near San Francisco

**Message from Ann Crawford:**

After covering military recreation and temporary military lodging for 33 years, it takes a lot to surprise me! This new lodging not only surprised me, it also delighted me. The reason for my excitement is that practically all temporary military lodging in San Francisco has been closed because of base closures.

Even though Novato is about a 25-minute drive from San Francisco, it is close enough to make this a very attractive option for military ID card holders who find themselves needing lower cost temporary lodging.

San Francisco, a popular vacation option, has been too expensive for some military folks to enjoy. Now, there's another option, and we suspect that you are hearing it first in Military Living's R&R Travel News. Another $aver - Shop at the military exchange and commissary near the waterfront at the "closed" Presidio of San Francisco. Novato is on the site of the old Hamilton Air Force Base.

These bases, Novato and the exchange and commissary stores at the Presidio, are just a couple of examples of never believing a base is closed completely until you see the locks on the front gate!

The information that follows was furnished to R&R Travel News by U.S. Coast Guard MWR. We thank them!

**New Lodging at Novato**

MWR at ISC Alameda, CA has ten
Novato Continued to Pg. 14

### IT'S HERE!

TEMPORARY Military Lodging AROUND THE WORLD

Save hundreds by staying at military facilities throughout the U.S. and the world.

This guide gives you all the vital information you need to travel more and spend less.

See Pg. 16 for ordering information.

### New Little Creek Navy Lodge Offers Modern Conveniences

Guests staying at Navy Lodge Little Creek have always had excellent service, a clean, comfortable room and a convenient location near area attractions. Now guests will find it even bigger and better with the grand opening of the new two-story Navy Lodge on March 26, 2001. Located on the original site of Seal Team 2 and the Seal Underwater Demolition Team, the new Navy Lodge is more modern than the Navy Lodge it replaces, which was built in 1971.

"Probably the biggest change our guests will notice is the new Navy Lodge has interior hallways, which means the rooms don't open to the outside," said Margaret Massie, Little Creek's Navy Lodge manager. "I think our guests will feel more comfortable entering their rooms through the lodge's hallway rather than from the outside."

The new Navy Lodge has 100 rooms, including 4 handicapped rooms, 16 Business Class rooms, which feature one queen-size bed, a "living room" area with a desk, and 80 standard rooms, all of which have two queen-size beds. Each room has a kitchenette, complete with stove, microwave, refrigerator, utensils and cookware as well as iron, ironing board, hair dryer and coffee maker. The Navy Lodge itself has a guest laundry facility, vending machines, playground, video rental service and complimentary coffee in the lobby every day. To make guests feel like they're at home, compli-
Continued to Pg. 15

### In This Issue

Report #178 May-June 2001 Volume 31, No. 3
- Surprise! New TML Near San Francisco
- New Navy Lodge in VA Beach, VA
- New NAS Norfolk, VA AMC Air Terminal
- Dos Rios Marine Corps Lodging Near Mexico
- Two New RV/Campgrounds: Fort Wainwright, AK; Wright-Patterson, OH

Our subscribers travel on less per day . . . the military way!™   1   R&R Travel News Report 178 May-June 2001 Volume 31, No. 3

---

## FREE GIFT with 5-year subscription-

Military Space-A Air Opportunities Air Route Map (a $12.95 mail order value)!

## 6 ISSUES PER YEAR

5 Yrs/$59   3 Yrs/$39
2 Yrs/$29   1 Yr/$19

## HOW TO ORDER

**CALL** 703-237-0203 or 1-888-691-0203 and place your credit card order by telephone.

**ORDER** at www.militaryliving.com

**FAX** the subscription form to 703-237-2233.

**MAIL** to P.O. Box 2347 Falls Church, VA 22042-0347

**SEE A SAMPLE ISSUE at www.militaryliving.com**
Click on R&R Travel News.

## Features of the R&R Travel News™

Be "In the Know" Sooner with R&R Travel News!™

Save $$$ on Military Lodging

Reader Trip Reports

Enjoy more Safety & Camaraderie

FLY FREE! Military Space-A Updates & News

Have Fun at Military RV & Camping Areas

Get the Latest News and Updates

# www.militaryliving.com

# CONTENTS

# CONTINENTAL UNITED STATES

## ALABAMA

### BIRMINGHAM INTERNATIONAL AIRPORT/AIR NATIONAL GUARD (BHM/KBHM)

117th ARW, Air National Guard
5401 Eastlake Blvd
Birmingham, AL 35217-3595

**LOCATION:** From east or west on I-59/20 take exit 128 north onto Tallapoosa Street, then north for one-half mile to a right on Eastlake Blvd and follow the airfield fence for approximately two miles northeast to main gate on the right (southeast) side of street. *USMRA: Page 36 (D, E-4). ML-ARM: (33°33'N/86°45'W).* LST: GMT-06:00. NMC: located in the northeast section of Birmingham. Main installation numbers: C-205-714-2000, D-312-778-2210.

**REGISTRATION INFO:** **C-205-714-2297, D-312-778-2297, Fax: C-205-714-2610, D-312-778-2610. WEB: www.albirm.ang.af.mil** Base Ops. Tue-Fri duty hours. Call for flight information.

**FOOD SERVICE: Restaurants:** 10 minutes by car. **Snack Bars:** Exchange, duty hours. **Snack Vending:** 24 hours daily.

**SUPPORT AVAILABLE: Exchange:** C-205-714-2348.

**TRANSPORTATION: Bus (Comm):** Birmingham IAP, C-205-252-7171/205-323-1678. **Car Rentals, Limo and Taxi:** Birmingham IAP; see telephone directory. **Parking:** None on ANG Base, use public parking at Birmingham IAP.

**TML:** Nearest TML is Bldg 157, 351 West Drive, Maxwell AFB, AL 36112-6024, 24 hours daily, C-1-888-235-6343, C-334-953-2055, D-312-493-2055, Fax: C-334-953-5696, D-312-493-5696; DV/VIP Protocol Office, Bldg 119, C-334-953-2095, 07+, Duty reservations anytime, Space-A reservations 24 hours in advance.

**TRAVELERS AID: Red Cross:** 2225 3rd Ave N, Hours: 0800-1200 daily, C-205-322-5661. **Security Police:** located at main gate, 24 hours daily, C-205-714-9240.

**OTHER INFORMATION:** U.S. Customs Service Airport.

**ATTRACTIONS:** Vulcan (iron man statue) on Red Mountain in city, zoo, Botanical Gardens, dog racing track, Museum of Flight, and largest shopping mall in southeast.

#### UNSCHEDULED FLIGHTS
Flight schedule is quarterly. Aircraft is KC-135E. Call for destinations, routings, and schedules.

### CAIRNS ARMY AIRFIELD (OZR/KOZR)

228th AVN
Cairns Army Airfield, Bldg 30501
Fort Rucker, AL 36362-5000

**LOCATION:** Eighty miles southeast of Montgomery, midway between the capital city and the Florida Gulf Coast, and seven miles south of Ozark, on US-231 to southwest on Al-249. Clearly marked. *USMRA: Page 36 (F,G-8). ML-ARM: (31°16'N/85°42'W).* LST: GMT-06:00. NMC: Dothan, 26 miles southeast. Main installation numbers: C-334-255-1030, D-312-558-1030.

**REGISTRATION INFO:** **C-334-255-8309, D-312-558-8309, Fax: C-334-255-8519, D-312-558-8519.** Bldg Hours: 0730-1630 daily. Directions: From the main gate (Daleville), continue on AL-85 to Air Traffic Control tower/Base Ops, right turn to Bldg 30501.

**PAX LOUNGES: General:** Bldg 3010, 24 hours daily, C-334-255-8361, D-312-558-8361. A/C, telephone (commercial), TV, O/S seats. Also, pilots' lounge. **DV/VIP:** Bldg 3010, 24 hours daily, C-334-255-8361, D-312-558-8361. A/C, telephones (commercial and defense), TV, restrooms, O/S seats. **Protocol Service:** D-312-558-3100.

**FOOD SERVICE: Cafeteria:** Bldg 30101, Hours: 0900-1700, C-334-598-0241, 3 miles away. **NCO/CPO Club:** Bldg 2908, C-334-598-2491. **O Club:** Bldg 113, C-334-598-2426. **Restaurants/Fast Food:** 2 miles outside Cairns AAF gate. **Snack Bars:** Hours: 0630-2000 Mon-Fri, C-334-598-8771.

**TRANSPORTATION: Bus (Comm):** Main gate; Greyhound, C-334-774-5500 (in Ozark); Trailways, C-334-598-2375 (Fort Rucker). **Limo Service:** in Dothan, C-334-792-8100. Dothan to Ozark. **Off Base Car Rental:** C-334-598-9390/3796, 2 miles away. **Off Base Taxi (Comm):** Located in Daleville, C-334-598-8771, 3 miles away. **Parking:** Very limited.

**TML:** Billeting, Bldg 308, 6th Ave, 24 hours daily, C-334-598-5216, D-312-558-2626, Fax: C-334-598-1242; DV/VIP Protocol, Bldg 114, Post Hq's, C-334-255-1134, D-312-558-1134, 06/GS-15, Retirees and lower ranks one night only.

**RVC:** Outdoor Recreation, Bldg 24236 Camper Shed, C-334-255-4305, D-312-558-4305.

**TRAVELERS AID: Chaplain:** Hours: 0800-1630, C-334-255-2989, D-312-558-2989, 3 miles away. **Medical/ Dental:** Hours: 0630-1730, C-334-255-7393, D-312-558-7393, 3 miles away. **Red Cross:** Bldg 5315, Hours: 0730-1600 Mon-Fri, C-334-255-1055, D-312-558-1055, 3 miles away. **Security Police:** 24 hours daily, C-334-255-2222, D-312-558-2222, 3 miles away. **Travelers Aid:** C-334-255-3643, D-312-558-3643.

**SUPPORT AVAILABLE: Bank/Currency Exchange:** Hours: 0900-1600, C-334-598-4411, 2 miles away. **Credit Union:** Hours: 0900-1630, C-334-598-2401, 2 miles away. **Exchange:** Hours: 0745-1615 daily, C-334-503-9044 ext 229, 3 miles away. **Laundry/Dry Cleaner:** Hours: 0745-1615 daily, C-334-503-9044 ext 276, 3 miles away. **Shoppette:** Hours: 0700-2100 daily, C-334-503-9044 ext 277, 3 miles away.

**ATTRACTIONS:** Eighty miles from beach (Panama City, FL), 20 miles from Dothan, and Waterworld.

#### UNSCHEDULED FLIGHTS
There are no unscheduled flights. All flights scheduled in advance. Most frequent destinations are: AL, VA, TX, OK, FL, NC, SC, GA and Washington, D.C. Call for destinations, routings, and schedules.

### MAXWELL AIR FORCE BASE (MXF/KMXF)

42nd TRNF/LGTRP
220 W. Ash Street, Bldg 844, Room 112
Maxwell AFB, AL 36112-5000

**LOCATION:** Take I-85 south to I-65 north to Herron Street (exit #172) west to right (north) on Dickerson Street two blocks to left (west) on Bell Street approximately 0.9 mile and follow signs to Bell Street Gate Visitor Center on right (north side of street). *USMRA: Page 36 (E-6). ML-ARM: (32°22'N/86°21'W).* LST: GMT-06:00. NMC: Montgomery, 1.5 miles southeast. Main installation numbers: C-334-953-1110, D-312-493-1110.

**REGISTRATION INFO:** **C-334-953-7372, D-312-493-7372, Rec: C-334-953-6760/6454, D-312-493-6760/6454, Fax: C-334-953-6114, D-312-493-6114.** Bldg 844, Hours: 0600-2000 Mon-Fri, weekends and holidays as needed. Schedule received 24 hours in advance. Directions: Day Street to left on Ash Street. Pax Service Office: C-334-953-7372/6454, D-312-493-7372/6454.

                    

**PAX LOUNGES: General:** Bldg 884, Hours: 0600-2000 Mon-Fri, C-334-953-7372/6454, D-312-493-7372/6454. A/C, telephones (commercial and defense), TV, restrooms, P/C seats. **DV/VIP:** Bldg 844, Hours: 0600-2200 daily, C-334-953-5374, D-312-493-5374. A/C, coffee/tea, telephones (commercial and defense), TV, restrooms, O/S seats (O6+, GS15+). **Protocol Service:** Bldg 800, Hours: 0800-1700 Mon-Fri, C-334-953-2095, D-312-493-2095.

**FOOD SERVICE: Dining Hall:** Bldg 668/1420. C-334-953-5127, D-312-493-5127. **Golf Course:** C-334-953-2209. **NCO Club:** Bldg 742, C-334-262-8364. **O Club:** Bldg 144, C-334-264-6423. **Snack Vending:** Bldg 844, C-334-953-5946.

**TRANSPORTATION:** Limo service and taxi (off base), telephone numbers at terminal. **Air Tickets:** SATO, Bldg 924, official travel, C-334-264-0076; leisure travel, C-334-263-5500. **On Base Car Rental:** Enterprise, C-334-264-7701. **On Base Bus (Comm):** Bldg 927, C-334-953-5038 (Maxwell AFB to Montgomery). **Off Base Bus (Comm):** Greyhound, C-334-286-0658, C-1-800-231-2222, 15 miles away. **On Base Taxi (Gov):** Bldg 927, C-334-953-5038 (duty passengers only). **Parking:** Bldg 843 (in front and across the street-short and long term).

**TML:** Bldg 157, 351 West Drive, Maxwell AFB, AL 36112-6024, C-1-888-235-6343, C-334-953-2055, D-312-493-2055, Fax: C-334-953-5696, D-312-493-5696; DV/VIP Bldg 119, C-334-953-2095, 06+ official duty or leave, Tel as above, duty reservations anytime, leave reservations 24 hours in advance.

**RVC:** FAMCAMP, Outdoor Recreation, March Road, Check-in FAMCAMP Office, C-334-953-5161, D-312-493-5161.

**TRAVELERS AID: Chaplain:** Bldg 155, C-334-953-2111. After duty hours, C-334-953-2862. **Emergency Relief:** Bldg 500, C-334-953-2353. **Medical:** Bldg 50, 24 hours daily, C-334-953-2333. **Red Cross:** Bldg 18, C-334-953-5626. After duty hours, C-334-953-7333. **Security Police:** Bldg 837, C-334-953-7222.

**SUPPORT AVAILABLE: Bank/Currency Exchange:** Bldg 1081, C-334-832-8190. **Credit Union:** C-334-260-2606. **Exchange:** Bldg 1090, C-334-834-5946. **Hair Styles:** Bldg 1090; Barber, C-334-263-3444; Beauty, C-334-263-3010. **Laundry/Dry Cleaning:** Bldg 1090, C-334-263-7826.

**ATTRACTIONS:** Air University, W.H. Gayle Planetarium, state capital and historical homes in Montgomery, the Zoo, and the First White House of the Confederacy.

**OTHER INFORMATION:** No regularly scheduled flights, below is merely a sample schedule. Weekends and holidays are on a standby basis.

**MAXWELL AIR FORCE BASE (MXF); REGION: ATL; OPERATOR: AMC; TYPE: CGO W/ PAX; ROUTE: OBJ5A; SAMPLE SCHEDULE: 1ST WED; EQUIPMENT: C130H**

{ MXF *NE* ➡ CHS (★) *SW* ➡ BZE *S* ➡ SAL ⇌ SAL *NE* ➡ TGU *NE* ➡ CHS (★) *SW* ➡ MXF}

| LI/ICAO | AIRPORT/STATION | CTRY/STA | DAYS EN ROUTE |
|---|---|---|---|
| MXF/KMXF | Maxwell AFB | AL | +0 |
| CHS/KCHS | Charleston AFB/IAP | SC | +1 |
| BZE/MZBZ | Belize IAP | BZ | +1 |
| SAL/MSLP | El Salvador IAP | SV | +1 |
| TGU/MHTG | Toncontin IAP | HN | +2 |
| CHS/KCHS | Charleston AFB/IAP | SC | +2 |
| MXF/KMXF | Maxwell AFB | AL | |

### UNSCHEDULED FLIGHTS

Frequent flights, via C-130H to: Andrews AFB, MD (**ADW**); Randoplh AFB, TX (**RND**); Langley AFB, VA (**LFI**); and Norfolk NS, VA (**NGU**) and other CONUS locations. ***Note: Baggage limit is 30 pounds on C-21s, C-12s and UC-35s.***

# MOBILE COAST GUARD AVIATION TRAINING CENTER (MOB/KMOB)

Commanding Officer
USCG Aviation Training Center
8501 Tanner Williams Road
Mobile, AL 36608-8322

**LOCATION:** From I-65 take Airport Boulevard (exit #3) west 5.8 miles, right (north) on Schillinger Road for 0.7 miles, to left (west) on Tanner Williams Road, 1 mile. Center in on left (south) side of road. Clearly marked. *USMRA: Page 36 (B-9). ML-ARM: (30°41'N/88°14'W).* LST: GMT-06:00. NMC: Mobile, 1 mile northwest. Main installation numbers: C-334-639-6110, D-312-436-3635, Flight Operations: D-312-436-3635.

**REGISTRATION INFO: C-334-441-6401, D-312-436-3635, Fax: C-334-639-6435.** Main hangar, Hours: 0800-1600 Mon-Fri, Directions: North side of Bates Municipal Airport, second floor deck on ramp side. No pax lounge. Restrooms, snack vending machines available.

**FOOD SERVICE: Enlisted Club:** C-334-639-6359.

**TRAVELERS AID: Medical:** C-334-639-6401.

**SUPPORT AVAILABLE: Exchange:** C-334-639-6390. **Hair Styles:** Barber, C-334-639-6494.

### UNSCHEDULED FLIGHTS

Infrequent flights only to East and Midwest. No overseas or helicopter Space-A.

# REDSTONE ARSENAL ARMY AIRFIELD (HUA/KHUA)

Flight Operations Division
Attn: AMSMI-RA-FO
Redstone Arsenal, AL 35898-5320

**LOCATION:** From I-565 east west take exit #14 south onto Rideout Road for 0.4 miles to gate #9. Or, from I-565 in city of Huntsville, exit south onto US-231 (Memorial Drive) for 4.5 miles to right (west) onto Martin Road to main gate (gate #1). Uniformed personnel may take I-565 to US-231 (Memorial Drive) south 1.0 mile to Drake exit west. Go west on Drake which becomes Goss Road to gate #8. *USMRA: Page 36 (E-1). ML-ARM: (34°39'N/86°37'W).* LST: GMT-06:00. NMC: Huntsville, adjacent north and east sides. Main installation numbers: C-256-876-2151, D-312-746-2151.

**REGISTRATION INFO: C-256-876-1916, D-312-746-4290, Fax: C-256-842-0562, D-312-788-0562.** Bldg 4809, Hours: 0700-1630 Mon-Fri, closed all national holidays. Directions: From Gate 8, take Goss Road to Rideout Road, left on Rideout Road to Hale Road, right on Hale Road to Base Ops. *Note: The limited unscheduled flights into Redstone make catching a Space-A flight very unlikely.*

**PAX LOUNGES:** Bldg 4809, Hours: 0700-1630 daily, C-256-876-4290, D-312-746-1916. A/C, read/write room, telephones (commercial and defense), TV, restrooms, O/S seats. **Protocol Service:** Bldg 5250, duty hours, C-256-876-7135 (O6+).

**FOOD SERVICE: None on Airfield. Cafeteria:** Bldg 4488, C-256-876-9973. **Enlisted Club:** Sports Haven, Bldg 3479, C-256-881-6595. **NCO/CPO Club:** Bldg 1500, C-256-837-0750. **O Club:** Bldg 130, C-256-830-2582. **Restaurants:** Bldg 3231, C-256-882-9631. **Snack Bars:** Bldg 3220, C-256-881-1591.

**TRANSPORTATION: Bus (Comm):** Main gate: Greyhound, C-256-536-5349; Trailways, C-256-534-1681. **On Base Taxi (Gov):** Bldg 3664, C-256-876-2261. Duty passengers only. **Car Rentals:** HUA Jetplex; Avis, C-256-772-9301; Hertz, C-256-772-9331; National, C-256-772-9336. **Parking:** limited, short term only.

**TML:** Billeting, Bldg 244, Goss Road, C-256-876-5713/8028, D-312-746-5713/8028, Fax: C-256-876-2929, D-312-746-2929, 24 hours daily, DV/VIP:Contact billeting above, 06+, Retirees and lower ranks Space-A.

**RVC:** Outdoor Recreation, Bldg 5132, Sportsman's Road, Check-in Camp, 0930-1700 hrs, C-256-876-4868/6854, D-312-746-4868/6854.

**TRAVELERS AID: Chaplain:** Bldg 376, C-256-876-2409. **Emergency Medical:** Fox Army Hospital, C-256-876-8621, D-312-746-8621. **Red Cross:** Bldg 3491, C-256-876-4427. **Security Police:** C-256-876-2222.

**SUPPORT AVAILABLE: Bank/Currency Exchange:** C-256-883-0173. **Exchange:** Bldg 3220, C-256-883-6100.

**ATTRACTIONS:** Space and Rocket Center on Highway 20, Tennessee River.

### UNSCHEDULED FLIGHTS

All flights are unscheduled. Missions are posted 24 hours in advance when possible. Most flights are to Andrews AFB, MD **(ADW)**. Call for availability of flights and seats. Baggage limit is 30 pounds.

# ARIZONA

## DAVIS-MONTHAN AIR FORCE BASE (DMA/KDMA)

355 TRNS/LGTTI
5275 E. Granite Street
Davis-Monthan AFB, AZ 85707-3017

**LOCATION:** From the east on I-10, exit #270 north onto Kolb Road, north 6 miles to Golf Links Road, left (west) to Craycroft Road, left (south) to main gate. From the west on I-10, exit #264 north onto Alvernon Way; turn left (north) following road to the main gate. (Alvernon Way turns into Golf Links Road at intersection with Ajo Way.) *USMRA: Page 108 (F-9). ML-ARM: (32°11'N/110°52'W).* LST: GMT-07:00. NMC: Tucson, 3 miles northwest. Main installation numbers: C-520-228-3900, D-312-228-3900.

**REGISTRATION INFO: C-520-228-2322, D-312-228-2322, Rec: C-520-228-3641, D-312-228-3641,Fax: C-520-228-7229, D-312-228-7229. E-mail: spaceatrns355@dm.af.mil WEB: www.dm.af.mil/355trans/lgtt/lgtta.htm** Bldg 4819, Hours: 0730-1630 Mon-Fri, Recording operated after hours. Directions: Continue on Craycroft Road to Tempe Street to right on Phoenix Street, Pax Term on left next to Base Ops. **Pax Service Office:** C-520-228-3641, D-312-228-3641.

**PAX LOUNGES:** No family lounge. **General:** Bldg 4819, Hours: 0700-1600 Mon-Fri, C-520-228-3641, D-312-228-3641. A/C, (commercial and defense) telephones, restrooms, TV, O/S seats. **DV/VIP:** Bldg 4820, 24 hours daily, C-520-228-4315, D-312-228-4315. A/C, TV, telephones (commercial and defense), showers, O/S seats, restrooms, coffee/tea served. Contact Base Ops in advance (O6+ and VIP). **Protocol Service:** Bldg 2300, Hours: 0700-1600 Mon-Fri, C-520-228-3600, D-312-228-3600 (O6+ and VIP). Air Combat Command sponsored.

**FOOD SERVICE: In-Flight Kitchen:** Bldg 5428, Hours: 1030-1330, 1730-2030 Mon-Fri, C-520-228-4096. **Fast Food:** Burger King, Bldg 2521, C-520-228-2878. **NCO Club:** Bldg 4455, C-520-228-3100, D-312-228-3100. **O Club:** Bldg 2050, C-520-228-3301. **Restaurants:** Cabana Pizza, Dine-in/Take-out/Delivery: C-520-747-3234; Desert Inn, Bldg 4100, C-520-228-3072, D-312-228-3072. **Snack Bars:** (AAFES) Bldg 2441, C-520-790-6150.

**TRANSPORTATION: Commercial Air Tickets:** SATO (Official Travel), Bldg 2300, Hours: 0700-1600 Mon-Fri, C-520-228-4841, D-312-228-4841; SATO (Leisure Travel), Bldg 4430, Hours: 0900-1800 Mon-Fri, 1000-1500 Sat, C-520-748-1942. **On Base Car Rental:** Enterprise, C-520-571-0886. **Off Base Bus Service:** Base Exchange parking lot, Bldg 2441, C-520-792-9222. **Car Rental:** Enterprise Rent-A-Car, (AAFES) Bldg 4432, C-520-571-0886. **Off Base Taxi:** ABC, C-520-623-7979; Allstate, C-520-881-2227; Checker, C-520-623-1133; Yellow Cab, C-520-624-6611. **Parking:** Bldg 4819, C-520-228-3641, D-312-228-3641.

**TML:** Inn on Davis-Monthan, Bldg 2350, 3375 South 10th Street, C-520-228-3230/3309, D-312-228-3230/3309, Fax: C-520-228-3312, D-312-228-3312, 24 hours daily, E-mail: lodging@dm.af.mil DV/VIP 355th Wing Protocol, C-520-228-3600, 06+, leave or official duty, Bldg 4065.

**RVC:** FAMCAMP, 5465 East Nuggat Street, Check-in Bldg 6015, C-520-747-9144, D-312-361-1110 (ask for FAMCAMP).

**TRAVELERS AID: Chaplain:** Bldg 3205, C-520-228-5411, D-312-228-5411. **Emergency Relief:** Family Support Center: (Air Force Aid Society) Bldg 3210, C-520-228-3891, D-312-228-3891. **Lost/Found:** Bldg 4819, C-520-228-3641, D-312-228-3641. **Medical:** Bldg 400, C-520-228-2828 (Clinic). **Red Cross:** Bldg 4300, C-520-228-3205, D-312-228-3205. **Security Police:** Bldg 4413, C-520-228-3517, D-312-228-3517.

**SUPPORT AVAILABLE: Exchange:** Bldg 2441, C-520-228-7887. **Bank/Currency Exchange:** Bank of America, Bldg 2317, C-520-228-7025. **Hair Styles:** Bldg 2441; Barber, C-520-228-1604; Beauty, C-520-228-8334. **Laundry:** Bldg 5000 (near Civilian Base Personnel Office [CBPO]), 24 hours daily. **Postal Service/Wire:** Bldg 2240; Military, C-520-228-4571, D-312-228-4571; Civilian, C-520-228-1651.

**ATTRACTIONS:** Old movie sets, Pima Air Museum, Arizona-Sonora Desert Museum, Zoo, Colossal Cave, Saguaro National Monument. Biosphere II, Kit Peak, great weather.

### EN ROUTE SCHEDULES

| AIRPORT/STATION | LI-MISSION (page #) |
| --- | --- |
| Travis AFB | SUU-456/MEDEVAC (13) |

### UNSCHEDULED FLIGHTS

Flight to Beale AFB, CA **(BAB)** via KC-135 on the first Fri of each month. Flight to Travis AFB, CA **(SUU)** via C-141B on the third Fri of each month. Other unscheduled flight notices are received 2-7 days in advance of flights to CONUS and OCONUS locations via C-005A/B, C-12, C-20, C-21, C-141B and KC-135E aircraft. Call for destinations, routings and schedules.

## LIBBY ARMY AIRFIELD (FHU/KFHU)

HQ Co 306 MI BN
Base Ops, Bldg 91251
Fort Huachuca, AZ 85613-6000

**LOCATION:** From I-10 take exit #302 south onto AZ-90 south approximately 28 miles to Sierra Vista and main gate to fort on right (west) side of road. *USMRA: Page 108 (F,G-9,10). ML-ARM: (31°33'N/110°17'W).* LST: GMT-07:00. NMC: Tucson, 75 miles northwest. Main installation numbers: C-520-538-7111, D-312-879-7111.

**REGISTRATION INFO: C-520-538-2860, D-312-879-2860.** Hours: 0600-1600 Mon-Fri. Call for flight information.

**FOOD SERVICE: NCO Club:** C-602-533-3802. **O Club:** C-602-533-2193. **Snack Bars:** C-602-533-5759.

**TRANSPORTATION: Off Base Car Rental:** C-520-458-2425, C-520-459-1296. **Off Base Taxi:** C-520-458-0027.

**TML:** Lodging Office, Bldg 43083, Service Road, C-520-533-2222, D-312-821-2222, 24 hours daily. DV/VIP C-520-533-1231, D-312-821-1231.

**RVC:** Check-in RV Park, 0800-1700 hours Mon-Fri, C-520-533-1335, D-312-879-1335, Fax: C-520-533-1349.

**TRAVELERS AID: Security Police:** Located at main gate, 24 hours daily, C-520-533-2181/3000.

**ATTRACTIONS:** Fort museum. Original cantonment a National Historical Landmark. Tombstone, 25 minute drive on Charleston Road.

### UNSCHEDULED FLIGHTS

**Operational support airlift center has closed.** Scheduling for all Operational Support Airlift (OSA) has been centralized at the OSA Center, Scott AFB, IL. Flights are limited to C-12A. Call for destinations, routings and schedules.

## LUKE AIR FORCE BASE (LUF/KLUF)

56 FW Transportation Squadron
7254 N. Fighter Country Ave, Suite 2, Bldg 453
Luke AFB, AZ 85309-1215

**LOCATION:** From Phoenix, west on I-10 to Litchfield Road, exit 128, north on Litchfield Road approximately five miles. Also, from Phoenix, north on I-17 to Glendale Avenue exit #205 west on Glendale Avenue to intersection of Glendale Avenue and Litchfield Road approximately 10 miles. *USMRA: Page 108 (D-6,7). ML-ARM: (33°32'N/112°20'W).* LST: GMT-07:00. NMC: Phoenix, 20 miles southeast. Main installation numbers: C-802-856-7411, D-312-896-1110.

**REGISTRATION INFO:** The 56 FW Transportation Squadron is the POC for processing passengers. At press time, there were no procedures for processing passengers. For update on registration, call **C-623-856-7035/7131, D-312-896-7035/7131.** Directions: From main gate west on Eagle Street to right on Fighter Country Ave to Terminal on flight line.

**PAX LOUNGES: General:** Bldg 453, Base Ops: 0600-2100 M-F; 0700-1600 Sat/Sun;  C-623-856-7131. A/C, baggage check, read/write room, telephones (commercial and defense), TV, restrooms, P/C seats. **DV/VIP:** Bldg 453, C-623-856-6087, D-312-896-6087. Located in the rear wing of the Base Ops. **Protocol Service:** Bldg 11, Hours: 0730-1630 Mon-Fri, D-312-853-5840 (O7+).

**FOOD SERVICE: Dining Hall:** Bldg 543, C-623-856-6420/7097, D-312-853-6420/7097. **Food Court:** Bldg 1540, C-623-935-4029. **NCO/CPO Club:** Bldg 161, C-623-856-7136. **O Club:** Bldg 750, C-623-856-6446. **Snack Vending:** Bldg 453, 0600-2100 M-F; 0700-1600 Sat/Sun; closed on Holidays C-623-269-5879. Many support services on and off base.

**TRANSPORTATION: Air Tickets:** SATO, Bldg 1150, Hours: 0730-1630 Mon-Fri, C-602-856-6891. **On Base Car Rental:** Enterprise, C-623-856-5005. **On Base Taxi (Gov):** Bldg 330, C-623-856-6866, other hours C-623-856-3702. **Parking:** Bldg 453, C-623-856-7131, D-312-853-7131. Limited parking; no overnight parking at Bldg 453.

**TML:** Fighter Country Inn, Bldg 660, 7012 N, Bong Lane, C-623-935-2641, D-312-896-3941, Fax: C-623-856-3332, 24 hours daily. DV/VIP C-623-856-5840.

**TRAVELERS AID: Chaplain:** Bldg 799, C-623-856-6211. **Medical:** Bldg 1130, Hours: 24 hours daily, C-623-856-7506, D-312-896-7506. **Red Cross:** Bldg 1150, C-623-856-7823. **Security Police:** Bldg 179, C-623-856-6322.

**SUPPORT AVAILABLE: Bank/Currency Exchange:** Armed Forces Bank, C-623-535-9766, across from main gate. **Credit Union:** Luke Federal Credit Union, C-623-631-3200, adjacent to main exchange. **Exchange:** Bldg 1540, C-623-935-2671, D-312-896-2671. **Hair Styles:** Bldg 1540; Barber, C-623-935-3466; Beauty, C-623-935-5850. **Laundry/Dry Cleaning:** Bldg 1540, C-623-935-9554. **Postal Service:** Bldg 550, C-623-935-1343.

**ATTRACTIONS:** Colorful Scottsdale nearby, fairgrounds and coliseum in Phoenix (state capital), Arizona State University in Tempe, Sun City - largest retirement center in the world.

### EN ROUTE SCHEDULES

| AIRPORT/STATION | LI-MISSION (page #) |
|---|---|
| Travis AFB | SUU-456/MEDEVAC (13) |

### UNSCHEDULED FLIGHTS

Flights to CONUS, OCONUS and foreign countries. Including flights to Travis AFB, CA (**SUU**); Yuma MCAS, AZ (**NYL**); Miramar MCAS, CA (**NKX**). Call for destinations, routings and schedules.

## SKY HARBOR INTERNATIONAL AIRPORT/PHOENIX AIR NATIONAL GUARD BASE (PHX/KPHX)

161st ARW/DO
3200 E. Old Tower Road
Phoenix, AZ 85034-7263

**LOCATION:** From I-10 in Phoenix, take the 24th street exit; go north one-quarter mile, turn east on Old Tower Road; follow Old Tower Road to the front gate of post. *USMRA: Page 108 (D-7). ML-ARM: (33°25'N/112°00'W).* LST: GMT-07:00. NMC: Phoenix, 5 miles northwest. Main installation numbers: C-602-302-9000, D-312-853-9000.

**REGISTRATION INFO: C-602-302-9162, D-312-853-9162, Rec: C-602-302-9058, D-312-853-9058, Fax: C-602-302-9411, D-312-853-9411.** Base Ops, Hours: 0630-1600 Mon-Thu.

**FOOD SERVICE:** Snack Vending available.

**TRANSPORTATION:** Local taxis available. All major car rental agencies available at airport.

**TML:** Nearest TML is at Luke AFB, Lodging Office, Bldg 660, 7012 N, Bong Lane, C-602-935-2644, 24 hours daily. DV/VIP C-623-856-5840.

**TRAVELERS AID: Security Police:** 24 hours daily, C-602-302-9133, D-312-853-9133.

**SUPPORT AVAILABLE:** Facilities of an IAP available. **SATO:** ANG Hq, Hours: 0730-1530 Mon-Fri, C-602-302-0774.

*Note: There are no meals, transportation or lodging available at this facility. Personnel must have adequate arrangements to leave the base as it is sometimes difficult to get a commercial taxi. The base is undergoing large amounts of construction and parking and will be very limited for the next two years.*

### UNSCHEDULED FLIGHTS

Space-A flights are available via KC-135E aircraft to CONUS and OCONUS locations. Call prior to arrival for flight info and specific directions.

## YUMA MARINE CORPS AIR STATION (YUM/KYUM)

Passenger Terminal
Bldg 151
Yuma MCAS, AZ 85369-5030

**LOCATION:** From I-8 east or west take exit #3 onto Avenue 3E south for one mile to base on right, adjacent to Yuma IAP. *USMRA: Page 108 (A-8). ML-ARM: (32°39'N/114°36'W).* LST: GMT-07:00. NMC: Yuma, 3 miles northwest. Main installation numbers: C-928-269-2011, D-312-269-2011.

**REGISTRATION INFO: C-520-269-2729, D-312-269-2729, Fax: C-520-269-3667, D-312-269-3667. Fax: C-520-341-3667, D-312-951-3667.** Bldg 151, Hours: 0730-1630 Mon-Fri, weekends as needed. Directions: From main gate straight on Quitter Street to a right on O'Neill Street. Pax Term is on the left. **Pax Service Office:** Bldg 151, Hours: 0730-1630 Mon-Fri, weekends as needed, C-520-341-2729. NCO on duty. **Pax Paging:** Bldg 151, Hours: 0700-1530 Mon-Fri, C-520-341-2729.

**PAX LOUNGES:** No family lounges. **GENERAL:** Bldg 151, Hours: 0600-1530 Mon-Fri, weekends as needed, C-520-341-2729. A/C, bag check, restrooms, P/C seats, telephones. **DV/VIP:** Bldg 151, Hours: 0600-1530 daily, C-520-341-2729. A/C, bag check, restrooms, P/C seats, telephones. **Protocol Service:** Bldg 980, Hours: 0600-1530 Mon-Fri, C-520-341-2252, D-312-951-2252.

**FOOD SERVICE: Cafeteria:** C-520-341-5183. **Enlisted Club:** C-520-341-2457. **Fast Food:** Burger King, C-520-341-0490. **O Club:** C-520-341-2711. **Restaurants:** Deli, C-520-725-5706; Godfather's Pizza, C-520-341-0150. **Snack Bars:** Bowling Alley, C-520-726-8320. **Snack Vending:** C-520-341-2294/5.

**TRANSPORTATION:** None on base. **Air Tickets:** C-520-341-2755. Major airline counters. **Car Rentals:** Enterprise, C-520-344-5444, Avis, C-520-344-5770. Additional car rental companies at Yuma IAP. **Taxi (Comm):** Yuma IAP, 24 hours daily, C-520-782-0111.

**TML:** Lodging Office, Bldg 1088, Martini Avenue, C-928-269-2262, D-312-269-2262, Fax: C-928-269-6639, 24 hours daily.

**TRAVELERS AID: Chaplain:** C-520-341-2371. **Emergency Relief:** C-520-341-2373/4 (Navy Relief). **Medical:** Bldg 1175, 24 hours daily, C-520-341-2772. **Red Cross:** C-520-341-2427. **Security Police:** Bldg 950, C-520-341-2205/2361.

**SUPPORT AVAILABLE: Bank/Currency Exchange:** First Interstate, C-520-343-7840. **Exchange:** C-520-341-2256. **Hair Styles:** Barber, C-520-341-2364; Beauty, C-520-341-2364. **Laundry/Dry Cleaning:** C-520-341-2356. **Postal Service:** C-520-341-2033. **Wire:** C-520-341-3567.

**ATTRACTIONS:** Desert climate, greyhound racing, major league baseball training, Territorial Prison, Yuma Crossing State Park.

### UNSCHEDULED FLIGHTS

Flights to: Beaufort MCAS, SC (**NBC**); Cherry Point MCAS, NC (**NKT**); El Toro MCAS, CA (**NZJ**) (weekly); Fallon NAS, NV (**NFL**); North Island NAS, CA (**NZY**); and other locations as needed. Call for destinations, routings, and schedules.

# ARKANSAS

## LITTLE ROCK AIR FORCE BASE (LRF/KLRF)

314th TRNS/LGTAP
3911 Ave B, B-430
Little Rock AFB, AR 72099-5000

**LOCATION:** From I-40 take exit #55 north on US-67/167 to Jacksonville, take exit #11 west to Vandenberg Blvd. Follow signs to main gate west of US-67/167. *USMRA: Page 76 (D,E-5). ML-ARM: (34°52'N/92°06'W).* LST: GMT-06:00. NMC: Little Rock, 18 miles southwest. Main installation numbers: C-501-987-1110, D-312-731-1110.

**REGISTRATION INFO: C-501-987-3342/3933, D-312-731-3342/3933, Rec: C-501-987-3684, D-312-731-3684, Fax: C-501-987-6726, D-312-731-6726.** Recording after hours. Bldg 430, Hours: 0730-1630 daily. Directions: Main gate on Vandenberg Blvd for 1.2 miles to a left on 3rd Street for a block to Thomas Ave. Pax Term located at the corner of Thomas and 3rd Streets. **Pax Service Office:** Bldg 430, Hours: 0730-1630 Mon-Fri, C-501-987-3933/3342, D-312-731-3933/3342.

**PAX LOUNGES:** Bldg 430. General lounge restricted to passengers awaiting processing. Lobby, A/C, couch, restrooms, TV. **DV/VIP:** Bldg 920, 24 hours daily, C-501-987-6123. A/C, restrooms, O/S seats.

**FOOD SERVICE: Dining Hall:** Bldg 864, Hours: 0530-1800 daily, C-501-987-6268/3427. **Enlisted Club:** Bldg 1080. Hours: 1000-2200 Sun, Tue-Thu, 1030-2300 Fri-Sat (closed Monday), C-501-987-4121. **O Club:** Bldg 1030, Hours: 1000-2200 Mon-Sat, 1000-1400 Sun, C-501-987-1111. **Snack Bars:** Bowling Alley, Bldg 956, Hours: 0900-2200 Sun-Thu, 0900-2400 Fri-Sat, C-501-987-3338; Champs Snack Bar, Bldg 868, Hours: 1100-2200 Mon-Fri, 1200-2400 Sat, 1200-2200 Sun, C-501-987-3908.

**TRANSPORTATION: Air Tickets:** SATO, Bldg 1255, Hours: 0730-1630 Mon-Fri, C-501-987-4117. **Car Rentals:** No car rentals on base. **Off Base Taxi (Comm):** 24 hours daily; Jacksonville Taxi Co, C-501-982-1500; Black and White, C-501-374-0333. $25+ to Little Rock. **On Base Taxi (Gov):** Bldg 551, 24 hours daily, C-501-987-6086 (duty passengers only). **Worldwide Travel:** C-501-982-7551. **Parking:** Bldg 430, 24 hours daily, short-term terminal; long term-contact Security Police, C-501-987-3221, or use unsecured long-term at Bldg 430.

**TML:** Bldg 1024, Cannon Circle, C-501-987-6652, D-312-731-6652, Fax: C-501-987-7769, D-312-731-7769, 24 hours daily. DV/VIP Bldg 1036, O6+, C-501-987-6828/8457.

**RVC:** FAMCAMP, Recreation Services, 1255 Vandenberg, Check-in FAMCAMP, C-501-987-3365, D-312-731-3365, Fax: C-501-987-6164, D-312-731-6164.

**TRAVELERS AID: Chaplain:** Bldg 950, Hours: 0730-1630 Mon-Fri, C-501-987-6014, after hours, call the operator. **Lost/Found:** Bldg 430, Hours: 0730-1630 daily, C-501-988-3933. **Medical/Dental:** Base Hospital, Hours: 0730-2000 daily, C-501-987-8811. **Red Cross:** Bldg 840, Hours: 0730-1630 Mon-Fri, C-501-987-3249, after hours, call the operator. **Security Police:** Bldg 480, 24 hours daily, C-501-987-3221.

**SUPPORT AVAILABLE: Bank/Currency Exchange:** Bldg 970, Hours: 0900-1600 Mon-Thu, 0900-1800 Fri, C-501-982-4521. **Exchange:** Bldg 940, Hours: 0900-2100 Mon-Sat, 1100-1800 Sun, C-501-988-1150. **Hair Styles:** Bldg 959, Hours: 1000-1800 Mon-Fri, 1000-1700 Sat-Sun, C-501-987-1150. **Laundry/Dry Cleaning:** Bldg 959, Hours: 0700-1800 daily, C-501-987-1150. **Postal Service:** Bldg 966, Hours: 0900-1630 Mon-Fri, 0830-1200 Sat, C-501-987-3695.

**ATTRACTIONS:** Little Rock, Governor's Mansion, Arkansas River, Ozark Mountains, Burns Park, Hot Springs and Lake Conway.

**OTHER INFORMATION:** All flights are unscheduled now except for Medevac.

### EN ROUTE SCHEDULES

| AIRPORT/STATION | LI-MISSION (page #) |
| --- | --- |
| Scott AFB | BLV-C-652/MEDEVAC (30) |

### UNSCHEDULED FLIGHTS

Flights via C-130H to CONUS and OCONUS locations, call for destinations, routings, and schedules.

# CALIFORNIA

## BEALE AIR FORCE BASE (BAB/KBAB)

9th TRNS/LGTR
19501 Edison Ave, Room 629
Beale AFB, CA 95903-1615

**LOCATION:** From CA-70 north or south, take Feather River Blvd. exit east (south of Marysville), follow to North Beale Road, take right (east), (follow signs to Beale), continue for 7 miles until road dead ends at main gate of AFB. *USMRA: Page 110 (C,D-5,6). ML-ARM: (39°05'N/121°21'W).* LST: GMT-08:00. NMC: Sacramento, 40 miles southwest. Main installation numbers: C-530-634-3000, D-312-368-1110.

**REGISTRATION INFO: C-530-634-2569/0403, D-312-368-2569/0403, Rec: C-530-634-2567, D-312-368-2567, Fax: C-530-634-2571, D-312-368-2571.** Bldg 1062, Hours: 0700-1600 Mon-Fri. Directions: 1 block north of ATC tower. Main gate: Beale Road to left on J Street, to left on Doolittle Drive to Base ops on left. **Pax Service Office:** C-530-634-2002/8388, D-312-368-2002/8388. **Pax Paging:** C-530-634-2002/8388, D-312-368-2002/8388.

**PAX LOUNGES:** Bldg 1062, Hours: 0700-1600 Mon-Fri, C-530-634-8387, D-312-368-8387. Bag check, telephones (commercial and defense), TV, restrooms. **Protocol Service:** Bldg 1086, Hours: 0730-1630 Mon-Fri, C-530-634-2564, D-312-368-2564.

**FOOD SERVICE: NCO/CPO Club:** Bldg 5800, C-530-788-0286 (Also EM Club). **O Club:** Bldg 2340, C-530-788-0292. **Snack Bars:** Bldg 1060, C-530-788-1550.

**TRANSPORTATION:** None. POV desirable. **Air Tickets:** SATO, Bldg 2432, C-530-634-2940. **On Base Bus/Shuttle:** Bldg 1060 (across street from Pax Term), C-530-634-2543. **Off Base Taxi (Comm):** Marysville, C-530-743-4661. **On Base Taxi (Gov):** Bldg 2491, C-530-634-2543. **Parking:** Bldg 1060, short and long term, adjacent to Term, C-530-634-8387.

**TML:** Gold Country Inn, 5786 A Street, C-530-634-2953/4, D-312-368-2953/4, Fax: C-530-634-3674, D-312-368-3674, 24 hours. DV/VIP Protocol Office, O6+, retirees, C-530-634-2120.

**TRAVELERS AID: Chaplain:** Bldg 5700, C-530-634-2306, after duty hours call Operator. **Lost/Found:** Bldg 1062, C-530-634-8387. **Medical:** Bldg 5700, 24 hours daily, C-530-634-4444/2333 (Emergency). **Red Cross:** Bldg 2179, C-530-634-2078, after duty hours, call Operator. **Security Police:** Bldg 2440, C-530-634-2131.

**SUPPORT AVAILABLE: Bank/Currency Exchange:** Bldg 2433, C-530-634-2251. **Exchange:** Bldg 2434, C-530-788-0221. **Hair Styles:** Bldg 2434, C-530-788-0053. **Laundry/Dry Cleaning:** Bldg 2434, C-530-788-0192. **Postal Service:** Bldg 2483, C-530-634-2766.

**ATTRACTIONS:** Sutter's Fort, Zoo, Old Sacramento (rebuilding Chinatown).

**UNSCHEDULED FLIGHTS**

Very infrequent flights to CONUS and OCONUS locations via KC-135E aircraft. Call for destinations, routings and schedules.

# CHANNEL ISLANDS AIR NATIONAL GUARD STATION (NTD/KNTD)

4146 Navalair Road
Port Hueneme, CA 93041-4002

**LOCATION:** From US-101 north or south to Camarillo, go south on South Las Posas Road to East Port Hueneme Road past CA-1, then left (southeast) on Navalair Road. ANG Station entrance is 200 yards on right (southwest) side of road. *USMRA: Page 111 (D,E-13). ML-ARM: (34°08'N/119°10'W).* LST: GMT-08:00. NMC: Oxnard, 1 mile south. NMI: Point Mugu NAS, adjacent. Main installation numbers: C-805-986-8000, D-312-893-7000.

**REGISTRATION INFO: C-805-986-7577, D-312-893-7577.** Base Ops, Bldg 106, Hours: 0700-2000 Tue-Fri.

**PAX LOUNGES:** Limited lounge facilities. For other services, see Point Mugu NAS.

**TML:** Nearest TML is Bldg 36, Point Mugu NAS, Missle Inn, Venture Country Naval Base, C-805-989-8251, D-312-351-8251, Fax: C-805-939-7470, D-312-351-7570, Mon-Thu, 0730-1630 hrs. DV/VIP C-805-989-8672, Fax: C-805-989-7470.

**ATTRACTIONS:** Beaches, Los Angeles, Disneyland within three hour drive.

**UNSCHEDULED FLIGHTS**

Frequent flights via C-130H to Davis-Monthan AFB, AZ (**DMA**); Kelly AFB, TX (**SKF**); Patrick AFB, FL (**COF**). Call for destinations, routings, and schedules.

# CHINA LAKE NAVAL AIR WEAPONS STATION (NID/KNID)

1 Administration Circle
Code 50000D
China Lake, CA 93555-6100

**LOCATION:** From north or south on US-395 or CA-14, go east on CA-178 to Ridgecrest to the main gate on Inyokern Road. *USMRA: Page 111 (G-10,11,12 and H-11). ML-ARM: (35°39'N/117°40'W).* LST: GMT-08:00. NMC: Los Angeles, 130 miles southwest. NMI: Fort Irwin, 70 miles south. Main installation numbers: C-760-939-9011, D-312-437-9011.

**REGISTRATION INFO: C-760-939-5301/5282, D-312-437-5308/5267, Fax: C-760-939-0320.** Bldg 20002, Hours: 0630-2200 Mon-Fri, 0730-1600 Sat-Sun, (only if flight ops are open, otherwise secured during non-flight ops hours). **Pax Service Office:** Bldg 20002, Hours: 0700-1600 Mon-Fri, C-760-939-5301/5282, D-312-437-5308/5267. General and DV/VIP lounge available.

**FOOD SERVICE: Cafeteria:** Hours: 0700-1800, 500 yards. Snack Vending available in terminal.

**TRANSPORTATION: On Base Taxi:** C-760-939-2280.

**TML:** China Lake Inn, Bldg 1395, C-760-939-3146/2383, D-312-437-3146/2383, Fax: C-760-939-2789, 24 hours daily. DV/VIP Bldg 02243, O6+, C-760-939-1364, D-312-437-1364, Fax: C-760-939-3152.

**SUPPORT AVAILABLE: Convenience Store:** Hours: 0900-2000, 5 miles. **Credit Union:** Hours: 1000-1730, 5 miles away. **Exchange:** Hours: 1000-1800, 5 miles away

**TRAVELERS AID: Chaplain:** 5 miles away. **Medical/Dental:** Hours: 0700-1700, C-760-939-8000, D-312-437-8000, 5 miles away. **Security Police:** 24 hours daily, C-760-939-3324, D-312-437-3324, 5 miles away.

**UNSCHEDULED FLIGHTS**

Daily flights to Point Mugu NAS, CA (**NTD**). Unscheduled flights to civilian and military locations in CA, NM, NV and AZ. Limited Space-A opportunity. Call for destinations, routings, and schedules.

# EL CENTRO NAVAL AIR FACILITY (NJK/KNJK)

Bldg 519
El Centro, CA 92243-5001

**LOCATION:** From east or west on I-8, two miles west of El Centro, to Forrester Road (S-30) exit, north one and a half miles to Evan Hewes Highway (S-80) left (west) for four miles, right on Bennet Road to main gate. *USMRA: Page 111 (H-15,16). ML-ARM: (32°47'N/115°33'W).* LST: GMT-08:00. NMC: El Centro, 7 miles east. Main installation numbers: C-760-339-2524, D-312-958-4935/4918.

**REGISTRATION INFO: C-760-339-2426/2524, D-312-958-2426/2524.** Bldg 519, Hours: 0700-2300 Mon-Fri, 0700-1800 Sat.

**FOOD SERVICE:** Dining, Bldg 227, C-760-339-2351, D-312-958-2351.

**TML:** Bldg 401, 24 hours daily, C-760-312-6000/6020, D-312-958-4918, Fax: C-760-337-4936, D-312-958-4936. Navy Lodge: C-760-339-2342, D-312-958-8341, Fax: C-760-352-4914. DV/VIP C-760-339-8535, Fax: C-760-353-1492.

**RVC:** MWR, Bldg 318, 0800-1630 hours Mon-Fri, Camp Host located at Space-43, Check-in Rec Equip Rental Bldg 318, C-760-339-2486, D-312-958-8481.

**SUPPORT AVAILABLE:** Pax lounge and full base support facilities.

**ATTRACTIONS:** Winter home (January-March) of the Navy's Blue Angels. Imperial Valley, near Mexico.

**UNSCHEDULED FLIGHTS**

Operations/air opportunities are largely from transient squadrons. Call for destinations, routings and schedules.

# LEMOORE NAVAL AIR STATION (NLC/KNLC)

Passenger Terminal
700 Avenger Ave
Lemoore NAS, CA 93246-5001

**LOCATION:** In south central part of state. From north or south on I-5, exit onto CA-198 east for approximately 24 miles to main gate on north (left) side of highway. Or, from north or south on CA-99, exit onto CA-198 west for approximately 27 miles to main gate on right (north) side of CA-198. *USMRA: Page 111 (D-10). ML-ARM: (36°33'N/119°95'W).* LST: GMT-08:00. NMC: Fresno, 40 miles north/northeast. Main installation numbers: C-559-998-5791, D-312-949-1110.

**REGISTRATION INFO: C-559-998-1680/1, D-312-884-1680/1, Fax: C-559-998-3046, D-312-884-3046.** Bldg 180, Hours: 0800-2400 daily. Directions: From main gate straight on Enterprise Ave, left on Franklin Ave for 5 miles to Ops area and Pax Term on right. **Pax Service Office:** C-559-998-1680/1/3, D-312-949-1680/1/3. **Pax Paging:** C-559-998-1680/1/3, D-312-949-1680/1/3.

**PAX LOUNGES:** Limited lounge space. No family lounge. **General:** Bldg 180, 24 hours daily, C-559-998-1680. Only for scheduled flights originating at NLC. A/C, P/C seats, pay commercial telephones. **Protocol Service:** Hangar 1, Hours: 0800-1700 Mon-Fri, C-559-998-3360, (O6+).

**FOOD SERVICE: Cafeteria:** C-559-998-3084, **Enlisted Club:** Bldg 920, C-559-998-3331. **In-flight Meals:** C-559-998-3236. **NCO/CPO Club:** C-559-998-3130. **O Club:** C-559-998-3550. **Snack Vending:** Bldg 184, 24 hours daily.

**TRANSPORTATION:** Limited on base. **Off Base Shuttle/Bus:** C-559-998-4196. **Off Base Taxi (Comm):** At main gate.

**TML:** Bldg 852, Hancock Circle, 24 hours daily, C-559-997-7000/1, D-312-949-4609. Navy Lodge: C-559-998-5791. DV/VIP C-559-998-3344.

**RVC:** Outdoor Adventure Center, Bldg 951, C-559-997-8983, D-312-949-8983, Fax: C-559-998-4040, D-312-949-4040.

**TRAVELERS AID: Chaplain:** C-559-998-3496. **Medical:** 911 (Emergency). **Navy Relief:** C-559-998-4045. **Red Cross:** C-559-998-3388/584-5015. **Security Police:** C-559-998-3306, 24 hours daily, at main gate.

**SUPPORT AVAILABLE: Exchange:** C-559-998-3611 (ask for information).

**ATTRACTIONS:** Sequoia National Park, 70 miles east. Ski areas nearby.

### UNSCHEDULED FLIGHTS

Frequent flights to: China Lake NWC, CA (**NID**); Fallon NAS, NV (**NFL**); Miramar MCAS, CA (**NKX**); North Island NAS, CA (**NZY**) and Whidbey Island NAS, WA (**NUW**). Call for destinations, routings, and schedules.

# LOS ALAMITOS ARMY AIRFIELD (SLI/KSLI)

11200 Lexington Drive, Bldg 1
Armed Forces Reserve Center (AFRC)
Los Alamitos AAF, CA 90720-5001

**LOCATION:** From I-405 (San Diego Freeway) north or south, take exit to I-605 (San Gabriel River Freeway) north approximately 1.5 miles to exit east onto East Katella Avenue, then east 1.7 miles to right (south) on Lexington Drive and proceed to main gate. Clearly marked. *USMRA: Page 117 (E-6,7). ML-ARM: (33°47'N/118°05'W).* LST: GMT-08:00. NMC: Los Angeles, 5 miles north. Main installation numbers: C-562-795-2000, D-312-972-2000.

**REGISTRATION INFO: C-562-795-2571, D-312-972-2571 ask for passenger service, Fax: C-562-795-2566.** Base Ops, Hours: 0600-2200 Tue-Fri, 0600-1630 Sat-Mon. Directions: From Main Gate proceed to first stop sign, go right around half circle drive to second stop sign. Pax Terminal is at the base of the Control Tower. **Pax Service Office:** C-562-795-2571, D-312-972-2571. *Note: No services available at terminal. No ground transportation available at terminal.*

**TRANSPORTATION: Air Tickets:** Carlson Wagonlit Travel, C-562-430-4936. or 1-800-828-8712

**TML:** Bldg 19, 4745 Yorktown Avenue, 0800-1630 hours, C-562-795-2124, D-312-972-2124, Fax: C-562-795-2125.

**SUPPORT AVAILABLE: Exchange:** C-562-430-1076/77. Military Clothing Sales 562-795-2059

**ATTRACTIONS:** Los Angeles, Hollywood, Long Beach, Seal Beach, Disneyland, and Orange County.

### UNSCHEDULED FLIGHTS

Frequent flights to southwest CONUS area. Space-A best on Reserve drill weekends. Call for destinations, routings and schedules.

# LOS ANGELES INTERNATIONAL AIRPORT (LAX/KLAX)

Det 1, 60th APS/TRO
200 Worldway, Box 2
Los Angeles, CA 90045-5810

**LOCATION:** From north or south on I-405 take Century Boulevard exit west, then drive 1.5 miles west to Terminal 2. Or, from I-105 east or west, take Sepulveda Blvd. exit north, the continue north one mile to Century Blvd. and turn left (west) to airport. Clearly marked. *USMRA: Page 117 (B-5). ML-ARM: (33°56'N/118°24'W).* LST: GMT-08:00. NMC: Los Angeles (downtown), 17 miles northeast. NMI: Los Angeles Air Force Base (LAAFB), 3 miles south of LAX at 200 Douglas Street. Main installation numbers: C-310-363-1110, D-312-833-1110.

**REGISTRATION INFO: C-310-363-0714, D-312-833-0714, Rec: C-310-363-0716, D-312-833-0716, Fax: C-310-363-2790, D-312-833-2790. E-mail: spacealax@travis.af.mil WEB: www.travis.af.mil/space_a** The AMC ticket/processing counter is located at the Los Angeles International Airport, Terminal 2 on the departure level. Hours: 0730-1600 daily, closed on holidays, located in terminal 2. **Pax Paging:** C-310-363-0714/0715/0716, D-312-833-0714/0715/0716. *Note: There is dual sign-up with Travis AFB, CA (SUU).*

**PAX LOUNGES:** No separate DV/VIP or family lounges. **General:** LAX Pax Term, 24 hours daily. All IAP facilities available. **Protocol Service:** Hours: 0730-2230 daily, C-310-363-2030, D-312-833-2030 (see passenger NCO). Also, a USO is located in terminal 4, lower level, C-310-642-0188, hours vary.

**FOOD SERVICE:** At LAX, Los Angeles AFB and off base. **Cafeteria:** Terms 1-7, Hours: 0600-2400 daily (these hours will vary by terminal), C-310-363-0715, see Pax Service for assistance. **Restaurants:** The Club, LAAFB Area A, Bldg 120, Hours: 0600-2000 daily, C-310-363-2230. **Snack Vending:** Terminal 4, 24 hours daily.

**TRANSPORTATION:** Extensive facilities and means at LAX and LAAFB. **Air Tickets:** SATO, LAAFB Area B, Bldg 243, Hours: 0800-1600 Mon-Fri, C-310-363-1130. **Off Base Bus Service (Comm):** City Bus, RTD, C-310-626-4455; Greyhound, C-310-620-1200. **Car Rentals:** Ajax, C-1-800-367-2529; Avis, C-310-646-5600; Budget, C-310-645-4500; Hertz, C-310-646-4861; Thrifty, C-310-645-1880; Tropical, C-310-216-9130. **Limo Service:** Airport Express, C-310-679-5603, 24 hours daily; Airport Limo Service, C-310-645-4346. **Taxi (Comm):** Airport Taxi Service, C-310-837-7252; A-1 Cab, C-310-222-1234; United Independent, C-310-653-5050; Red Top, C-310-822-4100. **Trains:** Los Angeles, AMTRAK, C-310-624-0171. **Parking:** As of 1 Jan 2001 long term parking at LAAFB has been discontinued. Only those assigned to LAAFB are exempt; all others must use commercial parking lots.

**TML:** Nearest TML located at Fort MacArthur Inn, Bldg 37, 2400 South Pacific Avenue, Los Angeles AFB, C-310-363-8296, D-312-833-8296.

**RVC:** FAMCAMP (Los Angeles AFB) 340 Challenger Way, Equip Rental Bldg 220, Check-in 0900-1500 hrs Mon-Fri, C-310-363-2081/2190, D-312-833-2081/2190.

**TRAVELERS AID: Chaplain:** LAAFB Bldg 219, duty hours, C-310-363-1956, after hours, C-310-363-0486. **Emergency Relief:** LAAFB Bldg 219, Hours: 0800-1600 Mon-Fri, C-310-363-1121 (Air Force Aid Society). **Lost/Found:** Terminal 4, Hours: daily 0730-2230, C-310-417-1603. **Medical:** LAAFB Bldg 200, Hours: 0700-1500 daily, C-310-363-0964, D-312-964. **Red Cross:** 100 Worldway, Room 330, Los Angeles, CA 90045,

C-310-646-2271. **Security Police:** LAAFB Bldg 241, 24 hours daily, C-310-363-2122/3 (Desk Sgt). **USO:** Terminal 4 (at American Airlines), hours vary, C-310-642-0188.

**SUPPORT AVAILABLE:** Most support services available at LAX or LAAFB. **Bank/Currency Exchange:** Pax Term, hours posted, check-cashing at LAAFB clubs and BX. **Exchange:** LAAFB Bldg 244, Hours: 1000-1730 Mon-Fri, 1000-1600 Sat-Sun, C-310-640-0129. **Hair Styles:** Unisex, BX at LAAFB Bldg 244, Hours: 0830-1730 Mon-Fri, C-310-640-0379. **Laundry/Dry Cleaning:** LAAFB Bldg 244, Hours: 0900-1700 Mon-Fri, 0900-1500 Sat, C-310-322-1333. **Postal Service/Wire:** LAX, Bradley International Terminal, USPS, Hours: 0800-1700 Mon-Fri. American Express, Hours: 0600-2100. **POV Shipment:** All State Auto Delivery, Inc., Hours: 0800-1700 Mon-Fri, C-310-678-5111.

**OTHER INFORMATION:** U.S. Customs Service Airport.

**ATTRACTIONS:** Disneyland, Universal Studios and City Walk, Magic Mountain, and Chinatown. Numerous attractions are available within the Los Angeles, Hollywood, and Orange County area.

*Note: Commercially contracted flights are now called Patriot Express.*

### LOS ANGELES IAP, CA (LAX); REGION: PAC; OPERATOR: COM; TYPE: PAX; ROUTE: 2W71B; SAMPLE SCHEDULE: MON; EQUIPMENT: MD011

{LAX *NW* ➡ SEA (★) *SW* ➡ OSN ⇌ OSN *S* ➡ DNA *NE* ➡ SEA (★)}

| LI/ICAO | AIRPORT/STATION | CTRY/STA | DAYS EN ROUTE |
|---|---|---|---|
| LAX/KLAX | Los Angeles IAP | CA | +0 |

| | | | |
|---|---|---|---|
| SEA/KSEA | Seattle/Tacoma IAP | WA | +0 |
| OSN/RKSO | Osan AB | KR | +1 |
| OSN/RKSO | Osan AB | KR | +1 |
| DNA/RODN | Kadena AB | JP | +1 |
| SEA/KSEA | Seattle/Tacoma IAP | WA | |

### LOS ANGELES IAP, CA (LAX); REGION: PAC; OPERATOR: COM; TYPE: PAX; ROUTE: 2W79A; SAMPLE SCHEDULE: FRI; EQUIPMENT: MD011

{LAX *NW* ➡ SEA (★) *SW* ➡ OKO ⇌ OKO *SW* ➡ DNA *NE* ➡ SEA (★) *SE* ➡ LAX}

| LI/ICAO | AIRPORT/STATION | CTRY/STA | DAYS EN ROUTE |
|---|---|---|---|
| LAX/KLAX | Los Angeles IAP | CA | +0 |
| SEA/KSEA | Seattle/Tacoma IAP | WA | +0 |
| OKO/RJTY | Yokota AB | JP | +1 |
| OKO/RJTY | Yokota AB | JP | +1 |
| DNA/RODN | Kadena AB | JP | +1 |
| SEA/KSEA | Seattle/Tacoma IAP | WA | +1 |
| LAX/KLAX | Los Angeles IAP | CA | |

### LOS ANGELES IAP, CA (LAX); REGION: PAC; OPERATOR: COM; TYPE: PAX; ROUTE: 2X87A; SAMPLE SCHEDULE: TUE; EQUIPMENT: L1011

{LAX *NW* ➡ SEA (★) *SW* ➡ OKO *SW* ➡ IWA *NE* ➡ MSJ ⇌ MSJ *NE* ➡ SEA *SE* ➡ LAX}

| LI/ICAO | AIRPORT/STATION | CTRY/STA | DAYS EN ROUTE |
|---|---|---|---|
| LAX/KLAX | Los Angeles IAP | CA | +0 |

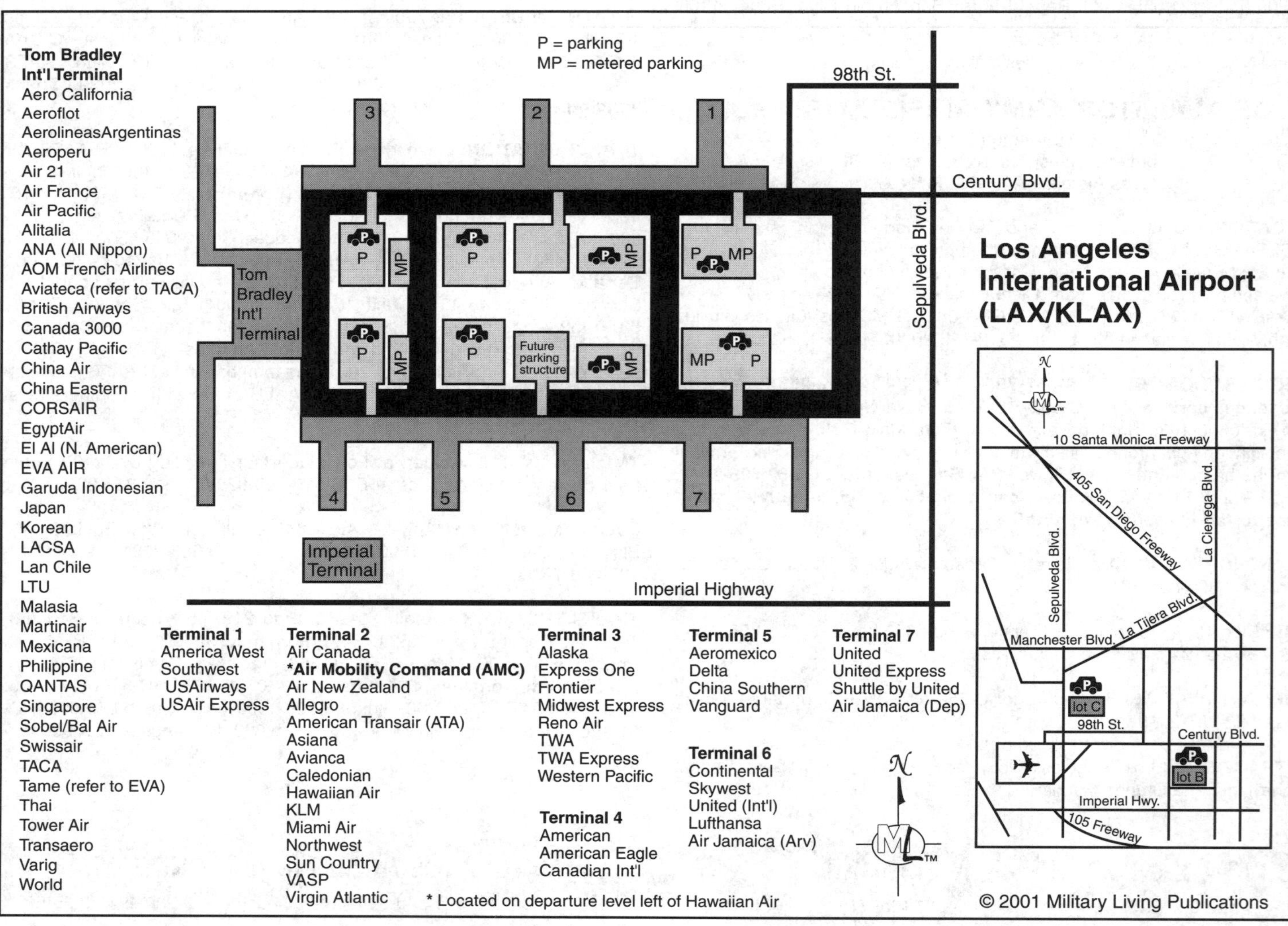

| | | | |
|---|---|---|---|
| SEA/KSEA | Seattle/Tacoma IAP | WA | +0 |
| OKO/RJTY | Yokota AB | JP | +1 |
| IWA/RJOI | Iwakuni MCAS | JP | +1 |
| MSJ/RJSM | Misawa AB | JP | +1 |
| MSJ/RJSM | Misawa AB | JP | +1 |
| SEA/KSEA | Seattle/Tacoma IAP | WA | +1 |
| LAX/KLAX | Los Angeles IAP | CA | |

# MARCH AIR RESERVE BASE (RIV/KRIV)

452nd Air Mobility Wing (AMW)
1141 Graeber Street, Suite 101
March ARB, CA 92518-2113

**LOCATION:** From north or south on I-215/CA-215 use March AFRB exit east onto Cactus Avenue. Continue east approximately 1.5 miles to traffic light at main gate on right (south) side of road. *USMRA: Page 111 (G-14). ML-ARM: (33°54'N/117°16'W).* LST: GMT-08:00. NMC: Riverside, 9 miles northwest. Main installation numbers: C-909-655-1110, D-312-947-1110.

**REGISTRATION INFO: C-909-655-2397, D-312-947-2397, Rec: C-909-655-2913, D-312-947-2913, Fax: C-909-655-3887, D-312-947-3887. E-mail: 452amw.apsf@riv.afrc.af.mil WEB: www.afrc.af.mil/march.** Bldg 265, Hours: 0730-1630 Mon-Fri and during flight processing. Directions: From West Gate, Ellsworth Street to left on Graeber Street to Base Ops on right. **Pax Service Office:** C-909-655-2397, D-312-947-2397.

**PAX LOUNGES:** Very limited lounge facilities. **General:** Bldg 265, Hours: 0730-1630 Tue-Sat and during flight processing, C-909-655-2913/4. Limit 25-40 people - most wait in snack bar next door. Restrooms, O/S seats. **Protocol Service:** Bldg 3403, Hours: 0800-1700 Mon-Fri, C-909-655-4520. **DV Lounge:** Bldg 1220, C-909-655-4401.

**FOOD SERVICE: All Ranks Club:** Bldg 110, Hours: 1100-2100 Tue-Sun, C-909-653-2121/655-4920. **Restaurants:** Hap Arnold Club, Hours: 1100-1300 Lunch, 1700-2030 Dinner, Tue-Sun; Backstreet Pizzeria, 1100-1300 Lunch, 1700-2000 Dinner daily. Fast Food is available just outside of the Main Gate.

**TRANSPORTATION:** No on base transportation. There are a limited number of UDI (you drive it) vehicles available for official business only, **Off Base Car Rental:** Alamo, C-1-800-327-9633; Budget, C-909-682-2610; Enterprise, C-909-486-8686 (pick up/drop off at terminal); Hertz, C-909-274-9380; Thrifty, C-909-243-7368. **Military Transportation:** C-909-655-3462. **Off Base Shuttle:** Airport Shuttle, C-909-626-6599 (all airports); Super Shuttle, C-909-467-9600 (all airports). **Off Base Taxi:** Yellow Cab, C-909-924-7172. **Parking:** Long term available across the street from the control tower. Contact the passenger terminal personnel for a parking permit. Parking up to 20 days is free. For storage in excess of 20 days, contact MWR at C-909-655-3128. If a parking permit is not obtained, the vehicle will be towed at the owner's expense.

**TML:** March Inn, 655 M Street, 24 hours daily, C-909-655-5241, Fax: C-909-655-4574, D-312-947-5241. DV/VIP O6+, C-909-655-3060.

**RVC:** FAMCAMP, Outdoor Rec Dept, Bldg 434, C-909-655-2816, D-312-947-2816, Fax: C-909-655-5221.

**TRAVELERS AID: Chaplain:** Bldg 468, Hours: 0800-1800 Mon-Fri, C-909-655-2715/2716. **Red Cross:** 8880 Magnolia Ave, Riverside, CA, Hours: 0800-1700 Mon-Fri, C-909-688-6440; after 1700 and on weekends, C-1-800-951-5600. **Security Police:** Bldg 317, 24 hours daily, C-909-655-2981. **USO:** LAX Terminal 4, 24 hours daily, C-909-642-0188.

**SUPPORT AVAILABLE: Exchange:** Bldg 758, Hours: 1000-1800 Mon-Sat, 1000-1700 Sun, C-909-653-2311. **Hair Styles:** Barber, Bldg 758, Hours: 0900-1630 Tue-Fri. **Laundry/Dry Cleaning:** Bldg 758, Hours: 1000-1630 Tue-Fri. **Postal Service/Wire:** Bldg 323, Hours: 0800-1500 Mon-Fri, C-909-655-3010.

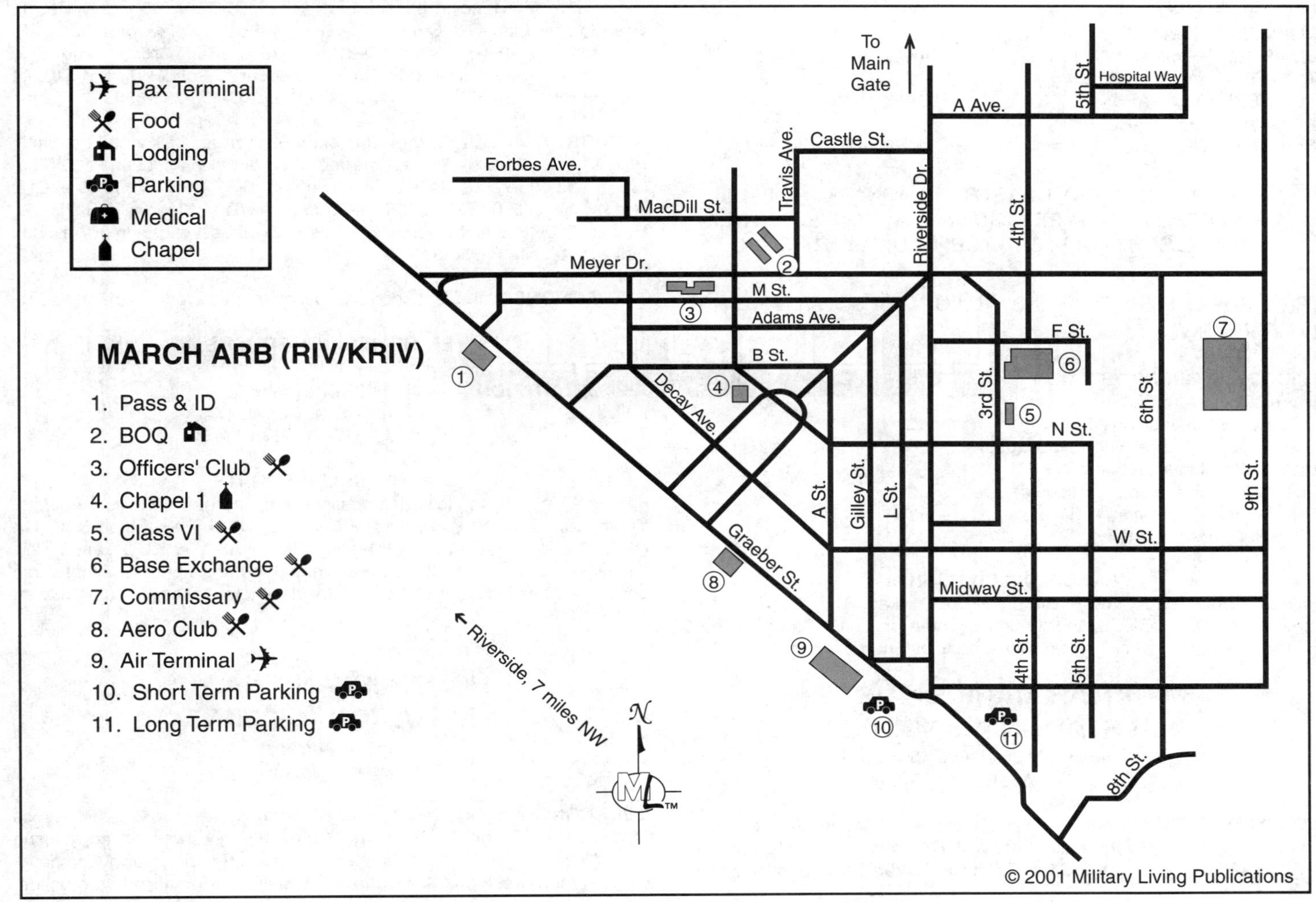

**OTHER INFORMATION:** U.S. Customs Service Airport.

**ATTRACTIONS:** Greater Los Angeles, Palm Springs resorts and golf courses.

### MARCH ARB, CA (RIV); REGION: PAC; OPERATOR: AMC; TYPE: MIXED; ROUTE: 5J43B; SAMPLE SCHEDULE: THU; EQUIPMENT: C141C

{RIV *NW* ➡ SUU (★) *SW* ➡ HIK *SW* ➡ KWA ⮀ KWA *NE* ➡ HIK *NE* ➡ SUU (★) *SE* ➡ RIV}

| LI/ICAO | AIRPORT/STATION | CTRY/STA | DAYS EN ROUTE |
|---|---|---|---|
| RIV/KRIV | March ARB | CA | +0 |
| SUU/KSUU | Travis AFB | CA | +0 |
| HIK/PHIK | Hickam AFB | HI | +1 |
| KWA/PKWA | Bucholz AAF/KMR (Kwajalein) | KA | +2 |
| KWA/PKWA | Bucholz AAF/KMR (Kwajalein) | KA | +2 |
| HIK/PHIK | Hickam AFB | HI | +3 |
| SUU/KSUU | Travis AFB | CA | +4 |
| RIV/KRIV | March ARB | CA | |

### MARCH ARB, CA (RIV); REGION: PAC; OPERATOR: AMC; TYPE:CGO W/ PAX; ROUTE: 9J97A/C; SAMPLE SCHEDULE: THU; EQUIPMENT: C141C

{RIV *NW* ➡ SUU *NW* ➡ TCM (★) *SE* EIL ⮀ EIL *S* ➡ EDF *NW* ➡ TCM (★) *SE* ➡ SUU *SE* ➡ RIV}

| LI/ICAO | AIRPORT/STATION | CTRY/STA | DAYS EN ROUTE |
|---|---|---|---|
| RIV/KRIV | March ARB | CA | +0 |
| SUU/KSUU | Travis AFB (✚) | CA | +1 |
| TCM/KTCM | McChord AFB | WA | +1 |
| EIL/PAEI | Eielson AFB | AK | +2 |
| EIL/PAEI | Eielson AFB | AK | +2 |
| EDF/PAED | Elmendorf AFB | AK | +2 |
| TCM/KTCM | McChord AFB | WA | +3 |
| SUU/KSUU | Travis AFB (✚) | CA | +3 |
| RIV/KRIV | March ARB | CA | |

Note: (✚) = MEDEVAC: SUU ➡ TCM ➡ EIL ➡ ED ➡ TCM ➡ SUU

### MARCH ARB, CA (RIV); REGION: PAC; OPERATOR: AMC; TYPE: CGO W/ PAX; ROUTE: 9JH1A; SAMPLE SCHEDULE: 3RD TUE; EQUIPMENT: C141C

{RIV *NE* ➡ CHS (★) *SW* ➡ UIO ⮀ UIO *NE* ➡ BOG *NW* ➡ CHS (★) *SW* ➡ RIV}

| LI/ICAO | AIRPORT/STATION | CTRY/STA | DAYS EN ROUTE |
|---|---|---|---|
| RIV/KRIV | March ARB | CA | +0 |
| CHS/KCHS | Charleston AFB/IAP | SC | +1 |
| UIO/SEQU | Mariscal Sucre Apt (Quito) | EC | +2 |
| UIO/SEQU | Mariscal Sucre Apt (Quito) | EC | +2 |
| BOG/SKBO | Eldorado IAP (Bogota) | CO | +2 |
| CHS/KCHS | Charleston AFB/IAP | SC | +3 |
| RIV/KRIV | March ARB | CA | |

### UNSCHEDULED FLIGHTS

Frequent flights on KC-135R and C-141B to Hickam AFB, HI (**HIK**). Also other CONUS, OCONUS and foreign country locations. Call after 1400 Friday for following week's destinations, routings and schedules.

## MIRAMAR MARINE CORPS AIR STATION (NKX/KNKX)

Operations Maintenance Division
Miramar MCAS, CA 92145-5399

**LOCATION:** From I-15 north of San Diego, take Miramar Way exit west which leads directly to the main gate. *USMRA: Page 118 (C,D-2,3,4; E,F-2,3). ML-ARM: (32°52'N/117°06'W).* LST: GMT-08:00. NMC: San Diego CA,

15 miles southwest. Main installation numbers: C-858-577-1011, D-312-267-1011.

**REGISTRATION INFO: C-858-577-4283/4284, D-312-267-4283/4284, Fax: C-858-577-4283, D-312-267-4283.** Bldg 476, Hours: Open 2 hours prior to scheduled departures. Directions: From main gate, straight on Miramar Way to left on Mitscher Way, right on Regulus Road and left at fork in road to front of Pax Term. **Pax Service Office:** C-858-577-4284, D-312-577-4284, NCO on duty. **Pax Paging:** C-858-577-4284, D-312-577-4284.

**PAX LOUNGES:** Limited facilities. No separate family lounge. **General:** Bldg 476, Hours: Open 2 hours prior to scheduled departures, restrooms, TV, and P/C seats. **DV/VIP:** Bldg K-211, Hours: 0700-2400 daily, C-858-577-4279, restrooms, TV, O/S seats. **Protocol Service:** Bldg 402, 24 hours daily, C-858-577-1657.

**FOOD SERVICE: Dining Hall:** Bldg M-305, C-858-577-7086. **Enlisted Club:** Bldg M-309, C-858-577-4821/20. **NCO/CPO Club:** Bldg M-309, C-858-577-4799. **O Club:** Bldg 472, C-858-577-4808. **Snack Bars:** Bldg K-211, C-858-695-7275 (Flight Line). **Snack Vending:** C-858-577-4808/4809.

**TRANSPORTATION:** Limited on base. No transportation from terminal except for taxi. **Air Tickets:** SATO, Bldg 524, Hours: 0800-1700 Mon-Fri, C-858-577-4396. **Off Base Bus (Comm):** Main gate, C-858-233-3004. **On Base Car Rentals:** Bldg 257, C-858-695-7549. **Off Base Limo Service:** San Diego, C-858-291-9002. **On Base Shuttle:** Bldg K-211, runs every 30 minutes, C-858-537-1142. **On Base Taxi:** Main gate, C-858-537-1142. **Parking:** Bldg K-211, C-858-537-4279, no restrictions.

**TML:** Bldg 4312, 19920 Schilt Avenue, 24 hours daily, C-858-577-4233/4235, D-312-267-4233/4235, Fax: C-858-577-4243, D-312-267-4243. Miramar Inn Bldg 2516, Newlin Lane, C-858-271-7111. DV/VIP O6+, C-858-537-1221.

**TRAVELERS AID: Chaplain:** Bldg 332, Hours: 0730-1600 daily, C-858-577-1333. **Emergency Relief:** Bldg 273, C-858-577-1807 (Navy Relief). **Lost/Found:** Bldg 476, C-858-577-4283. **Medical:** Bldg 495, Hours: 0730-1400 daily, C-858-577-4630, D-312-577-4630. **Red Cross:** Bldg 273, Hours: 0830-1800 daily, C-858-577-4107. **Security Police:** Bldg M-310, 24 hours daily, C-858-573-4059. **USO:** San Diego, C-858-235-6503.

**SUPPORT AVAILABLE: Bank/Currency Exchange:** California First Bank: Bldg 513, C-858-230-4717. **Exchange:** Bldg 660, Hours: 0900-2100 Mon-Fri, C-858-695-7200. **Hair Styles:** Barber, Bldg 600, C-858-695-7312; Beauty, Bldg 660, C-858-695-7227. **Laundry/Dry Cleaning:** Bldg 660, Hours: 0900-1800 daily, C-858-577-7238. **Postal Service:** Bldg 257, Hours: 0800-1530 daily, C-858-577-4578.

**ATTRACTIONS:** San Diego, beautiful beaches, Sea World, San Diego Zoo.

### EN ROUTE SCHEDULES

| AIRPORT/STATION | LI-MISSION (page #) |
|---|---|
| Kelly AFB | SKF-546/MEDEVAC (74) |
| Travis AFB | SUU-456/MEDEVAC (13) |

### UNSCHEDULED FLIGHTS

Frequent flights to the following destinations: Millington Municipal Apt/Mid-South NSA, TN (**NQA**); Pensacola NAS, FL (**NPA**); Point Mugu NAS, CA (**NTD**); Travis AFB, CA (**SUU**); Whidbey Island NAS, WA (**NUW**); and Willow Grove NAS/JRB, PA (**NXX**). Call Pax Term 1 to 3 days prior to flight for info on unscheduled flights and other Space-A information. C-009B aircraft stationed here.

## NORTH ISLAND NAVAL AIR STATION (NZY/KNZY)

Ops Air Terminal
San Diego, CA 92135-7035

**LOCATION:** From San Diego, take I-5 north or south to CA-75 across Coronado-San Diego Bay Bridge (toll) to CA-282 northwest directly to main gate. Also, take CA-75 north from Imperial Beach to downtown Coronado, then left (northwest) on CA-282 directly to main gate. Adjacent to Coronado.

*USMRA: Page 118 (B,C-6,7). ML-ARM: (32°41'N/117°0'W).* LST: GMT-08:00. NMC: San Diego, 4 miles northeast. Main installation numbers: C-619-545-1011, D-312-735-0444.

**REGISTRATION INFO: C-619-545-9567, D-312-735-9567, Rec: C-619-545-8278/8273, D-312-735-8278/8273, WEB: www.cnrswnavy.mil/airops/spacea.htm** Bldg 700, M-F 0600-2200 Sat, Sun: 0800-2200 hours. Directions: Main gate on McCain Blvd, left on Roosevelt Blvd to Pax Term on right. **Pax Service Office:** Bldg 700, 24 hours daily, C-619-545-9530. **Pax Paging:** Bldg 700, C-619-545-9530. D-312-735-9530.

**PAX LOUNGES:** No separate family lounge. **General:** Bldg 700, 24 hours daily, C-619-545-9567. A/C, bag check, restrooms, telephones, TV, O/S seats. **DV/VIP:** Bldg 516, 24 hours daily, C-619-545-8269, A/C, bag check, restrooms, local commercial and defense telephones, TV, O/S seats.

**Protocol Service:** Bldg 8, 24 hours daily, C-619-545-2017.

**FOOD SERVICE:** Bldg. 700. Navy Exchange Vending Machines **Dining Hall:** Bldg 794, C-619-545-7514. **Enlisted Club:** Bldg 417, C-619-545-2881 (Windjammer). **Fast Food:** McDonald's, C-619-435-0074 (on base). **NCO/CPO Club:** Bldg 864, C-619-545-7205. **O Club:** C-619-545-6945. **Restaurants:** Bldg 243, C-619-522-7267 (civilian cafe). **Snack Bars:** Bowling Alley, Bldg 772, C-619-545-7240. **Snack Vending:** Bldg 700, C-619-545-7438.

**TRANSPORTATION: Air Tickets:** Bldg 11, C-619-545-7199. **On Base Bus (Comm):** Bldg 700, C-619-233-3004. **On Base Shuttle/Bus:** Bldg 493, C-619-437-7731. **Off Base Taxi (Comm):** Coronado, C-619-435-6211. **Parking:** Bldg 700, (very limited), long term parking available.

**TML:** Bldg I, Officers, 24 hours daily, C-619-545-7545, D-312-735-7545; BEQ, C-619-545-9551, D-312-735-9551. Navy Lodge, Bldg 1402, 24 hours daily, C-619-435-0191, D-312-735-0191. DV/VIP, O6+, C-619-545-7545, Fax: C-619-545-9072.

**TRAVELERS AID: Chaplain:** Bldg 665, duty hours, C-619-545-8213. Other hours call OOD, C-619-545-8123. **Emergency Relief:** Bldg 607, C-619-437-7649 (Navy Relief Society). **Lost/Found:** Bldg 700, C-619-545-9530. **Medical:** Bldg 600, 24 hours daily, C-619-545-4263, D-312-735-4263; Ambulance, C-619-545-4380. **Red Cross:** Bldg 607, C-619-435-3195. **Security Police:** Main gate, C-619-545-9449. **USO:** 433 Harbor Dr, C-619-235-6503.

**SUPPORT AVAILABLE: Bank/Currency Exchange:** Bldg 318, C-619-435-5417/8 (Credit Union). **Exchange:** Bldg 483, C-619-522-7215. **Hair Styles:** Bldg 483, C-619-522-7272. **Laundry/Dry Cleaning:** Bldg 483, C-619-522-7231. **Postal Service:** Bldg 124, C-619-437-7698.

**ATTRACTIONS:** Beaches, Old San Diego, Sea World, Mexico nearby.

### UNSCHEDULED FLIGHTS

Frequent flights via C-009B and DC-009 aircraft to CONUS stations: Fallon NAS, NV (**NFL**); Lemoore NAS, CA (**NLC**); McChord AFB, WA (**TCM**); Whidbey Island NAS, WA (**NUW**). Call for destinations, routings and schedules.

## POINT MUGU NAVAL AIR STATION (NTD/KNTD)

Air Terminal, Code 85700E
11th Street, Bldg 339
Point Mugu, CA 93042-5000

**LOCATION:** Eight miles south of Oxnard and 40 miles north of Santa Monica on CA-1 (Pacific Coast Highway). From north or south on CA-1 take exit at Los Posas Road south onto Pacific Road directly to Gate 3 (Los Posas Gate). Take Frontage Road parallel to CA-1 northwest to Gate 1 and Main Gate (Gate 2). Or take exit onto Wood Drive southwest to Frontage Road and all three gates which will be on southwest (right) side of road. *USMRA: Page 111 (E-13). ML-ARM: (34°07'N/119°05'W).* LST: GMT-08:00. NMC: Los Angeles, 50 miles southeast. Main installation numbers: C-805-989-7209, D-312-351-7209.

**REGISTRATION INFO: NAVY: C-805-989-7731/7305, D-312-351-7731/7305, Fax: C-805-989-4085, D-312-351-4085.** Registration must e in person. Air Terminal, Hours: 0700-1700 Mon-Fri, closed every other Fri, Sat, Sun, and holidays. Reduced hours during Christmas and New Years. Enter gate 2, follow signs to Naval Air Station Air Terminal on 11th Street, Bldg 339. **Pax Service Office:** C-805-989-7731, D-312-351-7731. ***Note: In person sign up only.***

**PAX LOUNGES:** Limited lounge facilities. No DV/VIP lounge. **General:** Air Terminal, Hours: 0700-1700 Mon-Fri, C-805-989-7731. Bag check, rest-rooms, P/C seats. **Protocol Service:** Bldg 1, 24 hours daily, C-805-989-7209.

**FOOD SERVICE: CPO Club/Point Restaurant:** C-805-989-7517. **Restaurants:** Mugu's Pizza, C-805-989-8420/8714.

**TRANSPORTATION: Air Tickets:** Bldg 16, C-805-488-1084. **Shuttle/Bus:** Air Terminal, C-805-989-7406. **Car Rentals:** Avis, C-805-487-9429; Budget, C-805-483-2326. **Taxi (Comm):** C-805-483-2444. Commercial taxi only from NAWS. **Parking:** Security, C-805-989-7907.

**TML:** The Missile Inn, Bldg 27, C-805-989-8251, D-312-351-8251, Fax: C-805-989-7470, D-312-351-7470, Mon-Thu, 0730-1630 hrs. DV/VIP C-805-989-8672, Fax: C-805-989-7470.

**RVC:** MWR Dept, Bldg 774, 521 9th Street, Check-in Beach Motel, C-805-989-8407, D-312-351-8407, Fax: C-805-989-5413.

**TRAVELERS AID: Chaplain:** C-805-989-7967. **Emergency Relief:** C-805-989-8918 (Navy Relief). **Medical:** Dispensary, 24 hours daily, C-805-989-8815. **Red Cross:** Port Hueneme, C-805-989-4424. **Security Police:** Main gate, 24 hours daily, C-805-989-7907. **USO:** LAX IAP, Term 4, C-213-642-0188.

**SUPPORT AVAILABLE:** BX Complex has Hair Styles and Laundry/Dry Cleaning. **Bank/Currency Exchange:** Federal Credit Union: Mugu Road, C-805-989-8787. **Exchange:** BX Complex, C-805-989-7189. **Postal Service:** C-805-989-8707.

**ATTRACTIONS:** Beaches, Los Angeles, Disneyland within 3 hour drive.

### UNSCHEDULED FLIGHTS

Flights via P-003C and C-130 F/R aircraft to: Andrews AFB, MD (**ADW**); Kadena AB (Okinawa), JP (**DNA**); Rota NS, ES (**RTA**); Sigonella Airport, IT (**SIZ**); and Yokota AB, JP (**OKO**) via various contract aircraft. Call for destinations, routings and schedules.

## SAN DIEGO COAST GUARD AIR STATION (SAN/KSAN)

2710 N. Harbor Drive
San Diego, CA 92101-1079

**LOCATION:** From south on I-5, take exit south onto North Hawthorn Street which becomes N. Kettner Road. Continue southeast on N. Kettner Road to a right (west) on W. Laurel Street, which runs into N. Harbor Drive. Main entrance is approximately 0.1 mile on left (south) side of road. From north on I-5, exit west onto W. Hawthorn Street, continue southwest for 0.9 miles to right (northwest) on N. Harbor Drive for 1.1 miles to gate on left (south) side of road. Follow signs to Lindbergh Field. Ask for directions to the CG Hangar. *USMRA:Page 118 (C-6). ML-ARM: (32°43'N/117°10'W).* LST: GMT-08:00. NMC: San Diego, 2 miles east. Main installation numbers: C-619-683-6333.

**REGISTRATION INFO: C-619-557-6510, Fax: C-619-683-6338.** CG hangar, Hours: 0800-1600 Mon-Fri. Directions: East end of Lindbergh Field on Harbor Drive.

**TML:** Nearest TML at North Island Naval Air Station, Bldg I, Officers, 24 hours daily, C-619-545-7545, D-312-735-7545; BEQ, C-619-545-9551, D-312-735-9551. Navy Lodge, Bldg 1402, 24 hours daily, C-619-435-0191, D-312-735-0191. DV/VIP, O6+, C-619-545-8167, Fax: C-619-545-9072.

**SUPPORT AVAILABLE: Exchange:** C-619-557-6388. **Medical:** C-619-683-6380.

**ATTRACTIONS:** City of San Diego, Del Mar Racetrack, San Diego Zoo, Balboa Park, Sea World, Mission San Luis Rey.

### UNSCHEDULED FLIGHTS
Call for destinations, routings and schedules.

# TRAVIS AIR FORCE BASE (SUU/KSUU)
90 Ragsdale Street
Travis AFB, CA 94535-2941

**LOCATION:** Halfway between San Francisco and Sacramento, off I-80. From north or south on I-80 take Airbase Parkway exit east at Fairfield directly to main gate. Clearly marked. *USMRA: Page 110 (C-7). ML-ARM: (38°15'N/121°58'W).* LST: GMT-08:00. NMC: San Francisco, 45 miles southwest. Main installation numbers: C-707-424-1110, D-312-837-1110.

**REGISTRATION INFO: C-707-424-5703/5704, D-312-837-5703/5704, C-707-424-1854, D-312-837-1854 (updated 3 times daily), remote sign-up by Fax: C-707-424-2048/4021, D-312-837-2048/4021. E-mail: spacea@travis.af.mil**

**WEB: www.travis.af.mil/space_a** Bldg 3, 24 hours daily. Directions: From main gate take Travis Ave, turn right on Burgan Ave, Pax Term is 2.5 blocks on left, adjacent to control tower (Bldg 4). **Pax Paging:** C-1-800-787-2534, C-707-424-1854, D-312-837-1854. ***Note: There is dual sign-up with Los Angeles IAP, CA (LAX).***

**PAX LOUNGES: General:** Bldg 3, 24 hours daily, C-707-424-1854, D-312-837-1854. No smoking in terminal. Showers, free TV, bag check/lockers, restrooms. **DV/VIP:** Between Bldgs 3 and 4, Hours: 0600-2200 daily, C-707-424-3185, D-312-837-3185, O6+. Door locked all of the time. Request Passenger Service Supervisor for access. A/C, O/S seats, showers, restrooms, TV. **Family:** Bldg 3 (USO), Hours: 0800-2100 daily, C-707-424-3316, D-312-837-3316. A/C, O/S seats, crib room (24 hours daily), game rooms, restrooms, TV.

**FOOD SERVICE: Base Exchange Food Court:** Hours: 1030-2000 daily. **Cafeteria:** Bldg 3, open 24 hours. **Combined Club:** (Delta Breeze) Bldg 400, Hours: 1100-1700 Tue-Sun, closed Mon, C-707-424-5071/3711. **Dining Hall:** Bldg 1301, Hours: 0600-1830 Mon-Sat, 4th meal: 2300-0100 Mon-Fri, C-707-424-0906 (no retirees). **Fast Food:** Burger King, Bldg 685, Hours: 0630-2200 Mon-Sat, 0800-2130 Sun. **Snack Bars:** Bowling Alley, Bldg 214, Hours: 0800-2300 Mon-Sat, 0800-2200 Sun. **Snack Vending:** Bldg 3, 24 hours daily, C-707-437-4655.

**TRANSPORTATION: Air Tickets:** TMO, Bldg 3, Hours: 0730-1700 Mon-Fri; N&N Travel, C-707-437-7380, Hours: 0700-1700 Mon-Fri. **Car Rentals:** Budget, C-707-437-3366; Enterprise, C-707-425-5500; Rent-A-Wreck, C-707-422-9853; Thrifty, C-707-426-6000. **On Base Taxi (Comm):** Bldg 3, 24 hours daily, C-707-422-5555, C-707-446-1144, C-707-449-8294 (outside customs area). **Van Service (Comm):** Legacy Trans, C-707-449-3650; M&M Luxury, C-1-800-286-0303; Solano, C-1-800-304-2254 (to SanFrancisco/Oakland Airport and Bay Area). **Parking:** Short term available in front of Bldg 3 (2 hour limit); long

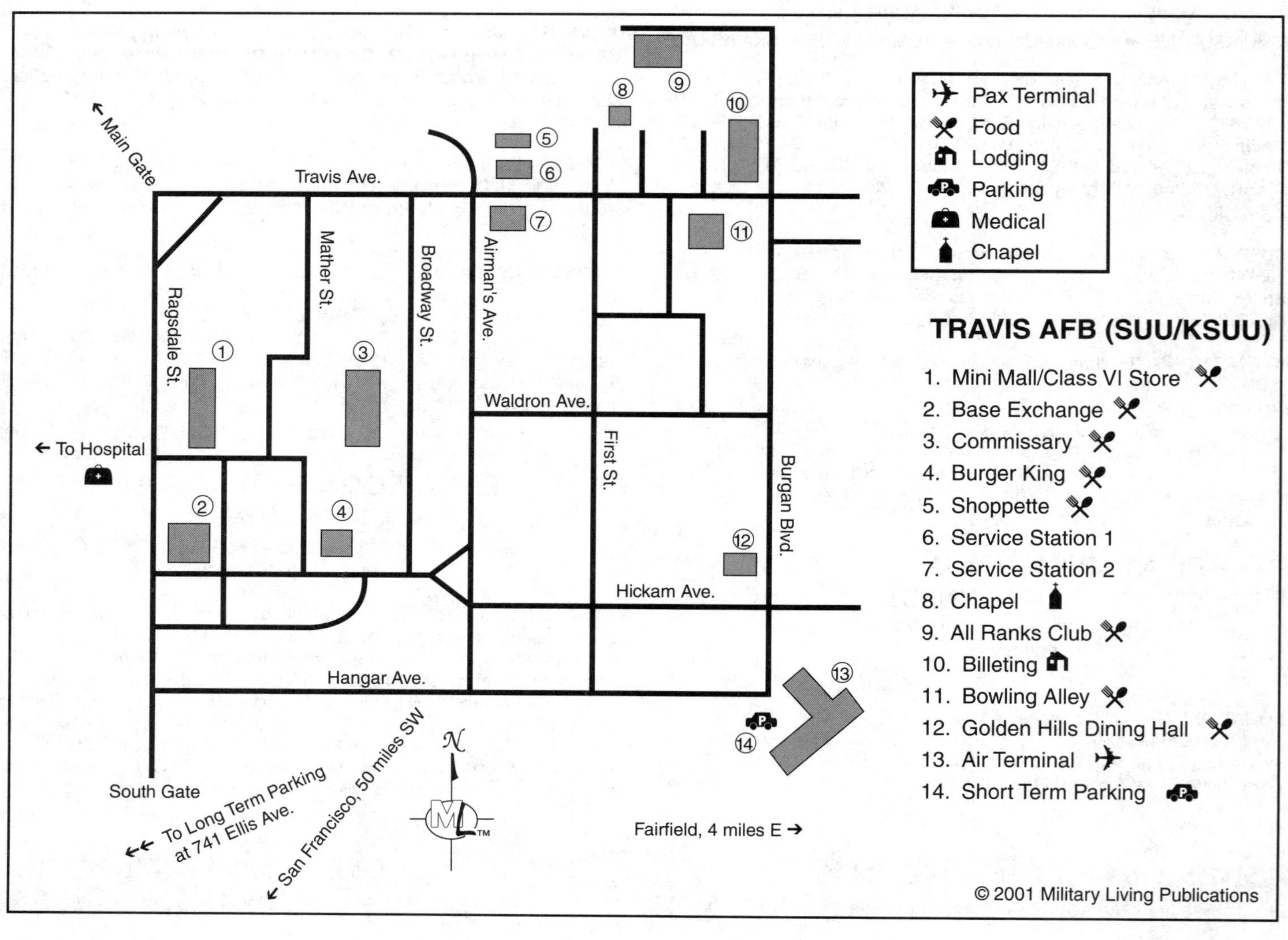

term parking ($7 a week automobiles, $9 a week RVs) available through Outdoor Rec, Bldg 863, Ellis Avenue. C-707-424-5659, D-312-837-5659.

**TML:** Bldg 404, 520 Sevedge Drive, 24 hours daily, C-707-437-0700, D-312-837-2987. Fax: C-707-424-5489, D-312-837-5489. DV/VIP C-707-424-3185, D-312-837-3185.

**RVC:** FAMCAMP, 273 Ellis St, Check-in FAMCAMP, 0830-1030 & 1530-1700 hours Mon-Fri, C-707-424-3583, D-312-837-3583, Fax: C-707-424-3583, D-312-837-3583.

**TRAVELERS AID: Chaplain:** Bldg 7766, Hours: 0730-1630, C-707-424-3217, after hours C-707-424-3293. **Emergency Relief:** Bldg 112, C-707-424-4349 (Air Force Aid Society). **Lost/Found:** Bldg 3, Hours: 0800-1700 Mon-Fri, C-707-424-5703/4, weekends/holidays C-707-424-1854. **Medical:** (David Grant), 24 hours daily, C-707-423-7300, D-312-837-7300. **Red Cross:** Bldg 107, Hours: 0800-1700 Mon-Fri, C-707-424-2261, after hours C-877-272-7337. **Security Police:** Bldg 850, 24 hours daily, C-707-424-3293, (Emergency - 911). **USO:** Bldg 3, Hours: 0800-2100 daily, C-707-424-3316.

**SUPPORT AVAILABLE: ATM:** Bldg 659, 24 hours daily. **Exchange:** Bldg 650, open daily, C-707-437-4634. **Hair Styles:** Barber, Bldg 4, C-707-437-9926; Beauty, Bldg 648, C-707-437-2848. **Laundry/Dry Cleaning:** Bldg 690, C-707-437-2733. **Laundromat:** Bldg 651, 24 hours daily. **Postal Service:** Bldg 645, Hours: 0800-1630 Mon-Fri, C-707-437-2889.

**ATTRACTIONS:** Marine World, Napa Valley wine country, San Francisco, Chinatown, Fisherman's Wharf, Golden Gate Bridge, and cable cars.

*Note: Commercially contracted flights are now called Patriot Express.*

### TRAVIS AFB (SUU/KSUU); MISSION 436/MEDEVAC; SAMPLE SCHEDULE: TUE; EQUIPMENT: C009A

{SUU/KSUU *NE* ➡ MUO/KMUO *NW* ➡ TCM/KTCM *E* ➡ SKA/KSKA *E* ➡ GTF/KGTF *E* ➡ MIB/KMIB *E* ➡ RDR/KRDR *SE* ➡ BLV/KBLV}

| LI | AIRPORT/STATION | CTRY/STA |
|---|---|---|
| SUU/KSUU | Travis AFB | CA |
| MUO/KMUO | Mountain Home AFB | ID |
| TCM/KTCM | McChord AFB | WA |
| SKA/KSKA | Fairchild AFB | WA |
| GTF/KGTF | Great Falls IAP/ANGB | MT |
| MIB/KMIB | Minot AFB | ND |
| RDR/KRDR | Grand Forks ARB | ND |
| BLV/KBLV | Scott AFB | IL |

### TRAVIS AFB (SUU/KSUU); MISSION 456/MEDEVAC; SAMPLE SCHEDULE: SUN; EQUIPMENT: C009A

{SUU/KSUU *S* ➡ NKX/KNKX *E* ➡ LUF/KLUF *SE* ➡ DMA/KDMA *NE* ➡ IKR/KIKR *E* ➡ CVS/KCVS *SW* ➡ BIF/KBIF *E* ➡ SKF/KSKF *NE* ➡ BLV/KBLV}

| LI | AIRPORT/STATION | CTRY/STA |
|---|---|---|
| SUU/KSUU | Travis AFB | CA |
| NKX/KNKX | Miramar MCAS | CA |
| LUF/KLUF | Luke AFB | AZ |
| DMA/KDMA | Davis-Monthan AFB | AZ |
| IKR/KIKR | Kirtland AFB | NM |
| CVS/KCVS | Cannon AFB | NM |
| BIF/KBIF | Biggs AAF | TX |
| SKF/KSKF | Kelly AFB | TX |
| BLV/KBLV | Scott AFB | IL |

### TRAVIS AFB, CA (SUU); REGION: PAC; OPERATOR: COM; TYPE: MIXED; ROUTE: ZJ43A; SAMPLE SCHEDULE: SUN; EQUIPMENT: DC862

{SUU (★) *SW* ➡ HIK *NW* ➡ KWA *SE* ➡ HIK *SW* ➡ JON *NE* ➡

HIK *NW* ➡ KWA ⇌ KWA *SE* ➡ HIK *NE* ➡ SUU (★)}

| LI/ICAO | AIRPORT/STATION | CTRY/STA | DAYS EN ROUTE |
|---|---|---|---|
| SUU/KSUU | Travis AFB | CA | +0 |
| HIK/PHIK | Hickam AFB | HI | +1 |
| KWA/PKWA | Bucholz AAF/KMR (Kwajalein) | KA | +2 |
| HIK/PHIK | Hickam AFB | HI | +2 |
| JON/PJON | Johnston Atoll | JO | +3 |
| HIK/PHIK | Hickam AFB | HI | +3 |
| KWA/PKWA | Bucholz AAF/KMR (Kwajalein) | KA | +4 |
| KWA/PKWA | Bucholz AAF/KMR (Kwajalein) | KA | +4 |
| HIK/PHIK | Hickam AFB | HI | +4 |
| SUU/KSUU | Travis AFB | CA | |

### TRAVIS AFB, CA (SUU); REGION: ATL; OPERATOR: AMC; TYPE: MIXED; ROUTE: GTA7B; SAMPLE SCHEDULE: 2ND & 4TH WED; EQUIPMENT: KC010A

{SUU *E* ➡ NGU (★) *E* ➡ RTA *E* ➡ SIZ *SE* ➡ DHF *N* ➡ FJR ⇌ FJR *NW* ➡ SIZ *W* ➡ RTA *W* ➡ NGU (★) *W* ➡ SUU}

| LI/ICAO | AIRPORT/STATION | CTRY/STA | DAYS EN ROUTE |
|---|---|---|---|
| SUU/KSUU | Travis AFB | CA | +0 |
| NGU/KNGU | Norfolk NS | VA | +1 |
| RTA/LERT | Rota NS | ES | +3 |
| SIZ/LICZ | Sigonella NAS/APT (Sicily) | IT | +3 |
| DHF/OMAM | Al Dhafra Airfield | AE | +4 |
| FJR/OMFJ | Al Fujayrah IAP | AE | +4 |
| SIZ/LICZ | Sigonella NAS/APT (Sicily) | IT | +5 |
| RTA/LERT | Rota NS | ES | +6 |
| NGU/KNGU | Norfolk NS | VA | +7 |
| SUU/KSUU | Travis AB | CA | |

### TRAVIS AFB, CA (SUU); REGION: PAC; OPERATOR: AMC; TYPE: MIXED; ROUTE: TTP5J; SAMPLE SCHEDULE: 4TH MON; EQUIPMENT: KC010A

{SSU (★) *NW* ➡ OKO *SW* ➡ QPG *SW* ➡ NKW ⇌ NKW *NE* ➡ QPG *NE* ➡ OKO}

| LI/ICAO | AIRPORT/STATION | CTRY/STA | DAYS EN ROUTE |
|---|---|---|---|
| SUU/KSUU | Travis AFB | CA | +0 |
| OKO/RJTY | Yokota AB | JP | +2 |
| QPG/WSAP | RSAF Paya Lebar (Singapore) | SG | +3 |
| NKW/FJDG | Diego Garcia Atoll | UK | +4 |
| NKW/FJDG | Diego Garcia Atoll | UK | +4 |
| QPG/WSAP | RSAF Paya Lebar (Singapore) | SG | +5 |
| OKO/RJTY | Yokota AB | JP | |

### TRAVIS AFB, CA (SUU); REGION: PAC; OPERATOR: AMC; TYPE: MIXED; ROUTE: TTP5J; SAMPLE SCHEDULE: 4TH MON; EQUIPMENT: KC010A

{SUU (★) *NW* ➡ OKO *SW* ➡ QPG *SW* ➡ NKW ⇌ NKW *NE* ➡ SIN *NE* ➡ OKO}

| LI/ICAO | AIRPORT/STATION | CTRY/STA | DAYS EN ROUTE |
|---|---|---|---|
| SUU/KSUU | Travis AFB | CA | +0 |
| OKO/RJTY | Yokota AB | JP | +2 |
| QPG/WSAP | RSAF Paya Lebar (Singapore) | SG | +3 |
| NKW/FJDG | Diego Garcia Atoll | UK | +4 |
| NKW/FJDG | Diego Garcia Atoll | UK | +4 |
| SIN/WSSS | Changi IAP (Singapore) | SG | +5 |
| OKO/RJTY | Yokota AB | JP | |

## TRAVIS AFB, CA (SUU); REGION: ATL;
### OPERATOR: AMC; TYPE: CGO W/ PAX; ROUTE: ATG3A;
### SAMPLE SCHEDULE: 1ST & 3RD THU; EQUIPMENT: KC010A

{SUU *E* ➡ DOV (★) *E* ➡ RTA *SE* ➡ TTH *NW* ➡ DHF ⮌ DHF *NW* ➡ SIZ *NW* ➡ RMS *SW* ➡ WRI (★) *W* ➡ SUU}

| LI/ICAO | AIRPORT/STATION | CTRY/STA | DAYS EN ROUTE |
|---|---|---|---|
| SUU/KSUU | Travis AFB | CA | +0 |
| DOV/KDOV | Dover AFB | DE | +1 |
| RTA/LERT | Rota NS | ES | +2 |
| TTH/OOTH | OAFB Thumrait | OM | +3 |
| DHF/OMAM | Al Dhafra Airfield | AE | +3 |
| SIZ/LICZ | Sigonella NAS/APT (Sicily) | IT | +4 |
| RMS/ETAR | Ramstein AB | DE | +5 |
| WRI/KWRI | McGuire AFB | NJ | +6 |
| SUU/KSUU | Travis AB | CA | |

## TRAVIS AFB, CA (SUU); REGION: PAC;
### OPERATOR: AMC; TYPE: CGO W/ PAX; ROUTE: P371C;
### SAMPLE SCHEDULE: THU; EQUIPMENT: C005B

{SUU (★) *SW* ➡ HIK *SW* ➡ UAM *NW* ➡ DNA *NW* ➡ OSN ⮌ OSN *SE* ➡ OKO *E* ➡ SUU(★)}

| LI/ICAO | AIRPORT/STATION | CTRY/STA | DAYS EN ROUTE |
|---|---|---|---|
| SUU/KSUU | Travis AFB | CA | +0 |
| HIK/PHIK | Hickam AFB | HI | +1 |
| UAM/PGUA | Andersen AFB | GU | +3 |
| DNA/RODN | Kadena AB | JP | +4 |
| OSN/RKSO | Osan ABl | KR | +4 |
| OKO/RJTY | Yokota AB | JP | +5 |
| SUU/KSUU | Travis AB | CA | |

## TRAVIS AFB, CA (SUU); REGION: PAC;
### OPERATOR: AMC; TYPE: CGO W/ PAX; ROUTE: P371F & G;
### SAMPLE SCHEDULE: FRI; EQUIPMENT: C005B

{SUU (★) *SW* ➡ HIK *SW* ➡ UAM *NW* ➡ OKO *NW* ➡ OSN ⮌ OSN *SE* ➡ OKO *E* ➡ SUU(★)}

| LI/ICAO | AIRPORT/STATION | CTRY/STA | DAYS EN ROUTE |
|---|---|---|---|
| SUU/KSUU | Travis AFB | CA | +0 |
| HIK/PHIK | Hickam AFB | HI | +1 |
| UAM/PGUA | Andersen AFB | GU | +2 |
| OKO/RJTY | Yokota AB | JP | +3 |
| OSN/RKSO | Osan AB | KR | +4 |
| OKO/RJTY | Yokota AB | JP | +5 |
| SUU/KSUU | Travis AB | CA | |

## TRAVIS AFB, CA (SUU); REGION: PAC;
### OPERATOR: AMC; TYPE: CGO W/ PAX; ROUTE: P371S & P371Z; SAMPLE SCHEDULE: 1ST, 2ND & 3RD WED; 4TH TUE; EQUIPMENT: C005B

{SUU (★) *SW* ➡ HIK *SW* ➡ UAM *NW* ➡ OKO *NW* ➡ OSN ⮌ OSN *SE* ➡ DNA *SE* ➡ UAM *NE* ➡ HIK *NE* ➡ SUU(★)}

| LI/ICAO | AIRPORT/STATION | CTRY/STA | DAYS EN ROUTE | |
|---|---|---|---|---|
| | | | P371S | |
| P371Z | | | | |
| SUU/KSUU | Travis AFB | CA | +0 | +0 |
| HIK/PHIK | Hickam AFB | HI | +1 | +1 |
| UAM/PGUA | Andersen AFB | GU | +2 | +2 |
| OKO/RJTY | Yokota AB | JP | +3 | +5 |
| OSN/RKSO | Osan ABl | KR | +4 | +5 |

---

| DNA/RODN | Kadena AB | JP | +4 | +6 |
|---|---|---|---|---|
| UAM/PGUA | Andersen AFB | GU | +5 | +7 |
| HIK/PHIK | Hickam AFB | HI | +6 | +8 |
| SUU/KSUU | Travis AB | CA | | |

## TRAVIS AFB, CA (SUU); REGION: PAC;
### OPERATOR: AMC; TYPE: CGO W/ PAX; ROUTE: P379A & P379B; SAMPLE SCHEDULE: 1ST,3RD,4TH & 5TH TUE; EQUIPMENT: C005B

{SUU (★) *SW* ➡ HIK *SW* ➡ UAM *NW* ➡ DNA ⮌ DNA *NE* ➡ OKO *SE* ➡ HIK *NE* ➡ SUU(★)}

| LI/ICAO | AIRPORT/STATION | CTRY/STA | DAYS EN ROUTE |
|---|---|---|---|
| SUU/KSUU | Travis AFB | CA | +0 |
| HIK/PHIK | Hickam AFB | HI | +1 |
| UAM/PGUA | Andersen AFB | GU | +2 |
| DNA/RODN | Kadena AB | JP | +3 |
| OKO/RJTY | Yokota AB | JP | +4 |
| HIK/PHIK | Hickam AFB | HI | +5 |
| SUU/KSUU | Travis AB | CA | |

## TRAVIS AFB, CA (SUU); REGION: PAC;
### OPERATOR: AMC; TYPE: CGO W/ PAX; ROUTE: P379D;
### SAMPLE SCHEDULE: 2ND TUE; EQUIPMENT: C005B

{SUU (★) *SW* ➡ HIK *SW* ➡ UAM *NW* ➡ DNA ⮌ DNA *NE* ➡ OKO *NE* ➡ EDF *SE* ➡ SUU(★)}

| LI/ICAO | AIRPORT/STATION | CTRY/STA | DAYS EN ROUTE |
|---|---|---|---|
| SUU/KSUU | Travis AFB | CA | +0 |
| HIK/PHIK | Hickam AFB | HI | +1 |
| UAM/PGUA | Andersen AFB | GU | +2 |
| DNA/RODN | Kadena AB | JP | +3 |
| OKO/RJTY | Yokota AB | JP | +4 |
| EDF/PAED | Elmendorf AFB | AK | +2 |
| SUU/KSUU | Travis AB | CA | |

## TRAVIS AFB, CA (SUU); REGION: PAC;
### OPERATOR: AMC; TYPE: CGO W/ PAX; ROUTE: PT03A; SAMPLE SCHEDULE: 2ND & 4TH SAT, 1ST & 3RD SUN, 2ND & 4TH MON, 1ST & 3RD WED, 2ND & 4TH THU AND 1ST & 3RD FRI; EQUIPMENT: KC010A

{SUU *NW* ➡ OKO ⮌ OKO *SE* ➡ SUU}

| LI/ICAO | AIRPORT/STATION | CTRY/STA | DAYS EN ROUTE |
|---|---|---|---|
| SUU/KSUU | Travis AFB | CA | +0 |
| OKO/RJTY | Yokota AB | JP | +1 |
| OKO/RJTY | Yokota AB | JP | +1 |
| SUU/KSUU | Travis AB | CA | |

## EN ROUTE SCHEDULES

| AIRPORT/STATION | LI-MISSION (page #) |
|---|---|
| Scott AFB | BLV-C-614/MEDEVAC (30) |
| Scott AFB | BLV-C-634/MEDEVAC (29) |
| Kelly AFB | SKF-546/MEDEVAC (74) |
| March ARB | RIV-5J43B (10) |
| March ARB | RIV-9J97A/C (10) |
| McGuire AFB | WRI-TQP5J (50) |
| Charleston AFB/IAP | CHS-P803R (68) |
| Charleston AFB/IAP | CHS-P803S (68) |
| Memphis IAP | MEM-IDB7B & 7D45A (70) |
| McChord AFB | TCM-T679F (92) |
| McChord AFB | TCM-TU79A (92) |
| McChord AFB | TCM-P6E1P (92) |
| McChord AFB | TCM-P6E7P (92) |

| McChord AFB | TCM-P6PXF (83) |
| McChord AFB | TCM-PUPXE (83) |
| Yokota AB | OKO-ZJ82A (128) |
| Yokota AB | OKO-TQP5V (128) |
| Yokota AB | OKO-TTP5V (128) |

### UNSCHEDULED FLIGHTS

Call for destinations, routings, and schedules. C-005A/B/C, KC-10A, C-141B aircraft stationed here.

## VANDENBERG AIR FORCE BASE
## (VBG/KVBG)

30 Transportation Squadron
1221 California Blvd
Vandenberg AFB, CA 93437-5079

**LOCATION:** From the north on US-101, exit westbound at Santa Maria onto Clark Avenue, then go west approximately 2.3 miles to left (south) on CA-135 which merges into CA-1. Continue southbound on CA-1 directly to main gate. Or, from the south, take US-101 north to Buelton. Exit northwest onto CA-246. Just before Lompoc, bear right on Purisima Road which runs into CA-1. Follow CA-1 northwest to the main gate on left. *USMRA: Page 111 (C-12).* LST: GMT-08:00. NMC: Lompoc, 6 miles south. Main installation numbers: C-805-606-1110, D-312-276-1110.

**REGISTRATION INFO: C-805-606-5749/1844, D-312-276-1844, Fax: C-805-606-5980.** Bldg 1749, Hours: 0800-1700 daily. Directions: From main gate on CA Blvd to right on 13th Street, left on Airfield Road. Pax Term is on the left. **Pax Service Office:** C-805-606-1854/7742, D-312-276-1854/7742.

**PAX LOUNGES:** Limited lounge facilities. **General:** Bldg 1749, Hours: 0800-1700 daily, C-805-866-7742.restrooms, P/C seats. **DV/VIP:** Adjacent to Bldg 1746, Hours: 0800-1700 daily, C-805-866-4129. Restrooms, TV, coffee/tea service, O/S seats. **Protocol Service:** Bldg 10577, 24 hours daily, C-805-606-3711.

**FOOD SERVICE: Dining Hall:** Bldg 13330, C-805-866-9571. **Enlisted Club:** Bldg 10252, C-805-734-4375. **Fast Food:** Burger King, Bldg 1749, C-805-734-4263; other fast food available, Hours: 0600-2100, 5 miles or 15 minutes. **O Club:** Bldg 11070, C-805-734-4311.

**TRANSPORTATION: Air Tickets:** Commercial Travel Office, Bldg 10364, Hours: 0730-1630 Mon-Fri. **On Base Bus (Gov):** Bldg 10004, C-805-606-1843. **On Base Car Rentals:** Bldg 10600, C-805-734-2185. **Parking:** Bldg 1749, C-805-734-8232 ext 6-7742.

**TML:** Bldg 13005, 24 hours daily, C-805-606-1844, D-312-276-1844. DV/VIP C-805-606-3711/2.

**RVC:** FAMCAMP, 1036 California Blvd, Check-in FAMCAMP Office, Bldg 5002, Duty hours, C-805-606-3911, D-312-276-8579, Fax: C-805-606-0410.

**TRAVELERS AID: Chaplain:** Bldg 16200, 24 hours daily, C-805-606-1859/6655. **Medical:** Bldg 13850, 24 hours daily, C-805-606-6206, D-312-276-6206. **Red Cross:** Bldg 11012, 24 hours daily, C-805-606-1855 or C-805-734-5110. **Security Police:** 24 hours daily, C-805-606-3911 (Desk Sgt).

**SUPPORT AVAILABLE: Bank/Currency Exchange:** Bldg 10375, C-805-734-4365. **Exchange:** Bldg 10400, C-805-734-5521. **Hair Styles:** Bldg 10400; Barber, C-805-734-1259; Beauty, C-805-734-1264. **Laundry/Dry Cleaning:** Bldg 11193, C-805-734-3039. **Postal Service:** Bldg 10373, C-805-606-3223. **Wire:** Bldg 10400, C-805-734-5521.

**ATTRACTIONS:** Great beaches, historic missions, and Hearst Castle.

### UNSCHEDULED FLIGHTS

Occasional unscheduled flights to Peterson AFB, CO (**COS**) and Offutt AFB, NE (**OFF**) via C-21 aircraft. Call for destinations, routings and schedules.

## Other California Installations
## with Possible Space-A Air Opportunities

**BICYCLE LAKE ARMY AIRFIELD (BYS/KBYS),** Fort Irwin, CA 92310-5000. **LOCATION:** From east or west on I-15, exit onto CA-58 at Barstow (approximately 2.5 miles northeast of junction with I-40). Go west on CA-58 approximately 2.6 miles to intersection with Irwin Road. Go north on Irwin Road, which becomes Fort Irwin Road, approximately 36 miles to fort. Watch for signs. *USMRA: Page 111 (G,H-11,12). ML-ARM: (35°17'N/116°38'W).* LST: GMT-08:00. **C-760-380-4111, D-312-470-4111. TML:** Landmark Inn, 39 Inter Loop, Road, 0800-1630 daily, C-760-386-4040, D-312-470-4040. DV/VIP C-760-380-3000. Full base support facilities available. Extremely limited Space-A.

**FORT HUNTER LIGGETT ARMY AIRFIELD (HGT/KHGT),** Fort Hunter Liggett, CA 93928-5000. **LOCATION:** From US-101 north or south, exit approximately one mile southwest of King City onto G-14 (Jolon Road), then south approximately 19 miles to main gate. *USMRA: Page 111 (C-10). ML-ARM: (36°0'N/121°14'W).* LST: GMT-08:00. **C-831-386-3000, D-312-686-3000. TML:** Bldg 229, 0800-1630 dialy, D-312-686-2511, 831-386-2025. Full base support facilities available. Very limited flights via helicopter. Call for destinations, routings and schedules.

**SACRAMENTO COAST GUARD AIR STATION (MCC/KMCC),** U.S. Coast Guard Air Station, Sacramento, 6037 Price Avenue, Sacramento, CA 95652-1260. **LOCATION:** Off I-80 N. From I-80 take Madison Ave exit. Clearly marked. *USMRA: Page 110 (C-6). ML-ARM: (38°40'N/121°24'W).* LST: GMT-08:00. NMC: Sacramento, 10 miles southwest. Main installation numbers: C-916-643-2081. **REGISTRATION INFO:** For information, call C-916-643-7659, Fax: 916-643-7702. No preregistration, same day only. Limited flights. Full base support available at Travis AFB.

# COLORADO

## BUCKLEY AIR FORCE BASE (BKF/KBKF)

19210 East Breckenridge Ave, Stop 74
Buckley AFB, CO 80011-9599

**LOCATION:** From north or south on I-225, take Exit #9 east onto East 6th Avenue (CO-30) 2.5 miles east to main gate on south (right) side of road. Clearly marked. *USMRA: Page 109 (G-3,4); Page 116 (C,D-3,4). ML-ARM: (39°43'N/104°46'W).* LST: GMT-07:00. NMC: Denver CO, 21 miles west. Main installation numbers: C-303-677-9011 or C-303-677-9155, D-312-877-9011 or D-312-877-9155 .

**REGISTRATION INFO:** Flight Ops, Hangar 909. Hours: 0600-2200 Mon-Fri, C-303-677-9847, D-312-877-9847. Very limited Space-A. ***Note: As of 2001 this base has become an Active Duty Air Force base, the airfield is the only part still run by the NG.***

**PAX LOUNGES:** No pax terminal, no pax services at this time.

**TRANSPORTATION:** Check with Security Police, C-303-677-9930, they must approve overnight/extended parking. Very limited off base transportation available to Space-A passengers. City bus schedule 3 hours in the morning until 0930 daily, bus resumes at 1530 until 1930 hours.

**TML:** Nearest TML at Bldg 1042, 125 E, Stewart Avenue, Peterson AFB, 24 hours daily, C-719-556-7851, D-312-834-7851, Fax: C-719-556-7852, DV/VIP C-719-554-3012.

**SUPPORT AVAILABLE:** Limited base support facilities. All Ranks Club and Shoppette available. Commissary and Exchange due to be finished by the end of 2001.

**ATTRACTIONS:** Denver nearby snow sports, snow. Pro sports teams. National Western Stock Show and Rodeo in January.

### UNSCHEDULED FLIGHTS

Very limited flights to CONUS locations as mission requires. Also host to Navy/USMC aircraft and reserve units, and ARNG and USAF units. The previous MEDEVAC flights now call at Peterson AFB, CO (**COS**). Call for destinations, routing and schedules.

## BUTTS ARMY AIRFIELD (FCS/KFCS)

Air Operations, Bldg 9601
Fort Carson, CO 80913-5000

**LOCATION:** From north or south on I-25, take exit #135 west onto CO-83 (Academy Blvd. for two miles to a left (south) on Co-115 for two miles to main gate on left (east) side of road. Clearly marked. *USMRA: Page 109 (F,G-5,6), Page 115 (C,D-6,7). ML-ARM: (38°45'N/104°47'W).* LST: GMT-07:00. NMC: Colorado Springs, 6 miles north. C-719-526-5811, D-312-691-3431.

**REGISTRATION INFO: C-719-526-7111/3762,** at Evans Community Hospital for MEDEVAC flights. AMC, MEDEVAC, flights, C009A are processed at Peterson AFB (COS). All other flights, C-719-556-4521.

**TML:** Colorado Inn, Bldg 7301, Woodfill Road, 24 hours daily, C-719-526-4832, D-312-691-4832, DV/VIP C-719-526-5811.

### UNSCHEDULED FLIGHTS

Call for destinations, routings and schedules.

## PETERSON AIR FORCE BASE (COS/KCOS)

21st LSS/LGTTS
621 W. Stewart Ave, Bldg 122
Peterson AFB, CO 80914-1628

**LOCATION:** Off US-24 (Platte Avenue) east of Colorado Springs. Eastbound from Colorado Springs on US-24, keep right onto CO-94 for 0.2 miles to right (south) on Peterson Blvd. directly to main gate. Clearly marked. Or, westbound on US-24, take exit south onto CO-94 then west for 0.2 miles to south (right) on Peterson Blvd. directly to main gate. *USMRA: Page 109 (G-5); Page 115 (D,E-5,6). ML-ARM: (38°49'N/104°41'W).* LST: GMT-07:00. NMC: Colorado Springs, 6 miles northwest. Main installation numbers: C-719-556-7321, D-312-834-7011.

**REGISTRATION INFO: C-719-556-4521/1638, D-312-834-4521/1638, Rec: C-719-556-4707, D-312-834-4707, Fax: C-719-556-4979, D-312-834-4979. E-mail: 21lslgtt@peterson.af.mil** Bldg 122, Hours: 0630-1630 Mon-Fri, weekends and federal holidays open for scheduled flights only. Directions: From main gate, straight on Peterson Blvd to flight line and Pax Term directly ahead. **Pax Service Office:** Bldg 122, Hours: 0600-2200 Mon-Fri. **Pax Paging:** Bldg 122, Hours: 0700-1600 Mon-Fri, C-719-556-4521. (Flight Line is closed 2200-0600, if flight comes in there is no service available).

**PAX LOUNGES:** No separate family lounge. **General:** Bldg 122, Hours: 0600-2200 Mon-Fri, weekends and federal holidays open for scheduled flights only, C-719-556-4707/4521. Telephones, TV, restrooms, O/S seats. **Protocol Service:** Bldg 122, Hours: 0700-1630 Mon-Fri, on call 24 hours daily, C-719-556-4225, D-312-834-4225, O-6+.

**FOOD SERVICE: Dining Hall:** Bldg 1160, Hours: 0530-1730 daily, C-719-556-4180 (In-flight meals). **Fast Food:** McDonald's, Bldg 1365, Hours: 0600-2100, C-719-597-4858. **NCO/CPO Club:** Bldg 725, Hours: 0700-2330 daily, C-719-556-4194/597-7876. **O Club:** Bldg 1013, Hours: 0630-2330 daily, C-719-574-4100. **Restaurants:** Bowling Alley, Bldg 406, Hours: 0900-2330 daily, C-719-556-4607; Golf, C-719-556-4454. **Snack Vending:** Bldg 122, 24 hours daily, C-719-591-2265.

**TRANSPORTATION: Air Tickets:** Bldg 365, Hours: 0730-1630 Mon-Fri, C-719-556-4199 (Professional Travel Corp). **On Base Bus (Comm):** Bldg 122, Hours: 0554-1722 daily, C-719-475-9733 (COS to Fort Carson). **On Base Bus (Gov):** Bldg 1229, 0600-2200 daily, C-719-556-4717. **Car Rentals:** Bldg 640; Avis, C-719-596-2751; Budget, C-719-574-7400; Enterprise, C-719-556-1733/4; Hertz, C-719-596-1863; National, C-719-596-1519. **On Base Taxi (Comm):** Bldg 1229, 24 hours daily, Airport, C-719-596-7300; Yellow, C-719-634-6601/5000. **On Base Taxi (Gov):** Bldg 1229, 0600-1800 Mon-Fri, C-719-556-4307 (duty passengers only). **Parking:** Short term available at Bldg 122, no long term parking.

**TML:** Bldg 1042, 125 E, Stewart Avenue, 24 hours daily, C-719-556-7851, D-312-834-7851, Fax: C-719-556-7852, DV/VIP C-719-554-3012.

**TRAVELERS AID:** On base at Fort Carson. **Chaplain:** Bldg 1410, Hours: 0730-1630 Mon-Fri, C-719-556-4442. After normal duty hours call security police at C-719-556-4000 and ask for the duty chaplain. **Emergency Relief:** Fort Carson, Hours: 0800-1600 Mon-Fri, C-719-579-2311 (Pax Services). **Medical :** Bldg 959, 24 hours daily, Emergency: C-719-556-4333, D-312-834-4333, Other: C-719-556-7712. **Red Cross:** Bldg 1470, Hours: 0800-1600 Mon-Fri, C-719-554-7590. **Security Police:** Bldg 1376, 24 hours daily, C-719-556-4000. **USO:** Colorado Springs Municipal Airport, C-719-574-9626.

**SERVICES AVAILABLE: Bank/Currency Exchange:** Bldg 1485, Hours: 0900-1500 Mon-Thu, 0900-1700 Fri, C-719-475-6387. **Exchange:** Bldg 1425, Hours: 0900-2100 Mon-Sat, 1000-1800 Sun, C-719-596-7270. **Hair Styles:** Bldg 1425, Hours: 0800-1730 Mon-Sat; Barber, C-719-597-0300; Beauty, C-719-596-0579. **Laundry/Dry Cleaning:** Bldg 1425, Hours: 0830-1730 Mon-Sat, C-719-597-3050. **Postal Service:** Bldg 1466, Hours: 0830-1630 Mon-Fri, 0830-1130 Sat, C-719-556-4596.

**OTHER INFORMATION:** U.S. Customs Service Airport.

**PETERSON AFB, CO (COS); REGION: ATL; OPERATOR: AMC; TYPE: CGO W/ PAX; ROUTE: OPN3B; SAMPLE SCHEDULE: 1ST TUE; EQUIPMENT: C130H**

{COS *SE* ➡ NGU (★) *SE* ➡ NRR *E* ➡ STX ⇌ STX *W* ➡ NRR *NW* ➡ NGU (★) *NW* ➡ COS}

| LI/ICAO | AIRPORT/STATION | CTRY/STA | DAYS EN ROUTE |
|---|---|---|---|
| COS/KCOS | Peterson AFB | CO | +0 |
| NGU/KNGU | Norfolk NS | VA | +1 |
| NRR/TJNR | Roosevelt Roads NS | PR | +1 |
| STX/TISX | Alexander Hamilton Apt (St Croix) | VI | +2 |
| NRR/TJNR | Roosevelt Roads NS | PR | +2 |
| NGU/KNGU | Norfolk NS | VA | +3 |
| POB/KPOB | Pope AFB | NC | |

**ATTRACTIONS:** Pikes Peak, Royal Gorge, Ski resorts, U.S. Olympic Training Center, Air Force Academy, Garden of the Gods, Seven Falls.

### EN ROUTE SCHEDULES

| AIRPORT/STATION | LI-MISSION (page #) |
|---|---|
| Scott AFB | BLV-C-635/MEDEVAC (30) |
| Scott AFB | BLV-C-656/MEDEVAC (30) |

### UNSCHEDULED FLIGHTS

Andrews AFB, MD (**ADW**) (3 per week); Kelly AFB, TX (**SKF**) (1 per week); Scott AFB, IL (**BLV**) (1 per week) and various destinations in CA once a week. Most flights utilize C-130H aircraft. No weekend flights. Call for destinations, routings and schedules. ***Note: 24 hour notice available on all scheduled and unscheduled flights.***

# DELAWARE

## DOVER AIR FORCE BASE (DOV/KDOV)

436th APS/TROP
505 Atlantic Avenue
Dover AFB, DE 19902-5501

**LOCATION:** From Philadelphia, take I-95 south to Route 13 south. Base is five miles south of Dover, on east side of DE-1 toll or US-13. Follow signs to base. Clearly marked. *USMRA: Page 42 (I-3). ML-ARM: (39°06'N/75°28'W).* LST: GMT-05:00. NMC: Dover, 5 miles northwest. Main installation numbers: C-302-677-3000, D-312-445-3000. Base Information: C-302-677-2113.

**REGISTRATION INFO: C-302-677-4088, D-312-445-4088, Rec: C-302-677-2854, D-312-445-2854, (updated 2000 daily), Fax: C-302-677-2953, D-312-445-2953. E-mail: 436aps.spacea@dover.af.mil WEB: www.dover.af.mil/spacea/index.html** Bldg 150, 24 hours daily. Directions: From North Gate: follow Atlantic Ave approximately 1.5 miles to Eagle Way. Make a left on Eagle Way then first right on Purple Heart Ave. Pax Term is on the left. **Pax Service Office:** Bldg 150, Hours: 0730-1630 Mon-Fri, C-302-677-4076/77/78 (Officer/Superintendent on duty). **Pax Paging:** Bldg 150, 24 hours daily, C-302-677-2854/4088.

**PAX LOUNGES:** USO Delaware. **General:** Bldg 150, first floor, 24 hours daily, C-302-677-6905. A/C, bag lockers, telephones (Commercial, defense and long distance), TV, restrooms, P/C seats. *Non-smoking building.* No sleeping in lounge area. **DV/VIP:** Bldg 150, 24 hours daily, C-302-677-4088. Not staffed. A/C, telephones (commercial and defense), TV, O/S seats (O6+). **Protocol Service:** Bldg 201, Hours: 0800-1600 Mon-Fri, C-302-677-4366, D-312-445-4366.

**FOOD SERVICE: Global Activities Center:** Bldg 425, Hours: 1100-1700 Mon-Fri, 0800-2400 Sat-Sun, C-302-677-6351. **Cafeteria:** Bldg 150, 24 hours daily, (closed 0430-0530 Mon-Fri), C-302-674-3380. **Combined Club:** Bldg 479, Hours: 1100-1300, 1700-2000 Mon-Fri. **Dining Hall:** Bldg 403, Hours: 0600-0045 daily, C-302-677-3923. **Fast Food:** Burger King, Hours: 0700-1830 Mon-Fri, 0800-1830 Sat, 1030-1600 Sun. **Snack Bars:** Bldg 266, Hours: 0900-1500 Mon-Sat, C-302-677-3380. In-Flight meals available at check-in.

**TRANSPORTATION: Air Tickets:** Rogers Travel Agency, Bldg 150, Hours: 0830-1630 Mon-Fri, C-302-736-1668. **Off Base Bus:** Trailways, Dover, C-302-734-1417, 24 hours daily. **Car Rentals:** Bldg 150, Hours: 0800-1700 daily; Avis, C-302-734-5550 or 1-800-331-1212; Budget, C-302-734-5688 or C-1-800-527-0700; Enterprise, C-302-674-5553 or 1-800-325-8007; Hertz, C-302-678-0700 or 1-800-654-3131; Kut Rate Car Rental, C-302-697-3000; National, C-302-734-5774 or 1-800-227-7368; Seacoast Limousine, C-302-834-7575 or 1-800-833-7575. **On/Off Base Limo Service:** C-1-800-717-1646, C-410-482-8522; Dover Limo, C-302-678-8090. **Off Base Taxi:** City Cab, 24 hours daily, C-302-734-5968. **Trains:** AMTRAK, Wilmington, 45 miles away, 24 hours daily, C-1-800-872-7245. **Parking:** Bldg 150, 24 hours daily, C-302-678-6892. Lot in front of Terminal limited to 12 hours (cars left longer will be towed at owner's expense). Long term lots 1, 2 and 3 are marked.

**TML:** Bldg 800, 14th Street, 24 hours daily, C-302-677-2844, D-312-445-2844, DV/VIP 302-677-4366, D-312-455-4366.

**RVC:** FAMCAMP, 262 Chad Street, Room 331, Check-in Equip Check out Bldg 124 after 1100 hrs, C-302-677-3959, D-312-445-3959.

**TRAVELERS AID: Chaplain:** Bldg 419, Hours: 0745-1645 Mon-Fri, C-302-677-3931/2. **Emergency Relief:** Bldg 263, Hours: 0800-1700 Mon-Fri, C-302-677-6930 (Air Force Aid). **Locator:** 677-3000. **Lost/Found:** Bldg 150, 24 hours daily, C-302-677-4088 (See Pax Term NCO). **Medical/Dental:** Bldg 300, Hours: 0700-1630, C-302-677-2500, D-312-445-2500 (Hospital). **Red Cross:** Bldg 447, Hours: 0730-1630 Mon-Fri, C-302-678-2855. After hours C-302-678-3000. **Retiree Desk:** Bldg 520, C-302-677-4612 (unique service-volunteers). **Security Police:** Bldg 910, 24 hours daily, C-302-677-6666 (see Security Police to park RVs).

**SUPPORT AVAILABLE: Exchange:** Bldg 266, Hours: 0900-2100 Mon-Fri, 0900-1600 Sat, C-302-674-4862. **Hair Styles:** Barber, Bldg 266, Hours: 0800-1800 Mon-Fri, 0800-1400 Sat, C-302-734-1747; Beauty, Bldg 266, Hours: 0830-1700 Mon-Fri, 0830-1500 Sat, C-302-734-1747. Locator: Bldg

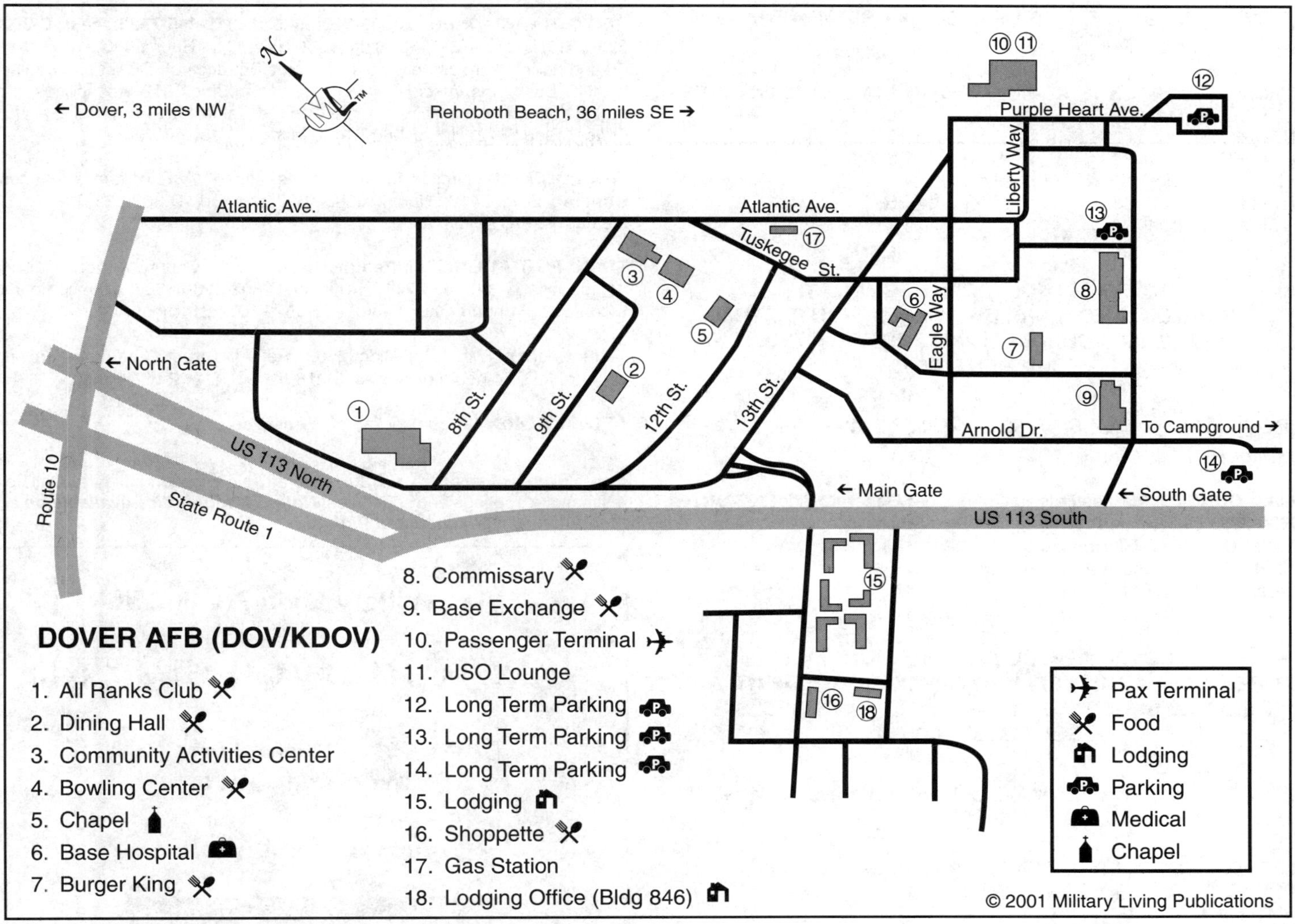

**DOVER AFB (DOV/KDOV)**

1. All Ranks Club
2. Dining Hall
3. Community Activities Center
4. Bowling Center
5. Chapel
6. Base Hospital
7. Burger King
8. Commissary
9. Base Exchange
10. Passenger Terminal
11. USO Lounge
12. Long Term Parking
13. Long Term Parking
14. Long Term Parking
15. Lodging
16. Shoppette
17. Gas Station
18. Lodging Office (Bldg 846)

Map legend:
- Pax Terminal
- Food
- Lodging
- Parking
- Medical
- Chapel

© 2001 Military Living Publications

442, duty hours, C-302-677-2841. **Postal Service:** Bldg 442, Hours: 0730-1630 Mon-Fri, C-302-677-6195. **Valet/Dry Cleaning:** Bldg 266, Hours: 0800-1800 Mon-Fri, 0900-1300 Sat, C-302-678-8835.

**OTHER INFORMATION:** Port of Entry and U.S. Customs Bldg 150.

**ATTRACTIONS:** State capital, great beaches, and the Delaware Bay.

*Note: Commercially contracted flights are now called Patriot Express.*

### DOVER AFB, DE (DOV); REGION: ATL; OPERATOR: AMC; TYPE: CGO W/ PAX; ROUTE:A201A & A2F5B; SAMPLE SCHEDULE: SUN; 2ND 3RD AND & 4TH THU; FRI; EQUIPMENT: C005B

{DOV (★) *NE* ➡ RMS ⇌ RMS *SW* ➡ DOV (★)}

| LI/ICAO | AIRPORT/STATION | CTRY/STA | DAYS EN ROUTE |
|---|---|---|---|
| DOV/KDOV | Dover AFB | DE | +0 |
| RMS/ETAR | Ramstein AB | DE | +1 |
| DOV/KDOV | Dover AFB | DE | |

### DOVER AFB, DE (DOV); REGION: ATL; OPERATOR: AMC; TYPE: CGO W/ PAX; ROUTE:A2F3R; SAMPLE SCHEDULE: 1ST, 3RD AND & 4TH WED; EQUIPMENT: C005B

{DOV *S* ➡ NGU (★) *E* ➡ RTA *E* ➡ SIZ ⇌ SIZ *W* ➡ RTA *W* ➡ NGU (★) *N* ➡DOV}

| LI/ICAO | AIRPORT/STATION | CTRY/STA | DAYS EN ROUTE |
|---|---|---|---|
| DOV/KDOV | Dover AFB | DE | +0 |
| NGU/KNGU | Norfolk NS | VA | +0 |
| RTA/LERT | Rota NS | ES | +1 |
| SIZ/LICZ | Sigonella NAS/APT (Sicily) | IT | +2 |
| RTA/LERT | Rota NS | ES | +3 |
| NGU/KNGU | Norfolk NS | VA | +3 |
| DOV/KDOV | Dover AFB | DE | +0 |

### DOVER AFB, DE (DOV); REGION: ATL; OPERATOR: AMC; TYPE: CGO W/ PAX; ROUTE:A2R3D; SAMPLE SCHEDULE: 2ND AND & 4TH THU; EQUIPMENT: C005B

{DOV (★) *NE* ➡ MHZ *SE* ➡ RMS ⇌ RMS *NW* ➡ MHZ *SW* ➡ ➡DOV (★)}

| LI/ICAO | AIRPORT/STATION | CTRY/STA | DAYS EN ROUTE |
|---|---|---|---|
| DOV/KDOV | Dover AFB | DE | +0 |
| MHZ/EGUN | RAF Mildenhall | UK | +1 |
| RMS/ETAR | Ramstein AB | DE | +1 |
| MHZ/EGUN | RAF Mildenhall | UK | +2 |
| DOV/KDOV | Dover AFB | DE | |

### DOVER AFB, DE (DOV); REGION: ATL; OPERATOR: AMC; TYPE: CGO W/ PAX; ROUTE:A2V1A & B; SAMPLE SCHEDULE: 2ND 3RD AND & 4TH WED, SAT; EQUIPMENT: C005B

{DOV (★) *NE* ➡RMS *SE* ➡ AVB ⇌ AVB *NW* ➡ MHZ *SW* ➡DOV (★)}

| LI/ICAO | AIRPORT/STATION | CTRY/STA | DAYS EN ROUTE |
|---|---|---|---|
| DOV/KDOV | Dover AFB | DE | +0 |
| RMS/ETAR | Ramstein AB | DE | +1 |
| AVB/LIPA | Aviano AB | IT | +1 |
| MHZ/EGUN | RAF Mildenhall | UK | +2 |
| DOV/KDOV | Dover AFB | DE | |

## EN ROUTE SCHEDULES

| AIRPORT/STATION | LI-MISSION (page #) |
|---|---|
| Travis AFB | SUU-ATG3A (14) |
| Westover ARB | CEF-OFR3A (41) |
| Westover ARB | CEF-OFV1A (41) |
| McGuire AFB | WRI-A7R1A (51) |
| McGuire AFB | WRI-AQ01A (51) |
| Stewart IAP/ANGB | SWF-IFV1A (54) |
| Stewart IAP/ANGB | SWF-IFV3A (54) |
| Wright-Patterson AFB | FFO-OER1A (62) |
| Charleston AFB/IAP | CHS-A8R1S & A8R1T (67) |

### UNSCHEDULED FLIGHTS

Flights via C-005A/B to Bangor ANGB, ME (**BGR**), Westover ARB, MA (**CEF**), Wright-Patterson AFB, OH (**FFO**), McGuire AFB, NJ (**WRI**), and other locations. Call for destinations, routings and schedules.

# NEW CASTLE COUNTY AIRPORT (ILG/KILG)
166th AG/ILG, (ANG)
New Castle, DE 19720-2495

**LOCATION:** From I-95 take exit 5 to DE-141 south for one mile to intersection of DE-37 (Corporate Commons Blvd). Turn right into Corporate Commons Blvd, then left onto Spruance Drive and follow to gate entrance. *USMRA: Page 42 (I-2). ML-ARM: (39°42'N/75°36'W).* LST: GMT-05:00. NMC: Wilmington DE, 7 miles northeast. Main installation numbers: C-302-323-3500, D-312-445-7500.

**REGISTRATION INFO: C-302-323-3525, D-312-445-7525, Fax: C-302-323-3330, D-312-445-7330.** Bldg 2812, Base Ops, Hours: 0800-1630 Mon-Fri and during flight processing. Directions: Entrance off DE-41 and straight to ANG Base Ops. Also, DE ANG Flight Ops, Bldg 2812. All facilities of a regional airport are available at the Commercial Airport Term. **Pax Service Office:** Bldg 2812, Hours: 0800-1630 Mon-Fri, C-302-323-3525.

**PAX LOUNGES:** Limited lounge facilities. No DV/VIP or family lounges. **General:** Bldg 2812, Hours: 0800-1630 Mon-Fri, C-302-323-3525. A/C, restrooms, P/C seats.

**TRANSPORTATION: Car Rentals:** New Castle County Airport. Call for hours. Dollar, C-302-655-7117; National, C-302-328-5636. **Parking:** Behind Bldg 2812, 24 hours daily, C-302-323-3525 (no restrictions).

**TML:** Nearest TML is at Bldg 2207, Bel Air Street, Aberdeen Proving Ground, MD, 24 hours daily, C-410-278-5148/9, D-312-298-5148/9.

**ATTRACTIONS:** Historic section of Wilmington.

### UNSCHEDULED FLIGHTS

Some flights to CONUS and OCONUS locations via C-130H aircraft. Call for destinations, routings and schedules.

# Military Living's™
# Mini-Guide

## Temporary Military Lodging
## RV Camping and Outdoor Recreation
## Commercial Airline and Hotel 800 Guide

Seward Resort, AK (left); Patton Hotel, Garmisch, DE (top right); Camp Darby, IT (bottom right)

# UNITED STATES

## ALABAMA

**Dauphin Island Coast Guard Recreational Facility** C-334-861-7113
**Fort Rucker** C-334-598-5216, DSN-312-558-2626
**Gunter Annex, Maxwell Air Force Base** C-334-416-3360/5501, DSN-312-596-3360
**Maxwell Air Force Base** C-334-953-2055, DSN-312-493-2055
**Redstone Arsenal** C-256-876-5713/8028, DSN-312-746-5713/8028

## ALASKA

**Clear Air Force Station** C-907-585-6224, DSN-317-585-6224
**Eielson Air Force Base** C-907-377-1844, DSN-317-377-1844
**Elmendorf Air Force Base** C-907-552-2454 ext 1118, DSN-317-552-2454 ext 1118
**Fort Greely** C-907-873-3285, DSN-317-873-3285
**Fort Richardson** C-907-384-0421, DSN-317-384-0436
**Fort Wainwright** C-907-353-7291/6294, DSN-317-353-7291/6294
**Kodiak Coast Guard Integrated Support Command** C-907-487-5446
**Seward Air Force Camp** C-1-800-501-5642 (18 May-4 Sep); C-907-552-5526 (1 Feb-14 May); DSN-317-552-5526
**Seward Resort** C-907-224-2654/2659/5559

## ARIZONA

**Davis-Monthan Air Force Base** C-520-228-3230/3309, DSN-312-228-3230/3309
**Fort Huachuca** C-520-533-2222, DSN-312-821-2222
**Fort Tuthill Recreation Area** C-1-800-552-6268, DSN-312-896-3401
**Gila Bend Air Force Auxiliary Field** C-520-683-6238, DSN-312-896-5238
**Luke Air Force Base** C-623-935-2641, DSN-312-896-3941
**Yuma Army Proving Ground** C-520-328-2129/2036, DSN-312-899-2129/2036
**Yuma Marine Corps Air Station** C-928-269-2262, DSN-312-269-2262

## ARKANSAS

**Camp Joseph T. Robinson** C-888-366-3205, C-501-212-5100/5274/5275, DSN-312-962-5100/5274/5275
**Fort Chaffee Maneuver Training Center** C-501-484-2252, DSN-312-962-2252
**Little Rock Air Force Base** C-501-987-6652, DSN-312-731-6652
**Pine Bluff Arsenal** C-870-540-3008, DSN-312-966-3008

## CALIFORNIA

**Barstow Marine Corps Logistics Base** C-760-577-6418, DSN-312-282-6418
**Beale Air Force Base** C-530-634-2953/2954, DSN-312-368-2953/2954
**Big Bear Recreation Facility** C-858-577-4126/4141
**Camp Pendleton Marine Corps Base** C-760-430-4701, DSN-312-365-3451/3718
**Camp Roberts** C-805-238-8312, DSN-312-949-8312
**Camp San Luis Obispo** C-805-594-6500, DSN-312-630-6500
**China Lake Naval Air Weapons Station** C-760-939-3146/2383, DSN-312-437-3146/2383
**Coronado Naval Amphibious Base** C-619-437-3494, DSN-312-577-3494
**Edwards Air Force Base** C-661-277-4101/3394, DSN-312-527-4101/3394
**El Centro Naval Air Facility** C-760-312-6000/6020, DSN-312-958-4918
**Fallbrook Naval Ordnance Detachment** C-760-731-3573, DSN-312-873-3573
**Fort Hunter Liggett** C-831-386-2511/2108, DSN-312-686-2511
**Fort Irwin National Training Center** C-760-386-4040, DSN-312-470-4040
**Fort MacArthur** C-310-363-8296, DSN-312-833-8296
**Fort Mason Officers' Club** C-415-441-7700
**Lake Tahoe Coast Guard Recreation Facilities** C-530-583-7438
**Lake Tahoe Condominiums** C-510-437-3573
**Lemoore Naval Air Station** C-559-997-7000/7001, DSN-312-949-4609
**Los Alamitos Joint Forces Training Base** C-562-795-2124, DSN-312-972-2124
**March Air Reserve Base** C-909-655-5241
**Marines' Memorial Club** 1-800-562-7463
**Miramar Marine Corps Air Station** C-858-577-4233/4235, DSN-312-267-4233/4235
**Moffett Federal Airfield/NASA Ames Research Center** C-650-603-7101
**Monterey Naval Postgraduate School** C-831-656-2060/9, DSN-312-878-2060/9
**North Island Naval Air Station** C-619-545-7545, DSN-312-735-7545
**Novato Temporary Quarters** C-415-506-3130
**Petaluma Coast Guard Training Center** C-707-765-7248
**Point Mugu Naval Air Station/Ventura County Naval Base** C-805-989-8251, DSN-312-351-8251
**Port Hueneme Naval Construction Battalion Center/Ventura County Naval Base** C-805-982-4497/4115, DSN-312-551-4497/4115
**Presidio of Monterey** C-888-719-8886, C-831-242-5091, DSN-312-878-5091
**San Clemente Island Naval Auxiliary Landing Field** C-619-524-9202
**San Diego Fleet Anti-Submarine Warfare Training Center** C-619-226-5382, DSN-312-524-5382
**San Diego Marine Corps Recruit Depot** C-619-524-4401, DSN-312-524-4401
**San Diego Naval Medical Center** C-619-532-6282, DSN-312-522-6282
**San Diego Naval Station** C-619-556-8672, DSN-312-526-8672
**San Diego Naval Submarine Base** C-619-553-9381, DSN-312-553-9381
**San Diego YMCA Inns** C-619-234-5252
**San Pedro Coast Guard Integrapport Command** C-310-732-7444
**Sierra Army Depot** C-530-827-4544, DSN-312-855-4544
**South Lake Tahoe Recreation Housing** C-831-242-5506/6133, DSN-312-878-5506/6133
**Travis Air Force Base** C-707-437-0700, DSN-312-837-2988
**Twentynine Palms Marine Corps Air/Ground Combat Center** C-760-830-7375, DSN-312-230-7375
**Vandenberg Air Force Base** C-805-606-1844, DSN-312-276-1844

## COLORADO

**Farish Recreation Area** C-719-687-9098/9306
**Fisher House, Denver** C-303-364-4616
**Fort Carson** C-719-526-4832, DSN-312-691-4832
**Peterson Air Force Base** C-719-556-7851, DSN-312-834-7851
**United States Air Force Academy** C-719-333-4910, DSN-312-333-4910

## CONNECTICUT

**Camp Rowland Army National Guard Training Site** C-860-691-4314, DSN-312-636-7314
**New London Naval Submarine Base** C-860-694-3416, DSN-312-694-3416
**United States Coast Guard Academy** C-860-444-8664

## DELAWARE

**Delaware Army National Guard** C-302-854-7902, DSN-312-440-7902
**Dover Air Force Base** C-302-677-2844, DSN-312-445-2844

## DISTRICT OF COLUMBIA

**Bolling Air Force Base** C-202-767-5316, DSN-312-297-5316
**Fort Lesley J. McNair** C-703-696-3576/77, DSN-312-226-3576/77
**United States Soldiers' and Airmen's Home** C-202-730-3044
**Walter Reed Army Medical Center** C-202-726-8700, DSN-312-662-3844
**Washington Naval Support Activity/Anacostia Annex** C-202-433-3862, DSN-312-288-3862
Washington Navy Lodge C-202-563-6950

## FLORIDA

**Camp Blanding/National Guard Post** C-904-682-3381, DSN-312-960-3381
**Corry Station Naval Technical Training Center** C-850-452-6541/6609, DSN-312-922-6541/6609
**Destin Army Infantry Center Recreation Area** C-1-800-642-0466, C-706-545-5600
**Eglin Air Force Base** C-850-882-8761/4534, DSN-312-872-8761/4534
**Fisher House, West Palm Beach** C-561-882-7180
**Homestead Air Reserve Base** C-1-800-330-8149 ext 7198, C-305-224-7198, DSN-312-791-7198
**Hurlburt Field** C-850-884-7115/6245, DSN-312-579-7115/6245
**Jacksonville Naval Air Station** C-904-542-3138/3139, DSN-312-942-3138
**Key West Naval Air Station** C-305-293-4142/4305, DSN-312-483-4142/4305
**MacDill Air Force Base** C-813-831-4804, 813-828-4259, DSN-312-968-4259/4804
**Marathon Recreation Cottages & RV Park** C-305-535-4565
**Mayport Naval Station** C-904-270-5423/5707, DSN-312-960-5423
**Oak Grove Park FAMCAMP** C-850-452-2535, DSN-312-922-2535
**Panama City Coastal Systems Station Naval Surface Warfare Center** C-850-236-2500, DSN-312-436-4217
**Patrick Air Force Base** C-321-494-2075/5428, DSN-312-854-2075/6590
**Pensacola Naval Air Station** C-850-452-7782, DSN-312-922-7782

**Shades of Green™ on Walt Disney World® Resort** C-407-824-3400/3600
**Tyndall Air Force Base** C-850-283-4211 ext 1, DSN-312-523-4211
**Whiting Field Naval Air Station** C-850-623-7605/6/7, C-877-627-9324, DSN-312-868-7605/6/7

**GEORGIA**
**Albany Marine Corps Logistics Base** C-229-639-5614, DSN-312-567-5614
**Athens Navy Supply Corps School** C-706-543-3033, DSN-312-588-7360
**Atlanta Naval Air Station** C-770-919-6393, DSN-312-925-6393
**Camp Frank D. Merrill** C-706-867-7748
**Dobbins Air Reserve Base** C-770-424-1352, DSN-312-925-1352
**Fort Benning** C-706-689-0067, DSN-312-835-3145
**Fort Gillem** C-404-464-3833/2253, DSN-312-367-3833
**Fort Gordon/United States Army Signal Center** C-706-791-2277, DSN-312-780-2277
**Fort Gordon Recreation Area** C-706-541-1057
**Fort McPherson** C-404-464-3833/2253, DSN-312-367-3833
**Fort Stewart** C-912-767-8384/4184, DSN-312-870-8384
**Grassy Pond Recreation Area** C-229-559-5840
**Hunter Army Airfield** C-912-352-5910/5834, DSN-312-971-5910/5834
**Kings Bay Naval Submarine Base** C-912-673-4971/4871, DSN-312-573-4971/4871
**Lake Allatoona Army Recreation Area** C-770-974-3413
**Moody Air Force Base** C-229-257-3893, DSN-312-460-3893
**Robins Air Force Base** C-912-926-2100, DSN-312-468-2100
**World Famous Navy Lake Site** C-770-974-6309

**HAWAII**
**Barbers Point Recreation Area** C-808-682-2019
**Barking Sands Pacific Missile Range Facility** C-808-335-4383, DSN-315-471-6752
**Bellows Air Force Station** C-1-800-437-2607 from U.S. Mainland, All Others, C-808-259-8080
**Fort Shafter** C-808-438-1685 or C-808-893-2336, DSN 315-839-2336
**Hale Koa Hotel AFRC** C-808-955-0555
**Hickam Air Force Base** C-808-448-5400, DSN-315-448-5400
**Kaneohe Bay Beach Cottages** C-808-254-2806, DSN-315-457-2409
**Kaneohe Bay Marine Corps Base** C-808-257-2409, DSN-315-457-2409
**Kilauea Military Camp JSRC** C-808-967-8333
**Pearl Harbor Naval Station** C-808-473-5210, DSN-315-473-5210
**Schofield Barracks** C-1-800-490-9638, C-808-624-9650/9640, DSN-315-655-5036
**Tripler Medical Center** C-808-839-2336
**Waianae Army Recreation Center** C-1-800-333-4158 (mainland), 1-800-847-6771 (outer island), C-808-696-4158 (Oahu)

**IDAHO**
**Boise Air Terminal/Gowen Field Airport/Air National Guard** C-208-422-4451, DSN-312-422-4451

**Mountain Home Air Force Base** C-208-828-5200, DSN-312-728-5200
**Yellowstone Country Trailers** C-208-828-6333, DSN-312-728-6333

**ILLINOIS**
**Great Lakes Naval Training Center** C-847-688-3777/2170/2241, DSN-312-792-3777/2170/2241
**Rock Island U.S. Army Armament & Chemical Acquisition & Logistics Activity** C-309-782-0833, DSN-312-793-0833
**Scott Air Force Base** C-618-256-1844, DSN-312-576-1844

**INDIANA**
**Camp Atterbury** C-812-526-1128, DSN-312-569-2128
**Crane Division Naval Surface Warfare Center** C-812-854-1176, DSN-312-482-1176
**Grissom Air Reserve Base** C-765-688-2844, DSN-312-928-2844

**IOWA**
**Camp Dodge/Army National Guard Base** C-515-252-4238 or C-1-800-294-6607 ext 4010, DSN-312-946-2238

**KANSAS**
**Fort Leavenworth** C-913-684-4091 or 1-800-854-8627, DSN-312-552-4091
**Fort Riley** C-785-239-2830, DSN-312-856-2830
**McConnell Air Force Base** C-316-759-6999, DSN-312-743-6999

**KENTUCKY**
**Fort Campbell** C-270-798-5618, DSN-312-635-5618
**Fort Knox** C-502-943-1000, DSN-312-464-3491

**LOUISIANA**
**Barksdale Air Force Base** C-318-456-3091, DSN-312-781-3091
**Camp Beauregard** C-318-641-5669, DSN-312-435-5669
**Fort Polk/Joint Readiness Training Center** C-337-531-9000/9200, DSN-312-863-9000/9200
**Jackson Barracks/Army National Guard Base** C-504-278-8364, DSN-312-485-8364
**New Orleans Naval Air Station/Joint Reserve Base** C-504-678-3419, DSN-312-678-3419
**New Orleans Naval Support Activity** C-504-678-2220/2252, DSN-312-678-2220/2252

**MAINE**
**Bangor International Airport/Air National Guard** C-207-942-2081
**Brunswick Naval Air Station** C-207-921-2386, DSN-312-476-2386
**Prospect Harbor Naval Satellite Operations Center** C-805-989-4212/4211, DSN 312-351-4212/4211
**Winter Harbor Naval Security Group Activity** C-207-963-5534 ext 223/203, DSN-312-476-9223/9203

**MARYLAND**
**Aberdeen Proving Ground** C-410-278-5148/5149, DSN-312-298-4373/5148
**Andrews Air Force Base** C-301-981-0785, DSN-312-858-0785
**Bethesda National Naval Medical Center** C-301-295-5856/0321/55, DSN-312-295-5855/56/0321

**Curtis Bay Coast Guard Yard** C-410-636-7373
**Fort Detrick Army Garrison** C-301-619-2154, DSN-312-343-2154
**Fort George G. Meade** C-301-677-6529/5884, DSN-312-923-5884
**Indian Head Division Naval Surface Warfare Center** C-301-743-4845, DSN-312-354-4845
**Patuxent River Naval Air Station** C-301-863-9343, DSN-312-342-3601
**Solomons Navy Recreation Center** C-410-326-5203/5204
**United States Naval Academy/Annapolis Naval Station** C-410-293-3906, DSN-312-281-3906
**Washington Naval Air Facility** C-240-857-2750, DSN-312-857-2750

**MASSACHUSETTS**
**Armed Services YMCA of Boston** C-1-800-495-9622, C-617-241-8400
**Camp Edwards** C-508-968-5915/16, DSN-312-557-5916/15
**Cuttyhunk Island Recreational Facility** C-617-223-3181
**Devens Reserve Forces Training Area** C-978-772-4300
**Fourth Cliff Recreation Area** C-1-800-468-9547, C-781-837-9269
**Hanscom Air Force Base** C-781-377-2112, DSN-312-478-2112
**Martha's Vineyard/Nantucket Vacation Houses**
**Otis Air National Guard Base/Cape Cod Coast Guard Air Station** C-508-968-6461
**Westover Air Reserve Base** C-413-557-2700, DSN-312-589-2700

**MICHIGAN**
**Camp Grayling/Army National Guard** C-517-344-6202
**Point Betsie Recreation Cottage** C-616-850-2510
**Selfridge Air National Guard Base** C-810-307-4062 DSN-312-273-4062

**MINNESOTA**
**Camp Ripley** C-320-632-7378, DSN-312-871-7378
**Minneapolis-St. Paul International Airport/Air Reserve Station** C-612-713-1983/1984, DSN-312-783-1983/1984

**MISSISSIPPI**
**Camp Shelby Training Site** C-601-558-2540, DSN-312-921-2540
**Columbus Air Force Base** C-662-434-2548/2372, DSN-312-742-2548/2372
**Gulfport Naval Construction Battalion Center** C-228-871-2505, DSN-312-868-2505
**Keesler Air Force Base** C-228-377-9986, DSN-312-597-9986
**Meridian Naval Air Station** C-601-679-2186, DSN-312-367-2186
**Pascagoula Naval Station** C-228-769-4627, DSN-312-457-4627

**MISSOURI**
**Fort Leonard Wood** C-1-800-677-8356, DSN-312-581-8356
**Lake of the Ozarks Recreation Area** C-573-346-5640, DSN-312-581-5640
**Marine Corps Activities at Richards-Gebaur Airport** C-816-843-3850/1/2, DSN-312-894-3850/1/2

**Whiteman Air Force Base** C-660-687-1844, DSN-312-660-975-1844

**MONTANA**
**Malmstrom Air Force Base** C-406-727-8600/731-3394, DSN-312-632-3394
**Timber Wolf Resort** C-406-387-9653 or toll free C-877-846-9653

**NEBRASKA**
**Camp Ashland** C-402-944-2479 ext 200
**Offutt Air Force Base** C-402-294-3671/9000, DSN-312-271-3671

**NEVADA**
**Fallon Naval Air Station** C-775-428-3003/3004, C-775-426-3199, DSN-312-890-3003/3004
**Indian Springs Air Force Auxiliary Field** C-702-652-0401, DSN-312-682-0401
**Nellis Air Force Base** C-702-652-2711, DSN-312-682-2711
**Stead Training Center/Army National Guard Base** C-775-677-5213, DSN-312-830-5213

**NEW HAMPSHIRE**
**Portsmouth Naval Shipyard** C-207-438-1513/2015, DSN-312-684-1513/2015

**NEW JERSEY**
**Cape May Coast Guard Training Center** C-609-898-6922, DSN-312-898-6922
**Earle Naval Weapons Station** C-732-866-2103, DSN-312-449-2167
**Fort Dix Army Garrison** C-609-562-3188/723-2026, DSN-312-944-3188
**Fort Monmouth** C-732-532-1092, DSN-312-992-5510
**Lakehurst Naval Air Engineering Station** C-732-323-2266, DSN-312-624-2266
**McGuire Air Force Base** C-609-754-3336/7, DSN-312-650-3336/7
**Picatinny Arsenal** C-973-724-8855/4014, DSN-312-880-8855/4014
**Townsends Inlet Recreation Facility** C-609-677-2028 (Nov-Feb), C-609-263-3722 (Mar-Oct)

**NEW MEXICO**
**Cannon Air Force Base** C-505-784-2918/2919, DSN-312-681-2918/2919
**Holloman Air Force Base** C-505-572-7160/3311, DSN-312-572-7160/3468
**Kirtland Air Force Base** C-505-846-9652/9653, DSN-312-246-9652/9653
**White Sands Missile Range** C-505-678-4559, DSN-312-258-4559

**NEW YORK**
**Fisher House, Albany** C-518-462-3311 ext 2800
**Fort Drum** C-315-772-5435, DSN-312-341-6011
**Fort Hamilton** C-718-630-4564, DSN-312-232-4564
**New York Coast Guard Activities** C-718-354-4407
**Niagara Falls International Airport/Air Reserve Station** C-716-236-2014, DSN-312-238-2014
**Soldiers', Sailors', Marines', and Airmen's Club** C-212-683-4353, toll free 1-800-678-8443
**Staten Island Navy Lodge** C-718-442-0413
**United States Military Academy, West Point** C-845-446-4731 or C-1-800-247-5047

**NORTH CAROLINA**
**Camp Lejeune Marine Corps Base** C-910-456-1070 ext 0, DSN-312-451-5655
**Cape Hatteras Coast Guard Group** C-252-995-3676
**Cherry Point Marine Corps Air Station** C-252-463-3061/252-466-3060, DSN-312-582-3060
**Elizabeth City Coast Guard Support Center** C-252-335-6397
**Fort Bragg** C-910-396-7700, DSN-312-236-7700
**Fort Fisher Air Force Recreation Area** C-910-458-6549/6546
**New River Marine Corps Air Station** C-910-937-5020, DSN-312-750-6621
**Pope Air Force Base** C-910-394-4131, DSN-312-424-4131
**Seymour Johnson Air Force Base** C-919-722-0385, DSN-312-722-0385

**NORTH DAKOTA**
**Camp Gilbert C. Grafton National Guard Training Site** C-701-662-0239
**Grand Forks Air Force Base** C-701-747-3070, DSN-312-362-3070
**Minot Air Force Base** C-701-723-6161, DSN-312-453-6161

**OHIO**
**Camp Perry Training Site** C-614-336-6214
**Columbus Defense Supply Center** C-614-692-4758, DSN-312-850-4758
**Rickenbacker International Airport/Air National Guard Base** C-614-409-2660, DSN-312-850-4451
**Wright-Patterson Air Force Base** C-937-879-5921 or C-937-257-3810, DSN-312-787-3451
**Youngstown-Warren Regional Airport/Air Reserve Station** C-330-609-1268, DSN-312-346-1268

**OKLAHOMA**
**Altus Air Force Base** C-580-481-7356, DSN-312-866-7356
**Fort Sill** C-580-442-5000, C-1-877-902-3607, DSN-312-639-5000
**Tinker Air Force Base** C-405-734-2822
**Vance Air Force Base** C-580-213-7358, DSN-312-448-7358

**OREGON**
**Camp Rilea Armed Forces Training Center** C-503-861-4048/4052, DSN-314-355-4048/4052
**Klamath Falls International Airport/Kingsley Field/Air National Guard** C-541-885-6365, D-312-830-6365

**PENNSYLVANIA**
**Carlisle Barracks** C-717-245-4245, DSN-312-245-4245
**Defense Distribution Center, Susquehanna** C-717-770-7035, DSN-312-977-7035
**Fort Indiantown Gap** C-717-861-2512/2540/8158, DSN-312-491-2512/ 2540/8158
**Pittsburgh International Airport/Air Reserve Station** C-412-474-8229/8230, DSN-312-277-8230
**Tobyhanna Army Depot** C-570-895-8529, DSN-312-795-7970
**Willow Grove Naval Air Station/Joint Reserve Base** C-215-442-5800/5801, DSN-312-991-5800, Toll-Free C-1-800-227-9472

**RHODE ISLAND**
**Newport Naval Station** C-401-841-7900, DSN-312-948-7900

**SOUTH CAROLINA**
**Beaufort Marine Corps Air Station** C-843-522-1663, DSN-312-335-7676
**Charleston Air Force Base** C-843-963-3806, C-843-552-9900, DSN-312-673-3806/8000
**Charleston Naval Weapons Station** C-843-764-7218, DSN-312-794-7218
**Fort Jackson** C-803-751-6223, DSN-312-734-6223
**Parris Island Marine Corps Recruit Depot** C-843-228-2744, DSN-312-335-2744
**Shaw Air Force Base** C-1-800-769-7429, C-803-895-3803, DSN-312-965-3801/3802
**Short Stay Navy Outdoor Recreation Area** C-1-800-447-2178 or C-843-761-8353
**Wateree Recreation Area** C-803-895-0449, DSN-312-965-0449

**SOUTH DAKOTA**
**Ellsworth Air Force Base** C-605-385-2844, DSN-312-675-2844

**TENNESSEE**
**Arnold Air Base** C-931-454-3099, DSN-312-340-3094
**Mid-South Naval Support Activity** C-901-872-0121

**TEXAS**
**Armed Services YMCA of El Paso** C-915-562-8461
**Belton Lake Recreation Area** C-254-287-2523, DSN-312-737-2523
**Brooks Air Force Base** C-210-536-1844, DSN-312-240-1844
**Canyon Lake Recreation Area** C-1-888-882-9878 or C-830-964-3318, DSN-312-471-3318
**Corpus Christi Naval Air Station** C-361-961-2388/89, DSN-312-861-2388/89
**Dyess Air Force Base** C-915-696-1874, DSN-312-461-1874/2681
**Fort Bliss** C-915-565-7777, DSN-312-978-7777
**Fort Hood** C-254-532-5157, DSN-312-737-3067
**Fort Sam Houston** C-210-357-2705, C-1-800-462-7691, DSN-312-471-2705
**Fort Worth Naval Air Station/Joint Reserve Base** C-817-782-5392/3, DSN-312-739-5392/3
**Goodfellow Air Force Base** C-915-654-3686, DSN-312-477-3686
**Ingleside Naval Station** C-361-776-4420, DSN-312-776-4420
**Kelly Air Force Base** C-210-925-1844/8279, DSN-312-945-1844
**Kingsville Naval Air Station** C-361-516-6321/6581, DSN-312-876-6581/6321
**Lackland Air Force Base** C-210-671-3622/4277/2556, DSN-312-473-3622/4277/2556
**Laughlin Air Force Base** C-830-298-5731, DSN-312-732-5731
**Randolph Air Force Base** C-210-652-1844, DSN-312-487-1844
**Red River Army Depot** C-903-334-2688/2254, DSN-312-829-2688/2254
**Sheppard Air Force Base** C-940-855-7370, DSN-312-736-1844
**Sheppard Air Force Base Recreation Annex** C-903-523-4613, DSN-312-736-4613

**UTAH**
**Camp W.G. Williams** C-801-253-5410, DSN-312-766-5410
**Dugway Proving Ground** C-431-831-2333, DSN-312-789-2333
**Hill Air Force Base** C-801-777-1844; DSN-312-777-0801
**Tooele Army Depot** C-435-833-2056, DSN-312-790-2056

**VIRGINIA**
**Camp Pendleton Army National Guard** C-757-491-5140 ext 20
**Cheatham Annex/Yorktown Naval Weapons Station** C-757-887-7224, DSN-312-953-7224
**Chesapeake Naval Security Group Activity Northwest** C-757-421-8282/83, DSN-312-564-1336
**Dahlgren Naval Surface Warfare Center** C-540-653-7671/72, DSN-312-249-7671/72
**Dam Neck Annex, Oceana Naval Air Station** C-757-492-6453, DSN-312-492-6453
**Fort A.P. Hill** C-804-633-8335, DSN-312-578-8335
**Fort Belvoir** C-1-800-295-9750 or 703-805-2333/2307, DSN-312-655-2333
**Fort Eustis** C-757-878-5807, DSN-312-927-5807
**Fort Lee** C-804-733-4100, DSN-312-687-6700
Fort Monroe C-757-788-2128, DSN-312-680-2128
**Fort Myer** C-703-696-3576/77, DSN-312-426-3576/77
**Fort Pickett** C-804-292-2443, DSN-312-438-2443
**Fort Story** C-757-422-8818
**Judge Advocate General's School** C-804-972-6450, DSN-312-934-6450
**Langley Air Force Base** C-757-764-4667, DSN-312-574-4667
**Little Creek Naval Amphibious Base** C-757-462-7522, DSN-312-253-7522
**Norfolk Naval Station** C-757-402-7005 or 1-877-986-9258, DSN-312-564-7005
**Norfolk Naval Shipyard** C-757-396-4449, DSN-312-961-4449
**Oceana Naval Air Station** C-757-433-2574, DSN-312-433-2574
**Quantico Marine Corps Base** C-703-784-3148/9 ext 221, DSN-312-278-3148/9 ext 221
**Richmond Defense Supply Center** C-804-279-3371 or 804-279-4198; DSN-312-695-4198
**Wallops Island Surface Combat Systems Center** C-757-824-2064
**Yorktown Coast Guard Reserve Training Center** C-757-898-2378, DSN-312-827-2378
**Yorktown Naval Weapons Station** C-757-887-7621, DSN-312-952-7621

**WASHINGTON**
**Bangor Naval Submarine Base** C-360-396-6581/4035, DSN-312-744-6581/4035
**Bremerton Naval Station** C-360-476-9527, C-360-476-7660 ext 5000, DSN-312-439-7660
**Clear Lake Recreation Area** C-509-299-5129
**Everett Naval Station** C-425-304-3111, DSN-312-727-3111
**Fairchild Air Force Base** C-509-247-5519, DSN-312-657-5519
**Fort Lewis** C-253-967-2815/6754/5051
**Madigan Army Medical Center** C-253-964-0211, DSN-312-357-5051

**McChord Air Force Base** C-1-800-847-3899. C-253-982-5613, DSN-312-382-5613
**Pacific Beach Resort and Conference Center** C-888-463-6697, C-360-276-4414
**Whidbey Island Naval Air Station** C-360-257-2529, DSN-312-820-2529

**WEST VIRGINIA**
**Camp Dawson Army Training Site** C-304-329-4420, DSN-312-623-4420
**Sugar Grove Naval Security Group Activity** C-304-249-6309, DSN-312-564-6309

**WISCONSIN**
**Fort McCoy** C-608-388-2107, DSN-312-280-2107

**WYOMING**
**Francis E. Warren Air Force Base** C-307-773-1844, DSN-312-481-1844
**Yellowstone Country Trailers** C-208-828-6333, DSN-312-728-6333

## UNITED STATES POSSESSIONS

**GUAM**
**Andersen Air Force Base** C-671-362-4444, DSN-315-362-4444
**Guam Naval Computer & Telecommunications Area Master Station** C-671-355-5793, DSN-315-355-5793
**Marianas U.S. Naval Forces** C-671-339-5259, DSN-315-339-5259

**PACIFIC ISLANDS**
**Wake Island Army Airfield** C-808-424-2210, DSN-314-424-2210

**PUERTO RICO**
**Borinquen Coast Guard Air Station** C-787-890-8492
**Fort Buchanan** C-787-792-7977, DSN-313-740-3633/3634/3635
**Roosevelt Roads Naval Station** C-787-865-4358
**Sabana Seca Naval Security Group Activity** C-787-261-8413

## FOREIGN COUNTRIES

**AUSTRALIA**
**Naval and Military Club** C-011-61-3-9650-4741

**BAHRAIN**
**Bahrain Administrative Support Unit** C-(USA) 011-973-724-716/762, DSN-318-439-4716, (BA) 318-439-4716

**BELGIUM**
**SHAPE/Chievres Air Base Community** C-(USA) 011-32-65-73-93-00/99, DSN-314-366-7211
**United States Embassy/Tri-Mission Association** C-(USA) 011-32-2-508-2481, DSN-314-365-9691

**CANADA**
**18th Wing Trenton** C-613-392-2811 ext 3402, DSN-312-827-7011, ext 3402
**19th Wing Gander** C-709-256-1703 ext 212, DSN-312-622-3212

**117th Wing Winnipeg** C-204-833-2500 ext 6416, DSN-312-257-6416

**CUBA**
**Guantanamo Bay Naval Station** C-(USA) 011-53-99-2400, DSN-313-564-8877

**CZECH REPUBLIC**
**Prague United States Embassy Apartments** C-011-420-2-5753-0663 ext 2096

**DENMARK (GREENLAND)**
**Thule Air Base** C-011-299-976-585 ext 3276, DSN-314-268-1110 ext 3276

**FRANCE**
**Cercle National des Armées** C-011-33-1-4490-26-26
**La Fondation Furtado Heine, Villa des Officiers** C-011-33-4-93-37-51-00, (FR) 04-93-37-51-00
**United Service Organizations (USO) - Paris** C-011-33-1-40-70-99-68

**GERMANY**
**Ansbach Community** C-(USA) 011-49-9802-83-2812, (DE) 09802-83-1700, DSN-314-467-2812 or DSN-314-468-1700
**Babenhausen Sub-Community** C-(USA) 011-49-6073-38-655, (DE) 06073-72-880, DSN-314-348-3655
**Bad Aibling Station** C-(USA) 011-49-8061-38-5778/3445, (DE) 08061-38-5778, DSN-314-441-1700
**Bamberg Community** C-(USA) 011-49-951-300-1700, (DE) 0951-300-1700, DSN-314-469-1700/8604,
**Baumholder Community** C-(USA) 011-49-6783-999300, (DE) 06783-999300, DSN-314-485-1700/7433
**Cassels House** C-011-49-2161-47-4234
**Chiemsee AFRC** C-(USA) 011-49-8821-72981, (DE) 08821-79081, DSN-314-440-2575
**Darmstadt Community** C-(USA) 011-49-6151-69-1700/7520 or C-011-49-6151-96430, DSN-314-348-1700/7520
**Friedberg Community** C-(USA) 011-49-6031-73380, or C-011-49-6031-81-1700, DSN-314-324-1700
**Garmisch AFRC** C-(USA) 011-49-8821-72981, (DE) 08821-79081, DSN-314-440-2575
**Garmisch Community** C-(USA) 011-49-8821-53396/750873, DSN-314-440-2876
**Geilenkirchen NATO Air Base** C-(USA) 011-49-2451-63-4962, (DE) 02451-63-4962
**Giessen Community** C-(USA) 011-49-641-402-1700, (DE) 0641-402-1700, DSN-314-343-1700
**Grafenwoehr Community** C-(USA) 011-49-9641-930103 or C-011-49-9641-83-1700, (DE) 09641-83-1700/6182, DSN-314-475-6182/1700
**Hanau Community** C-(USA) 011-49-6181-88-1700/8357, 011-49-6181-9550, DSN-314-322-1700/8357
**Heidelberg Community** C-(USA) 011-49-17-6221-1700 or C-011-49-6221-795100/795402, (DE) 06221-795100, DSN-314-370-6941/7979
**Hohenfels Community** C-(USA) 011-49-9472-950155/2 or C-(USA) 011-49-9472-83-1700, DSN-314-466-1700/2438
**Illesheim Community** C-011-49-9841-83-523, DSN-314-467-4523

**Kaiserslautern Community, Ramstein Air Base** C-(USA) 011-49-6371-45-4920, DSN-314-480-4920, (DE) 06371-45-4920

**Kitzingen Community** C-011-49-9321-31836, or C-011-49-9321-305-600, DSN-314-355-8311/8322

**Landstuhl Medical Center** C-(USA) 011-49-6371-45-4920, DSN-314-480-4920, (DE) 06371-45-4920

**Mannheim Community** C-(USA) 011-49-621-730-9218/1700, (DE) 0621-730-9218/1700, DSN-314-380-1700/9218

**Oberammergau Community** C-(USA) 011-49-8822-9160

**Ramstein Air Base** C-(USA) 011-49-6371-45-4920, (DE) 06371-45-4920, DSN-314-480-4920

**Rhein Main Air Base** C-(USA) 011-49-69-699-7265/6, (DE) 069-699-4630, DSN-314-330-6843/7265

**Schweinfurt Community** C-(USA) 011-49-9721-96-1700/7940, (DE) 09721-96-1700/7940, DSN-314-354-1700

**Sembach Air Base Annex, Ramstein Air Base** C-(USA) 011-49-6371-45-4920, (DE) 06371-45-4920, DSN-314-480-4920

**Spangdahlem Air Base** C-(USA) 011-49-6565-61-6504, DSN-314-452-6504, (DE) 06565-61-6504

**Stuttgart Community** C-(USA) 011-49-711-67840, (DE) 0711-67840, DSN-314-430-7181/4137

**Vilseck Community** C-(USA) 011-49-9662-83-441104 or C-011-49-9662-83-2555/1700, (DE) 09662-441104 or 09662-83-2555/1700, DSN-314-476-2555/1700

**Wiesbaden Community** C- (USA) 011-49-611-343136/343664, (DE) 0611-343664, DSN-314-337-7493/7212

**Wuerzburg Community** C-(USA) 011-49-931-70582-0 or C-011-49-931-889-1700/6648, (DE) 0931-70582-0 or 0931-889-1700/6648, DSN-314-350-1700/6648

### HONDURAS
**Soto Cano Air Base** C-(USA) 011-504-237-88-33, DSN-313-449-4000

### HONG KONG
**Hong Kong Community** C-(USA) 011-852-2-368-8261, (HK) 2368-8261

### ICELAND
**Keflavik NATO Base** C-(USA) 011-354-425-4333, DSN-314-450-4333

### ITALY
**Admiral Carney Park** C-(USA) 011-39-081-526-3396/1579, (IT) 081-526-3396/1579

**Aviano Air Base** C-(USA) 011-39-0434-66-5722/5041, (IT) 0434-66-5722/5041, DSN-314-632-5722/5041

**Camp Darby (Livorno)** C-(USA) 011-39-050-54-7225, (IT) 050-54-7225, DSN-314-633-7448/7225/7221

**Capodichino Airport (Naples)** C-(USA) 011-39-081-568-5250, (IT) 081-568-5250, DSN-314-568-5250

**La Maddalena Naval Support Activity** (Sardinia) C-(USA) 011-39-0789-798-297/416/417/418/419, (IT) 0789-798-297/416/417/418/419, DSN-314-623-8297/416/417/418/419

**Naples Naval Support Activity** C-(USA) 011-39-081-509-7120, (IT) 081-509-7120

**Sigonella Naval Air Station** C-(USA) 011-39-095-86-2300/6830/6508, (IT) 095-86-2300/6830/6508, DSN-314-624-2300/6830

**Vicenza Community** C-(USA) 011-39-0444-51-8034/35, (IT) 0444-51-8034/35, DSN-314-634-8034/35

### JAPAN
**Atsugi Naval Air Facility** C-(USA)-011-81-3117-64-3696, (JP) 3117-64-3696, DSN-315-264-3696

**Camp S.D. Butler Marine Corps Base** C-(USA) 011-81-98-892-2455, (JP) 098-892-2191, DSN-315-635-2191

**Camp Zama** C-(USA) 011-81-3117-63-3830/4474, DSN-315-263-3830/4474

**Iwakuni Marine Corps Air Station** C-(USA) 011-81-6117-53-3221 (TLF), (JP) 0827-21-4171 ext 3221, DSN-315-253-3221

**Kadena Air Base** C-(USA) 011-81-6117-32-1100/1101/1010/1050, DSN-315-632-1100/1101/1010/1050

**Misawa Air Base** C-(USA) 011-81-3117-62-1100 ext 3526, (JP) 0176-53-5181 ext 1100, DSN-315-222-1100

**New Sanno U.S. Forces Center** C-(USA) 011-81-3-3440-7871 ext 7121, (JP) 03-3440-7871 ext 7121, DSN-315-229-7121

**Okuma Joint Services Rec Facility (Okinawa)** C-(USA) 011-81-6117-34-4322, (JP) 098938-1110 ext 634-4322, DSN-315-634-4322

**Sasebo Fleet Activities** C-(USA) 011-81-956-24-6111 (BOQ ext 3794) (BEQ ext 3413), (JP) 095624-6111, DSN-315-252-3794 (BOQ), DSN-315-252-3413 (BEQ)

**Tama Hills Recreation Area** C-(USA) 011-81-423-77-7009, (JP) 042-377-7009, DSN-315-224-3421/3422

**Tokyo Administration Facility** C-(USA) 011-81-3117-29-3270, (JP) 03117-29-3270

**White Beach Recreation Services** C-(USA) 011-81-634-6952/6954, DSN-315-634-6952/6954/6342

**Yokosuka Fleet Activities** C-(USA) 011-81-6160-43-7317/5685, DSN-315-243-7317

**Yokota Air Base** C-(USA) 011-81-3117-55-7712/754-2002, C-(JP) 042-552-2510 ext 4-2000, DSN-315-224-2002

### KOREA
**Camp Carroll** C-(USA) 011-82-545-970-7823

**Camp Casey** C-(USA) 011-82-31-869-4247, (KR) 031-869-4247 DSN-315-730-4247

**Camp Henry** C-(USA) 011-82-53-470-7459, DSN-315-768-8171

**Camp Hialeah** C-(USA) 011-82-51-801-3668, DSN-315-763-3668

**Camp Humphreys** C-(USA) 011-82-333-690-7355/7269, DSN-315-753-7355/7269

**Camp Page** C-(USA) 011-82-33-259-5331, DSN-315-721-5331/5691

**Cheju-do Recreation Center (Camp McNabb)** C-011-82-53-470-4003, DSN-315-764-4403

**Chinhae Fleet Activities** C-(USA) 011-82-55-540-5336, DSN-315-762-5336

**Dragon Hill Lodge** C-(USA) 011-82-2-790-0016, (KR) 790-0016, DSN-315-738-2222

**Kunsan Air Base** C-(USA) 011-82-654-470-4604, (KR) 0654-470-4604, DSN-315-782-4604/4743

**Osan Air Base** C-(USA) 011-82-331-661-1844/4597, DSN-315-784-1844/4597

**Yongsan Army Garrison** C-(USA) 011-82-2-7914-8830/8810, (KR) 2-07914-8830, DSN-315-724-8830/8810

### NETHERLANDS
**Schinnen Community (NATO HQ AFNORTH)** C-(USA) 011-31-45-564-3188/6200, (NT) 045-564-3188/6200, DSN-314-360-3188

### PORTUGAL
**Lajes Field Air Base (Azores)** C-(USA) 011-351-295-57-4138/24146, DSN-(USA) 314-535-4138, DSN-(Europe) 314-245-3426

### SAUDI ARABIA
**Dhahran Community** C-(USA) 011-966-3-899-1119 ext 431-4018, DSN-318-435-7081/2

**Riyadh Community** C-(USA) 011-966-1-435-7837

### SINGAPORE
**Sembawang Community** C-(USA) 011-65-257-0256

### SPAIN
**Moron Air Base** C-(USA) 011-34-95-584-8098, (ES) 095-584-8098, DSN-314-722-8098

**Rota Naval Station** C-(USA) 011-34-956-82-1871/1752, (ES) 0956-82-1871/1752, DSN-314-727-1871/1752

### TURKEY
**Incirlik Air Base** C-(USA) 011-90-322-316-6786, (TR) 0322-316-6786. DSN-314-676-6786

**Izmir Community/Air Station** C-(USA) 011-90-232-489-4090, DSN-314-675-3379

### UNITED KINGDOM
**RAF Alconbury** C-(USA) 011-44-1480-82-6000, DSN-(USA) 314-268-6000, (UK) 01480-82-6000

**RAF Croughton** C-011-44-1280-708-394, DSN-314-236-8394

**Diego Garcia Atoll, U.S. Navy Support Facility** C-011-246-370-4830, DSN-315-370-4830

**RAF Fairford** C-(USA) 011-44-1285-716-100, (UK) 01285-716-100, DSN-314-247-4272

**RAF Lakenheath** C-(USA) 011-44-1638-52-6700/6713, (UK) 0638-52-6700/6713, DSN-314-226-6700/6713

**Menwith Hill Station** C-(USA) 011-44-1423-77-7895, DSN-314-262-7895

**RAF Mildenhall** C-(USA) 011-44-1-638-54-2655/3093/6001, DSN-314-238-2655/3093/6001, (UK) 01638-54-2655/2965

**The Naval Club** C-(USA) 011-44-20-7493-7672, (UK) 020-7493-7672

**Portsmouth Royal Sailors' Home Club** C-(USA) 011-44-23-92-824231

**Royal Fleet Club** C-(USA) 011-44-1752-562723

**The Royal Scots Club** C-(USA) 011-44-131-556-4270

**St. Mawgan Joint Maritime Facility** C-011-44-1637-85-3541/3597, DSN-314-234-3541/3597

**Union Jack Club** C-(USA) 011-44-20-7928-4814, (UK) 020-7928-4814

**Victory Services Club** C-(USA) 011-44-207-723-4474, (UK) 0207-723-4474

## UNITED STATES

### ALABAMA
**Dauphin Island Coast Guard Recreation Facility** C-334-861-7113
**Lake Martin Maxwell/Gunter Recreation Area** (Maxwell AFB) C-334-953-3509/3510, DSN-312-493-3510
**Maxwell/Gunter FAMCAMP** (Maxwell AFB) C-334-953-5161, DSN-312-493-5161
**Redstone Arsenal Campground** C-256-876-4868/6854, DSN-312-746-4868/6854
**Rucker Outdoor Recreation Area** (Fort Rucker) C-334-255-4305, DSN-312-558-4305

### ALASKA
**Birch Lake Recreation Area** (Eielson AFB) C-907-377-1232/1328/2769, DSN-317-377-1232
**Black Spruce Travel Camp** (Fort Richardson) C-907-384-1476 or C-907-428-0001
**Eielson FAMCAMP** (Eielson AFB) C-907-377-1232, DSN-317-377-1232
**Elmendorf FAMCAMP** (Elmendorf AFB) C-907-552-2023
**Glass Park** (Fort Wainwright) C-907-353-6349/6350, DSN-317-353-6349/6350
**Ravenwood Ski Lodge** (Eielson AFB) C-907-377-1232
**Seward Air Force Camp** (Elmendorf AFB) C-907-552-5526, DSN-317-552-5526
**Seward Resort** (Fort Richardson) C-800-770-1858 or C-907-224-5559/2659/2654, DSN-317-384-FISH (3474)/LINE (5463)

### ARIZONA
**Apache RV Park** (Fort Huachuca) C-520-533-1335, DSN-312-879-1335
**Davis-Monthan FAMCAMP** (Davis-Monthan AFB) C-520-747-9144, DSN-312-361-1110
**Desert Breeze Travel Camp** (Yuma Army Proving Ground) C-520-329-8710 or C-520-328-3989, DSN-312-899-3989
**Fort Tuthill Recreation Area** C-800-552-6268, C-520-774-3464 or C-623-856-3401
**Gila Bend FAMCAMP** (Gila Bend AF Auxiliary Field) C-520-683-6238/6211, DSN-312-896-5238/5211
**Lake Martinez Recreation Facility** (Yuma MCAS) C-520-269-2278, DSN-312-951-2278

### ARKANSAS
**Chaffee Trailer Park** (Fort Chaffee Maneuver Training Center) C-501-484-2252/2917, DSN-312-962-2252/2917
**Little Rock FAMCAMP** (Little Rock AFB) C-501-987-3365, DSN-312-731-3365

### CALIFORNIA
**Admiral Baker Field Campground** (San Diego Naval Station) C-619-556-5525
**Barstow RV Camp** (Barstow MCLB) C-760-577-6418
**Beale FAMCAMP** (Beale AFB) C-530-634-3382/2054, DSN-312-368-3382/2054
**Big Bear Recreation Facility** (Miramar MCAS) C-858-577-4141/4126, DSN-312-577-4141/4126
**Camp Roberts** C-805-238-8312, DSN-312-949-8312
**Camp San Luis Obispo RV Park** C-805-594-6500, DSN-312-630-6500

**Channel Islands Harbor Family Recreational Facility (Channel Islands CGS)** C-805-982-6123
**Del Mar Beach Cottages/Campsites** (Camp Pendleton MCB) C-760-725-2134
**Edwards FAMCAMP** (Edwards AFB) C-661-277-3456, DSN-312-527-3546
**El Centro NAF Campground** (El Centro NAF) C-760-339-2486, DSN-312-958-8486
**Fiddler's Cove RV Park** (Coronado Naval Amphibious Base) C-619-522-8681
**Fort Hunter Liggett Primitive Campground** C-831-386-2550
**Lake O'Neill Recreation Park** (Camp Pendleton MCB) C-760-725-4241, DSN-312-365-4241
**Lake Tahoe Coast Guard Recreation Facilities** (Lake Tahoe CGG) C-530-583-7438
**Lake Tahoe Rental Condominiums** (Alameda CGISC) C-510-437-3573
**Lemoore Naval Air Station Campground** C-559-997-8983, DSN-312-949-8983
**Los Angeles AFB FAMCAMP** C-310-363-2081/2190, DSN-312-833-2081/2190
**March ARB FAMCAMP** C-909-655-2816, DSN-312-947-2816
**Monterey Pines RV Campground** (Monterey Bay NSA) C-831-656-4029, DSN-312-878-4029
**Petaluma Lake Area Campsites** (Petaluma CGTC) C-707-765-7348
**Port Hueneme RV Park** (Port Hueneme NCBC) C-805-982-4392/6123
**Point Mugu Recreation Facilities** (Point Mugu NAS) C-805-989-8407, DSN-312-351-8407
**San Onofre Recreation Beach** (Camp Pendleton MCB) C-760-725-7935, DSN-312-365-7935
**Sharpe Travel Camp** (Defense Distribution Depot) C-209-982-2237, DSN-312-462-2237
**South Lake Tahoe Recreation Housing** (Presidio of Monterey) C-831-242-5506/6132/6133, DSN-312-878-5506/6132
**Travis FAMCAMP** C-707-424-3583, DSN-312-837-3583
**Vandenberg FAMCAMP** C-805-606-8579, DSN-312-276-8579

### COLORADO
**Farish Recreation Area** (USAF Academy) C-719-687-9098
**Peregrine Pines FAMCAMP** (USAF Academy) C-719-333-4356 or 719-333-4980, DSN-312-333-4356/4980

### CONNECTICUT
None

### DELAWARE
**Bethany Beach Training Site** (Delaware ANG) C-302-854-7900/7902, DSN-312-440-7900/2
**Dover AFB FAMCAMP** C-302-677-3959, DSN-312-445-3959

### DISTRICT OF COLUMBIA
None

### FLORIDA
**Blue Angel Naval Recreation Area** (Corry Station NTTC) C-850-453-9435/3798
**Camp Blanding RV Park and Campsites** C-904-682-3104, DSN-312-533-3104

**Choctaw Recreation Area** (Eglin AFB) C-850-882-6581
**Coon's Creek Recreation Area** (MacDill AFB) C-800-821-4982 or C-813-840-6919, DSN-312-968-4982
**Destin Army Infantry Center Recreation Area** (Fort Benning) C-800-642-0466 or C-850-837-2725
**Eglin FAMCAMP** C-850-882-6581
**Hurlburt FAMCAMP** C-850-884-6939, DSN-312-579-6939
**Jacksonville RV Park** (Jacksonville NAS) C-904-542-3227, DSN-312-942-3227
**Lake Pippin, Maxwell/Gunter Recreation Area** (Maxwell AFB) C-850-897-2411, DSN-312-493-3509
**Manatee Cove Campground & Recreational Lodging** (Patrick AFB) C-321-494-4787 or C-321-494-2042, DSN-312-854-4787
**Marathon Recreation Cottages and RV Park** (Marathon CGS) C-305-535-4565
**Oak Grove Park FAMCAMP** (Pensacola NAS) C-850-452-2535, DSN-312-922-2535
**Panama City CSS Outdoor Recreation/Marina** (Panama City CSS NSWC) C-850-234-4402, DSN-312-436-4402
**Pelican's Roost RV Park** (Mayport NS) C-904-270-5221
**Sigsbee RV Park** (Key West NAS) C-888-539-7697 or C-305-293-4432/4433
**Tyndall FAMCAMP** (Tyndall AFB) C-850-283-2798, DSN-312-523-2798

### GEORGIA
**Dobbins Lakeside FAMCAMP** (Dobbins ARB) C-770-919-4870, DSN-312-925-4870
**Fort Gordon Recreation Area** C-706-541-1057
**Grassy Pond Recreation Area** (Moody AFB) C-912-559-5840, DSN-312-460-1110 ext 559-5840
**Holbrook Pond Recreation Area and Campground** (Fort Stewart) C-912-767-2717/2771/5145, DSN-312-870-2717/2771/5145
**Lake Allatoona Army Recreation Area** (Fort McPherson) C-770-974-3413/9420
**Lotts Island Army Air Field Travel Camp** (Hunter AAF) C-912-352-5916/5722/5274, DSN-312-870-5722
**Robins FAMCAMP** (Robins AFB) C-912-926-4500 or 912-926-3193, DSN-312-468-3193
**Uchee Creek Army Campground/Marina** (Fort Benning) C-706-545-4053/7238/5600, DSN-312-835-4053/7238
**World Famous Navy Lake Site** (Atlanta NAS) C-770-974-6309

### HAWAII
**Barbers Point Recreation Area** (Barbers Point NAS) C-808-682-2019
**Barking Sands Beach Cottages** (Barking Sands Pacific Missile Range Facility) C-808-335-4752, DSN-315-471-6752
**Bellows Recreation Center** (Bellows AFS) C-800-437-2607, C-808-259-8080 for cottages C-808-529-4121 for camping
**Camp Smith Stables** C-808-484-9417
**Kaneohe Bay Beach Cottages and Campsites** (Kaneohe Bay MCAS) C-808-254-2716, DSN-315-430-7695
**Kilauea Military Camp, Joint Services Recreation Center** C-808-967-8343 or C-808-867-8343 (from Oahu only)

**Waianae Army Recreation Center** (Fort Shafter) C-800-333-4158 from mainland , C-800-847-6771 from outer islands or C-808-696-4158

### IDAHO
**Gowen Field**
C-208-422-4451, DSN-312-422-4451
**Mountain Home FAMCAMP** (Mountain Home AFB) C-208-828-6333, DSN-312-728-6333
**Strike Dam Marina** (Mountain Home AFB)
C-208-828-6333
**Yellowstone Country Trailers** (Mountain Home AFB) C-208-828-6333

### ILLINOIS
**Great Lakes Naval Training Center**
C-847-688-5417, DSN-312-792-5417
**Scott FAMCAMP** (Scott AFB)
C-618-256-2067, DSN-312-576-2067

### INDIANA
**Camp Atterbury Campgrounds**
C-812-526-1149, DSN-312-569-2149
**Crane MWR Campgrounds** (Crane Division NSWC) C-812-854-1368, DSN-312-482-1368

### IOWA
**None**

### KANSAS
**McConnell AFB FAMCAMP**
C-316-759-6999, DSN-312-743-6999

### KENTUCKY
**Camp Carlson Army Travel Camp** (Fort Knox)
C-502-624-4836, DSN-312-464-4836
**Destiny Parks & Pavilions** (Army Travel Camp) (Fort Campbell) C-270-798-5590/3126, DSN-312-635-5590/3126

### LOUISIANA
**Barksdale FAMCAMP** (Barksdale AFB)
C-318-456-2679, DSN-312-781-2679
**Magnolia Shade Recreational Vehicle Park** (New Orleans NSA) C-504-678-2527/2285, DSN-312-678-2527/2285
**New Orleans NAS/JRB Campground**
C-504-678-3142
**Toledo Bend Recreation Site** (Fort Polk)
C-888-718-9088 or C-318-565-4235
**Twin Lakes Recreation Area** (Camp Beauregard) C-318-641-8302/8269

### MAINE
**Gull Cottage** (Prospect Harbor Naval Satellite Operations Center) C-207-963-7700
**Winter Harbor Recreation Area** (Winter Harbor NSGA) C-207-963-5337 or C-207-963-5334 ext 287/288, DSN-312-476-9287/9288

### MARYLAND
**Andrews FAMCAMP** (Andrews AFB)
C-301-981-5663, DSN-312-858-4109
**Annapolis FAMCAMP** (U.S. Naval Academy/ Annapolis Naval Station) C-410-293-9200, DSN-312-281-9200
**Goose Creek/West Basin Recreation Area** (Patuxent NAS) C-301-342-3508, DSN-312-342-3508
**Skipper's Point Recreational Area** (Aberdeen Proving Ground) C-410-278-4124, DSN-312-298-4124

**Solomons Navy Recreation Center**
C-800-NAVY-230 (D.C. area) or C-410-326-1260

### MASSACHUSETTS
**Cape Cod Vacation Apartments** (Otis ANGB/ Cape Cod CGAS) C-508-968-6461, DSN-312-557-6461
**Cuttyhunk Island Recreational Housing Facility** (USCG Group Boston) C-617-223-3181
**Fourth Cliff Recreation Area** (Hanscom AFB)
C-800-468-9547 or C-781-837-9269
**Hanscom FAMCAMP** (Hanscom AFB)
C-781-377-4670, DSN-312-478-4670

### MICHIGAN
**Camp Grayling Trailer Park** (Camp Grayling MTC) C-517-348-9033
**Point Betsie Recreation Cottage** (Grand Haven CGG) C-616-850-2510
**Selfridge's Five Flags Campground** (Selfridge ANGB) C-810-307-5449, D-312-273-5499

### MINNESOTA
**None**

### MISSISSIPPI
**Keesler FAMCAMP** (Keesler AFB)
C-228-594-0543, DSN-312-597-3160/3186/0002
**Lake Walker Family Campground** (Mississippi ANG/Camp Shelby TS) C-601-558-2397, DSN-312-921-2397
**Shields Park FAMCAMP** (Gulfport NCBC)
C-228-871-5435, DSN-312-868-2231

### MISSOURI
**Lake of the Ozarks Recreation Area** (Fort Leonard Wood) C-573-346-5640

### MONTANA
**Gateway FAMCAMP** (Malmstrom AFB)
C-406-731-3263, DSN-312-632-3263
**Trailers at Timber Wolf Resort** (Malmstrom AFB)
C-406-731-3263, DSN-312-632-4202

### NEBRASKA
**Offutt FAMCAMP** (Offutt AFB)
C-402-294-2108, DSN-312-271-2108

### NEVADA
**Fallon RV Park and Recreation Area** (Fallon NAS) C-775-426-2598/2279, DSN-312-830-2598/2279
**Lucky Seven FAMCAMP** (Nellis AFB)
C-702-643-3060
**Rose Creek** (Fallon NAS) C-775-426-2598/2279, DSN-312-830-2598/2279

### NEW HAMPSHIRE
**New Boston Recreation Area** (New Boston AS) C-603-471-2234, DSN-312-489-2234

### NEW JERSEY
**Brindle Lake Travel Camp** (Fort Dix)
C-609-562-6667, DSN-312-944-6667
**Lake Laurie Campground** (Willow Grove NAS)
C-215-443-6082, DSN-312-991-6082
**Townsends Inlet Recreation Facility** (USCG Group Atlantic City) C-609-263-3722

### NEW MEXICO
**Holloman FAMCAMP** (Holloman AFB)
C-505-572-5369, DSN-312-867-5369

**Kirtland FAMCAMP** (Kirtland AFB)
C-505-846-0337, DSN-312-246-1275
**Volunteer Park Travel Camp Site** (White Sands Missile Range) C-505-678-1713, DSN-312-258-1713

### NEW YORK
**Remington Pond Recreation Area** (Fort Drum)
C-315-772-5169, DSN-312-341-5169
**Round Pond Recreation Area** (U.S. Military Academy, West Point) C-845-938-2503/3860, DSN-312-688-2503

### NORTH CAROLINA
**Cape Hatteras Recreational Quarters** (Cape Hatteras CGG) C-252-995-3676/6435
**Cherry Point MWR FAMCAMP** (Cherry Point MCAS) C-252-466-2197/2172, DSN-312-582-2197
**Elizabeth City Lodging** (Elizabeth City CG Support Center) C-252-335-6397
**Fort Fisher Air Force Recreation Area** (Seymour Johnson AFB) C-910-458-6549
**New River MCAS Marina**
C-910-451-6578, DSN-312-484-6578
**Onslow Beach Campsites and Recreation Area** (Camp Lejeune MCB) C-910-450-7473/7502, DSN-312-484-7473/7502
**Seymour Johnson FAMCAMP** (Seymour Johnson AFB) C-919-736-5405, DSN-312-488-5405
**Smith Lake Army Travel Campground** (Fort Bragg) C-910-396-5979, DSN-312-326-5979

### NORTH DAKOTA
**Grand Forks FAMCAMP** (Grand Forks AFB)
C-701-747-3688, DSN-312-362-3688
**Minot Air Force Base FAMCAMP**
C-701-723-3648, DSN-312-453-3648

### OHIO
**Wright-Patterson AFB FAMCAMP**
C-937-257-5327, DSN-312-787-5327

### OKLAHOMA
**Altus FAMCAMP** (Altus AFB)
C-580-481-6420/6704, DSN-312-866-6704
**Blackhawk Recreational Vehicle Park** (Camp Gruber TS) C-918-487-6065
**Lake Elmer Thomas Recreation Area** (Fort Sill) C-580-442-5858/9
**Murphy's Meadow** (McAlester Army Ammunition Plant) C-918-420-7484/6673, DSN-312-956-7484
**Tinker FAMCAMP** (Tinker AFB)
C-405-734-2289, DSN-312-884-2289

### OREGON
**Camp Rilea** (Camp Rilea AFTC)
C-503-861-4048, DSN-312-355-3972
**Kingsley Field RV Park** (Kingsley Field/Oregon ANG) C-541-885-6350 ext 645

### PENNSYLVANIA
**Letterkenny Army Travel Camp** (Letterkenny Army Depot) C-717-267-9494, DSN-312-570-9494

### RHODE ISLAND
**Carr Point Recreation Area** (Newport Naval Education and Training Center)
C-401-841-3116

## SOUTH CAROLINA

Falcon's Nest FAMCAMP (Shaw AFB)
C-803-895-0449/0450, DSN-312-965-0449/0450
**Shady Oaks Family Campground** (Charleston AFB) C-843-963-5270/1, DSN-312-673-5271
**Short Stay Navy Outdoor Recreation Area** (Charleston NWS) C-800-447-2178 or C-843-761-8353
**Wateree Recreation Area** (Shaw AFB)
C-803-895-0449/0450, DSN-312-965-0449/0450
**Weston Lake Recreation Area and Travel Camp** (Fort Jackson) C-803-751-LAKE (5253), DSN-312-734-LAKE

## SOUTH DAKOTA

**Ellsworth AFB FAMCAMP**
C-605-385-2997, DSN-312-675-2997

## TENNESSEE

**Arnold FAMCAMP** (Arnold AFB)
C-931-454-4520/6084, DSN-312-340-6084
**Navy Lake Recreation Area** (Mid-South Naval Support Activity) C-800-779-4252, C-901-872-3660, DSN-312-882-5163

## TEXAS

**Belton Lake Outdoor Recreation Area** (Fort Hood) C-254-287-2523/8308, DSN-312-737-2523
**Brooks FAMCAMP** (Brooks AFB)
C-210-536-1844, DSN-312-240-1844
**Elliott Lake Recreation Area** (Red River Army Depot) C-903-334-2254, DSN-312-829-2254
**Escondido Ranch** (Kingsville NAS)
C-830-373-4419
**Fort Bliss RV Park**
C-915-568-4693/0106, DSN-312-978-4693/0106
**Fort Sam Houston Army Travel Camp**
C-210-221-5502, DSN-312-471-5502
**Fort Sam Houston Recreation Area at Canyon Lake** C-888-882-9878, C-830-964-3318, DSN-312-471-3318
**Goodfellow AFB Recreation Camp**
C-915-944-1012, DSN-312-477-3217
**Lackland FAMCAMP** (Lackland AFB)
C-210-671-5179, DSN-312-473-5179
**Laughlin FAMCAMP** (Laughlin AFB)
C-830-298-5830, DSN-312-732-5830
**Nasking Recreation FAMCAMP** (Kingsville NAS) C-512-516-6443, DSN-312-861-6443
**Randolph Outdoor Recreation Area** - Canyon Lake (Randolph AFB) C-800-280-3466, C-830-964-4134
**Sheppard AFB Recreation Annex**
C-903-523-4613
**Shields Park NAS Recreation Area** (Corpus Christi NAS) C-361-961-1293/4/5, D-312-861-1293/4/5
**Southwinds Marina on Lake Amistad** (Laughlin AFB) C-830-775-5971/7800
**West Fort Hood Travel Camp**
C-254-288-9926, DSN-312-738-9926

## UTAH

**Carter Creek Camp** (Hill AFB)
C-801-777-3250/2225
**Hill FAMCAMP** (Hill AFB)
C-801-777-3250, DSN-312-458-3250
**Oquirrh Hills Travel Camp** (Tooele Army Depot)C-435-833-3129, DSN-312-790-3129

## VERMONT
**None**
## VIRGINIA
**Bethel Recreation Area-Park & FAMCAMP** (Langley AFB) C-757-766-3017 (Park) or C757-766-7627 (FAMCAMP)
**Cape Henry Inn** (Fort Story) C-757-422-8818
Cape Henry Travel Camp (Fort Story)
C-757-422-7601, DSN-312-438-7601
**Cheatham Annex Recreation Cabins and RV Park** (Cheatham Annex FISC) C-757-887-7224, DSN-312-953-7224
**The Colonies Travel Park** (Fort Monroe)
C-757-788-4305, DSN-312-680-4305
**Fort A.P. Hill Recreation Facilities**
C-804-633-8219, DSN-312-934-8219
**Little Creek MWR RV Park** (Little Creek NAB)
C-757-462-7282, DSN-312-253-7282
**Lunga Park** (Quantico MCB)
C-703-784-5270, DSN-312-278-5270
**Pickett Travel Camp** (Fort Pickett/Virginia ANG MTC) C-804-292-2443, DSN-312-438-2443
**Sea Mist Recreational Vehicle Campground** (Dam Neck FCTC, Atlantic) C-757-492-7545, DSN-312-757-7545
**Stewart Campground** (Chesapeake NSGA, Northwest) C-757-421-8262
**Yorktown CG Campground** (Yorktown CGRTC)
C-757-856-2100

## WASHINGTON
**Camp Murray Beach**
C-253-584-5411, C-800-588-6420, D-312-355-7610
**Clear Lake Recreation Area** (Fairchild AFB)
C-509-299-5129
**Cliffside RV Park** (Whidbey Island NAS)
C-360-257-2434, DSN-312-820-2434
**Fairchild AFB FAMCAMP**
C-509-247-2511/5366, DSN-312-657-2511
**Fort Lewis Travel Camp**
C-253-967-5415/7744, DSN-312-357-1110
**Holiday Park FAMCAMP** (McChord AFB)
C-253-982-5488
**Jim Creek Regional Outdoor Recreation Area** (Jim Creek Naval Radio Station)
C-425-304-5315/5363 or C-888-463-6697, DSN-312-727-5315
**Pacific Beach Resort and Conference Center** (Everett NS) C-888-463-6697 or C-425-276-4414
**Rocky Point RV Park** (Whidbey Island NAS)
C-360-257-2178, DSN-312-820-2178
**Westport Recreation Park** (Grays Harbor Coast Guard Station) C-360-268-0121

## WEST VIRGINIA
**Sugar Grove Cabins** (Sugar Grove NSGA)
C-304-249-6309, DSN-312-564-7276

## WISCONSIN
**Pine View Recreation Area** (Fort McCoy)
C-608-388-3517/2619, DSN-312-280-3517
**Rawley Point Cottage** (Milwaukee CGG)
C-414-747-7185
**Sherwood Point Cottage** (Milwaukee CGG)
C-414-747-7185

## WYOMING
**F.E. Warren FAMCAMP** (Francis E. Warren AFB) C-307-773-2988, DSN-312-481-2988

## UNITED STATES POSSESSIONS

### GUAM
**Andersen AFB Recreation**
C-671-366-5204
**Guam Naval Station Cabanas**
C-671-564-1826

### PUERTO RICO
**Borinquen Recreation Area** (Borinquen CGAS)
C-787-890-8492

## FOREIGN COUNTRIES

### CANADA
**Falls Lake Recreational Facility** (Canadian Forces Base) C-9877-325-5253 or C-902-798-6535, DSN-312-5341/5331
**Lake Pleasant Recreational Facility** (Canadian Forces Base) C-902-765-8165, DSN-312-568-5412
**Tee Pee Park/Air Force Beach** (Canadian Forces Base) C-250-339-8211 ext 8483, DSN-312-252-8211 ext 8483
**Twin Rivers Of Petawawa** (Canadian Forces Base) C-613-687-5331

### GERMANY
**Big Mike Travel Camp** (Vilseck Community)
C-011-49-9662-83-2563
**Chiemsee AFRC Travel Camp**
C-011-49-8821-72981, DSN-314-440-2575
**Garmisch AFRC Travel Camp**
C-011-49-8821-72981, DSN-314-440-2575/6
**Rhein-Main Recreation Area/Campground** (Rhein-Main AB) C-011-49-69-699-7274, DSN-314-330-7274
**Rolling Hills Travel Camp** (Baumholder Community) C-011-49-6783-6-7182, DSN-314-485-7182

### ITALY
**Admiral Carney Park** (Naples Naval Support Activity) C-011-39-081-526-1579
**Sea Pines Camp and Lodge** (Camp Darby)
C-011-39-050-54-7225, DSN-314-633-7225
**Vicenza Travel Camp** (Vincenza Community)
C-011-39-0444-517094, DSN-314-634-7094

### JAPAN
**Okuma Beach Resort—Okinawa** (Kadena AB)
C-011-81-611-734-4322, DSN-315-634-4322
**Tama Outdoor Recreation Area** (Yokota AB)
C-011-81-423-77-7009, DSN-315-224-3421/3422
**White Beach Recreation Services** (Kadena AB) C-011-81-6117-34-6952/6342, DSN-315-634-6952/6954/6342

## AIRLINES

**Air Canada**
888-247-2262
www.aircanada.ca
**Air France**
800-237-2747
www.airfrance.com/us
**Airtran Airways**
800-AIRTRAN (800-247-8726)
www.airtran.com
**Alaska Airlines**
800-ALASKAAIR (800-252-7522)
www.alaska-air.com
**Aloha Airlines**
800-367-5250
877-TRY-ALOHA (877-879-25642)
www.alohaairlines.com
**America West**
800-235-9292
www.americawest.com
**American Airlines/American Eagle**
800-433-7300
www.aa.com
**American Trans Air**
800-225-2995
www.ata.com
**British Airways**
800-247-9297
www.british-airways.com
**Continental Airlines**
800-523-3273 (Domestic)
800-231-0856 (International)
www.continental.com
**Delta Air Lines Inc.**
800-221-1212 (Domestic)
800-241-4141
www.delta.com
**Evergreen International Airlines**
800-382-2746
www.evergreenairlines.com
**Hawaiian Airlines**
800-367-5320
www.hawaiianair.com
**Icelandair**
800-223-5500
www.icelandair.is
**Japan Airlines**
800-JAL-FONE (800-525-3663)
www.japanair.com
**Lufthansa**
800-399-LUFT (800-399-5838)
www.lufthansa.com
**Midwest Express**
800-452-2022
www.midwestexpress.com
**Northwest Airlines/KLM**
800-225-2525 (Domestic)
800-447-4747 (International)
www.nwa.com
**Pan Am**
800-FLYPANAM (800-359-72626)
www.flypanam.com
**Qantas Airways**
800-227-4500
www.qantas.com
**Southwest Airlines**
800-435-9792
www.iflyswa.com
**Spanair**
888-545-5757
www.spanair.com

**Trans World Airlines**
800-221-2000
www.twa.com
**Tower Air**
800-WORLD50 (800-967-5350)
www.worldair.com
**United Airlines**
800-241-6522
www.ual.com
**US Airways**
800-428-4322
www.usairways.com

## HOTELS

**Best Western**
800-780-7234
www.bestwestern.com
**Choice Hotels International** (Includes Clarion, MainStay, Quality, Comfort Suites, Comfort Inn, Sleep, Rodeway Inn and Econo Lodge)
800-4-CHOICE
800-424-6423
www.choicehotels.com
**Concorde Plaza Hotels**
800-888-4747
www.concorde-hotels.com
**Bass Hotels and Resorts** (Includes Intercontinental, Crowne Plaza, Holiday Inn, Holiday Inn Express and Staybridge Suites)
800-HOLIDAY
www. basshotels.com
**Doubletree Hotels**
800-222-TREE
www.doubletree.com
**Drury Hotels**
800-Drury-Inn
www.drury-inn.com
**Embassy Suites**
800-EMBASSY (800-362-2779)
www.embassy-suites.com
**Fairmont Hotels and Resorts**
800-866-5577
www.fairmont.com
**Forte Travelodge**
800-578-7878
www.travelodge.com
**Four Seasons Hotels and Resorts**
800-819-5053
www.fourseasons.com
**Grand Heritage Hotels International**
888-93-GRAND
www.grandheritage.com
**Hampton Inn**
800-HAMPTON (800-426-7866)
www.hampton-inn.com
**Helmsley Hotels**
800-221-4982
www.helmsleyhotels.com
**Hilton**
800-774-1500
www.hilton.com
**Homewood Suites**
800-CALL-HOME (800-225-5466)
www.homewood-suites.com
**Hyatt Hotels & Resorts**
888-591-1234
www.hyatt.com
**Loews Hotels**
800-23-LOEWS
www.loewshotels.com

**Mandarin Oriental**
www.mandarin-oriental.com
**Marriott** (Includes Marriott Hotels, Resorts &Suites, Renaissance Hotels, Courtyard, Residence Inn, Fairfield Inn, ExecuStay, TownePlace Suites and SpringHill Suites)
888-236-2427
www.marriott.com
**Nikko Hotels International**
800-NIKKO-US (800-645-5687)
www.nikkohotels.com
**Omni Hotels**
800-The-Omni
www.omnihotels.com
**Pan Pacific Hotels & Resorts**
800-327-8585
www.panpac.com
**Radisson Hotels**
800-333-3333
www.radisson.com
**Ramada** (Includes Ramada Limited, Ramada Inn and Ramada Plaza Hotels)
888-298-2054
www.ramada.com
**Ritz-Carlton**
800-241-3333
www.ritzcarlton.com
**Sheraton Hotels and Resorts**
888-625-5144
www.sheraton.com
**Sofitel Hotels and Resorts**
800-221-4542
www.sofitel.com
**Sonesta Hotels, Resorts and Nile Cruises**
800-843-3311
www.sonesta.com
**St Regis Hotels**
800-325-3589
www.stregis.com
**Trump Hotels and Casino Resorts**
877-DJTRUMP
www.trump.com
**W Hotels**
877-W-HOTELS
www.whotels.com
**Westin**
888-625-5144
www.westin.com
**Wyndham Hotels and Resorts**
877-WWW-3223
www.wyndham.com

## OTHER HELPFUL HOTEL SITES

www.aaahotels.net
www.abotel.com (Paris)
www.asiahotels.net
www.asiatravel.com
www.chinesehotels.net
www.dataplace.to/twhdb/
www.eurotels.com
www.germancastles.com
www.hawaiihotels.com
www.hotel-discount.net
www.hotels-europe.com
www.hotelsitaly.com
www.paris.org/Hotels
www.srs-worldhotels.com/germany

**Hertz®**

CDP# 06592
Must appear on rental record

## ONE CAR CLASS UPGRADE

Mention this offer to enjoy a one car class upgrade while taking advantage of your Government savings. Reserve a compact 4-door through full-size car (Class B, C, D, or F) for a day, weekend or week. At the time of rental, present your U.S. Government ID or Hertz Member Discount Card for identification and surrender this coupon. If a car from the next higher class is available, you'll be driving it at the lower rate!

Call your travel agent or call:
1-800-654-2210 in the U.S.
1-800-263-0600 in Canada

---

**Hertz®**

CDP# 06592
Must appear on rental record

## $10 OFF A WEEKLY RENTAL

Take $10 off your weekly rental and then take advantage of your Government savings. Mention this offer when you reserve and rent a mid-size through full-size car (Class C, D, or F) for at least 5 consecutive days, including a Saturday night, at Hertz Standard, Leisure or Government Weekly Rates. At the time of rental, present your U.S. Government ID or Hertz Member Discount Card for identification and surrender this coupon.

Call your travel agent or call:
1-800-654-2210 in the U.S.
1-800-263-0600 in Canada

---

**Hertz®**

CDP CARD# 06592

### Member Discount Card

For worldwide reservations, call your travel agent or call Hertz. In Canada, call 1-800-263-0600. In the U.S., call 1-800-654-6511.

---

**Hertz®**

CDP# 06592
Must appear on rental record

## ONE CAR CLASS UPGRADE

Mention this offer to enjoy a one car class upgrade while taking advantage of your Government savings. Reserve a compact 4-door through full-size car (Class B, C, D, or F) for a day, weekend or week. At the time of rental, present your U.S. Government ID or Hertz Member Discount Card for identification and surrender this coupon. If a car from the next higher class is available, you'll be driving it at the lower rate!

Call your travel agent or call:
1-800-654-2210 in the U.S.
1-800-263-0600 in Canada

---

**Hertz®**

CDP# 06592
Must appear on rental record

## $10 OFF A WEEKLY RENTAL

Take $10 off your weekly rental and then take advantage of your Government savings. Mention this offer when you reserve and rent a mid-size through full-size car (Class C, D, or F) for at least 5 consecutive days, including a Saturday night, at Hertz Standard, Leisure or Government Weekly Rates. At the time of rental, present your U.S. Government ID or Hertz Member Discount Card for identification and surrender this coupon.

Call your travel agent or call:
1-800-654-2210 in the U.S.
1-800-263-0600 in Canada

---

**Hertz®**

CDP CARD# 06592

### Member Discount Card

For worldwide reservations, call your travel agent or call Hertz. In Canada, call 1-800-263-0600. In the U.S., call 1-800-654-6511.

---

**Hertz®**

CDP# 06592
Must appear on rental record

## ONE CAR CLASS UPGRADE

Mention this offer to enjoy a one car class upgrade while taking advantage of your Government savings. Reserve a compact 4-door through full-size car (Class B, C, D, or F) for a day, weekend or week. At the time of rental, present your U.S. Government ID or Hertz Member Discount Card for identification and surrender this coupon. If a car from the next higher class is available, you'll be driving it at the lower rate!

Call your travel agent or call:
1-800-654-2210 in the U.S.
1-800-263-0600 in Canada

---

**Hertz®**

CDP# 06592
Must appear on rental record

## $10 OFF A WEEKLY RENTAL

Take $10 off your weekly rental and then take advantage of your Government savings. Mention this offer when you reserve and rent a mid-size through full-size car (Class C, D, or F) for at least 5 consecutive days, including a Saturday night, at Hertz Standard, Leisure or Government Weekly Rates. At the time of rental, present your U.S. Government ID or Hertz Member Discount Card for identification and surrender this coupon.

Call your travel agent or call:
1-800-654-2210 in the U.S.
1-800-263-0600 in Canada

---

**Hertz®**

CDP CARD# 06592

### Member Discount Card

For worldwide reservations, call your travel agent or call Hertz. In Canada, call 1-800-263-0600. In the U.S., call 1-800-654-6511.

**IMPORTANT RENTAL INFORMATION**

Advance reservations are required as blackout periods may apply in some cities at some times, especially during periods of peak demand. If a blackout occurs, you're still entitled to your Hertz discount and can save this offer for another trip. The expiration date for this offer appears on the front of the coupon.

This offer is redeemable at participating Hertz locations in the U.S. and Canada subject to vehicle availability. Highest obtainable upgrade is to a Premium (Class G) car. This coupon has no cash value, must be surrendered on rental and may not be used with any other CDP#, coupon, discount, rate or promotion. This coupon may only be used with a GOVT. CDP#. Hertz standard age, driver and credit qualifications at the time and place of rental apply and the car must be returned to that location. Call for details.

**COUPON EXPIRES 12/31/01**

**U.S. PC# 901320**
**Canada PC# 901331**
**Puerto Rico PC# 901342**

Hertz rents Fords and other fine cars.

**IMPORTANT RENTAL INFORMATION**

Advance reservations are required as blackout periods may apply in some cities at some times, especially during periods of peak demand. If a blackout occurs, you're still entitled to your Hertz discount and can save this offer for another trip. The expiration date for this offer appears on the front of the coupon.

This offer is redeemable at participating Hertz locations in the U.S. and Canada subject to vehicle availability. Highest obtainable upgrade is to a Premium (Class G) car. This coupon has no cash value, must be surrendered on rental and may not be used with any other CDP#, coupon, discount, rate or promotion. This coupon may only be used with a GOVT. CDP#. Hertz standard age, driver and credit qualifications at the time and place of rental apply and the car must be returned to that location. Call for details.

**COUPON EXPIRES 12/31/01**

**U.S. PC# 901320**
**Canada PC# 901331**
**Puerto Rico PC# 901342**

Hertz rents Fords and other fine cars.

**IMPORTANT RENTAL INFORMATION**

Advance reservations are required as blackout periods may apply in some cities at some times, especially during periods of peak demand. If a blackout occurs, you're still entitled to your Hertz discount and can save this offer for another trip. The expiration date for this offer appears on the front of the coupon.

This offer is redeemable at participating Hertz locations in the U.S. and Canada subject to vehicle availability. Highest obtainable upgrade is to a Premium (Class G) car. This coupon has no cash value, must be surrendered on rental and may not be used with any other CDP#, coupon, discount, rate or promotion. This coupon may only be used with a GOVT. CDP#. Hertz standard age, driver and credit qualifications at the time and place of rental apply and the car must be returned to that location. Call for details.

**COUPON EXPIRES 12/31/01**

**U.S. PC# 901320**
**Canada PC# 901331**
**Puerto Rico PC# 901342**

Hertz rents Fords and other fine cars.

---

**IMPORTANT RENTAL INFORMATION**

Advance reservations are required as blackout periods may apply in some cities at some times, especially during periods of peak demand. If a blackout occurs, you're still entitled to your Hertz discount and can save this offer for another trip. The expiration date for this offer appears on the front of the coupon.

This offer is available at participating Hertz locations in the U.S. and Canada. This coupon has no cash value, must be surrendered on rental and may not be used with any other CDP#, coupon, discount, rate or promotion. This coupon may only be used with a GOVT. CDP#. The $10 off will be valued in local currency on redemption. Hertz standard age, driver and credit qualifications at the time and place of rental apply and the car must be returned to that location. Taxes and optional service charges, such as refueling, are not included and are not subject to discount. Call for details.

**COUPON EXPIRES 12/31/01**

**U.S. PC# 901320**
**Canada PC# 901331**
**Puerto Rico PC# 901342**

Hertz rents Fords and other fine cars.

**IMPORTANT RENTAL INFORMATION**

Advance reservations are required as blackout periods may apply in some cities at some times, especially during periods of peak demand. If a blackout occurs, you're still entitled to your Hertz discount and can save this offer for another trip. The expiration date for this offer appears on the front of the coupon.

This offer is available at participating Hertz locations in the U.S. and Canada. This coupon has no cash value, must be surrendered on rental and may not be used with any other CDP#, coupon, discount, rate or promotion. This coupon may only be used with a GOVT. CDP#. The $10 off will be valued in local currency on redemption. Hertz standard age, driver and credit qualifications at the time and place of rental apply and the car must be returned to that location. Taxes and optional service charges, such as refueling, are not included and are not subject to discount. Call for details.

**COUPON EXPIRES 12/31/01**

**U.S. PC# 901320**
**Canada PC# 901331**
**Puerto Rico PC# 901342**

Hertz rents Fords and other fine cars.

**IMPORTANT RENTAL INFORMATION**

Advance reservations are required as blackout periods may apply in some cities at some times, especially during periods of peak demand. If a blackout occurs, you're still entitled to your Hertz discount and can save this offer for another trip. The expiration date for this offer appears on the front of the coupon.

This offer is available at participating Hertz locations in the U.S. and Canada. This coupon has no cash value, must be surrendered on rental and may not be used with any other CDP#, coupon, discount, rate or promotion. This coupon may only be used with a GOVT. CDP#. The $10 off will be valued in local currency on redemption. Hertz standard age, driver and credit qualifications at the time and place of rental apply and the car must be returned to that location. Taxes and optional service charges, such as refueling, are not included and are not subject to discount. Call for details.

**COUPON EXPIRES 12/31/01**

**U.S. PC# 901320**
**Canada PC# 901331**
**Puerto Rico PC# 901342**

Hertz rents Fords and other fine cars.

---

**USING YOUR HERTZ DISCOUNT CARD**

Mention the CDP# on the face of this card when making your advance reservation and present this card for identification when you get to the Hertz counter to take advantage of the year-round discount program offered to your organization.

Hertz standard age, driver and credit qualifications in effect at the time and place of rental apply. In accordance with the applicable Hertz agreement with the organization identified on the face hereof, discounts are not transferable and are available at participating locations, which participation is subject to change without notice. Hertz discounts identified by the CDP# on the face of this card may not be combined or used with Travel Industry Discounts, Tour Rates, or other discounts or rates not included in your organization's discount program. Taxes and optional service charges, such as refueling, are not subject to discount. All discounts may be modified, amended, or terminated without notice to the holder hereof. CDP stickers/cards are NOT transferable. Minimum rental periods and other restrictions apply.

Hertz rents Fords and other fine cars.

FORM# 4118
REV. 11/96

**USING YOUR HERTZ DISCOUNT CARD**

Mention the CDP# on the face of this card when making your advance reservation and present this card for identification when you get to the Hertz counter to take advantage of the year-round discount program offered to your organization.

Hertz standard age, driver and credit qualifications in effect at the time and place of rental apply. In accordance with the applicable Hertz agreement with the organization identified on the face hereof, discounts are not transferable and are available at participating locations, which participation is subject to change without notice. Hertz discounts identified by the CDP# on the face of this card may not be combined or used with Travel Industry Discounts, Tour Rates, or other discounts or rates not included in your organization's discount program. Taxes and optional service charges, such as refueling, are not subject to discount. All discounts may be modified, amended, or terminated without notice to the holder hereof. CDP stickers/cards are NOT transferable. Minimum rental periods and other restrictions apply.

Hertz rents Fords and other fine cars.

FORM# 4118
REV. 11/96

**USING YOUR HERTZ DISCOUNT CARD**

Mention the CDP# on the face of this card when making your advance reservation and present this card for identification when you get to the Hertz counter to take advantage of the year-round discount program offered to your organization.

Hertz standard age, driver and credit qualifications in effect at the time and place of rental apply. In accordance with the applicable Hertz agreement with the organization identified on the face hereof, discounts are not transferable and are available at participating locations, which participation is subject to change without notice. Hertz discounts identified by the CDP# on the face of this card may not be combined or used with Travel Industry Discounts, Tour Rates, or other discounts or rates not included in your organization's discount program. Taxes and optional service charges, such as refueling, are not subject to discount. All discounts may be modified, amended, or terminated without notice to the holder hereof. CDP stickers/cards are NOT transferable. Minimum rental periods and other restrictions apply.

Hertz rents Fords and other fine cars.

FORM# 4118
REV. 11/96

# Features of Our Military International Calling Card

## SPECIAL SERVICES
- Toll Free Direct Access Number in 80 Countries
- Conference
- Speed Dial
- Voice Mail

## EXCELLENT INTERNATIONAL RATES
- Current Rates Are Available at: www.gphone.com/military
- Some Rates 24 Hours A Day
- 6-Second Increment Billing
- No Connection Charges

## MONTHLY BILLING
- Monthly Statement
- Charges Apply to Your Credit Card
- There are No Monthly Service Fees

---

### Add 60 Free Domestic Minutes to My Account and Activate My Global Phone Military International Calling Card

**4 EASY WAYS TO ACTIVATE YOUR CARD:**
1. Internet: www.gphone.com/military
2. Telephone: Call Toll-Free 1-866-840-0446
   Direct 1-703-242-3060
   See Reverse Side for Overseas Numbers
3. E-Mail: military@gphone.com
4. Fax: Fill out the This Form and Fax to 1-703-533-2445

Name_______________________________________
Address_____________________________________
____________________________________________
Telephone __________________________________
Fax_________________________________________
E-Mail______________________________________
Please Send My Calling Card Statement by ❑ Mail or ❑ E-Mail

Ad Code: GP50

# Global Phone Dialing Instructions

## Calling from a touch-tone phone:

1. Refer to the chart for the GlobalPhone direct access number for the country you are in.

2. If you are in a hotel, follow hotel instructions to get an outside line.

3. Dial the GlobalPhone direct access number.

4. Following the voice prompts, enter your ten digit account code and, if requested, your four digit PIN.

5. Dial your destination number.
   Calling to USA/Canada, dial:
   1 + Area Code + Number
   Calling to other countries, dial Country Code+ City Code + Number

## Calling tips:

- Press # after entering the number to speed the dialing process (optional).
- If you make an error when dialing, press * to start over.
- To place another call without hanging up, press # twice.
- For conference calls, dial your first party, then, press *#2 and dial the next party. Up to 16 people can be conferenced in.
- To obtain the Enhanced Services menu, press * and #. (speed dial, voice mail, redial, account balance)
- To immediately force termination of all connections, press * twice (optional).
- For fax calls, pick up the handset and follow steps 2-5. When ou hear the fax tone at the destination, press SEND and replace the hand set.
- **Toll Free in USA 1-866-840-0446**
  **Phone 1-703-242-3060     Fax 1-703-533-2445**
  137 N. Washington St, Falls Church, VA 22046
  E-Mail: military@gphone.com

## For Overseas Activation

**Call** the 800 number for the country you are in (see below) and press 999#5# to be transferred to customer service. Operators are standing by 7 am - 7 pm EST Monday-Saturday.

## INTERNATIONAL DIRECT ACCESS NUMBERS

| Country | Access Number | 661 |
|---|---|---|
| Antigua | 1800534220 | ● |
| Argentina | 08008880872 | ● |
| Australia | 1800706906 | |
| or | 001180045624562 | |
| Austria | 0800201480 | |
| or | 0080045624562 | |
| Bahrain | 800415 | |
| or | 800442 | ● |
| Barbados | 18005340244 | |
| or | 18005340257 | ● |
| Belarus | 8800114 | ● |
| or | 810800114 | ● |
| Belgium | 080075089 | |
| or | 0080045624562 | |
| Bermuda | 18006230089 | |
| Bolivia | 08000103 | ● |
| Brazil | 00081562016732 | |
| Brunei | 800013 | ● |
| Bulgaria | 008001300 | ● |
| Chile | 800570247 | |
| China | 108001400029 | |
| Colombia | 9809196735 | |
| Croatia | 0800220116 | ● |
| Cyprus | 08096052 | |
| Czech Republic | 0042000158 | ● |
| Denmark | 80881459 | |
| or | 0080045624562 | |
| Dominican Republic | 18881563036 | |
| Egypt | 3640083 | ● |
| Fiji | 0048901007 | ● |
| Finland | 0800115527 | |
| or | 0080045624562 | |
| or | 99080045624562 | |
| France | 0800911800 | |
| or | 0080045624562 | |
| French Antilles | 0800992016 | ● |
| Germany | 08001819123 | |
| or | 0080045624562 | |
| Ghana | 019211 | ● |
| Greece | 0080016122016745 | |
| Hong Kong | 800903421 | |
| or | 00180045624562 | |
| Hungary | 0680011821 | |
| Iceland | 8008258 | |
| India | 000168 | ● |
| Indonesia | 008800105104 | |
| Ireland | 1800550681 | |
| or | 0080045624562 | |
| Israel | 18009460020 | |
| or | 0080045624562 | |
| Italy | 800877217 | |
| Japan | 00531160166 | |
| or | 00180080308030 | |
| or | 006180080308030 | |
| Korea-South | 00308140131 | |
| or | 00280045624562 | |
| Korea-cont'd | 00180045624562 | |
| Lithuania | 880091000 | ● |
| Luxembourg | 08002932 | |
| Macedonia | 998004275 | ● |
| Malaysia | 1800800620 | |
| or | 0080045624562 | |
| Malta | 0800890112 | ● |
| Mexico | 0018005146783 | |
| Monaco | 80090141 | ● |
| Netherlands | 08000226968 | |
| or | 0080045624562 | |
| Nevis | 18007449200 | |
| New Zealand | 0800448321 | |
| or | 0080045624562 | |
| Nicaragua | 1551 | ● |
| Norway | 80012136 | |
| or | 0080045624562 | |
| Papua New Guinea | 050715181 | ● |
| Philippines | 180011100143 | |
| Poland | 008001114227 | |
| Portugal | 0800819162 | |
| Puerto Rico | 18887016766 | |
| Romania | 018005030 | ● |
| Russia | 8108001301012 | ● |
| Senegal | 3080 | ● |
| Singapore | 8001011139 | |
| or | 00180045624562 | |
| or | 8000100941 | ● |
| Slovak Republic | 0800000154 | ● |
| South Africa | 0800994931 | |
| Spain | 900991532 | |
| Sri Lanka | 451456 | ● |
| St. Kitts | 18007449120 | ● |
| St. Vincent | 18002016769 | |
| Sweden | 0200214614 | |
| or | 00780045624562 | |
| or | 00980045624562 | |
| Switzerland | 0800838543 | |
| or | 0080045624562 | |
| Syria | 0814 | ● |
| Taiwan | 0080126273 | |
| or | 00180045624562 | |
| Thailand | 00180018177 | ● |
| Trinidad/Tobago | 18002016775 | |
| Turkey | 0080018177 | ● |
| Ukraine | 8100180 | ● |
| United Kingdom | 08081000689 | |
| or | 0080045624562 | |
| United States | 18007053304 | |
| US- Washington DC | 7038522111 | |
| US Virgin Islands | 18887016780 | |
| Venezuela | 80011103 | ● |
| Yemen | 00800105 | ● |

● Dial 661 when you hear the long tone.
**Note:** Public phones may require coins or a phone card before allowing you to dial.

# Enjoy A Night On Us

## Marines' Memorial Club & Hotel
### Union Square, San Francisco

**Open to All Branches of the Armed Forces ~ Active Duty and Former**

Enjoy a night on us! Come to San Francisco and experience the sights and sounds of one of the world's most popular cities. Superior location, accommodations and rates. Stay five consecutive nights and enjoy the *sixth night free*. *(See reverse side for details on this offer.)*

## Reservations: 1-800-562-7463

# FLORIDA

## CLEARWATER COAST GUARD AIR STATION (PIE/KPIE)

Commanding Officer
15100 Rescue Way
Clearwater, FL 33762-2990

**LOCATION:** From I-275, take FL-60 west to FL-611 south. Follow signs to air station. *USMRA: Page 38 (E-8); Page 53 (C-3). ML-ARM: (27°54'N/82°41'W).* LST: GMT-05:00. NMC: St Petersburg, 5 miles south. Main installation numbers: C-727-535-1437.

**REGISTRATION INFO: C-727-535-1437 ext 1223, Fax: C-813-535-4256.** USCG Hangar, Hours: 0715-1515 Mon-Fri. Ask Security Police for directions.

**TRAVELERS AID: Medical:** C-727-535-1437 ext 1606.

**TML:** Nearest TML is at Bldg 411, 8604 Hanger Loop, MacDill AFB, 24 hours daily, C-813-828-4259, C-813-831-4804, D-312-968-4259/4804, DV/VIP C-813-828-2056.

**SUPPORT AVAILABLE: Exchange:** ext 1710. **Hair Styles:** Barber, ext 1712.

### UNSCHEDULED FLIGHTS
Administrative and logistical flights via C-130A-H and HU-25A aircraft to CONUS and OCONUS stations. Call for destinations, routings and schedules.

## EGLIN AIR FORCE BASE (VPS/KVPS)

96th TRANS/LGTRM
601 W. Choctawhatchee Ave, Suite 78
Eglin AFB, FL 32542-5000

**LOCATION:** Exit I-10 at Crestview. Follow signs to Niceville and Valparaiso (Eglin AFB). *USMRA: Page 39 (B,C,D-13); Page 53 (E,F,G,H-1,2,3,4). ML-ARM: (30°28'N/86°32'W).* LST: GMT-05:00. NMC: Fort Walton Beach, 7 miles south. Main installation numbers: C-850-882-1110, D-312-872-1110.

**REGISTRATION INFO: C-850-882-4757/3301, D-312-872-4757/3301, Rec: C-850-882-3332, D-312-872-3332, Fax: C-850-882-1461, D-312-872-1461. E-mail: wardg@eglin.af.mil** Bldg 60, Hours: 0800-1600 Mon-Fri. Directions: From west gate straight on Eglin Blvd to left on 7th Street to a left onto Choctawhatchee Ave to Pax Term on right. **Pax Service Office:** C-850-882-4757, D-312-872-4757 (NCO on duty). **Pax Paging:** C-850-882-5313.

**PAX LOUNGES:** No separate family lounge. **General:** Bldg 60, 24 hours daily, C-850-882-5732. A/C, restrooms, TV, P/C seats. **DV/VIP:** Bldg 60, 24 hours daily, C-850-882-5732 (no host). A/C, coffee/tea service, restrooms, separate read/write rooms, O/S seats. **Protocol Service:** Bldg 1, Hours: 0730-1630 Mon-Fri, C-850-882-3011.

**FOOD SERVICE: Cafeteria:** Bldg 1759, C-850-651-4821 ("Run-in-Chef"). **Dining Hall:** Bldg 18-D, C-850-882-5053. **Flight Kitchen:** C-850-882-5014. **NCO/CPO Club:** Bldg 860, C-850-678-5127. **O Club:** Bldg 10870, C-904-651-1010. **Snack Bars:** Bldg 100, C-850-678-5932.

**TRANSPORTATION: Air Tickets:** (Ortega) Bldg 350, C-850-882-8016. **On Base Taxi (Gov):** Bldg 509, C-850-882-3791 (passengers only); Bob's Airport Shuttle and Taxi Service: C-850-729-7771 (E-mail: bnmck@digitalexp.com). **Parking:** Bldg 60, C-850-882-2502 (in front of building).

**TML:** Bldg 11001, Boatner Road, 24 hours daily, C-850-882-8761/4534, D-312-872-8761/4534, Fax: C-850-882-2708, D-312-872-2708, DV/VIP C-850-882-3011/3238.

**RVC:** FAMCAMP, Outdoor Recreation, 404 North 7th Street, Suite 3, C-850-882-6581.

**TRAVELERS AID: Chaplain:** Bldg 868, C-850-882-2111. **Emergency Relief:** Bldg 210, C-850-882-4395. **Lost/Found:** Bldg 60, C-850-882-5732. **Red Cross:** Bldg 210, C-850-882-5848, after hours C-850-882-2485. **Security Police:** Bldg 272, C-850-882-2502.

**SUPPORT AVAILABLE: Bank/Currency Exchange:** Memorial Lake, C-850-651-1112. **Exchange:** Bldg 1757, C-850-651-2512. **Hair Styles:** Bldg 1757; Barber, C-850-651-5122; Beauty, C-850-651-5224. **Laundry/Dry Cleaning:** Bldg 12, C-850-651-4924. **Medical:** Bldg 2825, C-850-883-8242, D-312-872-8242. **Postal Service:** Bldg 10, C-850-882-3548.

**ATTRACTIONS:** Beaches, sport fishing, dog races.

### EN ROUTE SCHEDULES

| AIRPORT/STATION | LI-MISSION (page #) |
| --- | --- |
| Keesler AFB | BIX-226/MEDEVAC (44) |
| Scott AFB | BLV-C-626/MEDEVAC (30) |

### UNSCHEDULED FLIGHTS
Frequent flights via MC-130 and KC-135 to CONUS and OCONUS locations. Occasional flights via CK-10, C-005 and C-141. Call for destinations, routing and schedules.

## HOMESTEAD AIR RESERVE BASE (HST/KHST)

70th Aerial Port Squadron
29050 Coral Sea Blvd, Box 78
Homestead ARB, FL 33039-1299

**LOCATION:** Exit 5 (Biscayne Blvd/288th Street) off Florida Turnpike, left at bottom of ramp. Road leads straight to base. Or take exit 6 (Speedway Blvd) off Florida Turnpike, left at bottom of ramp. At first light take a left. Road leads straight to base. *USMRA: Page 39 (I-14). ML-ARM: (25°29'N/80°24'W).* LST: GMT-05:00. NMC: Miami, 25 miles northeast. Main installation numbers: C-305-224-7000, D-312-791-7000.

**REGISTRATION INFO: C-305-224-7518/7518, D-317-791-7518/7518, Fax: C-305-224-7491.** Pax Term/Lounge Bldg 178. Directions: From main gate: south on Coral Sea Blvd to right onto Bikini Blvd then continue for one block to Bldg 178. For Space-A information, go to Bldg 588 across from gas pump. General lounge available.

**FOOD SERVICE:** Snack Vending available.

**TML:** Homestead Inn, Bldg 476, 29050 Coral Sea Blvd, 0700-2100 hours daily, C-305-224-7198, D-312-791-7190, Fax: C-305-224-7290, D-312-791-7290.

**TRAVELERS AID: Chaplain:** C-305-224-7093, D-317-791-7093, 1 mile away. **Red Cross:** Hours: 0730-1630, C-305-224-4611, D-317-791-4611, 1 mile away. **Security Police:** 24 hours daily, C-305-257-7116, D-317-791-7116, 1 mile away. **Travelers Aid:** Hours: 0730-1630, C-305-257-1400, D-317-791-7051, 1 mile away.

**SUPPORT AVAILABLE: Bank/Currency Exchange:** Hours: 0900-0300, C-305-224-1800, 1.5 miles away. **Dry Cleaner:** Hours: 1000-1700, C-305-224-7095, 1.5 miles away. **Exchange:** Hours: 1000-1800, C-305-258-3881, 1.5 miles away.

**ATTRACTIONS:** Key West, Bayside, Metro Zoo, Monkey Jungle and Seaquarium.

### UNSCHEDULED FLIGHTS
Limited Space-A air opportunities - mostly MEDEVAC - call for destinations, routings and schedules. Weekend shuttle flight routes may include stops at Charleston AFB, SC (**CHS**); MacDill AFB, FL (**MCF**); Patrick AFB, FL (**COF**); Jacksonville NAS, FL (**NIP**).

## HURLBURT FIELD (HRT/KHRT)

Passenger Service Personnel, Base Operations
16 Transportation Squadron, Bldg 90761
Hurlburt Field, FL 32544-5844

**LOCATION:** Off US-98, five miles west of Fort Walton Beach, north of US-98. Clearly marked. *USMRA: Page 39 (C-13); Page 53 (H-4). ML-ARM: (30°22'N/86°40'W).* LST: GMT-05:00. NMC: Pensacola, 30 miles west. NMI: Eglin AFB, 13 miles northeast. Main installation numbers: C-850-884-1110, D-312-579-1110 (Hurlburt Field).

**REGISTRATION INFO: C-850-884-5781, D-312-579-5781, Fax: C-850-884-5020, D-312-579-5020.** Bldg 90761, Hours: 0730-1630 daily.

**FOOD SERVICE:** Fast Food: Burger King 0600-2000 M-F; (Sat: 0700-2000; Sun: 1000-1800) **Soundside** 1100-1300 M-F; Sunday Brunch: 1000-1300 hrs; **J.R. Rockers:** 1100-2100 M-F;(Sat:1400-2100; Sun:1400-2100 hrs.) **Mulligan's Snack Bar** 1100-1400 M-F (Sat, Sun 0630-1400); **Spartime Grill** 0600-2200 M-F;(Sat:0900-2200; Sun: Noon-2100) **Hurlburt Mini Mall** 1030-1800 M-F; (Sat,Sun: Closed) **Base Food Court** 1030-1700 M-F; (Sat: 1030-1700; Sun: closed); Flight Kitchen: 24 hours, seven days a week.

**TRANSPORTATION: Off Base Car Rental:** Budget, C-850-651-9600; Hertz, C-850-651-0612; National, C-850-651-1113. **On Base Taxi:** C-850-884-7223, D-312-579-7223. **Off Base Taxi:** C-850-654-0005. **Off Base Limo:** C-850-651-0404.

**TML:** Commando Inn, Bldg 90509, 301 Tully Street, 24 hours daily, C-850-580-6271, C-850-884-7115/6245, D-312-579-6245/7115, Fax: C-850-884-5043, D-312-579-5043. DV/VIP C-850-884-2308.

**RVC:** FAMCAMP, 345 Tully Street, Bldg 90505, Check-in Bldg 92473, after hours park and register next day, C-850-884-6939, D-312-579-6939.

**TRAVELERS AID: Chaplain:** 0730-1630, C-850-884-7795, D-312-579-7795, after hours, C-850-884-7774, D-312-579-7774, 3 miles away. **Medical/Dental:** 0730-1630, C-850-884-7882/7881, D-312-579-7882/81, 8 miles away; Emergency Room (Eglin AFB) 24 hours daily, C-850-883-8227, 18 miles away. **Red Cross:** 0730-1630, C-850-884-6107, D-312-579-6207, after hours, C-850-883-4020, 3 miles away. **Security Police:** 24 hours daily, C-850-884-6423/6666, D-312-579-6423/6666, 1 mile away.

**SUPPORT AVAILABLE: Bank/Currency Exchange:** Hours: 0830-1630, C-850-581-2222, 3 miles away. **Commissary:** Hours: 0900-1800, C-850-881-2139, D-312-579-2139, 8 miles away. **Credit Union:** Hours: 0830-1630, C-850-862-0111, 3 miles. **Exchange:** Hours: 1000-2100, C-850-581-0030, 8 miles away. **Laundry/Dry Cleaner:** Hours: 0900-1700, C-581-3614, 3 miles away. **Postal Service:** Hours: 0730-1630, C-850-884-6219, D-312-579-6219, 2 miles. **Shoppette:** 24 hours daily, C-850-581-0488, 4 miles away.

**ATTRACTIONS:** Beaches, Clubs, Deep-Sea fishing.

### UNSCHEDULED FLIGHTS

Mobility contingency flights to CONUS and overseas mostly via AC-130H/U, C-130E, ML-130E/H, ML-130P aircraft. Call for destinations, routings and schedules.

## JACKSONVILLE NAVAL AIR STATION (NIP/KNIP)

Box 7, Air Terminal
Jacksonville NAS, FL 32212-5000

**LOCATION:** Access from US-17 south, Roosevelt Blvd. Clearly marked. *USMRA: Page 38 (G-3); Page 50 (B,C-6,7). ML-ARM: (30°13'N/81°42'W).* LST: GMT-05:00. NMC: Jacksonville, 9 miles northeast. Main installation numbers: C-904-542-2345/2346, D-312-942-2345/2346.

**REGISTRATION INFO: C-402-458-1249, D-312-942-1249, Rec: C-904-542-3825, D-312-942-3825, Fax: C-904-542-3257.** Bldg 279, 0600-2300 hours daily. Directions: From main gate, straight on Yorktown Ave to a left on Wasp Street to a right on Albemarle Ave. Pax Term on left. General lounge available at Bldg 279; VIP lounge in Bldg 118. **Pax Service Office:** C-904-542-4257/8165, D-312-942-4257/8165. **Pax Paging:** C-904-542-3956/3825, D-312-942-3956/3825.

**FOOD SERVICE: O Club:** C-904-542-3041.

**TML:** Bldg 11, 24 hours daily, C-904-542-3138/9, Fax: C-904-542-5002, Navy Lodge: C-904-772-6000, Fax: C-904-977-1736, DV/VIP 904-542-3147/3138.

**RVC:** RV Park, MWR 584 Enterprise Ave, Check-in Bldg 622, Auto Hobby Shop, C-904-542-3227, D-312-942-3227, Fax: C-904-542-3742, E-mail: dahearn@nasjax.org

**TRAVELERS AID: Medical:** C-904-777-7300. **Security Police:** C-904-542-2661.

**SUPPORT AVAILABLE: Exchange:** C-904-777-7200. **SATO** Ticket Office, C-904-542-3703.

**ATTRACTIONS:** Golfing, Beaches, fishing, St Augustine, Orlando.

### EN ROUTE SCHEDULES

| AIRPORT/STATION | LI-MISSION (page #) |
|---|---|
| Keesler AFB | BIX-226/MEDEVAC (44) |
| Scott AFB | BLV-C-626/MEDEVAC (30) |
| Norfolk NS | NGU-HJM3A & B (79) |

### UNSCHEDULED FLIGHTS

Frequent flights via P-003C, TP-003A, UP-003A, C-009B to: Charleston AFB/IAP, SC (**CHS**); MacDill AFB, FL (**MCF**); Norfolk NS, VA (**NGU**); and Roosevelt Roads NS, PR (**NRR**). *Note: 3 days prior notice on flights.* Schedules subject to change. Most flights to East Coast destinations and some to OCONUS and foreign countries. Call for destinations, routings and schedules.

## KEY WEST NAVAL AIR STATION (NQX/KNQX)

Operations Dept, Field Services Division
P.O. Box 9031, Bldg A-244
Key West NAS, FL 33040-9001

**LOCATION:** Take Florida Turnpike, US-1 south to exit signs east for Key West Naval Air Station on Boca Chica Key, seven miles north of Key West. *USMRA: Page 39 (G-16). ML-ARM: (24°35'N/81°42'W).* LST: GMT-05:00. NMC: Miami, 150 miles north. NMI: Homestead ARB, 140 miles. Main installation numbers: C-305-293-2348, D-312-483-3700.

**REGISTRATION INFO: C-305-293-2769/2187, D-312-483-2769/2187, Rec: C-305-293-2751, D-312-483-2751, Fax: C-305-293-2779, D-312-483-2779.** Bldg NAS ATC tower, Hours: daily 0800-1600. Directions: On Boca Chica Key, easily visible. **Pax Service Office:** C-305-292-2770 (NCO on duty).

**PAX LOUNGES:** General and DV/VIP lounges available. All passenger processing handled at Ops/Field Services, C-305-293-2769. A/C, restrooms, TV, O/S and P/C seats.

**FOOD SERVICE: Cafeteria:** Boca Chica Key, Hours: 0630-1700, C-305-293-2435, D-312-483-2435, 2 blocks away. **Dining Hall:** Hours: 0630-1700 daily, C-305-292-2687. **Enlisted Club:** C-305-293-2495. **Fast Food:** Hours: 0700-2100, C-305-293-2495, 3 blocks away. **NCO/CPO Club:** C-305-293-2407. **O Club:** C-305-293-2480. **Snack Vending:** Hours: 0600-2200, in terminal.

**TRANSPORTATION: On Base Car Rentals:** Enterprise, C-305-293-0220, at BOQ, 7 miles away. **Off Base Car Rentals:** Key West IAP; Avis, C-305-296-8744; Hertz, C-305-294-1039; Other, C-305-296-6666. **Off Base Shuttle/Bus:** C-305-293-2268, D-312-483-2268. **Off Base Taxi:** C-305-296-6666, C-305-292-2000. **Parking:** Short term ATC/Ops, unlimited behind Ops building.

**TML:** CBQ, 24 hours daily, C-305-293-4142/4305, D-312-483-4142/4305, Fax: C-305-293-2084, D-312-483-4302, BOQ: C-305-293-5571, BEQ: C-305-293-2488, Navy Lodge: C-305-292-7556 or 1-800-NAVY INN. DV/VIP C-305-293-2095/2013.

**RVC:** Sigsbee RV Park, MWR Dept, Check-in Sigsbee Community Center, C-1-888-539-7697, C-305-293-4432/4433, Fax: C-305-293-4413.

**TRAVELERS AID: Chaplain:** Base Chapel Truman Annex, Hours: 0700-1600, C-305-293-2318, D-312-483-2318, 2 blocks away. **Emergency Relief:** Bldg 711, Hours: 0800-1600 Mon-Fri, C-305-293-2169, D-312-483-2169 (Navy Relief). **Medical:** 24 hours daily, C-305-293-4500, C-305-294-3500. **Red Cross:** 600 White Street, Key West, Hours: 0900-1700, C-305-296-3651, 7 miles away. **Security Police:** Main gate, 24 hours daily, C-305-293-2531, 1 block away.

**SUPPORT AVAILABLE: Bank/Currency Exchange:** C-305-294-1796 (US currency only). **Commissary:** C-305-239-4402. **Convenience Store:** Hours: 0700-1800, C-305-292-7226, 2 blocks away. **Exchange:** Hours: 1000-1900, C-305-292-7210, 6 miles away. **Hair Styles:** BX, C-305-292-7223. **Postal Service:** Bldg 305, Hours: 0900-1630, C-305-293-2406, 1 block away.

**OTHER INFORMATION:** Port of Entry and U.S. Customs Service Airport.

**ATTRACTIONS:** Water sports, Ernest Hemingway home.

### EN ROUTE SCHEDULES

| AIRPORT/STATION | LI-MISSION (page #) |
|---|---|
| Keesler AFB | BIX-226/MEDEVAC (44) |
| Scott AFB | BLV-C-626/MEDEVAC (30) |

### UNSCHEDULED FLIGHTS

Occasional flights to Keesler AFB, MS (**BIX**) and MacDill AFB, FL (**MCF**). Call for destinations, routings and schedules.

# MacDILL AIR FORCE BASE (MCF/KMCF)

6th TRANS/LGTTA
7813 Hangar Loop Drive, Room 101
MacDill AFB, FL 33621-5501

**LOCATION:** From I-75 north or south exit 57 to I-275 south, exit 23 at Dale Mabry Highway (US-92/573), south five miles to MacDill AFB main gate. *USMRA: Page 38 (E,F-8). ML-ARM: (27°51'N/82°29'W).* LST: GMT-05:00. NMC: Tampa, 5 miles north. Main installation numbers: C-813-828-1110, D-312-968-1110.

**REGISTRATION INFO: C-813-828-2440/2485, D-312-968-2440/2485, Rec: (updated daily) C-813-828-2310, D-312-968-2310, Fax: C-813-828-7844, D-312-968-7844. E-mail: spacea@macdill.af.mil (backlog sign up)** Hangar #4, Hours: 0830-1630 Mon-Fri, weekends as required. Directions: Enter Dale Mabry gate. Turn left on North Boundary Road to right on Hangar Loop Road, 4th Hangar on right. **Pax Service Office:** C-813-828-2485, D-312-968-2485. No Paging.

**PAX LOUNGES:** General lounge is also family lounge. **General:** Hangar #4, Room 101, Hours: 0730-1630 Mon-Fri, C-813-828-2485. A/C, bag check, telephones (local, long distance and defense), TV, restrooms, P/C seats. **DV/VIP:** Hangar #3, Hours: 0730-1630 daily, C-813-828-2350. A/C, read/write rooms, telephones (local, long distance and defense), TV,

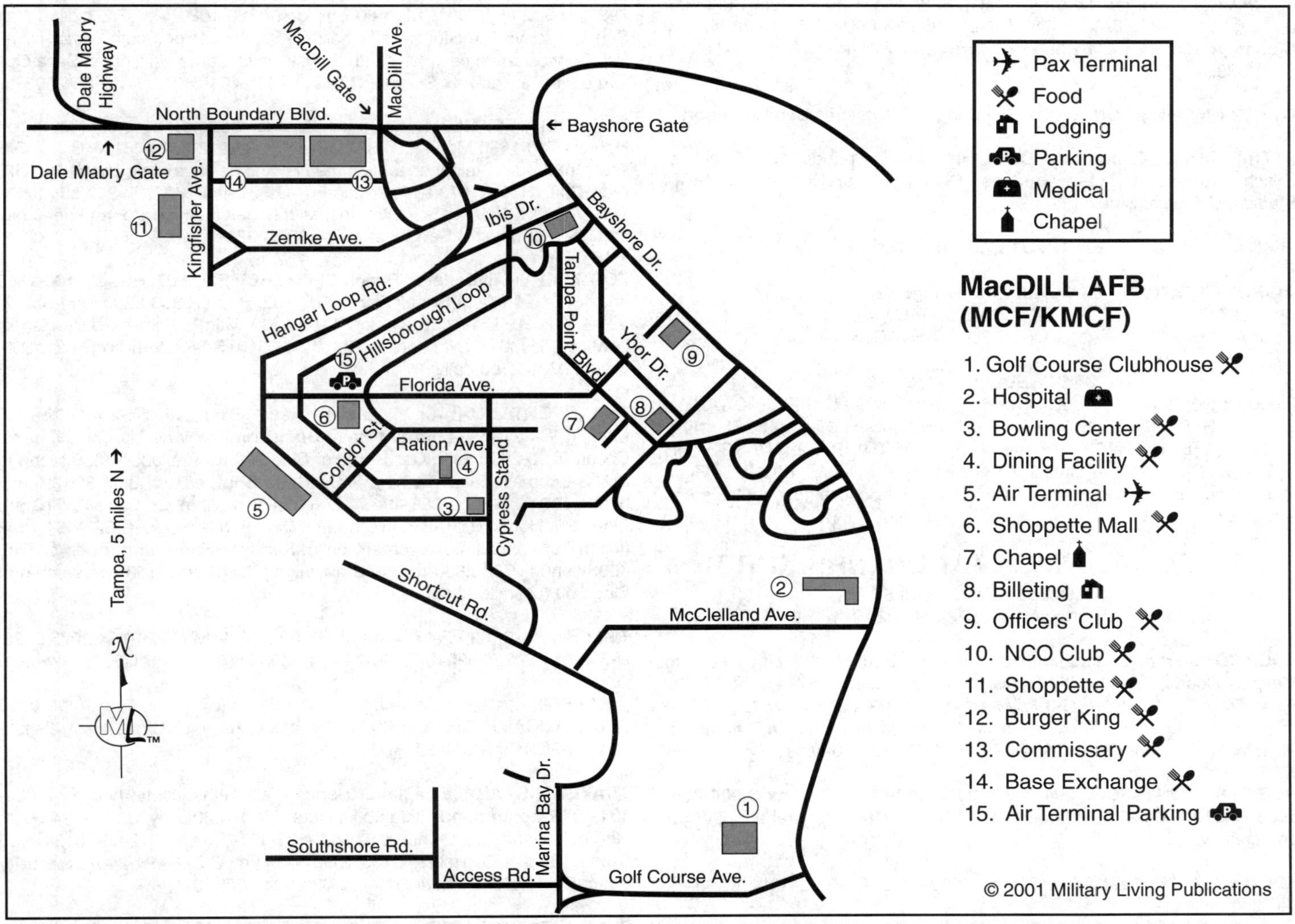

© 2001 Military Living Publications

restrooms, showers, O/S seats (O6+). **Protocol Service:** Bldg 9, Hours: 0730-1630 Mon-Fri, C-813-828-2056.

**FOOD SERVICE: Cafeteria:** Bldg 259, C-813-828-0511. **Enlisted Club:** Bldg 499, C-813-828-3357. **Fast Food:** Burger King, C-813-840-2992. **O Club:** Bldg 397, C-813-837-1031.

**TRANSPORTATION: Air Tickets:** SATO, Bldg 528, C-813-828-4327. **Off Base Car Rental:** Enterprise, C-813-840-2613. **On Base Shuttle/Bus (Comm):** Bldg 926, C-813-254-HART. **On Base Taxi (Gov):** Bldg 176, C-813-828-5281 (duty passengers only). **Off Base Taxi (Comm):** United, C-813-253-2424; Yellow, C-813-253-0121. **Parking:** Short term - Hangar #4, 24 hour limit, C-813-828-2485; long term - at Coons Creek Recreation Area, C-813-828-4982. Call Security Police for info, C-813-828-3322.

**TML:** Bldg 411, 8604 Hanger Loop, 24 hours daily, C-813-831-4259/4804, D-312-968-4259/4804, DV/VIP C-813-828-2056.

**RVC:** Coon's Creek Rec Area, Check-in Marina adjacent to Rec Area, C-1-800-821-4982, C-813-840-6919, D-312-968-4982/2162, Fax: C-813-828-7507.

**TRAVELERS AID: Chaplain:** Bldg 355, C-813-828-3621. **Emergency Relief:** Bldg 373, C-813-828-3311. **Lost/Found:** Bldg P-26, C-813-828-3322. **Medical:** Bldg 711, 24 hours daily, C-813-839-3344, D-312-968-3344. **Red Cross:** Hospital, Bldg 7011, C-813-828-3156. If no answer call C-813-832-2507. **Security Police:** Bldg P-26, C-813-828-3322.

**SUPPORT AVAILABLE: Bank/Currency Exchange:** Bldg 102, C-813-837-2451. **Exchange:** Bldg 926, C-813-828-0511. **Hair Styles:** Bldg 926; Barber, C-813-840-2154/3978; Beauty, C-813-840-0525. **Laundry/Dry Cleaning:** Bldg 17, C-813-840-2329. **Postal Service:** Bldg 17, C-813-828-4438.

**OTHER INFORMATION:** Port of Entry and U.S. Customs Service Airport.

**ATTRACTIONS:** Tampa Bay, Citrus Belt, Silver Springs, Gulf Beaches. Busch Gardens, Cypress Gardens, Disney World, Sea World, MGM Studios, Universal Studios.

### EN ROUTE SCHEDULES

| AIRPORT/STATION | LI-MISSION (page #) |
| --- | --- |
| Keesler AFB | BIX-226/MEDEVAC (44) |
| Scott AFB | BLV-C-626/MEDEVAC (30) |

### UNSCHEDULED FLIGHTS

Frequent flights via KC-135E AND KC-10A to: Andrews AFB, MD (**ADW**); Dover AFB, DE (**DOV**); Eglin AFB, FL (**VPS**); Jacksonville NAS, FL (**NIP**); McGuire AFB, NJ (**WRI**); Oceana NAS, VA (**NTU**); Pease IT/ANGS, NH (**PSM**); and Peterson AFB, CO (**COS**). Infrequent flights OCONUS. Flight information available one day in advance. Call for destinations, routings and schedules.

## MAYPORT NAVAL STATION (NRB/KNRB)

P.O. Box 280032, Bldg 54
Mayport, FL 32228-0032

**LOCATION:** From Jacksonville take Atlantic Boulevard (FL-10) east to Mayport Road (FL-A1A), left to Naval Station, east of FL-A1A. *USMRA: Page 38 (H-3), Page 50 (G-3,4). ML-ARM: (30°22'N/81°24'W).* LST: GMT-05:00. NMC: Jacksonville, 10 miles west. NMI: Jacksonville NAS, 40 miles. Main installation numbers: C-904-270-5011, D-312-960-5011.

**REGISTRATION INFO: C-904-270-6023, D-312-960-6023, Fax C-904-270-5254, D-312-960-5254.** Bldg 424, Hours: 0700-2100. General and DV/VIP Lounges available.

**FOOD SERVICE: Fast Food:** Hours: 0530-2300, C-904-241-1486. Snack Vending available.

**TML:** Davis Hall, Bldg 425, 24 hours daily, C-904-270-5423/5707, D-312-960-5423, Fax: C-904-270-5596. Navy Lodge: C-904-247-3964. DV/VIP:(EM) C-904-270-4501.

**TRAVELERS AID: Chaplain:** C-904-270-5401. **Medical/Dental:** Hours: 0730-1630, C-904-270-5400. **Red Cross:** C-904-246-1395. **Security Police:** C-904-270-6802.

**SUPPORT AVAILABLE: Convenience Store:** Hours: 0700-2100 Mon-Fri, 0800-2100 Sat-Sun, C-904-247-5715. **Exchange:** Hours: 0900-1900 Mon-Sat, 1100-1700 Sun, C-904-247-5715. **Laundry/Dry Cleaner:** Hours: 0900-1700 Mon-Fri, C-904-247-5301. **Postal Service:** Hours: 0900-1600 Mon-Fri, C-904-270-5560.

**OTHER INFORMATION: U.S.** Customs Service Airport.

### UNSCHEDULED FLIGHTS

Frequent flights to Dobbins ARB/Atlanta NAS, GA (**MGE/NCQ**), Key West NAS, FL (**NQX**), Oceana NAS,VA (**NTU**), Pensacola NAS, FL (**NPA**) and Norfolk NS, VA (**NGU**). Call for destinations, routings and schedules.

## PATRICK AIR FORCE BASE (COF/KCOF)

45th TRNS/LGTTB
930 South Patrick Drive, Bldg 800
Patrick AFB, FL 32925-3437

**LOCATION:** Take I-95 south to exit 73 east (Wickham Road), three miles to FL-404 (Pineda Causeway), left on South Patrick Drive, to Patrick AFB. *USMRA: Page 38 (I-8). ML-ARM: (28°15'N/80°36'W).* LST: GMT-05:00. NMC: Orlando, 45 miles northwest. Melbourne, Cocoa, and Merritt Island - all within 20 miles of base. Main installation numbers: C-321-494-1110, D-312-854-1110.

**REGISTRATION INFO: C-321-494-5631, D-312-854-5631, Fax: C-321-494-7991, D-312-854-7991.** Bldg 800, Hours: 0730-1630 Mon-Fri, closed Sat, Sun & holidays. Directions: 1 mile north of South Gate on South Patrick Drive. Pax Service entrance faces south Patrick Drive. Same building as Base Ops and control tower. **Pax Service Office:** C-321-494-5631, D-312-854-5631.

**PAX LOUNGES:** No separate family lounge. **General:** Bldg 800, first floor, Hours: 0730-1630 Mon-Fri, C-321-494-5631, D-312-854-5631. A/C, TV, O/S seats, restrooms, telephones (commercial and defense), bag check. **DV/VIP:** Bldg 800, Hours: 0730-1630 Mon-Fri, C-321-494-5631, D-312-854-5631, O6+. A/C, TV, O/S seats, restrooms, telephones (commercial and defense), bag check. **Protocol Services:** Bldg 423, C-321-494-4506, O7+.

**FOOD SERVICE: Enlisted Beach Club (EBC):** Bldg 967, Hours: 1100-1300 and 1700-1900 daily. **Snack Bars:** Bldg 732, Hours: 0800-2300 Mon-Sat, C-321-494-2598. Bldg 415, Hours: 1100-1300 Mon-Fri. Snack bars also at bowling alley and golf course C-321-494-6510. **Snack Vending:** Bldg 800, Hours: 0730-2300 daily.

**TRANSPORTATION: Air Tickets:** CI Travel, Bldg 546, Hours: 0900-1800 Mon-Fri, C-321-494-4155. **Off Base Bus (Comm):** Available in Melbourne/Cocoa 0730-2000 daily. **Car Rentals:** Bldg 720, Hours: 0800-1630 Mon-Fri, S & S Express, C-321-783-2424. **On Base Shuttle/Bus:** Bldg 800, Hours: 0730-1700 Mon-Fri, C-321-494-7247 (on base routing). **On Base Taxi (Gov):** Bldg 329, Hours: 0730-2300 Mon-Fri, 0730-1500 Sat-Sun, C-321-494-7247 (for military personnel on orders only). **Parking:** Short term, north of Bldg 800, Hours: 0730-2300 daily (no overnight); long term, 150 yards south of Bldg 800 (unlimited hours).

**TML:** Bldg 720, 820 Falcon Avenue, 24 hours daily, C-321-494-2075/5428, D-312-854-2075/6590, Fax: C-321-494-6093/7597. DV/VIP O6+, C-321-494-4511.

**RVC:** FAMCAMP, Check-in 0800-1600 hours daily, or Camp Host, C-321-494-4787/2042, D-312-854-4787.

**TRAVELERS AID: Chaplain:** Serving all faiths. Duty hours, C-321-494-4073. **Lost/Found:** Bldg 800, Hours: 0730-1630 daily, C-321-494-5631. **Medical:** Bldg 1380, 24 hours daily, C-321-494-8134, D-312-854-8134. **Red Cross:** Bldg 425, Hours: 0730-1630 Mon-Fri, C-321-494-2402. **Security Police:** Bldg 405, 24 hours daily, C-321-494-2008.

**SUPPORT AVAILABLE: Bank/Currency Exchange:** Bldg 720, Hours: 0900-1700 Mon-Fri, C-321-783-3411. **Exchange:** Off base. Hours: 0930-1800 Mon-Fri, 0930-1630 Sat-Sun, C-321-799-1300. **Hair Styles:** Bldg 415; Barber, C-321-784-2781; Beauty, C-321-784-1241. **Laundry/Dry**

**Cleaning:** Bldg 415, Hours: 0930-1800 Mon-Fri, 0930-1630 Sat-Sun, C-321-783-3625. **Postal Service:** Bldg 424. **Wire:** Western Union available at exchange cashier cage.

**ATTRACTIONS:** NASA Space Flight Center, Daytona Beach, Orlando-Disney World, Cocoa Beach.

*Note: Commercially contracted flights are now called Patriot Express.*

**PATRICK AFB, FL (COF); REGION: ATL;
OPERATOR: COM; TYPE: MIXED; ROUTE: HJL3A;
SCHEDULE: 1ST, 2ND & 3RD MON; EQUIPMENT: DC862**

{COF (★) *NE* ➡ SJH *NE* ➡ ASI ⇌ ASI *SW* ➡ SJH *SW* ➡ COF (★)}

| LI/ICAO | AIRPORT/STATION | CTRY/STA | | DAYS EN ROUTE |
|---|---|---|---|---|
| COF/KCOF | Patrick AFB | FL | | +0 |
| SJH/TAPA | V C Bird IAP (St John's) | AG | | +0 |
| ASI/FHAW | Ascension AUX AF (Georgetown) | GB | | +2 |
| ASI/FHAW | Ascension AUX AF (Georgetown) | GB | | +2 |
| SJH/TAPA | V C Bird IAP (St John's) | AG | | +2 |
| COF/KCOF | Patrick AFB | FL | | |

### EN ROUTE SCHEDULES

| AIRPORT/STATION | LI-MISSION (page #) |
|---|---|
| Keesler AFB | BIX-226/MEDEVAC (44) |
| Charleston AFB/IAP | CHS-G8L3A (67) |

### UNSCHEDULED FLIGHTS

Frequent flights via HC-130N/P to CONUS and OCONUS locations. Call for destinations, routings and schedules.

# PENSACOLA NAVAL AIR STATION (NPA/KNPA)

Air Operations/Air Terminal Services Bldg 1852
280 Skyhawk Drive
Pensacola NAS, FL 32508-5000

**LOCATION:** Four miles south of US-98, and 12 miles south of I-10. Take Navy Blvd from US-98 or US-29 directly to NAS. *USMRA: Page 39 (A,B-13); Page 53 (A,B-4,5). ML-ARM: (30°22'N/87°16'W).* LST: GMT-05:00. NMC: Pensacola, 8 miles north. Main installation numbers: C-850-452-0111, D-312-922-0111.

**REGISTRATION INFO: C-850-452-3311, D-312-922-3311, Rec: C-850-452-3311, Fax: C-850-452-8105, D-312-922-8105.** Bldg 1852, 24 hours daily. Directions: From main gate, straight on Duncan Road to right on Taylor Road to a right onto Radford Road to Air Ops on the right. **Pax Service Office:** C-850-452-3311, D-312-922-3311. **Pax Paging:** C-850-452-3311, D-312-922-3311.

**PAX LOUNGES:** No separate family lounge. **General/Family Lounge:** Bldg 1852, Room 105, 24 hours daily, C-850-452-3311. A/C, bag check, restrooms, TV. **DV/VIP:** Bldg 1852, Hours: 0600-2400, C-850-452-2431. Restrooms and showers available, A/C, coffee/tea served.

**FOOD SERVICE: Cafeteria:** Bldg 634, C-850-455-0932 ext 222. **Enlisted Club:** (Ducks/Gosalinos/Bleachers) Bldg 667, C-850-452-2443; Lighthouse Point Restaurant, Bldg 3558, C-850-452-3251. **Enlisted Dining Facility:** Bldg 601, C-850-452-3538, D-850-922-3538. **O Club:** Bldg 253, C-850-455-2276, (Mustin Beach); International Deli, Bldg 634, C-850-455-0932. **Snack Bars:** Bowling Center, C-850-452-3899; Golf Course, C-850-452-3859.

**TRANSPORTATION: Air Tickets:** ITT, Bldg 632, C-850-453-8922; SATO, Bldg 680, C-850-452-2589. **Bus (Comm):** ECAT-Fairfield Drive, C-850-436-9383. **Car Rentals:** Enterprise Rent-A-Car, C-850-456-7468, (will pick you up); Guardian, C-850-456-0351; Snappy, C-850-435-8808. **Taxi (Comm):** Crosstown, C-850-456-8294; Warrington, C-850-455-8506; Blue Angel, C-850-456-8294. **Parking:** Short and long term, Bldg 3585, C-850-452-3311.

**TML:** Bldg 3910, 24 hours daily, C-850-452-7782, D-312-922-7782, Fax: C-850-452-7784, D-312-922-7784. Navy Lodge: Bldg 3875, C-850-456-8676.

**RVC:** Oak Grove Park, Rec Dept, C-850-452-2535, D-312-922-2535.

**TRAVELERS AID: Chaplain:** Bldg 634, C-850-452-2341. **Emergency Relief:** Bldg 16, C-850-455-8574 (Navy Relief). **Lost/Found:** Bldg 1852. **Medical:** Naval Hospital, 24 hours daily, C-850-505-6601, D-312-922-6601; Pharmacy, C-850-505-6459. **Red Cross:** Bldg 25, C-850-452-2492, After hours C-850-452-6601. **Security Police:** Hq Bldg 1534, C-850-452-3753. Pass and Tag, main gate, C-850-452-4153. **Family Service Center:** Bldg 625, C-850-452-5990.

## PATRICK AIR FORCE BASE, FL (COF/KCOF)

1. Officers Club
2. Billeting Office/Visitors Quarters
3. Credit Union
4. Bowling Center
5. Service Station
6. Passenger Terminal Base Ops (Bldg 800)
7. NCO Club
8. Base Exchange
9. Commissary
10. Hospital



© 2001 Military Living Publications

**SUPPORT AVAILABLE: Bank/Currency Exchange:** First Navy Bank on base: Murray Road, C-850-453-3411; Pen Air FCU (on base), C-850-453-4341. **Exchange:** Bldg 634 (retail store), C-850-458-3224. NEX Mall, C-850-455-5311. **Hair Styles:** Barber, Bldg 3248, C-850-458-3339; Beauty, Bldg 470, C-850-458-3328. **Laundry/Dry Cleaning:** Bldg 634, C-850-458-3275. **Postal Service:** Bldg 223, C-850-452-2726. U.S. **Coast Guard Station:** C-850-452-2176. **Veterinarian:** Bldg 626A, C-850-452-3530.

**OTHER INFORMATION:** U.S. Customs Service Airport; 24 hour prior notice required, Military A/C only.

**ATTRACTIONS:** Sport fishing, dog races, golf course, tennis center, ice hockey, enlisted and officer pools, campground and RV park, Naval Aviation Museum, Blue Angels (NAVY Flight Demonstration Team) C-850-452-BLUE, Sailing Facility and Marina, Gulf Island National Seashore, Fort Pickens, Fort Redoubt, Fort Barrancas (on base), and Seville historical district.

### UNSCHEDULED FLIGHTS
Flights to: Dobbins ARB/Atlanta NAS, GA (**MGE/NCQ**), Corpus Christi NAS, TX (**NGP**), Fort Worth NAS/JRB, TX (**FWH**), Jacksonville NAS, FL (**NIP**), Millington Municipal Apt/ Mid-South NSA, TN (**NQA**), Meridian NAS, MS (**NMM**), Norfolk NS, VA (**NGU**) and Washington NAF, MD (**NSF**). Most flights are via C009A and C-12/21 aircraft. Call for destinations, routings and schedules.

## TYNDALL AIR FORCE BASE (PAM/KPAM)
445 Suwannee Road, Suite 101
Tyndall AFB, FL 32403-5541

**LOCATION:** Take I-10, exit to US-231 south to US-98 east. Tyndall AFB is southeast of US-98. Clearly marked. *USMRA: Page 39 (E-14). ML-ARM: (30°04'N/85°36'W).* LST: GMT-05:00. NMC: Panama City, 10 miles northwest. Main installation numbers: C-850-283-1113, D-312-523-1113.

**REGISTRATION INFO: C-850-283-4360, D-312-523-4244.** Base Ops.

**FOOD SERVICE: Enlisted Club:** C-850-283-4444. **O Club:** C-850-283-4357. **Snack Bars:** C-850-283-4110.

**TML:** Bldg 1332, 204 Oak Drive, 24 hours daily, C-850-283-44211 EX-1, D-312-523-4211, Fax: C-850-283-4811. DV/VIP C-850-283-2232.

**RVC:** FAMCAMP, 101 FAMCAMP Road, C-850-283-2798, D-312-523-2798.

**TRAVELERS AID: Chaplain:** C-850-283-2925. **Medical:** C-850-283-2778. **Security Police:** C-850-283-2558.

**SUPPORT AVAILABLE: Exchange:** C-850-283-4110.

**ATTRACTIONS:** Panama City and beautiful white sand beaches.

### UNSCHEDULED FLIGHTS
Infrequent flights to Jacksonville NAS, FL (**NIP**). Call for destinations, routings and schedules.

## Other Florida Installations with Possible Space-A Air Opportunities

**MIAMI COAST GUARD AIR STATION (NOM/KNOM),** Opa Locka Airport, Opa Locka, FL 33054-2397. **LOCATION:** Take exit 14 from I-95 onto NW 135th Street (Opa Locka Blvd., also FL-916) west to Lejeune Road, then north to the airport. Turn left (west) on Wright Road.  Air Station is at the end of the road. *USMRA: Page 39 (J-13), Page 51 (B-4). ML-ARM: (25°54'N/80°16'W).* LST: GMT-05:00. Extremely limited Space-A. **C-305-953-2130.** **TML:** Nearest TML is at Key West, CBQ, 24 hours daily, C-305-293-4142, D-312-483-4142, Fax: C-305-293-2084, D-312-483-4302, BOQ - C-305-293-5571, BEQ - C-305-293-2488, Navy Lodge - C-305-292-7556, DV/VIP 305-293-2095. Limited base support facilities available. Call for destinations, routings and schedules.

## GEORGIA

## BUSH FIELD AIRPORT (AGS/KAGS)
1501 Aviation Way
Augusta, GA 30906-9600

**LOCATION:** From I-20 east or west, exit 61 south, between US-78/278 and US-1. Gates are on both US-78 and US-1. Gate 2 and Gate 1 (McKenna Gate) on US-78 east-west. *USMRA: Page 37 (F,G-4). ML-ARM: (33°22'N/81°58'W).* LST: GMT-05:00. NMC: Augusta, 12 miles northeast. C-706-791-0110, D-312-780-0110.

**REGISTRATION INFO:** For MEDEVAC Space-A contact Dwight David Eisenhower Army Medical Center, 14 miles west of airport. **C-706-791-5811.** TML: Bldg 250, C-706-791-2277/3103. Fort Gordon, 10 miles west of airport, has full support facilities.

**PAX LOUNGES:** Follow signs to private aircraft terminal.

**FOOD SERVICE: Snack Bars:** Jerry's, C-706-790-4208, at airport. Limited snack vending available.

**TRANSPORTATION: Car Rental:** Avis, C-706-798-1383; Budget, 706-790-6902; Hertz, C-706-798-3970; National, C-706-798-5835. **Off Base Limo:** Old South Limo Service, C-706-828-7400. **Off Base Taxi:** City Cab, C-706-722-3501. **Parking:** Long-term parking, C-706-798-8950.

**TML:** Nearest TML is at Griffith Hall, Bldg 250, Chamberlain Avenue, Fort Gordon, 0730-2400 daily, C-706-791-2277, D-312-780-2277. Also at Fort Gordon: Stinson Hall, C-706-791-2277.

**TRAVELERS AID: Security Police:** Airport police C-706-793-1137, 24 hours daily.

**OTHER INFORMATION:** ATM machine available in airport terminal.

### EN ROUTE SCHEDULES

| AIRPORT/STATION | LI-MISSION (page #) |
|---|---|
| Keesler AFB | BIX-226/MEDEVAC (44) |
| Scott AFB | BLV-C-621/MEDEVAC (30) |
| Scott AFB | BLV-C-626/MEDEVAC (30) |

### UNSCHEDULED FLIGHTS
Call for destinations, routings and schedules. Most flights are MEDEVAC.

## DOBBINS AIR RESERVE BASE/ ATLANTA NAVAL AIR STATION (MGE/KNCQ)
94 OG/OGA
Base Operations, Bldg 737
1477 Mimosa Drive
Dobbins ARB, GA 30069-4821

**LOCATION:** From Atlanta take I-75 north to Windy Hill Exit (#260 west). Turn right (north) onto Highway 41. Follow signs to Dobbins main gate. *USMRA: Page 37 (B-3); Page 49 (A-1). ML-ARM: (33°54'N/84°30'W).* LST: GMT-05:00. NMC: Atlanta, 16 miles southeast. Main installation numbers: 770-919-5000, D-312-925-5000.

**REGISTRATION INFO: C-770-919-6359, D-312-925-6359, Fax: C-770-919-4915.** Bldg 737, Base Ops, Hours: 0700-2300 daily. Directions: From main gate, straight on Mimosa Drive to dead end at Base Ops. NAS Ops Bldg 352: C-770-919-6359, D-312-925-6359, Fax: C-770-919-6155, D-312-925-6155, 0630-2300 daily. **Pax Paging:** C-770-919-4903/6359, D-312-925-4903/6359.

**PAX LOUNGES:** Limited lounge facilities. **General:** Bldg 737, Hours: 0700-2300 daily, C-770-919-4903 (capacity 20). A/C, restrooms, P/C seats.

**DV/VIP:** Bldg 737, Hours: 0700-2300 daily. Commercial telephone in Pax Term (capacity 8). Key from dispatcher. A/C, telephones (commercial and defense), restrooms, O/S seats. **Protocol Service:** Bldg 729, Hours: 0730-1630 Mon-Fri, C-770-919-4520,O6+.

**FOOD SERVICE:** Limited services on base. **Combined Club:** Atlantic Ave, C-770-427-5551, C-770-919-4594, C-770-919-5040. **Dining Hall:** Bldg 60 NAS, C-770-919-6469. **O Club:** Take Two Club, Bldg 53 NAS, C-770-919-6393.

**TRANSPORTATION: Air Tickets:** SATO, MAG 42, Marine Corp. Hangar 1, Room 226 NAS, Hours: 0730-1615 Mon-Fri, C-770-919-4848 and C-770-425-2113. **Commercial Ticket Office:** Omega Travel, Bldg 812, C-770-919-5788, D-312-925-5788. **Off Base Bus (Comm):** Highway 41 N; Greyhound, C-770-427-3011; Tradewinds, C-770-429-0092. **Off Base Car Rentals:** The William B. Hartsfield Atlanta IAP; Avis, C-404-530-2700; Hertz, C-404-530-2900. **On Base Taxi (Gov):** Motor Pool, Hours: 0800-1600 Mon-Fri, C-770-919-4853 (duty passengers only). **Parking:** Bldg 827, short and long term.

**TML:** Dobbins Inn, Bldg 800, 1295 Barracks Court, 24 hours daily, C-770-424-1352, D-312-925-1352, Fax: C-770-919-5185. DV/VIP C-770-919-4520.

**TRAVELERS AID: Chaplain:** Bldg 32 NAS, Hours: 0730-1600 Wed-Sun, C-770-919-6955/6. **Medical:** NAS Clinic, 24 hours daily, C-770-919-5302, D-312-925-5302. **Security Police:** Main gate, C-770-919-4910. **USO:** The William B. Hartsfield Atlanta IAP, C-404-761-8061 (North Term).

**SUPPORT AVAILABLE: Exchange:** Bldg 530, C-770-428-3054. **Hair Styles:** Bldg 530, C-770-425-3092. **Postal Service:** Bldg 827, C-770-919-5049.

**ATTRACTIONS:** Stone Mountain, Six Flags, White Water.

### UNSCHEDULED FLIGHTS

Flights via C-130H, C-009B and DC-009 to Andrews AFB, MD (**ADW**); Charleston AFB/IAP, SC (**CHS**); Eglin AFB, FL (**VPS**); Jacksonville NAS, FL (**NIP**); Kelly AFB, TX (**SKF**); Keesler AFB. MS (**BIX**); New Orleans NAS, LA (**NBG**); Norfolk NS, VA (**NGU**); North Island NAS, CA (**NZY**); Pensacola NAS, FL (**NPA**); Pope AFB, NC (**POB**); Roosevelt Roads NAS, PR (**NRR**). Call for destinations, routings and schedules.

## HUNTER ARMY AIRFIELD (SVN/KSVN)

240 South Lightning Road, Bldg 1252
Savannah, GA 31409-5000

**LOCATION:** From I-95 north or south exit 16 to GA-204 east for 13 miles to Savannah. Turn left (north) onto Stephenson Avenue, proceed to Wilson Avenue gate to installation. *USMRA: Page 37 (H-7). ML-ARM: (32°01'N/81°07'W).* LST: GMT-05:00. C-912-352-6521, D-312-971-1110.

**REGISTRATION INFO:** C-912-352-5110, D-312-971-5110, Fax: C-912-352-6842, D-312-971-6842. Very limited Space-A. *Note: Telephone calls to Hunter now require dialing the entire prefix.*

**TML:** Bldg 6010, 525 Leonard Neal Streets, 0730-2400 Mon-Fri, 0800-1700 Sat, Sun, holidays, C-912-355-1060, C-912-352-5910/5834, D-312-971-5910/5834, other hours, Bldg 1201, C-912-352-5140. DV/VIP C-912-767-7742, D-312-870-7742.

**RVC:** Lotts Island Travel Camp, Outdoor Rec, Bldg 8454, Shooting Star Road, C-912-352-5916/5722/5274, D-312-870-5722.

**SUPPORT AVAILABLE:** Full base support facilities available.

**ATTRACTIONS:** Historic Savannah, period homes, General Sherman's headquarters, Cotton Exchange, Fort Pulaski and Fort McAllister.

### UNSCHEDULED FLIGHTS

Call for destinations, routings, and schedules.

## LAWSON ARMY AIRFIELD (LSF/KLSF)

DOT Aviation Division, Base Ops, Bldg 2485
Fort Benning, GA 31905-5593

**LOCATION:** Off I-85 north or south and US-27/280 east or west. South to Benning Blvd and main gate. *USMRA: Page 37 (B-6). ML-ARM: (32°20'N/85°00'W).* LST: GMT-05:00. NMC. Columbus, 5 miles northwest. NMI: Robins AFB, east. Main installation numbers: C-706-545-2011, D-312-835-2011.

**REGISTRATION INFO:** C-706-545-3524, D-312-835-3524, Fax: C-706-545-7249, D-312-835-7249. Base Ops, 24 hours daily. Ask Security Police for directions. Full base support available.

**PAX LOUNGES:** Pax and DV/VIP lounges.

**FOOD SERVICE:** Snack Vending at Base Ops. Burger King and pizza available on Main Post.

**TRANSPORTATION: On Base Car Rental:** Enterprise, C-706-686-0896. Post shuttle bus and commercial taxi available.

**TML:** Bldg 399, 24 hours daily, C-706-689-0067, D-312-835-3145. DV/VIP:C-706-545-1549, D-312-835-5724.

**TRAVELERS AID:** Duty hours for Red Cross, Medical, Travelers Aid, Chaplain, Security police.

**SUPPORT AVAILABLE:** Duty hours for Bank/Currency Exchange, Hair Styles, Postal Service, Laundry/Cleaning.

### UNSCHEDULED FLIGHTS

Flights to Andrews AFB, MD (**ADW**); Davison AAF, VA (**DAA**); Charleston AFB/IAP, SC (**CHS**); Cherry Point MCAS, NC (**NKT**); Bush Field Airport, GA (**AGS**); McGuire AFB, NJ (**WRI**); Norfolk NS, VA (**NGU**); Pope AFB, NC (**POB**); and Shaw AFB, SC (**SSC**). Call for destinations, routings and schedules.

## MOODY AIR FORCE BASE (VAD/KVAD)

347th TFW/Air Ops
8049 Robinson Road
Moody AFB, GA 31699-1511

**LOCATION:** On GA-125, 10 miles north of Valdosta, east of GA-125. Also, can be reached from I-75 north or south via GA-122 east to GA-125 south. *USMRA: Page 37 (D,E-9). ML-ARM: (30°57'N/83°11'W).* LST: GMT-05:00. NMC: Valdosta, 10 miles south. Main installation numbers: C-229-257-3395, D-312-460-3395.

**REGISTRATION INFO:** C-229-257-1776, D-312-460-1776, REC: C-229-257-1776; D-312-460-1776, Fax: C-229-257-4112 D-312-460-4112. **WEB:** www.moody.af.mil Bldg 8153, Hours: 0730-1630 Mon-Fri, Sat-Sun and holidays: Stand-by (contact through Base Ops). Directions: From main gate, straight on Mitchell Blvd (1/4 mile) Left on Robinson Road (1/2 mile). Pax Terminal is in Transportation Bldg. (8049) on the left. All passengers processed by Pax Term. **Pax Service Office:** C-229-257-1776, D-312-460-1776. Very limited Space-A flights available.

**FOOD SERVICE: Combined Club:** Hours: 1100-2000, C-229-257-4530, on base. **Dining Hall:** C-229-257-3031. **Fast Food:** Burger King, Hours: 0730-1800, C-229-245-8296, on base. **Snack Bars:** Bowling Alley, Hours: 0730-2100, C-229-257-3872, on base.

**TRANSPORTATION: Commercial Travel:** C-229-257-4278. **Taxi:** C-229-257-3461. **Parking:** ATC tower. No restrictions.

**TML:** Bldg 3131, Cooney Street, 24 hours daily, C-229-257-3893, D-312-460-3893, Fax: C-229-257-4971, D-312-460-4971. DV/VIP Protocol Office, Bldg 5113, C-229-257-2656.

**TRAVELERS AID: Chaplain:** C-229-257-3211. **Medical:** Bldg 900, 24 hours daily, C-229-257-3232, D-312-460-3232. **Red Cross:** C-229-257-3542. **Security Police:** Bldg 617, 24 hours daily, C-229-257-3108.

**SUPPORT AVAILABLE: Exchange:** C-229-257-3431.

**ATTRACTIONS:** Historic homes in Valdosta, Okefenokee Swamp, 50 miles east; Wild Adventures, 20 miles south.

**OTHER INFORMATION:** No scheduled flights.

### UNSCHEDULED FLIGHTS

Very limited. Call for destinations, routings and schedules.

# ROBINS AIR FORCE BASE (WRB/KWRB)

78th Air Base Wing (AFMC)
455 Byron Street, Suite 425
Robins AFB, GA 31098-1860

**LOCATION:** Off US-129 on GA-247 at Warner Robins. Go south on I-75. Get off exit 46. Go east on Hwy 247 (Watson Blvd) until dead-end at Robins AFB, east of US-129. *USMRA: Page 37 (D-6). ML-ARM: (32°37'N/83°35'W).* LST: GMT-05:00. NMC: Macon, 15 miles northwest. Main installation numbers: C-478-926-2137, D-312-468-1110.

**REGISTRATION INFO: C-478-926-3166/4915, D-312-468-3166/4915, Fax: C-478-926-4355, D-312-468-4355.** Bldg 127, Hours: 0800-1600 Mon-Fri. Directions: From Gate 2 (Visitor Center), straight on 2nd Street to a left onto Robins Parkway. Continue to Gate 31. **Pax Service Office:** C-478-926-3166, D-312-468-4915.

**PAX LOUNGES:** No separate family lounge. **General:** Bldg 127, Hours: 0800-1600 Mon-Fri, C-478-926-3166. A/C, telephones, TV, restrooms. **DV/VIP:** Bldg 110, 24 hours daily. A/C, showers, telephones, TV, read/write rooms, O/S seats. **Protocol Service:** Bldg 215, Hours: 0600-1800 with 24 hour voice mail daily, C-478-926-2761.

**FOOD SERVICE: Cafeteria:** Bldg 166, C-478-922-8635. **Dining Hall:** Bldg 757, C-478-7306. **Smith Community Center:** Bldg 767, C-478-926-2105. **NCO Club:** Bldg 956, C-478-923-5581. **O Club:** Bldg 542, C-478-922-3011. **Snack Vending:** Bldg 110, 24 hours daily, C-478-926-2114.

**TRANSPORTATION: Air Tickets:** Bay Area Travel, Leisure, Bldg 914, Hours: 0900-1700 Mon-Fri, C-912-329-0600 and Bldg 166, Hours: 0700-1500 Mon-Fri, C-478-918-3046. **On Base Bus (Gov):** Bldg 306, 24 hours daily, C-912-926-3493. **Off Base Bus (Comm):** Macon; Greyhound, C-478-743-5411. **On Base Shuttle/Bus:** Bldg 306, Hours: 0700-1730 daily, C-478-926-3493. **Taxi (Comm):** Warner Robins, 24 hours daily, C-478-923-6414. **Taxi (Gov):** Bldg 306, 24 hours daily, C-478-926-3493. **Parking:** Any unmarked space outside the controlled area (near gate 31).

**TML:** Bldg 557, Club Drive, 24 hours daily, C-478-926-2100, D-312-468-2100. DV/VIP Bldg 215, O6+, C-478-926-2761.

**RVC:** FAMCAMP, Outdoor Rec, Bldg 1305, Check-in 1330-1730 hrs, Wed-Sat, C-478-926-4500, C-478-926-3193, D-312-468-3193.

**TRAVELERS AID: Chaplain:** Bldg 769, C-478-926-2821. **Medical:** Bldg 700, C-478-926-3845, D-312-468-3845. **Red Cross:** Bldg 794, Hours: 0900-1300 Mon-Fri, C-478-926-5493. **Security Police:** Bldg 263, C-478-926-...

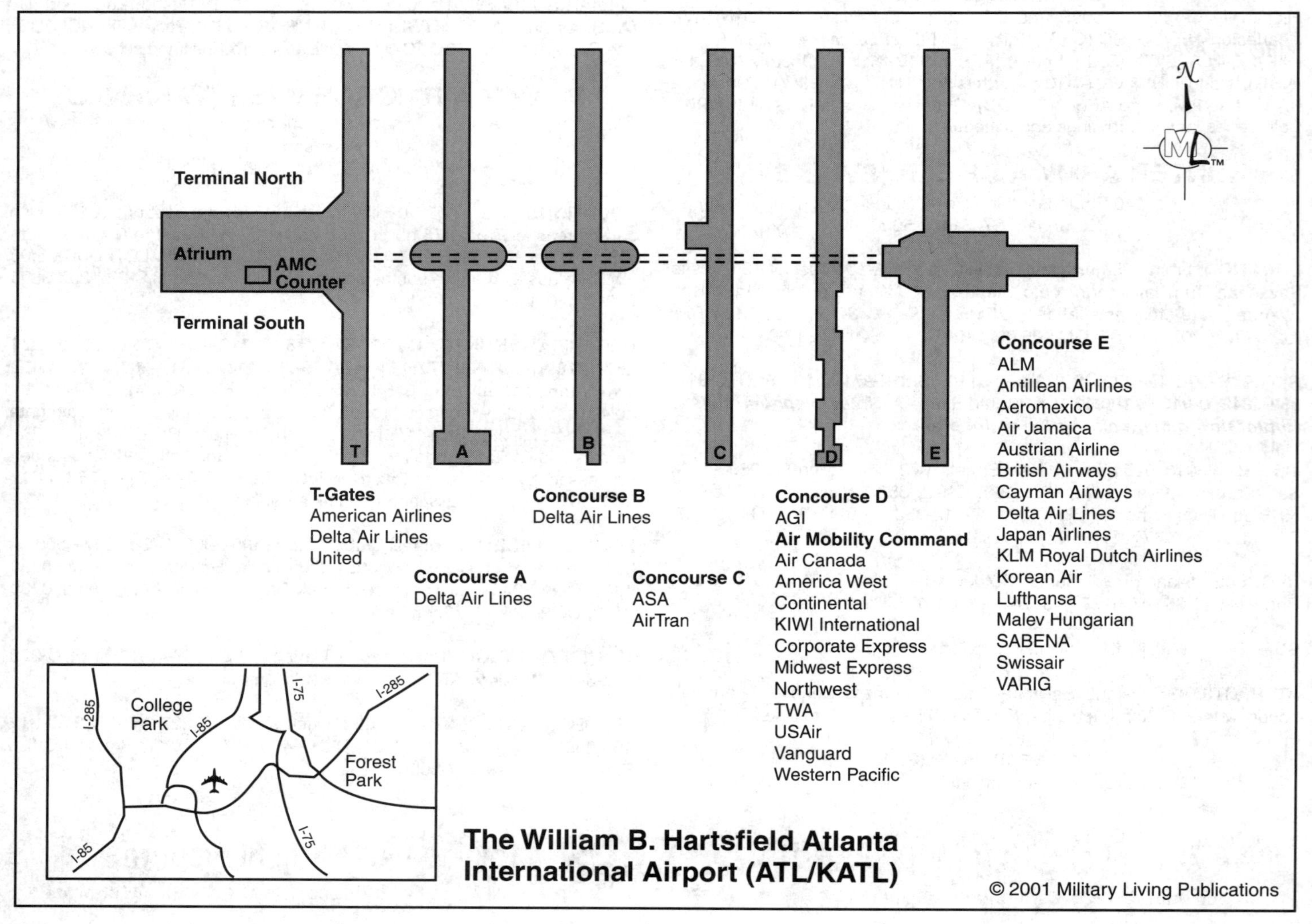


**The William B. Hartsfield Atlanta International Airport (ATL/KATL)**

926-2187. **USO:** Bldg 767, C-478-926-2105. Hours: 0900-1300 Wed, 0900-1700 Fri.

**SUPPORT AVAILABLE: Bank/Currency Exchange:** Bldg 911, Hours: 0900-1700 Mon-Fri, C-478-922-7786. **Exchange:** Bldg 914, Hours: 0900-2100 Mon-Sat, 0900-1700 Sun, C-478-923-5537. **Hair Styles:** Barber/Beauty, Bldg 914, C-478-923-7027. **Laundry/Dry Cleaning:** Bldg 914, C-478-922-2332. **Postal Service:** Bldg 910, C-478-926-3078

**ATTRACTIONS:** Andersonville Trail, Robins AFB Museum.

### UNSCHEDULED FLIGHTS

Flights via C-130E, KC-135E and C-005A. *Note: Missions are posted 24 hours in advance when possible.* Call for destinations, routings, and schedules.

## SAVANNAH INTERNATIONAL AIRPORT (SAV/KSAV)

165th ALW (ANG)
1401 Robert B. Miller Drive
Savannah, GA 31408-9001

**LOCATION:** From I-95 north or south, exit 18A east to Airways Avenue to IAP. *USMRA: Page 37 (H-7).* ML-ARM: *(32°07'N/81°12'W).* LST: GMT-05:00. NMC: Savannah, 4 miles southeast. Main installation numbers: C-912-966-8201/1941, D-312-860-8201.

**REGISTRATION INFO: C-912-964-1941, D-312-860-8201, Fax: C-912-966-8200.** ANG area during flight processing. **TML:** Nearest TML is at Bldg 6010, 525 Leonard Neal Streets, Hunter Army Airfield, 0730-2400 Mon-Fri, 0800-1700 Sat, Sun, holidays, C-912-355-1060, C-912-352-5910/5834, D-312-971-5910/5834, other hours, Bldg 1201, C-912-352-5140. DV/VIP C-912-767-7742, D-312-870-7742.

**SUPPORT AVAILABLE:** Services and facilities of an IAP available.

**OTHER INFORMATION:** U.S. Customs Service Airport.

### UNSCHEDULED FLIGHTS

Most flights on weekends via C-130H aircraft to CONUS and OCONUS locations.

## THE WILLIAM B. HARTSFIELD ATLANTA INTERNATIONAL AIRPORT (ATL/KATL)

Air Mobility Command (AMC)
437 APS/TRG
Charleston IAP
5500 International Blvd, Suite 124
Charleston, SC 29418-0308

**LOCATION:** Off I-285 east or west, exit 42, follow signs. *USMRA: Page 37 (B,C-4), Page 49 (B-4).* ML-ARM: *(33°38'N/84°26'W).* LST: GMT-05:00. Main installation numbers: (At press time all telephone inquiries should be made to Charleston) C-843-963-5794/5795. D-312-673-5794/5795.

**REGISTRATION INFO: C-843-963-5794/5795, D-312-673-5794/5795, Fax: C-843-963-3845, D-312-673-3845. E-mail: spacea@charleston.af.mil** Base Ops, Hours: flight days only, 4 hours prior to flight, 2 hours after flight. Directions: The AMC counter is located in the South Terminal of the William B. Hartsfield Atlanta IAP in Atlanta, GA (near Delta Baggage Claim). **Pax Paging:** C-404-714-7251.

**PAX LOUNGES: USO Lounge:** Located in Atlanta Hartsfield International, North Terminal, C-404-530-8061. Hours: 0930-2100 Mon-Fri, 1000-1900 Sat, 1000-2100 Sun.

**FOOD SERVICE:** All terminals have dining facilities.

**TRANSPORTATION: Train:** MARTA (regional transit authority) train is $1.25 for Atlanta area. Taxi service available. **Parking:** An alternative to paying long-term parking fees—park your car at Fort McPherson, GA. Contact Military Police: C-404-464-2281, park where directed, complete paperwork, short walk outside gate to MARTA station (light rail system) and a short ride to IAP.

**TML:** Nearest TML is at Fort McPherson, C-404-464-3833/2253, D-312-367-3833/2253. DV/VIP C-404-464-5388.

**TRAVELERS AID:** Personnel Assistance Point (Army), C-404-464-4254/5, D-312-367-4254/5 and USO Lounge, C-404-530-6771, Atrium upper-level. *Note: Personnel Assistance Point closed in Summer 1999.*

**SUPPORT AVAILABLE:** In the airport: Chapels, Post Office, Foreign Currency Exchange, Duty Free shops, etc.

**OTHER INFORMATION:** U.S. Customs Service Airport.

**ATTRACTIONS:** Six Flags over Georgia and the Atlanta area.

*Note: Commercially contracted flights are now called Patriot Express.*

### THE WM B. HARTSFIELD IAP, GA (ATL); REGION: ATL; OPERATOR: COM; TYPE: PAX; ROUTE: EX37A; SAMPLE SCHEDULE: THU; EQUIPMENT: L1011

{ATL (★) *NE* ➡ FRF ⮂ FRF *SW* ➡ ATL (★)}

| LI/ICAO | AIRPORT/STATION | CTRY/STA | DAYS EN ROUTE |
|---|---|---|---|
| ATL/KATL | The WM B Hartsfield IAP (Atlanta) | GA | +0 |
| FRF/EDDF | Rhein-Main AB (Frankfurt) | DE | +1 |
| FRF/EDDF | Rhein-Main AB (Frankfurt) | DE | +1 |
| ATL/KATL | The WM B Hartsfield IAP (Atlanta) | GA | |

### THE WM B. HARTSFIELD IAP, GA (ATL); REGION: ATL; OPERATOR: COM; TYPE: PAX; ROUTE: EXR5B; SAMPLE SCHEDULE: SUN; EQUIPMENT: L1011

{ATL (★) *NE* ➡ FRF ⮂ FRF *SW* ➡ BWI (★) *SW* ➡ CHS}

| LI/ICAO | AIRPORT/STATION | CTRY/STA | DAYS EN ROUTE |
|---|---|---|---|
| ATL/KATL | The WM B Hartsfield IAP (Atlanta) | GA | +0 |
| FRF/EDDF | Rhein-Main AB (Frankfurt) | DE | +1 |
| FRF/EDDF | Rhein-Main AB (Frankfurt) | DE | +1 |
| BWI/KBWI | Baltimore/Washington IAP | MD | +1 |
| CHS/KCHS | Charleston AFB/IAP | SC | |

## Other Georgia Installations with Possible Space-A Air Opportunities

**ATLANTA REGIONAL FLIGHT CENTER/FULTON COUNTY AIRPORT (Brown Field) (FTY/KFTY),** Fort McPherson, Fort McPherson, 4185 Martin Luther King Drive, Atlanta, GA 30336-1396. **C-404-691-2500, D-312-367-4271, Fax: C-404-505-9130/691-2409. TML:** Bldg T-22, C-404-464-3833/2253, Fax: C-404-464-3376. Full base support facilities available. Call for destinations, routings, and schedules.

**WRIGHT ARMY AIRFIELD (LHW/KLHW),** Fort Stewart, GA 31314-5000. On US-84. Accessible from US-17 or I-95. Also GA-119 or GA-144 crosses the post but may be closed occasionally. From I-95 north or south, exit 15 to GA-144 west and east. From I-16 east or west exit 29 to GA-119 south. *USMRA: Page 37 (G-7).* ML-ARM: *(31°52'N/81°37'W).* LST: GMT-0500. **C-912-767-1411, D-312-870-1411. TML:** Bldg 4951, 0730-2400 daily, C-912-767-8384/4184, D-312-870-8384, other hours, SDO, Bldg 1, C-912-767-8666. DV/VIP C-912-767-8610. **RVC:** Holbrook Pond Rec Area, Outdoor Rec, Bldg 622, Check-in Outdoor Rec or with Camp Host, C-912-767-2717/2771/5145, D-312-870-2717/2771/5145. Full base support facilities available.

## UNSCHEDULED FLIGHTS

Limited Space-A flights via C009A MEDEVAC and executive C-12 and C-21 aircraft. Call for destinations, routings, and schedules.

# IDAHO

## BOISE AIR TERMINAL/ GOWEN FIELD AIRPORT (BOI/KBOI)

124th APF
3787 Aeronca Street
Boise, ID 83705-5006

**LOCATION:** From I-84 east or west, take Orchard Street exit (exit 52 south). Turn left and remain on Gowen road as it goes behind the airport. Watch for "Gowen Field" sign near tanks. Turn left into Main Gate. *USMRA: Page 98 (B-8). ML-ARM: (43°33'N/116°13'W).* LST: GMT-07:00. NMC: Boise, 5 miles north. Main installation numbers: C-208-422-5011, D-312-422-5011.

**REGISTRATION INFO: C-208-422-5989, D-312-422-5989, Fax: C-208-422-6410, D-312-422-6410.** Hours: 0800-1600 Mon-Fri.

**TRANSPORTATION:** Taxi service and rental cars available.

**TML:** Bldg 669, 0800-1630 hours M-F, C-208-422-4451, D-312-422-4451, Fax: C-208-422-4452, D-312-422-4452. DV/VIP Protocol Office, C-208-422-6364, Fax: C-208-422-6179.

**TRAVELERS AID:** Chaplain, Red Cross, and Security Police available.

**ATTRACTIONS:** Boise (capital of Idaho), Bogos Basin Ski Resort, rodeos, fairs, fishing.

### UNSCHEDULED FLIGHTS

Frequent flights to CONUS and OCONUS locations via C-130A-H aircraft. Call for destinations, routings, and schedules.

## MOUNTAIN HOME AIR FORCE BASE (MUO/KMUO)

366th OSS/OSSA
665 Thunderbolt Ave, Bldg 262
Mountain Home AFB, ID 83648-3401

**LOCATION:** From Boise, take I-84 southeast, 39 miles to Mountain Home, exit 95 west, follow road through town to Airbase Road, (ID- 67 west), 10 miles to main gate on left. *USMRA: Page 98 (C-9). ML-ARM: (43°03'N/115°51'W).* LST: GMT-07:00. NMC: Boise ID, 51 miles northwest. Main installation numbers: C-208-828-2111, D-312-728-2111.

**REGISTRATION INFO: C-208-828-2222, D-312-728-2222, Fax: C-208-828-4128, D-312-728-4128.** Base Ops, Bldg 262, Hours: 0630-2330 Mon-Fri, 0800-1600 Sat, Sun and holidays.

**PAX LOUNGES:** No separate family lounge. **General:** Bldg 262, C-208-828-2304. A/C, bag check, telephones (local and defense), restrooms, P/C seats. **DV/VIP:** Bldg 262, C-208-828-2304, O6+. A/C, bag check, read/write rooms, telephones (defense), TV, restrooms, O/S seats. **Protocol Service:** Bldg 512, Hours: 0730-1630 Mon-Fri, C-208-828-4536.

**FOOD SERVICE: Dining Hall:** Bldg 2316, C-208-832-2313. **Gunfighters Club:** Bldg 195, C-208-828-2106. **NCO/CPO Club:** Bldg 195, C-208-828-2105. **Restaurants:** Community Activity Center: Bldg 2618, C-208-828-6546. **Soda Machine:** Bldg 262, C-208-832-2304.

**TRANSPORTATION: Air Tickets:** SATO, Bldg 512, Hours: 0730-1630 Mon-Fri, C-208-832-2276. **On Base Shuttle/Bus:** Bldg 1126, Hours: 0630-1720 daily, C-208-828-2339. **On Base Taxi:** Bldg 1126, 24 hours daily, C-208-343-2215/2239.

**TML:** Bldg 2604, Falcon Street, 24 hours daily, C-208-828-5200/5352, D-312-728-5200/5352, Fax: C-208-828-4797, D-312-728-4797. DV/VIP Bldg 1506, O6+, C-208-828-4536, D-312-728-4536.

**RVC:** FAMCAMP, 775 Pine Street, Bldg 2800, Check-in FAMCAMP, C-208-828-6333, D-312-728-6333, Fax: C-208-828-6317.

**TRAVELERS AID: Chaplain:** Bldg 2606, Hours: 0730-1630 Mon-Fri, C-208-828-6417, after hours C-208-828-2111. **Emergency Relief:** Bldg 278, Hours: 0900-1700 Mon-Fri, C-208-828-2503/6148. **Red Cross:** Bldg 1506, Hours: 0800-1700 Mon-Fri, C-208-828-6622/3. **Security:** Bldg 1013, 24 hours daily, C-208-828-2256.

**SUPPORT AVAILABLE: Bank/Currency Exchange:** Bldg 2620, C-208-832-7582; Federal Credit Union, C-208-832-4675. **Exchange:** Bldg 2607, C-208-832-4353. **Hair Styles:** Bldg 2607; Barber, C-208-832-7191; Beauty, C-208-832-4090. **Laundry:** Bldg 2700, C-208-832-7465. **Medical/Dental:** Bldg 6000, 24 hours daily, C-208-828-6274, D-312-728-7100 (Ambulance) C-208-828-2233. **Postal Service:** Bldg 2607, C-208-832-7008.

**ATTRACTIONS:** Snow skiing, hunting, fishing, camping and mountain biking.

### EN ROUTE SCHEDULES

| AIRPORT/STATION | LI-MISSION (page #) |
| --- | --- |
| Travis AFB | SUU-436/MEDEVAC (13) |
| Scott AFB | BLV-C-634/MEDEVAC (30) |

### UNSCHEDULED FLIGHTS

Limited scheduled flights to CONUS locations, via C-9 MEDEVAC aircraft. Call for destinations, routings, and schedules.

# ILLINOIS

## GREATER PEORIA REGIONAL AIRPORT (PIA/KPIA)

182nd Airlift Wing/ILANG
2416 Falcon Blvd
Peoria, IL 61607-1498

**LOCATION:** From I-474 north or south, take exit at 5 southwest to airport. Left on Airport Road to right on Smithville Road. Approximately three miles to base on right. *USMRA: Page 64, (D-4). ML-ARM: (40°40'N/89°36'W).* LST: GMT-06:00. NMC: Peoria 7 miles northeast. Main installation numbers: C-308-633-5210, D-312-724-5210.

**REGISTRATION INFO: C-309-633-5216, D-312-724-5216, Fax: C-309-633-5306.** Military Dispensary at the Airport. No other military support available. **TML:** Nearest TML is at Rock Island Arsenal, 65 miles northwest. Lodging Office Bldg 110, 0800-1600 hours, C-309-782-0833, D-312-793-0833, Fax: C-309-782-1706.

### UNSCHEDULED FLIGHTS

Frequent flights via ANG C-130E aircraft to CONUS and OCONUS locations. Call for destinations, routings and schedules.

## SCOTT AIR FORCE BASE (BLV/KBLV)

Scott Passenger Terminal
801 Hangar Road, Room 203
Scott AFB, IL 62225-1344

**LOCATION:** From I-64 east or west, take exit 19 east or 19-A west to IL-158 south, two miles and watch for signs to AFB entry. *USMRA: Page 64 (D-8). ML-ARM: (38°32'N/89°51'W).* LST: GMT-06:00. NMC: St Louis MO, 25 miles west. Main installation numbers: C-618-256-1110, D-312-576-1110.

**REGISTRATION INFO: C-618-256-2014/3017/4042, D-312-576-2014/3017/4042, Rec: C-618-256-1854, D-312-576-1854, Fax: C-618-256-1946, D-312-576-1946. E-mail: spacea@scott.af.mil or paxterminal @scott.af.mil** Bldg P-8, Hours: 0445-2200 daily (closed Christmas and New Years). Directions: Main gate, Scott Drive to left on Heritage Drive. Pax Term on right at corner of Heritage Drive and Hanger Road. **Pax Service Office:** Bldg P-8, Hours: 0730-1630 Mon-Fri, C-618-256-4042 (NCO on duty). **Pax Paging:** C-618-256-1854/2014, D-312-576-1854/2014. *Note: The new Mid-America*

*Airport will be used by Scott AFB as an alternate. At press time, very little information is known. Check Military Living's R&R Space-A Report (travel newsletter) for developments.*

**PAX LOUNGES:** No family lounge. **General:** Bldg P-8, Hours: 0445-2200 daily, C-618-256-1854. A/C, game room, telephones (commercial and defense), TV, restrooms. **Protocol Service:** Bldg 1600, duty hours, C-618-256-5555. DV lounge now available.

**FOOD SERVICE: Cafeteria:** Bldg P-8, Hours: 0530-1330 Mon-Fri, closed Sat and Sun and major holidays, C-618-746-4199. **Combined Club:** Bldg 1948, Hours: 0630-2030 Mon, Thurs, Fri, 0800-2100 Sat, closed Sun, Tue, Wed, C-618-744-0300. **Dining Hall:** Bldg 1800, Hours: 0600-1800 daily, C-618-256-4215 (Nightingale Inn). **O Club:** Bldg 1500, Hours: 1000-1315 Mon and Tue, closed Wed, Thurs, 1100-1315 Fri, Sat (dinner hours fluctuate 1630-1830), Sun brunch only, C-618-744-0444. **Snack Bars:** Pronto Pizza and Subs, Bldg 1930 (recreation center), C-618-256-3921; Burger King, C-618-744-1747. Snack Vending available within terminal area.

**TRANSPORTATION: Air Tickets:** Rogers Travel, Bldg P-8, Hours: 0730-1600 Mon-Fri , C-618-256-5397. **Bus (Gov):** (duty passengers only) Bldg 548, C-618-256-3201/3066. Bi-state transit (city bus) is also available. *Note: This can connect travelers to the mono-rail train which makes numerous stops in St Louis.* **Car Rentals:** Agency, C-800-321-1972; Alamo, C-800-327-9633; Auffenburg, C-800-424-0304; Auffenburg (local), C-744-0304; Avis, C-800-331-1212; Enterprise, C-800-325-8007; Hertz, C-800-654-3131; **Limo Service:** Bldg P-8, Hours: 0615-2000 Mon-Fri, 0845-1445 Sat, 1000-1600 Sun and holidays, C-618-256-3201/3066; Alton Airport Limo Service, C-1-800-946-0103, C-618-462-3313, or C-314-741-6650. **Off Base Shuttle:** The regular scheduled shuttle service was cancelled due to lack of usage. Other shuttle services are provided. At Your Service, C-1-800-586-9655 or C-618-234-9555; H&G Transportation, C-1-800-294-4427 or C-618-274-44727; Metro-East Shuttle Service, C-1-800-852-6810; Professional Taxi and Airport Transportation, C-1-800-991-8669. **Off Base Taxi:** Bldg P-8; Magic Carpet, C-618-744-1300; Professional, C-618-397-4334; Tri- County, C-618-277-1515. **Parking:** Long term, located south of Post Office. Notify Security Police.

**TML:** Scott Inn, Bldg 1510, Beech Street, 24 hours daily, C-618-256-1844, D-312-576-1844. DV/VIP O6+, C-618-229-2555, D-312-56-2555.

**RVC:** FAMCAMP, Outdoor Rec, Bldg 855, Room 203, Check-in, 0800-1600 M-F, 1700 hours , Sat 0800-1200 (summer), C-618-256-2067, D-312-576-2067.

**TRAVELERS AID: Chaplain:** Bldg 1620, Hours: 0730-1600 Mon-Fri, C-618-256-3303, After hours: C-618-256-1110. **Emergency Relief:** Air Force Aid Society, Bldg 1930, C-618-256-8668. **Lost/Found:** Bldg P-8, C-618-256-3017. **Red Cross:** Bldg 8, C-618-256-1855, D-312-576-1855, After hours: C-314-658-2000. **Security Police:** Bldg 1970, C-618-256-2223.

**SUPPORT AVAILABLE: Bank/Currency Exchange:** Bldg 1644, Hours: 0800-1700 Mon-Fri, 0900-1200 Sat, C-618-744-1144. **Clothing Sales:** Bldg 1961, C-618-256-2131, D-312-576-2131. **Commissary:** Bldg 1980, C-618-256-2783. **Exchange:** Bldg 1650, Hours: 0900-2100 Mon-Sat, 1000-1800 Sun, C-618-744-0888. **Hair Styles:** Bldg 1650; Barber, C-618-746-2899; Beauty, C-618-744-1544. **Laundry/Dry Cleaning:** Bldg 1650, C-618-746-2417. **Medical:** Bldg 1530, 24 hours daily, C-618-256-7595, D-312-576-7595. **Postal Service:** Bldg 1900, C-618-256-5942.

**ATTRACTIONS:** St Louis and the Arch are 20 miles away, Mississippi River, Six Flags Amusement Park, Cahokia Indian Mounds, numerous caves, Rod and Gun Club, Aero Club, golf course (18 holes, par 72). Call the Gateway Community Activities Center C-618-256-5919.

### SCOTT AFB (BLV/KBLV); MISSION C-634/MEDEVAC; SAMPLE SCHEDULE: SAT; EQUIPMENT: C009A

{BLV *NW* ➡ RDR *W* ➡ MIB *W* ➡ GTF *W* ➡ SKA *SW* ➡ TCM *SE* ➡ MUO *SW* ➡ SUU}

| LI | AIRPORT/STATION | CTRY/STA |
|---|---|---|
| BLV/KBLV | Scott AFB | IL |
| RDR/KRDR | Grand Forks ARB | ND |
| MIB/KMIB | Minot AFB | ND |
| GTF/KGTF | Great Falls IAP/ANGB | MT |
| SKA/KSKA | Fairchild AFB | WA |

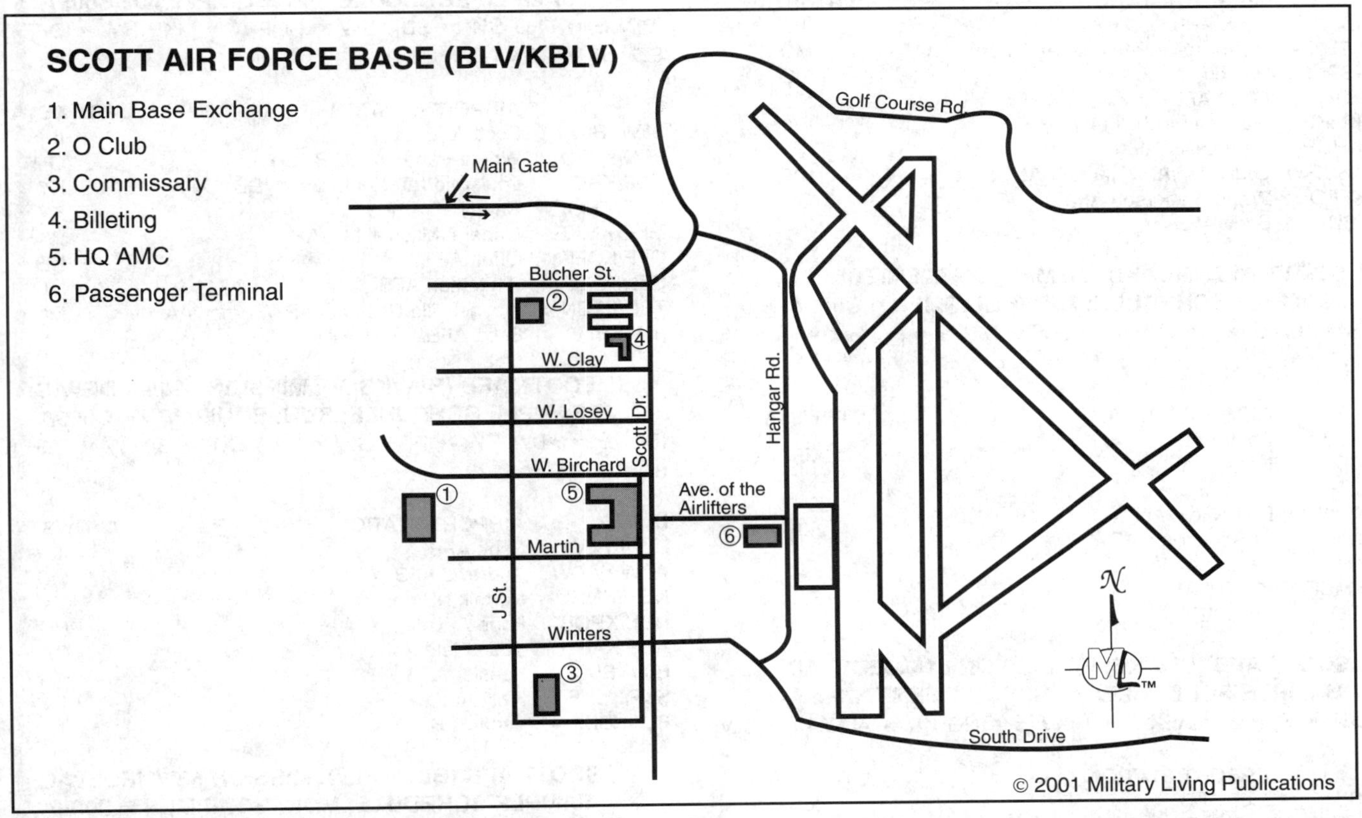

## SCOTT AIR FORCE BASE (BLV/KBLV)

1. Main Base Exchange
2. O Club
3. Commissary
4. Billeting
5. HQ AMC
6. Passenger Terminal



© 2001 Military Living Publications

| | | |
|---|---|---|
| TCM/KTCM | McChord AFB | WA |
| MUO/KMUO | Mountain Home AFB | ID |
| SUU/KSUU | Travis AFB | CA |

| | | |
|---|---|---|
| NGU/KNGU | Norfolk NS | VA |
| ADW/KADW | Andrews AFB | MD |
| BLV/KBLV | Scott AFB | IL |

## SCOTT AFB (BLV/KBLV); MISSION 614/MEDEVAC; SAMPLE SCHEDULE: MON; EQUIPMENT: C009A

{BLV *E* ➡ ADW *S* ➡ NGU *SW* ➡ SKF *NW* ➡ NKX *NW* ➡ SUU}

| LI | AIRPORT/STATION | CTRY/STA |
|---|---|---|
| BLV/KBLV | Scott AFB | IL |
| ADW/KADW | Andrews AFB | MD |
| NGU/KNGU | Norfolk NS | VA |
| SKF/KSKF | Kelly AFB | TX |
| NKX/KNKX | Miramar MCAS | CA |
| SUU/KSUU | Travis AFB | CA |

## SCOTT AFB (BLV/KBLV); MISSION 635/MEDEVAC; SAMPLE SCHEDULE: TUE; EQUIPMENT: C009A

{BLV *NW* ➡ RCA *W* ➡ CYS *S* ➡ COS *E* ➡ MHK *S* ➡ FLV *S* ➡ IAB *SW* ➡ SKF}

| LI | AIRPORT/STATION | CTRY/STA |
|---|---|---|
| BLV/KBLV | Scott AFB | IL |
| RCA/KRCA | Ellsworth AFB | SD |
| CYS/KCYS | Cheyenne Mun APT | WY |
| COS/KCS | Peterson AFB | CO |
| MHK/KMHK | Marshall AAF/Manhattan Mun APT | KS |
| MCI/KMCI | Kansas City IAP | MO |
| IAB/KIAB | McConnell AFB | KS |
| SKF/KSKF | Kelly AFB | TX |

## SCOTT AFB (BLV/KBLV); MISSION 666/MEDEVAC; SAMPLE SCHEDULE: WED; EQUIPMENT: C009A

{BLV *SW* ➡ TBN *W* ➡ SZL *NW* ➡ OFF *NE* ➡ MKE *S* ➡ HOP *NE* ➡ SDF *NE* ➡ FFO *SW* ➡ BLV}

| LI | AIRPORT/STATION | CTRY/STA |
|---|---|---|
| BLV/KBLV | Scott AFB | IL |
| TBN/KTBN | Waynesville Regional APT/Forney AAF | MO |
| SZL/KSZL | Whiteman AFB | MO |
| OFF/KOFF | Offutt AFB | NE |
| MKE/KMKE | General Mitchell IAP/ARS | WI |
| HOP/KHOP | Campbell AAF | KY |
| SDF/KSDF | Louisville IAP/Kentucky ANGB | KY |
| FFO/KFFO | Wright-Patterson AFB | OH |
| BLV/KBLV | Scott AFB | IL |

## SCOTT AFB (BLV/KBLV); MISSION 626/MEDEVAC; SAMPLE SCHEDULE: THU; EQUIPMENT: C009A

{BLV *S* ➡ BIX *E* ➡ VPS *NE* ➡ AGS *S* ➡ NIP *S* ➡ NQX *N* ➡ MCF *NW* ➡ BLV}

| LI | AIRPORT/STATION | CTRY/STA |
|---|---|---|
| BLV/KBLV | Scott AFB | IL |
| BIX/KBIX | Keesler AFB | MS |
| VPS/KVPS | Eglin AFB | FL |
| AGS/KAGS | Bush Field Apt | GA |
| NIP/KNIP | Jacksonville NAS | FL |
| NQX/KNQX | Key West NAS | FL |
| MCF/KMCF | MacDill AFB | FL |
| BLV/KBLV | Scott AFB | IL |

## SCOTT AFB (BLV/KBLV); MISSION 616/MEDEVAC; SAMPLE SCHEDULE: WED; EQUIPMENT: C009A

{BLV *SW* ➡ SKF *E* ➡ AEX *E* ➡ BIX *NE* ➡ NGU *N* ➡ ADW *W* ➡ BLV}

| LI | AIRPORT/STATION | CTRY/STA |
|---|---|---|
| BLV/KBLV | Scott AFB | IL |
| SKF/KSKF | Kelly AFB | TX |
| AEX/KAEX | Fort Polk | LA |
| BIX/KBIX | Keesler AFB | MS |

## SCOTT AFB (BLV/KBLV); MISSION 621/MEDEVAC; SAMPLE SCHEDULE: THU; EQUIPMENT: C009A

{BLV *SW* ➡ LAW *E* ➡ AGS *E* ➡ CHS *N* ➡ SSC *N* ➡ POB *NE* ➡ NKT *N* ➡ NGU *N* ➡ ADW}

| LI | AIRPORT/STATION | CTRY/STA |
|---|---|---|
| BLV/KBLV | Scott AFB | IL |
| LSF/KLSF | Lawson AAF | GA |
| AGS/KAGS | Bush Field Apt | GA |
| CHS/KCHS | Charleston AFB | SC |
| SSC/KSSC | Shaw AFB | SC |
| POB/KPOB | Pope AFB | NC |
| NKT/KNKT | Cherry Point MCAS | NC |
| NGU/KNGU | Norfolk NS | VA |
| ADW/KADW | Andrews AFB | MD |

## SCOTT AFB (BLV/KBLV); MISSION 656/MEDEVAC; SAMPLE SCHEDULE: THU; EQUIPMENT: C009A

{BLV *SW* ➡ SKF *N* ➡ LAW *N* ➡ TIK *NW* ➡ COS *E* ➡ MHK *E* ➡ FLV *E* ➡ BLV}

| LI | AIRPORT/STATION | CTRY/STA |
|---|---|---|
| BLV/KBLV | Scott AFB | IL |
| SKF/KSKF | Kelly AFB | TX |
| LAW/KLAW | Lawton/Fort Sill Regional APT | OK |
| TIK/KTIK | Tinker AFB | OK |
| COS/KCS | Peterson AFB | CO |
| MHK/KMHK | Marshall AAF/Manhattan Mun APT | KS |
| MCI/KMCI | Kansas City IAP | MO |
| BLV/KBLV | Scott AFB | IL |

## SCOTT AFB (BLV/KBLV); MISSION 666/MEDEVAC; SAMPLE SCHEDULE: FRI; EQUIPMENT: C009A

{BLV *E* ➡ FFO *SW* ➡ SDF *SW* ➡ HOP *N* ➡ MKE *SW* ➡ OFF *SE* ➡ SZL *SE* ➡ TBN *NE* ➡ BLV}

| LI | AIRPORT/STATION | CTRY/STA |
|---|---|---|
| BLV/KBLV | Scott AFB | IL |
| FFO/KFFO | Wright-Patterson AFB | OH |
| SDF/KSDF | Louisville IAP/Kentucky ANGB | KY |
| HOP/KHOP | Campbell AAF | KY |
| MKE/KMKE | General Mitchell IAP/ARS | WI |
| OFF/KOFF | Offutt AFB | NE |
| SZL/KSZL | Whiteman AFB | MO |
| TBN/KTBN | Waynesville Regional APT/Forney AAF | MO |
| BLV/KBLV | Scott AFB | IL |

## SCOTT AFB (BLV/KBLV); MISSION 626/MEDEVAC; SAMPLE SCHEDULE: SUN; EQUIPMENT: C009A

{BLV *E* ➡ ADW *SW* ➡ POB *SW* ➡ AGS *SW* ➡ BIX *W* ➡ SKF *NE* ➡ BLV}

| LI | AIRPORT/STATION | CTRY/STA |
|---|---|---|
| BLV/KBLV | Scott AFB | IL |
| ADW/KADW | Andrews AFB | MD |
| NGU/KNGU | Norfolk NS | VA |
| POB/KPOB | Pope AFB | NC |
| AGS/KAGS | Bush Field Apt | GA |
| BIX/KBIX | Keesler AFB | MS |
| SKF/KSKF | Kelly AFB | TX |
| BLV/KBLV | Scott AFB | IL |

## SCOTT AFB (BLV/KBLV); MISSION 652/MEDEVAC; SAMPLE SCHEDULE: MON; EQUIPMENT: C009A

{BLV *S* ➡ LRF *S* ➡ AEX *N* ➡ BAD *NW* ➡ TIK *SW* ➡ LAW *S* ➡ GRK *S* ➡ SKF *E* ➡ BIX}

| LI | AIRPORT/STATION | CTRY/STA |
|---|---|---|
| BLV/KBLV | Scott AFB | IL |
| LRF/KLRF | Little Rock AFB | AR |
| AEX/KAEX | Fort Polk | LA |
| BAD/KBAD | Barksdale AFB | LA |
| TIK/KTIK | Tinker AFB | OK |
| LAW/KLAW | Lawton/Fort Sill Regional APT | OK |
| GRK/KGRK | Robert Gray AAF | TX |
| SKF/KSKF | Kelly AFB | TX |
| BIX/KBIX | Keesler AFB | MS |

*Note: Schedules change slightly by season.*

### EN ROUTE SCHEDULES

| AIRPORT/STATION | LI-MISSION (page #) |
|---|---|
| Travis AFB | SUU-436/MEDEVAC (13) |
| Travis AFB | SUU-456/MEDEVAC (13) |
| Andrews AFB | ADW-116/MEDEVAC (37) |
| Keesler AFB | BIX-226/MEDEVAC (44) |
| Kelly AFB | SKF-546/MEDEVAC (74) |

### UNSCHEDULED FLIGHTS

Flights via C-009A/E to CONUS and OCONUS. Call for destinations, routings, and schedules.

# INDIANA

## GRISSOM AIR RESERVE BASE (GUS/KGUS)

434th OSF/ATB
Warthog Drive, Bldg 600
Grissom ARB, IN 46971-5000

**LOCATION:** On US-31, 15 miles north of Kokomo and 7 miles south of Peru. Turn at Grisson Aeroplex, proceed on Hoosier Blvd west of US-31 to main gate. Take a left onto Warthog Drive and proceed to Bldg 600. *USMRA: Page 65 (E-3). ML-ARM: (40°39'N/86°07'W).* LST: GMT-05:00. NMC Indianapolis, 64 miles south. NMI: Wright-Patterson AFB, OH, 120 miles. Main installation numbers: C-765-688-5211, D-312-928-1110.

**REGISTRATION INFO: C-765-688-2861, D-312-928-2861, Fax: C-765-688-3643, D-312-928-3643.** Bldg 28, Hours: 0700-2300 daily.

**PAX LOUNGES:** No separate family lounge. **General:** Bldg 600, Hours: 0700-2300 daily, C-765-688-2254/2861. A/C, bag check, telephones (commercial and defense), TV, restrooms, O/S seats. **DV/VIP:** Bldg 600, Hours: 0700-2300 daily, C-765-688-2254/2861, O6+ (separate room). Protocol Service: Bldg 28, Hours: 0700-2300 daily, C-765-689-2254.

**FOOD SERVICE: All Ranks Club:** Hours: 1100-2200 Mon-Fri, C-765-699-9151, 2 miles away. **Fast Food:** Burger King, Hours: 0530-2000, C-765-689-8776, 2 miles away. *Note: No in-flight meals.*

**TRANSPORTATION: Off Base Car Rentals:** Ace Rent-A-Car, C-765-453-3939; Enterprise Rent-A-Car, C-765-457-4980; National Rent-A-Car, C-765-455-0282.

**TML:** Grissom Inn, Bldg 333, Matador Street, 24 hours, C-765-688-2844, D-312-928-2844, Fax: C-765-688-8751, D-312-928-8751. DV/VIP C-765-688-2844.

**TRAVELERS AID: Security Police:** Bldg 430, 24 hours daily, C-765-688-2503, D-312-928-2503, 1 mile away.

**SUPPORT AVAILABLE: Credit Union:** Hours: 0800-1600 Mon-Fri, C-765-689-9181, D-312-928-9181, 1.5 miles away. **Shoppette:** Hours: 1100-1730, C-765-689-5270, .5 miles away.

**ATTRACTIONS:** Grissom Air Museum, City of Peru, Circus Hall of Fame,

Indianapolis Motor Speedway, 72 miles south.

### UNSCHEDULED FLIGHTS

Limited flights to CONUS, OCONUS and foreign country locations via KC-135R aircraft. Call for destinations, routings and schedules.

# KANSAS

## FORBES FIELD INTERNATIONAL AIRPORT/AIR NATIONAL GUARD BASE (FOE/KFOE)

190th Air Refueling Wing (ANG)
5920 SE Coyote Drive
Topeka, KS 66619-5370

**LOCATION:** From I-70 east or west, exit 361A, take US-75 south. Main gate located at second stoplight on US-75. Base is east of US-75 south. *USMRA: Page 78 (I-4). ML-ARM: (38°56'N/95°41'W).* LST: GMT-06:00. NMC: Topeka, 4 miles north. Main installation numbers: C-785-861-4210, D-312-720-4210.

**REGISTRATION INFO: C-785-861-4558, D-312-720-4558, Fax: C-785-861-4555, D-312-720-4555. WEB: www.ksfoe.ang.af.mil** Bldg 679 Base Ops, Hours: During flight processing. Directions: From the main gate proceed south to Bldg 679, first building on left with tunnels. Small shoppette is the only U.S. military base support facility. Hours: 1100-1600 Tue-Thu, C-785-862-2605, 2 blocks away. No other services provided. **TML:** Nearest TML is at Fort Riley, KS, Bldg 45, Barry Avenue, 24 hours daily, C-800-643-8991 or C-785-239-2830/3525, D-312-856-2830, Fax: C-785-239-8882. DV/VIP C-785-239-8843.

### UNSCHEDULED FLIGHTS

Air National Guard Unit Flying Training Missions to CONUS and OCONUS locations via KC-135R aircraft. Call for destinations, routings, and schedules.

## MARSHALL ARMY AIRFIELD/ MANHATTAN MUNICIPAL AIRPORT (FRI/KFRI, MHK/KMHK)

AOD/Bldg 743
Fort Riley, KS 66442-5000

**LOCATION:** Near Junction City. From east or west on I-70, take exit 301 (Fort Riley/Marshall Army Air Field) northwest onto Henry Drive directly to Main Post. Follow signs. *USMRA: Page 78 (G,H-3,4). ML-ARM: (39°04'N/96°46'W).* LST: GMT-06:00. NMC: Topeka, 70 miles east. Main installation numbers: C-785-239-3911, D-312-856-1110.

**REGISTRATION INFO: C-785-239-7740, D-312-856-7740, Fax: C-785-239-7405, D-312-856-7405. E-mail: sandra.mathews2@cen.amedd.army.mil** No Pax Term available. Flights through Irwin Army Community Hospital. MEDEVAC Office, Hospital Bldg 600, Fort Riley. Ask for directions and map at main gate. Located at base of Old Tower on AAF. NCO on duty.

**TML:** Bldg 45, Barry Avenue, 24 hours daily, C-800-643-8991 or C-785-239-2830/3525, D-312-856-2830, Fax: C-785-239-8882. DV/VIP C-785-239-8843.

**SUPPORT AVAILABLE:** Limited facilities. DV/VIP between Hangars 1 and 2 (O6+) on request from Pax Service NCO. Full base facilities available.

**OTHER INFORMATION:** Active Duty or Retirees (dependents not eligible) can call C-785-239-7740, D-312-856-7740 for information on flights. Passengers will report with patients to the hospital where they will undergo search procedures to be taken to the Manhattan Airport with patients for MEDEVAC. Passengers must come to the hospital MEDEVAC Office and their spouses and family members are not eligible for flights on the Nightingale in CONUS.

## EN ROUTE SCHEDULES

| AIRPORT/STATION | LI-MISSION (page #) |
|---|---|
| Scott AFB | BLV-C-635/MEDEVAC (30) |
| Scott AFB | BLV-C-656/MEDEVAC (30) |

# McCONNELL AIR FORCE BASE (IAB/KIAB)

McConnell AFB Passenger Terminal
22 OSS/OSAA 22ARW
53435 Kansas Court, Suite 104
Witchita, KS 67221-3720

**LOCATION:** Take I-35 north or south to Wichita, exit at Kellogg Street (US-54/400) west one block to Rock Road south and McConnell AFB, west of Rock Road. *USMRA: Page 78 (G-6). ML-ARM: (37°38'N/97°15'W).* LST: GMT-06:00. NMC: Wichita, 6 miles northwest. Main installation numbers: C-316-759-6100, D-312-743-1110.

**REGISTRATION INFO:** C-316-759-3701/3840, D-312-743-3840/3701, **Fax: C-316-759-4957, D-312-743-4957.** Bldg 1112, 24 hours daily. Directions: From east gate straight on Kansas Street for 1.5 miles to Base Ops on the right.

**PAX LOUNGES: General:** Bldg 1112, Hours: 24 hours daily. **DV/VIP:** Bldg 1112, 24 hours daily, C-316-759-6609. **Protocol Service:** Bldg 1112, 24 hours daily, C-316-759-3110.

**FOOD SERVICE: Dining Hall:** Bldg 408, C-316-759-4183; Bldg 421, C-316-759-4186 (In-flight). **Emerald City Food Court:** C-316-759-6114, D-312-743-6114. **Fast Food:** Burger King, C-316-683-7750. **O Club:** Bldg 197, C-316-685-2288.

**TRANSPORTATION:** Very limited transportation on base. No on-base shuttle service for Space-A passengers (only for duty passengers). **Air Tickets:** SATO, Bldg 334, Hours: 1100-2200 Mon-Sat, C-316-759-5263. **On Base Taxi:** Bldg 710, C-316-759-4051 ($15 to Wichita).

**TML:** Air Capital Inn, Bldg 196, 53050 Glen Elder, 24 hours daily, C-316-759-6999, D-312-743-6999, Fax C-316-759-4190, D-312-743-4190. DV/VIP Bldg 202, O6+, C-316-759-3110, D-312-743-3110.

**RVC:** FAMCAMP, 53050 Glen Elder, C-316-759-6999, D-312-743-6999.

**TRAVELERS AID: Chaplain:** Bldg 510, C-316-759-3562. **Dental:** Bldg 250, C-316-759-5182, D-312-743-5182, .5 miles away. **Medical:** Bldg 250, C-316-759-5020, D-312-743-5020, .5 miles away. **Red Cross:** C-316-265-6601, D-312-743-5202. **Security Police:** Bldg 1115, C-316-759-3796, D-312-743-3978. **Travelers Aid:** Bldg 732, C-316-759-6021, D-312-743-6021, .5 miles away.

**SUPPORT AVAILABLE: Bank/Currency Exchange:** Freedom First Federal Credit Union: Bldg 490, C-316-759-5457. **Exchange:** Bldg 352, C-316-685-0231. **Hair Styles:** Bldg 352; Barber, C-316-686-9971; Beauty, C-316-689-8716. **Laundry/Dry Cleaning:** Bldg 352/357, C-316-685-2439, .5 miles away. **Postal Service:** Bldg 327, C-316-759-4879, D-312-743-4879, .33 miles away. **Shoppette:** C-316-685-0291, .25 miles away.

**OTHER INFORMATION:** Port of Entry and U.S. Customs Service Airport.

**ATTRACTIONS:** Sedgewick County Zoo, Museum of Art and History, Old Towne, Warren Theater, Water Theme Park.

## EN ROUTE SCHEDULES

| AIRPORT/STATION | LI-MISSION (page #) |
|---|---|
| Scott AFB | BLV-C-635/MEDEVAC (30) |

## UNSCHEDULED FLIGHTS

Infrequent flights via KC-135R aircraft to OCONUS and overseas locations. Call for destinations, routings and schedules.

*Note: McConnell AFB is now a port of entry for anyone with a military ID and U.S. passport. Call for more information.*

# SHERMAN ARMY AIRFIELD (FLV/KFLV)

(Kansas City International Airport (MCI)
ATZL-GCT-A
1000 Chief Joseph Loop, Bldg 132
Fort Leavenworth, KS 66027-5071

**LOCATION:** From I-70 east or west, exit 223 to US-73 north to Leavenworth. From I-29 north or south, exit 19, KS-92 west to Leavenworth. Fort is adjacent to city of Leavenworth. Main gate on US-73 (Metropolitan Avenue). *USMRA: Page 78 (J-3). ML-ARM: (39°20'N/94°55'W).* LST: GMT-06:00. NMC: Kansas City KS/MO, 30 miles southeast. Main installation numbers: C-913-684-4021, D-312-552-4021.

**REGISTRATION INFO: C-913-684-6041, D-312-552-6041, Rec: C-913-684-6041, D-312-684-6041, Fax: C-913-684-6025, D-312-552-6025.** Bldg 132, Hours: 0700-1630 Mon-Fri. Directions: From main gate straight on Grant Ave for 2 miles to Riverside Ave, turn right on Riverside Ave, cross the railroad tracks, bear left into Chief Joseph Street. The airfield is approximately 1 mile ahead. The tower is visible and the passenger area is directly below the tower. **Pax Service Office:** C-913-684-2396, D-312-552-2396.

**PAX LOUNGES: General. DV/VIP:** Bldg 132, east side of Hangar 2, Hours: 0700-1630 Mon-Fri, C-913-684-2396 (O7+). A/C, coffee available, restrooms, telephone (local, long distance and defense), seats 5. **Protocol Services:** Bldg 22, Hours: 0730-1630 Mon-Fri, C-913-684-4604/4605.

**FOOD SERVICE: Cafeteria:** Hours: 0630-1500, C-913-684-6573, D-312-552-6573, 1 mile away. **Fast Food:** Hours: 0630-2100, C-913-651-9511, 2 miles away. **Snack Bars:** Hours: 0700-1400, C-913-651-6586, 1.5 miles away. **Snack Vending:** Soda machine in North Hangar. *(All food at least 1 mile from the airfield.)*

**TRANSPORTATION: Air Tickets:** C-913-651-7171. **Off Base Car Rental:** C-913-727-2222, 7 miles away. **Off Base Limo:** C-913-651-4649, 4 miles away. **Off Base Taxi:** C-913-682-1229/7200, 4 miles away. **Parking:** Short and long-term available near Bldg 132.

**TML:** Bldg 695, 210 Grant Avenue, 24 hours daily, C-913-684-4091 or 1-800-854-8627, D-312-552-4091, Fax C-913-684-4097, D-312-552-4097. DV/VIP Hours: 0730-1630, C-913-684-4065, D-312-552-4065, 1 mile away.

**TRAVELERS AID: Chaplain:** Hours: 0730-1630, C-913-684-2210/4154, D-312-552-2210/4154, 1 mile away. **Emergency Relief:** C-913-684-2800. **Lost/Found:** C-913-684-4967. **Medical/Dental:** Hours: 0730-1630, C-913-684-6110, D-312-552-6110, 1 mile away. **Red Cross:** Hours: 0730-1630, C-913-684-4383, D-312-552-4843, 1 mile away. **Security Police:** 24 hours daily, C-913-684-2111, D-312-552-2111, .5 miles away.

**SUPPORT AVAILABLE: Bank/Currency Exchange:** Hours: 0900-2000, C-913-682-9090, 2 miles away. **Dry Cleaner:** 0900-1800 Mon-Fri, 0900-1700 Sat, C-913-651-3923, 7 miles away. **Exchange:** 0900-2000 Mon-Sat, 1000-1800 Sun, C-913-651-7271, 2 miles away. **Laundry:** 0800-1700 Mon-Fri, C-913-684-4679, D-312-552-4679, 1 mile away. **Postal Service:** 0900-1700 Mon-Fri, 0900-1200 Sat, C-913-682-0052. **Shoppette: Hours:** 0630-2300 Mon-Fri, 0800-2300 Sat-Sun, C-913-651-7183/7175, 2 miles away.

**ATTRACTIONS:** Fort Leavenworth Museum, Harry S. Truman Library & Museum, Kansas City and their professional sports teams.

## EN ROUTE SCHEDULES

| AIRPORT/STATION | LI-MISSION (page #) |
|---|---|
| Scott AFB | BLV-C-635/MEDEVAC (30) |
| Scott AFB | BLV-C-656/MEDEVAC (30) |

*Note: At press time the MEDEVAC flights for Sherman AAF were operating out of Kansas City IAP (MCI/KMCI). See page 30 for schedule.*

## UNSCHEDULED FLIGHTS

One or more flights each month to the following destinations: Robert Gray AAF, TX (**GRK**); Davison AAF, VA (**DAA**); Langley AFB, VA (**LFI**). Limited other locations mostly in the midwest, east and Texas. Call for destinations, routings, and schedules.

# KENTUCKY

## CAMPBELL ARMY AIRFIELD (HOP/KHOP)

H Street, Bldg 7163, Base Operations
Fort Campbell, KY 42223-5030

**LOCATION:** In the southwest part of Kentucky, four miles south of intersection of US-41A and I-24, exit 86 on I-24, 10 miles northwest of Clarksville, TN. *USMRA: Page 40 (E,F-7). ML-ARM: (36°39'N/87°26'W).* LST: GMT-06:00. NMC: Hopkinsville, 15 miles north. Main installation numbers: C-270-798-2151, D-312-635-1110.

**REGISTRATION INFO: C-270-798-7146, D-312-635-7146, Fax: C-270-798-9288, D-312-635-9288.** Zone H/I, Bldg 7163, 24 hours daily. Directions: Gate 4- Turn right on Wickham. Take Wickham to Campbell Army Airfield, bear right. Turn left on Hedge Row. Turn right on "H" Street. Bldg 7163 on left.

**FOOD SERVICE:** Base Ops, vending machines. KFC, Taco Bell, Burger King on base but only commercial cabs for transportation.

**TRANSPORTATION: On Base Car Rental:** Enterprise, C-270-439-9988. **TML:** Turner Guest House, Bldg 1581 William C Lee Road, C-270-798-5818, D-312-635-5618, Fax: C-270-798-0602. DV/VIP C-270-798-9913, D-312-635-9913.

**RVC:** Destin Parks & Pavilions, Outdoor Rec Br, Check-in Travel Camp, C-270-798-5590/3126, D-312-635-5590/3126.

### EN ROUTE SCHEDULES

| AIRPORT/STATION | LI-MISSION (page #) |
|---|---|
| Scott AFB | BLV-C-666/MEDEVAC (30) |

### UNSCHEDULED FLIGHTS

Flights via Army executive aircraft, C-12A and C-21A to CONUS East Coast and Midwest locations. Call for destinations, routings and schedules.

## GODMAN ARMY AIRFIELD (FTK/KFTK)

AVN Div, 63/DPTM USAARMC & Fort Knox
5220 Pilot Street
Fort Knox, KY 40121-5000

**LOCATION:** From I-65 north or south, in Louisville, exit Gene Snyder Expressway west to US-31 west, go south to Fort Knox. From I-64, exit I-264 (Waterson Expressway west) to US-31 west, south to Fort Knox. Or from I-71, exit I-65 south to Gene Snyder Expressway to US-31 west then south to Fort Knox. *USMRA: Page 40-41 (H,I-3,4). ML-ARM: (37°54'N/85°57'W).* LST: GMT-06:00. NMC: Louisville, 25 miles north. NMI: Fort Knox, on base. Main installation numbers: C-502-624-1000/1181, D-312-464-1181.

**REGISTRATION INFO: C-502-624-5545/6047, D-312-464-5545/6047, Fax: C-502-624-2421, D-312-464-2421.** Bldg 5220, 24 hours daily. Directions: From US-31 W enter Fort on Chaffee Ave to left on Park Road, to left on Pilot Street. Air Ops on left.

**PAX LOUNGES:** General and DV/VIP available.

**FOOD SERVICE: Fast Food:** Burger King, KFC, Pizza, on post, .5 miles away. **Restaurants:** Club System, 1 mile away. **Snack Bar** at PX, 2 miles away. **Snack Vending** in lounge at Godman AAF.

**TRANSPORTATION: Air Tickets:** Carlson Wagonlit Travel, Hours: 0800-1630, C-502-942-4195, on post, 2 miles away. **Off Base Car Rental:** Budget, C-502-351-4777, 3 miles south; C-502-942-3368, 3 miles north; Enterprise, C-502-352-4088, 3 miles south *Note: No on base car rental, but off base will deliver to Godman AAF.* **Off Base Taxi:** Freddy's, C-502-942-0397, 3 miles south. **Off Base Limo:** Skaggs, C-502-765-7297, 7 miles south.

**TML:** Newgarden Tower, Bldg 4770, Dixie Hwy 31 west, 24 hours daily, C-502-943-1000, D-312-464-3491. Fax: C-502-942-8752, DV/VIP C-502-624-6951.

**TRAVELERS AID: Chaplain:** Hours: 0800-1730 Mon-Fri, C-502-624-5255, D-312-464-5255, on post, 1 mile away. **Medical/Dental:** Hours: 0800-1630 Mon-Fri, C-502-624-9290/9670/4-9333, D-312-464-9290/9670/4-9333, 1 mile away. **Red Cross:** Hours: 0800-1630 Mon-Fri, C-502-624-2163, D-312-464-2163, on post, 1 mile away. **Security Police:** 24 hours daily, C-502-624-2111, D-312-464-2111, Emergency 911, on post, 1 mile away.

**SUPPORT AVAILABLE: Bank/Currency Exchange:** Hours: 0900-1530 Mon-Fri, C-502-942-3000, on post, 1 mile away. **Convenience Store:** Hours: 0600-2400 daily, C-502-942-4262, on post, 2 miles away. **Credit Union:** Fort Knox Federal Credit Union, Hours: 0830-1530 Mon-Fri, 1000-1530 Sat, C-502-942-0254, on post, 1 mile away. **Exchange:** Hours: 0900-2100 Mon-Sat, 1000-1800 Sun, C-502-942-4200, on post, 2 miles away. **Postal Service:** Hours: 0830-1700 Mon-Fri, 0830-1200 Sat, C-502-942-1244, on post, 1 mile away. **Shoppette:** Hours: 0600-2400, C-502-942-0367/4200, on post, 1 mile away.

**ATTRACTIONS:** U.S. Bullion Depository-Highway 31W to Bullion Blvd, 1 mile south of Godman AAF-on post. No tours. Patton Museum on Post 1 mile away.

### UNSCHEDULED FLIGHTS

Flights via Army executive aircraft, C-12A and C-21A to CONUS East Coast and Midwest locations. Call for destinations, routings and schedules.

## LOUISVILLE INTERNATIONAL AIRPORT/ KENTUCKY AIR NATIONAL GUARD BASE (SDF/KSDF)

123rd AW
1011 Grade Lane
Louisville, KY 40213-2678

**LOCATION:** Take I-65 S to exit 130 to Grade Lane. Turn right then right into base. Take I-65 N to exit 130 to Preston Street. Turn left at the light and drive 1 block. Turn left at the 2nd light to Grade Lane. Follow Grade to the base. *USMRA: Page 41 (I-3). ML-ARM: (38°11'N/85°44'W).* LST: GMT-06:00. NMC: Louisville, Standiford Field in city. Main installation numbers: C-502-364-9400, D-312-989-4400, Fax: C-502-364-9605, D-312-989-4605.

**REGISTRATION INFO: C-502-364-9459 ext 1, D-312-989-4459 ext 1, Rec: C-502-364-9459 ext 3, D-312-989-4459 ext 3, Fax: C-502-364-9605, D-312-989-4605. E-mail: vance.fulkerson@kyloui.ang.af.mil (to request info), WEB: www. kyang.ang.af.mil/spacea** Air National Guard Base Ops, Hours: 0630-1630 Tue-Fri. All Space-A managed by Air National Guard Air Ops. *Note: MEDEVAC scheduled flights are scheduled thru the MEDEVAC section at Ireland Army Hospital, Fort Knox, KY, C-502-624-9273.*

**TRANSPORTATION:** Taxi available.

**TRAVELERS AID:** Security Police.

**TML:** Nearest TML is 25 miles south at Fort Knox, Newgarden Tower, Bldg 4770, Dixie Hwy 31 west, 24 hours daily, C-502-942-0490 or C-502-943-1000, D-312-464-3491. Fax: C-502-942-8752, DV/VIP C-502-624-6951.

**SUPPORT AVAILABLE: Credit Union:** Hours: 0830-1530 (closed 1200-1300 for lunch), C-502-364-4410. Full support of a metropolitan airport available.

**ATTRACTIONS:** Churchill Downs and Louisville Slugger Museum.

### EN ROUTE SCHEDULES

| AIRPORT/STATION | LI-MISSION (page #) |
|---|---|
| Scott AFB | BLV-C-666/MEDEVAC (30) |

### UNSCHEDULED FLIGHTS

Flights to CONUS, OCONUS and foreign countries via Air National Guard C-130H aircraft. Call for destinations, routings and schedules.

# LOUISIANA

# BARKSDALE AIR FORCE BASE (BAD/KBAD)

2 TRNS/LGTR, Air Operations
625 Davis Ave East, Bldg 5724
Barksdale AFB, LA 71110-2270

**LOCATION:** Exit I-20 east or west, at Airline Drive exit 22, go south to Old Minden Road (one quarter mile), left on Old Minden Road (one block), then right on North Gate Drive (one mile) to North Gate of AFB. *USMRA: Page 79 (B-2). ML-ARM: (32°31'N/93°43'W).* LST: GMT-06:00. NMC: Shreveport, 1 mile west. Co-located with Bossier City in Shreveport. Main installation numbers: C-318-456-1110, D-312-781-1110.

**REGISTRATION INFO:** C-318-456-8814/8815, D-312-781-5622, **Fax: C-318-456-2918, D-312-781-2918, Fax: 318-456-4989, D-312-781-4989** Bldg 6448, Hours: 0630-1630 Mon-Fri. Directions: From West Gate straight on Barksdale Blvd, Pax Term right at Hangar Line Road. **Pax Service Office:** Bldg 6448, Hours: 0630-1630 Mon-Fri, C-318-456-3738, NCO on duty. Many facilities on and off base.

**FOOD SERVICE:** Burger King, NCO Club and O Club.

**TRANSPORTATION:** Commercial Taxi/Bus service and several Rental Car Companies available.

**TML:** Bldg 5155, 555 Davis Avenue, 24 hours daily, C-318-456-3091, D-312-781-3091. Fax: C-318-456-1263/2267, D-312-781-1263, DV/VIP C-318-456-4228.

**RVC:** FAMCAMP, Bldg 7262 Red Horse Drive, Check-in FAMCAMP 0800-1700 hours Mon-Sat, after hours pick site and Check-in next day, C-318-456-2679, D-312-781-2679, Fax: C-318-742-5236.

**TRAVELERS AID: Chaplain:** C-318-456-2111/2151. **Law Enforcement Desk:** C-318-456-2552/2557. **Red Cross:** C-318-865-9545.

### EN ROUTE SCHEDULES

| AIRPORT/STATION | LI-MISSION (page #) |
|---|---|
| Scott AFB | BLV-C-652/MEDEVAC (30) |

### UNSCHEDULED FLIGHTS

Infrequent MEDEVAC to Scott AFB, IL (**BLV**) and Kelly AFB, TX (**SKF**). Occasional C-21 flights to CONUS locations. Call for destinations, routings and schedules.

# NEW ORLEANS NAVAL AIR STATION/ JOINT RESERVE BASE (NBG/KNBG)

Operations Department, Bldg 1
New Orleans NAS, LA 70143-7001

**LOCATION:** Take I-10 to US-90 Business West, cross the Crescent City Connection Bridge to the Westbank Expressway. Exit at Lafayette Street. Make a left turn at the traffic light. Keep straight on Belle Chasse Hwy LA-23. Go through a tunnel. At the traffic light after the tunnel, make a left turn to go in the back gate or stay on Hwy 23 (Belle Chasse Hwy) about 7-9 miles to go in the main gate. Clearly marked. *USMRA: Page 79 (H-7); Page 90 (F-6). ML-ARM: (29°49'N/90°02'W).* LST: GMT-06:00. NMC: New Orleans, 10 miles north. Main installation numbers: C-504-678-3292, D-312-678-3292.

**REGISTRATION INFO:** C-504-678-3213, D-312-678-3213, **Rec: 1-800-222-7549 or 504-678-3103, D-312-678-3103, Fax: C-504-678-3156, D-312-678-3156.** Bldg 1, Hours: 0630-2300 daily. Directions: From main gate on Russell Ave to a left on RADM Fowler Drive to a right on Coast Guard Road to Air Ops. **Pax Service Office:** Bldg 1, Hours: 0630-14300 Mon-Fri and after hours when needed, C-504-678-3213. **Pax Paging:** Bldg 1, Hours: 0630-2300 daily, C-504-678-3213.

**PAX LOUNGES:** No separate family lounge. **General:** Bldg 1, Hours: 0700-2300 daily, C-504-678-3213. A/C, telephones (local and defense), TV, restrooms, P/C seats. **DV/VIP:** Bldg 1, Hours: 0700-2300 daily, C-504-678-3100. A/C, coffee, read/write room, telephones (local and defense), TV, restrooms, O/S seats. **Protocol Service:** Base PAO, Hours: 0730-1000 Tue-Sat, C-504-678-3260, O6+.

**FOOD SERVICE: Dining Hall:** Bldg 23, C-504-678-3421. **Enlisted Club:** Bldg 410, Hours: 1000-2100 daily, C-504-678-3508. **NCO/CPO Club:** Bldg 300, Hours: 1100-2300 Tue-Sun, C-504-678-3844. **O Club:** Bldg 40, Hours: 1100-0100 Wed-Sun, C-504-678-3841. **Snack Vending:** Bldg 1, Hours: 0700-2300 daily.

**TRANSPORTATION: Air Tickets:** SATO, C-504-678-2208. **Car Rentals:** Enterprise, C-504-366-9400. **Taxi (Comm):** Bldg 1, 24 hours daily (various cab companies service base). **Parking:** Bldg 1, Hours: 0800-1600 daily **(short term-no overnight; long term-Fowler Drive)**.

**TML:** Bldg 40, 400 Russell Avenue, 24 hours daily, C-504-678-3419, D-312-678-3419, Fax: C-504-678-9745, D-312-638-9745. DV/VIP C-504-678-3260.

**RVC:** Campground, MWR 400 Russell Avenue, Check-in Auto Hobby Shop, Mon 1000-1800 hours, Tue 0800-1200 hours, Wed 0800-1800 hours, Thr/Fri 0700-1800 hours, C-504-678-3142, Fax: C-504-678-3552.

**TRAVELERS AID:** Many agencies at NAS and NSA. **Chaplain:** Bldg 403, Hours: 0730-1600 Tue-Sun, C-504-678-3525, D-312-678-3525, .5 miles away. **Lost/Found:** Bldg 1, Hours: 0700-2300 daily, C-504-678-3213. **Medical/Dental:** Hours: 0730-1600 Tue-Sat, C-504-678-3660, D-312-678-3660, .5 miles away. **Security Police:** Bldg 70, 24 hours daily, C-504-678-3827, D-312-678-3827, .5 miles away.

**SUPPORT AVAILABLE: Bank/Currency Exchange:** Bldg 300, Hours: 0900-1300 Tue-Sat, C-504-678-3527. **Exchange:** Bldg 300, Hours: 1000-1700 Tue-Sun, C-504-678-3527. **Hair Styles:** Barber, Bldg 300, Hours: 1000-1700 Tue-Sun, C-504-678-3510; Beauty, Bldg 300, Hours: 0730-1600 Tue-Sun, C-504-678-3511. **Laundry/Dry Cleaning:** Bldg 300, Hours: 1000-1700 Tue-Sun, C-504-678-3510. **Postal Service:** Bldg 46, Hours: 1000-1300 Tue-Sat, C-504-678-3204. **Wire:** Bldg 300, Hours: 1000-1730 Tue-Sun, C-504-678-3580.

**ATTRACTIONS:** French quarter and downtown New Orleans.

### UNSCHEDULED FLIGHTS

One to five flights daily to CONUS. Dobbins ARB/ Atlanta NAS, GA (**NCQ**) (2-3 per month); Corpus Christi NAS, TX (**NGP**) (5 per month); Texas ANG/Ellington Field Houston, TX (**EFD**) (3 per month); Jacksonville NAS, FL (**NIP**) (1-2 per month); Millington Municipal Apt/ Mid-South NSA, TN (**NQA**) (1-2 per month); Meridian NAS, MS (**NMM**); Norfolk NS, VA (**NGU**) (2-3 per month); North Island NAS, CA (**NZY**) (1 per month); Pensacola NAS, FL (**NPA**) (1-2 per month). Occasional flights to Lajes Field AB (Azores), PT (**LGS**); Sigonella NAS (Sicily), IT (**SIZ**); Rota NS, ES (**RTA**); Hickam AFB, HI (**HIK**); Atsugi NAF, JP (**NJA**); Roosevelt Roads NS, PR (**NRR**). No flights to Germany. Passenger, cargo, and mixed missions via P-003C and C-130T aircraft.

# POLK ARMY AIRFIELD (POE/KPOE)

HHG USAG DPTMS FLT DET, Bldg 4255
Fort Polk, LA 71459-5000

**LOCATION:** Off US-171 north or south, nine miles south of Leesville. East of US-171 south. *USMRA: Page 79 (C-4). ML-ARM: (31°03'N/93°12'W).* LST: GMT-06:00. NMC: Alexandria, 45 miles northeast. Main installation numbers: C-337-531-2911, D-312-863-1110.

**REGISTRATION INFO:** C-337-531-4831/7328, D-312-863-7328, **Fax: C-337-531-3033, D-312-863-3033.** Army Airfield Flight Ops, Hours: 0700-2200 Mon-Fri, closed Sat, Sun and holidays. General and DV/VIP lounges. AMC, MEDEVAC, missions, C009A are serviced at the Alexandria IAP (AEX), LA. Please contact, Bayne-Jones Army Community Hospital, C-377-531-3368/3361.

**FOOD SERVICE: Fast Food:** Hours: 0900-2200, C-337-537-3540/7948, 5 miles away. **Snack Vending** in Flight Ops Day Room.

**TRANSPORTATION: On Base Car Rental:** McCrae Auto Plaza, C-318-537-8694. **Off Base Shuttle/Bus:** C-337-537-0244, 3 miles.

**TML:** Magnolia House, Bldg 522, Utah Avenue, 24 hours daily, C-337-531-9200, D-312-863-9100/9200, Fax: C-337-535-0968. DV/VIP Protocol, C-337-531-1720/21, D-312-863-1720/21.

**RVC:** South Fort RV Park, c/o Magnolia Guest House, Bldg 522, 1300-1800 hrs, C-377-531-9200/9000, D-312-863-9200/9000.

**TRAVELERS AID: Red Cross:** C-377-531-1927.

**SUPPORT AVAILABLE: Credit Union:** Hours: 0900-1700, C-377-531-2996, 6 miles. Full base support facilities available.

### EN ROUTE SCHEDULES

| AIRPORT/STATION | LI-MISSION (page #) |
| --- | --- |
| Scott AFB | BLV-C-616/MEDEVAC (30) |
| Scott AFB | BLV-C-652/MEDEVAC (30) |

### UNSCHEDULED FLIGHTS

Limited flights. Call for destinations, routing and schedules.

# MAINE

## BANGOR INTERNATIONAL AIRPORT/ AIR NATIONAL GUARD BASE (BGR/KBGR)

101 ARW
102 Glenn Ave, Suite 491
Bangor IAP (ANG), ME 04401-3099

**LOCATION:** Located in Bangor city limits. Northbound from I-95 take exit 47, Ohio Street, drive west two blocks and turn left, one block to right turn on Union Street (ME-222), past Bangor IAP, turn left on Griffin Road; entrance is 300 yards on right. *USMRA: Page 18 (E-6,7). ML-ARM: (44°48'N/68°49'W).* LST: GMT-05:00. NMC: Bangor, in city limits. Main installation numbers: C-207-990-7700, D-312-698-7700.

**REGISTRATION INFO: C-207-990-7212, D-312-698-7212.** Must register in person. Bldg 540, Hours: 0730-1600 Mon-Fri. Directions: First left once inside gate to last building on Ashley Street, Bldg 540.

**FOOD SERVICE:** Fast food and restaurants located off base.

**TRANSPORTATION:** Off Base Taxi, Off Base Bus and Off Base Car Rental available. **Parking:** Short term, Bldg 417.

**TML:** Pine Tree Inn, Bldg 346, 22 Cleveland Avenue, 24 hours daily, C-207-942-2081, D-312-698-2081.

**SUPPORT AVAILABLE:** Facilities of an IAP available. Other facilities off base. **Commissary/Shoppette:** C-207-990-7751; **Exchange:** C-207-990-7233.

**OTHER INFORMATION:** Port of Entry and U.S. Customs Service Airport (at International Airport).

**ATTRACTIONS:** Lobster and other seafood, Bar Harbor, beaches and boating.

### EN ROUTE SCHEDULES

| AIRPORT/STATION | LI-MISSION (page #) |
| --- | --- |
| Andrews AFB | ADW-116/MEDEVAC (37) |

### UNSCHEDULED FLIGHTS

Flights to: CONUS, OCONUS (Europe and Pacific areas), and foreign countries via KC-135R Air National Guard aircraft. Call for destinations, routings and schedules.

## BRUNSWICK NAVAL AIR STATION (NHZ/KNHZ)

Air Operations
Brunswick NAS, ME 04011-5000

**LOCATION:** From I-95 north, exit Coastal Route 1 north. Take Route 1 four miles to Cooks Corner. Turn right to main gate of Brunswick NAS. *USMRA: Page 18 (C-9). ML-ARM: (43°54'N/69°55'W).* LST: GMT-05:00. NMC: Portland, 30 miles southwest. Main installation numbers: C-207-921-1110, D-312-476-1110.

**REGISTRATION INFO: C-207-921-2692/2682, D-312-476-2682, Rec: C-207-921-2689, D-312-476-2689, Fax: C-207-921-2827, D-312-476-2827.** Bldg 200, 24 hours daily. Directions: From Main Gate straight on Fitch Ave, right on Orion Street, Air Ops is on the left. **Pax Service Office:** C-207-921-2682 (NCO on duty).

**PAX LOUNGES:** Limited lounge facilities. DV/VIP lounge. **General:** Bldg 200, main lobby, 24 hours daily. Restrooms, telephones (commercial and defense), snack vending machines. **Protocol Service:** Bldg 4, Hours: 0800-1700 Mon-Fri, C-207-921-2214.

**FOOD SERVICE: Officer's Lounge (at BOQ):** Hours: 1530-2100 Fri only, no meals, C-207-921-2591. **Restaurants:** Dining Hall, Bldg 201, C-207-921-2293/2881; Nite Flight/Sportzone, Bldg 516; Deli/Pizza, Hours: 1100-1300/1600-2200 Tue-Fri, C-207-921-2121. No O Club.

**TRANSPORTATION:** Very limited transportation on base. **Off Base Bus Service:** C-207-725-5573, various taxi service. **Parking:** Short and long term, Bldg 41, C-207-921-2457.

**TML:** Lodging office, Building 512, 351 Sewall Street, 24 hours daily, C-207-921-2386, D-312-476-2386, Fax: C-207-921-2942. Navy Lodge, 1400 Burbank Ave, Bldg 31, 0800-2000 daily, other hours OD, C-207-725-6268, Fax: C-207-721-9028. Note: located seven miles from base. DV/VIP C-207-921-2206.

**TRAVELERS AID: Chaplain:** Bldg 585, C-207-921-2231/32. **Emergency Relief:** Bldg 3420, C-207-921-2414 (Navy Relief). **Medical:** Bldg 645, Emergency Service 24 hours daily, C-207-921-2991/2222. **Security Police:** Bldg 41, C-207-921-2457/2775.

**SUPPORT AVAILABLE: Exchange:** Bldg 11, C-207-921-2378. **Credit Union:** Bldg 20, C-207-729-1831. **Hair Styles:** Bldg 11; Barber, C-207-921-2346; Beauty, C-207-921-2248. **Laundry/Dry Cleaning:** Bldg 11, C-207-729-9253. **Postal Service:** Bldg 20, C-207-921-2518.

**ATTRACTIONS:** Snow skiing area, lobster/seafood, Maine Maritime Museum.

### UNSCHEDULED FLIGHTS

Frequent flights via P-003B/C, C-130T and EP-35 to: Andrews AFB, MD (**ADW**); Jacksonville NAS, FL (**NIP**); Norfolk NS, VA (**NGU**); and other CONUS, OCONUS and foreign locations. Call for destinations, routings and schedules.

# MARYLAND

*Note: As of 1 May 1997, Maryland's telephone system has changed to a 10-digit dialing system. Regardless of the originating location, all phone calls must include the area code (XXX), switch code (XXX) & line code (XXXX).*

# ANDREWS AIR FORCE BASE (ADW/KADW)

89th APS/TROP, 1245 Menoher Ave
Andrews AFB, MD 20762-5000

**LOCATION:** From I-95 north (east portion of Capital Beltway, I-495) take exit 9; first traffic light after leaving exit ramp turn left. At next traffic light turn right into main gate of AFB. Also, from I-395 north, exit South Capitol Street, cross Anacostia River bear left to Suitland Pkwy east, exit at Morningside on Suitland Road east to main gate of AFB. From I-495 south, take exit 9; turn right at stop sign, turn right at next light onto Allentown Road; turn left into main gate on Suitland Road. *USMRA: Page 42 (E-5); Page 55 (I,J-6,7).* *ML-ARM: (38°48'N/76°52'W).* LST: GMT-05:00. NMC: Washington, 6 miles northwest. NMI: Bolling AFB, 10 miles. Main installation number: C-301-981-1110, D-312-858-1110.

**REGISTRATION INFO: Toll free: C-888-360-8700. C-301-981-1854/3604, D-312-858-1854/3604, Rec: (updated: 0600 daily) Same Day: C-301-981-3527, D-312-858-3527, Next Day: C-301-981-5851, D-312-858-5851, Fax: C-301-981-4241, D-312-858-4241. E-mail: passenger@andrews.af.mil WEB: www.andrews.af.mil** Bldg 1245, Hours: 0600-2200 daily, open after hours for later flights. Directions: Left of Base Ops and ATC tower. Main gate, go through stop sign, take a left onto Westover Drive and a right onto Arnold Ave to stop sign, left to Pax Term. **Navy Ops: C-240-857-2740/4, D-312-857-2740/4,** Bldg 3198, 24 hours daily, (east side of Andrews AFB). No ground transportation provided to Navy Ops. See Washington Naval Air Facility MD (NSF) listing in this book. Also, **D.C. National Guard, C-301-981-5004. Pax Service Office:** Bldg 1245, Hours: 0730-1630 Mon-Fri. **Pax Paging:** Bldg 1245, Hours: 0600-2200 daily, C-301-981-3604, D-312-858-3604.

**PAX LOUNGES: General:** Bldg 1245, Hours: 0600-2200 daily. A/C, bag check, telephones (commercial, long distance and defense), TV, restrooms, P/C seats. **DV/VIP:** Bldg 1245, 24 hours daily, C-301-981-2100, D-312-858-2100. A/C, coffee/tea served, telephones (commercial, long distance and defense), TV, restrooms, O/S seats. Hostess (O6+). Active and retired. **Protocol Service:** Bldg 1245, Hours: 0800-1700 Mon-Fri, C-301-981-2100, D-312-858-2100,O6+. Active and retired. AMC sponsored.

**FOOD SERVICE: Dining Hall:** Bldg l628, Colorado Ave, Hours: 0330-0400, 0530-0800, 1100-1300, 1530-1800, 2300-0030 daily, C-301-981-6516. **Enlisted Club:** Bldg 1889, Hours: 0900-2200 Mon-Thu, 1000-2300 Fri-Sat, C-301-981-2325. **In-flight Meals:** Bldg 1201, 24 hours daily, C-301-981-3543. **NCO/CPO Club:** Bldg 1889, Hours: 1100-1300 daily, 1730-2100 Tue-Sat, C-301-568-3100. **O Club:** Bldg 1352, 0700-2300 Mon-Thu, 0700-0130 Fri-Sat, C-301-420-4744. **Snack Bars:** Bldg 1672, Hours: 0700-2300 Mon-Fri, 1000-2300 Sat-Sun, C-301-981-6452. **Snack Vending:** Bldg 1245, Hours: 0600-2200 daily.

**TRANSPORTATION: Air Tickets:** SATO, Bldg 1442, Hours: 0800-1630 Mon-Fri, C-301-817-2911; Official Travel, Bldg 1535, C-301-981-5362. **Off Base Bus (Comm):** Departs North Gate to Washington, D.C., Hours: daily 0600-2100, C-202-637-7000; Greyhound/Trailways, C-202-289-5160. **Car Rentals:** Bldg 1245, Hours: 0730-1900 Mon-Fri, 0900-1300 Sat, 0400-1700 Sun; Thrifty Car Rental, C-301-568-7900. **Limo Service:** Bldg 1245, 24 hours daily, C-301-599-1222 (Golden Touch Limo). **On Base Shuttle/Bus:** Bldg 1245, Hours: 0600-0900, 1100-1300, 1500-1700 Mon-Fri, C-301-981-4661. **On Base Taxi (Comm):** Bldg 1245, Hours: 0600-2200 daily, C-301-277-6000 (at Pax Term). **On Base Taxi (Gov):** Bldg 1568, 24 hours daily, C-301-981-2689/5458 (for official duty). **Trains:** AMTRAK, 24 hours daily, C-1-800-USA-RAIL (call for schedule). **Parking:** Bldg 1245, 24 hours daily, C-301-981-3528 (short term has 24 hour limit; long term at Bldg 1413 has 30 day limit).

**TML:** Gateway Inn, 1375 Arkansas Road, 24 hours daily, C-301-981-0785, D-312-858-0785, Fax: C-301-981-9277, D-312-858-9277 DV/VIP C-301-981-4525, D-312-858-4525, 06+.

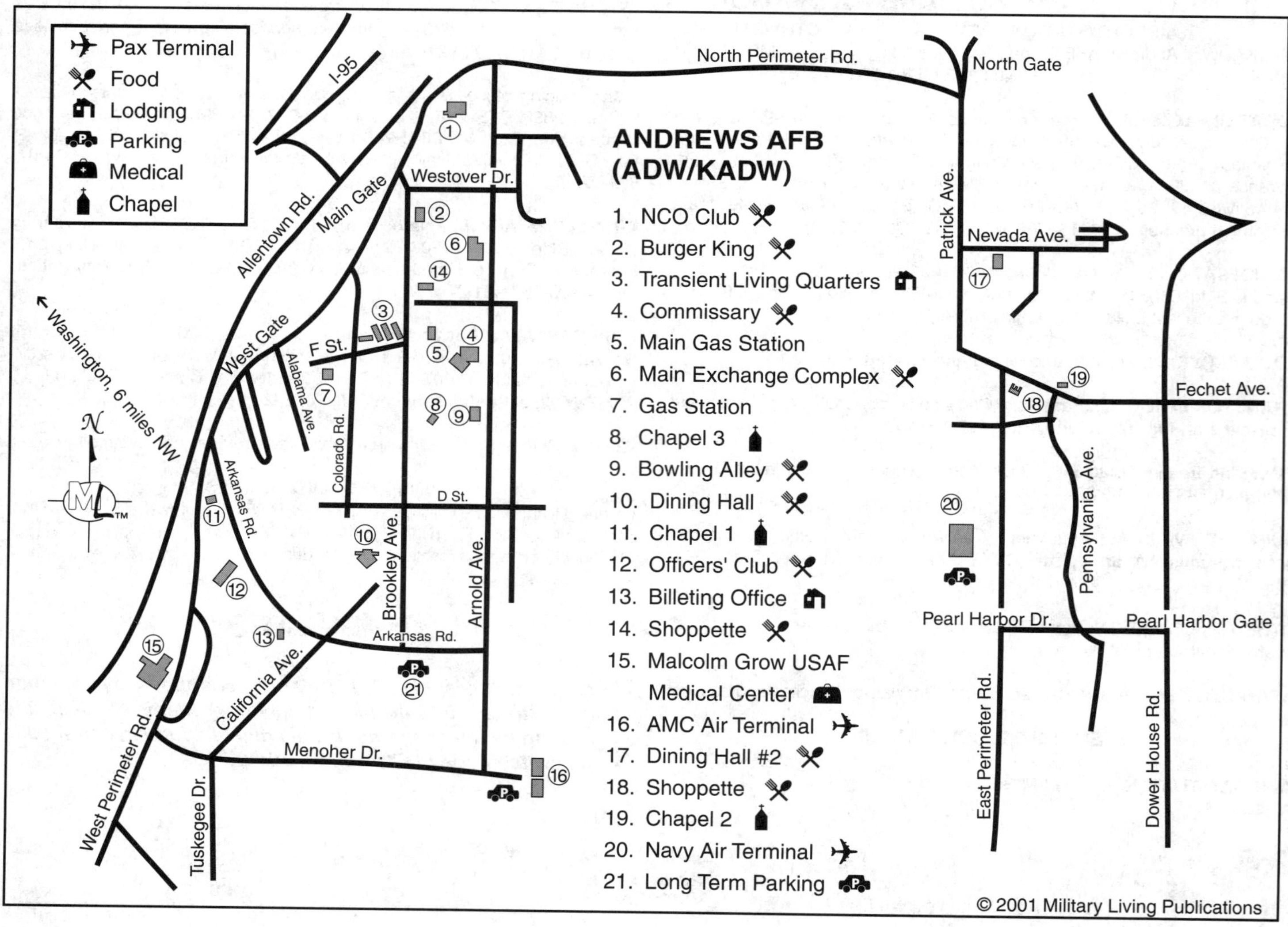

**RVC:** FAMCAMP, Camp Yocomico, Bldg 4520, Wheeling Road, Check-in after 1100 hrs, FAMCAMP, C-301-981-5663, D-312-858-4109.

**TRAVELERS AID: Air Force Aid:** C-301-981-7087/7088. **Chaplain:** Bldg 1345, 24 hours daily, C-301-981-2111 (Chapel #I). **Lost/Found:** Bldg 1245, Hours: 0600-2200 daily, C-301-981-3526 (Pax Term, NCO). **Medical:** Bldg 1050, 24 hours daily, daily, C-301-981-2333/2158 (hospital emergency). **Red Cross:** Bldg 1610, Hours: 0800-1600 Mon-Fri, C-301-981-6008, (hospital). **Security Police:** Bldg 1845, 24 hours daily, C-301-981-2001/2002 (main gate). **USO:** Bldg 1245, Hours: 0600-1800 Mon-Fri, C-301-981-2525.

**SUPPORT AVAILABLE: Bank/Currency Exchange:** Bldg 1677, Hours: 0900-1700 Mon-Fri, C-301-735-8100. **Exchange** Bldg 1811, Hours: 1000-2100 Mon-Sat, 1000-1800 Sun, C-301-568-1500. **Hair Styles:** Barber, Bldg 1245, Hours: 0800-1630 Mon-Fri, C-301-420-9383; Beauty, Bldg 1811, Hours: 0800-1800 Mon-Fri, 0800-1700 Sat, C-301-735-1988. **Laundry/Dry Cleaning:** Bldg 1668, Hours: 0830-2030 Mon-Fri, 0900-1700 Sun, C-301-568-2546. **Postal Service:** Bldg 1668, Hours: 0800-1615 Mon-Fri, 0830-1230 Sat, C-301-981-3539 (no wire service). **Shoppette:** Bldg 1348, Hours: 0900-2300 Sat-Sun, C-301-568-2364.

**OTHER INFORMATION:** Port of Entry and U.S. Customs Service Airport.

**ATTRACTIONS:** Aerial gateway to Washington, D.C.; home of "Air Force One" (the President's aircraft); monuments, White House, parks and more.

### ANDREWS AFB (ADW/KADW); MISSION 116/MEDEVAC; SAMPLE SCHEDULE: FRI; EQUIPMENT: C009A

{ADW/KADW *NE* ➡ WRI/KWRI *N* ➡ SWF/KSWF *E* ➡ PVD/KPVD *N* ➡ BED/KBED *NE* ➡ BGR/KBGR *W* ➡ GTB/KGTB *S* ➡ ADW/KADW *W* ➡ BLV/KBLV}

| LI | AIRPORT/STATION | CTRY/STA |
|---|---|---|
| ADW/KADW | Andrews AFB | MD |
| WRI/KWRI | McGuire AFB | NJ |
| SWF/KSWF | Stewart IAP/ANGB | NY |
| PVD/KPVD | Theodore Francis Green State Apt | RI |
| BED/KBED | Hanscom AFB | MA |
| BGR/KBGR | Bangor IAP/ANGB | ME |
| GTB/KGTB | Wheeler-Sack AAF | NY |
| ADW/KADW | Andrews AFB | MD |
| BLV/KBLV | Scott AFB | IL |

**Note:** (✚) = MEDEVAC: ADW to ADW

### EN ROUTE SCHEDULES

| AIRPORT/STATION | LI-MISSION (page #) |
|---|---|
| Scott AFB | BLV-C-614/MEDEVAC (30) |
| Scott AFB | BLV-C-616/MEDEVAC (30) |
| Scott AFB | BLV-C-621/MEDEVAC (30) |
| Scott AFB | BLV-C-626/MEDEVAC (30) |
| Allen C Thompson (Jackson) | JAN-IKM3A (44) |
| Allen C Thompson (Jackson) | JAN-IKX3A (44) |
| McGuire AFB | WRI-A7R1A (51) |
| McGuire AFB | WRI-A7R3A (51) |
| McGuire AFB | WRI-A7X3C (51) |
| Wright-Patterson AFB | FFO-OEM3A (61) |
| Wright-Patterson AFB | FFO-OER1A (62) |
| Charleston AFB/IAP | CHS-A4M3A (67) |
| Charleston AFB/IAP | CHS-A4X3A (67) |

### UNSCHEDULED FLIGHTS

All unscheduled flights operate with 24 hour notice. Frequent flights (once a week) to Guantanamo Bay NAS, CU (**GAO**); Kelly AFB, TX (**SKF**); Norfolk NS, VA (**NGU**); Roosevelt Roads NS, PR (**NRR**); Scott AFB, IL (**BLV**). Infrequent flights to: Langley AFB, VA (**LFI**); Maxwell AFB, AL (**MXF**); Randolph AFB, TX (**RND**) via C-21; Eglin AFB, FL (**VPS**); Wright-Patterson AFB, OH (**FFO**). Other destinations vary widely. Equipment is C-135B, 137,

C-009C and C-141B in most cases. Baggage on these aircraft limited to 2 pieces, not more than 40 lbs combined except C009A MEDEVAC which is 45 lbs and C-21, which is 30 lbs.

# BALTIMORE/WASHINGTON INTERNATIONAL AIRPORT (BWI/KBWI)

305 APS/Det 1 (AMC)
P.O. Box 8613
Baltimore, MD 21240-5000

**LOCATION:** From I-95 north or south, take the BWI exit 47 east, I-95 and airport. Also I-295 north or south exit 2 east, I-195 and airport. *USMRA: Page 49 (A,B-4,5).* ML-ARM: (39°10'N/76°40'W). LST: GMT-05:00. NMC: Baltimore, 5 miles north. Main installation number: C-410-918-6900 or C-1-877-429-4262.

**REGISTRATION INFO: Toll-free: C-877-429-4262. C-410-918-6900, D-312-243-6902, Rec: C-410-918-6900, Fax: C-410-918-6932, D-312-243-6932. E-mail: bwipax@mcguire.af.mil** Hours: 0800-1600 Mon-Fri. AMC is located in the new International Pier (connected to the terminal near Pier D). **Pax Paging:** C-1-800-435-9294. Support of an international airport. **Processing Counter:** C-410-918-6900.

**FOOD SERVICE: Restaurants:** CK's, Wild Goose Ale House. **Fast Food:** Burger King, Pizza Hut, Roy Rogers, Taco Bell. Starbucks and other snack places also throughout the terminal.

**TRANSPORTATION: Car Rentals:** Lower Level near baggage claim. Avis, C-410-859-1680; Alamo, C-410-850-5011; Budget, C-410-859-0850; Dollar, C-410-684-3316; Hertz, C-410-850-7400; National, C-410-859-8860; Thrifty, C-410-859-1136. **Off Base Limo Service:** Pick up at service area. C-410-519-0000, C-301-912-0000, C-202-737-2600. **On Base Shuttle/Bus:** C-1-800-258-3826. **Off Base Taxi:** Outside the baggage claim area. C-410-859-1100. **Trains:** AMTRAK, 24 hours daily, C-1-800-USA-RAIL; BWI Amtrak Station, C-410-672-6167; MARC (commuter train), C-1-800-325-RAIL. **Parking:** C-1-800-468-6294, C-410-859-9230. Garage, $2.00/half hour, $15/day; ESP (with shuttle service), $4.00/hour, $13/day; Daily Express (with shuttle service), $2.00/hour, $7/day; Satellite (with shuttle service), $1.00/hour, $5/day with every 7th day free. ***Note:*** An alternative to paying long-term parking fees—park your car at Fort George G. Meade, MD. Contact Military Police: C-301-677-6622, park where directed, fill out "Quarters Watch Request," take commercial taxi to BWI (approx 8 miles north) or contact Security Police at Curtis Bay Coast Guard Yard, C-410-636-3695 for parking availablility, 5 miles NW of BWI.

**TML:** Nearest TML is at Curtis Bay Coast Guard Yard, Family Transient Lodging, 2401 Hawkins Point Road, Bldg 143, C-410-636-7373, Fax: C-410-636-7496, 0900-1500 Mon-Fri, other hours, OOD/JOOD, Building 33, C-410-636-7493.

**TRAVELERS AID: Currency Exchange:** C-410-859-5997. **Lost/Found:** C-410-691-2701. **Security Police:** C-410-859-7040. **USO:** Located between Pier C and D, next to Burger King, C-410-859-4425. (This is a temporary location until the new USO is completed. New USO on Pier E' lower level.)

**ATTRACTIONS:** Baltimore Orioles (Major League Baseball), Baltimore Ravens (National Football League), Inner Harbor, Baltimore Aquarium.

***Note: Commercially contracted flights are now called Patriot Express.***

### BALTIMORE/WASHINGTON IAP, MD (BWI); REGION: ATL; OPERATOR: COM; TYPE: PAX; ROUTE: EXG5A; SAMPLE SCHEDULE: 1ST FRI, 2ND, 3RD & 4TH WED; EQUIPMENT: L1011

{BWI (★) *NE* ➡ LGS *SE* ➡ AVB *SE* ➡ KWI ⮌ KWI *NW* ➡ AVB *NW* ➡ LGS *SW* ➡ BWI (★)}

| LI/ICAO | AIRPORT/STATION | CTRY/STA | DAYS EN ROUTE |
|---|---|---|---|
| BWI/KBWI | Baltimore/Washington IAP | MD | +0 |
| LGS/LPLA | Lajes Field AB (Azores) | PT | +0 |
| AVB/LIPA | Aviano AB | IT | +0 |
| KWI/OKBK | Kuwait IAP | KW | +1 |
| KWI/OKBK | Kuwait IAP | KW | +1 |
| AVB/LIPA | Aviano AB | IT | +1 |
| LGS/LPLA | Lajes Field AB (Azores) | PT | +1 |
| BWI/KBWI | Baltimore/Washington IAP | MD | |

### BALTIMORE/WASHINGTON IAP, MD (BWI); REGION: ATL; OPERATOR: COM; TYPE: PAX; ROUTE: LZ27A; SAMPLE SCHEDULE: 3RD MON, 1ST WED, 4TH THU, 2ND FRI; EQUIPMENT: B747

{BWI (★) *NE* ➡ FRF *SE* ➡ EKJ ⇌ EKJ *NW* ➡ FRF *SW* ➡ BWI (★)}

| LI/ICAO | AIRPORT/STATION | CTRY/STA | DAYS EN ROUTE |
|---|---|---|---|
| BWI/KBWI | Baltimore/Washington IAP | MD | +0 |
| FRF/EDDF | Rhein-Main AB (Frankfurt) | DE | +0 |
| EKJ/OEKJ | Prince Sultan AB | SA | +1 |
| EKJ/OEKJ | Prince Sultan AB | SA | +1 |
| FRF/EDDF | Rhein-Main AB (Frankfurt) | DE | +1 |
| BWI/KBWI | Baltimore/Washington IAP | MD | |

### BALTIMORE/WASHINGTON IAP, MD (BWI); REGION: ATL; OPERATOR: COM; TYPE: PAX; ROUTE: LX19A; SAMPLE SCHEDULE: SAT; EQUIPMENT: L1011

{BWI (★) *NE* ➡ FRF *SE* ➡ AVB *SE* ➡ ADA ⇌ ADA *NW* ➡ AVB *NW* ➡ FRF *SW* ➡ BWI (★)}

| LI/ICAO | AIRPORT/STATION | CTRY/STA | DAYS EN ROUTE |
|---|---|---|---|
| BWI/KBWI | Baltimore/Washington IAP | MD | +0 |
| FRF/EDDF | Rhein-Main AB (Frankfurt) | DE | +0 |
| AVB/LIPA | Aviano AB | IT | +0 |
| ADA/LTAG | Incirlik AB | TR | +0 |
| ADA/LTAG | Incirlik AB | TR | +0 |
| AVB/LIPA | Aviano AB | IT | +1 |
| FRF/EDDF | Rhein-Main AB (Frankfurt) | DE | +1 |
| BWI/KBWI | Baltimore/Washington IAP | MD | |

### BALTIMORE/WASHINGTON IAP, MD (BWI); REGION: ATL; OPERATOR: COM; TYPE: PAX; ROUTE: LX27A; SAMPLE SCHEDULE: 2ND & 4TH SAT; EQUIPMENT: L1011

{BWI (★) *NE* ➡ SNN *SE* ➡ CAI *SE* ➡ KWI ⇌ KWI *SE* ➡ EKJ *NW* ➡ CAI *NW* ➡ SNN *SW* ➡ BWI (★)}

| LI/ICAO | AIRPORT/STATION | CTRY/STA | DAYS EN ROUTE |
|---|---|---|---|
| BWI/KBWI | Baltimore/Washington IAP | MD | +0 |
| SNN/EINN | Shannon APT* | IE | +1 |
| CAI/HECA | Cairo IAP | EG | +1 |
| KWI/OKBK | Kuwait IAP | KW | +1 |
| EKJ/OEKJ | Prince Sultan AB | SA | +1 |
| CAI/HECA | Cairo IAP | EG | +2 |
| SNN/EINN | Shannon APT* | IE | +2 |
| BWI/KBWI | Baltimore/Washington IAP | MD | |

**Note:** * = refueling and crew rest. No Space-A embarking or debarking.

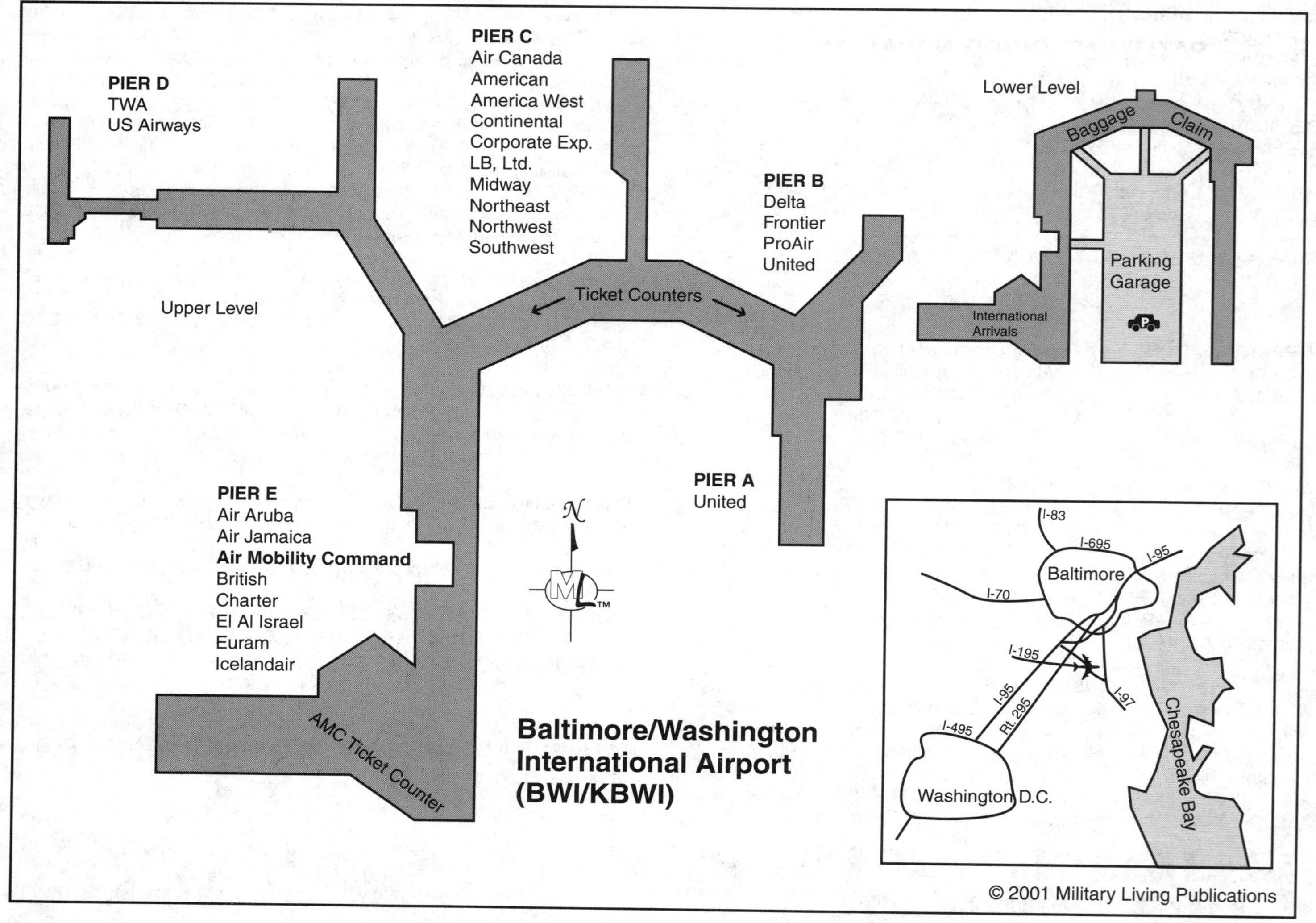

## EN ROUTE SCHEDULES

| AIRPORT/STATION | LI-MISSION (page #) |
| --- | --- |
| WM B Hartsfield IAP (Atlanta) | ATL-EXR5B (27) |
| McGuire AFB | WRI-HJX1A (49) |
| McGuire AFB | WRI-HJX5A (50) |
| Charleston AFB/IAP | CHS-HJJ7A (69) |
| Norfolk NS | NGU-EX13DM & EX23A (78) |

# MARTIN STATE AIRPORT (MTN/KMTN)

175th WG/C-130 OPS (ANG)
2701 Eastern Blvd
Baltimore, MD 21220-2899

**LOCATION:** From US-40 east, exit to MD-702 east and continue east to MD-150. Follow signs to airport. *USMRA: Page 42 (F,G-3). ML-ARM: (39°20'N/76°25'W).* LST: GMT-05:00. NMC: Baltimore, 8 miles southwest. Main installation numbers: C-410-918-6210, D-312-243-6210.

**REGISTRATION INFO: C-410-918-6381, D-312-243-6381, Rec: C-410-918-6551, D-312-243-6551. Note: Pax Service personnel will not provide flight info over the telephone, only in person. Parking:** Check with Security Police.

**TML:** Nearest TML is at Aberdeen Proving Ground, Lodging office, Building 2207, Bel Air Street, 24 hours daily, C-410-278-5148/9, D-312-298-4373/5148, Fax: C-410-278-5515.

### UNSCHEDULED FLIGHTS

Flights via C-130A-H aircraft to CONUS, OCONUS and foreign country locations. **Note: This organization is not staffed to process requests for Space-A travel on a regular basis.**

# PATUXENT RIVER NAVAL AIR WARFARE CENTER (NHK/KNHK)

Aircraft Division,
Air Operations Department
Patuxent River NAWC, MD 20670-5409

**LOCATION:** From I-95 (east portion of Capital Beltway, I-495) take exit 7-A to Branch Avenue (MD-5) south. Follow MD-5 until it becomes MD-235 near Oraville, on to Lexington Park, and the NAS. Main gate is on MD-235 and MD-246 (Cedar Point Road). *USMRA: Page 42 (F,G-6,7). ML-ARM: (38°17'N/76°26'W).* LST: GMT-05:00. NMC: Washington, D.C., 65 miles northwest. Main installation numbers: C-301-342-3000, D-312-326-3000.

**REGISTRATION INFO: C-301-342-3836/7, D-312-342-3836/7. Fax: 301-342-5961, D-312-342-5961 WEB: www.nawcad.navy.mil/pax/** Bldg 103, Hours: 0700-2300 daily. Directions: From main gate straight on Cedar Point Road for 2.5 miles. Air Ops sign on the right. **Pax Service Office:** C-301-342-3836/7, D-312-326-3836/7 (NCO on duty). **Pax Paging:** C-301-342-3836/7, D-312-326-3836/7.

**FOOD SERVICE: O Club:** C-301-342-3656. **Commissary:** 301-342-3789 **Patuxent Landing:** C-301-342-3940; Subway, McDonald's available.

**TRANSPORTATION: Car Rental:** Enterprise, C-301-737-0100. Ford Rent-A-Car 301-863-8111; Hertz 301-863-0033; Thrifty Car Rental 301-737-1304; Base Taxi 301-342-5088. On Base Shuttle/Bus available.

**TML:** Lodging Office, Bldg 406, C-301-863-9343, D-312-342-3601, Fax: C-301-342-1015, DV/VIP C-301-342-1108, Navy Lodge C-301-737-2400, 1-800-NAVY-INN, Fax: C-301-862-7866.

**RVC:** Goose Creek/West Basin, Rec Office, Bldg 458, 47382 Keane Road, Check-in 0800-1630 hours Mon-Fri, at Drill Hall, Bldg 458, C-301-342-3508, D-312-342-3508, Fax: C-301-342-3232, D-312-342-3232.

**TRAVELERS AID: Chaplain:** C-301-342-3812. **Medical:** C-301-342-1506.

**SUPPORT AVAILABLE: Exchange:** C-301-863-8814; **SATO:** C-301-342-1060 Many facilities available on base.

**ATTRACTIONS:** Calvert Cliffs Nuclear Power Plant Museum, Calvert Marine Museum, Naval Air Test & Evaluation Museum, Potomac River-St Clement's Island Museum, St Mary's City, Sotterley Plantation, Cecil's Mill, Point Lookout State Park, Seafood Festivals.

### UNSCHEDULED FLIGHTS

Extremely limited flights. Equipment: P-003C, UP-003A, NP-003C/D, KC-130F, NC-130H. Call for destinations, routings and schedules.

# WASHINGTON NAVAL AIR FACILITY (NSF/KNSF)

1 San Diego Loop, Bldg 3198
Andrews Air Force Base, MD 20762-5518

**LOCATION:** From I-95 (east part of Capital Beltway, I-495) N or S, Exit 9. At first traffic light after leaving exit ramp, turn right into main gate of Andrews AFB. Also, from I-395 N, exit South Capital Street, cross Anacostia River on South Capital Street, bear left to Suitland Parkway East, exit Parkway at Morningside on Suitland Road east to main gate of Andrews AFB. Follow signs to east side of Andrews AFB, Bldg 3198, north of Hangar #12. Clearly marked. *USMRA: Page 42 (E-5); Page 55 (I,J-6,7). ML-ARM: (38°21'N/76°06'W).* LST: GMT-05:00. NMC: Washington, D.C., 6 miles northwest. Main installation numbers: C-240-857-9111, D-312-857-9111.

**REGISTRATION INFO: C-240-857-2740/2744, D-312-857-2740/2744, Rec: C-240-857-3473, D-312-857-3473.** Bldg 3198, Hours: 0600-2200 daily, closed Thanksgiving, Christmas and New Year's Day. Directions: Left at 4-way stop to second left onto North Perimeter Road, then right at light onto Patrick Ave. Follow to Fetchet Ave. to right onto East Perimeter Road. PAX just past firehouse on right. Report to Flight Services desk, first floor south end of building. **Note: Space-A seats not used by Washington NAF are offered to Andrews AFB and vice versa.**

**PAX LOUNGES:** Bldg 3198, Hours: 0600-2200 daily, closed Thanksgiving, Christmas and New Year's Day, C-240-857-2740/2744, D-312-857-2744/2740. No overnight use by passengers. Lounge in building lobby. A/C, telephones (commercial), restrooms, P/C seats, TV. **DV/VIP:** Bldg 3198, Hours: 0600-2200 daily, closed Thanksgiving, Christmas and New Year's Day, C-240-857-2740, D-312-857-2740 (O6+). Off lobby. A/C, telephones (commercial and defense), restrooms, O/S seats. **Protocol Service:** Bldg 3198, Hours: 0600-2200 daily, closed Thanksgiving, Christmas and New Year's Day, C-240-857-2740, D-312-857-2740.

**FOOD SERVICE: Restaurants:** Denny's BBQ, Hours: 1000-1500 Mon-Fri, .5 blocks east of Bldg 3198. **Snack Vending:** Bldg 3198. See Andrews AFB for complete services.

**TRANSPORTATION:** Bldg 3198. See Andrews AFB listing for complete services. **Parking:** Bldg 3198, 24 hours daily. Short and long term available. Contact ATC, C-240-857-2740/2744. No parking in lot next to Bldg 3198.

**TML:** Lodging Office, Bldg 1384, 1 San Diego Loop, 24 hrs, C-240-857-2750, C-312-857-2750, Fax: C-240-857-3588. No family quarters. More lodging available at Andrews AFB, Gateway Inn, Building 1375, Arkansas Road, 24 hours daily, C-301-981-40785, D-312-858-0785, Fax: C-301-981-9277. DV/VIP C-301-981-4525, D-312-858-4525, 06+.

**SUPPORT AVAILABLE:** See Andrews AFB listing for other services.

### UNSCHEDULED FLIGHTS

There are no scheduled flights from the Washington NAF. Most flights are planned 48 hours prior to departure. Call for information. There are unscheduled flights to the following locations: Beaufort MCAS, SC (**NBC**); Brunswick NAS, ME (**NHZ**); Cherry Point MCAS, NC (**NKT**); Jacksonville NAS, FL (**NIP**); Millington Municipal Apt/ Mid-South NSA, TN (**NQA**); New

Orleans NAS/JRB, LA (**NBG**); New River MCAS, NC (**NCA**); Norfolk NS, VA (**NGU**); Oceana NAS, VA (**NTU**); and Pensacola NAS, FL (**NPA**). Equipment flown varies with flights and distances. Most aircraft used are C-20D/G and C-130T. Call for destinations, routings and schedules.

# MASSACHUSETTS

## HANSCOM AIR FORCE BASE (BED/KBED)

66 ABW/LGTF
Attn: Passenger Lounge
3 Robbins Street
Hanscom AFB, MA 01731-1711

**LOCATION:** From I-95 south take exit 30 B (MA-2A) west for two miles then turn right at the Hanscom Field Sign. From I-95 north take exit 31B, keep to right, follow signs to base, two miles. *USMRA: Page 17 (J-3); Page 24 (A-2). ML-ARM: (42°27'N/71°16'W).* LST: GMT-05:00. NMC: Boston, 17 miles southeast. Main installation numbers: C-781-377-4441, D-312-478-5980.

**REGISTRATION INFO: C-781-377-1143/3333, D-312-478-1143/3333, Fax: C-781-377-2383, D-312-478-2383.** Recording after hours ext 3333. Bldg 1721, Hours: 0730-1600 Mon-Fri, for Space-A sign up. Terminal will open 2 hours prior to all advertised flight departures for Space-A passengers. Open for any unscheduled late night or weekend flights. Closed on most federal holidays.

**PAX LOUNGES:** General and DV/VIP lounges available. A/C, restrooms, telephones, TV and vending machines. No inflight meals available. **Protocol Service:** POC C-781-377-5151, D-312-478-5151.

**FOOD SERVICE: Enlisted Club:** C-781-377-2123, D-312-478-2123. **NCO Club:** C-781-377-2123. **O Club:** C-781-377-3799, D-312-478-3799. **USO (Boston):** C-781-720-4949. **Restaurants:** C-781-274-0133. **Snack Vending:** Bldg 1721, Hours: 0700-2300 Mon-Fri.

**TRANSPORTATION: Air Tickets:** C-781-274-6050. **Off Base Shuttle:** To/from Woburn Mon-Fri. Community Bus Service from there to Logan IAP; cost is approximately $6. **On Base Car Rentals:** Avis, C-781-274-7488 or C-1-800-331-1212; Budget, C-781-497-1800, C-1-800-527-0700; Enterprise, C-781-643-1558, C-1-800-325-8007; Hertz, C-781-273-1650, C-1-800-654-3131. **Off Base Bus/Subway:** Massachusetts Transit Authority (bus and subway), C-1-800-392-6100. **Off Base Taxi:** Arlex Taxi, C-781-862-4600; Bedford town Taxi, C-781-275-6200; Patriot Express, C-781-275-8009; Red Cab, C-781-275-5000. **On Base Taxi:** Hours: 0630-1930 Mon-Fri, C-781-377-2588. **Parking:** Short and Long-Term, Bldg 1721, D-312-478-1143. Overnight/long term parking is available at the west end (the end closest to the BX) of the Commissary parking lot. Vehicles parked overnight outside the Passenger Terminal will be towed at the owner's expense. For long-term parking, notify Security Police at D-312-478-2314.

**TML:** Hanscom Inn, Building 1427, Kirtland Street, 24 hours daily, C-781-377-2112, D-312-478-2112. Fax: C-781-377-4961. DV/VIP 781-377-5151, 07+.

**TRAVELERS AID: Air Force Aid Society:** C-781-377-4222, D-213-478-4222. **Red Cross:** C-781-375-0700, C-800-462-2705.

**SUPPORT AVAILABLE: Exchange:** C-781-377-5258. **Hair Styles:** Barber, C-781-377-5127; Beauty, C-781-274-6634. **Laundry:** C-781-274-8581. **Medical/Dental:** C-781-377-4988. **Postal Service:** C-781-377-2242. **Valet/Dry Cleaning:** C-781-377-5139. **Wire:** C-781-377-4441.

**ATTRACTIONS:** Hanscom AFB is located in the historical towns of Lexington, Concord, Bedford, and Lincoln which offer a number of historical sights such as the north bridge.

### EN ROUTE SCHEDULES

| AIRPORT/STATION | LI-MISSION (page #) |
| --- | --- |
| Andrews AFB | ADW-116/MEDEVAC (37) |


Limited flights to Andrews AFB, MD (**ADW**); Wright-Patterson AFB, OH (**FFO**) and other East Coast locations. Call for destinations, routings and schedules after 1400 for the 24-48 hour departure schedule.

## OTIS AIR NATIONAL GUARD BASE/ CAPE COD COAST GUARD AIR STATION (FMH/KFMH)

102 FW/OTM
158 Reilly Street, Bldg 165
Otis ANGB, MA 02542-5028

**LOCATION:** South of Plymouth, from MA-28 north or south take MA Military Reservation exit, south on Connley Avenue approximately two miles to Bourne Gate. *USMRA: Page 17 (M-7). ML-ARM: (41°39'N/70°31'W).* LST: GMT-05:00. NMC: New Bedford, 30 miles southwest. Boston is 45 miles north on Route 3 over Sagamore Bridge. NMI: Hanscom AFB, 60 miles north. Main installation numbers: C-508-968-4667, D-312-557-4667.

**REGISTRATION INFO: C-508-968-4831/4832, D-312-557-4831/4832, Fax: C-508-968-4690, D-312-557-4690.** Base Ops/Pax Term Bldg 165, Hours: 0730-1600 Mon-Fri.

**PAX LOUNGES:** Small, General pax lounges with snack machines.

**FOOD SERVICE: Commissary:** C-508-968-6662, D-312-557-6662, on base (sandwiches). **Snack Vending:** Hours: 0730-1600 Mon-Fri, Pax Lounge. Local establishments are 6-10 miles off base.

**TRANSPORTATION:** No commercial or military bus on base. Bus connections can be made from rotary coming in to main gate. Commercial taxi and rental car available in Falmouth, MA 10 miles south of base. **Off Base Car Rental:** U Save, C-508-457-1700, C-508-540-4910, 10 miles; will deliver automobiles to the base.

**TML:** Temporary quarters, Building 5204, C-508-968-6461, Fax: C-508-968-6337, Mon - Fri 0800-1600 hours, Sat - Sun 0900-1400 hours.

**TRAVELERS AID:** Security Police.

**SUPPORT AVAILABLE: Emergency Medical:** C-508-968-4111, D-312-557-4111. BX, barber shop, small dispensary (Mon-Fri), post office, laundry, gas station available.

**ATTRACTIONS:** Cape Cod has numerous attractions and is one of the largest tourist areas in New England from May to October.


Very limited Space-A, no advance schedules published. Call for destinations, routings and schedules.

## WESTOVER AIR RESERVE BASE (CEF/KCEF)

439th CCU-RAO
570 Patriot Ave
Space-A Travel, Box 42
Westover ARB, Chicopee, MA 01022-1634

**LOCATION:** From Boston take I-90 west (Massachusetts Turnpike) to exit 5 in Chicopee; bear right after toll booth to traffic light; take a left onto Memorial Drive (Route 33) and follow signs to Westover ARB. *USMRA: Page 16 (F-4). ML-ARM: (42°10'N/72°33'W).* LST: GMT-05:00. NMC: Springfield, 8 miles south. Main installation numbers: C-413-557-1110, D-312-589-1110.

**REGISTRATION INFO: C-413-557-2622, D-312-589-2622, Rec: C-413-557-2549, Fax: (Attn: Space-A) C-413-557-3147. WEB: www.afrc.af.mil/ units/439aw/default.htm** Hangar 3, Suite 109. Pax Service office will provide flight schedules daily by calling C-413-557-2549. The actual signing up for a flight will be done only on Mon, Wed and Fri, 1000-1200 and 1300-1500. This may be accomplished by calling C-413-557-2622. Many facilities available on base.

**PAX LOUNGES:** General facility to accommodate 60-70; DV/VIP facility to accommodate 10.

**FOOD SERVICE:** No inflight kitchen on base. **Snack Bars:** C-413-557-3896.

**TRANSPORTATION:** None available on base. Taxi service, bus station, and train station nearby in Springfield. Bradley International Airport located in Windsor Locks, CT (20 miles from Westover).

**TML:** Lodging office: Flyers Inn, Building 2201, 650 Airlift Drive. (VOQ) C-413-557-2700, D-312-589-2700, Fax: C-413-557-2835, D-312-589-2835, 24 hours daily. SDO, 557-3557. DV/VIP Bldg. 2200. C-413-557-5421.

**TRAVELERS AID:** Chaplain: C-413-557-3031. **Family Readiness Center** on base, C-413-593-1431. **Medical:** C-413-557-3565. **Security Police:** C-413-557-3557.

**SUPPORT AVAILABLE: Exchange:** C-413-593-5941/5413. **Retiree Services:** C-413-557-3424/3918. **Shoppette:** C-413-593-3288. **USO:** C-413-593-6395.

**ATTRACTIONS:** Air Museum (Bradley Field, CT), Basketball Hall of Fame (Springfield), Indian Motorcycle Museum (Springfield), Military Museum (Danbury, CT).

### WESTOVER ARB, MA (CEF); REGION: ATL; OPERATOR: AMC; TYPE: CGO W/ PAX; ROUTE: OFF3A; SAMPLE SCHEDULE: 2ND WED; EQUIPMENT: C005A

{CEF *SW* ➡ NGU (★) *E* ➡ RTA *E* ➡ SIZ ⮀ SIZ *W* ➡ RTA *W* ➡ NGU (★) *N* ➡ CEF}

| LI/ICAO | AIRPORT/STATION | CTRY/STA | DAYS EN ROUTE |
| --- | --- | --- | --- |
| CEF/KCEF | Westover ARB | MA | +0 |
| NGU/KNGU | Norfolk NS | VA | +1 |
| RTA/LERT | Rota NS | ES | +2 |

| LI/ICAO | AIRPORT/STATION | CTRY/STA | DAYS EN ROUTE |
| --- | --- | --- | --- |
| SIZ/LICZ | Sigonella NAS/APT (Sicily) | IT | +2 |
| RTA/LERT | Rota NS | ES | +3 |
| NGU/KNGU | Norfolk NS | VA | +3 |
| CEF/KCEF | Westover ARB | MA | |

### WESTOVER ARB, MA (CEF); REGION: ATL; OPERATOR: AMC; TYPE: CGO W/ PAX; ROUTE: OFR3A; SAMPLE SCHEDULE: 1ST THU; EQUIPMENT: C005A

{CEF *SW* ➡ DOV (★) *NE* ➡ RMS *SE* ➡ NAP ⮀ NAP *W* ➡ RTA *SW* ➡ NGU (★) *NE* ➡ CEF}

| LI/ICAO | AIRPORT/STATION | CTRY/STA | DAYS EN ROUTE |
| --- | --- | --- | --- |
| CEF/KCEF | Westover ARB | MA | +0 |
| DOV/KDOV | Dover AFB | DE | +0 |
| RMS/ETAR | Ramstein AB | DE | +1 |
| NAP/LIRN | Capodichino APT (Naples) | IT | +1 |
| NAP/LIRN | Capodichino APT (Naples) | IT | +1 |
| RTA/LERT | Rota NS | ES | +2 |
| NGU/KNGU | Norfolk NS | VA | +2 |
| CEF/KCEF | Westover ARB | MA | |

### WESTOVER ARB, MA (CEF); REGION: ATL; OPERATOR: AMC; TYPE: CGO W/ PAX; ROUTE: OFV1A; SAMPLE SCHEDULE: 3RD WED; EQUIPMENT: C005A

{CEF *SW* ➡ DOV (★) *NE* ➡ RMS *SE* ➡ AVB ⮀ AVB *NW* ➡ MHZ *SW* ➡ DOV (★) *NE* ➡ CEF}

| LI/ICAO | AIRPORT/STATION | CTRY/STA | DAYS EN ROUTE |
| --- | --- | --- | --- |
| CEF/KCEF | Westover ARB | MA | +0 |
| DOV/KDOV | Dover AFB | DE | +0 |
| RMS/ETAR | Ramstein AB | DE | +1 |
| AVB/LIPA | Aviano AB | IT | +1 |

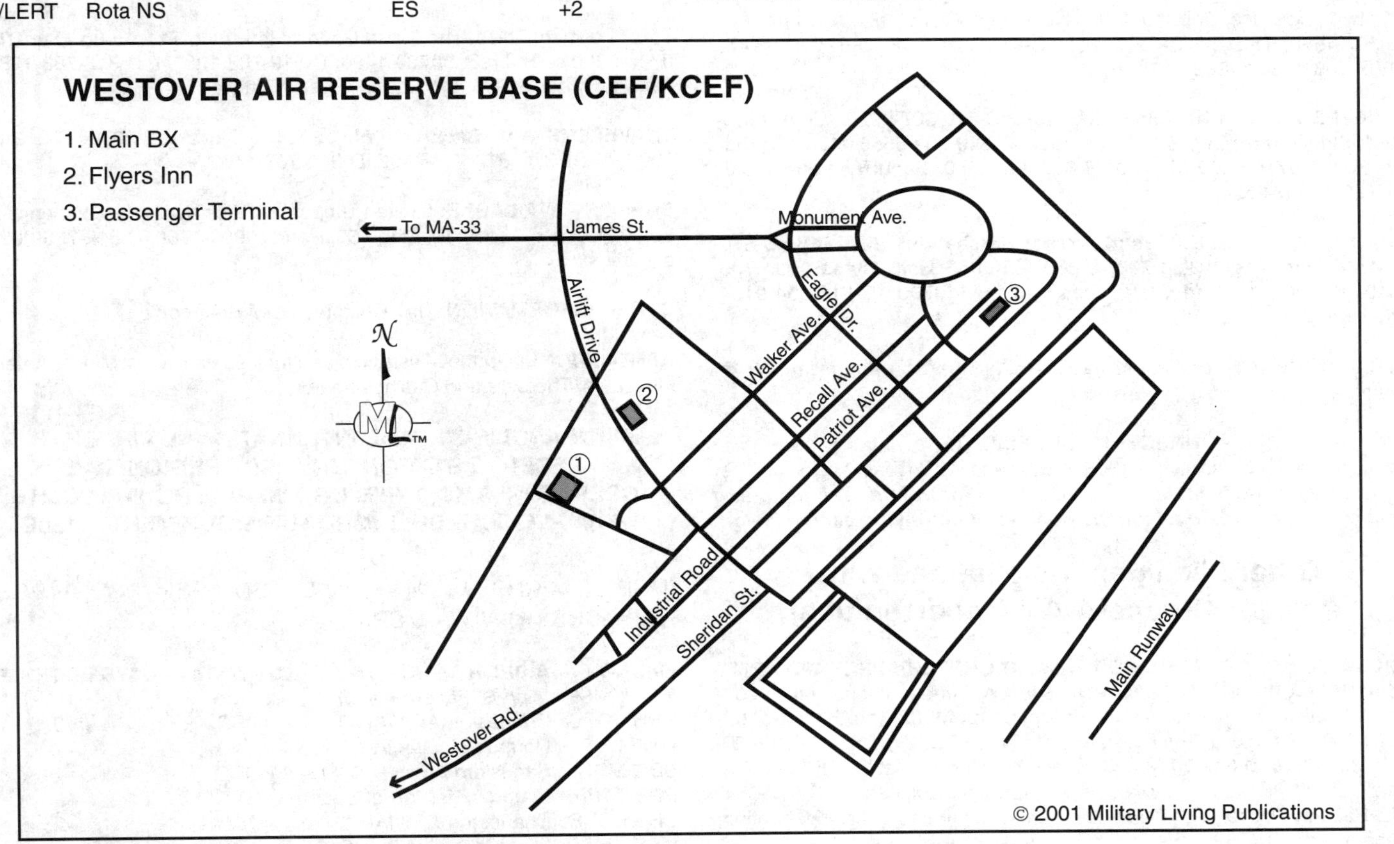

| AVB/LIPA | Aviano AB | IT | +1 |
| MHZ/EGUN | RAF Mildenhall | GB | +2 |
| DOV/KDOV | Dover AFB | DE | +3 |
| CEF/KCEF | Westover ARB | MA | |

### UNSCHEDULED FLIGHTS

Flights via C-005A/B to CONUS and OCONUS via C-005A. Call for destinations, routings and schedules.

# MICHIGAN

## SELFRIDGE AIR NATIONAL GUARD BASE (MTC/KMTC)

127th WG/OTM
29080 Wilbur Wright Blvd
Selfridge ANGB, MI 48045-5207

**LOCATION:** Take I-94 north from Detroit to Selfridge exit 240, then east on MI-59 to main gate of base. *USMRA: Page 66 (G-9); Page 70 (G-1). ML-ARM: (42°37'N/82°49'W).* LST: GMT-05:00. NMC: Detroit, 25 miles southwest. Main installation numbers: C-810-307-5110, D-312-273-5110.

**REGISTRATION INFO: C-810-307-5322, D-312-273-5322, Rec: C-810-307-5884, D-312-273-5884.** At this time there is no Pax Term.

**PAX LOUNGES:** No lounges. Flights are processed by individual units.

**FOOD SERVICE:** Limited services on base. **All Ranks Club:** C-810-307-4785. **Snack Bars:** Bldg 700 (BX), C-810-307-6062.

**TRANSPORTATION: Air Tickets:** SATO, Bldg B-128, C-810-307-4931. **On Base Bus (Comm):** Bldg B-50, C-313-962-5515. **Parking:** Across from Base Ops.

**TML:** Lodging office, Building 410, 410 George Avenue, 24 hours daily, C-810-307-4062, D-312-273-4062. Fax: C-810-307-6102. D-312-273-6102, DV/VIP C-810-307-4062.

**TRAVELERS AID: Chaplain:** Bldg 168, C-810-307-4020. **Emergency Relief:** Bldg 780 (Army), C-810-307-4514, C-810-739-6558. **Medical:** Bldg 310, Hours: 0715-1600 Mon-Fri, C-810-307-4650. **Security Police:** Bldg 300, C-810-307-2621.

**SUPPORT AVAILABLE: Bank/Currency Exchange:** Bldg 718, C-810-307-4744. **Exchange:** Bldg 700, C-810-465-0960. **Hair Styles:** Bldg 700, C-810-468-8009. **Laundry/Dry Cleaning:** Bldg 700, C-810-954-9134. **Postal Service:** Bldg 178.

**ATTRACTIONS:** City of Detroit, Lake St Clair, Canada approximately 40 minutes away.

### UNSCHEDULED FLIGHTS

A few flights each week via KC-135E to East and West Coast and Southeast CONUS. Flights are processed by ANG and AFRES. *Note: Call recording number for appropriate telephone number of unit flying each mission.*

## Other Michigan Installations with Possible Space-A Air Opportunities

**ALPENA COMBAT READINESS TRAINING CENTER/ALPENA COUNTY REGIONAL AIRPORT (APN/KAPN),** 5884 A Street, Alpena, MI 49707-8125. **LOCATION:** Five miles west of Alpena on MI-32, (north side of MI-32). *USMRA: Page 66 (F-4). ML-ARM: (45°04'N/83°38'W).* LST: GMT-05:00. **C-517-354-6305, D-312-741-3305.** Snack Vending available. Off Base Car Rental: C-517-354-3222, civilian airport terminal. Exchange: C-517-354-6272. Security Police: C-517-354-6210. Lake Huron shore, fishing, hunting, and camping.

### UNSCHEDULED FLIGHTS

Flights available during National Guard and Reserve training periods. Call for destinations, routings and schedules.

# MINNESOTA

## MINNEAPOLIS-ST PAUL INTERNATIONAL AIRPORT/ AIR RESERVE STATION (MSP/KMSP)

| 133rd AW (ANG) | 934th AW (AFRC) |
| 133 OSF/DO | 934 OSF/OSA |
| 641 Spitfire Ave | 760 MilitaryHighway |
| St Paul, MN 55111-4122 | Minneapolis ARS, MN 55450-2000 |

**LOCATION:** From I-35 west or MN-55 south to crosstown MN-62, exit at 34th Avenue and entrance. Or I-495 east to exit 1A on MN-5 and entrance west to airport. *USMRA: Page 89 (C-3). ML-ARM: (44°53'N/93°13'W).* LST: GMT-06:00. NMC: Minneapolis-St Paul, in city limits. Main installation numbers: ANG: C-612-713-2501, D-312-783-2501; AFRES: C-612-713-1110, D-312-783-1000.

**REGISTRATION INFO: ANG: C-612-713-2461/2474, D-312-783-2461/2474, Rec: C-612-713-2450, D-312-783-2450.** Bldg 641, Base Ops, Hours: 0730-1600 daily. **AFRES: C-612-713-1701, D-312-783-1701, Rec: C-612-713-1741, D-312-783-1741, Fax: 612-713-1747, D-312-783-1747.** Bldg 821, Base Ops, Hours: daily 0630-1515. Directions: From main gate make a left and follow road. Passenger processing on left. Separate facilities maintained by ANG and AFRES.

**PAX LOUNGES:** No lounges. All passengers wait in and are processed by Base Ops.

**FOOD SERVICE: NCO Club:** C-612-713-1655. **O Club:** C-612-713-3670. Snack Vending available.

**TRANSPORTATION: Off Base Car Rental:** C-612-830-2345, C-612-727-200, C-800-331-1212, 5 minutes away. **Off Base Limo Service:** 612-726-5479, 5 minutes away. **Off Base Taxi:** C-612-721-6566, 5 minutes away. **Off Base Train Station:** Amtrak, C-800-872-7245, 25 minutes away.

**TML:** Lodging Office: The North Country Inn, Bldg 711, Hours: Sun-Thurs 0700-2200 daily, Fri/Sat 0700-1400, C-612-783-1983/4, D-312-783-1983/4, Fax: C-612-713-1966, C-312-783-1966. All ranks.

**TRAVELERS AID: Security Police:** ANG: C-612-713-2002, D-312-783-2002; AFRES: C-612-713-1102, D-312-783-1102.

**SUPPORT AVAILABLE:** Limited support facilities available. **Exchange:** Air Force Reserve, 934th AW, Bldg 755, Hours: 0900-1700, C-612-726-9023, 2 minutes away.

**OTHER INFORMATION:** U.S. Customs Service Airport.

**ATTRACTIONS:** On the Mississippi and Minnesota Rivers. Mall of America. Museums, Theaters and Casinos nearby.

**MINNEAPOLIS-ST PAUL INTERNATIONAL AIRPORT/AIR RESERVE STATION, MN (MSP); REGION: PAC; OPERATOR: AMC; TYPE: CGO W/ PAX; ROUTE: 9QM1B; SAMPLE SCHEDULE: 3RD TUE; EQUIPMENT: C130E**

{MSP *SE* ➡ CHS (★) *SW* ➡ KIN *E* ➡ SDQ *SE* ➡ POS ⇌ POS *NW* ➡ CHS (★) *NW* ➡ MSP}

| LI/ICAO | AIRPORT/STATION | CTRY/STA | DAYS EN ROUTE |
|---|---|---|---|
| MSP/KMSP | Minn-St Paul IAP/ARS | MN | +0 |
| CHS/KCHS | Charleston AFB/IAP | SC | +0 |
| KIN/MKJP | Norman Manley IAP | JM | +1 |
| SDQ/MDSI | San Isidro AB | DO | +1 |
| POS/TTPP | Piarco APT (Port-of-Spain) | TT | +2 |
| CHS/KCHS | Charleston AFB/IAP | SC | +2 |
| MSP/KMSP | Minn-St Paul IAP/ARS | MN | |

### UNSCHEDULED FLIGHTS

Flights to CONUS locations via ANG C-130H and AFRES C-130E aircraft. Most flights on weekends. Call for destinations, routings and schedules.

# MISSISSIPPI

## COLUMBUS AIR FORCE BASE (CBM/KCBM)

14th Flight Training Wing
Columbus AFB, MS 39710-1000

**LOCATION:** From Columbus north on US-45, five miles north and west of US-45. *USMRA: Page 43 (G-3). ML-ARM: (33°36'N/88°26'W).* LST: GMT-06:00. NMC: Columbus, 10 miles south. Main installation numbers: C-662-434-7322, D-312-742-1110.

**REGISTRATION INFO: C-662-434-2862/7322, D-312-742-2861/7322.** Hours: 0700-1200 Mon-Fri, 1000-1700 Sat-Sun.

**TML:** Magnolia Inn, 79 F St, Suite 1607, 24 hours daily, C-662-434-2548/2372, D-312-742-2548. Fax: C-662-434-277, DV/VIP 662-434-7002.

### UNSCHEDULED FLIGHTS

Infrequent flight via MEDEVAC and C-141B aircraft to CONUS locations. Call for destinations, routings and schedules.

## JACKSON INTERNATIONAL AIRPORT/ ALLEN C. THOMPSON FIELD (JAN/KJAN)

172 APF
141 Military Drive, Bldg 181
Jackson, MS 39208-8874

**LOCATION:** Off I-20 east or west and US-80. From I-20 exit 52 north to IAP. Clearly marked. *USMRA: Page 43 (D-6). ML-ARM: (32°18'N/90°04'W).* LST: GMT-06:00. NMC: Jackson, 5 miles west. Main installation numbers: C-601-936-8730, D-312-731-9730.

**REGISTRATION INFO: C-601-936-8761, D-312-731-7319 (Rec after hours), Fax: C-601-936-8698, D-312-731-9698. E-mail: 172aw.spacea@ msjack.ang.af.mil (to sign up) WEB: 172aw.ang.af.mil** Bldg 181, Hours: 0730-1600 Mon-Fri, No separate Pax Term, Space-A desk is open every other Monday and every Tues-Thur 0930-1200 hours. Passengers are to wait in the dining hall. No military support facilities. All the support of a commercial airport provided.

**TML:** Nearest TML is at Meridian NAS, Lodging office, 24 hours daily. Building 218 (CBQ), Fuller Road, BEQ C-601-679-2186, D-312-637-2186, Fax: C-601-679-2745.

**OTHER INFORMATION:** U.S. Customs Service Airport.

**ATTRACTIONS:** Historic homes.

**ALLEN C. THOMPSON FIELD, MS (JAN); REGION: ATL; OPERATOR: AMC; TYPE: CGO W/ PAX; ROUTE: IKB7A; SAMPLE SCHEDULE: 1ST WED; EQUIPMENT: C141B**

{JAN *NE* ➡ CHS (★) *SW* ➡ SJO (★) *SE* ➡ SCL *N* ➡ LPB *SE* ➡ VIU ⇌ VIU *NW* ➡ CUR *NE* ➡ CHS(★) *SW* ➡ JAN}

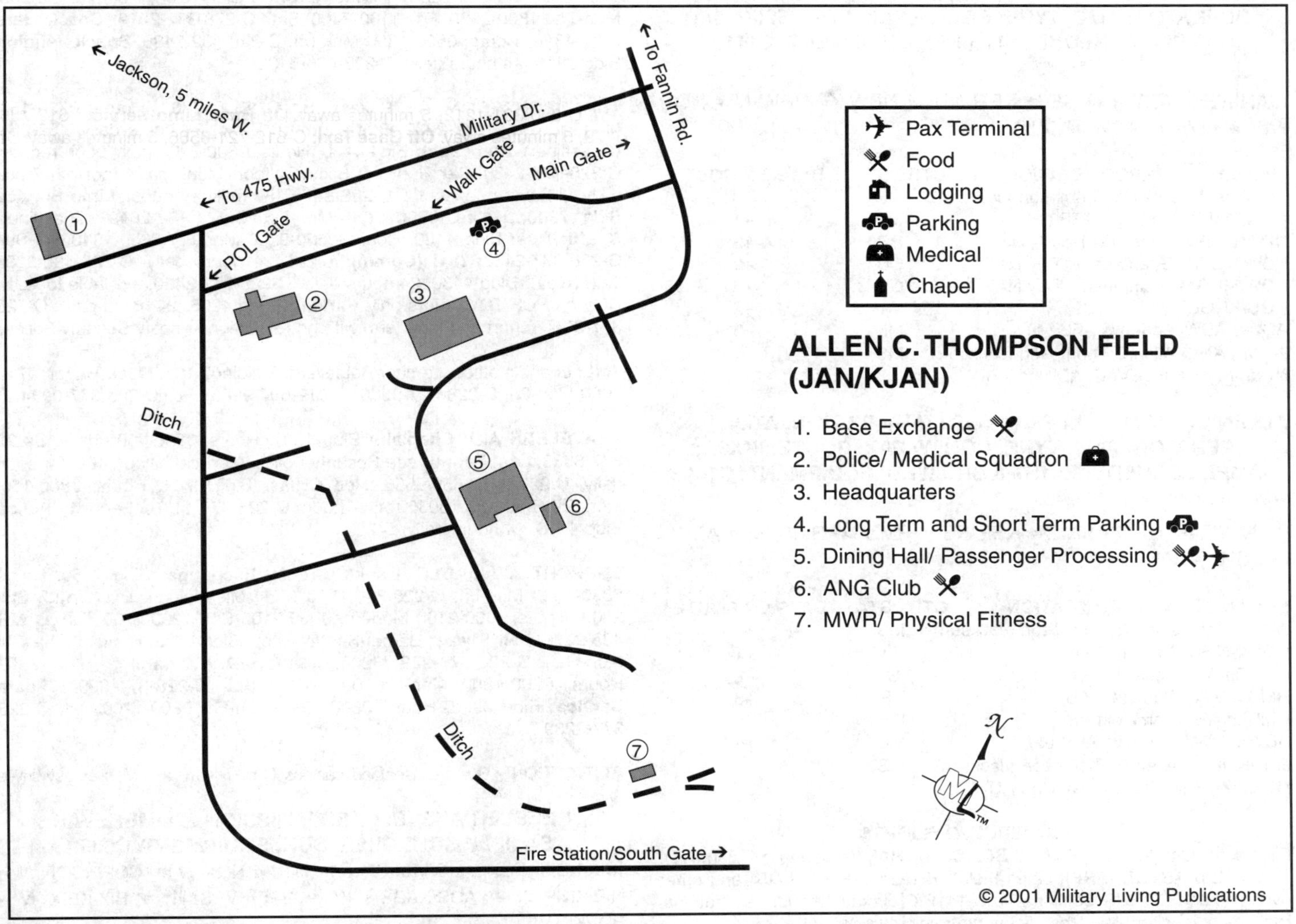

### ALLEN C. THOMPSON FIELD (JAN/KJAN)

1. Base Exchange
2. Police/ Medical Squadron
3. Headquarters
4. Long Term and Short Term Parking
5. Dining Hall/ Passenger Processing
6. ANG Club
7. MWR/ Physical Fitness

© 2001 Military Living Publications

| LI/ICAO | AIRPORT/STATION | CTRY/STA | DAYS EN ROUTE |
|---|---|---|---|
| JAN/KJAN | Allen C Thompson (Jackson) | MS | +0 |
| CHS/KCHS | Charleston AFB/IAP | SC | +0 |
| SJO/MROC | Juan Santamaria IAP (San Jose) | CR | +1 |
| SCL/SCEL | Arturo Merino Benitez IAP (Santiago) | CL | +2 |
| LPB/SLLP | JF Kennedy IAP (La Paz) | BO | +2 |
| VVI/SLVR | Viru Viru IAP (Santa Cruz) | BO | +3 |
| CUR/TNCC | Hato | AN | +4 |
| CHS/KCHS | Charleston AFB/IAP | SC | +4 |
| JAN/KJAN | Allen C Thompson (Jackson) | MS | |

### ALLEN C. THOMPSON FIELD, MS (JAN); REGION: ATL; OPERATOR: AMC; TYPE: CGO W/ PAX; ROUTE: IKH5A; SAMPLE SCHEDULE: 3RD WED; EQUIPMENT: C141B

{JAN *NE* ➡ CHS (★) *SE* ➡ STX *SE* ➡ RIO ⮂ RIO *NW* ➡ BSB *NW* ➡ STX *NW* ➡ CHS (★) *SW* ➡ JAN}

| LI/ICAO | AIRPORT/STATION | CTRY/STA | DAYS EN ROUTE |
|---|---|---|---|
| JAN/KJAN | Allen C Thompson (Jackson) | MS | +0 |
| CHS/KCHS | Charleston AFB/IAP | SC | +0 |
| STX/TISX | Alexander Hamilton Apt (St Croix) | VI | +1 |
| RIO/SBGL | Rio de Janeiro IAP (Brazil) | BR | +1 |
| BSB/SBBR | Brasilia APT | BR | +2 |
| STX/TISX | Alexander Hamilton Apt (St Croix) | VI | +4 |
| CHS/KCHS | Charleston AFB/IAP | SC | +4 |
| JAN/KJAN | Allen C Thompson (Jackson) | MS | |

### ALLEN C. THOMPSON FIELD, MS (JAN); REGION: ATL; OPERATOR: AMC; TYPE: CGO W/ PAX; ROUTE: IKM3A; SAMPLE SCHEDULE: 4TH FRI; EQUIPMENT: C141B

{JAN *NE* ➡ ADW (★) *SE* ➡ NRR *NW* ➡ NBW ⮂ NBW *N* ➡ NGU *NW* ➡ ADW (★) *SW* ➡ JAN}

| LI/ICAO | AIRPORT/STATION | CTRY/STA | DAYS EN ROUTE |
|---|---|---|---|
| JAN/KJAN | Allen C Thompson (Jackson) | MS | +0 |
| ADW/KADW | Andrews AFB (✚) | MD | +1 |
| NRR/TJNR | Roosevelt Roads NS | PR | +2 |
| NBW/MUGM | Guantanamo Bay NAS | CU | +2 |
| NBW/MUGM | Guantanamo Bay NAS | CU | +2 |
| NGU/KNGU | Norfolk NS | VA | +2 |
| ADW/KADW | Andrews AFB (✚) | MD | +3 |
| JAN/KJAN | Allen C Thompson (Jackson) | MS | |

**Note:** (✚) = MEDEVAC: ADW to ADW

### ALLEN C. THOMPSON FIELD, MS (JAN); REGION: ATL; OPERATOR: AMC; TYPE: CGO W/ PAX; ROUTE: IKX3A; SAMPLE SCHEDULE: 1ST & 3RD WED; EQUIPMENT: C141B

{JAN *NE* ➡ NGU (★) *NE* ➡ KEF *SE* ➡ RMS ⮂ RMS *W* ➡ ADW (★) *SW* ➡ JAN}

| LI/ICAO | AIRPORT/STATION | CTRY/STA | DAYS EN ROUTE |
|---|---|---|---|
| JAN/KJAN | Allen C Thompson (Jackson) | MS | +0 |
| NGU/KNGU | Norfolk NS (✚) | VA | +1 |
| KEF/BIKF | Keflavik APT | IS | +2 |
| RMS/ETAR | Ramstein AB | DE | +3 |
| RMS/ETAR | Ramstein AB | DE | +3 |
| ADW/KADW | Andrews AFB (✚) | MD | +4 |
| JAN/KJAN | Allen C Thompson (Jackson) | MS | |

**Note:** (✚) = MEDEVAC: NGU to ADW

### UNSCHEDULED FLIGHTS

Flights to: Charleston AFB/IAP, SC (**CHS**); RAF Mildenhall, GB (**MHZ**); Rhein-Main AB, DE (**FRF**); Lajes Field AB (Azores), PT (**LGS**) and other overseas and CONUS locations via C-141B/C aircraft. Call for destinations, routings and schedules. Most flights on training weekends.

# KEESLER AIR FORCE BASE (BIX/KBIX)

45 AS/AOFAM
817 H Street, Suite 102
Keesler AFB, MS 39534-2452

**LOCATION:** From I-10 exit 46 south on I-110 to base, west of I-110. From US-90, north on White Avenue to main gate. *USMRA: Page 43 (F-10). ML-ARM: (30°41'N/88°92'W).* LST: GMT-06:00. NMC: Biloxi, in the city. Main installation numbers: C-228-377-1110, D-312-597-1110.

**REGISTRATION INFO:** C-228-377-2120, D-312-597-4538, **Rec:** C-228-377-4538, D-312-597-4538, (Updated daily 0800), Fax: C-228-377-2459, D-312-597-2459. Bldg 0233, Hours: 0700-2300 daily. Closed all Federal holidays. Directions: From main gate straight on Larcher Blvd, left on Meadows Drive, right on Hangar Road to H Street, Terminal faces H Street.

**PAX LOUNGE:** Base Ops, located on H Street and Hangar Road. **General:** Bldg 0233, Hours: 0700-2300 Mon-Fri, C-228-377-2120. A/C, read/write rooms, telephone (local and defense), TV, restrooms, P/C and O/S seats. **DV/VIP:** Bldg 0233, Hours: 0700-2300 Mon-Fri, C-228-377-2215. Coffee/tea, telephones (long distance). **Protocol Service:** Bldg 2816, Hours: 0700-1630 Mon-Fri, O7+, C-228-377-3359 (Air Education and Training Command).

**FOOD SERVICE: Cafeteria:** Bldg 2001, Hours: 0415-0730,1030-1315, 1645-1930 daily, C-228-377-3854 (Gulf Breeze). **Enlisted Club:** Bldg 7503, Hours: 0800-2200 Mon-Thu, 0800-2400 Fri, 1100-2400 Sat, C-228-377-2424. **NCO/CPO Club:** Bldg 2221, Hours: 0630-1030, 1100-1330, 1700-2100 daily, C-228-377-3439. **O Club:** Bldg 3208, Hours: 1730-2030 Mon-Thu,1800-2130 Fri, 1100-2400 Sat, C-228-377-2219. **Snack Bars:** Bldg 4328, Hours: 0630-1300 Mon-Fri, C-228-432-7488. **Snack Vending:** Bldg 3216, 24 hours daily, C-228-435-5130.

**TRANSPORTATION: Air Tickets:** SATO, Bldg 2303, Hours: 0730-1600 Mon-Fri, C-228-377-2230. **Bus (Comm):** Biloxi, 24 hours daily, 432-2649 (Coastliner). **Bus (Gov):** Bldg 4430, Hours: 0600-2300 daily upon request, C-228-377-2430. **Car Rentals:** Biloxi/Gulfport Municipal Airport, 24 hours daily, U-Save Auto Rental, C-228-864-5181 (military rates). **Limo Service:** Bldg 7303, Hours: 0800-1700 Mon-Fri, C-228-432-2649 (Coastliner). **Shuttle/Bus:** Bldg 4430, Hours: 0630-2200 Mon-Fri, 0630-1940 Sat-Sun, C-228-377-2430. **Taxi (Comm):** Biloxi, 24 hours daily, C-228-436-3788. **Taxi (Gov):** Bldg 4430, 24 hours daily, C-228-377-2430, available to Active Duty on PCS/TDY orders only. **Parking:** Bldg 4205, 24 hours daily, C-228-377-3040 (short and long term with no restrictions - notify Security Police).

**TML:** Lodging office, Larcher Boulevard, Building 2101, Muse Manor, 0715-1600 Mon-Fri, C-228-377-9886, D-312-597-9986, Fax: C-228-377-0084.

**TRAVELERS AID: Chaplain:** Bldg 1901, Hours: 0730-1600 daily, C-228-377-8633. **Lost/Found:** see Security Police. **Medical:** Bldg 0468, 24 hours daily, C-228-377-6555/6556. **Red Cross:** Bldg 0701, Hours: 0800-1600 Mon-Fri, C-228-377-3030 (other hours C-228-377-1110). **Security Police:** Bldg 4703, 24 hours daily, C-228-377-2878.

**SUPPORT AVAILABLE: Bank/Currency Exchange:** Bldg 1550, Hours: 0830-1500 Mon-Fri, C-228-374-1740 (First Mississippi). **Exchange:** Bldg 2303, Hours: 0900-2100 Mon-Fri, 0900-2100 Sat, 1200-1700 Sun, C-228-435-2216. **Hair Styles:** Barber/Beauty Shop, Bldg 2303, Hours: 0900-1700 Mon-Sat, C-228-377-2221/3200. **Laundry/Dry Cleaning:** Bldg 2303, Hours: 0900-1800 Mon-Fri, 0900-1700 Sat, C-228-374-6994. **Postal Service:** Bldg 3913, Hours: 0800-1630 Mon-Fri, 0800-1200 Sat, C-228-377-2289.

**ATTRACTIONS:** Beaches, seafood, casinos, New Orleans and Mobile easy drives.

### KEESLER AFB (BIX/KBIX); MISSION 226/MEDEVAC; SAMPLE SCHEDULE: SUN; EQUIPMENT: C009A

{BIX/KBIX *SE* ➡ MCF/KMCF *S* ➡ NQX/KNQX *N* ➡ COF/KCOF *N* ➡ NIP/KNIP *N* ➡ AGS/KAGS *SW* ➡ VPS/KVPS *W* ➡ BIX/KBIX *N* ➡ BLV/KBLV}

| LI | AIRPORT/STATION | CTRY/STA |
|---|---|---|
| BIX/KBIX | Keesler AFB | MS |
| MCF/KMCF | MacDill AFB | FL |
| NQX/KNQX | Key West NAS | FL |
| COF/KCOF | Patrick AFB | FL |
| NIP/KNIP | Jacksonville NAS | FL |
| AGS/KAGS | Bush Field Apt | GA |
| VPS/KVPS | Eglin AFB | FL |
| BIX/KBIX | Keesler AFB | MS |
| BLV/KBLV | Scott AFB | IL |

### EN ROUTE SCHEDULES

| AIRPORT/STATION | LI-MISSION (page #) |
|---|---|
| Scott AFB | BLV-C-616/MEDEVAC (30) |
| Scott AFB | BLV-C-626/MEDEVAC (30) |
| Scott AFB | BLV-C-652/MEDEVAC (30) |

### UNSCHEDULED FLIGHTS

Flights to CONUS and OCONUS via C-130E and WC-130H aircraft. Call for destinations, routings and schedules.

## KEY FIELD AIRPORT (MEI/KMEI)

186th Air Refueling Wing (ARW)
6225 M Street, Bldg 308, Room 114B
Meridian, MS 39307-7112

**LOCATION:** From I-20 west, take US-45 south, Air National Guard signs clearly marked. Field is east of US-45. *USMRA: Page 43 (F-6). ML-ARM: (32°18'N/88°46'W).* LST: GMT-06:00. NMC: Meridian 3 miles northeast. NMI: Meridian NAS 20 miles north of airport. Main installation numbers: C-601-484-9000, D-312-778-9000.

**REGISTRATION INFO: C-601-484-9730, D-312-778-9730, Rec: C-601-484-9730, D-312-778-9730; Fax: C-601-484-9470, D-312-778-9470.** No military support at Key Field Airport.

**PAX LOUNGE:** Available in Ops Bldg. Directions: Located in OPS Bldg 308, one block south of main gate.

**FOOD SERVICE:** Vending machines in Ops Bldg.

**TRANSPORTATION:** Off Base Taxi and Car Rental available.

**TML:** Nearest TML is at Meridian NAS, Lodging office, 24 hours daily. Building 218 (CBQ), Fuller Road, BEQ C-601-679-2186, D-312-367-2186, Fax: C-601-679-3174.

**OTHER INFORMATION:** Frequent flights via Ang KC-135R to CONUS and OCONUS locations. Call for destinations, routing and schedules. No recurring scheduled OCONUS flights at this time.

### UNSCHEDULED FLIGHTS

Frequent flights via ANG KC-135R aircraft to CONUS and OCONUS locations. Call for destinations, routings and schedules.

## MERIDIAN NAVAL AIR STATION (NMM/KNMM)

Operations Duty Officer, Box 2, ATCF
Meridian NAS, 100 Fuller Road
Meridian, MS 39305-5000

**LOCATION:** Take MS-39 north from Meridian, for 12 miles to four-lane access road. Clearly marked. Right for three miles to NAS main gate. *USMRA: Page 43 (G-6). ML-ARM: (32°55'N/88°56'W).* LST: GMT-06:00. NMC: Meridian, 15 miles southwest. Main installation numbers: C-601-679-2211, D-312-367-2211.

**REGISTRATION INFO: C-601-679-2505, D-312-367-2505, Fax: C-601-679-2038, D-312-367-2038.** Bldg 1, Hours: 0700-2300 Mon-Fri, closed Sat and Sun. Directions: From main gate straight on Whitaker Blvd to a right on Fuller Road for 3 miles to Base Ops on the left. **Pax Service Office:** Base Ops, Hours: 0700-2300 Mon-Thu, 0700-2300 Fri, C-601-679-2505 (NCO on duty).

**PAX LOUNGES:** Limited lounge facilities. Pax Term Information, Hours: 0700-2300 Mon-Fri. **General:** Base Ops, Hours: 0700-2300 Mon-Fri, C-601-679-2505. A/C, bag check, restrooms, P/C seats. **DV/VIP:** Base Ops, Hours: 0700-2300 Mon-Thu, 1300-2200 Fri, C-601-679-2505 (O6+ - on request). **Protocol Service:** Bldg 200, Hours: 1300-1800 Mon-Fri, D-312-367-2318.

**FOOD SERVICE: Cafeteria:** Bldg 1, Hours: 0700-1800 Mon-Fri, C-601-679-2681. **Fast Food:** McDonald's, Hours: 0700-2000 daily. **All Hands Recreation Club:** Bldg 365, Hours: 1600-0400 Mon-Sat:, C-601-679-2650. **Restaurants:** Bldg 1, Hours: 0630-1900 Mon-Fri, C-601-679-2505. **Snack Bars:** Bldg 1, Hours: 1400-2300 Mon-Fri, C-601-679-2505. **Snack Vending:** Bldg 1, Hours: 0700-2300 Mon-Fri:, C-601-679-2505.

**TRANSPORTATION: Off Base Taxi:** Meridian city cab is available for off base transportation. **Parking:** Short term, Base Ops, Hours: 1400-0300 Mon-Thu, 1400-2200 Fri-Sun, C-601-679-2454 (across street - 1 week limit).

**TML:** Lodging office, 24 hours daily. Building 218 (CBQ), Fuller Road, BEQ C-601-679-2186, D-312-367-2186, Fax: C-601-679-3173.

**TRAVELERS AID: Chaplain:** Bldg 211, Hours: 0800-1700 Mon-Fri, C-601-679-2475. **Emergency Relief:** Bldg 362, Hours: 1000-1300 Mon-Fri, C-601-679-2504 (Navy Relief). **Red Cross:** Bldg 362, Hours: 0800-1300 Mon,Wed,Fri, C-601-679-2679. **Security Police:** Main gate, 24 hours daily, C-601-679-2361.

**SUPPORT AVAILABLE: Bank/Currency Exchange:** NEX Mall, Hours: 0900-1500 Mon-Fri, C-601-679-2501 (NFCU). **Exchange:** NEX Mall, Hours: 1000-1800 Mon-Fri, C-601-679-2725. **Hair Styles:** NEX Mall, Hours: 1000-1800 Mon-Sat; Barber, C-601-679-2569; Beauty, C-601-679-8411. **Laundry:** NEX Mall, Hours: 1000-1800 Mon-Sat:, C-601-679-2632. **Medical/Dental:** Map #50, 24 hours daily, C-601-679-2444. **Postal Service:** Map #30, Hours: 0800-1600 Mon-Fri, C-601-679-2211.

**ATTRACTIONS:** Fishing, hunting, swimming, stables, Jimmy Rogers Country Music Museum in downtown Meridian.

### UNSCHEDULED FLIGHTS

Call for destinations, routings and schedules.

## VICKSBURG MUNICIPAL AIRPORT (VKS/KVIKS

5855 Highway 61 S
Vicksburg, MS 39180-5000

**LOCATION:** Take US-61 south from I-20 east or west for six miles, exit west to airport. *USMRA: Page 43 (C-6). ML-ARM: (32°23'N/90°92'W).* LST: GMT-06:00. NMC: Vicksburg, 6 miles north. Main installation numbers: C-601-638-6550.

**REGISTRATION INFO: C-601-638-6550, Fax: C-601-636-0681.** Army Reserve, Hours: 0730-1600 daily. Army Reserve Hangar is the largest hangar on south end of field. No Pax Term. All passengers processed through Base Ops. Commercial facilities available at Commercial Pax Term. **TML:** Nearest TML is at Meridian NAS, Lodging office, 24 hours daily. Building 218 (CBQ), Fuller Road, BEQ C-601-679-2186, D-312-367-2186, Fax: C-601-679-2745.

### UNSCHEDULED FLIGHTS

Flights via UH-IH aircraft to: Birmingham IAP, AL (**BHM**); Cairns AAF, AL (**OZR**) and Lawson AAF, GA (**LSF**). Call for other destinations, routings and schedules.

# MISSOURI

## ROSECRANS MEMORIAL AIRPORT
## (STJ/KSTJ)

139th AW, 705 Memorial Drive
St Joseph, MO 64503-9307

**LOCATION:** From US-36 east or west exit west of I-229 on MO-238. Straight 1.5 miles to airport entrance. *USMRA: Page 81 (B-3). ML-ARM: (39°46'N/94°53'W).* LST: GMT-06:00. NMC: St Joseph, 4 miles southeast. NMI: Fort Leavenworth, KS, 28 miles south. Main installation numbers: C-816-236-3300, D-312-956-3300. ***Note: Limited airport services. Commercial taxi to Kansas City IAP is only available transportation.***

**REGISTRATION INFO: C-816-236-3260, D-312-956-3260, Rec: C-816-236-3472, D-312-956-3472, Fax: C-816-236-3239, D-312-956-3239.** No Pax Term. Base Ops handles Pax Term duties on time available basis. Bldg 17, Squadron Operations, Hours: 0730-1600 daily. Ask Security Police for ANG facility. All support facilities of a regional airport. Main gate open 24 hours daily.

**FOOD SERVICE: Cafeteria:** Hours: 0600-1500, C-816-364-0319. **Tower Restaurant:** Hours: 0600-1500, C-816-364-0319. **Snack Vending:** Bldg 17, Base Ops.

**TRANSPORTATION: Heartland Express:** 3801 Oakland, C-816-279-7800. **Off Base Taxi:** Yellow Cab Co., C-816-279-2777. **Taylor's Transportation KCI:** 2826 Oakland, C-16-233-8753. ***Note: It is best to get several people to share the transportation cost to Kansas City IAP. It can take an hour or more for any form of transportation to arrive and the cost is high. After hours (1800) and on weekends it is difficult to get transportation unless prior arrangements have been made.***

**TML:** Nearest TML is at Fort Leavenworth, KS, Lodging office, Building 695, 210 Grant Avenue, 24 hours daily, C-913-684-4091, D-312-552-4091, Fax: C-913-684-4097. DV/VIP C-913-684-4065.

**ATTRACTIONS:** In St Joseph, Pony Express museums, Jesse James' home, National Military Heritage Museum and St Joseph River Boat Casino.

### UNSCHEDULED FLIGHTS
Flights via C-130H aircraft to CONUS stations. Call for destinations, routings and schedules.

## WAYNESVILLE REGIONAL AIRPORT
## AT FORNEY ARMY AIRFIELD (TBN/KTBN)

2579 Iowa Avenue
Fort Leonard Wood, MO 65473-8948

**LOCATION:** Two miles south of I-44 exit 161 south, adjacent to St. Robert & Waynesville, at Fort Leonard Wood exit. *USMRA: Page 81 (E-6). ML-ARM: (37°73'N/92°14'W).* LST: GMT-06:00. NMC: Springfield, 85 miles southwest. NMI: Fort Leonard Wood, on base. Main installation numbers: C-573-596-0131, D-312-581-0110.

**REGISTRATION INFO: C-573-596-0165, D-312-581-0165, Fax: C-573-596-0166, D-312-581-0166. WEB: www.wood.army.mil** Base Ops, Hours: 0730-1630 Mon-Fri, closed Sat, Sun and holidays. Directions: From south gate straight on Iowa Ave to left exit to WRAAF. Commercial Pax Term and commercial flights at WRAAF. Commercial number is C-314-329-3400. All the support of a large fort available at nearby Fort Leonard Wood.

**FOOD SERVICE: Fast Food:** Hours: 0600-2200, C-573-329-5677, 2 miles north. Snack Vending available.

**TRANSPORTATION: On Base Bus:** Greyhound, C-573-329-4232, 2 miles north. **On Base Car Rental:** Hertz, C-573-329-6688, 2 miles north in Main PX. **On Base Taxi:** C-573-596-1927. **Off Base Taxi:** C-573-329-2100. Off Base Limo service available.

**TML:** Lodging office, Building 470, Missouri Avenue, 24 hours daily, C-573-596-0999, or 1-800-677-8356. D-312-581-8356, DV/VIP C-593-596-8070/1.

**SUPPORT AVAILABLE: Bank:** Hours: 0900-1630, C-573-329-2000, 2 miles north. **Credit Union:** Hours: 0900-1700, C-573-329-3151, 2 miles north. **Exchange:** Hours: 0900-2100, C-573-329-2200, 2 miles north. **Laundry/Dry Cleaner:** Hours: 0900-1800, C-573-329-3490, Main PX. **Postal Service:** Hours: 0800-1600, C-573-329-2717, 2 miles north. **Shoppette:** Hours: 0600-2300, C-573-329-6200, 1 mile north.

**ATTRACTIONS:** U.S. Army Engineer Museum, 1000-1700 Mon-Sat, admission is free and open to the public. For more information, call C-573-596-4249.

### EN ROUTE SCHEDULES

| AIRPORT/STATION | LI-MISSION (page #) |
|---|---|
| Scott AFB | BLV-C-666/MEDEVAC (30) |

### UNSCHEDULED FLIGHTS
Flights to east and southeast CONUS via C-12A, C-009A/E MEDEVAC and C-21A aircraft. Baggage limit 30 lbs. Call for destinations, routings, and schedules.

## WHITEMAN AIR FORCE BASE (SZL/KSZL)

745 Arnold Ave, Suite 2A
Whiteman AFB, MO 65305-5026

**LOCATION:** From I-70 east exit 49 south to US-13 south to US-50 east for ten miles, Hwy 23 (south) which leads to base, south of US-50 and east of MO-23. *USMRA: Page 81 (C-5). ML-ARM: (38°42'N/93°34'W).* LST: GMT-06:00. NMC: Kansas City, 60 miles northwest. Main installation numbers: C-660-687-1110, D-312-975-1110.

**REGISTRATION INFO: C-660-687-3101, D-312-975-3101, Fax: C-660-687-6106, D-312-975-6106.** Bldg 35. Full base support available.

**PAX LOUNGES:** DV/VIP lounges available.

**TML:** Whiteman Inn, Building 325, Spirit Boulevard, 24 hours daily, C-660-687-1844, D-312-975-1844, Fax: C-660-687-3052. DV/VIP, Protocol Office, O6/GS15+, C-660-687-7144.

**SUPPORT AVAILABLE:** Exchange available.

### EN ROUTE SCHEDULES

| AIRPORT/STATION | LI-MISSION (page #) |
|---|---|
| Scott AFB | BLV-C-666/MEDEVAC (30) |

### UNSCHEDULED FLIGHTS
Infrequent MEDEVAC and flights of opportunity to midwest areas. Call for destinations, routings and schedules.

# MONTANA

## GREAT FALLS INTERNATIONAL AIRPORT/
## AIR NATIONAL GUARD BASE (GTF/KGTF)

Attn: Holman Aviation Co
Malmstrom AFB
1940 Airport Court
P.O. Box 2228
Great Falls, MT 59403-2228

**LOCATION:** Great Falls International Airport exit 277 is off I-15, and is one mile south of the 10th Avenue south exit. Follow Airport Drive to intersection with Airport Court. Follow Airport Court to old terminal building. *USMRA: Page 99 (D,E-4). ML-ARM: (47°29'N/111°21'W).* LST: GMT-06:00. NMC: Great Falls, 3 mile est. NMI: Malmstrom AFB, 10 miles east. Main installation numbers: C-406-791-6285, D-312-279-2285.

**REGISTRATION INFO:** C-406-731-4622 or 406-453-7613, D-312-632-4622, **Fax:** 406-731-4312 or 406-453-7204, D-312-632-4312. **E-mail:** dan.littleton@malmstrom.af.mil, john.robbins@malmstrom.af.mil, ryan.pokorny@malmstrom.af.mil Directions: see above. **Pax Service Office:** C-406-453-7613.

**PAX LOUNGES: General:** 1940 Airport Court, C-406-453-7613.

**FOOD SERVICE: Restaurant:** 24 hours daily, C-406-771-1828, 1 miles away. **Snack Vending:** 24 hours daily, C-406-453-7613.

**TRANSPORTATION: Car Rental:** Avis, C-406-761-7610, .5 miles away; Hertz, C-406-761-6641, .5 miles away; National, C-406-453-4386, .5 miles away. **Taxi Off Base:** C-406-453-3241.

**TML:** Nearest TML is at Malmstrom AFB, Lodging office, Malmstrom Inn, Building 1860, 7028 4th Avenue N, 24 hours daily C-406-727-8600; D-632-3394.

**RVC:** FAMCAMP, Outdoor Rec, 500 76th Street N, Bldg 1222, Check-in FAMCAMP, on site fee station, 24 hours daily, C-406-731-3263, D-312-632-3263, Fax: C-406-453-6684.

**TRAVELERS AID: Chaplain:** C-406-731-3721, Malmstrom AFB, 10 miles away. **Emergency Relief:** C-406-731-4881. **Medical:** C-406-731-3483, Malmstrom AFB, 10 miles away. **Red Cross:** C-406-727-2212, 7 miles away. **Security Police:** C-406-727-4747, .5 miles away; C-406-731-3895 Malmstrom AFB, 10 miles away.

**SUPPORT AVAILABLE: Exchange:** C-406-454-1301. **Laundry/Dry Cleaning:** C-406-453-1031. **Postal Service:** C-406-454-0716.

**OTHER INFORMATION:** Port of Entry and U.S. Customs Service Airport.

**ATTRACTIONS:** C.M. Russell Museum, Ulm Pishkin Interpretive Center, Lewis and Clark Interpretive Center, Yellowstone National Park, Glacier National Park.

### EN ROUTE SCHEDULES

| AIRPORT/STATION | LI-MISSION (page #) |
|---|---|
| Travis AFB | SUU-436/MEDEVAC (13) |
| Scott AFB | BLV-C-634/MEDEVAC (30) |

### UNSCHEDULED FLIGHTS

Flights via KC-135R aircraft to CONUS and overseas stations. Call for destinations, routings and schedules.

# NEBRASKA

# LINCOLN MUNICIPAL AIRPORT/NEBRASKA AIR NATIONAL GUARD BASE (LNK/KLNK)

2420 West Butler Ave
Lincoln, NE 68524-1897

**LOCATION:** Adjacent to Lincoln Municipal Airport, right on I-80. From I-80 east or west, exit 399 west to airport. *USMRA: Page 82 (I-5). ML-ARM: (40°50'N/96°45'W).* LST: GMT-06:00. NMC: Lincoln, 2 miles east. Main installation numbers: C-402-458-1234, D-312-946-1234.

**REGISTRATION INFO:** C-402-458-1249, D-312-946-1249, **Fax:** C-402-458-1272, D-312-946-1272. 155th Air Refueling Group (ANG). BX-474-3454, All Ranks Club-458-1125, Police-473-1348. **TML:** Nearest TML is at Offutt AFB, Lodging office, Building 44, 105 Grants Pass Street, 24 hours daily, **C-402-291-9000, D-312-271-3621,** Fax: C-402-294-3199, D-312-271-3199. DV/VIP C-402-294-4212, D-312-271-4212.

### UNSCHEDULED FLIGHTS

Frequent flights via ANG KC-135R aircraft to CONUS and OCONUS locations. Call for destinations, routing and schedules.

# OFFUTT AIR FORCE BASE (OFF/KOFF)

55th TRANS/LGTRP
Bldg T-47, Suite 2N3
Offutt AFB, NE 68113-2084

**LOCATION:** From I-80 east or west, exit to US-75 south to AFB exit, 6.5 miles south of I-80/US-75 interchange, on east side of US-75. *USMRA: Page 82 (I,J-5). ML-ARM: (41°07'N/95°55'W).* LST: GMT-06:00. NMC: Omaha, 8 miles north. Main installation numbers: C-402-294-1110, D-312-271-1110.

**REGISTRATION INFO:** C-402-294-7111/8510, D-312-271-7111/8510, **Rec:** C-402-294-6235, D-312-271-6235, **Fax:** C-402-232-4070, D-312-271-4070. Bldg T-47, Hours: 0500-1700 Mon-Fri, closed weekends and holidays. There are 5 gates. Ask Security Police for directions. From SAC gate, straight on Lincoln Highway to Pax Term on right. **Pax Service Office:** C-402-294-7111, D-312-271-7111 (NCO on duty).

**PAX LOUNGES:** No separate family lounge. **General:** Bldg T-47, Hours: 0500-1700 Mon-Fri, Sat-Sun, closed holidays, C-402-294-7111. A/C, telephones (local and long distance), TV, read/write rooms, restrooms, P/C seats. **DV/VIP:** Base Ops, C-402-294-3207. **Protocol Service:** Bldg 500, Hours: 0730-1630 Mon-Fri, C-402-294-4212/6411, D-312-271-4212/6411, O7+.

**FOOD SERVICE: Dining Hall:** Bldg 324, C-402-294-3980, D-312-371-3980 (will serve retirees). **Enlisted Club:** Bldg 418, C-402-292-6785. **Food Court:** Bldg 165, C-402-291-9596. **NCO/CPO Club:** Bldg 132, C-402-292-1600. **O Club:** Bldg 462, C-402-292-1560. **Snack Bars:** Bldg 64, C-402-291-9596; Bldg T-47, C-402-294-7111. **Snack Vending:** Bldg T-47, C-402-294-6235.

**TRANSPORTATION: Air Tickets:** SATO, Bldg 500, Room 188, C-402-291-3333; Bldg T-47, C-402-294-2228. **On Base Car Rental:** Bldg 165, Cheepers, C-402-292-9676. **Limo Service:** Bldg T-47, C-402-342-8000. **Shuttle/Bus:** Bldg T-47, C-402-294-4375 (every 30 minutes). **Taxi (Comm):** Corhusker; Yellow, C-402-341-9000. **Taxi (Gov):** Bldg T-47, C-402-294-4375/6 (duty passengers only).

**Parking:** Bldg T-47, (short term - 30 minutes at Pax Term; long term - 24 hours daily). **Security Police:** C-402-294-6110, D-312-271-6110.

**TML:** Lodging office, Building 44, 105 Grants Pass Street, 24 hours daily, C-402-291-9000, D-312-271-3671, Fax: C-402-294-3199, D-312-271-3199. DV/VIP C-402-294-4212, D-312-271-4212.

**TRAVELERS AID: Chaplain:** Chapel (Air Combat Command), C-402-294-6244, After hours C-402-294-1110. **Emergency Relief:** Bldg C, C-402-294-4329 (Air Force Aid). **Medical:** Bldg 4000, 24 hours daily, C-402-294-3000, D-312-271-3000. **Red Cross:** Bldg C, C-402-294-3600. **Security Police:** Main gate, C-402-294-6110.

**SUPPORT AVAILABLE: Bank/Currency Exchange:** BX area, Bellevue: C-402-291-1400. **Exchange:** Bldg 165, C-402-291-9100. **Hair Styles:** Bldg 162; Barber, C-402-291-8521; Beauty, C-402-292-1520. **Laundry/Dry Cleaning:** Bldg 162, C-402-292-1232. **Postal Service:** Bldg 137, C-402-294-3523.

**ATTRACTIONS:** City of Omaha, steaks, zoo, museums, riverboat casinos, art and music.

### EN ROUTE SCHEDULES

| AIRPORT/STATION | LI-MISSION (page #) |
|---|---|
| Scott AFB | BLV-C-666/MEDEVAC (30) |

### UNSCHEDULED FLIGHTS

Frequent flights to: Andrews AFB, MD (**ADW**); Peterson AFB, CO (**COS**); Scott AFB, IL (**BLV**); Wright-Patterson AFB, OH (**FFO**); Langley AFB, VA

(**LFI**). Equipment: OC-135B, RC-135S/U/V/W, TC-135S/W, WC-135W. *Note: New flight schedules received daily. Flights confirmed 24 hours in advance.* Flights to other CONUS destinations. Call for destinations, routings and schedules.

# NEVADA

## FALLON NAVAL AIR STATION (NFL/KNFL)

Air Field Services
4755 Pasture Road
Fallon NAS, NV 89496-5000

**LOCATION:** From Reno take I-80 east or west to Fernley (exit 48). Go to stop light and turn left (southeast) onto US Highway alternate 50 to Fallon. Once through Fallon, turn right on Crook Road, then left on Wildes Road, then right on Pasture Road to main gate. *USMRA: Page 113 (C-4). ML-ARM: (39°25'N/118°43'W).* LST: GMT-08:00. NMC: Reno, 72 miles west. Main installation numbers: C-775-426-5161, D-312-890-5161.

**REGISTRATION INFO: C-775-426-3415, D-312-890-3415, Fax: C-775-426-3452.** Hangar 7, Hours: 0630-2245 Mon-Fri, 0745-1815 Sat, 1000-1800 Sun. Directions: From main gate to 4-way stop, right for 2 miles to a left at the stop sign. **Pax Service Office:** C-775-426-3415, D-312-890-3415. **Pax Paging:** C-775-426-3415, D-312-890-3415.

**PAX LOUNGES: General:** Bldg Hangar 7, Hours: Mon-Fri: 0630-2245, Sat: 0745-1815, Sun: 1000-1800, C-775-426-3415. A/C, coffee served, telephones (local, long distance and defense), TV, restrooms.

**FOOD SERVICE: Cafeteria:** C-775-426-2501. **All Ranks Club:** Silver State, C-775-426-2453. **Galley:** C-775-426-2520. **Restaurant:** Sportsline Bar & Grill, C-775-426-2445.

**TRANSPORTATION:** Limited on and off base. **Car Rentals:** C-775-426-2592. **K-T Bus Lines:** C-775-423-6622. **On Base Taxi:** C-775-426-2792. **Off Base Taxi (Comm):** C-775-423-9333. **Parking:** C-775-426-3415.

**TML:** Lodging office, 24 hours daily, BOQ C-775-428-3003, BEQ C-775-426-2515, D-312-890-2515. DV/VIP C-775-428-2859, Fax: C-775-426-2408. Navy Lodge: C-775-428-2818 or 1-800-NAVY INN. Fax: C-775-423-3720.

**RVC:** Fallon RV Park and Rec Area, MWR Dept, Pony Express Outfitters, Check-in Equip rental, Bldg 393, 0700-1800 hours Mon-Fri 1600 hours Sat-Sun, C-775-426-2598/2279, D-312-830-2598/2279.

**TRAVELERS AID: Chaplain:** C-775-426-2813. **Emergency Relief:** C-775-426-2739. **Lost/Found:** C-775-426-3415. **Medical:** C-775-426-3110. **Security Police:** C-775-426-2803.

**SUPPORT AVAILABLE: Bank/Currency Exchange:** C-775-426-2673. **Exchange:** C-775-426-2400. **Hair Styles:** C-775-426-2547. **Postal Service:** C-775-426-2738.

**ATTRACTIONS:** Reno and Lake Tahoe nearby.

### UNSCHEDULED FLIGHTS
Frequent flights to: China Lake NWC, CA (**NID**); Jacksonville NAS, FL (**NIP**); Lemoore NAS, CA (**NLC**); Miramar MCAS, CA (**NKX**); Norfolk NS, VA (**NGU**); North Island NAS, CA (**NZY**); Oceana NAS, VA (**NTU**); Point Mugu NAS, CA (**NTD**); Whidbey NAS, WA (**NUW**). Flights are via C-009B, C-12A and T-39. Call for destinations, routings and schedules.

## NELLIS AIR FORCE BASE (LSV/KLSV)

99 TRANS/LGTRA
0255 Depot Road, Bldg 809
Nellis AFB, NV 89191-7224

**LOCATION:** Off I-15. Also accessible from US-93/95. Exit 48 east on Craig Road to north on Las Vegas Blvd to main gate on right. Clearly marked. *USMRA: Page 113 (G-9). ML-ARM: (36°15'N/115°00'W).* LST: GMT-08:00.

NMC: Las Vegas, 8 miles southwest. Main installation numbers: C-702-652-1110, D-312-682-1110.

**REGISTRATION INFO: C-702-652-2562, D-312-682-2562, Fax: C-702-652-2561.** Bldg 809, Hours: 0800-1600 daily. Directions: From main gate straight on Fitzgerald Blvd to a left on D Street, right on Depot Road to Base Ops (Air Field Management) C-702-652-4600. **Pax Service Office:** C-702-652-6099/2562, D-312-682-6099/2562 (NCO on duty). **Pax Paging:** C-702-652-6099/2562, D-312-682-6099/2562.

**PAX LOUNGES:** Limited lounge facilities. No separate family lounge. **General:** Bldg 809, Hours: 0700-1600 daily, C-702-652-1854. A/C, bag check, restrooms, telephones, TV, wood seats. **DV/VIP:** Bldg 805, 24 hours daily, C-702-652-4600. A/C, lockers, restrooms, telephones, TV. **Protocol Service:** Bldg 620, Hours: 0800-1700 Mon-Fri, C-702-652-2987.

**FOOD SERVICE: Dining Hall:** Bldg 705, C-702-652-2880. **Enlisted Club:** Bldg 555, C-702-652-9733/4218. **Fast Food:** Burger King, Bldg 350, C-702-644-3374. **In-flight Meals:** Bldg 567, 24 hours daily, C-702-652-5112. **Enlisted Club:** C-702-652-9733/4218 **O Club:** Bldg 541, C-702-652-9188. Time Out Sports Lounge C-702-652-2880; Dining Hall: (Mt. View) C-702-652-4764 (or Crosswinds) C-702-652-6741 **Snack Bars:** Golf Club C-702-652-8571 Bowling Center C-702-652-8823 **Snack Vending:** Bldg 340, C-702-644-4425.

**TRANSPORTATION: Air Tickets:** SATO, Bldg 282, C-702-644-5400. **Car Rentals:** Bldg 340, Allstate Car Rental, C-702-644-5567/6180. **Limo Service:** C-702-739-8414. **On Base Shuttle/Bus (Gov):** Bldg 837, C-702-652-8305 (duty passengers only). **Off Base Shuttle/Bus (Comm):** Across from Main Gate, Hours: 0600-2100 daily. **On Base Taxi (Gov):** Bldg 837, C-702-652-8305. **Off Base Taxi (Comm):** North Las Vegas, C-702-643-1041. **Parking:** Bldg 809, 7 day limit.

**TML:** Lodging office, Building 780, 5990 Fitzgerald Boulevard, Nellis AFB NV 89191-6514, 24 hours daily, C-702-643-2711, D-312-682-2711. DV/VIP C-702-652-2525.

**TRAVELERS AID: Chaplain:** Bldg 615, C-702-652-2950. **Emergency Relief:** Bldg 20, C-702-652-3327 (Air Force Aid). **Lost/Found:** Bldg 2, C-702-652-8088. **Medical:** Base Hospital 24 hours daily, C-702-653-2260, D-312-682-2333. **Red Cross:** Bldg 115, C-702-652-2106. **Security Police:** Bldg 2, C-702-652-2311.

**SUPPORT AVAILABLE: Bank/Currency Exchange:** Bldg 374, C-702-651-8228 **Exchange:** (Main) Exchange 702-644-2044 Base Exchange (Personnel) 702-644-4425; Base Exchange (Home & Gardens) C-702-643-3526 **Postal Service:** Bldg 320, C-702-652-4679.

**ATTRACTIONS:** Las Vegas, Lake Mead, Thunderbirds, Mt Charleston, Red Rock.

### UNSCHEDULED FLIGHTS
Many unscheduled flights, especially during exercise weekends, to various locations throughout CONUS. Call for destinations, routings and schedules.

## RENO/TAHOE INTERNATIONAL AIRPORT (RNO/KRNO)

152nd Airlift Wing (ANG)/Base Ops
Reno/Tahoe IAP, NV 89502-5000

**LOCATION:** Reno/Tahoe International Airport exit 64/65 east off I-395. Co-located with the IAP. NMC: Reno is 5 miles northwest. *USMRA: Page 113 (B-4). ML-ARM: (39°30'N/119°46'W).* LST: GMT-08:00. NMI: Fallon NAS, 70 miles east. Main installation numbers: C-775-788-4500, D-312-830-4500.

**REGISTRATION INFO:** Base Ops, Bldg 84, **C-775-788-4709, D-312-830-4709, Fax: C-775-788-4727, D-312-830-4727.** General Pax Lounge.

**FOOD SERVICE:** Snack vending available.

**TRANSPORTATION: Off Base Car Rental:** Budget C-775-785-2545; Dollar, C-775-348-2800; Hertz, C-775-785-2554. All car rental agencies are one and one half miles west. **Off Base Taxi:** Available at IAP.

**TML:** Nearest TML is at Fallon NAS, Lodging office, 24 hours daily, BOQ C-

775-428-3003/4, BEQ C-775-426-2515, D-312-890-2515. DV/VIP C-775-428-2859, Fax: C-775-426-2408. Navy Lodge: C-775-428-2818 or 1-800-NAVY INN. Fax: C-775-423-3720.

### UNSCHEDULED FLIGHTS

Flights to CONUS and OCONUS locations via C-130H aircraft. Call for destinations, routings and schedules.

# NEW HAMPSHIRE

## PEASE INTERNATIONAL TRADEPORT/ AIR NATIONAL GUARD STATION (PSM/KPSM)

157th ARW/DOBO
302 Newmarket Street
Pease IT/ANGS, NH 03803-0157

**LOCATION:** From I-95 north to Spaulding Turnpike NH-3 northwest exit 1, then follow signs. Base is at intersection of Spaulding Turnpike and Gosling Road. *USMRA: Page 23 (H-9). ML-ARM: (43°04'N/70°49'W).* LST: GMT-05:00. NMC: Portsmouth, 3 miles northeast. Main installation numbers: C-603-430-2453, D-312-852-2453.

**REGISTRATION INFO: C-603-430-3323, D-312-852-3323, Rec:C-603-430-3323, D-312-852-3323; Fax: C-603-430-3335, D-312-852-3335; E-mail: spaceA@nhpeas.ang.af.mil WEB: www.nhpeas.ang.af.mil** Bldg 257. *Note: Sign up must be in person on Wednesdays from 0900-1100, 1300-1500 hours only.* There are limited support facilities available on base for Space-A flyers.

**PAX LOUNGES:** Operations lounge: Coffee/vending machine. C-603-430-3323, D-312-852-3323. Directions: New Market Street to Bldg 257 (Operations) 1/8 mile from gate on the right is the Pax Term.

**TRANSPORTATION: Off Base Bus (Comm):** Portsmouth, Greyhound and Trailways to all locations and from Park Square Bus Terminal in Boston MA. **Off Base Car Rentals:** Portsmouth, Manchester, and Boston. **Limo Service:** Main Gate, C-608-431-2424 (local service to Logan IAP, Boston, $17 one way, $31 round trip). **Taxi (Gov):** C-603-430-3588, **Off Base Taxi:** C-603-436-7500/0008/7111/7777. **Parking:** Short term - in front of Operations Bldg (257); long term - main gate parking lot. Pick up parking form at main gate.

**SUPPORT AVAILABLE: Bank/Currency Exchange:** C-603-436-0302. **Exchange:** C-608-436-0302. **Hair Styles:** Barber, C-608-436-2903.

**TML:** Nearest TML is at Portsmouth Naval Shipyard, Helmsman Inn, C-207-438-1513/2015, D-312-684-1513/2015, Fax C-207-438-3580.

**ATTRACTIONS:** Portsmouth, sea coast, snow skiing, camping, fishing.

**OTHER INFORMATION:** All inbound military traffic should contact Pease Command Post C-603-430-2459, D-852-2459 with numbers and types of passengers 24 hours prior.

### UNSCHEDULED FLIGHTS

The ANG has some flights to U.S. and overseas destinations, via KC-135R. Call for destinations, routings and schedules.

# NEW JERSEY

## McGUIRE AIR FORCE BASE (WRI/KWRI)

305th APS/TROP
1706 Vandenberg Ave
McGuire AFB, NJ 08641-5507

**LOCATION:** From New Jersey Turnpike (I-95), exit 7 to NJ-206 south to Route 68 south, then to Route 537, turn left. Take Route 537 northeast to intersection (traffic light) of Routes 545 and 680, turn right. Take Route 680 to base's main gate, about two miles. Clearly marked. *USMRA: Page 19 (E-6). ML-ARM: (40°02'N/74°35'W).* LST: GMT-05:00. NMC: Trenton, 18 miles northwest. Main installation numbers: C-609-754-1100, D-312-650-1100.

**REGISTRATION INFO: C-609-754-2864, D-312-650-3070, Rec: C-1-800-569-8284 ext 754-9950, Fax: C-609-754-4621, D-312-650-4621. E-mail: wripax@mcguire.af.mil WEB: www.mcguire.af.mil** Bldg 1706, 24 hours daily. Directions: From main gate straight on McGuire Blvd. Road ends at Pax Term. Space-A desk, lst floor. **Pax Service Office:** Bldg 1706, 24 hours daily, C-609-754-5023, D-312-650-5023. **Pax Paging:** C-609-754-5023, D-312-650-5023.

**PAX LOUNGES: General:** Bldg 1706, lst floor, Hours: 0700-0130 daily, C-609-754-5023. A/C, telephones (commercial and defense), TV, restrooms, showers, P/C seats. **DV/VIP:** Bldg 1706, lst floor, 24 hours daily, C-609-754-2812, D-312-650-2812. A/C, telephones (commercial and defense), TV, restrooms, O/S seats. Check with counter #1 for access to lounge/Protocol Service. **Dependent:** Now available, includes nursery.

**FOOD SERVICE: Dining Hall:** Bldg 2501, Hours: 0600-0800, 1100-1330, 1800-1930, 2300-0100 daily, C-609-754-3784 (active duty only). **NCO Club:** Bldg 2508, Hours: 1000-2330 daily, C-609-754-3296. **O Club:** Bldg 2705, Hours: 1130-1300 daily, C-609-754-3296. **Golf Course:** Bldg 2003, Hours: 0730-1400 daily, C-609-754-2169.

**TRANSPORTATION: Air Tickets:** Rodger's Travel, Bldg 1706, Hours: 0730-1630 Mon-Fri, C-609-723-1323. **Off Base Bus:** NJ Transit, C-800-772-2222, C-201-762-5100. **Car Rentals:** B&J Rental (outside main gate), Hours: 0800-1730 Mon-Fri, 0800-1630 Sat, C-609-723-1313/8366; Enterprise, Hours: 0800-1800 Mon-Fri, 0800-1200 Sat, C-609-291-1112; Hertz, Hours: 0700-1830 Mon-Fri, 0800-1600 Sat-Sun, C-609-298-8585; Town Ford, inc, C-609-723-4419. **Off Base Taxi:** Eagle Transportation, Hours: 0730-1830 Mon-Fri, C-609-723-2001. United Cab Company, 24 hours daily, C-609-723-3000. **Trains:** AMTRAK, Newark NJ, C-1-800-523-5700. **Parking:** Short and long term, Bldg 1706, 24 hours daily.

**TML:** All American Inn, Building 2717, C-609-754-3336/7, D-312-650-3336/7. Fax C-609-754-2035, D-312-650-2035, 24 hours daily. DV/VIP C-609-754-2405.

**RVC:** Bridle Lake Travel Camp (Fort Dix), Outdoor Rec, Bldg 6045, Doughboy Loop, C-609-562-6667, D-312-944-6667, Fax: C-609-562-2354.

**TRAVELERS AID: Chaplain:** Bldg 1706, Hours: 0730-1630 Mon-Fri, C-609-754-3811 (after duty hours C-609-754-2001). **Emergency Relief:** Bldg 2916, Hours: 0800-1700 Mon-Fri, C-609-754-4353. **Lost/Found:** Bldg 1706, Hours: 0730-1630 Mon-Fri, C-609-754-7618, D-312-650-8618 (after duty hours C-609-754-5023). **Medical:** Bldg 5201, Hours: 0730-1630 Mon-Fri, C-609-562-9200. **Red Cross:** Fort Dix: C-609-562-2258. **Retired Affairs:** Bldg 2916, Hours: 0900-1500 Mon-Fri, C-609-754-2459. **Security Police:** Bldg 1738, 24 hours daily, C-609-754-2001.

**SUPPORT AVAILABLE: ATM:** outside bank, 24 hours daily. **Bank/Currency Exchange:** Bldg 2914, Hours: 0900-1500 Mon-Fri, C-609-758-1500. **Exchange:** Bldg 3452, Hours: 1000-2100 Mon-Sat, 1000-1730 Sun, C-609-723-6100. **Hair Styles:** Barber, Bldg 1706, Hours: 0900-1700 Mon-Fri, C-609-723-4449. **Postal Service:** Bldg 2907, Hours: 0900-1700 Mon-Fri, C-609-754-6012.

**ATTRACTIONS:** Philadelphia, Liberty Bell, Atlantic City and Manhattan, NY.

*Note: Commercially contracted flights are now called Patriot Express.*

**McGUIRE AFB, NJ (WRI); REGION: ATL;
OPERATOR: COM; TYPE: MIXED; ROUTE: HJX1A;
SAMPLE SCHEDULE: THU; EQUIPMENT: DC862**

{WRI *SW* ➡ BWI (★) *NE* ➡ THU ⮀ THU *SW* ➡ BWI (★) *NE* ➡ WRI}

| LI/ICAO | AIRPORT/STATION | CTRY/STA | DAYS EN ROUTE |
|---|---|---|---|
| WRI/KWRI | McGuire AFB | NJ | +0 |
| BWI/KBWI | Baltimore/Washington IAP | MD | +0 |
| THU/BGTL | Thule AB | GL | +0 |
| THU/BGTL | Thule AB | GL | +0 |
| BWI/KBWI | Baltimore/Washington IAP | MD | +0 |
| WRI/KWRI | McGuire AFB | NJ | +0 |

### McGUIRE AFB, NJ (WRI); REGION: ATL; OPERATOR: COM; TYPE: MIXED; ROUTE: HJX5A; SAMPLE SCHEDULE: SAT; EQUIPMENT: DC862

{WRI *SW* ➡ BWI (★) *NE* ➡ LGS ⇌ LGS *W* ➡ BWI (★) *NE* ➡ WRI}

| LI/ICAO | AIRPORT/STATION | CTRY/STA | DAYS EN ROUTE |
|---|---|---|---|
| WRI/KWRI | McGuire AFB | NJ | +0 |
| BWI/KBWI | Baltimore/Washington IAP | MD | +0 |
| LGS/LPLA | Lajes Field AB (Azores) | PT | +1 |
| LGS/LPLA | Lajes Field AB (Azores) | PT | +1 |
| BWI/KBWI | Baltimore/Washington IAP | MD | +1 |
| WRI/KWRI | McGuire AFB | NJ | +0 |

### McGUIRE AFB NJ (WRI); REGION: ATL; OPERATOR: AMC; TYPE: MIXED; ROUTE: A7W7B; SAMPLE SCHEDULE: 1ST & 2ND SAT; EQUIPMENT: KC010A

{WRI *SW* ➡ NGU (★) *E* ➡ SIZ *NE* ➡ SKP ⇌ SKP *NW* ➡ MHZ *SW* ➡ WRI}

| LI/ICAO | AIRPORT/STATION | CTRY/STA | DAYS EN ROUTE |
|---|---|---|---|
| WRI/KWRI | McGuire AFB | NJ | +0 |
| NGU/KNGU | Norfolk NS | VA | +0 |
| SIZ/LICZ | Sigonella NAS/APT (Sicily) | IT | +2 |
| SKP/LWSK | Skopje* | MK | +2 |
| MHZ/EGUN | RAF Mildenhall | UK | +3 |
| WRI/KWRI | McGuire AFB | NJ | |

* Space-A passengers can not go through Skopje. We list this schedule because many people may wish to use the McGuire to Norfolk to Sigonella & the Mildenhall to McGuire leg of this flight.

### McGUIRE AFB, NJ (WRI); REGION: ATL; OPERATOR: AMC; TYPE: MIXED; ROUTE: TQP5J; SAMPLE SCHEDULE: 4TH SUN; EQUIPMENT: KC010A

{WRI *SW* ➡ SUU (★) *SW* ➡ HIK *SW* ➡ OKO *SW* ➡ QPG *NE* ➡ NKW ⇌ NKW *SW* ➡ SIN *NE* ➡ OKO}

| LI/ICAO | AIRPORT/STATION | CTRY/STA | DAYS EN ROUTE |
|---|---|---|---|
| WRI/KWRI | McGuire AFB | NJ | +0 |
| SUU/KSUU | Travis AFB | CA | +0 |
| HIK/PHIK | Hickam AFB | HI | +1 |
| OKO/RJTY | Yokota AB | JP | +3 |
| QPG/WSAP | RSAF Paya Lebar (Singapore) | SG | +4 |
| NKW/FJDG | Diego Garcia Atoll | GB | +5 |
| NKW/FJDG | Diego Garcia Atoll | GB | +5 |
| SIN/WSSS | Changi IAP (Singapore) | SG | +6 |
| OKO/RJTY | Yokota AB | JP | |

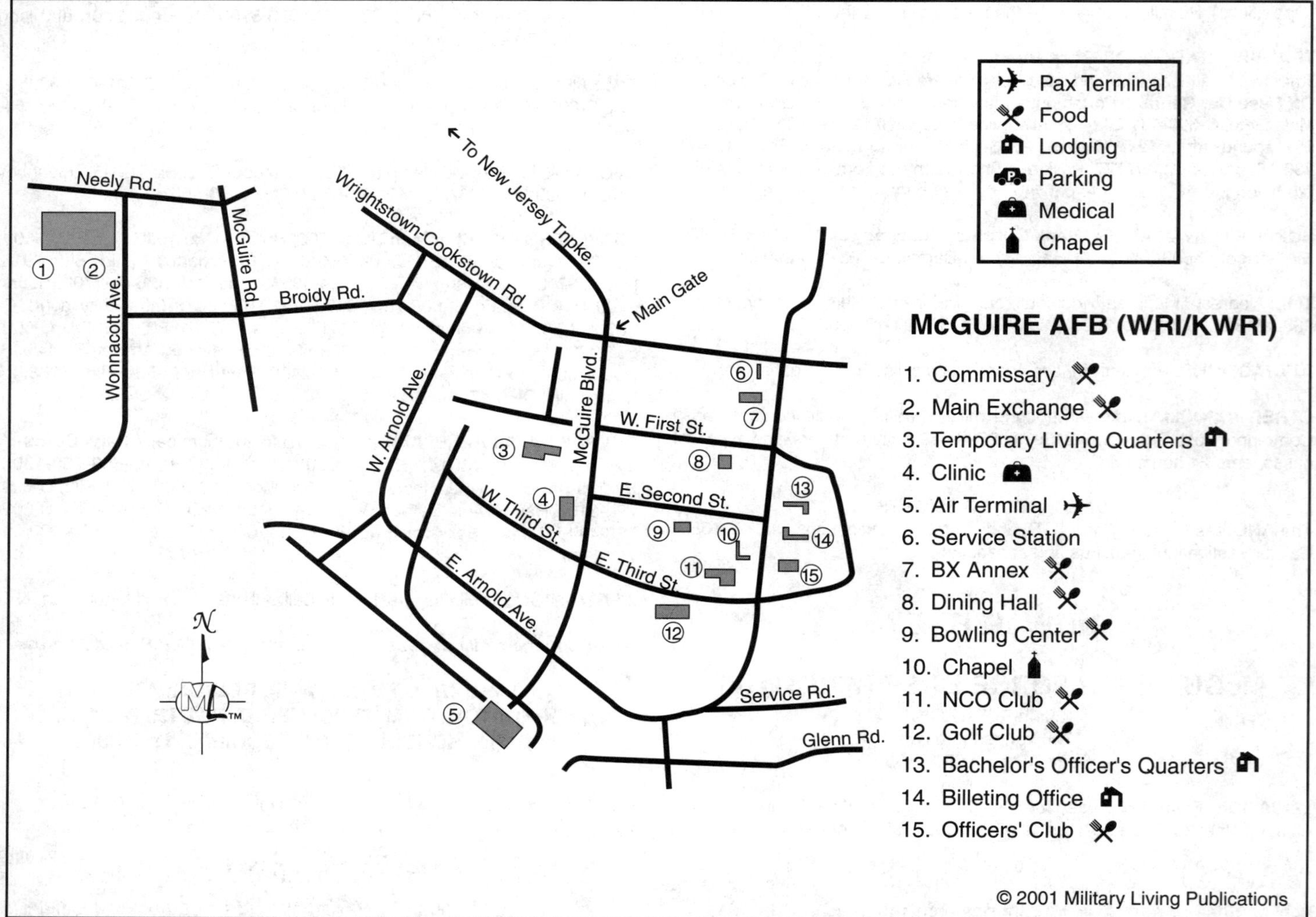


## McGUIRE AFB (WRI/KWRI)

1. Commissary 🍴
2. Main Exchange 🍴
3. Temporary Living Quarters 🏠
4. Clinic 🧰
5. Air Terminal ✈
6. Service Station
7. BX Annex 🍴
8. Dining Hall 🍴
9. Bowling Center 🍴
10. Chapel ⛪
11. NCO Club 🍴
12. Golf Club 🍴
13. Bachelor's Officer's Quarters 🏠
14. Billeting Office 🏠
15. Officers' Club 🍴

### McGUIRE AFB, NJ (WRI); REGION: ATL; OPERATOR: AMC; TYPE: CGO W/ PAX; ROUTE: A7F3A; SAMPLE SCHEDULE: 3RD & 4TH TUE; EQUIPMENT: C141B

{WRI *SW* ➡ NGU (★) *NE* ➡ RTA *NE* ➡ SIZ *SE* ➡ BAH ⮂ BAH *NW* ➡ SIZ *SW* ➡ RTA *SW* ➡ NGU (★) *NE* ➡ WRI}

| LI/ICAO | AIRPORT/STATION | CTRY/STA | DAYS EN ROUTE |
|---|---|---|---|
| WRI/KWRI | McGuire AFB | NJ | +0 |
| NGU/KNGU | Norfolk NS | VA | +0 |
| RTA/LERT | Rota NS | ES | +1 |
| SIZ/LICZ | Sigonella NAS/APT (Sicily) | IT | +2 |
| BAH/OBBI | Bahrain IAP | BH | +2 |
| BAH/OBBI | Bahrain IAP | BH | +2 |
| SIZ/LICZ | Sigonella NAS/APT (Sicily) | IT | +3 |
| RTA/LERT | Rota NS | ES | +3 |
| NGU/KNGU | Norfolk NS | VA | +4 |
| WRI/KWRI | McGuire AFB | NJ | |

### McGUIRE AFB, NJ (WRI); REGION: ATL; OPERATOR: AMC; TYPE: CGO W/ PAX; ROUTE: A7N1B; SAMPLE SCHEDULE: 4TH FRI; EQUIPMENT: C141B

{WRI *SW* ➡ NGU (★) *S* ➡ NBW *E* ➡ STX ⮂ STX *W* NRR *N* ➡ NGU (★) *NE* ➡ WRI}

| LI/ICAO | AIRPORT/STATION | CTRY/STA | DAYS EN ROUTE |
|---|---|---|---|
| WRI/KWRI | McGuire AFB | NJ | +0 |
| NGU/KNGU | Norfolk NS | VA | +1 |
| NBW/MUGM | Guantanamo Bay NAS | CU | +1 |
| STX/TISX | Alexander Hamilton Apt (St Croix) | VI | +2 |
| NRR/TJNR | Roosevelt Roads NS | PR | +2 |
| NGU/KNGU | Norfolk NS | VA | +2 |
| WRI/KWRI | McGuire AFB | NJ | |

### McGUIRE AFB, NJ (WRI); REGION: ATL; OPERATOR: AMC; TYPE: CGO W/ PAX; ROUTE: A7R1A; SAMPLE SCHEDULE: 1ST & 4TH TUE; EQUIPMENT: C141B

{WRI *SW* ➡ DOV (★) *NE* ➡ RMS ⮂ RMS *W* ➡ ADW (★) *NE* ➡ WRI}

| LI/ICAO | AIRPORT/STATION | CTRY/STA | DAYS EN ROUTE |
|---|---|---|---|
| WRI/KWRI | McGuire AFB | NJ | +0 |
| DOV/KDOV | Dover AFB | DE | +0 |
| RMS/ETAR | Ramstein AB (✚) | DE | +1 |
| RMS/ETAR | Ramstein AB (✚) | DE | +1 |
| ADW/KADW | Andrews AFB (✚) | MD | +2 |
| WRI/KWRI | McGuire AFB | NJ | |

**Note:** (✚) = MEDEVAC: RMS to ADW

### McGUIRE AFB, NJ (WRI); REGION: ATL; OPERATOR: AMC; TYPE: CGO W/ PAX; ROUTE: A7R3A; SAMPLE SCHEDULE: 1ST & 3RD MON; EQUIPMENT: C141B

{WRI *SW* ➡ ADW (★) *NE* ➡ LGS *NE* ➡ RMS ⮂ RMS *SW* ➡ ADW (★) *NE* ➡ WRI}

| LI/ICAO | AIRPORT/STATION | CTRY/STA | DAYS EN ROUTE |
|---|---|---|---|
| WRI/KWRI | McGuire AFB | NJ | +0 |
| ADW/KADW | Andrews AFB (✚) | MD | +0 |
| LGS/LPLA | Lajes Field AB (Azores) | PT | +1 |
| RMS/ETAR | Ramstein AB | DE | +2 |
| RMS/ETAR | Ramstein AB | DE | +2 |
| ADW/KADW | Andrews AFB (✚) | MD | +3 |

| WRI/KWRI | McGuire AFB | | NJ |
|---|---|---|---|

**Note:** (✚) = MEDEVAC: ADW to ADW

### McGUIRE AFB, NJ (WRI); REGION: ATL; OPERATOR: AMC; TYPE: CGO W/ PAX; ROUTE: A7X1A; SAMPLE SCHEDULE: TUE; EQUIPMENT: C141B

{WRI (★) *NE* ➡ THU ⮂ THU *SW* ➡ WRI (★)}

| LI/ICAO | AIRPORT/STATION | CTRY/STA | DAYS EN ROUTE |
|---|---|---|---|
| WRI/KWRI | McGuire AFB | NJ | +0 |
| THU/BGTL | Thule AB | GL | +1 |
| THU/BGTL | Thule AB | GL | +1 |
| WRI/KWRI | McGuire AFB | NJ | |

### McGUIRE AFB, NJ (WRI); REGION: ATL; OPERATOR: AMC; TYPE: CGO W/ PAX; ROUTE: A7X3C; SAMPLE SCHEDULE: 1ST FRI; EQUIPMENT: C141B

{WRI *SW* ➡ ADW (★) *NE* ➡ LGS *NE* ➡ KEF ⮂ KEF *SW* ➡ ADW (★) *NE* ➡ WRI}

| LI/ICAO | AIRPORT/STATION | CTRY/STA | DAYS EN ROUTE |
|---|---|---|---|
| WRI/KWRI | McGuire AFB | NJ | +0 |
| ADW/KADW | Andrews AFB | MD | +1 |
| LGS/LPLA | Lajes Field AB (Azores) | PT | +2 |
| KEF/BIKF | Keflavik APT | IS | +2 |
| KEF/BIKF | Keflavik APT | IS | +2 |
| ADW/KADW | Andrews AFB | MD | +3 |
| WRI/KWRI | McGuire AFB | NJ | |

**Note:** (✚) = MEDEVAC: ADW to ADW

### McGUIRE AFB, NJ (WRI); REGION: ATL; OPERATOR: AMC; TYPE: CGO W/ PAX; ROUTE: AQ01A; SAMPLE SCHEDULE: SAT & TUE; EQUIPMENT: KC010A

{WRI *SW* ➡ DOV (★) *NE* ➡ RMS ⮂ RMS *SW* ➡ WRI (★)}

| LI/ICAO | AIRPORT/STATION | CTRY/STA | DAYS EN ROUTE |
|---|---|---|---|
| WRI/KWRI | McGuire AFB | NJ | +0 |
| DOV/KDOV | Dover AFB | DE | +0 |
| RMS/ETAR | Ramstein AB | DE | +1 |
| RMS/ETAR | Ramstein AB | DE | +1 |
| WRI/KWRI | McGuire AFB | NJ | |

### McGUIRE AFB, NJ (WRI); REGION: ATL; OPERATOR: AMC; TYPE: MIXED; ROUTE: G7X5A; SAMPLE SCHEDULE: THU; EQUIPMENT: C141B

{WRI (★) *NE* ➡ LGS ⮂ LGS *SW* ➡ WRI (★)}

| LI/ICAO | AIRPORT/STATION | CTRY/STA | DAYS EN ROUTE |
|---|---|---|---|
| WRI/KWRI | McGuire AFB | NJ | +0 |
| LGS/LPLA | Lajes Field AB (Azores) | PT | +1 |
| LGS/LPLA | Lajes Field AB (Azores) | PT | +1 |
| WRI/KWRI | McGuire AFB | NJ | |

## EN ROUTE SCHEDULES

| AIRPORT/STATION | LI-MISSION (page #) |
|---|---|
| Andrews AFB | ADW-116/MEDEVAC (37) |
| Travis AFB | SUU-ATG3A (14) |
| Charleston AFB/IAP | CHS-A8X5S (68) |
| Yokota AB | OKO-TQP5V (128) |

### UNSCHEDULED FLIGHTS

Unscheduled flights via C-141B, KC-10A and KC-135R aircraft to: Andrews AFB, MD (**ADW**); Charleston AFB/IAP, SC (**CHS**); V.C. Bird IAP (St. John's), Antigua (**SJH**); Dover AFB, DE (**DOV**); Guantanamo Bay NAS, CU (**GAO**); Pope AFB, NC (**POB**); and Roosevelt Roads NS, PR (**NRR**). Call for destinations, routings and schedules.

## Other New Jersey Installations with Possible Space-A Air Opportunities

**LAKEHURST NAVAL AIR ENGINEERING STATION (NEL/KNEL),** ATC Facility, Naval Air Engineering Station, Highway 547, Lakehurst, NJ 08733-5085. **LOCATION:** Take the Garden State Parkway south to NJ-70, west to junction of NJ-547, turn right and proceed one mile to base. *USMRA: Page 19 (F-6).* ML-ARM: (40°01'N/74°18'W). LST: GMT-05:00. **REGISTRATION INFO: C-732-323-2438. D-312-624-2438 FAX: C-732-323-5316; D-312-624-5316; WEB: www.lakehurst.navy.mil** Bldg 307 **TML:** Lodging office, Building 480-481, 24 hours daily, CBQ/DV/VIP C-732-323-2266, D-312-624-2266, Fax: C-732-323-4371. **TRAVELERS AID: Security Police:** Bldg 8, 24 hours daily, C-732-323-2332 (Emergency Only) or C-732-323-2457 (Non-Emergency).

### UNSCHEDULED FLIGHTS

Infrequent flights via Army and Navy administrative aircraft to CONUS East Coast locations. All flights leaving/arriving NEL are military or official business only. Call for destinations, routings and schedules.

# NEW MEXICO

## CANNON AIR FORCE BASE (CVS/KCVS)

27th TRANS/TRTM
511 N Torch Blvd, Bldg 300
Cannon AFB, NM 88103-5328

**LOCATION:** From Clovis, near the Texas border, west on US-60/84 for seven miles to AFB south of US-60/84. From NM-467 north or south enter the Portales gate. *USMRA: Page 114 (H-5).* ML-ARM: (34°24'N/103°20'W). LST: GMT-07:00. NMC. Clovis, 7 miles east. Main installation numbers: C-505-784-3311, D-312-681-1110.

**REGISTRATION INFO: C-505-784-2978, D-312-681-2978, Fax: C-505-784-4320, D-312-681-4320.** Bldg 300, Hours: 0700-2300 Mon-Fri, 0700-2100 Sat-Sun. Ask Security Police for directions.

**PAX LOUNGES:** Limited, General: Bldg 300, Hours: 0700-2300 Mon-Fri, 0700-2100 Sat-Sun, C-505-784-2935, D-312-681-2935.

**FOOD SERVICE: Cafeteria:** C-505-784-3621. **O Club:** C-505-784-2477. **Snack Bars:** C-505-784-2280.

**TRANSPORTATION: Air Tickets:** SATO, C-505-784-2304.

**TML:** Lodging office, Caprock Inn, Building 1801, 401 S Olympic Blvd, 24 hours daily, C-505-784-2918/9, D-312-681-2918/9, Fax: C-505-784-4833, D-312-681-4833. DV/VIP C-505-784-2727. Advance reservations C-505-784-2935, Fax: C-505-784-4833.

**TRAVELERS AID: Chaplain:** C-505-784-2507, D-312-681-2507

**SUPPORT AVAILABLE: Exchange:** C-505-784-3387. Full Base support available.

**ATTRACTIONS:** Carlsbad Caverns, Sierre Blanca Ski Resort.

### EN ROUTE SCHEDULES

| AIRPORT/STATION | LI-MISSION (page #) |
| --- | --- |
| Travis AFB | SUU-456/MEDEVAC (13) |

### UNSCHEDULED FLIGHTS

Infrequent flights to Midwest and West Coast stations. Call for destinations, routings and schedules.

## HOLLOMAN AIR FORCE BASE (HMN/KHMN)

49th OSS/OSAA
1081 8th Street
Holloman AFB, NM 88310-8023

**LOCATION:** Exit US-70, eight miles southwest of Alamogordo. Route to AFB north of US-70 is clearly marked. *USMRA: Page 114 (D, E-7).* ML-ARM: (32°28'N/106°25'W). LST: GMT-07:00. NMC: Las Cruces, 50 miles southwest. Main installation numbers: C-505-572-5406, D-312-572-5406.

**REGISTRATION INFO: C-505-572-5411, D-312-572-5411, Fax: C-505-572-7627, D-312-572-7627.** Base Ops, Hours: 0600-2400 Mon-Fri, 0700-2100 Sat-Sun, holidays.

**PAX LOUNGES:** Aircrew lounge for crew members and Space-A passengers. VIP lounge at Base Ops, O6+.

**FOOD SERVICE: Cafeteria:** C-505-572-2698. **NCO Club:** C-505-572-3226. **O Club:** C-505-572-3611. **Snack Bars:** C-505-572-2779. McDonald's, and other dining facilities available.

**TRANSPORTATION:** Car rental, such as Avis, Hertz, and Enterprise, is available. There is a shuttle service to and from El Paso as well as a local and military taxi service.

**TML:** Billeting Office, Building 583, 1040 New Mexico Avenue, 24 hours daily, C-505-572-7160/3311, D-312-572-7160/3468. Fax: C-505-572-7753, D-312-572-7753. DV/VIP C-505-572-5573/5574.

**TRAVELERS AID: Chaplain:** C-505-475-7211/7024. **Dental:** C-505-572-3742. **Medical:** C-505-572-3260. **Security Police:** C-505-475-7171.

**SUPPORT AVAILABLE: Commissary:** C-505-475-5127. **Convenience Store:** C-505-479-2381. **Exchange:** C-505-479-6164. **Shoppette:** C-505-479-2381.

**ATTRACTIONS:** White Sands National Park, Space Hall of Fame and Museum, are ski lodges.

### UNSCHEDULED FLIGHTS

Transient and MEDEVAC aircraft provide limited Space-A air opportunities to CONUS locations. Call for destinations, routings and schedules.

## KIRTLAND AIR FORCE BASE (IKR/KIKR)

377th Transportation Squadron
377 LGT/LGTR
1551 First Street SE
Kirtland AFB, NM 87117-5616

**LOCATION:** From I-40 east or west exit on Wyoming Boulevard, south for two miles to Wyoming gate to AFB. *USMRA: Page 114 (D-4).* ML-ARM: (35°03'N/106°35'W). LST: GMT-07:00. NMC: Albuquerque, one mile northeast. Main installation numbers: C-505-846-0011, D-312-246-0011.

**REGISTRATION INFO: C-505-846-7000/7001, D-312-246-7000/7001, Fax: C-505-846-6184, D-312-246-6184.** Bldg 333, Hours: 0700-1600 Mon-Fri, 0800-1700 Sat-Sun. Directions: From Carlisle gate straight on Carlisle Ave to a right on Clark Ave to Pax Term on left. Carlisle gate 0600-1700. Truman gate after 1700. Ask for directions. **Pax Service Office:** C-505-846-1652/2075, D-312-246-1652/2075. **Pax Paging:** Bldg 333, C-505-846-8335/9070 (Base Operations).

**PAX LOUNGES:** Adequate lounge facilities. General lounge available. **DV/VIP:** Bldg 333, Hours: 0600-2200 daily, C-505-846-8336 (next to Base Ops desk). A/C, coffee/tea served, separate read/write rooms, restrooms, TV, O/S seats. **Protocol Service:** Bldg 333, Hours: 0600-2200 daily, C-505-846-9070, O6+.

**FOOD SERVICE:** Thunder Bird Inn: C-505-846-8048; **Dining Hall:** Bldg 923W, C-505-846-0011. **Enlisted Club:** Bldg 20255, C-505-846-5611. **NCO/CPO Club:** Bldg 20255, C-505-846-7512; Bldg 201, C-505-846-3488. **O Club:** Bldg 22000, C-505-856-5165; Bldg 1900, C-505-846-3488. **Snack**

**Bars:** Bldg 20170, C-505-265-3679/7301. **Snack Vending:** Bldg 333, C-505-265-3679/7301.

**TRANSPORTATION: Air Tickets:** Rodgers Travel Leisure C-505-846-2914, Office: 505-846-7171 Bldg.20245. **On Base Car Rental:** Enterprise. Contact base info for new number: C-505-846-0011. **Off Base Bus:** Albuquerque-Greyhound. **Trains:** Albuquerque is a major AMTRAK stop. **Parking:** Bldg 333, C-505-846-4618 (west side of Pax Term).

**TML:** Lodging office, Building 22016, Club Drive, 24 hours daily, C-505-846-9653, D-312-246-9653, Fax: C-505-846-4142. DV/VIP C-505-846-4119.

**RVC:** FAMCAMP, Outdoor Rec, 2000 Wyoming Blvd SE, Bldg 20410, Check-in FAMCAMP 0900-1130 hrs, C-505-846-0337, D-312-246-1275.

**TRAVELERS AID: Chaplain:** Bldg 20107, C-505-846-5691;. **Emergency Relief:** Bldg 20245, C-505-846-0741 (AF Aid). **Medical:** Bldg 1501, 24 hours daily, C-505-846-3200, D-312-244-4611. **Security Police:** Bldg 20219, C-505-846-4618.

**SUPPORT AVAILABLE: Bank/Currency Exchange:** Kirtland Federal Credit Union: Bldg 6440 C-505-254-4369. **Exchange:** Bldg 20170, C-505-262-1703. **Hair Styles:** Bldg 20170, C-505-266-6430. **Laundry/Dry Cleaning:** Bldg 24404, C-505-266-8116;. **Postal Service:** Bldg 1400, C-505-346-0560.

**ATTRACTIONS:** National Atomic Museum, Albuquerque.

### EN ROUTE SCHEDULES

| AIRPORT/STATION | LI-MISSION (page #) |
| --- | --- |
| Travis AFB | SUU-456/MEDEVAC (13) |

### UNSCHEDULED FLIGHTS

Frequent flights via MC-130E/H to: Andrews AFB, MD (**ADW**); Davis-Monthan AFB, AZ (**DMA**); Hill AFB, UT (**HIF**); Kelly AFB, TX (**SKF**); Offutt AFB, NE (**OFF**); Randolph AFB, TX (**RND**); Scott AFB, IL (**BLV**); Travis AFB, CA (**SUU**); Wright-Patterson AFB, OH (**FFO**). Several flights weekly to each location. Other flights to CONUS locations. An AMC training base. Call for destinations, routings and schedules.

## Other New Mexico Installations with Possible Space-A Air Opportunities

**CONDRON ARMY AIRFIELD (WSD/KWSD),** Bldg 122, Augusta Street, AVN SEC, White Sands Missile Range, NM 88002-5047. **LOCATION:** From US-70 north or south, 18 miles south of Alamogordo, follow signs to Visitors Center and White Sands Missile Range, north of US-70. Clearly marked. *USMRA: Page 114 (D-6,7,8).* ML-ARM: *(32°20'N/106°24'W).* LST: GMT-07:00. **C-505-678-2121. TML:** Billeting Office, Mon-Thu, 0700-1630; Alternate Fri: 0700-1530, C-505-678-4559, D-312-258-4559. DV/VIP C-505-678-1028. **RVC:** Volunteer Park Travel Camp, Outdoor Rec, Bldg 445, Flagler Street, Check-in camp duty hrs and Bldg 384 after hours, C-505-678-1713, D-312-258-1713. Infrequent flights. Call for destinations, routings and schedules.

# NEW YORK

## FRANCIS S. GABRESKI INTERNATIONAL AIRPORT/ AIR NATIONAL GUARD (FOK/KFOK)

Gabreski Airport (ANG)
Bldg 369
Westhampton Beach, NY 11978-1201.

**LOCATION:** On Long Island, one mile south of NY-27 (Sunrise Highway), exit 63 onto Old Riverhead Road. *USMRA: Page 20 (F-2).* ML-ARM: *(40°49'N/72°36'W).* LST: GMT-05:00. NMC: Southampton, 12 miles east. Main installation numbers: C-631-288-7400, D-312-456-7300.

**REGISTRATION INFO: C-631-288-7362, D-312-456-7362, Fax: C-631-288-7420, D-312-457-7420.** Bldg 369, Hours: 0730-1600 Mon-Fri. Directions: Between large hangars, 0.13 miles from main gate. All facilities of a regional airport. Limited military support facilities. Exchange: C-631-288-7557, Combined Club: C-631-288-7481. Police (Security) C-631-288-7478

### UNSCHEDULED FLIGHTS

Flights via MC-130P aircraft to CONUS locations. Call for destinations, routings and schedules.

## NIAGARA FALLS INTERNATIONAL AIRPORT/AIR RESERVE STATION (IAG/KIAG)

| | |
| --- | --- |
| 914 Airlift Wing 105A | 107th Air Refueling Wing |
| 10460 Wagner Drive | 9910 Blewett Avenue |
| Niagara Falls IAP/ARS | Niagra Falls NYANG |
| Niagara Falls, NY 14304-5010 | Niagra Falls, NY 14304-6001 |

**LOCATION:** Take I-190 north or south to Niagara Falls, exit 23 Porter Packard Road east. Turn right onto Porter Road (Route 182) east and stay on it past five traffic lights until it becomes Lockport Road. After one mile on Lockport, turn right at main gate. *USMRA: Page 20 (D-6).* ML-ARM: *(43°10'N/78°59'W).* LST: GMT-05:00. NMC: Niagara Falls, 5 miles west. Main installation numbers: C-716-236-2000, D-312-238-2000.

**REGISTRATION INFO: IAP: C-716-236-2534, D-312-238-2534, Rec: C-716-236-2475, D-312-238-2475, Fax: C-716-236-2391, D-312-238-2391.** Bldg 912, room 163. **ANG: C-716-236-2474, D-312-238-2474. E-mail: kurt.novak@iag.afres.af.mil** Bldg 807 (SQ OPS), Hours: 0800-1600 Mon-Fri. Ask guard at gate for directions. 107th Air Wing ANG:107 Air Refueling Wing, 107 Operations Support Flight, 10055 Guardian Street, Bldg 912, Room 163, Niagara Falls IAP, NY 14304-6011.

**PAX LOUNGES:** Family lounge with baby changing station available; Hours: limited to scheduled Space-A flights. Minimum essentials. Restrooms. **Protocol Service:** Bldg 800, Hours: 0800-1600 Mon-Fri, C-716-236-2138.

**FOOD SERVICE: Consolidated Open Mess:** C-716-297-6604. **Snack Bars:** Rec Center: C-716-236-2329. **Snack Vending:** Bldg 807, Hours: 0800-1600 Mon-Fri.

**TRANSPORTATION:** Limited. No commercial bus service to/from base. Taxi service is available. Car rental available at commercial side of IAP. **Parking:** Limited. Overnight and long term by arrangement with Security Police.

**TML:** Niagara Falls Lodge, Bldg. 312, 10780 Kinross Street, 0700-2300 daily, C-716-236-2014, D-312-238-2014, Fax: C-716-236-6348, D-312-238-6348. DV/VIP C-716-236-2136/2139.

**TRAVELERS AID: Security Police:** Main gate, C-716-236-2279.

**SUPPORT AVAILABLE: Exchange:** Bldg 805, C-716-236-2100. **Retiree Activities:** Bldg 800, C-716-236-2389.

**OTHER INFORMATION:** Port of Entry and U.S. Customs Service Airport.

**ATTRACTIONS:** Greater Buffalo/Niagara Falls area, Lake Erie, Lake Ontario, Niagara River, Canada, Festival of Lights.

**NIAGARA FALLS IAP/ARS, NY (IAG); REGION: ATL; OPERATOR: AMC; TYPE: CGO W/ PAX; ROUTE: OHN3C; SAMPLE SCHEDULE: 4TH WED; EQUIPMENT: C130E**

{IAG *SE* ➡ NGU (★) *SE* ➡ NRR *SE* ➡ STX ⇌ NRR *NW* ➡ NGU (★) *NW* ➡ IAG}

| LI/ICAO | AIRPORT/STATION | CTRY/STA | DAYS EN ROUTE |
|---------|-----------------|----------|---------------|
| IAG/KIAG | Niagara Falls IAP/ARS | NY | +0 |
| NGU/KNGU | Norfolk NS | VA | +1 |
| NRR/TJNR | Roosevelt Roads NS | PR | +1 |
| STX/TISX | Alexander Hamilton IAP (St Croix) | VI | +2 |
| NRR/TJNR | Roosevelt Roads NS | PR | +2 |
| NGU/KNGU | Norfolk NS | VA | +3 |
| IAG/KIAG | Niagara Falls IAP/ARS | NY | |

### UNSCHEDULED FLIGHTS

Frequent flights via C-130H and KC-135R to CONUS and OCONUS locations. Call for destinations, routings and schedules.

# STEWART INTERNATIONAL AIRPORT/ AIR NATIONAL GUARD BASE (SWF/KSWF)

105 OSF/DOTM
218 Militia Way
Newburgh, NY 12550-5043

**LOCATION:** From I-84 or I-87 take exit 17 Union Avenue south to Route 17-K west for three miles. Follow signs to Stewart ANG Base, colocated with Stewart IAP. *USMRA: Page 21 (M-10).* ML-ARM: (41°30'N/74°05'W). LST: GMT-05:00. NMC: New York City, 60 miles south. Main installation numbers: C-845-563-2001, D-312-636-2001.

**REGISTRATION INFO: USMC OPS: C-845-563-2965/2968, D-312-636-2965/2968, Fax: C-845-563-2988, D-312-636-2988, Bldg 300. AIR GUARD OPS: C-845-563-2226, D-312-636-2226, Fax: C-845-563-2228, D-312-636-2228.** Full base support at U.S. Military Academy (West Point) 15 miles south. Limited pax facilities. **Stewart ANG has Space-A availability on C-0058 aircraft; however, a maximum of 19 seats will be released for flights out of Stewart.**

**PAX LOUNGES:** Very limited services and accommodations available in passenger lounge. No VIP lounge available.

**FOOD SERVICE:** Snack Vending in pax lounge and local business food service establishments are available.

**TRANSPORTATION:** Local area transportation is available.

**TML:** Nearest TML is at U.S. Military Academy, West Point, Hotel Thayer, Building 674, 24 hours daily, C-845-446-4731, D-312-688-2632 or 1-800-247-5047. DV/VIP C-845-938-4315/4316, Five Star Inn, C-845-446-4731, D-312-688-4731.

**TRAVELERS AID: Chapel:** C-845-564-3310. **Dental:** C-845-563-3438. **Medical:** C-845-563-2113. **Security Police:** C-845-567-6031.

**SUPPORT AVAILABLE: Exchange:** C-845-564-7601. **Laundry/Dry Cleaner:** Available.

**OTHER INFORMATION:** United States Port of Entry.

**STEWART IAP/ANGB, NY (SWF); REGION: ATL; OPERATOR: AMC; TYPE: CGO W/ PAX; ROUTE: IFV1A; SAMPLE SCHEDULE: 1ST WED; EQUIPMENT: C005A**

{SWF *SE* ➡ DOV (★) *NE* ➡ RMS *SE* ➡ AVB ⇌ AVB *NW* ➡ MHZ *SW* ➡ DOV (★) *NW* ➡ SWF}

| LI/ICAO | AIRPORT/STATION | CTRY/STA | DAYS EN ROUTE |
|---------|-----------------|----------|---------------|
| SWF/KSWF | Stewart IAP/ANGB | NY | +0 |
| DOV/KDOV | Dover AFB | DE | +0 |
| RMS/ETAR | Ramstein AB | DE | +1 |
| AVB/LIPA | Aviano AB | IT | +1 |
| AVB/LIPA | Aviano AB | IT | +1 |
| MHZ/EGUN | RAF Mildenhall | GB | +2 |
| DOV/KDOV | Dover AFB | DE | +3 |
| SWF/KSWF | Stewart IAP/ANGB | NY | |

**STEWART IAP/ANGB, NY (SWF); REGION: ATL; OPERATOR: AMC; TYPE: CGO W/ PAX; ROUTE: IFV3A; SAMPLE SCHEDULE: 1ST MON; EQUIPMENT: C005A**

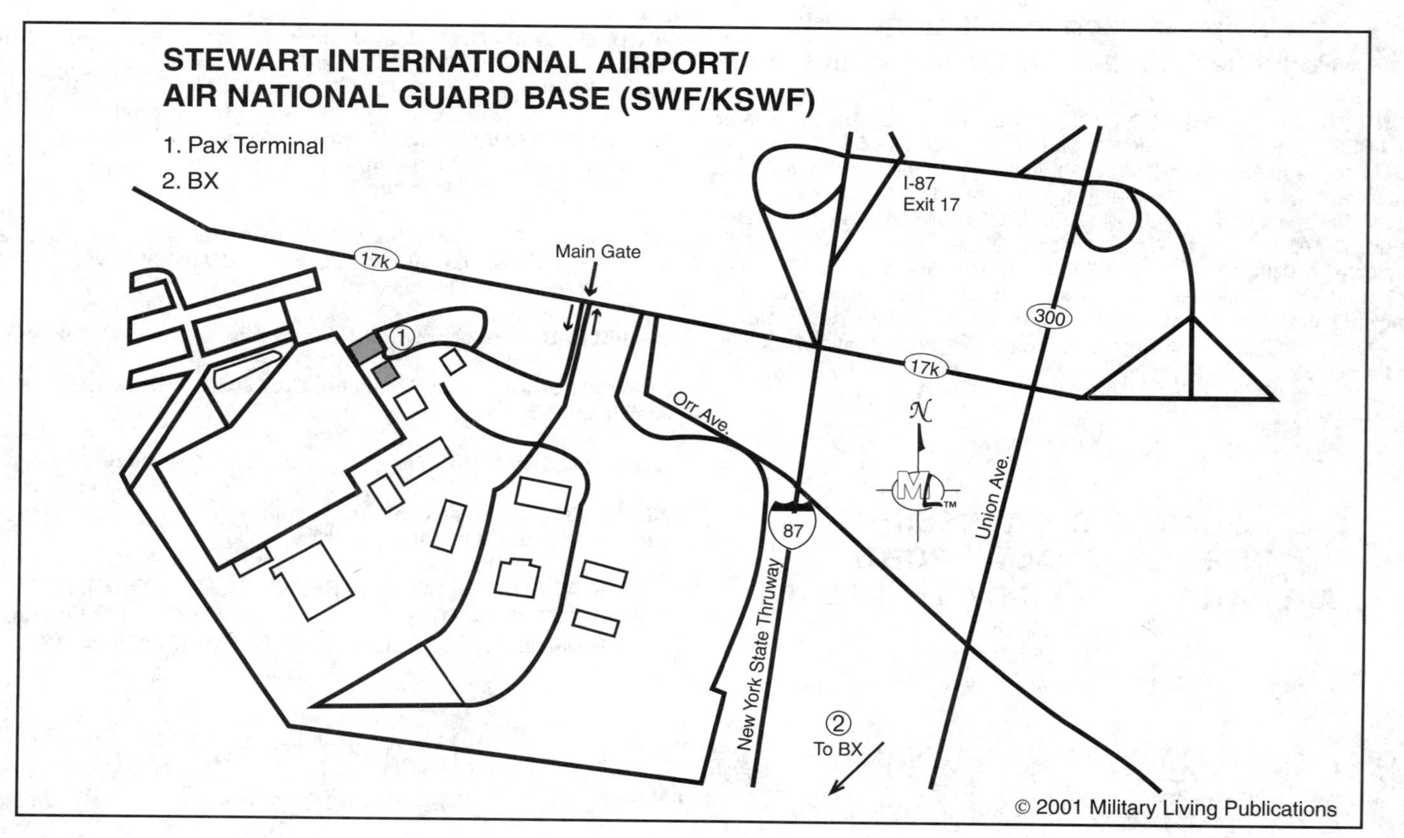

{SWF *SE* ➡ DOV (★) *NE* ➡ MHZ *SE* ➡ RMS ⇌ RMS *NW* ➡ MHZ *SW* ➡ DOV (★) *NE* ➡ SWF}

| LI/ICAO | AIRPORT/STATION | CTRY/STA | DAYS EN ROUTE |
|---|---|---|---|
| SWF/KSWF | Stewart IAP/ANGB | NY | +0 |
| DOV/KDOV | Dover AFB | DE | +1 |
| MHZ/EGUN | RAF Mildenhall | UK | +2 |
| RMS/ETAR | Ramstein AB | DE | +2 |
| MHZ/EGUN | RAF Mildenhall | UK | +3 |
| DOV/KDOV | Dover AFB | DE | +3 |
| SWF/KSWF | Stewart IAP/ANGB | | |

### EN ROUTE SCHEDULES

| AIRPORT/STATION | LI-MISSION (page #) |
|---|---|
| Andrews AFB | ADW-116/MEDEVAC (37) |

### UNSCHEDULED FLIGHTS

Some flights via C-005A/B aircraft. Flights to CONUS and OCONUS. Call for destinations, routings and schedules.

## STRATTON AIR NATIONAL GUARD BASE (SCH/KSCH)

109 AW/DOCP
1 Air National Guard Road
Scotia, NY 12302-9752

**LOCATION:** From I-87 north or south, exit 89 to NY-146 west (Mechanicville Road). Continue on, as it changes to Glenridge Road, to Maple Avenue, left (south) onto Air National Guard Road and gate. *USMRA: Page 21 (M,N-6).* *ML-ARM: (42°51'N/73°54'W).* LST: GMT-05:00. NMC: Schenectady, 3 miles south. Main installation numbers: C-518-344-2300 D-312-974-2300.

**REGISTRATION INFO: C-518-344-2420, D-312-974-9420, Fax: C-518-344-2520, D-312-974-9520.** ANG Ops Bldg. 2A, 24 hours daily. First building past gate on left, enter from parking lot. All the support facilities of a regional airport. Commissary: C-518-370-5935. NEX: C-518-377-6640.

**TRANSPORTATION:** AMTRAK, 5 miles away. Rental cars at Ramada Inn Schenectady, 4 miles away. Albany IAP, 15 miles away.

**ATTRACTIONS:** Saratoga Racecourse, 25 miles away. Saratoga Performing Arts Center, 24 miles away. Downtown Albany (State Capital), 20 miles away.

### UNSCHEDULED FLIGHTS

Flights via C-130H aircraft to CONUS and OCONUS locations on training missions. Call for destinations, routings and schedules.

## Other New York Installations with Possible Space-A Air Opportunities

**SYRACUSE-HANCOCK FIELD INTERNATIONAL AIRPORT (SYR/KSYR),** 174th FW, 6001 E Malloy Road, Syracuse, NY 13211-7099. C-315-454-6100 D-312-489-9100. **LOCATION:** From I-81 north or south, take exit 27 north of Syracuse, east to IAP/ANGB. *USMRA: Page 21 (I-6).* *ML-ARM: (43°07'N/76°06'W).* LST: GMT-05:00. MEDEVAC flights only. Call for destinations, routings and schedules. **TML:** Nearest TML is approximately 90 miles away at Fort Drum, Lodging office, Building T-227, 24 hours daily, C-315-772-5435, D-312-341-6011. DV/VIP C-315-772-5010. Also, the Inn at Fort Drum at 4205 Po Valley Road, C-315-773-7777.

**WHEELER-SACK ARMY AIRFIELD (GTB/KGTB),** 10th Mountain Division, Fort Drum, NY 13602-5000. **LOCATION:** From I-81 north or south take exit 48 (north of Watertown) east, and follow signs to Fort Drum. *USMRA: Page 21 (J-3).* *ML-ARM: (44°03'N/75°43'W).* LST: GMT-05:00. NMC: Watertown, eight miles southwest. **REGISTRATION INFO: C-315-772-5681, D-312-341-5681.** Bldg P-2065, 0700-1730 hrs. MEDEVAC flights. Call for destinations, routings and schedules. **TML:** Lodging office, Building T-227, 24 hours daily, C-315-772-5435, D-312-341-6011. DV/VIP C-315-772-5010. Also, the Inn at 4205 Po Valley Road, C-315-773-7777. **RVC:** Remington Pond Recreational Area, C-315-772-5169, D-312-341-5169. **SUPPORT AVAILABLE:** Full base support facilities at Fort Drum.

### EN ROUTE SCHEDULES

| AIRPORT/STATION | LI-MISSION (page #) |
|---|---|
| Andrews AFB | ADW-116/MEDEVAC (37) |

# NORTH CAROLINA

## CHARLOTTE/DOUGLAS INTERNATIONAL AIRPORT (CLT/KCLT)

145th AW/LGT
5225 Morris Field Drive, Bldg 1
Charlotte, NC 28208-5797

**LOCATION:** From I-77 north or south take exit 6 A/B to Billy Graham Parkway (US-521) north to Morris Field Drive (3.5 miles), turn left. Base is on your right. From I-85 take Billy Graham Parkway Exit 33 south to Morris Field Drive, turn right. *USMRA: Page 44 (G-4).* *ML-ARM: (35°13'N/80°56'W).* LST: GMT-05:00. NMC: Charlotte, 6 miles east. Main installation numbers: C-704-391-4100, D-312-583-9210.

**REGISTRATION INFO: C-704-391-4177, D-312-583-9177, Fax: C-704-391-4322.** ANG, Hours: 0730-1600 Mon-Fri. No pax facilities. All pax processed by Base Ops. Full support of an IAP available. **TML:** Nearest TML is at Fort Bragg, Lodging office, Building D-3601 (Moon Hall), Room 101, 24 hours daily, C-910-396-7700, D-312-236-7700. DV/VIP C-910-396-2804. Limited military base support. Commercial transportation available.

**ATTRACTIONS:** Carowinds Amusement Park, Charlotte Coliseum home of the Hornets.

### UNSCHEDULED FLIGHTS

Flights via C-130H aircraft to CONUS and OCONUS locations on training missions. Call for destinations, routings and schedules.

## CHERRY POINT MARINE CORPS AIR STATION (NKT/KNKT)

Transient Services Division, Bldg 199
Cherry Point, NC 28533-5079

**LOCATION:** On NC-101 between New Bern and Morehead City. US-70 connects with NC-101 at Havelock. *USMRA: Page 45 (M,N-4).* *ML-ARM: (34°35'N/76°54'W).* LST: GMT-05:00. NMC: Jacksonville, 30 miles southwest. Main installation numbers: C-252-466-2811, D-312-582-1110.

**REGISTRATION INFO: C-252-466-3232/3279, D-312-582-3232, Rec: C-252-466-3225, Fax: C-252-466-4518/6526.** Bldg 199, 24 hours daily. Directions: From main gate take Roosevelt Blvd to a right on A Street to end. Pax Service in ATC tower building. **Pax Service Office:** Bldg 199, Hours: 0730-1630 daily, C-252-466-2379, D-312-582-2379. **Pax Paging:** C-252-466-3232/2379, D-312-582-3232/2379 (NCO on duty).**PAX LOUNGES:** No family lounge. **General:** Bldg 199, 24 hours daily, C-252-466-2379. A/C, bag check, restrooms, O/S seats, telephones (local and long distance). **DV/VIP:** Bldg 199, 24 hours daily, C-252-466-2379. A/C, bag check, coffee/tea served, restrooms, O/S seats, separate reading/writing rooms, telephones (local, long distance and defense), TV.

**FOOD SERVICE: Cafeteria:** C-252-466-4381. **O Club:** C-252-447-2395. **Snack Bars:** Hours: 0800-1400 Mon-Fri, C-252-447-7041 ext 285, Topside. **SNCO Club:** C-252-466-3087. Snack Vending available.

**TRANSPORTATION: Air Tickets:** SATO, C-252-466-2016. **Off Base Bus:** C-252-466-9287, D-312-582-9287, front gate. **Off Base Car Rental:** C-252-240-0218, C-1-800-325-8007, 16 miles away. **On Base Shuttle/Bus:** C-252-466-2787. **On Base Taxi:** C-252-466-3505, D-312-582-3505, .5 miles away. **Off Base Taxi:** C-252-447-7744, 1 mile away. **Taxi (Gov):** C-252-466-2808 (duty passengers only).

**TML:** Lodging office, 24 hours daily, Building 3673 (EM), 24 hours daily, C-252-463-3061, D-312-582-3060. DV/VIP C-252-466-2848, 24 hours daily.

**RVC:** MWR FAMCAMP, ITT Dir, MWR, C-252-466-2197/2172, D-312-582-2197.

**TRAVELERS AID: Chaplain:** C-252-466-4001, D-312-582-4001. **Emergency Relief:** C-252-447-2074. **Lost and Found:** C-252-466-3445. **Medical:** C-252-466-0266, D-312-582-4419. **Red Cross:** C-252-466-3613, D-312-582-3613. **Security Police:** C-252-466-3615, D-312-582-3615.

**SUPPORT AVAILABLE: Bank/Currency Exchange:** C-252-447-2077. **Credit Union:** C-252-447-0692. **Dry Cleaner:** C-252-447-2130. **Exchange:** C-252-447-7041. **Hair Styles:** Barber, C-252-447-7041; Beauty, C-252-447-1857. **Laundry:** C-252-466-5203, D-312-582-5203. **Postal Service:** C-252-466-2496, D-312-582-2496. **Shoppette:** C-252-447-4233.

**OTHER INFORMATION:** Port of Entry and U.S. Customs Service Airport.

**ATTRACTIONS:** Outer Banks, Kitty Hawk.

### EN ROUTE SCHEDULES

| AIRPORT/STATION | LI-MISSION (page #) |
|---|---|
| Scott AFB | BLV-C-621/MEDEVAC (30) |

### UNSCHEDULED FLIGHTS
Frequent CONUS flights to: Beaufort MCAS, SC (**NBC**); Norfolk NS, VA (**NGU**); and Washington NAF, MD (**NSF**) via C-009B aircraft on passenger missions. Occasional OCONUS and foreign flights. Call for destinations, routings and schedules, usually available 1 week in advance.

## ELIZABETH CITY COAST GUARD AIR STATION (ECG/KECG)
Flight Services
Elizabeth City CGAS, NC 27909-5006

**LOCATION:** Take I-64 east to US-17 south to Elizabeth City, left on Halstead Boulevard, three miles to main gate of Center; or from I-95 north or south, exit 176 east on US 158 to Elizabeth City. *USMRA: Page 45 (O-1). ML-ARM: (36°15'N/76°11'W).* LST: GMT-05:00. NMC: Elizabeth City, 4 miles north. Main installation numbers: C-252-335-6886, D-312-935-1520.

**REGISTRATION INFO: C-252-335-6333, D-312-935-6333.** Bldg 49, base of ATC tower, Hours: 0800-1600 Mon-Fri. Ask gate guard for directions. **Pax Service Office:** C-252-335-6333, D-312-935-1520 (Duty Officer). **PAX LOUNGES:** No pax lounges. Pax assemble at Air Ops Center located at base of ATC tower for processing.

**FOOD SERVICE: All Ranks Club:** C-252-335-6301. **Dining Hall:** C-252-335-6281. **Snack Vending:** Bldg 55, 24 hours daily.

**TRANSPORTATION: Air Tickets:** AAA Travel, C-252-335-6321. **Off Base Bus:** Elizabeth City; Trailways, C-252-335-5183. **Car Rentals:** Elizabeth City; National, C-252-335-1860. **Off Base Taxi:** In Elizabeth City. **Parking:** ATC tower, 24 hours daily, (limited/some reserved spaces).

**TML:** Lodging office, Building 5, 0800-1630 daily, C-252-335-6397. Six two-bedroom trailers, reservations required, C-252-335-6397.

**RVC:** MWR Office, Bldg 5, Check-in main gate. C-252-335-6397, Fax: C-252-335-6296.

**TRAVELERS AID: Chaplain:** C-252-335-6202. **Medical:** Bldg 41, 24 hours daily, C-252-335-6460. **Red Cross:** C-252-335-2185. **Security Police:** Main gate, 24 hours daily, C-252-335-6398.

**SUPPORT AVAILABLE: Bank/Currency Exchange:** C-252-335-6237. **Exchange:** C-252-335-6207. **Hair Styles:** Barber, C-252-335-6403; Beauty, C-252-335-6382. **Laundry:** C-252-335-2797. **Postal Service:** (Off base) C-252-338-3869.

**ATTRACTIONS:** North Carolina's Outer Banks, fresh seafood, beaches, deep-sea fishing, hang gliding at Jockey's Ridge, Wright Brothers Memorial.

### UNSCHEDULED FLIGHTS
Infrequent flights via C-130H aircraft to Borinquen CGAS, PR (**BQN**); Clearwater CGAS, FL (**PIE**) and other destinations. Call for destinations, routings and schedules.

## NEW RIVER MARINE CORPS AIR STATION (NCA/KNCA)
Commanding Officer
MCAS New River Ops Dept
PSC Box 21001
Jacksonville, NC 28545-1001.

**LOCATION:** Off US-17 north or south, two miles south of Jacksonville, on east side of US-17. Clearly marked. *USMRA: Page 45 (L,M-5). ML-ARM: (39°43'N/77°28'W).* LST: GMT-05:00. NMC: Jacksonville, 2 miles northeast. NMI: Camp Lejeune, 10 miles east. Main installation numbers: C-910-451-1113 D-312-751-1113.

**REGISTRATION INFO: C-910-450-6316, D-312-750-6316.** Directions: Straight on Curtis Road to Bldg AS-843 on left across from airfield. Helicopters only - very limited Space-A.

**FOOD SERVICES:** Snack Vending available.

**TRANSPORTATION:** Off Base Car Rental and Taxi available.

**TML:** Lodging office, Building 705, Flounder Road, duty hours, C-910-937-5020, D-312-750-6621. Fax: C-910-450-6969.

**RVC:** Marina, MWR, Check-in marina, C-910-451-6578, D-312-484-6578, Fax: C-910-450-6907.

**TRAVELERS AID: Chaplain:** C-910-450-6801. **Medical:** C-910-450-6511. **Security Police:** C-910-450-6111.

**SUPPORT AVAILABLE: Dry Cleaner:** C-910-450-0593, D-312-750-0593. **Exchange:** C-910-450-0539, D-312-750-0539. **Postal Service:** C-910-450-6397, D-312-750-6397.

**ATTRACTIONS:** Great North Carolina beaches. Cape Lookout National Seashore to the northeast.

### UNSCHEDULED FLIGHTS
Frequent flights to Andrews AFB, MD (**ADW**); Beaufort MCAS, SC (**NBC**); Cherry Point MCAS, NC (**NKT**); and Norfolk NS, VA (**NGU**). Call for destinations, routings and schedules.

## POPE AIR FORCE BASE (POB/KPOB)
3rd APS/TRP
718 Manchester Street
Pope AFB, NC 28308-2087

**LOCATION:** Take I-95, exit to NC-87/24 west. Follow signs northwest for 15 miles to Pope AFB and Fort Bragg. *USMRA: Page 45 (J-4). ML-ARM: (35°10'N/78°59'W).* LST: GMT-05:00. NMC: Fayetteville, 12 miles southeast. Main installation numbers: C-910-394-1110, D-312-424-1110.

**REGISTRATION INFO: C-910-394-6527, D-312-424-6527, Rec: C-910-394-6525, D-312-424-6525, Fax: C-910-394-6526, D-312-424-6526. E-mail: spacea@pope.af.mil WEB: www.pope.af.mil/43og/3aps/pax.htm** Bldg 704, Hours: 0715-2400 Mon-Fri, 0900-1700 Sat. Directions: From gate 3, straight on Manchester Road to a right on Booster Street to Pax Term on right. Signs at all gates give directions to Pax Term. **Pax Service Office:** Bldg 708, Hours: 0715-1615 Mon-Fri. *Note: the Pax Term will be moving to a new building soon; an exact date has not been determined due to construction delays. Call for more information.*

**PAX LOUNGES:** No separate family lounge. **General:** Bldg 718, Hours: 0715-1615 daily, C-910-394-4429. A/C, baggage check, restrooms, TV, P/C seats. **Protocol Service:** Bldg 309, Hours: 0715-1615 Mon-Fri, C-910-394-4739, D-312-424-4739.

**FOOD SERVICE: Cafeteria:** 505 Virgin Street, C-910-394-4377. **In-flight Meals:** 736 Armistead Street, C-910-394-2671. **Pope Club:** 5504 Reilly Road, C-910-394-2154. **Snack Vending:** Bldg 708, 24 hours daily.

**TRANSPORTATION:** No base shuttle. No on base transportation. **Car Rentals:** Fort Bragg, Hours: 0800-1800 Mon-Sat, 1200-1800 Sun; Continental Car Rental, 1-888-374-6466, C-910-436-5200. SATO Pope AFB.

**TML:** Lodging office, Carolina Inn, 302 Ethridge Street, 24 hours daily, C-910-394-4131, D-312-424-4131. Fax: C-910-394-4912. DV/VIP C-910-394-4739.

**TRAVELERS AID: Chaplain:** Bldg 317, Hours: 0800-1700 Mon-Fri, C-910-394-2677, After hours C-910-394-0111. **Emergency Relief:** Bldg 308, Hours: 0715-1615 Mon-Fri, C-910-394-2470 (AF Aid), C-910-394-2800. **Medical:** Bldg 307, 24 hours daily, C-910-394-2232/4421. **Red Cross:** Bldg 1-1139, Hours: 0800-1630 Mon-Fri, C-910-396-1234, After hours C-910-394-0111. **Security Police:** Bldg 378, 24 hours daily, C-910-394-2808. **USO:** 333 Ray Ave, Fayetteville.

**SUPPORT AVAILABLE: Bank/Currency Exchange:** Bldg 346, Hours: 0900-1700 Mon-Fri, C-910-497-6161. **Exchange:** Bldg 355, Hours: 1030-1730 Mon-Fri, 1030-1300 Sat, C-910-497-2111. **Hair Styles:** Bldg 355, Hours: 0700-1700 Mon-Fri, C-910-497-5119. **Laundry/Dry Cleaning:** Bldg 355, Hours: 0900-1700 Mon-Fri, 0900-1500 Sat, C-910-497-2111 **Postal Service:** Bldg 381, Hours: 0715-1630 Mon-Fri, 0715-1000 Sat, C-910-394-2828. Also nearby Fort Bragg.

**ATTRACTIONS:** Raleigh, Durham, Chapel Hill Triangle, 2 hours from Atlantic Ocean, Battleship USS North Carolina is 2 hours away in Willington, several museums in nearby Raleigh, Wrigh Brothers Memorial.

### POPE AFB, NC (POB); REGION: ATL; OPERATOR: AMC; TYPE: CGO W/ PAX; ROUTE: ACN1A; SAMPLE SCHEDULE: 2ND THU; EQUIPMENT: C130E

{POB *NE* ➡ NGU (★) *SE* ➡ NRR ⇌ NRR *NW* ➡ NGU (★) *SW* ➡ POB}

| LI/ICAO | AIRPORT/STATION | CTRY/STA | DAYS EN ROUTE |
| --- | --- | --- | --- |
| POB/KPOB | Pope AFB | NC | +0 |
| NGU/KNGU | Norfolk NS | VA | +1 |
| NRR/TJNR | Roosevelt Roads NS | PR | +2 |
| NGU/KNGU | Norfolk NS | VA | +1 |
| POB/KPOB | Pope AFB | NC | +0 |

### POPE AFB, NC (POB); REGION: ATL; OPERATOR: AMC; TYPE: CGO W/ PAX; ROUTE: ACN1B; SAMPLE SCHEDULE: 1ST WED; EQUIPMENT: C130E

{POB *NE* ➡ NGU (★) *SE* ➡ NRR *NW* ➡ NGU *SE* ➡ NBW ⇌ NBW *NW* ➡ NGU (★) *SW* ➡ POB}

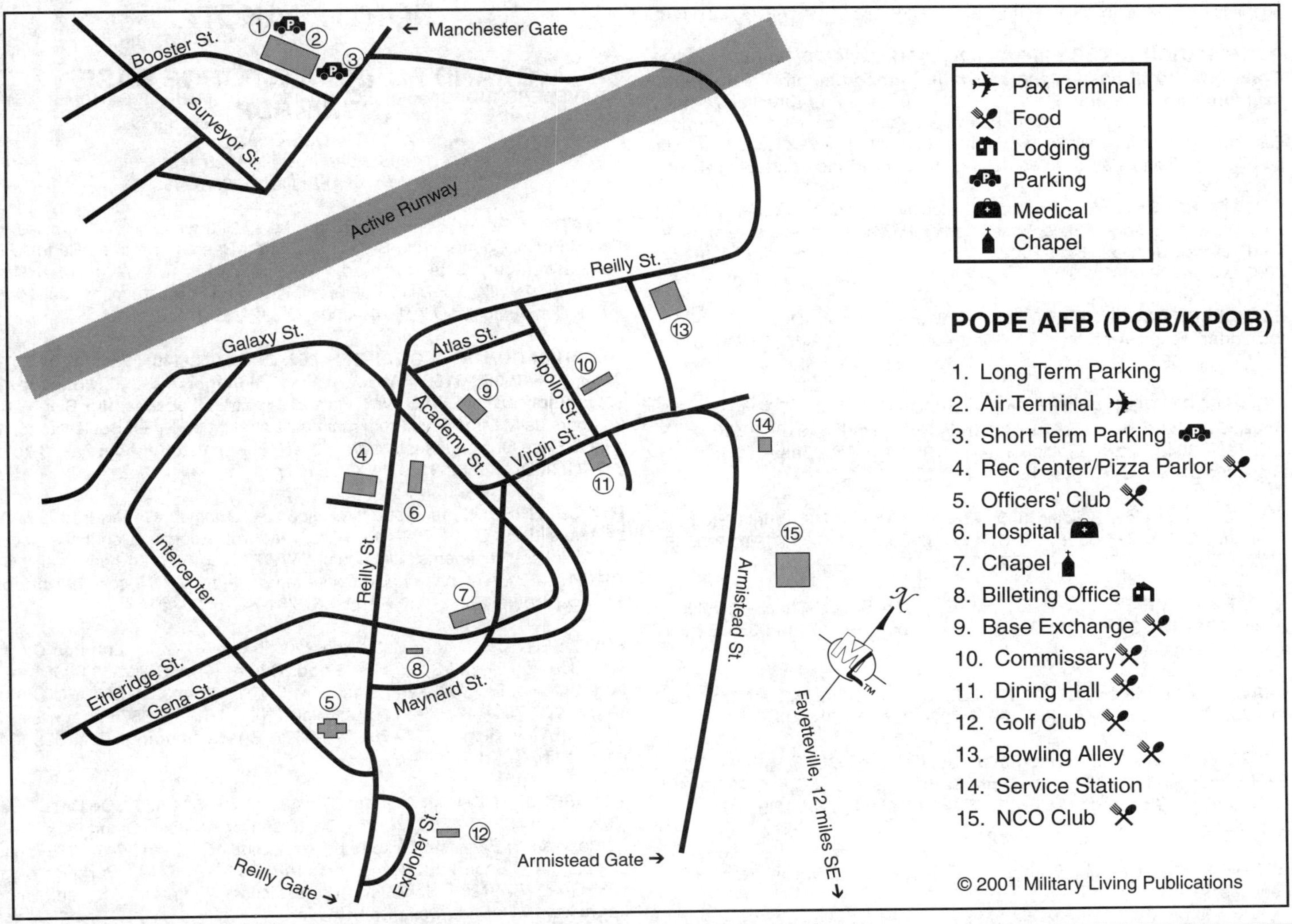

| LI/ICAO | AIRPORT/STATION | CTRY/STA | DAYS EN ROUTE |
|---|---|---|---|
| POB/KPOB | Pope AFB | NC | +0 |
| NGU/KNGU | Norfolk NS | VA | +1 |
| NRR/TJNR | Roosevelt Roads NS | PR | +2 |
| NGU/KNGU | Norfolk NS | VA | +1 |
| NBW/MUGM | Guantanamo Bay NAS | CU | +1 |
| NGU/KNGU | Norfolk NS | VA | +1 |
| POB/KPOB | Pope AFB | NC | +0 |

## EN ROUTE SCHEDULES

| AIRPORT/STATION | LI-MISSION (page #) |
|---|---|
| Scott AFB | BLV-C-621/MEDEVAC (30) |
| Scott AFB | BLV-C-626/MEDEVAC (30) |
| Peterson AFB | COS-OPN3B (16) |

### UNSCHEDULED FLIGHTS

Flights via C-130H aircraft. Call for destinations, routings and schedules.

# SEYMOUR JOHNSON AIR FORCE BASE (GSB/KGSB)

4th TFW/LGTT
1280 Flightline Road, Bldg 4012
Seymour Johnson AFB, NC 27531-5270

**LOCATION:** From US-70 Bypass east or west, take Seymour Johnson AFB exit east onto Berkeley Boulevard to main gate. Clearly marked. *USMRA: Page 45 (L-3). ML-ARM: (35°20'N/77°59'W).* LST: GMT-05:00. NMC: Raleigh, 50 miles west. Main installation numbers: C-919-722-1110, D-312-722-1110.

**REGISTRATION INFO: C-919-722-4170, D-312-722-4170; Fax: C-919-722-4162. Email: 4trans.spacea@seymourjohnson.af.mil WEB: www.seymourjohnson.af.mil** Hours: 0800-1600 Mon-Fri, Directions: From Berkeley Gate straight on Wright Brothers Avenue to a left on Vermont Garrison, to a right on Blakeslee Avenue, to a left on Tower Road to a right on Flightline Road. Pax Term on right at end of Flightline Road, Bldg. 4743.

**PAX LOUNGES:** Limited, no separate family lounge. No General/DV/VIP Lounge. A/C, bag check, telephones (local), P/C bleacher seats, restrooms, TV. **Protocol Service:** Bldg 2902, Hours: 0730-1630 Mon-Fri, C-919-722-0003 D-312-722-0003.

**FOOD SERVICE: Dining Hall:** C-919-722-1244; D-312-722-1244. **Expanded Flight Kitchen:** C-919-722-4085; D-312-722-4085 **NCO Club:** C-919-734-2993 **O Club:** C-919-722-1340; D-312-722-1340.

**TRANSPORTATION: Air Tickets:** C-919-722-4036; D-312-722-4036; . **Off Base Bus:** Goldsboro, C-919-734-3811. **Bus (Gov):** C-919-722-1304; D-312-722-1304. **Limo:** Goldsboro, C-919-751-0525. **Base Taxi:** (duty passengers only). C-919-722-1304 D-722-1304.

**TML:** Lodging office, Building 3804, 24 hours daily, 1235 Wright Brothers Avenue, C-919-722-0385, D-312-722-0385, Fax: C-919-722-0375, DV/VIP:C-919-722-0003, D-312-722-0003.

**RVC:** FAMCAMP, Outdoor Rec, 1515 Goodson Street, Check-in Outdoor Rec, C-919-736-5405, D-312-488-5405, Fax: C-919-731-4035, E-mail: sjoutrec@esn.net

**TRAVELERS AID: Chaplain:** C-919-722-0315; D-722-0315. **Red Cross:** C-919-735-7201. **Security Police:** C-919-722-1211, D-722-1211.

**SUPPORT AVAILABLE: Bank: Seymour Johnson FCU:** C-919-734-8224. **Exchange:** C-919-735-8512. **Hair Styles:** Barber, C-919-735-9442; **Laundry/Dry Cleaning:** C-919-734-7436. **Medical:** TRICARE C-1-800-931-9501.

**ATTRACTIONS:** Raleigh, Durham, and Chapel Hill Triangle, New Bern, beaches within 2 hour drive.

### UNSCHEDULED FLIGHTS

Unscheduled flights via KC-135R aircraft to various CONUS and OCONUS locations. Call for destinations, routings and schedules.

## Other North Carolina Installations with Possible Space-A Air Opportunities

**SIMMONS ARMY AIRFIELD (FBG/KFBG),** Readiness Business Center, ATTN: Aviation Branch, Bldg #P4541 Parham Blvd, Simmons AAF, Fort Bragg, NC 28307-5000. **LOCATION:** From I-95 north or south, exit 52 to NC-24 west for 15 miles. NC-24 runs through Post as Bragg Boulevard. From US-401 (Fayetteville Bypass) exit to All American Expressway, west five miles to Fort. *USMRA: Page 45 (I,J-4). ML-ARM: (35°07'N/78°56'W).* LST: GMT-05:00. **REGISTRATION INFO: C-910-396-7804, D-312-236-7804, Fax: C-910-396-5730, D-312-236-5730.** Pax Lounge: DV/VIP lounge available. **TRANSPORTATION: Off Base Taxi,** 910-488-5555. **Off Base Car Rental,** 910-436-5200. **TML:** Lodging office, Building D-3601 (Moon Hall), Room 101, 24 hours daily, C-910-396-7700, D-312-236-7700. DV/VIP C-910-396-2804. **TRAVELERS AID: Red Cross:** Hours: 0800-1700, C-910-867-8151. **SUPPORT AVAILABLE: Credit Union:** Hours: 0930-1700, C-910-864-2232, 3 miles away. **Dry Cleaner:** Hours: 0900-2000, C-910-497-0305, 3 miles away. **Exchange:** Hours: 0900-2200 Mon-Sat, 0900-2000 Sun, C-910-436-4888, 2 miles away. **Postal Service:** 0800-1700 Mon-Fri, 0800-1300 Sat, C-910-436-0763, 4 miles away. **Shoppette:** Hours: 0600-2000 Mon-Fri, 0900-1700 Sat-Sun, C-910-436-1600, 2 miles away.

### UNSCHEDULED FLIGHTS

Limited Space-A air opportunities via executive C-12 and UC-35 aircraft to CONUS locations. Call for destinations, routings and schedules.

# NORTH DAKOTA

# GRAND FORKS AIR FORCE BASE (RDR/KRDR)

319th OSS/OSAA
695 Steen Ave, Bldg 528
Grand Forks AFB, ND 58205-6245

**LOCATION:** From I-29 north or south, take US-2 west exit for 14 miles to Grand Forks, County Road B-3 (Emeraldo/Air Base) north one mile to AFB on east (right) side of road. *USMRA: Page 83 (I-3). ML-ARM: (47°55'N/97°23'W).* LST: GMT-06:00. NMC: Grand Forks, 15 miles east. Main installation numbers: C-701-747-3000, D-312-362-1110.

**REGISTRATION INFO: C-701-747-4403, D-312-362-4403, Fax: C-701-747-3169, D-312-362-3169 (Attn: Airfield Manager). E-mail: baseops2 @grandforks.af.mil WEB: www.grandforks.af.mil/spacea.htm** Bldg 528, 24 hours daily. Directions: From main gate straight on Steen Boulevard for 1 mile to Base Ops on the left under old ATC Tower. **Pax Service:** Fax: C-701-747-3169, D-312-362-3169 (NCO on duty).

**PAX LOUNGES:** General and family lounge combined. **General:** Bldg 528, 24 hours daily, C-701-747-4409. A/C, read/write rooms, telephones (local and defense), restrooms, P/C seats. **DV/VIP:** Bldg 528, 24 hours daily, C-701-747-4409. A/C, bag check, coffee/tea served, TV, O/S seats. **Protocol Service:** Hours: 0730-1630 Mon-Fri, C-701-747-5055.

**FOOD SERVICE: Dining Hall:** Bldg 220, C-701-747-3276. **Enlisted Club:** Bldg 309, C-701-747-3392. **Fast Food:** Burger King, C-701-594-8581. **In-Flight Meals:** Bldg 697, 24 hours daily, C-701-747-4439. **NCO/CPO Club:** Bldg 309, C-701-747-3392. **O Club:** Bldg 118, C-701-747-5576 **Snack Bars:** Bowling Alley, Bldg 202, C-701-594-2695. **Snack Vending:** Bldg 528, 24 hours daily, C-701-747-4409.

**TRANSPORTATION: Air Tickets:** Bldg 409, C-701-594-5507. **On Base Bus (Gov):** Bldg 459, C-701-747-3976. **Off Base Car Rentals:** Grand Forks IAP, 9 miles east of Base. **On Base Taxi (Gov):** Bldg 459, C-701-747-3976 (duty pax only). **Off Base Taxi:** Grand Forks IAP, C-701-746-7433. **Parking:** Bldg 528, C-701-747-4283. Short term no restrictions; long term - 3 week limit. Leave keys with Base Ops dispatch desk.

**TML:** Warrior Inn, Building 117, Holzapple & 6th Avenue, 24 hours daily, C-701-747-3070, D-312-362-3070. Fax: C-701-747-3069. DV/VIP C-701-747-5055; D-312-362-5055.

**RVC:** FAMCAMP, 201 Steen Avenue, Bldg 129, Check-in Outdoor Rec, Bldg 129, 0800-1700 hours or use registration envelope other hrs, C-701-747-3688, D-312-362-3688.

**TRAVELERS AID: Chaplain:** Bldg 109, C-701-747-3076. **Emergency Relief:** Bldg 101, C-701-747-6437 (AF Aid). **Lost/Found:** Bldg 103, C-701-747-5378. **Medical:** Bldg 109, 24 hours daily, C-701-747-5601, D-312-362-5601. **Red Cross:** Bldg 101, C-701-747-3855; after hours, C-701-747-3000. **Security Police:** Bldg 103, C-701-747-5351.

**SUPPORT AVAILABLE: Bank/Currency Exchange:** Bldg 207, C-701-795-3355. **Exchange:** Bldg 105, C-701-594-5542. **Hair Styles:** Bldg 105, Barber, C-701-594-2124; Beauty, C-701-594-4531. **Laundry/Dry Cleaning:** Bldg 211, C-701-594-2331. **Postal Service:** Bldg 230, C-701-747-3339.

**ATTRACTIONS:** Outdoor sports and recreation, Canada easy drive north via I-29.

### EN ROUTE SCHEDULES

| AIRPORT/STATION | LI-MISSION (page #) |
|---|---|
| Travis AFB | SUU-436/MEDEVAC (13) |
| Scott AFB | BLV-C-634/MEDEVAC (30) |

### UNSCHEDULED FLIGHTS

Frequent KC-135R flights to CONUS and foreign country locations. Call for destinations, routings and schedules.

# MINOT AIR FORCE BASE (MIB/KMIB)

5th OSS/OSAA
221 Flightline Drive, Bldg 746
Minot AFB, ND 58705-5049

**LOCATION:** On US-83 north or south, 13 miles north of Minot. *USMRA: Page 83 (D-2)*. ML-ARM: (48°25'N/101°17'W). LST: GMT-07:00. NMC: Minot, 15 miles south. Main installation numbers: C-701-723-6212, D-312-453-6212.

**REGISTRATION INFO: C-701-723-1854, D-312-453-1854, Fax: C-701-723-3637, D-312-453-3637. WEB: www.minot.af.mil** Bldg 746, Base Ops, 0600-2359 Mon-Thu, 0600-2200 Fri, 0800-1700 Sat, closed Sun and holidays. Directions: From main gate straight on Missile Ave to a left on Peacekeeper Place to Base Ops on the left. **Pax Service Office:** C-701-723-2348, D-312-453-2348.

**PAX LOUNGES:** Limited lounge facilities. **General:** Bldg 746, 0600-2359 Mon-Thu, 0600-2200 Fri, 0800-1700 Sat, closed Sun and holidays, C-701-723-2347. TV, restrooms, P/C seats. **Protocol Service:** Bldg 167, Hours: 0730-1630 Mon-Fri, C-701-723-3474, O6+.

**FOOD SERVICE: Base Exchange Food Court:** C-701-727-4706, 2 minutes away. **Cafeteria:** Bldg 587, C-701-727-4462; Kelly's (Bowling Lanes), C-701-727-4714, 5 minutes away. **Dining Hall:** Bldg 213, C-701-723-3550. **Fast Food:** Burger King, Hours: 0900-2100; Sub Shop, C-701-723-6707/6718, 5 minutes away. **In-flight Meals:** Bldg 846, Hours: 0001-2200 Mon-Fri, C-701-723-3079, after hours C-701-723-3503. **NCO/CPO Club:** Bldg 292, C-701-727-6156. **O Club:** Bldg 174, C-701-727-3731. **Restaurants:** Buffalo Bill's BBQ, Bldg 292, C-701-727-6156; Rough Rider's Pizza, Bldg 202, C-701-727-4377. **Snack Bars:** Pride Bldg, C-701-727-9312, 2 minutes away. **Snack Vending:** Bldg 746, C-701-727-4627.

**TRANSPORTATION: Air Tickets:** SATO, Bldg 475, C-701-723-2108, Bldg 202, Rec Center, C-701-727-6575. **On Base Bus:** C-701-723-3121. **Off Base Bus:** C-701-852-2477, Bus Depot in Minot. **Off Base Car Rental:** Avis, C-701-838-7665; Enterprise, C-701-838-3800; Hertz, C-701-852-0104; Rent-A-Wreck, C-701-838-0098. **Off Base Limo:** C-701-858-0790 or 852-8998. **Taxi (Gov):** C-701-723-3121. **Off Base Taxi:** C-701-852-8000. **Off Base Train Station:** International Travel, C-701-852-6445; Amtrak, C-701-852-0358. **Parking:** Short term parking available at Base Ops. Get parking pass from dispatch.

**TML:** Lodging office, Building 173, Summit Drive. C-701-723-6161, D-312-453-6161, Fax: C-701-723-1844, D-312-453-1844, 24 hours. DV/VIP Protocol Office, 201 Summit Drive, C-701-723-3474, D-312-453-3474.

**RVC:** FAMCAMP, 315 Bomber Boulevard, Check-in at Outdoor Rec, C-701-723-3648, D-312-453-3648, Fax: C-701-723-2175.

**TRAVELERS AID: Chaplain:** C-701-723-3633. **Red Cross:** C-701-727-2477. **Security/Police:** C-701-723-3096 (Desk Sgt).

**SUPPORT AVAILABLE: Bank/Currency Exchange:** Bomber Blvd, C-701-727-6228. **Exchange:** Bldg 437, C-701-727-4717. **Hair Styles:** Bldg 437, Barber, C-701-727-4868; Beauty, C-701-727-9799. **Laundry/Dry Cleaning:** Bldg 437, C-701-727-6800. **Medical:** Bldg 194, 24 hours daily, C-701-727-5304, D-312-453-5304 (clinic). **Postal Service:** Bldg 135, C-701-727-4887. **Shoppette:** 24 hours daily, C-701-727-4973, 5 minutes away.

**ATTRACTIONS:** Turtle Mountain Ski Area.

### EN ROUTE SCHEDULES

| AIRPORT/STATION | LI-MISSION (page #) |
|---|---|
| Travis AFB | SUU-436/MEDEVAC (13) |
| Scott AFB | BLV-C-634/MEDEVAC (30) |

### UNSCHEDULED FLIGHTS

Infrequent flights to CONUS and OCONUS destinations. Call for destinations, routings and schedules.

# OHIO

# MANSFIELD LAHM AIRPORT (MFD/KMFD)

179th AW (ANG)
1947 Harrington Memorial Road
Mansfield Lahm Airport, OH 44903-0179

**LOCATION:** From I-71, take US-30 east or west exit to Route 13 north for one mile. Turn left (west) on Harrington Memorial Road to airport. *USMRA: Page 67 (E-4,5)*. ML-ARM: (40°48'N/82°31'W). LST: GMT-05:00. NMC: Mansfield, 3 miles south. Main installation numbers: C-419-521-0100, D-312-696-6210.

**REGISTRATION INFO: C-419-521-0488, D-312-696-6488.** Bldg 101, Hours: 0730-2230 Tue-Thu, 0730-1630 Fri. Directions: Main gate straight. Limited military support. **Pax Service Office:** C-419-521-0488, D-312-696-6488 (NCO on duty). Coast Guard Exchange just off base at 2100 Harrington Memorial Rd., within walking distance, C-419-526-5358.

**PAX LOUNGES:** General lounge only. **General:** Bldg 101, Hours: 0730-2230 Tue-Thu, 0730-1630 Fri, C-419-521-0165. A/C, coffee/tea served, TV, restrooms, O/S seats.

**TRANSPORTATION:** Rental cars and taxi available (limited).

**TML:** Nearest TML is approximately 90 miles away at Rickenbacker IAP/ANGB, The Buckeye Inn: C-614-409-2660, D-314-850-4451, Fax: C-614-409-2657, D-312-850-3390.

**ATTRACTIONS:** Mid-Ohio Sports Car Course, Kingwood Center, Mohican State Park.

### UNSCHEDULED FLIGHTS

Flights via C-130H aircraft to CONUS, OCONUS and foreign country locations. Infrequent destinations in AK, HI, PR, VI, PA, DE, and GB. Call for destinations, routings and schedules up to 20 days in advance.

# RICKENBACKER IAP/ AIR NATIONAL GUARD BASE (LCK/KLCK)

121st OSS/OM
7556 South Perimeter Road
Bldg 911, Base Ops
Rickenbacker IAP, OH 43217-5910

**LOCATION:** From I-270 south take Alum Creek Road exit 49 south to Rickenbacker IAP. Also accessible off US-23 south onto OH 317 east. Clearly marked. *USMRA: Page 67 (D-7). ML-ARM: (39°49'N/82°56'W).* LST: GMT-05:00. NMC: Columbus, 13 miles southeast. NMI: Wright-Patterson AFB, 73 miles. Main installation numbers: C-614-492-4468, D-312-950-4468.

**REGISTRATION INFO: C-614-492-4595, D-312-950-4595, Fax: C-614-492-3580, D-312-950-3580, Rec: C-614-492-3143, D-312-950-3143. WEB: www.ohcolu.ang.af.mil** Bldg 911, Base Ops, Hours: 0700-1500 Mon, 0700-2200 Tue-Fri, C-614-492-4595. Directions: Exit I-270, 4 miles south on Alum Creek Drive to a right on Port Road then left on Second Avenue to left on Rickenbacker Drive. Follow to guard gate where maps to Base Ops are available **Pax Service Office:** C-614-492-4595, D-312-950-4595. **Pax Paging:** C-614-492-4595, D-312-950-4595. Facilities available off base, on base BX only.

**TML:** Lodging Office: C-614-409-2660, D-312-850-4451, Fax: C-614-409-2657, D-312-850-3390.

**TRAVELERS AID: Security Police:** 24 hours daily, C-614-492-4321, D-312-950-4321.

**OTHER INFORMATION:** Port of Entry and U.S. Customs Service Airport.

## UNSCHEDULED FLIGHTS

Flights to CONUS, OCONUS and foreign country locations via KC-135R aircraft. Call recording, C-614-492-3143, D-312-950-3143, for destinations, routings and schedules.

# WRIGHT-PATTERSON AIR FORCE BASE (FFO/KFFO)

88th Transportation Squadron
5215 Thurlow, Suite #1
Wright-Patterson AFB, OH 45433-5541

**LOCATION:** South of I-70, off I-675 at Fairborn. Also access from OH-4 north or south. AFB clearly marked. *USMRA: Page 67 (B-7). ML-ARM: (39°48'N/84°02'W).* LST: GMT-05:00. NMC: Dayton, 10 miles southwest. Main installation numbers: C-937-257-1110, D-312-787-1110 (Areas A, B and C).

**REGISTRATION INFO: C-937-257-7741, D-312-787-7741, Rec: C-937-257-6235, D-312-787-6235, Fax: C-937-656-1580, D-312-986-1580. E-mail: spacea@wpafb.af.mil (sign up for Retirees only) WEB: www.wpafb.af.mil/flight** Bldg 206, Area C, Hours: 0630-1630 Mon-Fri, weekends and holidays check in with Base Ops. Directions: Enter Gate 8C, right on Skeel Ave, Pax Term on left. **Pax Service Office:** Bldg 206, Hours: 0730-1630 Mon-Fri, C-937-257-7741 (NCO on duty). **Pax Paging:** C-937-257-7741, D-312-787-7741.

**PAX LOUNGES:** No separate family lounge. **General:** Bldg 206, Hours: 0630-1630 Mon-Fri, C-937-257-7741. A/C, restrooms, TV, card tables, plush seating. **DV/VIP:** Bldg 206, 24 hours daily, C-937-257-6202, O7+. A/C, coffee/tea served, read/write rooms, telephones (commercial, long distance and defense), TV, restrooms, showers, O/S seats. **Protocol Service:** Aeronautical Systems Center, Hours: 0800-1600 Mon-Fri, C-937-255-3334.

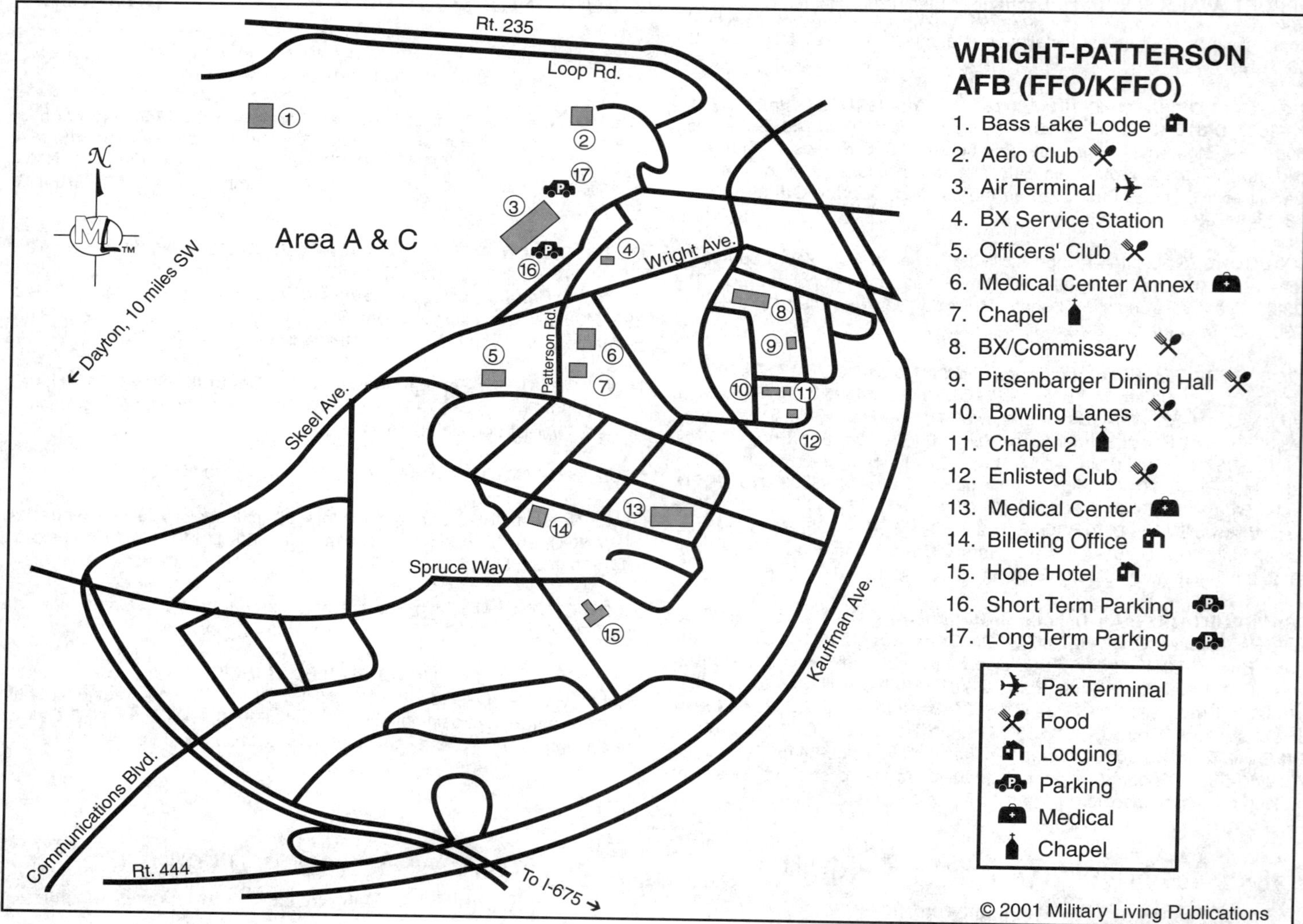

**FOOD SERVICE: Dining Hall:** Bldg 1214, Hours: 0530-0100 daily, C-937-257-2117 (In-Flight Kitchen, 24 hours daily). **NCO/CPO Club:** Bldg 1214, Hours: 0630-0100 daily, C-937-257-7292. **O Club:** Bldg 800, Hours: 0700-0100 daily, C-937-257-9742. **Restaurants:** Bldg 1, Hours: 0700-1330 daily, C-937-257-4902. **Snack Bars:** Bldg 262, Hours: 0700-1315 daily C-937-257-6052. **Snack Vending:** C-937-257-4616.

**TRANSPORTATION: Air Tickets:** Bldg 11A and 262, Hours: 0800-1630 daily, C-937-257-6611. **On Base Car Rental:** Enterprise, C-937-879-0023. **On Base Bus:** Bldg 262, Hours: 0800-1630 Mon-Fri, C-937-257-3755. **Off Base Bus:** C-800-231-2222, 5 miles away. **Off Base Car Rentals:** C-1-800-659-4471, 10 miles away. **Limo Service:** Bldg 146, Hours: 0605-2005 Mon-Fri, C-937-898-7171. **On Base Taxi:** Bldg 262, 24 hours daily, C-937-257-3755, D-312-787-3755, 2 miles away (area not covered by bus). **Off Base Taxi:** C-800-533-8320, 5 miles away. **Parking:** Bldg 206, 24 hours daily (short term - front of Term; long term - overnight parking at north end of building).

**TML:** Lodging office, Building 825, Schlatter Drive & Childlaw Road, 24 hours daily, C-937-879-5921, C-937-257-3810, D-312-787-3451. DV/VIP Protocol, Building 10, C-937-257-3110.

**RVC:** FAMCAMP, Outdoor Rec, 5215 Thurlow Street, Check-in Outdoor Rec, C-937-257-5327, D-312-787-5327, Fax: C-937-656-2107, D-312-486-2107.

**TRAVELERS AID: Chaplain:** Bldg 150, Hours: 0730-1630 Mon-Fri, C-937-257-7941. **Emergency Relief:** Bldg 2, Hours: 0730-1630, C-937-656-0994 (AF Aid). **Medical:** Bldg 830, 24 hours daily, C-937-656-0994, D-312-787-2968. **Red Cross:** Bldg 830, 24 hours daily, C-937-257-9875 or C-937-222-6711. **Security Police:** Gate 12-A, 24 hours daily, C-937-257-1097; Gate 9-A 24 hours daily C-937-257-1091; Gate 38-C 24 hours daily C-937-257-1083. **USO:** Port Columbus IAP, Room 102-A, C-614-231-7300.

**SUPPORT AVAILABLE: Base Exchange:** Bldg 1250, Hours: 1000-2100 Mon-Sat, 1100-1700 Sun: C-937-879-5730. **Hair Styles:** Bldg 1250; Barber, C-937-879-5171; Beauty, C-937-879-5281. **Laundry/Dry Cleaning:** Bldg 1250, Hours: 1000-1800 Mon-Sat, C-937-879-5790. **Postal Service:** Bldg 1044, C-937-257-6523.

**ATTRACTIONS:** U.S. Air Force Museum, Wright Brothers Memorial in Dayton.

### WRIGHT-PATTERSON AFB, OH (FFO); REGION: ATL; OPERATOR: AMC; TYPE: CGO W/ PAX; ROUTE: OEB1D; SAMPLE SCHEDULE: 3RD TUE; EQUIPMENT: C141C

{FFO *SE* ➡ CHS (★) *SE* ➡ MIQ *SW* ➡ LIM ⮀ LIM *NE* ➡ STX *NW* ➡ CHS (★) *NW* ➡ FFO}

| LI/ICAO | AIRPORT/STATION | CTRY/STA | DAYS EN ROUTE |
|---|---|---|---|
| FFO/KFFO | Wright-Patterson AFB | OH | +0 |
| CHS/KCHS | Charleston AFB/IAP | SC | +1 |
| MIQ/SEGU | Simon Bolivar IAP | VE | +2 |
| LIM/SPIM | Jorge Chavez IAP | PE | +2 |
| LIM/SPIM | Jorge Chavez IAP | PE | +2 |
| STX/TISX | Alexander Hamilton IAP (St Croix) | VI | +3 |
| CHS/KCHS | Charleston AFB/IAP | SC | +3 |
| FFO/KFFO | Wright-Patterson AFB | OH | |

### WRIGHT-PATTERSON AFB, OH (FFO); REGION: ATL; OPERATOR: AMC; TYPE: CGO W/ PAX; ROUTE: OEH3B; SAMPLE SCHEDULE: 2ND TUE; EQUIPMENT: C141C

{FFO *SE* ➡ CHS (★) *SE* ➡ BGI *SE* ➡ MIQ ⮀ MIQ *SE* ➡ PBM *NW* ➡ STX *NW* ➡ CHS(★) *NW* ➡ FFO}

| LI/ICAO | AIRPORT/STATION | CTRY/STA | DAYS EN ROUTE |
|---|---|---|---|
| FFO/KFFO | Wright-Patterson AFB | OH | +0 |
| CHS/KCHS | Charleston AFB/IAP | SC | +1 |

| BGI/TBPB | Grantley Adams IAP (Bridgetown) | BB | +1 |
|---|---|---|---|
| MIQ/SEGU | Simon Bolivar IAP (Carasco) | VE | +2 |
| MIQ/SEGU | Simon Bolivar IAP (Carasco) | VE | +2 |
| PBM/SMJP | Johan A Pengel IAP (Paramaribo) | SR | +2 |
| STX/TISX | Alexander Hamilton IAP (St Croix) | VI | +3 |
| CHS/KCHS | Charleston AFB/IAP | SC | +3 |
| FFO/KFFO | Wright-Patterson AFB | OH | |

### WRIGHT-PATTERSON AFB, OH (FFO); REGION: ATL; OPERATOR: AMC; TYPE: CGO W/ PAX; ROUTE: OEK5C; SAMPLE SCHEDULE: 1ST TUE; EQUIPMENT: C141C

{FFO *SE* ➡ CHS (★) *SE* ➡ GUA *SW* ➡ MGA *SE* ➡ SJO ⮀ SJO *NE* ➡ STX *NW* ➡ CHS (★) *NW* ➡ FFO}

| LI/ICAO | AIRPORT/STATION | CTRY/STA | DAYS EN ROUTE |
|---|---|---|---|
| FFO/KFFO | Wright-Patterson AFB | OH | +0 |
| CHS/KCHS | Charleston AFB/IAP | SC | +1 |
| GUA/MGGT | La Aurora APT (Guatemala City) | GT | +2 |
| MGA/MNMG | Augusto C Sandino IAP (Managua) | NI | +2 |
| SJO/MROC | Juan Santamaria IAP (San Jose) | CR | +2 |
| SJO/MROC | Juan Santamaria IAP (San Jose) | CR | +2 |
| STX/TISX | Alexander Hamilton IAP (St Croix) | VI | +3 |
| CHS/KCHS | Charleston AFB/IAP | SC | +4 |
| FFO/KFFO | Wright-Patterson AFB | OH | |

### WRIGHT-PATTERSON AFB, OH (FFO); REGION: ATL; OPERATOR: AMC; TYPE: CGO W/ PAX; ROUTE: OEM3A; SAMPLE SCHEDULE: 2ND FRI; EQUIPMENT: C141C

{FFO *SE* ➡ ADW (★) *SE* ➡ NRR *NE* ➡ NBW ⮀ NBW *N* ➡ NGU (★) *NE* ➡ ADW *NW* ➡ FFO}

| LI/ICAO | AIRPORT/STATION | CTRY/STA | DAYS EN ROUTE |
|---|---|---|---|
| FFO/KFFO | Wright-Patterson AFB | OH | +0 |
| ADW/KADW | Andrews AFB (✚) | MD | +1 |
| NRR/TJNR | Roosevelt Roads NS | PR | +2 |
| NBW/MUGM | Guantanamo Bay NAS | CU | +2 |
| NBW/MUGM | Guantanamo Bay NAS | CU | +2 |
| NGU/KNGU | Norfolk NS | VA | +3 |
| ADW/KADW | Andrews AFB (✚) | MD | +3 |
| FFO/KFFO | Wright-Patterson AFB | OH | |

**Note: (✚)** = MEDEVAC: ADW to ADW

### WRIGHT-PATTERSON AFB, OH (FFO); REGION: ATL; OPERATOR: AMC; TYPE: CGO W/ PAX; ROUTE: OEM3B; SAMPLE SCHEDULE: 2ND SUN; EQUIPMENT: C141C

{FFO *SE* ➡ NGU (★) *SE* ➡ NRR *NW* ➡ NBW ⮀ NBW *N* ➡ NGU (★) *NW* ➡ FFO}

| LI/ICAO | AIRPORT/STATION | CTRY/STA | DAYS EN ROUTE |
|---|---|---|---|
| FFO/KFFO | Wright-Patterson AFB | OH | +0 |
| NGU/KNGU | Norfolk NS | VA | +1 |
| NRR/TJNR | Roosevelt Roads NS | PR | +2 |
| NBW/MUGM | Guantanamo Bay NAS | CU | +2 |
| NBW/MUGM | Guantanamo Bay NAS | CU | +2 |
| NGU/KNGU | Norfolk NS | VA | +3 |
| FFO/KFFO | Wright-Patterson AFB | OH | |

### WRIGHT-PATTERSON AFB, OH (FFO); REGION: ATL; OPERATOR: AMC; TYPE: CGO W/ PAX; ROUTE: OEN1B; SAMPLE SCHEDULE: 1ST FRI; EQUIPMENT: C141C

{FFO *SE* ➡ NGU (★) *SE* ➡ NBW ⇌ NBW *E* ➡ NRR *NW* ➡ NGU (★) *NW* ➡ FFO}

| LI/ICAO | AIRPORT/STATION | CTRY/STA | DAYS EN ROUTE |
|---|---|---|---|
| FFO/KFFO | Wright-Patterson AFB | OH | +0 |
| NGU/KNGU | Norfolk NS | VA | +1 |
| NBW/MUGM | Guantanamo Bay NAS | CU | +1 |
| NBW/MUGM | Guantanamo Bay NAS | CU | +1 |
| NRR/TJNR | Roosevelt Roads NS | PR | +2 |
| NGU/KNGU | Norfolk NS | VA | +2 |
| FFO/KFFO | Wright-Patterson AFB | OH | |

**WRIGHT-PATTERSON AFB, OH (FFO); REGION: ATL; OPERATOR: AMC; TYPE: CGO W/ PAX; ROUTE: OER1A; SAMPLE SCHEDULE: 2ND MON; EQUIPMENT: C141C**

{FFO *SE* ➡ DOV (★) *NE* ➡ RMS ⇌ RMS *SW* ➡ ADW (★) *NW* ➡ FFO}

| LI/ICAO | AIRPORT/STATION | CTRY/STA | DAYS EN ROUTE |
|---|---|---|---|
| FFO/KFFO | Wright-Patterson AFB | OH | +0 |
| DOV/KDOV | Dover AFB | DE | +1 |
| RMS/ETAR | Ramstein AB | DE | +2 |
| ADW/KADW | Andrews AFB | MD | +3 |
| FFO/KFFO | Wright-Patterson AFB | OH | |

### EN ROUTE SCHEDULES

| AIRPORT/STATION | LI-MISSION (page #) |
|---|---|
| Scott AFB | BLV-C-666/MEDEVAC (30) |

### UNSCHEDULED FLIGHTS

Frequent flights to: Barksdale AFB, LA (**BAD**) (weekly); Eglin AFB, FL (**VPS**) (twice weekly); Kelly AFB, TX (**SKF**) (once/twice weekly); Langley AFB, VA (**LFI**) (once/twice weekly); Maxwell AFB, AL (**MXF**) (weekly); Norfolk NS, VA (**NGU**) (once/twice weekly); Offutt AFB, NE (**OFF**) (twice weekly); Peterson AFB, CO (**COS**) (monthly); Randolph AFB, TX (**RND**) (once/twice weekly); Robins AFB, GA (**WRB**) (weekly); Tinker AFB, OK (**TIK**) (three times monthly) and other CONUS locations utilizing C-17A and C-130E/H aircraft. Call for destinations, routings and schedules. Also flights via C-141B to CONUS and OCONUS destinations.

# YOUNGSTOWN-WARREN REGIONAL AIRPORT/AIR RESERVE STATION (YNG/KYNG)

757 AS/DOO
Youngstown Air Reserve Station
3976 King Graves Road
Vienna, OH 44473-0910

**LOCATION:** From OH-11 north or south, exit to King Graves Road  Hwy 82 east to Hwy 193 north at signs pointing to base, main gate left (west) one mile. Base is clearly marked. *USMRA: Page 67 (H-3).* ML-ARM: *(41°16'N/80°40'W).* LST: GMT-05:00. NMC: Youngstown, 8 miles south. Main installation numbers: C-330-609-1000, D-312-346-1000.

**REGISTRATION INFO: C-330-609-1767, D-312-346-1769, Fax: C-330-609-1371, D-312-346-1097.** Ask Security Police for directions. No Pax Term. No pax lounge, or comfort facilities. Base ops and command post. After duty hours call the Security Police Law Enforcement Desk: C-330-609-1277. Provides service to neighboring Youngstown Municipal Airport and support to transient U.S. government aircraft. Military support available for transient aircrews and government/military personnel on orders to Youngstown Air Reserve Base. Combined Club: C-330-609-1295, Exchange: C-330-609-1393.

**TML:** Eagles Nest Inn, 3976 King Graves Road, C-330-609-1268, D-312-346-1268, Fax: C-330-609-1120, D-312-346-1120.


Flights via C-130H aircraft to CONUS and OCONUS locations. Space-A opportunities infrequent. Connecting flight opportunities virtually non-existent. Call for destinations, routings and schedules.

# OKLAHOMA

## ALTUS AIR FORCE BASE (LTS/KLTS)

97th TRNS/ LGTAP
516 S. Sixth Street
Altus AFB, OK 73523-5270

**LOCATION:** From US-62 traveling west from Lawton, turn right (north) at first traffic light in Altus and follow the road to the main gate on Falcon Road. *USMRA: Page 84 (E-5).* ML-ARM: *(34°39'N/99°17'W).* LST: GMT-06:00. NMC: Lawton, 56 miles east. Main installation numbers: C-580-4481/82-8100, D-312-866-1110.

**REGISTRATION INFO: C-580-481-6428, D-312-866-6428, Rec: C-580-481-6350, D-312-866-6350, Fax: C-580-481-6826, D-312-866-6826.** Bldg 185, Hours: 0730-1630 Mon-Fri, Directions: From main gate left on First Street, right on East Ave to Pax Term on the left across from tower. **Pax Service Office:** C-580-481-6428, D-312-866-6428.

**PAX LOUNGES:** Limited. No separate DV/VIP or family lounges. **General:** Bldg 185, Hours: 0730-1630 Mon-Fri, C-580-481-6350. A/C, bag check limited, telephone (commercial and defense), TV, restrooms, O/S seats. **Protocol Service:** Bldg 1, Hours: 0800-1600 Mon-Fri, C-580-481-7044.

**FOOD SERVICE: Dining Hall:** Solar Inn, C-580-481-6169. **Enlisted Club:** C-580-481-6295. **O Club:** C-580-481-6224. **Snack Bars:** Golf Course, C-580-481-6411, Bowling Alley, C-580-481-6420, two blocks away. **Snack Vending:** Bldg 185.

**TRANSPORTATION: Air Tickets:** C-580-482-0611; SATO, Bldg 52, C-580-477-0733. **Off Base Bus:** Southwest Transit, C-405-483-5043 (Altus to Lawton - 3 times a week- Mon, Wed and Fri), C-580-482-5503. **Off Base Taxi:** 24 hours daily, C-580-482-0383/3300. **Taxi (Gov):** C-580-481-6272 (duty passengers only). **Parking:** Bldg 185, 24 hours daily. Long term designated areas and daily parking.

**TML:** Red River Inn, 308 North First Street, 24 hours daily, C-580-481-7356, D-312-866-7356, Fax: C-580-481-5704, D-312-866-5704. DV/VIP C-580-481-7044.

**RVC:** FAMCAMP, Bldg 418, Check-in Bowling Center, 24 hours daily, C-580-481-6420/6704, D-312-866-6704.

**TRAVELERS AID: Chaplain:** Bldg 301, C-580-481-7485. **Lost/Found:** C-580-481-6428/6614. **Medical:** Bldg 46, C-580-481-7171, Non emergency, Bldg 46, C-580-481-5222, D-312-866-5222. **Red Cross:** Bldg 46, C-580-481-6526. **Security Police:** Bldg 130, 24 hours daily, C-580-401-7444.

**SUPPORT AVAILABLE: Exchange:** Bldg 18, C-580-482-7441 **Hair Styles:** Bldg 18, Barber, C-580-482-8221; Beauty, C-580-482-4051. **Laundry/Dry Cleaning:** Bldg.18 C-580-477-2213. **Postal Service:** Bldg 120, C-580-481-6403.

**ATTRACTIONS:** Western prairie country, outdoor sports.

### UNSCHEDULED FLIGHTS

Infrequent flights via KC-135R, C-005A/B, C-17A and C-141B to: Dover AFB, DE (**DOV**); Hickam AFB, HI (**HIK**); RAF Mildenhall, GB (**MHZ**); and Travis AFB, CA (**SUU**). *Note: Flight schedules are received on a weekly basis.* Call for destinations, routings and schedules.

## HENRY POST ARMY AIRFIELD (FSI/KFSI)

Airfield Operations
Post Road, Bldg 4907, Room 206
Fort Sill, OK 73503-5100

**LOCATION:** From Lawton, take I-44 north to Exit #41, then west on Sheridan Road to Key Gate. Clearly marked. *USMRA: Page 84 (E,F-5).* ML-ARM: *(34°38'N/98°23'W).* LST: GMT-06:00. NMC: Wichita Falls, TX, 50 miles south. Main installation numbers: C-580-442-8111, D-312-639-7090.

**REGISTRATION INFO: C-580-442-5808/3385, D-312-639-5808/3385, Fax: C-580-442-5643.** Bldg 4907, Hours: 0730-1630 Mon-Fri. Directions: I-44 north to Gate 2 exit. In the Air Ops building. DV/VIP lounge available.

**TML:** Billeting Office, Building 5676, Fergusson Road, 24 hours daily, C-580-442-5000/353-5007, D-312-639-5000, Fax: C-580-442-7033, D-312-639-7033.

**SUPPORT AVAILABLE:** Full base support available.

### UNSCHEDULED FLIGHTS

Flights via C-12 aircraft to Midwest and East Coast locations. Call for destinations, routings and schedules.

## TINKER AIR FORCE BASE (TIK/KTIK)

72 Air Base Wing, Bldg 268
Tinker AFB, OK 73145-5000

**LOCATION**: Southeast Oklahoma City, off I-40. Use Tinker gate exit 157A off South Air Depot Boulevard. Clearly marked. *USMRA: Page 84 (G-4). ML-ARM: (35°25'N/97°24'W).* LST: GMT-06:00. NMC: Oklahoma City, 12 miles northwest. Main installation numbers: C-405-732-7321, D-312-884-1110.

**REGISTRATION INFO: C-405-739-4339, D-312-339-4339, Rec: C-405-739-4360, D-312-339-4360; Fax: C-405-739-3826 D-312-339-3826.** E-mail: **spacea@tinker.af.mil** WEB: **www.tinker.af.mil** Bldg 268, Hours: 0715-1600 Mon-Fri. Directions: Gate 1 to a left at first light, 1 more light to a right on H Street then to Sentry Blvd and turn left. Going east on Sentry Blvd go thru stop sign and turn right past Bldg 224. Park in parking lot North Bldg 268. 24 hours notice on flights. **Pax Service Office:** Bldg 268, Hours: 0715-1600 Mon-Fri, C-405-739-2106 (NCO on duty). **Pax Paging:** C-405-739-4339/60, D-312-339-4339/60.

**PAX LOUNGES:** Family and General lounge combined. **General:** Bldg 268, Hours: 0715-1600 Mon-Fri, C-405-739-4339/4360, D 312-339-4339/4360. A/C, bag check, read/write rooms, telephones (commercial and defense), TV, restrooms, P/C seats. **DV/VIP:** Bldg 240, 24 hours daily, C-405-734-2191, D 312-884-2191. A/C, bag check, read/write rooms, telephones (commercial and defense), TV, restrooms, O/S seats. **Protocol Service:** Bldg 460, 24 hours daily, C-405-739-3900.

**FOOD SERVICE: Dining Hall:** Bldg 5905, Hours: 0530-0100 daily, C-405-734-MENU. **Fast Food:** 3 blocks west. **Inflight kitchen:** Bldg 240, 24 hours daily, C-405-734-3795, D 312-884-3795. **NCO/CPO Club:** Bldg 6001, Hours: 1100-2100 daily, C-405-734-3418. **Snack Vending:** Bldg 268, Hours: 0715-1600 Mon-Fri.

**TRANSPORTATION: Air Tickets:** SATO, Bldg 1, Hours: 0715-1600 Mon-Fri, C-405-739-5057, D 312-339-5057. **Car Rentals:** OKC Airport, 24 hours daily; Hertz, C-405-732-0366.On Base Shuttle/Bus: Bldg 260, C-405-734-2803, D-312-334-2803. **Off Base Taxi:** Gate 1, 24 hours daily, C-405-235-1431 (Safeway). **On Base Taxi (Gov):** Bldg 2101, 24 hours daily, C-405-734-2803 (on Base only). **Parking:** Short term, North of terminal; long term, Bldg 591, unlimited, C-405-734-3737. Register with Security Police.

**TML:** Indian Hills Inn, 72nd SPTG/SVML, 4002 Mitchell Avenue, Tinker AFB, OK 73145-8101. C-405-734-2822, D-312-884-2822. Fax: C-405-734-7426, D-312-884-7426, 24 hours daily. DV/VIP Bldg. 3001, C-405-739-5511.

**RVC:** FAMCAMP, Check-in 0800-1700 hours, Outdoor Rec, Bldg 5935, after hrs, site host #10, C-405-734-2289, D-312-884-2289.

**TRAVELERS AID: Chaplain:** Bldg 5701, duty hours, C-405-734-2111. **Medical:** Bldg 581, 24 hours daily, C-405-734-8249, D-405-884-8249; Ambulance, C-405-734-8223. **Red Cross:** Bldg 3067, Hours: 0800-1630 Mon-Fri, C-405-232-7121. **Security Police:** Bldg 591, 24 hours daily, C-405-734-2000/3737.

**SUPPORT AVAILABLE: Bank/Currency Exchange:** Bldg 478, Hours: 0900-1500 Mon-Fri, C-405-736-2717. **Exchange:** Bldg 478, Hours: 1000-1800 Mon-Fri, 0900-1600 Sat-Sun, C-405-734-3035. **Hair Styles:** Bldg 478, Hours: 0800-1700 Mon-Fri, 0800-1600 Sat; Barber, C-405-732-5032; Beauty: C-405-732-6509. **Laundry/Dry Cleaning:** Bldg 478, Hours: 0900-1730 Mon-Fri, C-405-734-5225. **Postal Service:** Bldg 758, Hours: 0845-1600 Mon-Fri, 0845-1045 Sat, C-405-734-3611.

**ATTRACTIONS:** Oklahoma City, National Cowboy Hall of Fame, Oklahoma City Zoo, Remington Park Race Track, Firefighters Museum, Myriad Botanical Gardens, Frontier City Theme Park, Kirkpatrick Center.

### EN ROUTE SCHEDULES

| AIRPORT/STATION | LI-MISSION (page #) |
| --- | --- |
| Scott AFB | BLV-C-652/MEDEVAC (30) |
| Scott AFB | BLV-C-656/MEDEVAC (30) |

### UNSCHEDULED FLIGHTS

Flights to Andrews AFB, MD (**ADW**); Kelly AFB, TX (**SKF**); Offutt AFB, NE (**OFF**); Peterson AFB, CO (**COS**); Scott AFB, IL (**BLV**); Wright-Patterson AFB, OH (**FFO**); plus other CONUS bases. Flights are scheduled on a 1 day advance notice. Seldom any overseas flights. Only regularly scheduled flight is to Scott AFB, IL (**BLV**) on Thu and Sat. Flights to CONUS and OCONUS via KC-135R.

## VANCE AIR FORCE BASE (END/KEND)

Vance Base Operations
624 Elam Road, Suite 112
Vance AFB, OK 73705-5413

**LOCATION:** Off of US-81 south of Enid (on west side of US-81). Clearly marked. *USMRA: Page 84 (F-3). ML-ARM: (36°21'N/97°53'W).* LST: GMT-06:00. NMC: Oklahoma City, 80 miles southeast. NMI: Tinker AFB, 90 miles south. Main installation numbers: C-580-213-7111, D-312-448-7110.

**REGISTRATION INFO: C-580-213-7425, D-312-448-7425.** Base Ops, 0700-1900 Mon-Fri, 1300-1700 Sat-Sun.

**TML:** Lodging office, Building 714, 426 Goad St, Suite 131, 24 hours daily, C-580-213-7358, D-312-448-7358, Fax: C-580-213-6278, D-312-448-6278.

**TRAVELERS AID: Air Force Aid:** C-580-213-6288. **Chaplain:** C-580-213-7211. **Medical:** C-580-213-7416. **Red Cross:** C-580-213-5994. **Security Police:** C-580-213-7155.

**SUPPORT AVAILABLE: Bank/Currency Exchange:** C-580-213-3535. **Exchange:** C-580-213-7366.

**ATTRACTIONS:** Leonardo's Discovery Warehouse, Canton Little Salt Plains Dam and Lake.

### UNSCHEDULED FLIGHTS

Very infrequent flights via MEDEVAC and transient aircraft to CONUS locations. Call for destinations, routings and schedules.

## WILL ROGERS WORLD AIRPORT/ AIR NATIONAL GUARD BASE (OKC/KOKC)

137th TAW/DOO (ANG)
Will Rogers ANGB, OK 73179-1040

**LOCATION:** From I-40 east or west, exit 144 south 2.5 miles to airport. *USMRA: Page 84 (G-4). ML-ARM: (35°24'N/97°35'W).* LST: GMT-06:00. NMC: Oklahoma City, 7 miles northeast. Main installation numbers: C-405-686-5210, D-312-940-5210.

**REGISTRATION INFO: C-405-686-5550, D-312-940-5550, Rec: 405-686-5563, D-312-940-5563.** Bldg 1040, Hours: 0630-1700 Mon-Thu. Directions: From the main gate drive straight for 4 blocks south, then 2 blocks west.

**PAX LOUNGES:** No pax lounge. Canteen and restrooms available.

**TML:** Nearest TML is at Tinker AFB, Indian Hills Inn, 72nd SPTG/SVML, 4002 Mitchell Avenue, Tinker AFB, OK 73145-8101. C-405-734-2822, D-312-884-2822. Fax: C-405-734-7426, D-312-884-7426, 24 hours daily. DV/VIP Bldg. 3001, C-405-739-5511.

**SUPPORT AVAILABLE: NCO Club:** D-312-940-5279. **Security Police:** 24 hours daily, C-405-686-5300.

**OTHER INFORMATION:** U.S. Customs Service Airport.

### UNSCHEDULED FLIGHTS

Flights to CONUS and OCONUS via ANG C-130H aircraft. Call for destinations, routings and schedules.

## Other Oklahoma Installations with Possible Space-A Air Opportunities

**LAWTON/FORT SILL REGIONAL AIRPORT (LAW/KLAW),** Fort Sill, OK. *USMRA: Page 84 (E,F-5).* ML-ARM: (34°34'N/98°24'W). LST: GMT-06:00. AMC, MEDEVAC, flights, C-009A are serviced here. Contact Reynolds Army Community Hospital, **C-580-442-2815/2215. TML:** Billeting Office, Building 5676, Fergusson Road, 24 hours daily, C-580-442-5000/353-5007, D-312-639-5000, Fax: C-580-442-7033, D-312-639-7033. Full base support facilities available.

### EN ROUTE SCHEDULES

| AIRPORT/STATION | LI-MISSION (page #) |
| --- | --- |
| Scott AFB | BLV-C-652/MEDEVAC (30) |
| Scott AFB | BLV-C-656/MEDEVAC (30) |

# OREGON

## KINGSLEY FIELD (LMT/KLMT)

1730G/D00F
243 Vandenberg Drive, Suite 22
Klamath Falls, OR 97603-1935

**LOCATION:** Take I-5 north or south through Medford to Hwy 140 E 5.5 miles to southside bypass. Go east approximately four and a half miles to the airport. *USMRA: Page 100 (D-8).* ML-ARM: (42°09'N/121°44'W). LST: GMT-08:00. NMC: Medford, 80 miles west. Main installation numbers: C-541-885-6350, D-312-830-6350.

**REGISTRATION INFO: C-541-885-6686, D-312-830-6686.** General pax lounge available. ***Note: Very limited Space-A travel; 1-2 flights annually, call for information.***

**FOOD SERVICE:** Snack Vending available in Base Ops.

**TRANSPORTATION:** Car rental, off base taxi and train station available.

**TML:** Billeting Office, Kingsley Lodge, Building 208, McConnell Circle, 0800-1600 Mon-Fri (closed 1200-1300), C-541-885-6365, D-312-830-6365.

**TRAVELERS AID: Red Cross:** C-541-884-4125. **Security/Police:** 24 hours daily, C-541-885-6663.

**SUPPORT AVAILABLE: Shoppette:** Hours: 0930-1630 Mon-Fri, C-541-885-6371, D-312-830-6371, 100 yards away.

**ATTRACTIONS:** Crater Lake National Park, 60 miles north.

### UNSCHEDULED FLIGHTS

Infrequent flights. Call for destinations, routings and schedules.

## PORTLAND INTERNATIONAL AIRPORT/ AIR NATIONAL GUARD BASE (PDX/KPDX)

142nd FW/OSA (Air National Guard)
6801 N.E. Cornfoot Road
Portland, OR 97218-2797

**LOCATION:** Go south on I-205 to NE Airport Way exit, west on NE Airport Way to Alderwood, south on Alderwood to NE Cornfoot Road. Co-located with Portland International Airport.. *USMRA: Page 100 (C-2); Page 103 (C-1).* ML-ARM: (45°35'N/122°35'W). LST: GMT-08:00. NMC: Portland, 10 miles southwest. Main installation numbers: C-503-335-4020, D-312-638-4020.

**REGISTRATION INFO: C-503-335-4390/4421, D-312-638-4390.** Air National Guard Ops: 24 hours daily. Ask Security Police for directions (C-503-335-4229). All the support of an IAP.

**SUPPORT AVAILABLE: Exchange:** C-503-249-0997. **TML:** Nearest TML is at Camp Rilea, C-861-1018/4052.

### UNSCHEDULED FLIGHTS

Space-A opportunities are from transient aircraft and HC-130N/P aircraft. Call for destinations.

# PENNSYLVANIA

## PITTSBURGH INTERNATIONAL AIRPORT/ AIR RESERVE STATION (PIT/KPIT)

911th AW (AFRES)
2475 Defense Ave
Coraopolis, PA 15108-4475

**LOCATION:** Take I-279 west, which merges into PA-60 (Airport Parkway), then take exit 3 Business Route 60 to Thorn Run Interchange, follow signs to Air Reserve Station. *USMRA: Page 22 (A-5,6).* ML-ARM: (40°29'N/80°12'W). LST: GMT-05:00. NMC: Pittsburgh, 15 miles southeast. Main installation numbers: C-412-474-8000, D-312-277-8000.

**REGISTRATION INFO: AFRES: C-412-474-8163, D-312-277-8163, Fax: C-412-474-8156, D-312-277-8156.** AFRES Base Ops, Hours: 0730-1600 Mon-Fri, and flight times. **ANGB: C-412-269-7350, D-312-277-7350, Fax: C-412-474-8156, D-312-277-8156.** ANGB Ops, Hours: 0800-1700 Mon-Fri, and flight times. All the support of an IAP. Limited military support. BX: C-412-424-8207.

**TML:** 2875 Defense Avenue, Bldg 206, 0700-2400, C-412-474-8229/8230, D-312-277-8230, Fax: C-412-474-8752, D-312-277-8752.

**OTHER INFORMATION:** U.S. Customs Service Airport.

### UNSCHEDULED FLIGHTS

Limited flights via AFRES C-130H and ANG KC-135R aircraft to CONUS, OCONUS and foreign country locations. Weekly C-130 MEDEVAC flights to Caribbean. Call for destinations, routings and schedules.

## WILLOW GROVE NAVAL AIR STATION/ JOINT RESERVE BASE (NXX/KNXX)

Air Operations Department
Bldg 780
Willow Grove NAS, PA 19090-5010

**LOCATION:** Six miles north of Philadelphia. Take PA Turnpike (I-76) to Willow Grove exit 27 north approximately three or four miles on PA-611 to NAS. *USMRA: Page 22 (I,J-6).* ML-ARM: (40°12'N/75°08'W). LST: GMT-05:00. NMC: Philadelphia, 23 miles south. Main installation numbers: C-215-443-1050, D-312-991-1050.

**REGISTRATION INFO: C-215-443-6215/6/7, D-312-991-6215/6/7, Rec: C-215-443-6216, D-312-991-6216, Fax: C-215-443-6188, D-312-991-6188.** Bldg 780, Hours: 0630-2300 daily. Directions: From main gate circle to the far left, make first right toward control tower. **USAF: C-215-443-1076/1173. Pax Service Office:** C-215-443-6215/6/7, D-312-991-6215/6/7. E-mail: wgairter@enrf.navy.mil

**PAX LOUNGES:** DV only; no separate family lounge available. Terminal seats 90. **General:** A/C, TV, bag check, telephones (local and defense), restrooms, snack vending machines, cargo area. Protocol Services: **DV/VIP:** PAO, Bldg 1, top deck, C-215-443-1776/77, Hours: 0800-1600 Tue-Sat.

**FOOD SERVICE:** Several off base facilities have delivery services to Bldg 780. **Fast Food:** Subway, Hours: 0800-2000, within walking distance. **Navy Galley:** 3 meals daily, standard hours, surcharge applies.

**TRANSPORTATION:** Local bus or cab to Greyhound Terminal or local train. Local train to PHL or AMTRAK. Limo to-from PHL available via local hotels, $20. Car rentals: C&C Ford across from base. Enterprise will pick up and deliver to terminal. Parking: adjacent to main gate (notify Security Department C-215-443-6067/68).

**TML:** Lodging office, Building 609, 24 hours daily, C-215-442-5800/5801, D-312-991-5800/5801, Fax: C-215-442-5817. DV/VIP C-215-443-1776.

**TRAVELERS AID: Chaplain:** C-215-443-6002/3/4. **Emergency Relief:** C-215-443-6002 (Navy Relief). **Medical:** Bldg 37, C-215-443-6360, Hours: 0800-1600 daily. After hours medical available at local hospitals. **Security Police:** Bldg 1, 24 hours daily, C-215-443-6067/68. **USO:** C-215-336-0908.

**SUPPORT AVAILABLE: Bank:** NFCU Automated teller. **Exchange:** Hours: 1000-1700 Tue-Sun, C-215-443-6025. **Hair Styles:** Barber, C-215-443-6030. **Postal Service:** C-215-443-6055.

**ATTRACTIONS:** Philadelphia, New Jersey beaches, and Pocono Mountain area.

### UNSCHEDULED FLIGHTS

Frequent flights via Navy C-009 and P-003C, and AFRES C-130E aircraft to: Andrews AFB, MD (**ADW**); Brunswick NAS, ME (**NHZ**); Jacksonville NAS, FL (**NIP**); Lajes Field AB, (Azores), PT (**LGS**); New Orleans NAS/JRB, LA (**NBG**); Norfolk NS, VA (**NGU**); Roosevelt Roads, PR (**NRR**), and Rota NS, ES (**RTA**). Call for destinations, routings and schedules.

## Other Pennsylvania Installations with Possible Space-A Air Opportunities

**MUIR ARMY AIRFIELD (MUI/KMUI),** Fort Indiantown Gap, Dept of Military Affairs, Army Aviation Support Facility #1, Attn: Flight Operations, Annville, PA 17003-5000. **LOCATION:** From I-81 north or south, take exit 29 B north on PA-934 to post. *USMRA: Page 22 (G-6). ML-ARM: (40°26'N/76°34'W).* LST: GMT-05:00. **C-717-861-2000, D-312-491-2000 TML:** Lodging office, Building 11-7 Hours: 0800-1630 daily, C-717-861-2512/2540/8158, D-312-491-8158. DV/VIP C-717-861-2512/2540. Limited base support facilities available **under PA National Guard. Call ahead.**

### UNSCHEDULED FLIGHTS

Limited Space-A air opportunities via executive C-12 and C-23-B aircraft to CONUS locations: Coordination for Space-A travel must be with operational support Support Airlift Command, Det 22, at C-717-861-8920 or D-312-491-8920. Call for destinations, routings and schedules.

# RHODE ISLAND

## QUONSET STATE AIRPORT (OQU/KOQU)

143rd AG/CP (Air National Guard)
7 Flightline Drive
North Kingston, RI 02852-7548

**LOCATION:** From US-1 exit to RI-403 south or I-95 north or south, exit 9 to RI-4 south to exit 7 on RI-403 southwest. Airport is clearly marked. *USMRA:*

Page 17 (J-7). ML-ARM: (41°33'N/71°25'W). LST: GMT-05:00. NMC: Providence, 20 miles north. Main installation numbers: C-401-885-3960, D-312-476-3210.

**REGISTRATION INFO: C-401-886-1420, D-312-476-3405/3422/3420 Fax: C-401-886-1412.** Air National Guard area, Hours: 0700-1730 Tue-Fri. Ask Security Police for directions. No military support facilities.

**TML:** Nearest TML is at Newport NS, Lodging office, 24 hours daily; Building 684 (Officers) C-401-841-3156; Building 447 (EM), C-401-841-4410. Navy Lodge, Building 685, 0700-2300 daily, C-401-849-4500. DV/VIP C-401-841-3715, Fax: C-401-849-3906.

**OTHER INFORMATION:** U.S. Customs Service Airport.

### UNSCHEDULED FLIGHTS

Flights via ANG C-130H aircraft to CONUS and OCONUS locations. Call for destinations, routings and schedules.

## Other Rhode Island Installations with Possible Space-A Air Opportunities

**THEODORE FRANCIS GREEN STATE AIRPORT (PVD/KPVD),** Newport Naval Education and Training Center, 61 Capodanno Drive, Newport, RI 02841-1513. **LOCATION:** The airport is located in south Providence, RI off I-95 and US-1. *USMRA: Page-17 (J-7). ML-ARM: (41°43'N/71°26'W).* LST: GMT-05:00. NMC: Providence 5 miles north. **This location only services AMC MEDEVAC flights, C009A.** For passenger application contact, Naval Hospital, Newport Naval Education and Training Center, **C-401-841-3409** (ask for MEDEVAC flights). **TML:** Nearest TML is at Newport NS, Lodging office, 24 hours daily; Building 684 (Officers) C-401-841-3156; Building 447 (EM), C-401-841-4410. Navy Lodge, Building 685, 0700-2300 daily, C-401-849-4500. DV/VIP C-401-841-3715, Fax: C-401-849-3906.

### EN ROUTE SCHEDULES

| AIRPORT/STATION | LI-MISSION (page #) |
| --- | --- |
| Andrews AFB | ADW-116/MEDEVAC (37) |

# SOUTH CAROLINA

## BEAUFORT MARINE CORPS AIR STATION (NBC/KNBC)

H&HS, Traffic Management Office
P.O. Box 55010
Beaufort, SC 29904-5010

**LOCATION:** From I-95 take Beaufort exit 33 to SC-21 southeast and follow signs. Sixteen miles to MCAS east of SC-21. Clearly marked. *USMRA: Page 44 (G-9). ML-ARM: (32°27'N/80°43'W).* LST: GMT-05:00. NMC: Savannah GA, 40 miles south. Main installation numbers: C-843-228-7100, D-312-335-7100.

**REGISTRATION INFO: C-843-228-7143, D-312-335-7143.** Bldg 860, Hours: 0800-1630 Mon-Fri. Directions: From main gate straight on Geiger Blvd to a left on Drayton Street to Pax Term on the left. **Pax Service Office:** C-843-228-7143, D-312-335-7143 (NCO on Duty). Many facilities on and off base.

**FOOD SERVICE: Cafeteria:** Hours: 0700-1500, C-843-228-7895, 2 miles away. **O Club:** C-843-228-7541, 3 miles away. **Snack Bars:** Hours: 0700-1500, C-843-228-7895. **Snack Vending:** Hours: 0700-2300, 100 yards away.

**TRANSPORTATION: Off Base Car Rental:** Enterprise, C-843-228-0494; Thrifty, C-843-228-9996. **On Base Taxi:** C-843-228-7550. **Off Base Taxi:** Yellow Cab, C-843-228-1121.

**TML:** Building 1108, Delalio, 24 hours daily, C-843-522-1663, D-312-335-7676. DV/VIP C-843-228-7158. DeTreville House C-843-228-1663.

**TRAVELERS AID: Chaplain:** Hours: 0700-1600, C-843-228-7775, 50 yards away. **Medical/Dental:** C-843-228-7051. **Red Cross:** Hours: 0800-1600, C-843-228-7252/6105, 1 mile away. **Security/Police:** 24 hours daily, C-843-228-7589.

**SUPPORT AVAILABLE: Credit Union:** C-843-846-2266, 3 miles away. **Exchange:** C-843-228-7751, 2 miles away. **Laundry/Dry Cleaner:** C-843-228-6107, 2 miles away. **Postal Service:** C-843-228-7003, 3 miles away. **Shoppette:** C-843-228-7751, 2 miles away.

### UNSCHEDULED FLIGHTS

Frequent flights to East Coast and Mid-Atlantic areas. Call for destinations, routings and schedules.

# CHARLESTON AIR FORCE BASE (CHS/KCHS)

437th APS/TRP
105 South Bates Street, Bldg 164, Passenger Terminal
Charleston AFB, SC 29404-5006

**LOCATION:** From I-26 east or west, exit 211 to West Aviation Avenue to traffic light, continue through light to second light right, follow perimeter road around end of runway to gate 2 (Rivers Gate). *USMRA: Page 44 (H-8,9). ML-ARM: (32°51'N/80°04'W).* LST: GMT-05:00. NMC: Charleston, 5 miles southeast. Main installation numbers: C-843-963-6000, D-312-673-1110.

**REGISTRATION INFO: C-843-963-3083/3048, D-312-673-3082/3048, Rec: C-843-963-3082, D-312-673-3082, Fax: C-843-963-3060, D-312-673-3060/5808. E-mail: spacea@charleston.af.mil WEB: www.charleston. af.mil** Bldg 164, 24 Hours: 7 days a week. West side across from commercial airport and ATC tower. Directions: From Rivers Gate, take Arthur Drive to a left on Hill Blvd to a right on Bates Ave. Pax Term on left.

Check-in manned 0500-2300 daily. After hours information call C-843-963-3082. **Pax Service Office:** Bldg 164, Hours: 0500-2300 Mon-Fri, C-843-963-3082, D-312-673-3082. **Pax Paging:** Bldg 164, Hours: 0500-2300 daily, C-843-963-3082, D-312-673-3082. ***Note: There is multi-station sign-up between Charleston AFB and Charleston IAP, and the Wiliiam B. Hartsfield Atlanta IAP.***

**PAX LOUNGES:** Dependents lounge and nursery. See Pax Shift Supervisor. **General:** Bldg 164 (adjacent to check-in scales), Hours: 0500-2300 daily, C-843-963-3082. A/C, bag lockers, telephones (commercial and defense), TV lounge, restrooms, P/C seats. **USO/Dependent Lounge:** Bldg 164 (right of main entrance), Hours: 0500-2300 daily, C-843-963-3082. **DV/VIP:** Bldg 164, Hours: 0500-2300 daily, C-843-963-3082, D-312-673-3082. Flight line at end of building (unmanned). See Pax Service Shift Supervisor. A/C, telephones (commercial and defense), TV, rest-rooms, O/S seats. **Protocol Service:** Bldg 103, Hours: 0730-1630 Mon-Fri, C-843-963-5644, D-312-673-5644. **FOOD SERVICE: Dining Hall:** Bldg 250, Hours: 0530-0800 Breakfast, 1030-1300 Lunch, 1630-1900 Dinner, 2200-0100 Midnight daily, C-843-963-2395/3590. **Fast Food:** Burger King: Bldg 502, Hours: 0800-2000 daily, C-843-963-1533. **In-flight Meals:** Bldg 166, 24 hours daily, C-843-963-3103. **NCO/CPO Club:** Bldg 325, Hours: 0630-2300 daily, C-843-963-2930. **O Club:** Bldg 355, Hours: 1100-1300 Mon-Fri, lunch, 1730-2100 Tue-Sat, dinner, 1730-2330 daily, sandwiches. C-843-963-3921. **Restaurants:** Anthony's Pizza, Bldg 1900, Hours: 1100-1800 daily, C-843-963-9415; Frank's Frank, Bldg 1900, Hours: 1100-1700 Mon-Sat, C-843-963-9415; Reef Restaurant, Bldg 221, 1100-1500 Mon-Fri, C-843-963-3339. **Snack Bars:** Bldg 214, Hours: 0900-2300 Mon-Fri, 1200-2300 Sat, 1300-1900 Sun, C-843-963-3315 (sandwiches, salad, pizza); Golf Course, Bldg 370, Hours: 0700-1800 daily, C-843-963-4176 (breakfast, sandwiches); Robin Hood, Bldg 1990, Hours:

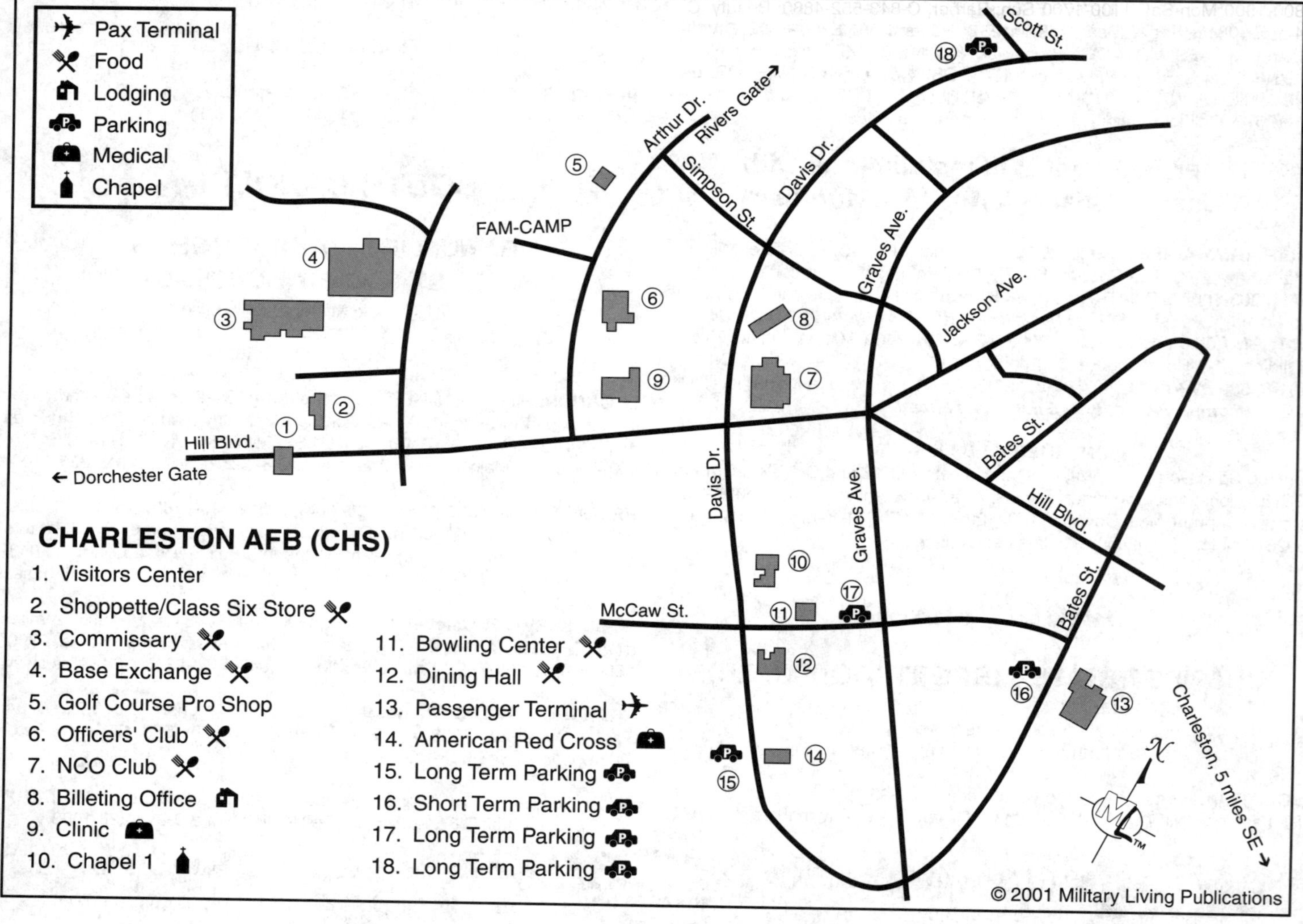


## CHARLESTON AFB (CHS)

1. Visitors Center
2. Shoppette/Class Six Store
3. Commissary
4. Base Exchange
5. Golf Course Pro Shop
6. Officers' Club
7. NCO Club
8. Billeting Office
9. Clinic
10. Chapel 1
11. Bowling Center
12. Dining Hall
13. Passenger Terminal
14. American Red Cross
15. Long Term Parking
16. Short Term Parking
17. Long Term Parking
18. Long Term Parking

0900-1700 Mon-Sat, 1000-1600 Sun, C-843-963-9415 (snack bar/ice cream). **Snack Vending:** Bldg 164, 24 hours daily, C-843-963-2610.

**TRANSPORTATION: Air Tickets:** ORTEGA, Bldg 164, Hours: 0800-2000 Mon-Fri, call for weekend hours, C-843-963-3092. **Off Base Bus:** Charleston, Hours: 0630-1000 daily; Greyhound, C-843-744-4245; Trailways, C-843-723-8649. **Car Rentals:** Alamo, 1-800-327-9633; Avis, 1-800-831-2847; Budget, 1-800-527-0700; Hertz, 1-800-654-3131; National, 1-800-227-7368; Thrifty, 1-800-367-2277. **Taxi (Comm):** Bldg 164, 24 hours daily, C-843-963-7575. **Taxi (Gov):** Bldg 408, 24 hours daily, C-843-963-3361 (duty only). **Parking:** Long term located at Scott Street and Davis Drive across from child care center.

**TML:** Lodging office, Building 322, Simpson Street & Davis Drive, 24 hours daily, C-843-963-3806, (552-9900-room number after duty hours), D-312-673-3806, Fax: C-843-963-3394.

**DV/VIP:** Hours: 0800-1700 daily, C-843-963-5644, O6+.

**TRAVELERS AID: Chaplain:** Bldg 217, Hours: 0730-1630 Mon-Fri, C-843-963-3327 (on call after hours); Bldg 1005, Hours: 0730-1630 Mon-Fri, C-843-963-2536 (on call after hours). **Emergency Relief:** Bldg 503, Hours: 0730-1630 Mon-Fri, C-843-963-2457. **Lost/Found:** Bldg 164, Hours: 0730-1630 Mon-Fri, C-843-963-2369. After hours C-843-963-2348. **Medical:** Bldg 1000, 24 hours daily, (Emergency) C-911. **Red Cross:** Bldg 500, Hours: 0800-1700 Mon-Fri, C-843-963-3377/8, Emergency C-843-963-3552. After hours C-843-744-3552. **Security Police:** Bldg 263, 24 hours daily, C-911. **USO:** C-843-767-3963 (call for hours).

**SUPPORT AVAILABLE: Bank/Currency Exchange:** South Carolina National, Bldg 306, Hours: 0900-1630 Mon-Fri, C-843-724-5055, closed 1300-1500. **Exchange:** Bldg 1990, Hours: 0900-1800 Mon-Fri, 0900-1900 Thu, Sat, 1100-1700 Sun, C-843-552-5000. **Hair Styles:** Bldg 1990, Hours: 0800-1800 Mon-Sat, 1100-1700 Sun; Barber, C-843-552-4880; Beauty, C-843-552-0812; Barber/Beauty, Bldg 237, Hours: 1000-1800 daily, C-843-760-2315. **Laundry/Dry Cleaning:** Bldg 1990, Hours: 1000-1800 Mon-Sat, C-843-767-3412. **Postal Service/Wire:** Bldg 306, Hours: 0900-1600 Mon-Fri, C-843-963-2370 (Western Union in town). **Porter:** Commercial Term (during commercial contract mission processing only). **POV Shipment:** Airport Auto Processing, C-843-744-7412/767-8900; Carolina Auto Processing, C-843-554-7253/747-0144, Gibson Auto Processing, C-843-553-8180; Owner Processing: C-843-743-5470.

**OTHER INFORMATION:** Port of Entry and U.S. Customs Service Airport. Flights via C-17A AND C-141B aircraft.

**ATTRACTIONS:** Historic Charleston, Beaches, period homes.

*Note: Commercially contracted flights are now called Patriot Express.*

### CHARLESTON AFB/IAP, SC (CHS); REGION: ATL; OPERATOR: AMC; TYPE: MIXED; ROUTE: G4M5A; SAMPLE SCHEDULE: TUE & THU; EQUIPMENT: C141B

{CHS (★) *SW* ➠ PAP ⮂ PAP *NE* ➠ CHS (★)}

| LI/ICAO | AIRPORT/STATION | CTRY/STA | DAYS EN ROUTE |
|---|---|---|---|
| CHS/KCHS | Charleston AFB/IAP | SC | +0 |
| PAP/MTPP | Port-Au-Prince IAP | HT | +0 |
| PAP/MTPP | Port-Au-Prince IAP | HT | +0 |
| CHS/KCHS | Charleston AFB/IAP | SC | |

### CHARLESTON AFB/IAP, SC (CHS); REGION: ATL; OPERATOR: AMC; TYPE: MIXED; ROUTE: G8L3A; SAMPLE SCHEDULE: 4TH SUN; EQUIPMENT: C017A

{CHS *SW* ➠ COF (★) *SE* ➠ SJH *SE* ➠ ASI ⮂ ASI *NW* ➠ SJH *NW* ➠ COF (★) *NE* ➠ CHS}

| LI/ICAO | AIRPORT/STATION | CTRY/STA | DAYS EN ROUTE |
|---|---|---|---|
| CHS/KCHS | Charleston AFB/IAP | SC | +0 |
| COF/KCOF | Patrick AFB | FL | +1 |
| SJH/TAPA | V C Bird IAP | AG | +2 |
| ASI/FHAW | Ascension AUX AF | GB | +3 |
| ASI/FHAW | Ascension AUX AF | GB | +3 |
| SJH/TAPA | V C Bird IAP | AG | +3 |
| COF/KCOF | Patrick AFB | FL | +3 |
| CHS/KCHS | Charleston AFB/IAP | SC | |

### CHARLESTON AFB/IAP, SC (CHS); REGION: ATL; OPERATOR: AMC; TYPE: CGO W/ PAX; ROUTE: A4M3A; SAMPLE SCHEDULE: 1ST FRI; EQUIPMENT: C141B

{CHS *NE* ➠ ADW (★) *SE* ➠ NRR *NW* ➠ NBW ⮂ NBW *NW* ➠ NGU (★) *NE* ➠ ADW *SW* ➠ CHS}

| LI/ICAO | AIRPORT/STATION | CTRY/STA | DAYS EN ROUTE |
|---|---|---|---|
| CHS/KCHS | Charleston AFB/IAP | SC | +0 |
| ADW/KADW | Andrews AFB | MD | +1 |
| NRR/TJNR | Roosevelt Roads NS | PR | +2 |
| NBW/MUGM | Guantanamo Bay NAS | CU | +2 |
| NBW/MUGM | Guantanamo Bay NAS | CU | +2 |
| NGU/KNGU | Norfolk NS | VA | +3 |
| ADW/KADW | Andrews AFB | MD | +3 |
| CHS/KCHS | Charleston AFB/IAP | SC | |

### CHARLESTON AFB/IAP, SC (CHS); REGION: ATL; OPERATOR: AMC; TYPE: CGO W/ PAX; ROUTE: A4P3A; SAMPLE SCHEDULE: 4TH WED; EQUIPMENT: C141B

{CHS (★) *SE* ➠ DKR *SE* ➠ NDJ *SW* ➠ NSI *SE* ➠ NBO ⮂ NBO *S* ➠ FAWK *SW* ➠ ASI *NW* ➠ STX *NW* ➠ CHS (★)}

| LI/ICAO | AIRPORT/STATION | CTRY/STA | DAYS EN ROUTE |
|---|---|---|---|
| CHS/KCHS | Charleston AFB/IAP | SC | +0 |
| DKR/GOOY | Dakar Yoff APT | SE | +1 |
| NDJ/FTTJ | N'Djamena IAP | TD | +1 |
| NSI/FKYS | Yaounde/Nsimalen IAP | CM | +2 |
| NBO/HKJK | Jomo Kenyatta IAP | KE | +2 |
| NBO/HKJK | Jomo Kenyatta IAP | KE | +2 |
| LMB/FAWK | Waterkloof AB | ZA | +3 |
| ASI/FHAW | Ascension AUX AF | GB | +4 |
| STX/TISX | Alexander Hamilton APT (St Croix) | VI | +5 |
| CHS/KCHS | Charleston AFB/IAP | SC | |

### CHARLESTON AFB/IAP, SC (CHS); REGION: ATL; OPERATOR: AMC; TYPE: CGO W/ PAX; ROUTE: A4X3A; SAMPLE SCHEDULE: 4TH THU; EQUIPMENT: C141B

{CHS *NE* ➠ NGU (★) *NE* ➠ KEF *SE* ➠ RMS ⮂ RMS *SW* ➠ ADW (★) *SW* ➠ CHS}

| LI/ICAO | AIRPORT/STATION | CTRY/STA | DAYS EN ROUTE |
|---|---|---|---|
| CHS/KCHS | Charleston AFB/IAP | SC | +0 |
| NGU/KNGU | Norfolk NS | VA | +0 |
| KEF/BIKF | Keflavik APT | IS | +1 |
| RMS/ETAR | Ramstein AB | DE | +2 |
| RMS/ETAR | Ramstein AB | DE | +2 |
| ADW/KADW | Andrews AFB | MD | +3 |
| CHS/KCHS | Charleston AFB/IAP | SC | |

### CHARLESTON AFB/IAP, SC (CHS); REGION: ATL; OPERATOR: AMC; TYPE: CGO W/ PAX; ROUTE: A8R1S &

**A8R1T; SAMPLE SCHEDULE: 2ND & 4TH TUE, 2ND & 4TH SUN; EQUIPMENT: C017A**

{CHS *NE* ➡ DOV (★) *NE* ➡ RMS ⇌ RMS *W* ➡ YQX *SW* ➡ CHS (★)}

| LI/ICAO | AIRPORT/STATION | CTRY/STA | DAYS EN ROUTE |
|---|---|---|---|
| CHS/KCHS | Charleston AFB/IAP | SC | +0 |
| DOV/KDOV | Dover AFB | DE | +1 |
| RMS/ETAR | Ramstein AB | DE | +16** |
| YQX/CYQX | Gander IAP * | CA | +16 |
| CHS/KCHS | Charleston AFB/IAP | SC | |

**Note:** * = refueling and crew rest. No Space-A embarking or debarking.
**Scheduled maintenance

### CHARLESTON AFB/IAP, SC (CHS); REGION: ATL; OPERATOR: AMC; TYPE: CGO W/ PAX; ROUTE: A8X5S; SAMPLE SCHEDULE: 1ST & 3RD FRI; EQUIPMENT: C017A

{CHS *NE* ➡ WRI (★) *E* ➡ LGS *NE* ➡ RMS ⇌ RMS *SW* ➡ LGS *SW* ➡ CHS (★)}

| LI/ICAO | AIRPORT/STATION | CTRY/STA | DAYS EN ROUTE |
|---|---|---|---|
| CHS/KCHS | Charleston AFB/IAP | SC | +0 |
| WRI/KWRI | McGuire AFB | NJ | +0 |
| LGS/LPLA | Lajes Field AB (Azores) | PT | +1 |
| RMS/ETAR | Ramstein AB | DE | +16* |
| LGS/LPLA | Lajes Field AB (Azores) | PT | +16 |
| CHS/KCHS | Charleston AFB/IAP | SC | |

*Scheduled maintenance

### CHARLESTON AFB/IAP, SC (CHS); REGION: PAC; OPERATOR: AMC; TYPE: CGO W/ PAX; ROUTE: P803R; SAMPLE SCHEDULE: SAT; EQUIPMENT: C017A

{CHS *NW* ➡ SUU (★) *NW* ➡ EDF *SW* ➡ OKO ⇌ OKO *NE* ➡ EDF *SE* ➡ TCM (★) *SE* ➡ CHS}

| LI/ICAO | AIRPORT/STATION | CTRY/STA | DAYS EN ROUTE |
|---|---|---|---|
| CHS/KCHS | Charleston AFB/IAP | SC | +0 |
| SUU/KSUU | Travis AFB | CA | +1 |
| EDF/PAED | Elmendorf AFB | AK | +2 |
| OKO/RJTY | Yokota AB | JP | +13* |
| OKO/RJTY | Yokota AB | JP | +13* |
| EDF/PAED | Elmendorf AFB | AK | +13 |
| TCM/KTCM | McChord AFB | WA | +14 |
| CHS/KCHS | Charleston AFB/IAP | SC | |

*Maintenance

### CHARLESTON AFB/IAP, SC (CHS); REGION: PAC; OPERATOR: AMC; TYPE: CGO W/ PAX; ROUTE: P803S; SAMPLE SCHEDULE: MON; EQUIPMENT: C017A

{CHS *NW* ➡ SUU (★) *NW* ➡ EDF *SW* ➡ OKO ⇌ OKO *NE* ➡ EDF *SE* ➡ TCM (★) *SE* ➡ CHS}

| LI/ICAO | AIRPORT/STATION | CTRY/STA | DAYS EN ROUTE |
|---|---|---|---|
| CHS/KCHS | Charleston AFB/IAP | SC | +0 |
| SUU/KSUU | Travis AFB | CA | +1 |
| EDF/PAED | Elmendorf AFB | AK | +2 |
| OKO/RJTY | Yokota AB | JP | +8* |
| OKO/RJTY | Yokota AB | JP | +8* |
| EDF/PAED | Elmendorf AFB | AK | +8 |
| TCM/KTCM | McChord AFB | WA | +9 |
| CHS/KCHS | Charleston AFB/IAP | SC | |

*Maintenance

## EN ROUTE SCHEDULES

| AIRPORT/STATION | LI-MISSION (page #) |
|---|---|
| Scott AFB | BLV-C-621/MEDEVAC (30) |
| Maxwell AFB | MXF-OBJ5A (2) |
| Travis AFB | SUU-ZJ43A (13) |
| WM B Hartsfield IAP (Atlanta) | ATL-EXR5B (27) |
| Minn-St Paul IAP/ARS | MSP-9QM1B (42) |
| Allen C Thompson (Jackson) | JAN-IKB7A (43) |
| Allen C Thompson (Jackson) | JAN-IKH5A (44) |

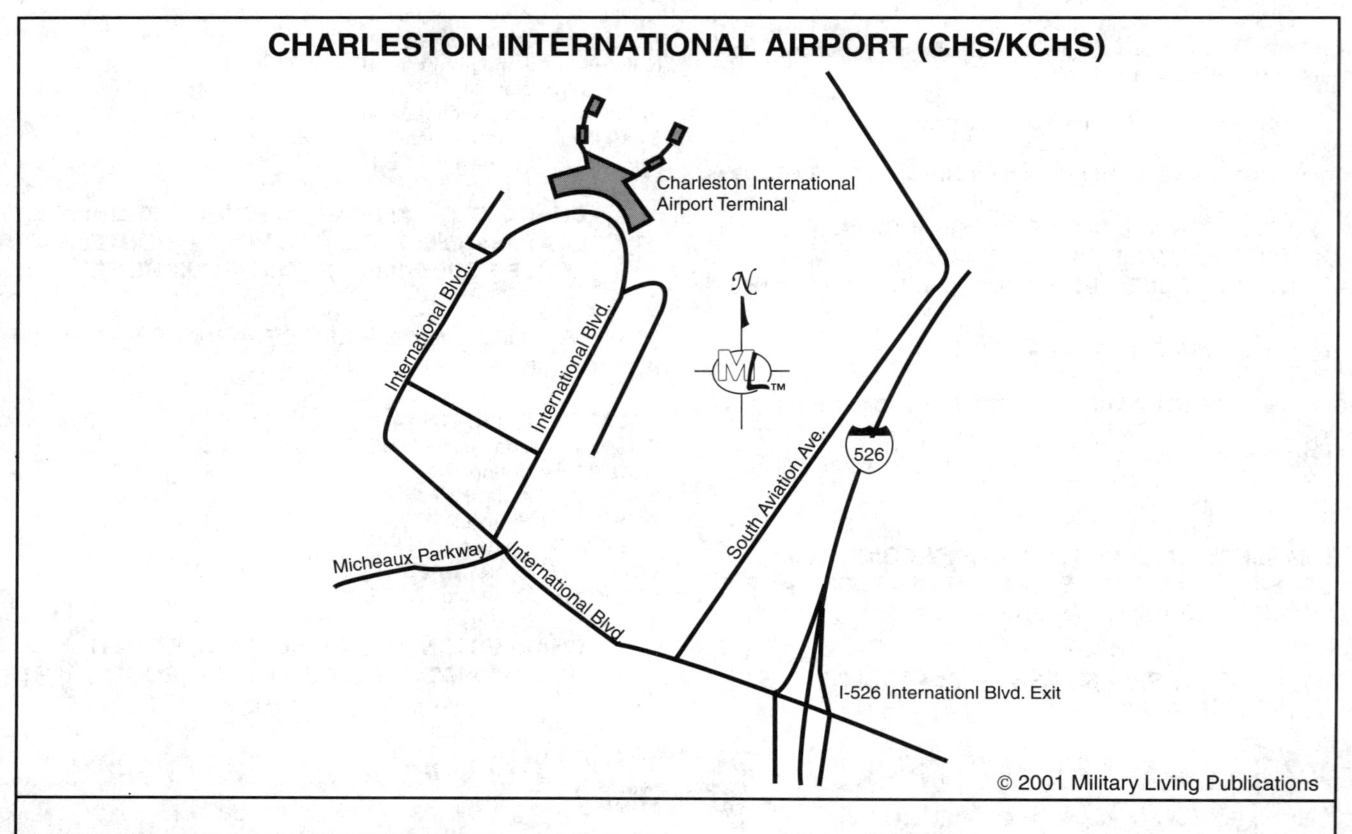

# CHARLESTON INTERNATIONAL AIRPORT (CHS/KCHS)

| | |
|---|---|
| Wright-Patterson AFB | FFO-OEB1D (61) |
| Wright-Patterson AFB | FFO-OEH3B (61) |
| Wright-Patterson AFB | FFO-OEK5C (61) |
| Memphis IAP | MEM-IDB3B (71) |
| Memphis IAP | MEM-IDB5A (71) |

## CHARLESTON INTERNATIONAL AIRPORT (CHS/KCHS)

437th APS/TRG
5500 International Blvd, Suite 124
Charleston IAP, SC 29418-6924

**LOCATION:** From I-26 take I-526 west one mile to airport exit. Turn right onto International Blvd, follow signs to airport. *USMRA: Page 44 (H-8,9). ML-ARM: (32°53'N/80°01'W).* LST: GMT-05:00. NMC: Charleston, 5 miles southeast. Main installation numbers: C-843-963-5794/95, D-312-673-5794/95.

**REGISTRATION INFO:** **C-843-963-5794/5795, D-312-673-5794/5795, Rec: C-843-963-5794 (during non-operation hours), Fax: C-843-963-3845, D-312-673-3845. E-mail: spacea@charleston.af.mil** Main ticket lobby, Hours: 0800-1900 on Mondays; 0800-1600 Tue-Fri; closed on weekends. **Pax Service Office:** Main lobby, C-843-963-5795/5794. **Pax Paging:** C-843-963-5795/5794 or Airport Paging: C-843-767-7009. ***Note: There is multi-station sign-up between Charleston AFB and Charleston IAP, and the William B. Hartsfield Atlanta IAP.***

**PAX LOUNGES:** No separate DV/VIP or family lounges. **General:** Commercial facilities in IAP. USO Lounge on ground floor, under domestic baggage claim, C-843-767-3963 See Charleston AFB listing.

**TML:** BEQ/BOQ C-843-764-7646. Also, see Charleston AFB listing, C-843-556-3806, D-312-673-3806.

**RVC:** FAMCAMP (Shady Oaks Family Campground), Check-in Outdoor Rec Center, Bldg 647, 0900-1700 hours daily, C-843-963-5270/1, D-312-673-5271.

**SUPPORT AVAILABLE:** See Charleston Air Force Base listing.

***Note: Commercially contracted flights are now called Patriot Express.***

### CHARLESTON AFB/IAP, SC (CHS); REGION: ATL; OPERATOR: COM; TYPE: MIXED; ROUTE: HJJ7A; SAMPLE SCHEDULE: THU; EQUIPMENT: DC863

{CHS (★) *SW* ➡ PLA ⇌ PLA *NE* ➡ CHS (★)}

| LI/ICAO | AIRPORT/STATION | CTRY/STA | DAYS EN ROUTE |
|---|---|---|---|
| CHS/KCHS | Charleston AFB/IAP | SC | +0 |
| PLA/MHSC | Soto Cano AB | HN | +0 |
| CHS/KCHS | Charleston AFB/IAP | SC | |

### CHARLESTON AFB/IAP, SC (CHS); REGION: ATL; OPERATOR: COM; TYPE: PAX; ROUTE: MX31C; SAMPLE SCHEDULE: TUE; EQUIPMENT: L1011

{CHS *NE* ➡ BWI (★) *NE* ➡ FRF ⇌ FRF *SW* ➡ BWI (★) *SW* ➡ ATL}

| LI/ICAO | AIRPORT/STATION | CTRY/STA | DAYS EN ROUTE |
|---|---|---|---|
| CHS/KCHS | Charleston AFB/IAP | SC | +0 |
| BWI/KBWI | Baltimore/Washington IAP | MD | +0 |
| FRF/EDDF | Rhein-Main AB (Frankfurt) | DE | +1 |
| FRF/EDDF | Rhein-Main AB (Frankfurt) | DE | +1 |
| BWI/KBWI | Baltimore/Washington IAP | MD | +1 |
| ATL/KATL | The WM B Hartsfield Atlanta IAP | GA | |

## McENTIRE AIR NATIONAL GUARD STATION (MMT/KMMT)

1325 South Carolina Road
Eastover, SC 29044-5000

**LOCATION:** On US-76/378 between Sumter and Columbia, south side of US-76/378. *USMRA: Page 44 (G-6, 7). ML-ARM: (33°54'N/80°48'W).* LST: GMT-05:00. NMC: Columbia, 15 miles west. NMI: Fort Jackson, 10 miles northwest. Main telephone numbers. C-803-647-8300, D-312-583-8201.

**REGISTRATION INFO: C-803-647-8231, D-312-583-8231, Fax: C-803-647-8479, D-312-583-8479.**

**FOOD SERVICE:** Available only on Tuesday, Wednesday and Thursday. Fast Food: Hours: 1100-1300. **Snack Vending:** Hours: 0730-1100.

**TRAVELERS AID: Medical/Dental:** C-803-647-8295, D-312-583-8295 **Security Police:** 24 hours daily, C-803-647-8284, D-312-583-8284, 2500 yards away.

**TML:** Nearest TML is at Shaw AFB, Carolina Pines Inn, Building 930, 471, 24 hours daily, C-803-895-3803, D-312-965-3801/2. Switchboard, C-803-895-3658, D-312-965-3803. DV/VIP C-803-668-2156/2311, D-312-965-2156/2311.

**SUPPORT AVAILABLE: Credit Union:** Hours: 0900-1600, C-843-647-8212, D-312-583-8212, 25 feet. **Exchange:** Hours: 1000-1700, C-843-647-8517, D-312-583-8517.

### UNSCHEDULED FLIGHTS
Very limited Space A Travel. Call for destinations, routings and schedules.

## SHAW AIR FORCE BASE (SSC/KSSC)

20th Fighter Wing
590 Killian Avenue
Shaw AFB, SC 29152-5000

**LOCATION:** Off US-76/378, eight miles west of Sumter, north side of US-76/378. Clearly marked. *USMRA: Page 44 (H-6). ML-ARM: (33°57'N/80°29'W).* LST: GMT-05:00. NMC: Columbia, 35 miles west. Main installation numbers: C-803-895-1110, D-312-965-1110.

**REGISTRATION INFO: C-803-895-1741/1738, D-312-965-1741/1738, Fax: C-803-895-4156, D-312-965-2796.** Base operations, Bldg 1578, Hours: daily 0800-1500 hours.

**PAX LOUNGES:** General lounge, Bldg 1518, Hours 0800-1500 daily, C-803-895-3818, D-312-965-3818.

**TML:** Nearest TML is at Shaw AFB, Carolina Pines Inn, Building 930, 471, 24 hours daily, C-803-895-3803, D-312-965-3801/2. Switchboard, C-803-895-3658, D-312-965-3803. DV/VIP C-803-668-2156/2311, D-312-965-2156/2311.

**RVC:** FAMCAMP (Falcon's Nest), Check-in, Outdoor Rec, 1 FAMCAMP Drive, duty hours, late arrivals check in next morning, C-803-895-0449/0450, D-312-965-0449/0450.

### EN ROUTE SCHEDULES

| AIRPORT/STATION | LI-MISSION (page #) |
|---|---|
| Scott AFB | BLV-C-621/MEDEVAC (30) |

### UNSCHEDULED FLIGHTS
Infrequent flights via MEDEVAC and transient aircraft. Call for destinations, routings and schedules.

## Other South Carolina Installations with Possible Space-A Opportunities

**COLUMBIA OWENS DOWNTOWN AIRPORT (CUB),** Midlands Aviation Corporation, 1400 Jim Hamilton Blvd, Columbia, SC 29205-5000. **LOCATION:** From I-20 east or west, exit US-1 (Two Notch Road) southwest, to south on Millwood Avenue to right (west) on Rosewood Drive to left (south) on South Holly Street and Airport. *USMRA: Page 44 (F-6,7). ML-ARM: (33°58'N/80°59'W).* LST: GMT-05:00. **C-803-771-7915, Fax: C-803-256-9425.** Call or fax for more information. **TML:** Nearest TML is at Fort Jackson, Kennedy Hall, Building 2785, Semmes & Lee Road, 24 hours daily, C-803-751-6223/6149, D-312-734-6223/6149. Palmetto Lodge, Building 6000: C-803-751-5205/4429, D-312-734-5205/4429. DV/VIP C-803-751-6618, D-312-734-5218.

### UNSCHEDULED FLIGHTS

Very limited flights. Call for destinations, routings and schedules.

# SOUTH DAKOTA

## ELLSWORTH AIR FORCE BASE (RCA/KRCA)

28 OSS/OSAA
1820 Vandenberg Court, Suite 2
Ellsworth AFB, SD 57706-4708

**LOCATION:** Two miles north of I-90. Seven miles east of Rapid City. From I-90 take exit 66 north approximately two miles to gate. Clearly marked. *USMRA: Page 85 (B-5). ML-ARM: (44°07'N/103°03'W).* LST: GMT-07:00. NMC: Rapid City, 10 miles west. Main installation numbers: C-605-385-5056, D-312-675-5056.

**REGISTRATION INFO: C-605-385-1181, D-312-675-1181, Fax: C-605-385-1181, D-312-675-1181.** Bldg 7510 (Traffic Management Office), Hours: 0730-1630 Mon-Fri. Directions: From main gate straight on Davis Drive to a right on Ellsworth Drive. Turn left at 4-way stop onto LeMay Blvd to Bldg 7510 which will be on the right after crossing second set of railroad tracks. For after hours flight information, call Base Ops, C-605-385-1052, D-312-675-1052.

**PAX LOUNGES:** No separate family lounge. **General:** Bldg 7506, 24 hours daily, C-605-385-1052. A/C, restrooms, showers, limited lobby seats. **DV/VIP:** Bldg 7506, 24 hours daily, C-605-385-1052 A/C, restrooms, showers, coffee/soda available/in-flight kitchen. **Protocol Service:** Bldg 7925, C-605-385-1205.

**FOOD SERVICE: Dining Hall:** Bandit Inn, Bldg 2106, C-605-385-1625. **NCO/CPO Club:** Dakota's, Bldg 5903, C-605-385-1764. **Food Court:** Burger King, Anthony's Pizza, and Robin Hood Deli located in BX, Bldg 4001. **Snack Bars:** Bowling Center, Bldg 4500.

**TRANSPORTATION:** Very limited on base. **Taxi (Gov):** Bldg 104, C-605-385-2907 (duty passengers only). Car Rental and Off Base Taxi service available in Rapid City. **Parking:** Bldg 7506, in front of Base Ops, C-605-385-1052.

**TML:** Billeting Office, Building 1103, 2349 Risner Drive, 24 hours daily, C-605-385-2844, D-312-675-2844: Fax: C-605-385-2718. DV/VIP C-605-385-1205, D-312-675-1205.

**RVC:** FAMCAMP, Outdoor Rec, 2750 George Drive, Check-in FAMCAMP, C-605-385-2997, D-312-675-2997, Fax: C-605-385-2997, D-312-675-2997.

**TRAVELERS AID: Chaplain:** Bldg 2009, C-605-385-1598. **Lost/Found:** Bldg 7506, C-605-385-1052. **Medical:** Bldg 6000, 24 hours daily, C-605-385-7630, D-312-675-7630. **Red Cross:** Bldg 1107, C-605-385-1381, after hours C-605-385-1000. **Security Police:** Bldg 4400, C-605-385-4010.

**SUPPORT AVAILABLE: Credit Union:** Bldg 4005, C-605-923-1405. **Exchange:** Bldg 4001, C-605-923-4774; services include barber and beauty shop, laundry/dry cleaning, optical shop and food court. **Postal Service:** Bldg 3602, C-605-385-6229. **Shoppette:** Bldg 5912, Hours: 0530-1200 Mon-Fri, 0700-1200 Sat-Sun, C-605-923-5231.

**ATTRACTIONS:** Black Hills and Mt Rushmore nearby; Badlands National Park, Custer State Park and Wind Cave National Park. Other area attractions include Reptile Gardens, Museum of Geology and several caves. Ideal location for outdoor summer and winter recreational enthusiasts.

### EN ROUTE SCHEDULES

| AIRPORT/STATION | LI-MISSION (page #) |
| --- | --- |
| Scott AFB | BLV-C-635/MEDEVAC (30) |

### UNSCHEDULED FLIGHTS

Flights to Midwest and West Coast areas. Call for destinations, routings and schedules.

# TENNESSEE

## McGHEE TYSON AIR NATIONAL GUARD BASE (TYS/KTYS)

134th ARW/OTB
102 Briscoe Drive
McGhee Tyson ANGB, TN 37777-6203

**LOCATION:** Exit north or south form US-129 onto Air Base Road. There is a large national guard sign at the exit. Proceed on Air Base Road approximately two miles to main gate. *USMRA: Page 41 (L-8). ML-ARM: (35°52'N/83°57'W).* LST: GMT-05:00. NMC: Knoxville, 10 miles northeast. Main installation numbers: C-865-985-3200, D-312-266-8200.

**REGISTRATION INFO: C-865-985-4404/4419, D-312-266-4404/4419, Rec: C-865-985-4403, D-312-266-4403, Fax: C-865-985-4397, D-312-266-4397.** Air National Guard area, Hours: 0700-1630 Mon-Fri. Closed every other Monday. Limited support on base. Dispensary: C-865-985-4277; BX: C-865-985-3400.

**ATTRACTIONS:** Knoxville.

### UNSCHEDULED FLIGHTS

Flights to CONUS and OCONUS locations via ANG KC-135E aircraft. Call for destinations, routings and schedules.

## MEMPHIS INTERNATIONAL AIRPORT/ AIR NATIONAL GUARD BASE (MEM/KMEM)

164th AW (ANG)
2815 Democrat Road
Memphis, TN 38181-1510

**LOCATION:** From I-55 north or south, exit 5A (Brooks Road) east, two miles to IAP, left on Airways on Democrat Road, right to 164th Air National Guard Base (north side of IAP), go to Aerial Port building. *USMRA: Page 40 (A-10). ML-ARM: (35°02'N/89°58'W).* LST: GMT-05:00. NMC: Memphis, in city limits. Main installation numbers: C-901-541-7111, D-312-966-8120.

**REGISTRATION INFO:** Contact Aerial Port **C-901-541-7221, D-312-966-8221, Rec: C-901-541-7202, D-312-966-8202, Fax: C-901-541-7230, D-312-966-8230.** Air National Guard area, Hours: 0730-1530 Mon-Fri. Ask Security Police for directions. All the facilities of an IAP. For other support services see Mid-South Naval Support Activity, C-901-873-5111, D-312-966-5111.

**TML:** Nearest TML is at Mid-South NSA, All ranks: C-901-874-5459. Navy Lodge: C-1-800-NAVY-INN, C-901-872-0121, Fax: C-901-873-1695.

**OTHER INFORMATION:** Weekly flight to Charleston AFB, SC. Equipment: C-141C. U.S. Customs Service Airport.

**MEMPHIS IAP/ANGB, TN (MEM); REGION: PAC; OPERATOR: AMC; TYPE: MIXED; ROUTE: IDB7B & 7D45A; SAMPLE SCHEDULE: THU & 1ST WED; EQUIPMENT: C141C**

{MEM *NW* ➠ SUU (★) *SW* ➠ HIK *SW* ➠ JON ⮂ JON *NE* ➠ HIK *NE* ➠ SUU (★) *SE* ➠MEM}

| LI/ICAO | AIRPORT/STATION | CTRY/STA | DAYS EN ROUTE |
|---|---|---|---|
| MEM/KMEM | Memphis IAP | TN | +0 |
| SUU/KSUU | Travis AFB | CA | +0 |
| HIK/PHIK | Hickam AFB | HI | +1 |
| JON/PJON | Johnston Atoll | JO | +2 |
| HIK/PHIK | Hickam AFB | HI | +3 |
| SUU/KSUU | Travis AFB | CA | +3 |
| MEM/KMEM | Memphis IAP | TN | |

### MEMPHIS IAP/ANGB, TN (MEM); REGION: ATL; OPERATOR: AMC; TYPE: CGO W/ PAX; ROUTE: IDB3B; SAMPLE SCHEDULE: 1ST WED; EQUIPMENT: C141C

{MEM *SE* ➡ CHS SE (★) ➡ STX *SE* ➡ BSB *SW* ➡ ASU ⇄ ASU *NW* ➡ STX *NW* ➡ CHS *NW* (★) ➡ MEM}

| LI/ICAO | AIRPORT/STATION | CTRY/STA | DAYS EN ROUTE |
|---|---|---|---|
| MEM/KMEM | Memphis IAP | TN | +0 |
| CHS/KCHS | Charleston AFB/IAP | SC | +0 |
| STX/TISX | Alexander Hamilton Apt (St Croix) | VI | +1 |
| BSB/SBBR | Brasilia APT | BR | +2 |
| ASU/SGAS | Silvio Pettirossi IAP | PY | +3 |
| STX/TISX | Alexander Hamilton Apt (St Croix) | VI | +4 |
| CHS/KCHS | Charleston AFB/IAP | SC | +4 |
| MEM/KMEM | Memphis IAP | TN | |

### MEMPHIS IAP/ANGB, TN (MEM); REGION: ATL; OPERATOR: AMC; TYPE: CGO W/ PAX; ROUTE: IDB5A; SAMPLE SCHEDULE: 4TH WED; EQUIPMENT: C141C

{MEM *SE* ➡ CHS *SE* (★) ➡ STX *SE* ➡ BSB *SW* ➡ MVD *W* ➡ BUE ⇄ BUE *NW* ➡ STX *NW* ➡ CHS *NW* (★) ➡ MEM}

| LI/ICAO | AIRPORT/STATION | CTRY/STA | DAYS EN ROUTE |
|---|---|---|---|
| MEM/KMEM | Memphis IAP | TN | +0 |
| CHS/KCHS | Charleston AFB/IAP | SC | +0 |
| STX/TISX | Alexander Hamilton Apt (St Croix) | VI | +1 |
| BSB/SBBR | Brasilia APT | BR | +2 |
| MVD/SUMU | Carrasco IAP (Montevideo) | UY | +2 |
| BUE/SAEZ | Ezeiza APT (Buenos Aires) | AR | +3 |
| STX/TISX | Alexander Hamilton Apt (St Croix) | VI | +4 |
| CHS/KCHS | Charleston AFB/IAP | SC | +4 |
| MEM/KMEM | Memphis IAP | TN | |

### UNSCHEDULED FLIGHTS

Fights to CONUS and OCONUS locations via ANG C-141B aircraft. Call for destinations, routings and schedules.

## MILLINGTON MUNICIPAL AIRPORT/ MID-SOUTH NAVAL SUPPORT ACTIVITY (NQA/KNQA)

7800 3rd Ave, Bldg N-126
Millington, TN 38054-5060

**LOCATION:** From Memphis, take Route 51 north to Millington. Turn right (east) on Navy Road 205. Go approximately two miles to base entrance on north side of road. *USMRA: Page 40 (B-9,10). ML-ARM: (35°35'N/89°86'W).* LST: GMT-05:00. NMC: Memphis, 20 miles south. Main installation numbers: C-901-874-5111, D-312-882-5111.

**REGISTRATION INFO: C-901-873-1818. REC: C-901-874-5111, D-312-966-5111.**

**PAX LOUNGES:** General accommodations available.

**FOOD SERVICE: Fast Food:** 2-4 miles away. **Restaurants**: 2-4 miles away. Snack Vending available at airport.

**TRANSPORTATION:** Off Base Taxi available in Millington.

**TML:** Lodging Office: 24 hours daily, C-901-874-5459, D-312-882-5459. All ranks. DV/VIP C-901-874-5101. Navy Lodge: Bldg N-931, C-901-872-0121 or 1-800-NAVY-INN, Fax: C-901-873-1695, all ranks, 1 mile away.

**RVC:** Navy Lake Rec Area, MWR Dept, Check-in Rec Area, C-1-800-779-4252, C-901-874-5163, D-312-882-5163, Fax: C-901-874-5690, D-312-882-5690, Rec Area C-901-872-3660.

**TRAVELERS AID: Chaplain:** C-901-874-5341, D-312-882-5341, 1-2 miles away. **Medical/Dental:** C-901-874-6100, D-312-882-6100, 1-2 miles away. **Red Cross:** C-901-874-5607, D-312-882-5607, .5 miles away. **Security Police:** C-901-874-5533/4, D-312-882-5533/4, 1-2 miles away.

**SUPPORT AVAILABLE: Convenience Store:** C-901-872-1334, on base, 2 miles away. **Credit Union:** C-901-873-2300, on base, 1.5 miles away. **Exchange:** Hours: 0900-1800, C-901-872-0139, D-312-882-0139, on base, 1.5 miles away. **Laundry/Dry Cleaner:** Hours: 0900-1800. C-901-872-7259, D-312-882-7259, on base, 1.5 miles away. **Postal Service:** C-901-874-5577, on base, 1.5 miles away.

### UNSCHEDULED FLIGHTS

Flights to Midwest and East Coast areas. Call for destinations, routings and schedules.

## NASHVILLE INTERNATIONAL AIRPORT/TENNESSEE AIR NATIONAL GUARD BASE (BNA/KBNA)

118th AW (ANG)
240 Knapp Blvd
Nashville, TN 37217-0267

**LOCATION:** From I-40 east to exit 216 B, from I-40 west to exit 216 south on Donelson Pike for two miles, right on Knapp Blvd. *USMRA: Page 40 (G,H-8). ML-ARM: (36°07'N/86°40'W).* LST: GMT-05:00. NMC: Nashville, 4 miles northwest. Main installation numbers: C-615-399-5410, D-312-778-6210.

**REGISTRATION INFO: C-615-399-5807, D-312-778-6407.** Bldg 721, Hours: 0700-1530 Mon-Fri. *Note: In-person sign up only.* Ask Security Police for directions. All the support facilities of a regional airport. **TML:** Nearest TML is at Fort Campbell, KY, Turner Guest House, Building 82, Texas Avenue & Indiana, C-270-798-5618. Fax: C-270-798-0602. DV/VIP: C-270-798-9913.

**ATTRACTIONS:** General Jackson Steamboat, Music City Row, Music City Hall of Fame, Ryman Auditorium. Call for destinations, routings and schedules.

### UNSCHEDULED FLIGHTS

Flights to CONUS and OCONUS locations via ANG C-130H aircraft. Must show ID for schedules.

# TEXAS

## BIGGS ARMY AIRFIELD (BIF/KBIF)

Commander, USAADACENFB
ATTN: ATZC-GC-AV
Bldg 11210, Room 112
Fort Bliss, TX 79916-6816

**LOCATION:** From I-10 take exit 25 Airport Road to north. Airport Road will turn to the west. After first traffic light, look for gradual right turn below second traffic light. Heading north on Airport Road pass three traffic lights

(not counting military crossing). Entrance to Biggs AAf is on right. Or from US-54 southbound, take Fred Wilson Drive exit. At first traffic light turn left (east) and continue to fifth traffic light, turn left into Biggs AAF. *USMRA: Page 86 (B-6)*. *ML-ARM: (31°51'N/106°22'W)*. LST: GMT-06:00. NMC: El Paso, in northeast section of the city limits. Main installation numbers: C-915-568-2121, D-312-978-2121.

**REGISTRATION INFO: C-915-568-8097, D-312-978-8097.** Bldg 11210, Hours: 0600-2200 Mon-Fri, 0800-1600 Sat, closed Sun and holidays. Northeast of main post off Wilson Road. Limited facilities. Personnel may not stay in building during closure periods.

**PAX LOUNGES: General:** Bldg 11210 near south entrance, same hours and phone as above. A/C, restrooms, P/C and O/S seats. **DV/VIP:** Bldg 11210 opposite dispatch counter, same hours and phone as above. **Protocol Service:** Hours: 0730-1630 Mon-Fri, C-915-568-5330.

**FOOD SERVICE: Dining Hall:** Hours: 1100-1300 Mon-Fri. **NCO Club:** Bldg 11199, C-915-562-55659. **O Club:** Bldg 250, C-915-562-2040. Pizza and sub delivery available. Snack Vending available.

**TRANSPORTATION:** No post taxi service but commercial taxis available. **Car Rentals:** Enterprise, C-915-562-5400; Avis, C-915-779-2700; Budget, C-915-778-5287; Dollar, C-915-778-5445; Hertz, C-915-772-4255.

**TML:** Lodging office, Fort Bliss Inn, 24 hours daily, C-915-565-7777, Fax: C-915-565-7778; DV/VIP: C-915-568-5319/5330. New YMCA Residence Center on William Beaumont Medical Center, C-915-562-8461.

**RVC:** Fort Bliss RV Park, Bldg 4130, Check-in Office, C-915-568-4693/0106, D-312-978-4693/0106, Fax: C-915-568-2028, D-312-978-2028.

**TRAVELERS AID: Chaplain:** C-915-568-1519. **Medical:** William Beaumont Army Medical Center: C-915-567-2121. Veterans Affairs Health Care Center: C-915-564-6100. **Red Cross:** C-915-568-5085/4898. **Security Police:** C-915-568-2115.

**SUPPORT AVAILABLE: Bank:** Armed Forces Bank, C-915-562-7778; Texas Commerce Bank, C-915-546-6500; Northwest Bank of El Paso NA, C-915-532-9922. **Credit Union:** C-915-562-1172. **Exchange:** Bldg 1735, Hours: 0900-2200 Mon-Sat, 1000-2100 Sun, C-915-562-9951. **Laundry:** C-915-568-5405. **Postal Service:** C-915-562-4036. **Shoppettes:** C-915-562-8442 or C-915-562-7200.

**ATTRACTIONS:** Museums: Art C-915-541-4040; History C-915-858-1928; Wilderness Park C-915-755-4332. Chamizal National Memorial, Rio Grande River, Tigua Indian Reservation. Tourist information center: C-915-534-0698. Numerous Golf Courses.

### EN ROUTE SCHEDULES

| AIRPORT/STATION | LI-MISSION (page #) |
| --- | --- |
| Travis AFB | SUU-456/MEDEVAC (13) |
| Kelly AFB | SKF-546/MEDEVAC (74) |

### UNSCHEDULED FLIGHTS

Limited flights via C-12A and C-21A aircraft. Some transient aircraft activity via C-141B and C-005A/B. Call for destinations, routings and schedules.

# CORPUS CHRISTI
# NAVAL AIR STATION (NGP/KNGP)

Air Operations, Hangar #58
Flight Clearance/Pax Term
Corpus Christi NAS, TX 78419-5021

**LOCATION:** From San Antonio, take Interstate 37 southeast to exit 4 A, Highway 358 southeast. Exit northwest for NAS after 12 miles. *USMRA: Page 87 (K-8)*. *ML-ARM: (27°40'N/97°16'W)*. LST: GMT-06:00. NMC: Corpus Christi, 10 miles north. Main installation numbers: C-361-961-2811, D-312-861-2811.

**REGISTRATION INFO: C-361-961-2505, D-312-861-2505, Rec: C-361-961-3385, D-312-861-3385. Fax: C-361-961-3301, D-312-861-3301.** Hangar 58, first floor, Hours: 0800-1700 Mon-Fri. Directions: From South Gate straight on Lexington Blvd to a left on First Street to a left on Ave D to Pax Term on the left. **Pax Service Office:** C-361-961-2505 (POIC on duty).

**PAX LOUNGES:** Limited facilities. No separate DV/VIP or family lounges. **General:** C-361-961-2505. A/C, restrooms, P/C seats. **Protocol Service:** Bldg 1, Hours: 0800-1600 Mon-Fri, C-361-961-2284.

**FOOD SERVICE: Cafeteria:** Hours: 0700-2000 Mon-Fri, C-361-961-8265, Hangar #57, 200 feet from Pax Term. **Restaurants:** C-361-961-2249, C-361-961-3360. **Club:** C-361-961-2541. Snack Vending available in pax lounge.

**TRANSPORTATION: Taxi:** Available. **Off Base Car Rental:** Available. **Parking:** At Hangar 58 (must have tag from Security Police).

**TML:** Lodging office, 24 hours daily, Building 1281, 11801 Ocean Drive, C-361-961-2388/89, D-312-861-2388/89. Fax: C-361-961-3275. Navy Lodge, Building 1281, 0800-1800 Mon-Fri, 0900-1800 Sat-Sun, C-361-937-6361. DV/VIP Protocol Office, Building 1281, C-361-961-2388/89, Fax: C-361-961-3275.

**RVC:** Shields Park, Outdoor Rec, Bldg 39, Code 22, Check-in Park, C-512-937-5071.

**TRAVELERS AID: Chaplain:** C-361-961-3751. **Medical:** C-361-961-2688. **Navy Relief:** C-361-961-2560. **Red Cross:** C-361-961-3751. **Security Police:** C-361-961-2480. **USO:** C-361-961-2391.

**SUPPORT AVAILABLE: Bank/Currency Exchange:** C-361-961-3113. **Exchange:** C-361-961-2033. **Hair Styles:** Barber, C-361-961-8880; Beauty, C-361-961-8901. **Laundry/Dry Cleaning:** C-361-961-8942. **Postal Service:** C-361-961-2984.

**OTHER INFORMATION:** Port of Entry.

**ATTRACTIONS:** Bay and gulf water sports, historic homes, Texas State Aquarium, USS Lexington Museum.

### UNSCHEDULED FLIGHTS

Various flights to: Pensacola NAS, FL (**NPA**); New Orleans NAS/JRB, LA (**NBG**); and other CONUS, Midwest, West Coast, and OCONUS locations via USN T-44A, USCG HU-25, and transient aircraft. Call for destinations, routings and schedules.

# DYESS AIR FORCE BASE (DYS/KDYS)

7th TRNS/LGTR
198 2nd Street, Bldg 7040, Room 214A
Dyess AFB, TX 79607-1244

**LOCATION:** Turn left off of I-20/US-277 west onto Arnold Blvd. Main gate will be up three miles on the right. *USMRA: Page 87 (I-3)*. *ML-ARM: (32°24'N/99°47'W)*. LST: GMT-06:00. NMC: Abilene, 6 miles northeast. Main installation numbers: C-915-696-2864, D-312-461-2864.

**REGISTRATION INFO: C-915-696-4505, D-312-461-4505, Fax: C-915-696-2943, D-312-461-2943.** Bldg 9001, 24 hours daily. Directions: From Main Gate: Continue past the traffic circle until you get to 2nd St., and take a left. Bldg.198 will be the first on your right. **Pax Service Office:** Bldg 7008, Hours: 0730-1630 Mon-Fri, C-915-696-3108 (NCO on duty).

**PAX LOUNGES:** Limited lounge facilities. Bldg 198, Hours: 0730-1630 daily, C-915-696-3108. A/C, bag check/lockers, restrooms, P/C seats. **DV/VIP:** Bldg 9001, 24 hours daily, C-915-696-3108. **Protocol Service:** Bldg 8030, C-915-696-5610.

**FOOD SERVICE: Dining Hall:** 349 3rd Street, C-915-696-2421. **Enlisted Club** 357 Ave B, Hours: 0630-2300 Mon-Fri, 1200-0300 Sat, 1200-1800 Sun, C-915-696-4311. **Fast Food:** Burger King, 290 Theatre Road, Hours: 0630-2000 Mon-Fri, 0830-2000 Sat, 1030-2000 Sun. **O Club:** 217 5th Street, Hours: 1100-1300 Mon-Fri, C-915-696-2405. **Snack Vending:** Bldg 9001, 24 hours daily, C-915-696-3108.

**TRANSPORTATION: Air Tickets:** SATO, 466 5th Street, Hours: 0800-1600 Mon-Fri, C-915-696-4743. **On Base Car Rental:** Enterprise. Contact base info for new number - 915-696-0212. **On Base Bus (Gov):** 690 Ave E, C-915-696-2265 (limited). **Off Base Car Rental:** C-915-692-9500 ext 201, C-915-677-9240, C-915-690-9338. **Off Base Limo:** C-915-677-5466. **Off Base Shuttle/Bus:** C-915-676-6287. **On Base Taxi (Gov):** C-915-696-2265. **Off Base Taxi:** C-915-677-8294. **Off Base Train Station:** C-915-677-8161. **Parking:** Across from Bldg 198 2nd Street (no restrictions).

**TML:** Lodging office, 441 Fifth Street, Dyess Inn, 24 hours daily, C-915-696-1874, D-312-461-1874/2681. Fax-C-915-696-2836. DV/VIP C-915-696-5610.

**TRAVELERS AID: Bank/Currency Exchange:** Bldg 7206, Hours: 0900-1430 Mon-Fri, C-915-692-9797. **Chaplain:** 158 Ave B, Hours: 0800-1700 Mon-Fri, C-915-696-4224. After hours C-915-636-3203. **Emergency Relief:** Ask the Commander, C-915-696-3355. **Medical:** Bldg 9201, 24 hours daily, C-915-696-4677, D-312-461-4677. **Security Police:** Bldg 6117, 24 hours daily, C-915-696-2131.

**SUPPORT AVAILABLE: Bank/Currency Exchange:** 7338 Commissary Road, Hours: 0900-1900 Mon-Fri, 1000-1900 Sat, and 1200-1700 Sun. C-915-690-6220. **Exchange:** Bldg 7338, Hours: 0900-1900 Mon-Fri, 1000-1900 Sat, 1200-1800 Sun, C-915-692-8996. **Hair Styles:** Bldg 7338, Barber, C-915-692-9974; Beauty, C-915-692-9257. **Postal Service:** Bldg 7332, Hours: 0830-1700 Mon-Fri, C-915-696-2655. **Valet/Dry Cleaning:** Bldg 7324, C-915-695-0231.

**ATTRACTIONS:** Dyess Air Park Museum, Abilene Zoo and outdoor sports.

### DYESS AFB,TX  (DYS); REGION: PAC; OPERATOR: AMC; TYPE: CGO W/ PAX; ROUTE: A1N1B; SAMPLE SCHEDULE: 4TH TUE; EQUIPMENT: C130H

{DYS *NE* ➡ NGU (★) *SE* ➡ NRR *NW* ➡ NGU (★) *S* ➡ NBW ⮌ NBW *N* ➡ NGU (★) *SW* ➡DYS}

| LI/ICAO | AIRPORT/STATION | CTRY/STA | DAYS EN ROUTE |
|---|---|---|---|
| DYS/KDYS | Dyess AFB | TX | +0 |
| NGU/KNGU | Norfolk NS | VA | +1 |
| NRR/TJNR | Roosevelt Roads NS | PR | +2 |
| NGU/KNGU | Norfolk NS | VA | +3 |
| NBW/MUGM | Guantanamo Bay | CU | +3 |
| NGU/KNGU | Norfolk NS | VA | +4 |
| DYS/KDYS | Dyess AFB | TX | |

### UNSCHEDULED FLIGHTS

Infrequent flights via C-130H to: Charleston AFB, SC (**CHS**); Norfolk NS, VA (**NGU**); and Pope AFB, NC (**POB**). Call for destinations, routings and schedules.

## FORT WORTH NAVAL AIR STATION/ JOINT RESERVE BASE (NFW/KNFW)

Bldg 1423
Fort Worth, TX 76127-5000

**LOCATION:** On TX-183. From Fort Worth, west on I-30, exit at 78 north on TX 183, 1.5 miles to gate on left/north of TX-183. *USMRA: Page 88 (A,3).* *ML-ARM: (32°40'N/97°25'W).* LST: GMT-6:00. NMC: Fort Worth, 7 miles east. Main installation numbers: C-817-782-5000, D-312-739-1110.

**REGISTRATION INFO:** C-817-782-6288, D-312-739-6288, Rec: C-817-782-6289/6071, D-312-739-6289/6071. Fax: C-413-294-6331 E-mail: **spacea@cnrs.nola.navy.mil** WEB: **nasftw.cnrf.nola.navy.mil** Bldg 1423, Hours: Daily, 0630-2300. General, Family lounge in Pax Term. DV/VIP lounge in Bldg 1425. A/C, restrooms, P/C seats, commercial and defense phone service.

**FOOD SERVICE:** Full service galley. Pizza and sub shops available on base. Bowling alley has a full service grill. **Snack Vending** at Pax Term.

**TRANSPORTATION: Off Base Bus:** City bus runs on base. **Off Base Car Rental:** Enterprise delivers and picks up cars on base. **Parking:** Short and long term parking available.

**TML:** Lodging office, Building 1324 Military Parkway, 24 hours daily, C-817-782-5392/3, DSN-312-739-5392/3 Fax: C-817-782-5391. DV/VIP Protocol, Building 1324, C-817-782-7614. CBQ: 817-782-5483.

**TRAVELERS AID:** Chapel, Family Service Center, Medical and Security Police.

**SUPPORT AVAILABLE:** Bank, Commissary, Exchange, Hair Styles, and Postal Service are all available.

**ATTRACTIONS:** Ripley's Believe It or Not and wax museum, Dallas Cowboys Football, Glen Rose Dinosaur Park, Six Flags over Arlington, Wet-N-Wild (Arlington), Fort Worth Stockyards.

### UNSCHEDULED FLIGHTS

Weekly flights/schedules received 3 days prior to departure. Flights via C-130H, C-009B AND DC-009 aircraft. Call for destinations, routings and schedules.

## KELLY AIR FORCE BASE (SKF/KSKF)

76th LG/LGTTHP
407 S Luke Drive, Suite 3
Kelly AFB, TX 78241-5312

**LOCATION:** All of the following, I-10, I-35, I-37, I-410 intersect with US-90 in southwest San Antonio. From US-90 take either the Gen. Hudnell or Gen. McMullen exit and go south to AFB. *USMRA: Page 91 (B-3,4).* *ML-ARM: (29°23'N/98°33'W).* LST: GMT-06:00. NMC: San Antonio, 7 miles northeast. Main installation numbers: C-210-925-1110, D-312-945-1110.

**REGISTRATION INFO:** C-210-925-8714/5, D-312-945-8714/5, Rec: C-210-925-1854, D-312-945-1854 (updated 0730 daily), Fax: C-210-925-2732, D-312-945-2732, E-mail: **spacea@lackland.af.mil** Bldg 1614, Hours: 0700-1900 daily. Directions: From Gate 1 straight on Duncan Drive to a right on Luke Drive to Pax Term on the left. **Pax Service Office:** Bldg 1614, C-210-925-8714/5 (NCO on duty). **Pax Paging:** Bldg 1614, C-210-925-8714/5. ***Note: Kelly AFB has realigned with Lackland AFB but all Space-A facilities and contacts will remain the same.***

**PAX LOUNGES: General:** Bldg 1614, Hours: 0730-1630 daily, C-210-925-8714. A/C, telephones (local and defense), TV, restrooms, P/C seats. **DV/VIP:** Bldg 1610, as needed. See Pax Service NCO, C-210-925-8714/5. **Protocol Service:** Post Commander, 24 hours daily, C-210-925-6906 (SAT-Air Logistics Center).

**FOOD SERVICE: Cafeteria:** Bldg 1614, Hours: 0600-1300 Mon-Fri, C-210-925-5021, D-312-945-5021. **La Hacienda Dining Hall:** Bldg 1650, C-210-925-5791, C-210-925-8350 (in-flight meals). **NCO/CPO Club:** Bldg 1700, C-210-924-4511. **O Club:** Bldg 1676, C-210-924-7127. **Snack Bars:** Bowling Alley; Pizza, Sandwich, Sub Shop, Bldg 1614, Hours: 0600-1300 Mon-Thu, 1500-2100 Fri-Sat, 1300-1900 Sun, C-210-925-5021, free delivery available. **Snack Vending:** Bldg 1614.

**TRANSPORTATION: Air Tickets** SATO, Bldg 1614, C-210-925-7371. **Off Base Bus:** San Antonio; Greyhound, C-210-227-8351; Trailways, C-210-226-6136; Bldg 1614, City Bus, (VIA) C-210-227-2020. **On Base Limo Service:** Bldg 1614, C-210-671-3555 (Lackland Taxi). **Off Base Taxi:** Bldg 1614; Checker, C-210-222-2151; Yellow, C-210-226-4242. **On Base Taxi (Gov):** Motor Pool, C-210-925-6372. **Trains:** AMTRAK, C-210-223-3226. **Parking:** Bldg 1614, 24 hours daily. Short term, Lot 718, across from Pax Term, 15 days max; long term, Lot 105 near main gate. Off base car rental also available.

**TML:** Kelly Inns, Building 1650, 24 hours daily, C-210-925-1844, D-312-945-1844, Fax: C-210-925-9556. DV/VIP 210-925-7678. (Protocol).

**RVC:** FAMCAMP, 250 Goodrich Drive, Check-in Bldg 3503, 299 Offutt Street, C-210-925-5725, D-312-975-5725.

**TRAVELERS AID: Chaplain:** Bldg 1669, C-210-925-7874. **Emergency Relief:** Bldg 1650, C-210-925-7114/6 (AF Aid). **Family Services:** Bldg 147, C-210-925-4181. **Red Cross:** Bldg 9016, C-210-671-3381; after hours, C-210-671-4225. **Security Police:** Bldg 105, C-210-925-6811. **USO:** I410 South Alamo, San Antonio, C-210-227-9373.

**SUPPORT AVAILABLE: Exchange:** Bldg 1637, C-210-924-9247. **Medical:** Bldg 1740, 24 hours daily, C-210-925-4544. **Postal Service:** Bldg 1650, C-210-925-8255. **Weather:** Bldg 1610, C-210-925-1115.

**OTHER INFORMATION:** U.S. Customs Service Airport.

**ATTRACTIONS:** Alamo, River Walk, Tower of the Americas, Sea World of Texas, Six Flags, Ripley's Believe It Or Not Wax Museum.

### KELLY AFB (SKF/KSKF); MISSION 546/MEDEVAC; SAMPLE SCHEDULE: WED; EQUIPMENT: C009A

{SKF/KSKF *W* ➡ BIF/KBIF *NW* ➡ SUU/KSUU *S* ➡ NKX/KNKX *NE* ➡ BLV/KBLV}

| LI | AIRPORT/STATION | CTRY/STA |
|---|---|---|
| SKF/KSKF | Kelly AFB | TX |
| BIF/KBIF | Biggs AAF | TX |
| SUU/KSUU | Travis AFB | CA |
| NKX/KNKX | Miramar MCAS | CA |
| BLV/KBLV | Scott AFB | IL |

### EN ROUTE SCHEDULES

| AIRPORT/STATION | LI-MISSION (page #) |
|---|---|
| Travis AFB | SUU-456/MEDEVAC (13) |
| Scott AFB | BLV-C-614/MEDEVAC (30) |
| Scott AFB | BLV-C-616/MEDEVAC (30) |
| Scott AFB | BLV-C-626/MEDEVAC (30) |
| Scott AFB | BLV-C-635/MEDEVAC (30) |
| Scott AFB | BLV-C-652/MEDEVAC (30) |
| Scott AFB | BLV-C-656/MEDEVAC (30) |

### UNSCHEDULED FLIGHTS

Various flights to CONUS, Pacific and European areas including but not limited to: Andersen AFB, GU (**UAM**); Dover AFB, DE (**DOV**); Hickam AFB, HI (**HIK**); Kadena AB, JP (**DNA**); Norfolk NS, VA (**NGU**); Ramstein AB, DE (**RMS**); Rhein-Main AB, DE (**FRF**); Roosevelt Roads NS, PR (**NRR**); Travis AFB, CA (**SUU**);Yuma MCAS, AZ (**YUM**) on C-005A/B AND C-17A aircraft. Call for destinations, routings and schedules.

# LAUGHLIN AIR FORCE BASE (DLF/KDLF)

47th OSS/OSAB, Bldg 306
541 First Street, Suite 1
Laughlin AFB, TX 78843-4333

**LOCATION:** Take US-90 west from San Antonio, 150 miles or US-277 south from San Angelo, 150 miles to Del Rio area, or exit I-10 east or west to US-277 south. The AFB is clearly marked off US-90. *USMRA: Page 86 (H-9). ML-ARM: (29°22'N/100°47'W).* LST: GMT-06:00. NMC: Del Rio, 6 miles northwest. Main installation numbers: C-830-298-3511, D-312-732-1110.

**REGISTRATION INFO: C-830-298-5308/5309, D-312-732-5308/5309.** Bldg 306, Hours: 0600-1900 Mon-Fri, 0900-1500 Sat, 1100-1700 Sun, closed holidays. Directions: From main gate straight on Liberty Drive to a left on Florida Ave to Base Ops on the left.

**TML:** Lodging Office: Laughlin Manor, Bldg 470, 416 Liberty Drive, C-830-298-5731, D-312-732-5731, Fax: C-830-298-5272, D-312-732-5272. DV/VIP Bldg 338, Room 1, C-830-298-5041, O6+.

**RVC:** FAMCAMP, 416 Liberty Drive, Check-in FAMCAMP, C-830-298-5830, D-312-732-5830, Fax: C-830-298-5554, D-312-732-5554.

### UNSCHEDULED FLIGHTS

Extremely limited flights to CONUS locations via Air Force administrative aircraft. Call for destinations, routings and schedules.

# RANDOLPH AIR FORCE BASE (RND/KRND)

12th TRNS/LGTT
5th Street East, Bldg 399, Room B-36
Randolph AFB, TX 78150-4424

**LOCATION:** From I-35 north or south take exit 172 south on TX-1604 to AFB or I-10 exit 587 north on TX-1604 to AFB. *USMRA: Page 91 (E-2). ML-ARM: (29°31'N/98°15'W).* LST: GMT-06:00. NMC: San Antonio, 20 miles southwest. Main installation numbers: C-210-652-1110, D-312-487-1110.

**REGISTRATION INFO: C-210-652-5287/3725, D-312-487-5287, Fax: C-210-652-5718, D-312-487-5718. REC: C-210-652-1854, D-312-487-1854. WEB: www.randolph.af.mil (go to Base Support link).** Bldg 399, Room B36, Hours: 0730-1615 Mon-Fri, Sat-Sun as required. Expected to move to Bldg 8 by end of 2001. Directions: From main gate turn left on First Ave East, right on 5th Street East for .75 miles to Pax Term on the right. **Pax Service Office:** C-210-652-3725, D-312-487-5287 (NCO on duty).

**PAX LOUNGES:** Limited lounge facilities. No separate family lounge. **General:** Bldg 399, Room B36, Hours: 0730-1615 Mon-Fri, C-210-652-1854. A/C, telephones (local, long distance and defense), TV, restrooms, O/S seats. **DV/VIP:** Bldg 8, Base Operations, Hours: 0600-2200 Mon-Fri, C-210-652-1861. A/C, coffee/tea served, telephones (local, long distance and defense), TV, restrooms, O/S seats. No host. **Protocol Service:** Bldg 100, Hours: 0800-1700 Mon-Fri, C-210-652-1110.

**FOOD SERVICE: Cafeteria:** Bldg 11, Hours: 0545-0745 Breakfast, 1030-1300 Lunch, 1630-1830 Dinner, 2300-0100 Midnight, C-210-652-8976, D-312-487-8976. **Dining Hall:** Bldg 860, Hours: 0500-1800 daily, C-210-652-1110. **NCO/CPO Club:** Bldg 598, C-210-658-3557. **O Club:** Bldg 500, C-210-658-7445. **Snack Vending:** Base Ops/ Pax Term. Anthony's Pizza, Frank's Franks, Robin Hood available outside main gate.

**TRANSPORTATION: Air Tickets:** Bldg 399, Hours: 0730-1615 Mon-Fri, C-210-652-2650. **On Base Taxi:** Bldg 172, 24 hours daily, C-210-652-8294, D-312-487-8294. **On Base Shuttle/Bus:** C-210-652-8294. Enterprise, off base car rental. **Parking:** Hangar 7, 24 hours daily, C-210-652-5700 (See Security Police for long term).

**TML:** Lodging office, Building 113, 415 B Street E, 24 hours daily, C-210-652-1844, D-312-487-1844. Fax: C-210-652-2616, DSN-312-487-2616. DV/VIP Protocol, Building 900, C-210-652-4126.

**TRAVELERS AID: Chaplain:** Bldg 103, Hours: 0730-1615 Mon-Fri, C-210-652-6121. **Medical:** Bldg 1040, 24 hours daily, C-210-652-2743, D-312-487-2743. **Red Cross:** Bldg 662, Hours: 0830-1600 Mon-Fri, C-210-652-1855, after hours C-210-652-1859. **Security Police:** Bldg 235, 24 hours daily, C-210-652-5700. **USO:** 410 South Alamo, San Antonio, C-210-227-9373.

**SUPPORT AVAILABLE: Bank/Currency Exchange:** Bldg 1074, Hours: 0800-1600 Mon-Fri, C-210-658-7427. **Exchange:** Bldg 1073, Hours: 0930-1730 Mon-Sat, 0930-1600 Sun, C-210-658-2681. **Hair Styles:** Bldg 1073, Hours: 0800-1730 Mon-Fri, 1600 Sat; Barber, C-210-658-0581; Beauty, C-512-658-7755. **Laundry:** Bldg 1073, Hours: 0800-1730 Mon-Fri, C-210-659-4260. **Postal Service:** Bldg 220, Hours: 0830-1630 Mon-Fri, C-210-652-2606.

**ATTRACTIONS:** San Antonio, New Braunfels, Canyon Lake, Sea World, Six Flags, Fiesta Texas.

### UNSCHEDULED FLIGHTS

Frequent flights to: Andrews AFB, MD (**ADW**); Maxwell AFB, AL (**MXF**); Wright-Patterson AFB, OH (**FFO**); and other CONUS locations utilizing C-21 aircraft. Call for destinations, routing and schedules.

# ROBERT GRAY ARMY AIRFIELD (GRK/KGRK)

Bldg 90049
West Fort Hood, TX 76544-5000

**LOCATION:** From US-190 take the West Fort Hood exit. Clearly marked. *USMRA: Page 87 (K-4,5). ML-ARM: (31°03'N/97°49'W).* LST: GMT-06:00.

NMC: Killeen, 10 miles northwest. NMI: Fort Hood, 8 miles northwest. Main installation numbers: C-254-287/288-1110, D-312-737/738-1110.

**REGISTRATION INFO: C-254-288-9200, D-312-738-9200,** Bldg 90049, Hours: 1800-2400 Mon-Fri. Pax Service is administered by Flight Operations.

**FOOD SERVICE: Snack Bars:** Hours: 0730-1430 Mon-Fri, C-254-539-6199, within Airfield Operations.

**TRANSPORTATION: On Base Car Rental:** C-254-532-3615, Fort Hood. **On Base Car Rental:** Enterprise, C-254-532-7333. **On Base Taxi:** C-254-287-2154, Fort Hood. **Off Base Taxi:** C-254-699-8294/2227, 10 miles away in Killeen. **Parking:** Limited parking available in lot adjacent to Bldg 90049.

**TML:** Lodging office, Building 36006, Wratten Drive, 24 hours daily, C-254-532-5157, D-312-738-3067, Fax: C-254-288-7604. DV/VIP C-254-287-5001.

**TRAVELERS AID: Medical/Dental:** Darnall Army Community Hospital, 24 hours daily, C-254-288-8156, D-312-738-8156, Fort Hood.

**SUPPORT AVAILABLE:** Barber, Exchange, Laundry/Dry Cleaner, Postal Service and Shoppette available; within 1 mile on West Fort Hood.

**ATTRACTIONS:** First Cavalry Division and Fourth Infantry Division museums located on Fort Hood.

### EN ROUTE SCHEDULES

| AIRPORT/STATION | LI-MISSION (page #) |
| --- | --- |
| Scott AFB | BLV-C-652/MEDEVAC (30) |

### UNSCHEDULED FLIGHTS
Infrequent flights to CONUS and OCONUS locations via transient Air Force C-130A-H, C-17A, C-141B and C-005B aircraft. Operations receive little advance notice of aircraft or Space-A seats available. Call for destinations, routings and schedules.

## SHEPPARD AIR FORCE BASE (SPS/KSPS)
82nd Training Wing
Ave J, Bldg 1360, Suite 2
Sheppard AFB, TX 76311-5000

**LOCATION:** Take US-281 north from Wichita Falls, exit to TX 325 which leads to main gate. Clearly marked. *USMRA: Page 87 (J-1).* ML-ARM: *(33°35'N/98°31'W).* LST: GMT-06:00. NMC: Wichita Falls, 5 miles southwest. Main installation numbers: C-940-676-2511, D-312-736-1001.

**REGISTRATION INFO: C-940-676-7119/2180/6474, D-312-736-7119/2180/6474.** Main gate right on First Street to a left on Ave J to Base Ops on the right. Airfield Management (Base Ops) processes passengers. Extremely limited.

**PAX LOUNGES:** No lounge facilities. **General:** Bldg 1360, Hours: 0800-1900 Mon-Fri, 0800-1700 Sat and Sun, C-940-676-6474. A/C, bag check, telephones (local and defense), restrooms. **DV/VIP:** Bldg 1360, Hours: 0800-2000 daily, C-940-676-6474 (O6+). A/C, bag check, coffee available, read/write rooms, telephones (local and defense), restrooms, O/S seats. **Protocol Service:** Bldg 400, Hours: 0730-1630 Mon-Fri, C-940-676-2123.

**FOOD SERVICE: O Club Lounge:** Dinner Mon-Fri. **Enlisted Club:** Breakfast, lunch, and dinner Mon-Fri. Several snack bars around base except in Bldg 1360.

**TRANSPORTATION:** Official business - base taxi ext 1843. Rental car agencies in nearby Wichita Falls.

**TML:** Sheppard Inn, Lodging office, Building 1600, Avenue J, 24 hours daily, C-940-855-7370, D-312-736-1864 Fax: C-940-676-7434, D-312-736-7434.

DV/VIP, Building 332, O6+, C-940-676-2707/2970.

**SUPPORT AVAILABLE:** Full base support facility available.

### UNSCHEDULED FLIGHTS
Extremely limited and infrequent flights via C-21A and CT-39 aircraft to CONUS locations. Infrequent MEDEVAC. Call for destinations, routings and schedules.

## TEXAS AIR NATIONAL GUARD/ ELLINGTON FIELD (EFD/KEFD)
Current Operations, Bldg 1193
14657 Sneider Street
Houston, TX 77034-5586

**LOCATION:** Take I-45 south from Houston exit 32 to Ellington Field. TX-1959, proceed 2.5 miles east of I-45 to base. *USMRA: Page 89 (D-4,5).* ML-ARM: *(29°36'N/95°10'W).* LST: GMT-06:00. NMC: Houston, 15 miles northwest. Main installation numbers: C-281-929-2142.

**REGISTRATION INFO: C-281-929-2142/3, D-312-954-2142/3, Fax: C-281-929-2442.** Bldg 1193, Hours: 0800-1600 Mon-Fri. Ask Security Police for directions. No pax lounge. Base Ops processes all pax. Barber shop available. **TML:** Nearest TML is at Fort Hood, Lodging office, C-245-532-5157.

**ATTRACTIONS:** Six Flags Astroworld in Houston.

### UNSCHEDULED FLIGHTS
Very limited flights available. **Houston CGAS does not report any Space-A flights.** Call for destinations, routings and schedules.

## Other Texas Installations with Possible Space-A Opportunities

**KINGSVILLE NAVAL AIR STATION (NQI/KNQI),** 311 N Mitscher Ave, Suite 101, Kingsville, TX 78363-5054. **LOCATION:** Off US-77 north or south, exit to TX-141 southeast to main gate. *USMRA: Page 87 (K-9).* ML-ARM: *(27°29'N/97°49'W).* LST: GMT-06:00. **C-361-516-6108, D-312-876-6108. RVC:** Nasking Rec FAMCAMP, Outdoor Rec, 3765 Nimitz Ave, Check-in FAMCAMP, C-512-516-6443, D-312-861-6443. **TML:** Lodging office, Building 3729, 1140 Moffett Avenue, duty hours, C-361-516-6321, D-312-876-6321, Fax: C-361-516-6428. DV/VIP C-361-516-6321. **Limited Space-A air opportunities. Call for destinations, routings and schedules.**

# UTAH

## HILL AIR FORCE BASE (HIF/KHIF)
649th ABG LGTTP
7439 Wardleigh Road
Ogden, UT 84056-5999

**LOCATION:** Adjacent to I-15 between Ogden and Salt Lake City. From I-15, take exit 334, go north to UT-232 to south gate on South Gate Drive; or exit 338 to west gate. *USMRA: Page 112 (D-3).* ML-ARM: *(41°06'N/111°55'W).* LST: GMT-07:00. NMC: Salt Lake City, 30 miles south. Main installation numbers: C-801-777-7221, D-312-458-1110.

**REGISTRATION INFO: C-801-777-2887/3088, D-312-777-2887/3088, Rec: C-801-775-1854, D-312-777-1854, Fax: C-801-775-2677, D-312-775-2677.** Bldg 900, Hours: 0800-1600 Mon-Fri. **Pax Service Office:** Bldg 900, Hours: 0800-1600 Mon-Fri.

**PAX LOUNGES:** Limited facilities. **General:** Bldg 900, Hours: 0800-1600 Mon-Fri. A/C, restrooms, TV, P/C seats. **DV/VIP:** Bldg 1, 0600-2200 hours daily, C-801-777-1861 (O6+). A/C, restrooms, read/write rooms, TV, O/S seats. **Protocol Service:** Bldg 1102, Area 2, Hours: 0700-1630 Mon-Fri, C-801-777-5565.

**FOOD SERVICE: Cafeteria:** Hours: 0600-1300 Mon-Fri, C-801-777-4165, 1 mile away. **Dining Hall:** C-801-777-3428. **Enlisted Club:** C-801-777-3428. **In-Flight Meals:** C-801-777-1010. **NCO/CPO Club:** C-801-777-3841. **O Club:** C-801-773-4924. **Restaurants:** Hours: 0600-1300, C-801-777-8161, 2 miles. **Snack Bars:** C-801-777-7947. Fast food available 0700-1800, C-801-773-1207, .5 miles away.

**TRANSPORTATION: Air Tickets:** C-801-777-4677. **On Base Car Rental:** Enterprise, C-801-825-0080. **Limo Service:** Classic Limo, C-801-774-6027. **On Base Shuttle/Bus:** C-801-777-1843, 2 miles away (20 minutes schedule). **On Base Taxi:** C-801-777-1843, 2 miles away. **Off Base Taxi:** C-801-394-9411, 15 miles away. **Parking:** C-801-777-3056. Short and long term, see Security Police. Pick up and discharge only.

**TML:** Lodging office, Mountain View Inn, Building 146, 5847 D Avenue, 24 hours daily, C-801-777-1844/0801, D-312-777-1844/0801, Fax: C-801-942-2014. DV/VIP C-801-777-5565.

**RVC:** FAMCAMP, Outdoor Rec, Check-in FAMCAMP 11th Street, C-801-777-3250, D-312-458-3250.

**TRAVELERS AID: Chaplain:** C-801-777-2106, after hours C-801-777-3007. **Emergency Relief:** C-801-777-4681 (AF Aid), after hours C-801-777-3007. **Medical/Dental:** Bldg 570, 24 hours daily, C-801-777-1846, **Red Cross:** C-801-777-1855, after hours C-801-927-3533. **Security Police:** Bldg 1219, 24 hours daily, C-801-777-3056.

**SUPPORT AVAILABLE: Bank/Currency Exchange:** C-801-773-1806, .5 miles away. **Convenience Store:** C-801-777-2300, .5 miles away. **Credit Union:** C-801-778-8705, .5 miles away. **Dry Cleaner:** C-801-773-3823, .5 miles away. **Exchange:** C-801-773-1207, .5 miles away. **Hair Styles:** Barber, C-801-773-4602; Beauty, C-801-773-4076. **Postal Service:** C-801-777-3507, .5 miles away. **Shoppette:** C-801-773-4673, .5 miles away.

**ATTRACTIONS:** Salt Lake City, snow skiing, Park City, Temple Square.

### UNSCHEDULED FLIGHTS

Flights via C-141B/M AFRES to McChord AFB, WA (**TCM**) and other CONUS west and southwest locations and returning to **HIF** largely on weekends. Flights via C-130E to CONUS locations. Call for destinations, routings and schedules.

# SALT LAKE CITY INTERNATIONAL AIRPORT (SLC/KSLC)

151st Air Refueling Wing
Utah Air National Guard
Air Operations/DOTA
765 North 2200 West
Salt Lake City, UT 84116-2999

**LOCATION:** From I-215 north or south take exit 26, go west one block, turn right on McDonnell Douglas Way (2200 West). ANG is on the immediate left. *USMRA: Page 112 (D-3); Page 116 (B-2). ML-ARM: (40°46'N/111°58'W).* LST: GMT-07:00. NMC: Salt Lake City, 5 miles southeast. NMI: Hill AFB, 30 miles south. Main installation numbers: C-801-595-2200, D-312-924-9200.

**REGISTRATION INFO: Base Ops: C-801-595-2274, D-312-924-9274, Rec: C-801-595-2415, D-312-924-9415, Fax: C-801-595-2271, D-312-924-9271.** ANG area, Bldg 40, Room 121, Hours: 0700-1545 Mon-Fri. Ask Gate Sentry for directions.

**FOOD SERVICE: Restaurants:** Vern & Carols, Hours: 0630-1500 Mon-Thu, C-801-595-2269.

**TRANSPORTATION: Car Rentals:** Alamo, C-801-575-2232; Avis, C-801-575-2847; Budget, C-801-575-2500; Enterprise, C-801-487-7555; Hertz, C-801-575-2683. **Off Base Shuttle/Bus:** C-801-287-4636. **Taxi:** City Cab Co, C-801-363-5014/5550; Elite Yellow Hub, C-801-262-6556; Murray Cab Co, C-801-328-5704; South Salt Lake Cab, C-801-328-5704; Yellow Cab, C-801-521-2100.

**TML:** Nearest TML is at Hill AFB, Lodging office, Mountain View Inn, Building 146, 5847 D Avenue, 24 hours daily, C-801-777-1844/0801, D-312-777-1844/0801, Fax: C-801-942-2014. DV/VIP C-801-777-5565.

**TRAVELERS AID: Medical:** C-801-595-2337. **Security Police:** C-801-595-2410, D-312-924-9410.

**SUPPORT AVAILABLE:** Full support of IAP. **Base NCO Club:** C-801-595-2269. **Base Exchange:** Trailer Size, Hours: 0900-1500, C-801-355-1923, **Hair Styles:** Barber, C-801-595-2500. Base dispensary, Enlisted/O Club, Exchange and other services available at Hill AFB.

**OTHER INFORMATION:** U.S. Customs Service Airport.

### UNSCHEDULED FLIGHTS

Flights via KC-135R ANG aircraft to CONUS and OCONUS locations. Call for destinations, routings and schedules.

## Other Utah Installations with Possible Space-A Opportunities

**MICHAEL ARMY AIRFIELD (DPG/KDPG),** STEDP-CO, AVN SEC, Dugway, UT 84022-5000. **LOCATION:** Isolated, but can be reached from I-80. Take exit 77 south, UT-196, Skull Valley Road for 40 miles south to Dugway and entrance to Proving Ground. *USMRA: Page 112 (B,C-4,5). ML-ARM: (40°12'N/112°56'W).* LST: GMT-07:00. **C-435-831-5322, Fax: C-435-831-5207. TML:** Lodging office, Building 5228, Valdez Circle, 0730-1845 Mon-Thu, 0700-1545 Fri. C-435-831-2333, D-312-789-2333. DV/VIP C-435-831-2020. **Infrequent flights. Call for destinations, routings and schedules.**

# VIRGINIA

# DAVISON ARMY AIRFIELD (DAA/KDAA)

E Co, 12th AVN BN
6970 Britton Drive, Bldg 3136, Suite 301
Fort Belvoir, VA 22060-5726

**LOCATION:** From Washington, D.C., take I-95 South to Belvoir/Newington exit 166. Turn right, connect with the southern leg of Fairfax County Pkwy. Take Pkwy to the end at Richmond Highway. Turn left. At the first light, Tulley Gate is on right. At second light, Pence Gate (main entrance) is to the right. Visitor Center is just inside Pence Gate. *USMRA: Page 47 (L,M-5). ML-ARM: (38°71'N/77°18'W).* LST: GMT-05:00. NMC: Washington, D.C., 10 miles northeast. Main installation numbers: C-703-806-7224/7225, D-312-656-7224/7225.

**REGISTRATION INFO: C-703-806-7225/7224/7682, D-312-656-7225/7224/7628, Fax: C-703-806-7178, D-312-656-7178.** Bldg 3136, 24 hours daily. Directions: On main road inside Highway 1, gate sign points to DAAF. **Pax Service Office:** Bldg 3136, 24 hours daily, C-703-806-7792 (NCO on duty).

**PAX LOUNGES:** General Lounge with DV/VIP in separate room. **General:** Bldg 3136, 24 hours daily, C-703-806-7535, D-312-656-7535. A/C, read/write room, telephones (commercial and defense), TV, restrooms, P/C and O/S seats.

**TRANSPORTATION: On Base Car Rental:** Enterprise, C-703-781-0480.

**TML:** Lodging office, Building 470, 9775 Gaillard Road, 24 hours daily, C-703-805-2333 or 1-800-295-9750, D-312-655-2333, Fax: C-703-805-3566. DV/VIP C-703-805-2333.

**SUPPORT AVAILABLE:** Enterprise Rent-A-Car: C-703-660-1331; Thrifty Rent-A-Car: C-703-360-3400. Full support facilities available. See Military Living's *Assignment Washington Military Road Atlas; Maps and Charts of Washington Area Military Installations* for full details on more than 18 military installations in the Washington, D.C. area.

### UNSCHEDULED FLIGHTS

Frequent flights via C-12A/P and U-21A/P aircraft to Langley AFB, VA (**LFI**) and other CONUS East Coast, Southeast and Midwest locations. There is usually no more than a two-day advanced notice on flights. Call for destinations, routings and schedules.

# LANGLEY AIR FORCE BASE (LFI/KLFI)

1 TRNS/LGTR
Bldg. 371, Juniper Street
Langley AFB, VA 23665-5000

**LOCATION:** From I-64 east or west in Hampton take Armistead Avenue exit 205B northeast, keep right to stop light; right into LaSalle Avenue and enter AFB. *USMRA: Page 47 (N-9); Page 52 (E-3). ML-ARM: (37°01'N/76°21'W).* LST: GMT-05:00. NMC: Hampton, 1 mile west. Main installation numbers: C-757-764-9990, D-312-574-7170.

**REGISTRATION INFO:** C-757-764-4311, D-312-574-4311, **Rec:** C-757-764-5807, D-312-574-5807, **Fax:** C-757-764-3722, D-312-574-3722. Bldg 371, Hours: 0700-1600 Mon-Fri. Directions: From LaSalle gate (I-64) right on Nealy Ave to left on Sweeney, and then right on Juniper to Pax Terminal is on the right. **Pax Service Office:** Pax Term, Hours 0500-1900 Mon-Fri, C-757-727-3707, D-312-680-3707.

**PAX LOUNGES:** General and family lounges combined. **General:** Bldg 371, Hours: 0730-1630 Mon-Fri, C-757-764-4311/4698. A/C, telephones (commercial and defense), TV, restrooms, P/C seats. **DV/VIP:** Bldg 754, as required, C-757-764-2504 (O6+). A/C, bag check, read/write rooms, telephones (commercial and defense), TV, restrooms. **Protocol Service:** Bldg 693, Hours: 0645-1900 Mon-Fri, C-757-764-5044, O7+.

**FOOD SERVICE: Cafeteria:** C-757-766-1255. **Dining Hall:** C-757-764-3694. **NCO/CPO Club:** C-757-766-1220. **O Club:** C-757-766-1361. **Snack Bars:** C-757-766-1237.

**TRANSPORTATION: Air Tickets:** Bldg 15, C-757-764-5989. **Car Rentals:** Avis, C-757-877-0291; Hertz, C-757-877-9229. **Limo Service:** C-757-877-9477. **Taxi (Gov):** C-757-764-8294. **Off Base Taxi:** C-757-723-3377. **Parking:** Bldg 754B. Short and long term near Pax Term.

**TML:** Lodging office, Building 75, Nealy Avenue, 24 hours daily, C-757-764-4667, D-312-574-4667. DV/VIP C-757-764-3467.

**TRAVELERS AID: Chaplain:** C-757-764-7847 (After hours C-757-764-9990). **Emergency Relief:** C-757-764-3991 (Air Force Aid). **Lost/Found:** C-757-764-5092. **Medical:** C-757-764-6800, D-312-574-6800. **Red Cross:** C-757-764-6161 (After hours C-757-838-7320). **Security Police:** C-757-764-5091. **USO:** C-757-827-1063.

**SUPPORT AVAILABLE: Bank/Currency Exchange:** C-757-827-7200. **Exchange:** C-757-766-1253. **Hair Styles:** Barber, C-757-766-1805; Beauty, C-757-766-1283. **Laundry/Dry Cleaning:** C-757-766-1287. **Postal Service:** C-757-764-3136.

**ATTRACTIONS:** Tidewater area, Williamsburg, Norfolk, Virginia Beach.

### UNSCHEDULED FLIGHTS

Frequent Air Force flights via C-12A and C-21A aircraft to: Andrews AFB, MD (**ADW**); Davison AAF, VA (**DAA**); Eglin AFB, FL (**VPS**); Maxwell AFB, AL (**MXF**); Randolph AFB, TX (**RND**); Scott AFB, IL (**BLV**); and Wright-Patterson AFB, OH (**FFO**). Call for destinations, routings and schedules. Also flights to: Cairns AAF, AL (**OZR**); Godman AAF, KY (**FTK**); Redstone Arsenal AAF, AL (**HUA**); and Simmons AAF, NC (**FBG**). Call for destinations, routings and schedules.

# NORFOLK NAVAL STATION (NGU/KNGU)

Naval Air Terminal
8225 Patrol Road, Bldg LP-210
Norfolk Naval Station, VA 23511-4497

**LOCATION:** From north take I-64 east, Naval Station exit 276 for I-564 northwest, follow signs. From south take I-64 exit I-564 northwest to Gate 3A. *USMRA: Page 52 (F-5,6). ML-ARM: (36°59'N/76°29'W).* LST: GMT-05:00. NMC: Norfolk, in city limits. Main installation numbers: C-757-444-0000, D-312-564-0111.

**REGISTRATION INFO:** C-757-444-4118/4148, D-312-564-4118/4148, **Fax:** C-757-445-7501, D-312-565-7501. Bldg LP-210, 24 hours daily. Directions: From Gate 22, left on Patrol Road. Pax terminal on right. *Note: Sign up for additional Navy and Marine Corps Space-A flights at LP-1 (Control Tower), C-757-444-2780.* **Pax Service Office:** Bldg LP-210, 24 hours daily, C-757-444-4118/4148, D-312-564-4118/4148 (duty NCO). **Pax Paging:** Bldg LP-210, 24 hours daily, C-757-444-4118/4148, D-312-564-4118/4148 (Space-A desk).

**PAX LOUNGES:** Bldg LP-210 USO lounge equipped for children. **General:** Bldg LP-210, 24 hours daily, C-757-444-4118, D-312-564-4118/4148. A/C, nursery, free TV, restrooms. **DV/VIP:** Bldg LP-210, 24 hours daily, C-757-444-4118/4148, D-312-564-4118/4148. A/C, showers, TV, restrooms, game room. **Protocol Service:** Bldg LP-1, 24 hours daily, C-757-444-2780 (Base Ops), C-757-444-2442 (SDO).

**FOOD SERVICE: Cafeteria:** Bldg LP-210, Hours: 0600-2200 daily, C-757-444-4118 (AMC Term grill). **Dining Hall:** Bldg I-AA (NS), Hours: 0530-1730 Mon-Fri, C-757-444-7024 (call for meal hours); Bldg U-16 (NS), Hours: 0700-1730 Mon-Fri, C-757-444-3744 (call for meal hours). **Enlisted Club:** Bldg X-360, Hours: 0600-2400 daily, C-757-440-5483. **NCO/CPO Club:** Hours vary, C-757-440-5483. **O Club:** Bldg SP-45 (NS), Th-Fri: 1400-1900 bar only, C-757-444-0773; Bldg SC-400 (AFSC), Hours: 0600-2400 daily, C-757-423-4713. **Snack Vending:** Bldg LP-210, 24 hours daily. Pay telephone also available. Many clubs, messes, and dining halls on Naval Station complex.

**TRANSPORTATION:** Facilities and means throughout Naval Base complex. **Off Base Bus:** Greyhound/Trailways, C-757-625-2500 in Norfolk. **Car Rentals:** Bldg LP-210, Enterprise, C-757-489-2006, Hours: Mon-Fri 0800-1800, Tues 0800-1930, Sat 0900-1600, Sun 1200-1600. **Limo Service:** Bldg LP-210, Hours: on call 0600-2200 daily, C-757-857-1231 (to Norfolk IAP). **Shuttle/Bus:** Bldg LP-210, Hours: 0700-2100 daily, C-757-444-4118/4148/3947 (from Pax Term to major points). **Off Base Taxi:** Bldg LP-210, 24 hours daily; BW, C-757-489-7777; Green & White, C-757-855-3333; Yellow, C-757-622-3232. Front of Bldg LP-210. **Trains:** AMTRAK; Norfolk, 24 hours daily, C-800-872-7245. **Parking:** Bldg LP-210, 24 hours daily, C-757-444-4118. Short term, 2 hours; long term, 30 days. For long term parking, get parking permit from Pax Service Center.

**TML:** Lodging office, 877-986-9258, Building R-63 (BEH), Wall Manor, 24 hrs, C-757-402-4553, Fax: C-757-444-0797. Building A-128 (BOH), 1756 Powhattan Street, 24 hours daily, C-757-402-7005, Fax: C-757-445-9888. Navy Lodge, 7811 Hampton Blvd, 24 hours daily, C-757-489-2656. DV/VIP:C-757-402-7005.

**TRAVELERS AID: Personal Service Center:** 7920 Hampton Blvd, 24 hours daily, C-757-622-3111. **Chaplain:** Bldg U-53/SP-108, 24 hours daily, C-757-444-7361 (all faiths). **Emergency Relief:** 7920 Hampton Blvd, 24 hours daily, C-757-444-6289; Navy-ML Relief, C-757-423-8830. **Lost/Found:** Bldg LP-210, Hours: 0600-2200 daily, C-877-417-1695 and Pax Service office. **Medical:** Bldg CD-2, 24 hours daily, C-757-314-6516; Portsmouth Naval Hospital, C-757-953-5008. **Red Cross:** Bldg A-67, 24 hours daily, C-757-444-4356; Norfolk: 24 hours daily, C-757-446-7700. **Security Police:** Bldg CEP-161, 24 hours daily, C-757-444-2324 (Desk Sgt). **USO:** Lounge Bldg LP-210. C-757-440-0939; open 0600-2100.

**SUPPORT AVAILABLE:** Throughout Naval Base complex. **Bank/Currency Exchange:** ATM available. **Credit Union:** NFCU, C-757-480-1777. **Exchange:** Bldg U-40 (NS), hours vary, C-757-440-6528. **Postal Service:** Bldg U-20. Lockers are not available. Check cashing, Clubs.

**ATTRACTIONS:** MacArthur Memorial, Norfolk NS tour, Colonial Williamsburg, Virginia Beach.

**EQUIPMENT:** C-009B, B-757, L-1011, DC-863, others.

*Note: Commercially contracted flights are now called Patriot Express.*

### NORFOLK NS, VA (NGU); REGION: ATL; OPERATOR: COM; TYPE: PAX; ROUTE: EX11E; SAMPLE SCHEDULE: 1ST SUN; EQUIPMENT: B757

{NGU (★) *E* ➡ LGS *E* ➡ RTA *NE* ➡ NAP *SE* ➡ SIZ *SE* ➡ BAH *SE* ➡ NKW *NE* ➡ SIN *NE* ➡ CRK ⇌ CRK *SW* ➡ SIN *SW* ➡ NKW *NW* ➡ BAH *NW* ➡ SIZ *NW* ➡ NAP *SW* ➡ RTA *NW* ➡ LGS *W* ➡ NGU (★)}

| LI/ICAO | AIRPORT/STATION | CTRY/STA | DAYS EN ROUTE |
|---|---|---|---|
| NGU/KNGU | Norfolk NS | VA | +0 |
| LGS/LPLA | Lajes Field AB (Azores) | PT | +0 |
| RTA/LERT | Rota NS | ES | +0 |
| NAP/LIRN | Capodichino APT (Naples) | IT | +0 |
| SIZ/LICZ | Sigonella NAS/APT (Sicily) | IT | +0 |
| BAH/OBBI | Bahrain IAP | BH | +1 |
| NKW/FJDG | Diego Garcia Atoll | UK | +2 |
| SIN/WSSS | Changi IAP (Singapore) | SG | +2 |
| CRK/RPLC | Clark IAP* | PH | +3 |
| SIN/WSSS | Changi IAP (Singapore) | SG | +3 |
| NKW/FJDG | Diego Garcia Atoll | UK | +4 |
| BAH/OBBI | Bahrain IAP | BH | +4 |
| SIZ/LICZ | Sigonella NAS/APT (Sicily) | IT | +5 |
| NAP/LIRN | Capodichino APT (Naples) | IT | +5 |
| RTA/LERT | Rota NS | ES | +5 |
| LGS/LPLA | Lajes Field AB (Azores) | PT | +5 |
| NGU/KNGU | Norfolk NS | VA | |

**Note:** * = refueling and crew rest. No Space-A embarking or debarking.

### NORFOLK NS, VA (NGU); REGION: ATL; OPERATOR: COM; TYPE: PAX; ROUTE: EX13DM & EX23A; SAMPLE SCHEDULE: SAT; EQUIPMENT: L1011

{NGU *N* ➡ BWI (★) *NE* ➡ KEF *SE* ➡ MHZ ⇌ MHZ *NW* ➡ KEF *SW* ➡ BWI (★) *S* ➡ NGU}

| LI/ICAO | AIRPORT/STATION | CTRY/STA | DAYS EN ROUTE |
|---|---|---|---|
| NGU/KNGU | Norfolk NS | VA | +0 |
| BWI/KBWI | Baltimore/Washington IAP | MD | +0 |
| KEF/BIKF | Keflavik APT | IS | +0 |
| MHZ/EGUN | RAF Mildenhall | UK | +1 |
| KEF/BIKF | Keflavik APT | IS | +1 |
| BWI/KBWI | Baltimore/Washington IAP | MD | +1 |
| NGU/KNGU | Norfolk NS | VA | |

### NORFOLK NS, VA (NGU); REGION: ATL; OPERATOR: COM; TYPE: PAX; ROUTE: EX17B; SAMPLE SCHEDULE: SUN; EQUIPMENT: B757

{NGU (★) *NE* ➡ LGS *SE* ➡ RTA *NE* ➡ NAP *SE* ➡ SIZ *SE* ➡ BAH ⇌ BAH *NW* ➡ SIZ *NE* ➡ NAP *SW* ➡ RTA *NW* ➡ LGS *SW* ➡ NGU (★)}

| LI/ICAO | AIRPORT/STATION | CTRY/STA | DAYS EN ROUTE |
|---|---|---|---|
| NGU/KNGU | Norfolk NS | VA | +0 |
| LGS/LPLA | Lajes Field AB (Azores) | PT | +1 |
| RTA/LERT | Rota NS | ES | +1 |
| NAP/LIRN | Capodichino APT (Naples) | IT | +1 |

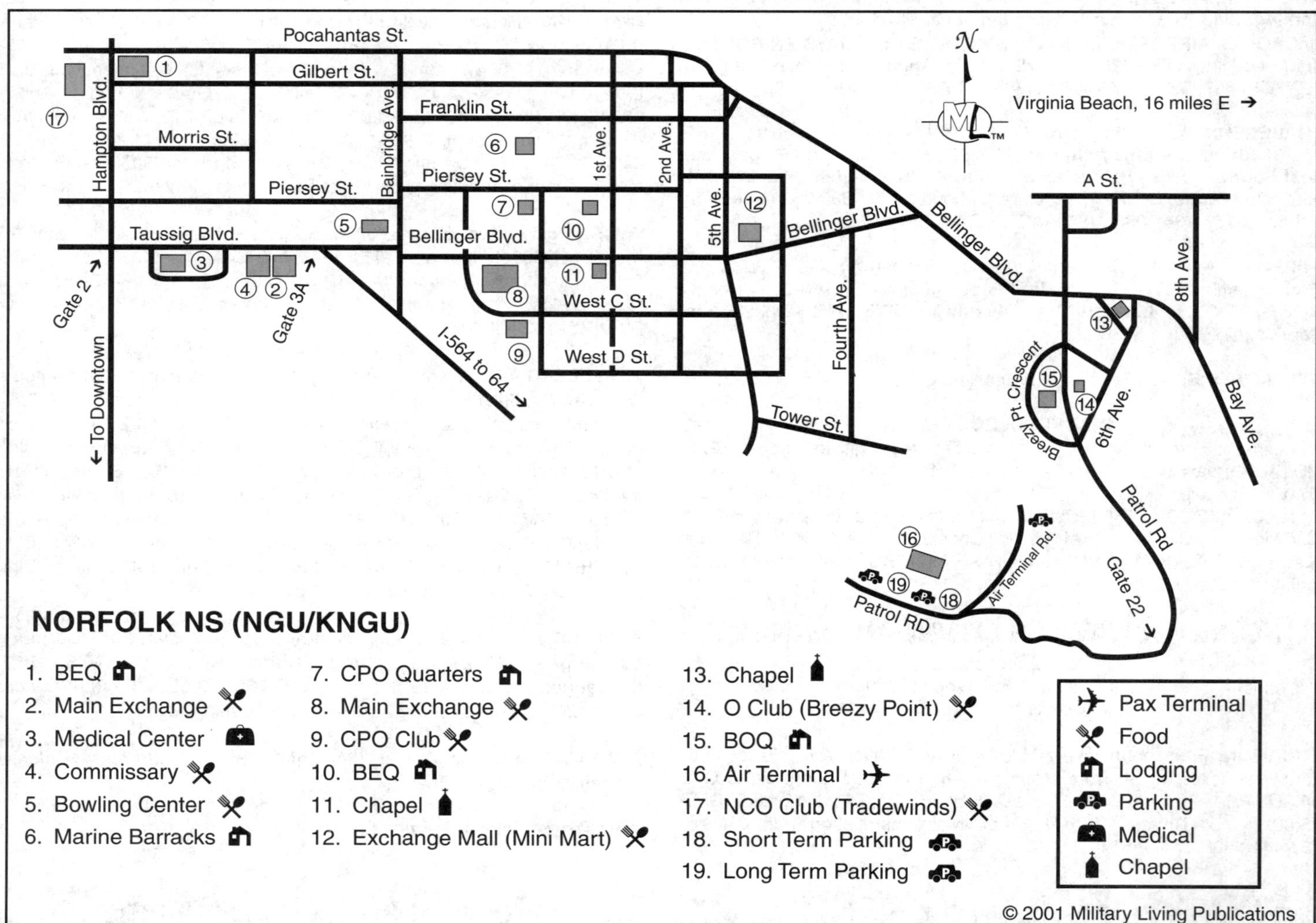


## NORFOLK NS (NGU/KNGU)

1. BEQ
2. Main Exchange
3. Medical Center
4. Commissary
5. Bowling Center
6. Marine Barracks
7. CPO Quarters
8. Main Exchange
9. CPO Club
10. BEQ
11. Chapel
12. Exchange Mall (Mini Mart)
13. Chapel
14. O Club (Breezy Point)
15. BOQ
16. Air Terminal
17. NCO Club (Tradewinds)
18. Short Term Parking
19. Long Term Parking

Pax Terminal
Food
Lodging
Parking
Medical
Chapel

© 2001 Military Living Publications

| SIZ/LICZ | Sigonella NAS/APT (Sicily) | IT | +1 |
|---|---|---|---|
| BAH/OBBI | Bahrain IAP | BH | +1 |
| BAH/OBBI | Bahrain IAP | BH | +1 |
| SIZ/LICZ | Sigonella NAS/APT (Sicily) | IT | +2 |
| NAP/LIRN | Capodichino APT | IT | +2 |
| RTA/LERT | Rota NS | ES | +2 |
| LGS/LPLA | Lajes Field AB (Azores) | PT | +2 |
| NGU/KNGU | Norfolk NS | VA | |

### NORFOLK NS, VA (NGU); REGION: ATL; OPERATOR: COM; TYPE: MIXED; ROUTE: HJM3A/B; SAMPLE SCHEDULE: WED & FRI; EQUIPMENT: DC863

{NGU *SW* ➡ NIP (★) *SE* ➡ NBW ⮂ NBW *N* ➡ NIP (★) *NE* ➡ NGU}

| LI/ICAO | AIRPORT/STATION | CTRY/STA | DAYS EN ROUTE |
|---|---|---|---|
| NGU/KNGU | Norfolk NS | VA | +0 |
| NIP/KNIP | Jacksonville NAS | FL | +0 |
| NBW/MUGM | Guantanamo Bay NAS | CU | +0 |
| NBW/MUGM | Guantanamo Bay NAS | CU | +0 |
| NIP/KNIP | Jacksonville NAS | FL | +0 |
| NGU/KNGU | Norfolk NS | VA | +0 |

### NORFOLK NS, VA (NGU); REGION: ATL; OPERATOR: COM; TYPE: MIXED; ROUTE: HJS1G; SAMPLE SCHEDULE: SUN; EQUIPMENT: DC863

{NGU *NE* (★) ➡ KEF *SE* ➡ RMS *SE* ➡ SKP ⮂ SKP *NW* ➡ RMS *NW* ➡ KEF *SW* ➡ NGU(★)}

| LI/ICAO | AIRPORT/STATION | CTRY/STA | DAYS EN ROUTE |
|---|---|---|---|
| NGU/KNGU | Norfolk NS | VA | +0 |
| KEF/BIKF | Keflavik APT | IS | +0 |
| RMS/ETAR | Ramstein AB | DE | +1 |
| SKP/LWSK | Skopje* | MK | +1 |
| RMS/ETAR | Ramstein AB | DE | +2 |
| KEF/BIKF | Keflavik APT | IS | +2 |
| NGU/KNGU | Norfolk NS | VA | |

* Space-A passengers cannot go through Skopje. We list this schedule because many people may wish to use the Norfolk to Keflavik to Ramstein & Ramstein to Keflavik to Norfolk legs of this flight.

### EN ROUTE SCHEDULES

| AIRPORT/STATION | LI-MISSION (page #) |
|---|---|
| Scott AFB | BLV-C-616/MEDEVAC (30) |
| Scott AFB | BLV-C-621/MEDEVAC (30) |
| Travis AFB | SUU-GTA7B (13) |
| Peterson AFB | COS-OPN3B (16) |
| Dover AFB | DOV-A2F3R (18) |
| Westover ARB | CEF-OFF3A (41) |
| Westover ARB | CEF-OFR3A (41) |
| Allen C Thompson (Jackson) | JAN-IKM3A (44) |
| Allen C Thompson (Jackson) | JAN-IKX3A (44) |
| McGuire AFB | WRI-A7W7B (50) |
| McGuire AFB | WRI-A7F3A (51) |
| McGuire AFB | WRI-A7N1B (51) |
| Pope AFB | POB-ACN1A (57) |
| Pope AFB | POB-ACN1B (57) |
| Wright-Patterson AFB | FFO-OEM3A (61) |
| Wright-Patterson AFB | FFO-OEM3B (61) |
| Wright-Patterson AFB | FFO-OEN1B (61) |
| Charleston AFB/IAP | CHS-A4M3A (67) |
| Charleston AFB/IAP | CHS-A4X3A (67) |
| Dyess AFB | DYS-A1N1B (73) |
| General Mitchell IAP/ARS | CMY-OTN3C (86) |

## OCEANA NAVAL AIR STATION (NTU/KNTU)

Air Terminal,
1750 Tomcat Blvd., Bldg 100
Virginia Beach, VA 23460-2191

**LOCATION:** From I-64 east or west exit to Norfolk-Virginia Beach Expressway (VA-44 E), east on Virginia Beach Boulevard. Bordered by Oceana Boulevard (VA-615) and London Bridge Road. Also bordered by Potters and Harpers Roads. *USMRA: Page 47 (O-9); Page 52 (I,J-7). ML-ARM: (36°47'N/76°00'W).* LST: GMT-05:00. NMC: Virginia Beach, in city limits. Main installation numbers: C-757-433-2366, D-312-433-2366.

**REGISTRATION INFO: C-757-433-2903, D-312-433-2903, Fax: C-757-433-2711, D-312-433-2711.** Registration in person only. Bldg 100, 24 hours daily. Directions: From main gate straight on Princess Anne Road to a right on London Bridge Road to the end, then left on First Street and follow around to Pax Term. **Pax Service Office:** Bldg 100, 24 Hours, 7 days a week. **Air Operations Duty Office:** Bldg 100, 24 hours daily, C-757-433-2162, D-312-433-2162.

**PAX LOUNGES:** No separate family lounge. **General:** Bldg 100, 24 hours daily, A/C, restrooms, passenger lounge with television. **DV/VIP:** Bldg 100, Room 119 (as required), A/C, restrooms, TV, O/S seats.

**FOOD SERVICE: Enlisted Club:** C-757-433-2122/2453. **NCO/CPO Club:** C-757-433-2637. **O Club:** C-757-428-0036. McDonald's available.

**TRANSPORTATION:** Very limited on Base. **Car Rentals:** C-757-855-1921. **Parking:** No Parking at Bldg 100. Long term, notify Security Police C-757-433-3123.

**TML:** Lodging office, Building 460, G Street, 24 hours daily, C-757-433-2574, D-312-433-2574. Fax: C-757-433-3351.

**TRAVELERS AID: Chaplain:** C-757-433-2871. **Medical:** C-757-433-2221, D-312-433-2221. **Navy Relief:** C-757-425-5789. **Red Cross:** C-757-425-8955. **Security Police:** C-757-433-3123. **USO:** C-757-838-4182.

**SUPPORT AVAILABLE: Bank/Currency Exchange:** C-757-473-2834. **Exchange:** C-757-491-4260. **Hair Styles:** C-757-491-4260. **Laundry/Dry Cleaning:** C-757-491-4260. **Postal Service:** Bldg 531.

### UNSCHEDULED FLIGHTS

Frequent flights via Navy UC-12B and other administrative aircraft to Charleston AFB/IAP, SC (**CHS**); El Centro NAF, CA (**NJK**); Jacksonville NAS, FL (**NIP**); Key West NAS, FL (**NQX**); Los Angeles IAP, CA (**LAX**); Mayport NS, FL (**NRB**); North Island NAS, CA (**NZY**); Pensacola NAS, FL (**NPA**) and Roosevelt Roads NS, PR (**NRR**). Call for destinations, routings and schedules.

## Other Virginia Installations with Possible Space-A Air Opportunities

**BLACKSTONE ARMY AIRFIELD (BKT/KBKT),** AFRC-FMP-C, AVN SEC, Blackstone, VA 23854-5000. *USMRA: Page 47 (K-9). ML-ARM: (37°04'N/77°57'W).* LST: GMT-05:00. **C-804-292-8621.** Limited Space-A opportunities. **TML:** Lodging office, Building T-469, Military Road, 0730-1600 duty days, C-804-292-2443, D-312-438-2443. **RVC:** Travel Camp, Check-in Mon-Fri 0730-1600 hours Billeting Office, Bldg T-469, C-804-292-2443, D-312-438-2443. Training flights by Seahawk helicopter only. Call for destinations, routings and schedules.

**FELKER ARMY AIRFIELD (FAF/KFAF),** Fort Eustis, VA 23604-5000. **LOCATION:** From I-64 east or west, exit 250A to VA-105, west to Fort Eustis. *USMRA: Page 47 (N-9); Page 52 (B,C-2,3). ML-ARM: (37°10'N/76°34'W).* LST: GMT-05:00. **C-757-878-2139.** Extremely limited Space-A opportunities. Call for destinations, routings and schedules. **TML:**

Lodging office, Building 2110, Pershing Avenue, 24 hours daily, C-757-878-5807, D-312-927-5807. DV/VIP C-757-878-6030.

**QUANTICO MARINE CORPS BASE (NYG/KNYG),** Quantico, VA 22134-5001. *USMRA: Page 101 (I-4). ML-ARM: (38°30'N/77°18'W).* LST: GMT-05:00. C-703-784-2121, D-312-278-2121. Flight Ops: **C-703-784-2979, D-312-278-2979. TML:** Lodging Office: C-703-784-3148 ext 221, D-312-278-3148/9, Fax: C: 703-784-5940. Full base support facilities available. Extremely limited Space-A air opportunities. Call for destinations, routings and schedules.

# WASHINGTON

## FAIRCHILD AIR FORCE BASE (SKA/KSKA)

92nd OSS/OSAA
901 West Boston Ave, Bldg 1
Base Operations
Fairchild AFB, WA 99011-5000

**LOCATION:** From I-90 west of Spokane take exit 277 which leads to US-2. Follow US-2 through Airway Heights, after two miles turn left to base main gate and visitors' control center. *USMRA: Page 101 (I-4). ML-ARM: (47°38'N/117°38'W).* LST: GMT-08:00. NMC: Spokane, 12 miles east. Main installation numbers: C-509-247-1212, D-312-657-1110.

**REGISTRATION INFO: C-509-247-5435, D-312-657-5435, Rec: C-509-247-4636 ext 531, D-312-657-4636 ext 531, Fax: C-509-247-4909, D-312-657-4909. WEB: fsgjlkwinet.fairchild.af.mil** Bldg 1, Base Ops, 24 hours daily. Directions: From main gate straight on Mitchell Ave to a right on Bong Street to a left on Seattle Avenue to a right on Arnold Street to a left on O'Malley

Avenue to Pax Term on the right. **Pax Service Office:** Bldg 1, 24 hours daily, C-509-247-5481, NCO on duty (days).

**PAX LOUNGES:** Limited Lounge facilities. **General:** Bldg 1, 24 hours daily, C-509-247-5435. Bag check, telephones (commercial and defense), restrooms, O/S seats. **DV/VIP:** Bldg 1, 24 hours daily, C-509-247-5435. Coffee/tea served, telephones (commercial), TV, restrooms, O/S seats. **Protocol Service:** Hq Bldg, Hours: 0730-1630 Mon-Fri, C-509-247-2127.

**FOOD SERVICE: Cafeteria:** Bldg 2262, Hours: 0530-0800 Breakfast, 1100-1300 Lunch, 1530-1800 Dinner daily, C-509-247-5348, D-312-657-5348. **In-flight Meals:** Bldg 2262, 24 hours daily, C-509-247-5140. **Enlisted Club:** Bldg 2452, Hours: 1100-2300 Mon-Sat, C-509-247-3622. **NCO/CPO Club:** Bldg 2452, Hours: 1100-2300 Mon-Sat, C-509-247-3622. **O Club:** Bldg 2452, Hours: 1100-2300 Mon-Sat, C-509-244-3622. **Burger King:** Bldg 2459, Hours: 0630-2100 daily, C-509-244-2680. **Snack Bars:** Fun Spot Bowling Center, Bldg 2245, Hours: 1000-1600 summer, 1000-2300 winter, C-509-244-2162, 1.5 miles. away **Snack Vending:** Bldg 1, 24 hours daily, C-509-247-5435. Multiple restaurants in Airway Heights, approximately 5 miles away.

**TRANSPORTATION: Air Tickets:** TRAVCO, Bldg 2245, Hours: 0730-1630 Mon-Fri, C-509-244-0599. **Off Base Bus:** Main gate, Spokane Transit System, C-509-328-9336. **Bus (Gov):** Motor Pool, 24 hours daily, C-509-247-2244. **Car Rentals:** Spokane, 24 hours daily; Avis, C-509-747-8081; National, C-509-624-8995; Thrifty, C-509-838-8223. **Taxi (Gov):** Motor Pool, 24 hours daily, C-509-247-2244. **Off Base Taxi:** Bldg 1, 24 hours daily; Checker, C-509-624-8995; Yellow, C-509-624-4321. **Parking:** Short and long term, lot northeast of Base Ops off of O'Malley Ave, 24 hours daily, C-509-247-5435.

**TML:** Lodging office, Fairchild Inn, 300 N. Short Street, 24 hours daily, C-509-247-5519; D-312-657-5519, Fax: 509-247-2307. DV/VIP Bldg 2392, C-509-247-2127.

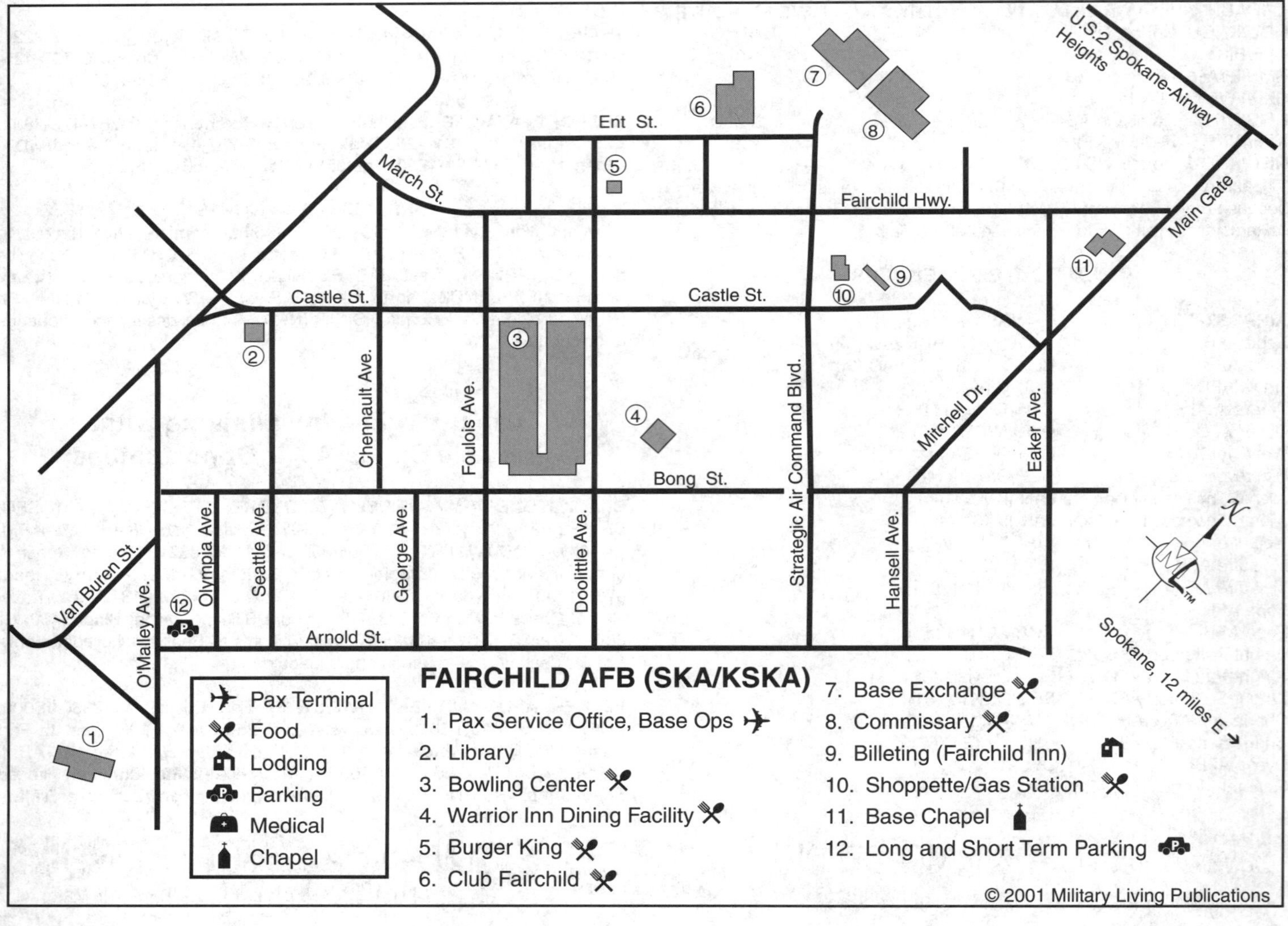

**RVC:** FAMCAMP, 120 North Foulois, Check-in FAMCAMP, host or Equip Check-out, C-509-247-2511/5366, D-312-657-2511, Fax: C-509-247-4495.

**TRAVELERS AID: Chaplain:** Bldg 4200, Hours: 0730-1630 Mon-Fri, C-509-247-2264. **Emergency Relief:** Bldg 3505, Hours: 0730-1630 Mon-Fri, C-509-247-5081 (Air Force Aid). **Lost/Found:** Bldg 325, 24 hours daily, C-509-247-5496. **Red Cross:** Bldg 2245, Hours: 0730-1130 Mon-Fri, C-509-247-5650; After hours, C-509-326-3330. **Medical:** Bldg 9000, 24 hours daily, C-509-247-5661 (emergency room), D-312-657-5661. **Security Police:** Bldg 2525, 24 hours daily, C-509-247-5493.

**SUPPORT AVAILABLE: Bank/Currency Exchange:** Bldg 2464, 24 hours daily (Money Machine). **Exchange:** Bldg 2264, Hours: 0900-2100 Mon-Fri, 0900-1800 Sat-Sun, C-509-244-2832. **Hair Styles:** Bldg 2452, call for hours; Barber, C-509-244-3968; Beauty, C-509-244-2848. **Laundry:** Bldg 644, 24 hours daily. **Postal Service:** Bldg 644, Hours: 1000-1630 Mon-Fri, C-509-244-5879 (civilian); C-509-244-5368 (military). **Valet/Dry Cleaning:** Bldg 2264, Hours: 1000-1630 Mon-Fri, C-509-244-9786. **Wire:** Bldg 2264, Hours: 0900-2100 Mon-Fri, 0900-1600 Sat-Sun, C-509-244-2832 (ask for customer service).

**ATTRACTIONS:** Spokane, Mt Spokane, Expo Site, parks.

### EN ROUTE SCHEDULES

| AIRPORT/STATION | LI-MISSION (page #) |
| --- | --- |
| Travis AFB | SUU-436/MEDEVAC (13) |
| Scott AFB | BLV-C-634/MEDEVAC (30) |

### UNSCHEDULED FLIGHTS

Flights via KC-135R. Call for destinations, routings and schedules.

## GRAY ARMY AIRFIELD (GRF/KGRF)

Air Operations, Bldg 3082
Fort Lewis, WA 98433-0085

**LOCATION:** On I-5 in north or south, exit 120 in Puget Sound area, 14 miles northeast of Olympia, 12 miles southwest of Tacoma. Clearly marked. *USMRA: Page 101 (C-5); Page 103 (A,B-7). ML-ARM: (47°06'N/122°35'W).* LST: GMT-08:00. NMC: Tacoma, 12 miles north. Main installation numbers: C-253-982-1910, D-312-382-1110.

**REGISTRATION INFO: C-253-967-6628/5998, D-312-357-6628/5998, Fax: C-253-967-6002.** Bldg 3082, 24 hours daily. Directions: Enter main gate on 41st Division Drive, go left on Stryker then left on 18th Street straight to Bldg 3082. **Pax Service Office:** C-253-967-6628/5998, D-312-357-6628/5998 (NCO on duty).

**TRANSPORTATION: On Base Car Rental:** U-Save, C-253-964-1331.

**TML:** Lodging Office: Bldg 2111, between Utah Ave and Pendleton Ave, C-253-967-2815/5051/6754, D-312-357-2815, Fax: C-253-967-2253, D-312-357-2253. DV/VIP Protocol Office, Bldg 2025, C-253-967-5834, D-312-357-5834, O7+.

**SUPPORT AVAILABLE:** Full base support facilities available. See Military Living's *U.S. Forces Travel Guide to U.S. Military Installations* for details.

### UNSCHEDULED FLIGHTS

Limited fwlights via Army C-12A, U-21 and CH-47 aircraft to CONUS West Coast and Midwest locations. Call for destinations, routings and schedules.

## McCHORD AIR FORCE BASE (TCM/KTCM)

62 APS/TRP
1422A Union Ave
McChord AFB, WA 98438-1003

**LOCATION:** From I-5, take exit 125 east onto Bridgeport Way. One mile to main gate. Clearly marked. *USMRA: Page 101 (C-5); Page 103 (B-7).ML-ARM: (47°08'N/122°28'W).* LST: GMT-08:00. NMC: Tacoma, 9 miles north. Main installation numbers: C-253-982-1910, D-312-382-1110.

**REGISTRATION INFO: C-253-982-7260/7259, D-312-382-7260/7259, Rec: C-253-982-7268, D-312-382-7268, Fax: C-253-982-6815, D-312-382-6815. E-mail: eagle@mcchord.af.mil WEB: www.mcchord.af.mil/aps** Bldg 1179, 24 hours daily. Directions: From main gate, left on Memorial Grove Ave, 1 block to A Street, left at stop sign, 1 mile to Pax Term. **Pax Service Office:** Bldg 1179, duty hours, C-253-982-7259. **Pax Paging:** C-253-512-4270/4265 D-312-982-4270/4265

**PAX LOUNGES: USO lounge:** Bldg 1183, Hours: 0600-1800 daily, cribs and restrooms, C-253-512-4254, D-312-982-4254. **General:** Bldg 1179, 24

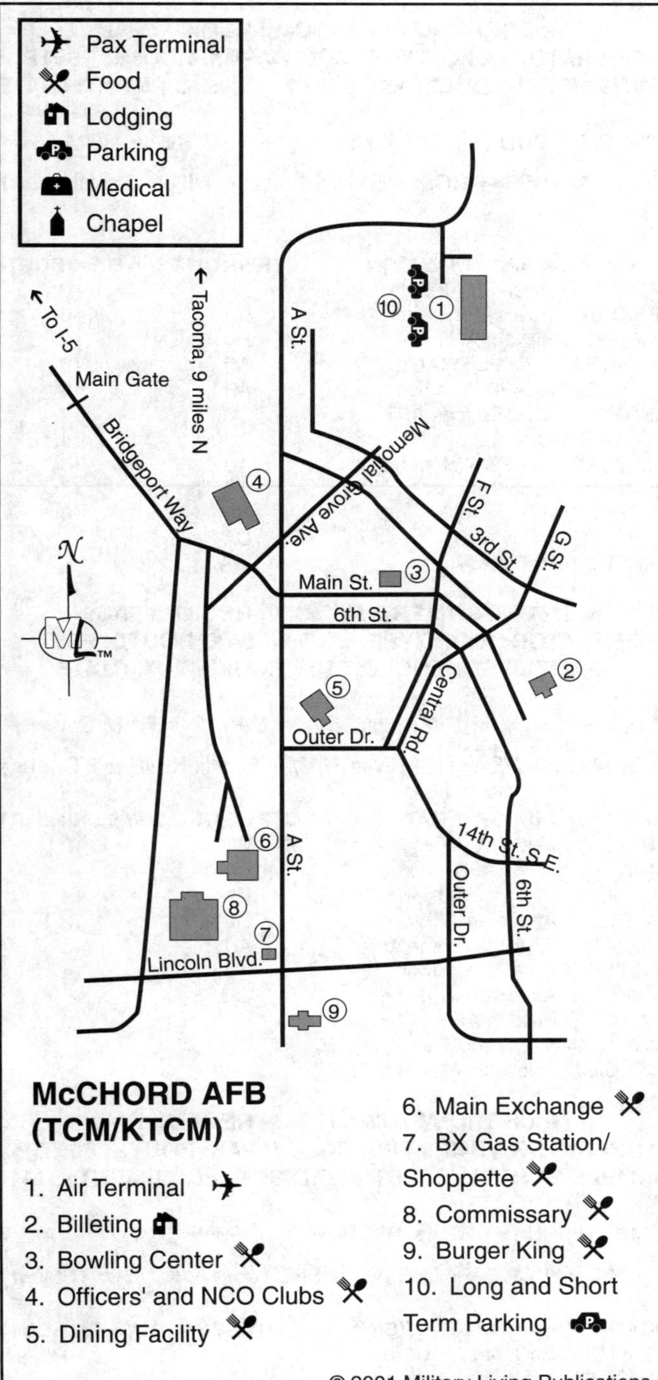

hours daily, C-253-512-4260, D-312-982-4260. Free TV, restrooms, P/C seats, vending machines, telephones. **DV/VIP:** Bldg 1179, 24 hours daily, C-253-512-4238/9, D-312-982-4238/9. Rear of Terminal behind Pax Service office. A/C, private office, shower, stereo, free TV, restrooms, O/S seats. **Protocol Service:** Bldg 100, Hours: 0800-1600 daily, C-253-512-2788, D-312-982-2788.

**FOOD SERVICE: Olympic Dining Hall:** Bldg 548, C-253-984-2145, D-312-984-2795. **Enlisted Club:** Bldg 746, C-253-512-5134. **O Club:** Bldg 746. **Snack Bars:** Bowling Alley, Bldg 737, C-253-512-2892. **Burger King:** Bldg 510, C-253-582-1188.

**TRANSPORTATION: Air Tickets:** N & N Travel and Tours, Inc: Bldg 1179, Hours: 0730-1700 Mon-Fri, C-253-512-4317, D-312-982-4317. **Base Transportation (Gov):** official business only, C-253-984-2684. **On Base Car Rentals:** AAFES; U-SAVE, hotline outside Pax Term, Hours: 0900-1800 Mon-Fri, 0900-1700 Sat, 1000-1600 Sun. **Off Base Car Rentals:** Budget, C-253-582-5900; Enterprise, C-253-531-4552; Thrifty, C-253-535-1122, all three deliver rentals to base. **SEA-TAC Airporter:** C-800-562-7948, leaves at 0520, last run 2250, two-hour intervals, reservations required, $10 one way. **On Base Shuttle/Bus:** Hours: 0530-0730, 1100-1300, 1430-1900, 2300-0100 Mon-Fri. **Off Base Taxi:** Bldg 1179, 24 hours daily, C-253-512-3331. **Parking:** Short term, in front of Pax Term, 24 hour limit; long term, in walking distance, 60 day maximum. You will be towed if you do not remove your car on a timely basis.

**TML:** Lodging office, Building 166, Main Street, 24 hours daily, C-1-800-847-3899, C-253-982-5613, D-312-382-5613; DV/VIP C-253-982-3591.

**RVC:** FAMCAMP, Holiday Park, Bldg 739, Check-in Office, C-253-982-5488.

**TRAVELERS AID: Chaplain:** Bldg 746, Hours: 0730-1630 Mon-Fri, C-253-512-5556/7. **Lost/Found:** Bldg 1179, In Pax Service Office: 24 hours daily, C-253-512-5658. **Medical:** Bldg 164, 24 hours daily, C-253-512-5601/3. **Red Cross:** Bldg 521, Hours: 0800-1600 daily, C-253-512-5577, After hours, C-253-967-7686. **Security Police:** Main gate, C-253-512-2119/2347. **USO:** SEA-TAC International Airport: 24 hours daily, C-253-512-4255/6, D-312-982-4255/6; McChord Terminal: Hours: 0600-1800 daily, C-253-512-2400.

**SUPPORT AVAILABLE: Bank/Currency Exchange:** Armed Forces Bank, Bldg 550, C-253-593-5772. Harborstone Credit Union: Bldg 530, C-253-584-5413. **Exchange:** Main BX: Bldg 543, C-253-582-9450/9451. **Hair Styles:** Bldg 543, Barber, C-253-588-2345; Beauty, C-253-584-1595. **Laundry/Dry Cleaning:** Bldg 506, C-253-584-7038. **Postal Service:** Bldg 735, C-253-512-5198. **Shoppette:** Bldg 545, C-253-589-4734.

**OTHER INFORMATION:** Port of Entry and U.S. Customs Service Airport.

**ATTRACTIONS:** Seattle (30 miles north), Cascade Mountains (Mt Rainier), State Ferries, Olympic Mountains, and Puget Sound

### McCHORD AFB, WA (TCM); REGION: PAC; OPERATOR: AMC; TYPE: MIXED; ROUTE: T679F; SAMPLE SCHEDULE: 1ST & 3RD THU; EQUIPMENT: C141B

{TCM *SE* ➡ SUU (★) *SW* ➡ HIK *SW* ➡ AWK *NW* ➡ DNA ⮌ DNA *SE* ➡ AWK *NE* ➡ HIK *NE* ➡ TCM (★)}

| LI/ICAO | AIRPORT/STATION | CTRY/STA | DAYS EN ROUTE |
|---|---|---|---|
| TCM/KTCM | McChord AFB | WA | +0 |
| SUU/KSUU | Travis AFB | CA | +0 |
| HIK/PHIK | Hickam AFB | HI | +1 |
| AWK/PWAK | Wake IS AAF | WK | +2 |
| DNA/RODN | Kadena AB | JP | +17 |
| DNA/RODN | Kadena AB | JP | +17 |
| AWK/PWAK | Wake IS AAF | WK | +18 |
| HIK/PHIK | Hickam AFB | HI | +18 |
| TCM/KTCM | McChord AFB | WA | |

### McCHORD AFB, WA (TCM); REGION: PAC; OPERATOR: AMC; TYPE: MIXED; ROUTE: TU79A; SAMPLE SCHEDULE: 2ND & 4TH THU; EQUIPMENT: C017A

{TCM *SW* ➡ SUU (★) *SW* ➡ HIK *E* ➡ AWK *NW* ➡ DNA ⮌ DNA *W* ➡ AWK *W* ➡ HIK *NW* ➡ TCM (★)}

| LI/ICAO | AIRPORT/STATION | CTRY/STA | DAYS EN ROUTE |
|---|---|---|---|
| TCM/KTCM | McChord AFB | WA | +0 |
| SUU/KSUU | Travis AFB | CA | +0 |
| HIK/PHIK | Hickam AFB | HI | +1 |
| AWK/PWAK | Wake IS AAF | WK | +2 |
| DNA/RODN | Kadena AB | JP | +17* |
| AWK/PWAK | Wake IS AAF | WK | +18 |
| HIK/PHIK | Hickam AFB | HI | +18 |
| TCM/KTCM | McChord AFB | WA | |

*Scheduled maintenance.

### McCHORD AFB, WA (TCM); REGION: PAC; OPERATOR: AMC; TYPE: CGO W/ PAX; ROUTE: P6E1P; SAMPLE SCHEDULE: 1ST & 3RD FRI; EQUIPMENT: C141B

{TCM *SE* ➡ SUU (★) *SW* ➡ HIK *SW* ➡ PPG *SW* ➡ RCM *NW* ➡ ASP ⮌ ASP *SE* ➡ RCM *NE* ➡ PPG *NE* ➡ HIK *NE* ➡ SUU (★) *NW* ➡ TCM}

| LI/ICAO | AIRPORT/STATION | CTRY/STA | DAYS EN ROUTE |
|---|---|---|---|
| TCM/KTCM | McChord AFB | WA | +0 |
| SUU/KSUU | Travis AFB | CA | +0 |
| HIK/PHIK | Hickam AFB | HI | +2 |
| PPG/NSTU | Pago Pago IAP | AS | +2 |
| RCM/YSRI | RAAFB Richmond | AU | +3 |
| ASP/YBAS | Alice Springs APT | AU | +4 |
| ASP/YBAS | Alice Springs APT | AU | +4 |
| RCM/YSRI | RAAFB Richmond | AU | +5 |
| PPG/NSTU | Pago Pago IAP | AS | +5 |
| HIK/PHIK | Hickam AFB | HI | +6 |
| SUU/KSUU | Travis AFB | CA | +6 |
| TCM/KTCM | McChord AFB | WA | |

### McCHORD AFB, WA (TCM); REGION: PAC; OPERATOR: AMC; TYPE: CGO W/ PAX; ROUTE: P6E7P; SAMPLE SCHEDULE: SUN; EQUIPMENT: C141B

{TCM *S* ➡ SUU (★) *SW* ➡ HIK *SW* ➡ UAM *S* ➡ RCM *SW* ➡ UMR ⮌ UMR *NE* ➡ RCM *N* ➡ UAM *NE* ➡ HIK *NE* ➡ TCM (★)}

| LI/ICAO | AIRPORT/STATION | CTRY/STA | DAYS EN ROUTE |
|---|---|---|---|
| TCM/KTCM | McChord AFB | WA | +0 |
| SUU/KSUU | Travis AFB | CA | +0 |
| HIK/PHIK | Hickam AFB | HI | +1 |
| UAM/PGUA | Andersen AFB | GU | +2 |
| RCM/YSRI | RAAFB Richmond | AU | +3 |
| RCM/YSRI | RAAFB Richmond | AU | +4 |
| UAM/PGUA | Andersen AFB | GU | +5 |
| HIK/PHIK | Hickam AFB | HI | +6 |
| TCM/KTCM | McChord AFB | WA | |

*Scheduled to close 31 Mar 2000.

### McCHORD AFB, WA (TCM); REGION: PAC; OPERATOR: AMC; TYPE: CGO W/ PAX; ROUTE: P6E7P; SAMPLE SCHEDULE: 1ST & 3RD SUN; EQUIPMENT: C141B

{TCM *S* ➡ SUU (★) *SW* ➡ HIK *W* ➡ UAM *S* ➡ RCM *NW* ➡ UMR *SE* ➡ RCM *SE* ➡ CHC ⮌ CHC *NE* ➡ PPG *NE* ➡ HIK *NE* ➡ TCM (★)}

| LI/ICAO | AIRPORT/STATION | CTRY/STA | DAYS EN ROUTE |
|---|---|---|---|
| TCM/KTCM | McChord AFB | WA | +0 |
| SUU/KSUU | Travis AFB | CA | +0 |
| HIK/PHIK | Hickam AFB | HI | +1 |
| UAM/PGUA | Andersen AFB | GU | +2 |
| RCM/YSRI | RAAFB Richmond | AU | +3 |

| RCM/YSRI | RAAFB Richmond | AU | +4 |
|---|---|---|---|
| CHC/NZCH | Christchurch IAP | NZ | +5 |
| CHC/NZCH | Christchurch IAP | NZ | +5 |
| PPG/NSTU | Pago Pago IAP | AS | +6 |
| HIK/PHIK | Hickam AFB | HI | +7 |
| TCM/KTCM | McChord AFB | WA | |

### McCHORD AFB, WA (TCM); REGION: PAC;
### OPERATOR: AMC; TYPE: CGO W/ PAX; ROUTE: P6PXF;
### SAMPLE SCHEDULE: 2ND & 4TH FRI; EQUIPMENT: C141B

{TCM *SE* ➡ SUU (★) *SW* ➡ HIK *NW* ➡ OKO ⇌ OKO *SE* ➡ HIK *NE* ➡ SUU (★) *NW* ➡ TCM}

| LI/ICAO | AIRPORT/STATION | CTRY/STA | DAYS EN ROUTE |
|---|---|---|---|
| TCM/KTCM | McChord AFB | WA | +0 |
| SUU/KSUU | Travis AFB | CA | +1 |
| HIK/PHIK | Hickam AFB | HI | +2 |
| OKO/RJTY | Yokota AB | JP | +4 |
| OKO/RJTY | Yokota AB | JP | +4 |
| HIK/PHIK | Hickam AFB | HI | +4 |
| SUU/KSUU | Travis AFB | CA | +5 |
| TCM/KTCM | McChord AFB | WA | |

### McCHORD AFB, WA (TCM); REGION: PAC;
### OPERATOR: AMC; TYPE: CGO W/ PAX; ROUTE: PUPXE; SAMPLE SCHEDULE: 1ST & 3RD FRI; EQUIPMENT: C017A

{TCM *SE* ➡ SUU (★) *SW* ➡ HIK *NW* ➡ OKO ⇌ OKO *SE* ➡ HIK *NE* ➡ SUU (★) *NW* ➡ TCM}

| LI/ICAO | AIRPORT/STATION | CTRY/STA | DAYS EN ROUTE |
|---|---|---|---|
| TCM/KTCM | McChord AFB | WA | +0 |
| SUU/KSUU | Travis AFB | CA | +1 |
| HIK/PHIK | Hickam AFB | HI | +2 |
| OKO/RJTY | Yokota AB | JP | +18 |
| OKO/RJTY | Yokota AB | JP | +18 |
| HIK/PHIK | Hickam AFB | HI | +18 |
| SUU/KSUU | Travis AFB | CA | +19 |
| TCM/KTCM | McChord AFB | WA | |

### EN ROUTE SCHEDULES

| AIRPORT/STATION | LI-MISSION (page #) |
|---|---|
| Travis AFB | SUU-436/MEDEVAC (13) |
| Scott AFB | BLV-C-634/MEDEVAC (30) |
| March ARB | RIV-9J97A/C (10) |
| Charleston AFB/IAP | CHS-P803R (68) |
| Charleston AFB/IAP | CHS-P803S (68) |

### UNSCHEDULED FLIGHTS

Frequent CONUS flights via C-141B and C-17A aircraft available but scheduled on a day-to-day basis as needed. Call **C-253-512-4260, D-312-982-4260** for status information. Flight schedules change month to month. Call for destinations, routings and schedules.

# SEATTLE/TACOMA
# INTERNATIONAL AIRPORT (SEA/KSEA)

Det 1, 62 APS (AMC)
SEATAC International Airport, Room 5445
17801 Pacific Highway S
Seattle, WA 98158-5000

**LOCATION:** From I-5 take exit 152 west. Clearly marked. *USMRA: Page 103 (C-4).* ML-ARM: (47°26'N/122°17'W). LST: GMT-08:00. NMC: Seattle, 15 miles north. Main installation number: C-206-444-9096.

**REGISTRATION INFO: C-1-877-863-1463 ext 258/259 or C-253-982-0555, D-312-382-0555, Fax: C-253-982-0557, D-312-382-0557. E-mail: eagle@mcchord.af.mil** or **seataccsb@yahoo.com WEB: www.mcchord.af.mil/aps** Dual sign-up with McChord AFB: Fax: C-253-984-5659, D-312-984-5659. AMC is located on the ticketing level of the main terminal between Northwest and British Airlines. Hours: 0800-1600 daily. See McChord AFB for support. **Pax Service Office: C-206-444-9096, D-312-382-0555.**

**FOOD SERVICE: Fast Food:** Burger King, concourse D; China First Express, concourse B; Taco Bell, just past concourse C/D checkpoint. **Restaurants:** Carvery, center of main terminal, C-206-433-5622; Pizza Hut, main terminal. Other snack places also throughout the terminal

**TRANSPORTATION: Airport Information:** C-800-544-1965, C-206-431-4444. **On/Off Base Bus:** Grayline, C-206-626-6088; Greyhound, C-1-800-231-2222; Metro, C-206-553-3000. **On Base Car Rental:** Advantage, C-206-824-0161; Alamo, C-206-433-0182; Avis, C-206-433-5231; Budget, C-206-243-2400; Dollar, C-206-433-5825; Hertz, C-206-248-1300; National, C-206-433-5501; Thrifty, C-206-246-7565. **Off Base Car Rental:** Century/Rent Rite, C-206-246-5039; Enterprise, C-206-248-9013; E-Z Rental, C-206241-4688; Holiday Rent-A-Car, C-206-248-3452; Reliable Auto Rental, C-206-243-3211; Rent-A-Wreck, C-206-246-8486; U Save, C-206-242-9778; Xtracar, C-206-248-3452. **On/Off Base Limo:** Available at the baggage claim area (lower) drive and outside Doors 6 and 26, C-1-800-303-3243. **On/Off Base Shuttle:** Pick-up at both ends of the baggage claim area (lower) drive and outside Doors 6 and 26. Airporter Shuttle, C-1-800-235-5247, reservations; Bremerton-Kitsap Airporter, C-1-800-562-7948; Capital Aeroporter, C-1-800-962-3579, C-360-754-7113, C-206-838-7431, C-206-927-6179, reservations; Centalia Sea-Tac Airporter, C-1-800-773-9490, reservations; Fort Lewis/McChord, C-1-800-562-7948; Olympic Van Tours, C-360-452-3858. Shuttle Express, C-1-800-487-7433. **On/Off Base Taxi:** Available at the baggage claim area (lower) drive and outside Doors 6 and 26, C-206-246-9999. All Star Transportation Service, C-206-623-6074. **Parking:** Disabled, garage 4th floor, C-206-433-5308; General, garage, C-206-433-5308; Meter, garage 4th floor; Valet, garage, pre-paid, C-206-248-6882/6887.

**TML:** Nearest TML is at McChord AFB, Lodging office, Building 166, Main Street, 24 hours daily, C-253-982-5613, D-312-984-5613; DV/VIP C-253-984-3591.

**TRAVELERS AID: Travelers Aid:** Center of main terminal, C-206-433-5288. **Lost/Found:** 0800-1600 hours daily, C-206-444-9112, D-312-382-0555 ext 2. **Medical:** Madigan Army Medical, C- 253-968-1390. **Police:** C-206-433-5400. **USO:** Main terminal, 2nd floor, 24 hours daily, snack bar, TV, showers, telephone, infant supplies, C-206-433-5438

**OTHER INFORMATION:** Port of Entry and U.S. Customs Service Airport.

**ATTRACTIONS:** Seattle professional sports teams, Seattle Aquarium, Space Needle, Pacific Science Center, Pike Place Market, Museum of Flight, Mount Rainier National Park and Mount St. Helens National Monument.

### SEATTLE/TACOMA IAP, WA (SEA); REGION: PAC;
### OPERATOR: COM; TYPE: PAX; ROUTE: 3W77A;
### SAMPLE SCHEDULE: WED; EQUIPMENT: MD011

{SEA (★) *SW* ➡ OSN *SW* ➡ KUZ *NE* ➡ OSN ⇌ OSN *NE* ➡ SEA (★)}

| LI/ICAO | AIRPORT/STATION | CTRY/STA | DAYS EN ROUTE |
|---|---|---|---|
| SEA/KSEA | Seattle/Tacoma IAP | WA | +0 |
| OSN/RKSO | Osan AB | KR | +1 |
| KUZ/RKJK | Kunsan AB | KR | +1 |
| OSN/RKSO | Osan AB | KR | +1 |
| OSN/RKSO | Osan AB | KR | +1 |
| SEA/KSEA | Seattle/Tacoma IAP | WA | |

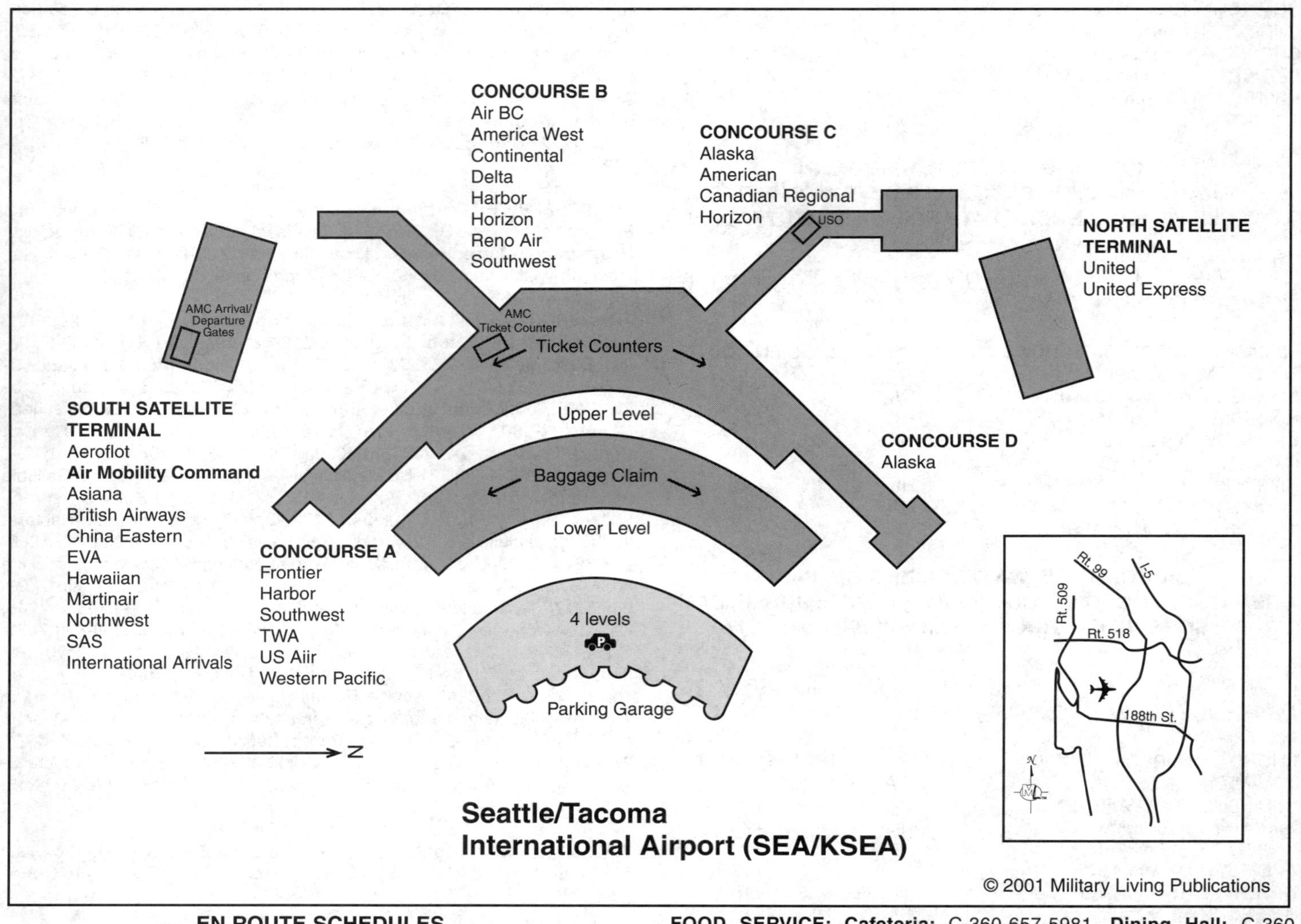


## EN ROUTE SCHEDULES

| AIRPORT/STATION | LI-MISSION (page #) |
|---|---|
| Los Angeles IAP | LAX-2W71B (8) |
| Los Angeles IAP | LAX-2W79A (8) |
| Los Angeles IAP | LAX-2X87A (8) |

# WHIDBEY ISLAND NAVAL AIR STATION (NUW/KNUW)

Air Terminal, N-32
3730 N Charles Porter Ave
Oak Harbor, WA 98278-5300

**LOCATION:** From I-5 north or south, exit 230, take WA-20 southwest to Whidbey Island, three miles west of WA-20 on Ault Field Road. *USMRA: Page 101 (C-2,3). ML-ARM: (48°19'N/122°38'W).* LST: GMT-08:00. NMC: Seattle, 90 miles southeast. Main installation numbers: C-360-257-2211, D-312-820-0111.

**REGISTRATION INFO:** C-360-257-2604, D-312-820-2604, Rec: C-360-257-2328, D-312-820-2328, after hours, Fax: C-360-257-6792, D-312-820-6792. WEB: www.naswi.navy.mil (Go to the Space-A Link) E-mail: web-airterm@naswi.navy.mil Bldg 2734, Hours: 0700-1900 daily. Directions: From main gate straight on Langley Blvd, left on Charles Porter Ave to a right on Lexington Street to Pax Term on left.

**PAX LOUNGES:** No family lounge. **General:** Bldg 2734, Hours: 0700-1900 M-F; Weekends: for inbound/outbound traffic only., C-360-257-2604. TV, restrooms, O/S seats. **DV/VIP:** Bldg 2734, Hours: 0700-1900 daily, C-360-257-2604. (O6+). **Base Operator:** Bldg 113, Hours: 0730-1630 Mon-Fri, C-360-257-2211.

**FOOD SERVICE: Cafeteria:** C-360-657-5981. **Dining Hall:** C-360-257-2211. **Enlisted Club:** C-360-257-3308. **NCO/CPO Club:** C-360-257-2829. **O Club:** C-360-257-2521; Admiral Nimitz Hall, C-360-257-2717; McDonald's, C-360-257-8888. **Snack Bars:** C-360-675-8598. **Snack Vending:** C-360-257-2604.

**TRANSPORTATION: Air Tickets:** SATO, C-360-679-4415. **Car Rentals:** C-360-675-1244. **Taxi (Gov):** C-360-257-3133. **Off Base Taxi:** C-360-675-1244. **Parking:** Short and long term, Bldg 117, C-360-257-3121 (near base gym).

**TML:** Lodging office: Building 973, McCormick Lodge, Midway Boulevard, C-360-257-2529. Navy Lodge, Building 2125 N Coral Sea Avenue, Oak Harbor, WA 98278, C-1-800-NAVY-INN, C-360-675-0633. DV/VIP C-360-257-2037.

**RVC:** Cliffside RV Park, Outdoor Rec Center, 1130 West Storm Lane, Check-in RV Park, C-360-257-2434, D-312-820-2434.

**TRAVELERS AID: Chaplain:** C-360-257-2414. **Navy Relief:** C-360-657-5177/2728. **Medical/Dental:** C-360-257-9500, D-312-820-9500. **Red Cross:** C-360-257-2096 (After hours C-360-257-2631). **Security Police:** C-360-257-3122. **YMCA:** C-360-675-2771.

**SUPPORT AVAILABLE: Exchange:** C-360-257-0503. **Hair Styles:** C-360-257-0511. **Laundry/Dry Cleaning:** C-360-257-0522.

**OTHER INFORMATION:** Port of Entry and U.S. Customs Service Airport.

**ATTRACTIONS:** Beautiful island setting. Summer: hiking, mountain biking, fishing, golfing, whale watching; winter: skiing, snowboarding, snowmobiling.

## UNSCHEDULED FLIGHTS

Flights via EP-003E, P-003C, UP-003A/B and DC-009 to: Atsugi NAF, JA (**NJA**); Elmendorf AFB, AK (**EDF**); Fallon NAS, NV (**NFL**); Kaneohe Bay MCB, HI (**NGF**); March ARB, CA (**RIV**); McChord AFB, WA (**TCM**); Mountain Home AFB, ID (**MUO**); Norfolk NS, VA (**NGU**); North Island NAS, CA (**NZY**). Call for destinations, routings and schedules.

# WEST VIRGINIA

## EASTERN WEST VIRGINIA REGIONAL AIRPORT (MRB/KMRB)

West Virginia Air National Guard
167th Airlift Wing
222 Sabre Jet Blvd
Martinsburg, WV 25401-7720

**LOCATION:** From US-11, 3 miles south of Martinsburg, turn left on Paynes Ford Road, 1 mile to sign for Air National Guard Base, at next intersection turn right. From I-81 N, take exit 8, make a right and continue to stop sign; turn left. Continue on for approximately 2 miles and make a right at the Global Gas Station. Go 1.5 miles, turn right. From I-81 S, take exit 12, make a left then a right at the second traffic signal. Continue on for approximately 1.5 miles and make a left at the Global Gas Station. Go 1.5 miles, turn right. *USMRA: Page 47 (K-3,4). ML-ARM: (39°24'N/77°58'W).* LST: GMT-05:00. NMC: Martinsburg, 3 miles north. Main installation numbers: C-304-262-5100, D-312-242-9210.

**REGISTRATION INFO: C-304-262-5250, D-312-242-5250.** To sign up must register in person with ID. Bldg 120, 2nd Floor, Hours: 0730-1600 Tues-Fri. Ask Security Police for directions. **Pax Service Office:** Bldg 120, Hours: 0730-1600 Tues-Fri, C-304-262-5250 (scheduling NCO). **PAX LOUNGES:** Limited. **General:** Bldg 120, Hours: 0730-1600 Tue-Fri, C-304-262-5250. A/C, restrooms, showers.

**FOOD SERVICE: Combined Club:** C-304-262-5298. Snack Vending available.

**TRANSPORTATION:** Located approximately 100 miles from Washington National Airport; 60 miles from Dulles International Airport; 20 miles from Hagerstown, MD Airport. No commercial Airlines/Bus service available at Martinsburg WV. AMTRAK has commuter service to Washington, D.C. each AM and PM Mon-Fri.

**TRAVELERS AID: Medical:** C-304-262-5244. **Red Cross:** C-304-263-5241, after hours: C-304-263-3311. **Security Police:** C-304-262-5300, D-312-242-9300.

**TML:** Nearest TML is at Fort Detrick, MD, Lodging office, Building 810, Schreider Street, 0745-1630 Mon-Fri, C-301-619-2154, D-312-343-2154. DV/VIP C-301-619-7114.

**SUPPORT AVAILABLE: Credit Union:** Hours: 1000-1400, C-304-262-5262, D-312-9262, .5 miles away. **Exchange:** C-304-262-5204.

**ATTRACTIONS:** Harpers Ferry National Park, Antietam Battlefield, Civil War Battlefields, and malls.

## UNSCHEDULED FLIGHTS

Flights to other CONUS and OCONUS locations via C-130H aircraft. Call for destinations, routings and schedules.

## YEAGER AIRPORT (CRW/KCRW)

130 AW/APS WVANG
1679 Coonskin Drive, Bldg 131
Charleston, WV 25311-5000

**LOCATION:** From I-77 north or south, take exit 99 north, Greenbrier Street, WV-114 to airport. *USMRA: Page 46 (E-6). ML-ARM: (38°22'N/81°34'W).*

LST: GMT-05:00. NMC: Charleston, 4 miles southwest. Main installation numbers: C-304-341-6000, D-312-366-6210.

**REGISTRATION INFO: C-304-341-6185, D-312-366-6185, Fax: C-304-341-6047, D-312-366-6047.** Air National Guard area, Hours: 0730-1600 Mon-Fri. Ask Security Police for directions. All support of regional airport.

**FOOD SERVICE: Fast Food:** 2 miles away. **Restaurants:** 2 miles away. Snack Vending available in terminal.

**TRANSPORTATION: Off Base Car Rental:** Avis, 1-800-831-2847; Hertz, C-1-800-654-3131; National, C-1-800-227-7368, all at Yeager Airport, 2 miles away. **On Base Taxi:** C-304-341-6222, D-312-366-6222, 1 mile away. **Off Base Taxi:** C-304-343-7522, 4 miles away.

**TRAVELERS AID: Security/Police:** 24 hours daily, C-304-341-6238, D-312-366-6238, 1.5 miles away.

**SUPPORT AVAILABLE: Exchange:** Hours: 0900-1630, C-304-346-4957.

## UNSCHEDULED FLIGHTS

Flights via ANG C-130H aircraft to CONUS and OCONUS locations. Call for destinations, routings and schedules.

# WISCONSIN

## FORT McCOY AVIATION SUPPORT FACILTY (CMY/KCMY)

B Company 2/228th AVN
Bldg 6058, South Post
Fort McCoy, WI 54656-5000

**LOCATION:** From I-90/94, exit 143 west to WI-21 northeast to fort. Main gate on north side of WI-21. *USMRA: page 68 (C,D/7). ML-ARM: (43°57'N/X94°44'W).* LST: GMT-06:00. NMC: La Crosse, 15 miles east. Main installation numbers: C-608-388-2222, D-312-280-1110.

**REGISTRATION INFO: C-608-388-5641, D-312-280-5641.** Bldg 6058, South Post. General and DV/VIP lounges available.

**FOOD SERVICE: Snack Vending:** Hours: 0730-1600, near Bldg 6058.

**TRANSPORTATION: On Base Car Rental:** National Car Rental, C-608-269-7692. On Base Shuttle/Bus and Off Base Taxi service are available.

**TML:** Lodging office, Building 2168, 8th Street, 24 hours daily, C-608-388-2107, D-312-280-2107, Fax: C-608-388-3946. DV/VIP C-608-388-3607, D-312-280-3607.

**SUPPORT AVAILABLE: Exchange:** Hours: 0730-19100, C-608-388-4134, 7 miles away.

**ATTRACTIONS:** Army Reserve Training Center, hunting, fishing, snow and water skiing. Close to the Mall of America and the Mississippi River.

## UNSCHEDULED FLIGHTS

Flights via C-12R aircraft. Call for destinations, routings and schedules.

## GENERAL MITCHELL INTERNATIONAL AIRPORT/AIR RESERVE STATION (MKE/KMKE)

128 Air Refueling Wing (ANG)
OSA, Bldg 552 Rm 31
1839 E. Grange Avenue
Milwaukee, WI 53207-6143

440 Airlift Wing (AFRC)
OSA, Bldg 224
300 E. College Avenue
Milwaukee, WI 53207-6143

**LOCATION:** From I-94 N or S, exit 318 (east) College Avenue. For 128 ARW (ANG): From the north, proceed to fifth stoplight and turn left on Pennsylvania Avenue. (From the south, proceed to the fourth stop light.) At next stoplight, turn left onto Grange Avenue. Follow road around to the main gate. For 440 AW (AFRC): Exiting from the north, proceed left on College to fourth stoplight. Exiting from the south, proceed to the third stoplight. Turn left and proceed to main gate.*USMRA: Page 68 (G-9).* ANG *ML-ARM: (42°56'N/82°53'W).* AFRES *ML-ARM: (42°55'N/87°54'W).* LST: GMT-06:00. NMC: Milwaukee, 3 miles north. Main installation numbers: ANG: C-414-944-8241, D-312-580-88241; AFRC: C-414-482-5000, 1-800-647-1638, D-312-950-5000.

**REGISTRATION INFO: 128 ARW (ANG): Rec: C-414-944-8732, D-312-580-8732.** Bldg 522, very limited hours of operations (call). Directions: East side of building. Ask at gate. Limited base support. No TML available. Very little transportation available. Small lounge with snack vending machines. **440 AW (Air Reserve Station): C-877-412-0126 ext 5586, Rec: ext 5167, D-312-950-5167, Fax: 414-482-5930. WEB: www.mke.afres.af.mil or www.afres.af.mil**

**Pax Lounges:** Small waiting area with vending machines.

**Attractions:** Summer festivals throughout the Milwaukee area. Chicago, IL within a one hour 45 minute drive south.

**GENERAL MITCHELL FIELD, WI (MKE); REGION: ATL; OPERATOR: AMC; TYPE: CGO W/ PAX; ROUTE: OTN3C; SAMPLE SCHEDULE: 4TH WED; EQUIPMENT: C130H**

{MKE *SE* ➡ NGU (★) *SE* ➡ NRR *E* ➡ STX ⮂ STX *W* ➡ NRR *NW* ➡ NGU (★) *NW* ➡ MKE}

| LI/ICAO | AIRPORT/STATION | CTRY/STA | DAYS EN ROUTE |
|---|---|---|---|
| MKE/KMKE | General Mitchell IAP/ARS | WI | +0 |
| NGU/KNGU | Norfolk NS | VA | +1 |
| NRR/TJNR | Roosevelt Roads NS | PR | +2 |
| STX/TISX | Alexander Hamilton Apt (St Croix) | VI | +1 |
| NRR/TJNR | Roosevelt Roads NS | PR | +2 |
| NGU/KNGU | Norfolk NS | VA | +4 |
| MKE/KMKE | General Mitchell IAP/ARS | WI | |

### EN ROUTE SCHEDULES

| AIRPORT/STATION | LI-MISSION (page #) |
|---|---|
| Scott AFB | BLV-C-666/MEDEVAC (30) |

### UNSCHEDULED FLIGHTS

Flights via ANG KC-135R and AFRC C-130H aircraft to CONUS, OCONUS, and foreign country locations. Call for destinations, routings and schedules.

## VOLK FIELD AIR NATIONAL GUARD BASE (VOK/KVOK)

Air Operations, CRTC/OTM
Camp Douglas, WI 54618-5001

**LOCATION:** From Madison take I-90/94 northwest, 85 miles to Camp Douglas exit northeast. From Lacrosse, take I-90 east to I-94 south to Camp Douglas exit (55 miles). *USMRA: Page 68 (D-7). ML-ARM: (43°55'N/90°15'W).* LST: GMT-06:00. NMC: La Crosse, 50 miles west. Main installation numbers: C-608-427-1210, D-312-946-3210.

**REGISTRATION INFO: C-608-427-1205, D-312-946-3205, Fax: C-608-427-1266.** Bldg 511, Base Ops, Hours: 0800-1600 Mon-Fri. **Pax Service Office:** Bldg 511, Hours: 0800-1600 Mon-Fri, C-608-427-1205 (NCO).

**PAX LOUNGES:** Limited. **General:** Bldg 511, Hours: 0800-1600 Mon-Fri. A/C, coffee available, telephones (commercial and defense), restrooms, O/S seats. **Protocol Service:** Bldg 100, Hours: 0800-1600 Mon-Fri, C-608-427-1204, D-312-946-3204.

**FOOD SERVICE: Restaurants:** Good off base. **Snack Vending:** Bldg 511.

**TRANSPORTATION: Off Base Bus:** Tomah, Greyhound, C-608-372-4466. **Off Base Taxi:** Tomah, C-608-372-2345. **Parking:** Bldg 511 (no restrictions).

**TML:** Nearest TML is at Fort McCoy, Lodging office, Building 2168, 8th Street, 24 hours daily, C-608-388-2107, D-312-280-2107, Fax: C-608-388-3946. DV/VIP C-608-388-3607, D-312-280-3607.

**TRAVELERS AID: Security Police:** C-608-427-1210 (ask for security).

### UNSCHEDULED FLIGHTS

Air National Guard Training Site. Flights via transient ANG aircraft. Call for destinations, routings and schedules.

# WYOMING

## CHEYENNE MUNICIPAL AIRPORT(CYS/KCYS)

153rd AW, Wyoming Air National Guard
217 Dell Range Blvd, Bldg 16, Room 122
Cheyenne, WY 82009-4799

**LOCATION:** From I-25 north or south, exit on Central Avenue exit 12 east to airport. Turn onto Yellowstone Road to first light. Turn onto Dell Range Blvd, first right into guard base. *USMRA: Page 102 (I-8). ML-ARM: (41°09'N/104°49'W).* LST: GMT-07:00. NMC: Cheyenne, 1 mile south. Main installation numbers: C-307-772-6132, D-312-943-6132.

**REGISTRATION INFO: Rec: C-307-772-6347, ext 71, C-1-800-832-1957, ext 71, D-312-943-6347, Fax: C-307-772-6000, D-312-943-6000.** Bldg 116, Hours: 0730-1630 Mon-Fri.

**FOOD SERVICE:** Snack Vending available.

**TML:** Nearest TML is at F.E. Warren AFB, Lodging Office: Crow Creek Inn, 7103 Randall Street, 24 hours daily, C-307-773-1844, D-312-481-1844. DV/VIP C-307-773-2137/3052.

**SUPPORT AVAILABLE:** Full support of a regional airport. No military facilities.

**OTHER INFORMATION:** U.S. Customs Service Airport.

### EN ROUTE SCHEDULES

| AIRPORT/STATION | LI-MISSION (page #) |
|---|---|
| Scott AFB | BLV-C-635/MEDEVAC (30) |

### UNSCHEDULED FLIGHTS

Flights to CONUS and OCONUS locations via ANG C-130H aircraft. Call for destinations, routings and schedules.

## F.E. WARREN AIR FORCE BASE (FEW/KFEW)

90th Transportation Squadron
7300 Saber Road, Bldg 1274
Cheyenne, WY 82005-2630

**LOCATION:** Off I-25, exit 11 west on Randall Avenue; main gate two miles north of I-80. Clearly marked. *USMRA: Page 102 (I-8). ML-ARM: (41°08'N/104°50'W).* LST: GMT-07:00. Off I-25, Warren Gate, exit 11. NMC: Cheyenne, adjacent. Main installation numbers: C-307-773-1110, D-312-481-1110.

**REGISTRATION INFO: C-307-773-3275, D-312-481-3275. E-mail: roger.vigen@warren.af.mil** *Note: There is not a building for passengers to wait in. One is being proposed at the Wyoming Air National Guard area.*

**FOOD SERVICE:** Dining, C-307-778-8272; Fast Food, C-307-773-2399.

**TML:** Lodging Office: Crow Creek Inn, 7103 Randall Street, 24 hours daily, C-307-773-1844, D-312-481-1844. DV/VIP C-307-773-2137/3052.

**RVC:** FAMCAMP, Outdoor Rec, 7103 Randall Ave, Check-in FAMCAMP, or Outdoor Rec, Bldg 316, C-307-773-2988, D-312-481-2988. Full base support facilities available.

**TRAVELERS AID: Chaplain:** C-307-773-3434, **Medical/Dental:** C-307-773-2277, C-307-773-1846, **Security Police:** C-307-773-3501.

**SUPPORT AVAILABLE: Credit Union:** C-307-634-9685, **Exchange:** C-307-634-1593, **Dry Cleaner:** C-307-638-0311, **Hair Styles:** C-307-634-7149, **Shoppette:** C-307-634-7432.

**ATTRACTIONS:** Cheyenne, historic Governer's Mansion, National First Day Cover Museum, State Capital.

### UNSCHEDULED FLIGHTS

Operational support aircraft flights to Midwest and West Coast areas. MEDEVAC available. Weekly C-130 MEDEVAC flights to Peterson AFB **(COS)**, CO. Call for destinations, routings and schedules.



---

# Going to Europe?

## Take Military Living's New Atlas with you and $ave!

## Look for Military Living's European U.S. Military Road Atlas at your military exchange, military clothing sales store, or shoppette.

If not available, you may order online through our secure web order system at www.militaryliving.com or call 703-237-0203 to place a credit card order by phone. You may also order by fax at 703-237-2233. Be sure to give the name on the credit card, card number, expiration date and credit card billing address, as well as ship-to address and daytime phone number.

## Visit us online at www.MilitaryLiving.com
### and learn more about our money-saving publications!

# OUTSIDE CONTINENTAL UNITED STATES (OCONUS)

## ALASKA

### EIELSON AIR FORCE BASE (EIL/PAEI)

Contract Air Terminal Operations
1220 Flightline Ave, Bldg 1190, Suite 1
Eielson AFB, AK 99702-1870

**LOCATION:** On east side of Richardson Highway (AK-2) at mile post 341. AFB is clearly marked. *USMRA: Page 128 (F,G-4). ML-ARM: (64°30'N/147°05'W).*LST: GMT-09:00. NMC: Fairbanks AK, 30 miles northwest. Main installation numbers: C-907-377-1110, D-317-377-1110.

**REGISTRATION INFO: C-907-377-1250/1854, D-317-377-1250/1854, Fax: C-907-377-2287, D-317-377-2287. Rec: C-907-377-1623, D-317-377-1623. WEB: www.eielson.af.mil** Bldg 1138, Hours: 0730-1630 Mon-Fri, other hours as required. Directions: From main gate to a right on North Street. Pax Term on left after crossing Flightline Avenue. **Pax Service Office:** C-907-377-1854/1250, D-317-377-1854/1250. Twenty-four hour self-sign up in entryway of terminal.

**PAX LOUNGES:** Bldg 1138. No separate **DV/VIP** or family lounges. **General:** Bldg 1138, Hours: 0730-1630 daily, C-907-377-1854. Telephones (defense), TV, restrooms, P/C seats. **Protocol Service:** Bldg 3112, duty hours, C-907-377-6101 (ask for Wing Executive Officer).

**FOOD SERVICE: Cafeteria:** Bldg 2216, Hours: 1100-2100 Mon-Fri, 1200-1800 Sat, C-907-377-1126. **Dining Hall:** Bldg 2207, Hours: 0600-1800 daily, C-907-377-2563. **Fast Food:** Burger King, Bldg 3315, Hours: 0600-2200 Mon-Thu, 0600-2300 Fri, 0800-2300 Sat, 0800-2200 Sun. **In-flight Meals:** Bldg 2207, 24 hours daily, C-907-377-1444. **NCO Club:** Bldg 2225, Hours: 1000-2300 Mon-Sat, C-907-377-2635. **O Club:** Bldg 5223, Hours: 0800-2100 Mon-Fri, C-907-377-1121. **Restaurants:** The Club, C-907-377-2051, D-312-377-2051. **Snack Bars:** Bowling Alley, Bldg 3301, C-907-377-5154. **Snack Vending:** Bldg 1221, Hours: 0730-1600 Mon-Fri, C-907-377-1854.

**TRANSPORTATION: Air Tickets:** SATO, Bldg 3112, Hours: 0800-1630 Mon-Fri, C-907-372-2288. **On Base Taxi** (Official use only) Bldg 3425, 24 hours daily, C-907-377-2197/1843. **Off Base Taxi:** North Pole Taxi Service, 24 hours daily, C-907-488-7900, 10 miles away.

**TML:** Gold Rush Inn, Bldg. 2270, Central Avenue, Eielson AFB, AK 99702-1870, 24 hours daily, C-907-377-1844, D-317-377-1844. Fax: C-907-377-2559. DV/VIP: C-907-377-7686. Availability low during summer.

**RVC:** FAMCAMP, 3112 Broadway Ave, Unit 6-B, Check-in Outdoor Rec,

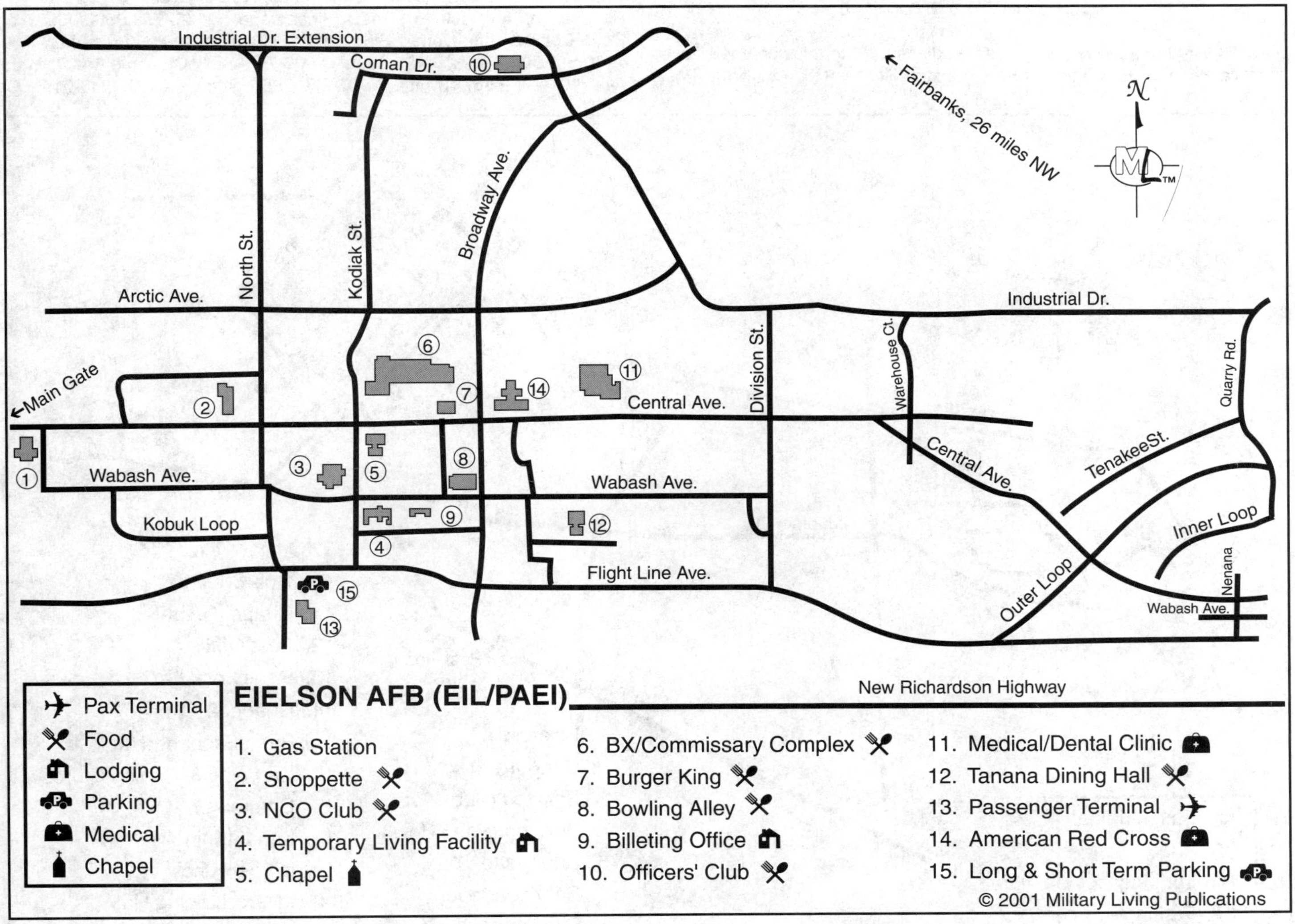

**EIELSON AFB (EIL/PAEI)**

- ✈ Pax Terminal
- ✕ Food
- 🏠 Lodging
- 🚓 Parking
- ⊞ Medical
- ⚕ Chapel

1. Gas Station
2. Shoppette ✕
3. NCO Club ✕
4. Temporary Living Facility 🏠
5. Chapel ⚕
6. BX/Commissary Complex ✕
7. Burger King ✕
8. Bowling Alley ✕
9. Billeting Office 🏠
10. Officers' Club ✕
11. Medical/Dental Clinic ⊞
12. Tanana Dining Hall ✕
13. Passenger Terminal ✈
14. American Red Cross ⊞
15. Long & Short Term Parking 🚓

© 2001 Military Living Publications

Bldg 6214, 0800-1700 hours, C-907-377-1232, D-317-377-1232, Fax: C-907-377-2770.

**TRAVELERS AID: Chaplain:** Bldg 3307, C-907-377-2130. **Emergency Relief:** Bldg 3125, C-907-377-2178 (Air Force Aid). **Medical:** C-907-377-1847. **Red Cross:** Bldg 3347, C-907-377-1855. **Security Police:** Bldg 2222, C-907-377-5130.

**SUPPORT AVAILABLE: Credit Union:** C-907-372-6111. **Exchange:** C-907-377-1454. **Postal Service:** Bldg 2216, C-907-372-1234. **Wire:** Bldg 3310, Hours: 0900-1800 Mon-Fri, 0930-1730 Sat, 1100-1700 Sun (Western Union).

**ATTRACTIONS:** Fairbanks, North Pole (Santa Claus House), outdoor sports and recreation.

### EN ROUTE SCHEDULES

| AIRPORT/STATION | LI-MISSION (page #) |
|---|---|
| March ARB | RIV-9J97A/C (10) |

### UNSCHEDULED FLIGHTS

Flights to CONUS and OCONUS via KC-135R aircraft. Call for destinations, routings and schedules.

## ELMENDORF AIR FORCE BASE (EDF/PAED)

732nd AMS/TROP
10-364 Fighter Drive
Elmendorf AFB, AK 99506-3935

**LOCATION:** Off Glenn Highway (AK-1) adjacent to north Anchorage. Take Boniface Parkway Exit. Take either Elmendorf Access Road or North Post Road. The base is adjacent to Fort Richardson. *USMRA: Page 128 (F-5) and Page 131 (B,C,D,E-1). ML-ARM: (61°22'N/150°00'W).* LST: GMT-09:00. NMC: Anchorage AK, 2 miles southwest. Main installation numbers: C-907-552-1110, D-317-552-1110.

**REGISTRATION INFO:** C-907-552-8588/4616, D-317-552-8588/4616, Fax: C-907-552-3996, D-317-552-3996. E-mail spacea@ elmendorf.af.mil WEB: www.elmendorf.af.mil Bldg 10-364, 24 hours daily. Directions: From Post Road gate to a left on 6th Street to dead end at Pax Term. **Pax Service Office:** Bldg 32-233, 24 hours daily, **Pax Paging:** C-907-552-3781/4616, D-317-552-3781/4616.

**PAX LOUNGES: Nursery lounge:** restricted to families with infants. **General:** Bldg 32-233, 24 hours daily. Bag check, game room, restrooms, telephone (local and long distance), P/C and O/S seats, TV. **DV/VIP:** Bldg 32-233, 24 hours daily, C-907-552-3781, O6+. Restrooms, telephones (local and long distance), O/S seats, TV. **Family:** Bldg 32-233, 24 hours daily, C-907-552-3781. TV, O/S seats. Armed Services YMCA Lounge located in inbound section TV/Info area.

**FOOD SERVICE: Cafeteria:** Bldg 32-233, 0500-1700, C-907-753-6146, inside Pax Term. **Dining Hall:** Bldg 8088, Hours: 0530-1800 daily, C-907-552-2469. **Enlisted Club:** Bldg 7135, C-907-753-6131. **O Club:** Bldg 9387, C-907-753-3131. **Fast Food:** Burger King, C-907-753-4486, 1-1.5 miles away. **Snack Bars:** Bldg 31-148, Hours: Vary with season, C-907-552-3669 (PolarBowl). **Snack Vending:** Bldg 31-233, C-907-552-3781. Facilities also available at Fort Richardson.

**TRANSPORTATION:** Local ground transportation also available at Fort Richardson. **Air Tickets:** SATO, Anchorage, C-907-753-3592/0509. **On Base Car Rentals:** Denali, Bldg 32-233, Hours: 0700-2000 Mon-Fri, 0800-1700 Sat-Sun, C-1-800-757-1230, C-907-753-2178. **Off Base Car Rentals:** Avis: 907-277-4567; Thrifty: C-907-276-2855; Budget: C-907-243-0150. **On**

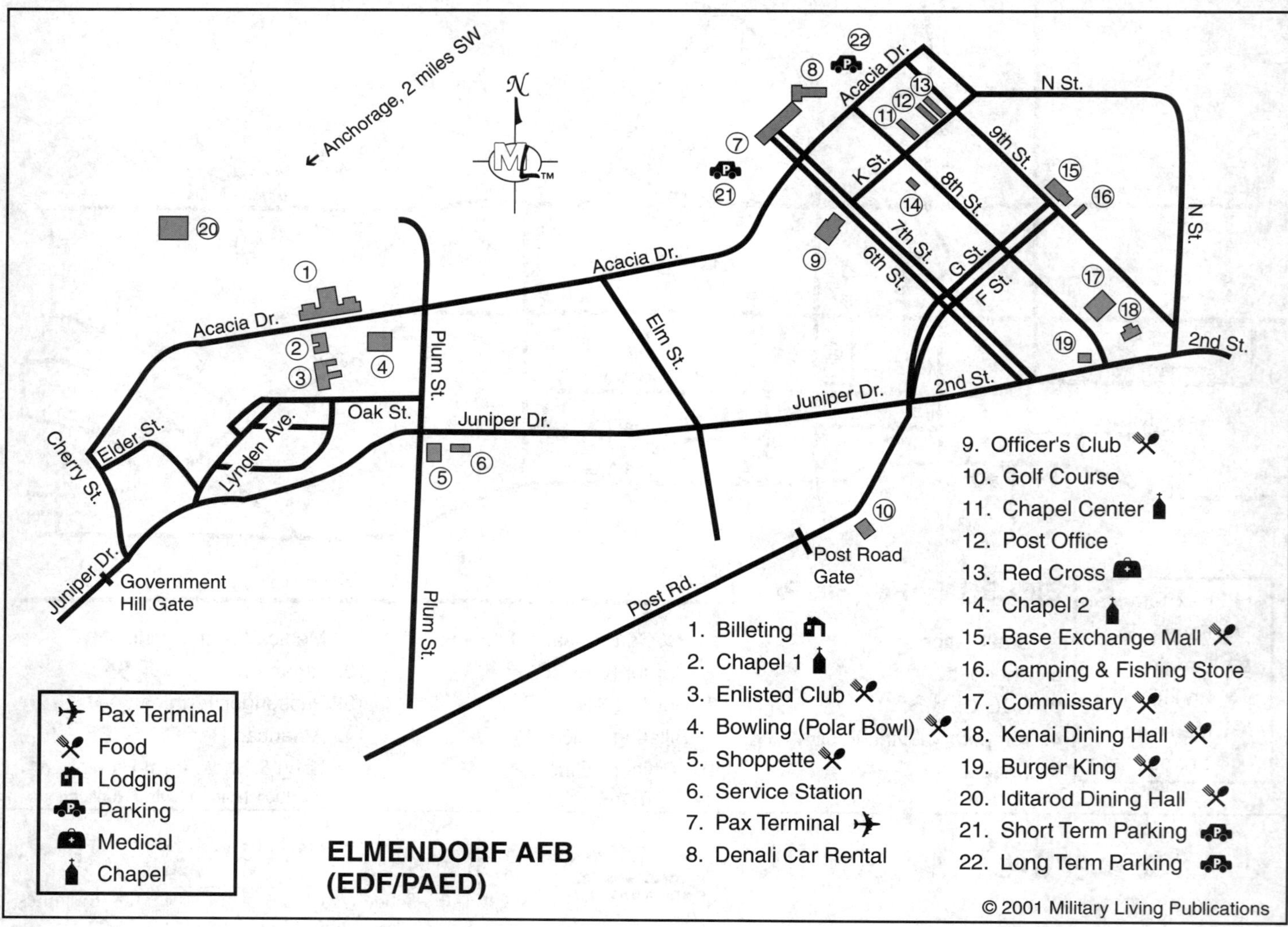

**Base Shuttle/Bus:** Bldg 32-233, Hours: 0600-1700 Mon-Fri, C-907-552-2454/4526 (schedule at billeting). **Off Base Shuttle/Bus:** Only at hospital. C-907-343-6543. **Off Base Taxi:** Checker: C-907-276-1234; Yellow: C-907-272-2422; Anchorage: C-907-278-8000; Alaska: C-907-563-5353. **Off Base Train Station:** C-901-265-2494/2688, 15-20 miles. **Parking:** Bldg 32-233, 24 hours daily, C-907-552-3781. Limit 60 days, fill out pass at Pass Counter.

**TML:** Lodging office, North Star Inn, Building 7153, Fighter Drive, 24 hours daily, C-907-552-2454 ext 118, D-317-552-2454 ext 118, Fax: C-907-552-8276. DV/VIP C-907-552-3517, DSN-317-552-3517.

**RVC:** FAMCAMP, Bldg 7301 13th Street, Check-in Camp Host, Space-2, C-907-552-2023, Fax: C-907-753-2498.

**TRAVELERS AID: Chaplain:** Bldg 24-800, 24 hours daily, C-907-552-4422, D-317-552-4422. **Lost/Found:** Pax Term, C-907-552-4616. **Medical:** Bldg 24-800, 24 hours daily, C-907-552-2778 (emergency), D-317-552-2778, C-907-552-2748 (appointment). **Red Cross:** Bldg 2-864, C-907-552-5253/4824, D-317-552-5253/4824. **Security Police:** Bldg 6-900, 24 hours daily, C-907-552-3421 (Desk Sgt), D-317-552-3421.

**SERVICES AVAILABLE:** Full range of support available at EDF and Fort Richardson. **Bank/Currency Exchange:** Bldg 3-850, Hours: 1000-1700, C-907-753-1179/1149 (First National Bank), 2-3 miles away. **Credit Union:** Hours: 1000-1700, C-907-753-0505. **Exchange:** Bldg 4-932, 24 hours daily, C-907-753-4260/7180, 2-3 miles away. **Hair Styles:** Bldg 4-932, C-907-753-3044. **Laundry/Dry Cleaner:** Bldg 31-160, Hours: 0930-1700, C-907-552-2266, 2-3 miles away. **Postal Service:** Bldg 9-854, Hours: 0900-1700, C-907-753-1049, 1-1.5 miles away. **Shoppette:** Hours: 0630-2200, C-907-753-1291, 1-1.5 miles away.

**OTHER INFORMATION:** Port of Entry and U.S. Customs Service Airport when called prior to aircraft arrival.

**ATTRACTIONS:** City of Anchorage and a full range of seasonal activities: fishing, hunting, hiking, camping, skiing, biking, etc.

*Note: Commercially contracted flights are now called Patriot Express.*

### ELMENDORF AFB, AK (EDF); REGION: PAC; OPERATOR: COM; TYPE: MIXED; ROUTE: ZQ93B; SAMPLE SCHEDULE: FRI & TUE; EQUIPMENT: B727

{EDF *SW* ➡ AKN *NW* ➡ SYA ⇌ SYA *SE* ➡ AKN *NE* ➡ EDF}

| LI/ICAO | AIRPORT/STATION | CTRY/STA | DAYS EN ROUTE |
|---|---|---|---|
| EDF/PAED | Elmendorf AFB | AK | +0 |
| AKN/PAKN | King Salmon APT | AK | +0 |
| SYA/PASY | Eareckson AS | AK | +0 |
| SYA/PASY | Eareckson AS | AK | +0 |
| AKN/PAKN | King Salmon APT | AK | +1 |
| EDF/PAED | Elmendorf AFB | AK | |

### EN ROUTE SCHEDULES

| AIRPORT/STATION | LI-MISSION (page #) |
|---|---|
| March ARB | RIV-9J97A/C (10) |
| Travis AFB | SUU-P379D (14) |
| Charleston AFB/IAP | CHS-P803R (68) |
| Charleston AFB/IAP | CHS-P803S (68) |

### UNSCHEDULED FLIGHTS

Flights each Wed via C-130H aircraft to Galena Apt, AK (**GAL**) and King Salmon Apt, AK (**AKN**). Flights each Mon and Fri via B-737 aircraft to Eareckson AS, AK (**SYA**). There is a C-141B MEDEVAC mission to Travis AFB, CA (**SUU**) on Sat. There are frequent flights to Eielson AFB, AK (**EIL**) and McChord AFB, WA (**TCM**) via C-12, C-130 A-H and C-141B.

## KODIAK COAST GUARD AIR STATION (ADQ/PADQ)

P.O. Box 190033
Kodiak, AK 99619-0033

**LOCATION:** From Kodiak City, take Chiniak Highway southwest for seven miles. Base is on left (southeast) side. *USMRA: Page 128 (E-7). ML-ARM: (57°44'N/152°29'W).* LST: GMT-10:00. NMC: Kodiak, 9 miles northeast. Main installation numbers: C-907-487-5267, D-317-487-5267.

**REGISTRATION INFO: C-907-487-5149, D-317-487-5149.** Hangar #1, first floor, Hours: 0900-1100 Mon, 0900-1100 Thu. Directions: From Rezanof Drive West turn left on 6th Street and proceed through the Front Gate. Take the 2nd right onto Albatross Road. Hangar 1 is located at the end on the left. **Pax Service Office:** Room 222.

**PAX LOUNGE:** General lounge available at Hangar 1, first floor, room 120.

**FOOD SERVICE: Cafeteria:** C-907-487-5710, 0.5 miles away. **Enlisted Club:** Kings Inn, C-907-487-5109. **Restaurants:** Golden Anchor (All Ranks), Hours: C-907-487-5440 Thu-Sun, 0.5 miles away. **Snack Bars:** Family Pizza Parlor, C-907-487-5988, 0.33 miles away.

**TRANSPORTATION: Air Tickets:** Kodiak Apt, (see directory for major airlines). **Off Base Car Rentals:** Avis, C-907-487-2264, airport; Budget, C-907-487-2220, airport. **On Base Shuttle/Bus:** C-907-487-5471. **Off Base Taxi:** Ace Mecca, C-907-486-3211, downtown Kodiak.

**TML:** Guest house, Building N-30, 24 hours daily, C-907-487-5446, D-317-487-5446. PCS or official duty, all others Space-A. DV/VIP C-907-487-5446.

**TRAVELERS AID: Chaplain:** Support Center, C-907-487-5730/5731, 0.5 miles away. **Lost/Found:** C-907-487-5267. **Medical:** Support Center, 24 hours daily, C-907-487-5757, D-317-487-5757. **Red Cross:** Support Center at Elmendorf AFB, C-907-552-1110, C-907-552-5253 (after hours). **Security Police:** Main Gate, C-907-487-5266.

**SUPPORT AVAILABLE: Convenience Store:** Hours: 0700-2100 Mon-Fri, 1000-2100 Sat-Sun, C-907-487-5475, 0.125 miles away. **Credit Union:** Tue-Sat, C-907-487-2138, 0.33 miles away, 5th floor of PAC Bldg. **Exchange:** Wed-Sun, C-907-487-5370 Support Center (PAC Bldg), 0.33 miles away. **Laundry/Dry Cleaner:** C-907-487-5450. **Postal Service:** Tue-Sat, C-907-487-5263 PAC Bldg, 0.33 miles away.

**ATTRACTIONS:** Hunting and fishing paradise and flight seeing tours.

### UNSCHEDULED FLIGHTS

Flights Mon and Wed, alternating every other week, to Elmendorf AFB, AK (**EDF**) via C-130A-H (MEDEVAC), Fri and Sun monthly to Elmendorf AFB, AK (**EDF**) via C-130A-H (Training flight). Also frequent flights to North Island NAS, CA (**NZY**) via C-009A and C130 A-H aircraft. Call for destinations, routings and schedules.

## KULIS AIR NATIONAL GUARD BASE/ ANCHORAGE INTERNATIONAL AIRPORT (ANC/PANC)

176 OSF, Bldg 21, Room 130
5005 Raspberry Road
Anchorage, AK 99502-1998

**LOCATION:** From downtown Anchorage, go south on Minnesota Thruway to right (west) on International Airport Road to left (south) on Jewel Lake Road, turn right onto Raspberry Road. Main gate is approximately one mile on right (north) side of road. *USMRA: Page 128 (F-5) and Page 131 (A-4). ML-ARM: (61°10'N/149°59'W).* LST: GMT-09:00. NMC: Anchorage, 5 miles northeast. Main installation numbers: C-907-249-1176, D-317-626-1176.

**REGISTRATION INFO: C-907-249-1225, D-317-626-1225, Rec: C-907-249-1000, D-317-626-1000, Fax: C-907-249-1477, D-317-626-1477.** Base Ops, Bldg 21, Hours: 0700-1600 Mon-Fri, All facilities of an IAP. See Elmendorf AFB listing for support. **TML:** Nearest TML is at Elmendorf AFB, Lodging office, North Star Inn, Building 31-250, Acacia Street, 24 hours daily, C-907-552-2454, D-317-552-2454, Fax: C-907-552-8276. DV/VIP C-907-552-3210.

**ATTRACTIONS:** Glacier. Outdoor sports such as fishing and hunting in the summer and cross country skiing in the winter.

### UNSCHEDULED FLIGHTS

ANG via C-130H and HC-130R flights to CONUS and OCONUS destinations including Eielson AFB, AK (**EIL**). Call for destinations, routings and schedules.

## WAINWRIGHT ARMY AIRFIELD/ FORT WAINWRIGHT (FBK/PAFB)

ATTN: APVR-WPTM-AO
1060 Gaffney Road
Fort Wainwright, AK 99703-5200

**LOCATION:** From Fairbanks, take Airport Way (AK-3) east which changes to Gaffney Road and leads to the Main Gate of the post. Turn right on Marks Road, and at stop sign turn left. Bldg 1558 is on immediate right. *USMRA: Page 128 (F-4). ML-ARM: (64°50'N/147°36'W).* LST: GMT-09:00. NMC: Fairbanks, 3 miles north. NMI: Eielson AFB, 20 miles north.

**REGISTRATION INFO: C-907-353-6514/7212, D-317-353-6514/7212, Fax: C-907-353-9941, D-317-353-9941.** General pax lounge available.

**FOOD SERVICE: Fast Food:** Burger King, Hours: 0630-2200, on post, 2 miles away. **Snack Bar,** Hours: 0730-1700, on post, 2 miles away. Various restaurants available off post, 2 or more miles away.

**TRANSPORTATION:** Various Car Rentals, Limo and Off Base Taxis available.

**TML:** Lodging office, Building 1045 (Murphy Hall), Gaffney Road, 24 hours, C-907-353-6294/7291, D-317-353-6294/7291, Fax: C-907-353-7409, D-317-353-7409. DV/VIP: C-907-353-6679.

**RVC:** Glass Park, 1555 Gaffney Road, Check-in Outdoor Rec, Bldg 2062 (Rec Center), C-907-353-6349/6350, D-317-353-6349/6350.

**SUPPORT AVAILABLE: Bank/Currency Exchange:** Hours: 0900-1700, C-1-800-856-4362, 3 miles away. **Credit Union:** Hours: 0900-1600, C-907-356-1262/1253, 2 miles away. **Dry Cleaner:** Hours: 1000-1700, C-907-356-1359, 2 miles away. **Exchange:** Hours: 0700-1900, C-907-356-1345/1357, 2 miles away. **Laundry:** Hours: 1000-1700, C-907-356-1359, 2 miles away. **Postal Service:** Hours: 1000-1700, 1-800-275-8775, 1 mile away. **Shoppette:** Hours: 0730-2200, C-907-356-2349, D-317-353-7259, 2 miles away.

### UNSCHEDULED FLIGHTS

Flights to Alaska stations via Administrative Aircraft. Call for destinations, routings and schedules.

## ALASKA ISOLATED STATIONS
### (Not listed separately in this book)

The stations listed below have Space-A air opportunities. Base support facilities are very limited. Lodging is not available except at Fort Greely. Camping, fishing, hiking, hunting and all outdoor recreation are outstanding. Permission of the station Commander is required for all visitors except for Allen AAF, Fort Greely.

**ALLEN ARMY AIRFIELD, (BIG/PABI)**, USAG AVN Det, Unit 45816, APO AP 96508-5816. **LOCATION:** West of AK-4 six miles south of junction of AK-2 and AK-4. Five miles south of Delta Junction. Located 1.5 miles from post (Fort Greely). *USMRA: Page 128 (F,G-4). ML-ARM: (63°59'N/145°43'W).* LST: GMT-09:00. **C-907-873-4172, D-317-873-4172, Fax: C-907-873-3725, D-317-873-3725.** Small pax lounge available. Contact C-12 scheduling office, C-907-384-7888, D-317-384-7888, Fax: C-907-384-7881, D-907-384-7881 for reservations. Support facilities available at Fort Greely. **TML:** Limited availability with TDY and new arrivals having priority. Lodging office, Building 663, First Street, 0730-1530 Mon, Tue, Thurs & Fri, 0730-1130 Wed, C-907-873-3285, D-317-873-3285, Fax: C-907-873-3003. Other hours, SDO, Building 501, C-907-873-4720.

**CLEAR AIR STATION, (CLF/PACL)**, 13 SWS, 200 A Street Stop 40013, Clear AS, AK 99704-0013. **LOCATION:** From Fairbanks, 80 miles southwest on Fairbanks/Anchorage Highway (AK-3). Located on east side of highway. *USMRA: Page 128 (F-4). ML-ARM: (64°45'N/148°56'W).* LST: GMT-09:00. NMC: Fairbanks, 80 miles northeast. NMI: Fort Wainwright, 75 miles. **REGISTRATION INFO: C-907-585-6409, D-317-585-6416.** There is no Pax Term at Clear AS. **TRANSPORTATION: On Base Shuttle/Bus:** C-907-585-6218, D-317-585-6218. **TML:** Lodging office, Building 200, C-907-585-6224. **TRAVELERS AID: Chaplain:** C-907-585-6485, D-312-585-6485. **Security Police:** C-907-585-6313, D-317-585-6313. **SUPPORT AVAILABLE: Postal Service:** Hours: 0900-1500 Mon-Fri, C-907-585-6268, D-317-585-6268. **Shoppette:** Hours: 1000-2000 Mon-Fri, 1200-1600 Sat-Sun, C-907-582-2691. **ATTRACTIONS:** Denali National Park. ***Note: This is a remote station with no flight line or aircraft assigned.***

**EARECKSON AIR STATION, (SYA/PASY)**, c/o Elmendorf AFB, 632nd AMSS/TROP, 42-525 Burns Road, Elmendorf AFB, AK 99506-3565. **LOCATION:** At the western tip of the Aleutian Islands chain. Accessible only by air. Visits require prior approval by the base commander. *USMRA: Page 128 (F-7). ML-ARM: (52°30'N/174°10'E).* LST: GMT-10:00. NMC: Anchorage, 1800 air miles northeast. **C-907-392-3401/3471/3064. TML: Very, very limited. C-907-392-3240.**

### EN ROUTE SCHEDULES

| AIRPORT/STATION | LI-MISSION (page #) |
| --- | --- |
| Elmendorf AFB | EDF-ZQ93B (91) |

**KING SALMON AIRPORT, (AKN/PAKN)**, 611 Air Support Squadron, King Salmon Program Office, 6900 9th Street, Suite 225, Elmendorf AFB, AK 99506-5000. Accessible only by air and water. *USMRA: Page 128 (D-6). ML-ARM: (58°30'N/156°30'W).* LST: GMT-10:00. NMC: Anchorage, 275 miles northeast. Main installation numbers: C-907-721-3750, D-317-721-3750. Limited support facilities available. ***Note: Pax must first acquire a site notification authorization by calling C-907-552-8744, D-317-552-8744, Fax: C-907-552-3474, D-317-552-3474.***

### EN ROUTE SCHEDULES

| AIRPORT/STATION | LI-MISSION (page #) |
| --- | --- |
| Elmendorf AFB | EDF-ZQ93B (91) |

**SITKA COAST GUARD AIR STATION, (SIT/PADQ)**, 611 Airport Road, Sitka, AK 99835-6500. **LOCATION:** At end of Airport Road, on Japonski Island, 0.5 miles north of airport terminal. *USMRA: Page 128 (I-7). ML-ARM: (57°02'N/135°21'W).* LST: GMT-09:00. **C-907-966-5580, D-None, Fax: C-907-966-5428. CGX: C-907-966-5436. TRAVELERS AID:** Medical/Dental: Hours: 0800-1600, C-907-966-5438. **SUPPORT AVAILABLE:** All-Hands Club, C-907-966-5516.

## UNSCHEDULED FLIGHTS

Flights to: Kulis ANGB/Anchorage IAP, AK (**ANC**); Elmendorf AFB, AK (**EDF**); McChord AFB, WA (**TCM**); and Eareckson AS, AK (**SYA**). Call for destinations, routings and schedules.

# AMERICAN SAMOA

## PAGO PAGO INTERNATIONAL AIRPORT (PPG/NTSU)

P.O. Box 50018
Pago Pago, American Samoa 96799-5000

**LOCATION:** On the south coast of the Island of Tutuila in American Samoa. Approximately 2,630 miles southwest of Honolulu HI, and 2,660 miles northeast of Christchurch NZ. *ML-ARM: (14°00'S/172°00'W).* LST: GMT-11:00. NMC: Village of Utulei, main U.S. Government offices, 9 miles from IAP. Main installation numbers: C-011-684-699-4262.

**REGISTRATION INFO: C-011-684-699-4262, Fax: C-011-684-699-9991/4260.** Pax Term, 24 hours daily. At IAP. One gate for departures. Contact AMC rep, C-011-684-699-4262. Basic refuel station. **Pax Service Office:** GCA International, Inc., IAP Trailer office 0800-1300 Mon-Fri, other times as scheduled; AMC Contractor: GCA International, Inc. C-011-684-699-4262; FAX: C-011-684-699-4262. AMC Control: GCA International, Inc.

**PAX LOUNGES:** Pax Term, 24 hours daily. Commercial IAP lounges available for Space-A pax. **General:** Pax Term, 24 hours daily, C-011-684-699-4262. Bag check/lockers, restrooms, wood seats. **DV/VIP:** Pax Term, 24 hours daily, C-011-684-699-4262. A/C, restrooms, O/S seats. No hostess. Advance notice through AMC rep. required.

**FOOD SERVICE:** At IAP, **Restaurant** open for AMC flights. C-011-684-699-6070 **Snacks:** Airport shops; C-011-684-633-4241. **Post Exchange:** 500 meters from airport terminal. Open M-F 1000-1700 hrs, C-011-634-699-2241. **Enlisted Club:** 4 blocks from PPG, Vet's Club open to Space-A passengers.

**TRANSPORTATION: Air Tickets:** Hawaiian Airlines at IAP Pax Term, C-011-684-699-1875/2184. **Bus (Comm):** P/U at Pax Term, C-011-684-699-4262. **Bus (Gov):** Pax Term, C-011-684-699-4262 (AMC rep). **Car Rentals:** PPG/hotels, C-011-684-699-1456, 011-684-699-2746 (PAVITTS/AVIS). **Taxi (Comm):** P/U at Pax Term, C-011-684-699-1169 (PPG to hotels $10). **Parking:** At IAP $1/day.

**TML:** No military or government TML. Pago Airport Inn C-011-684-699-6333. Rainmaker Hotel C-011-684-633-4241.

**TRAVELERS AID: Medical:** LBJ Medical Center, 24 hours daily, C-011-684-633-6222 (emergency). **Red Cross:** LBJ Medical Center, C-011-684-633-6222. **Security Police:** Pax Term, C-011-684-699-9101.

**ATTRACTIONS:** Beautiful tropical islands, beaches and fishing.

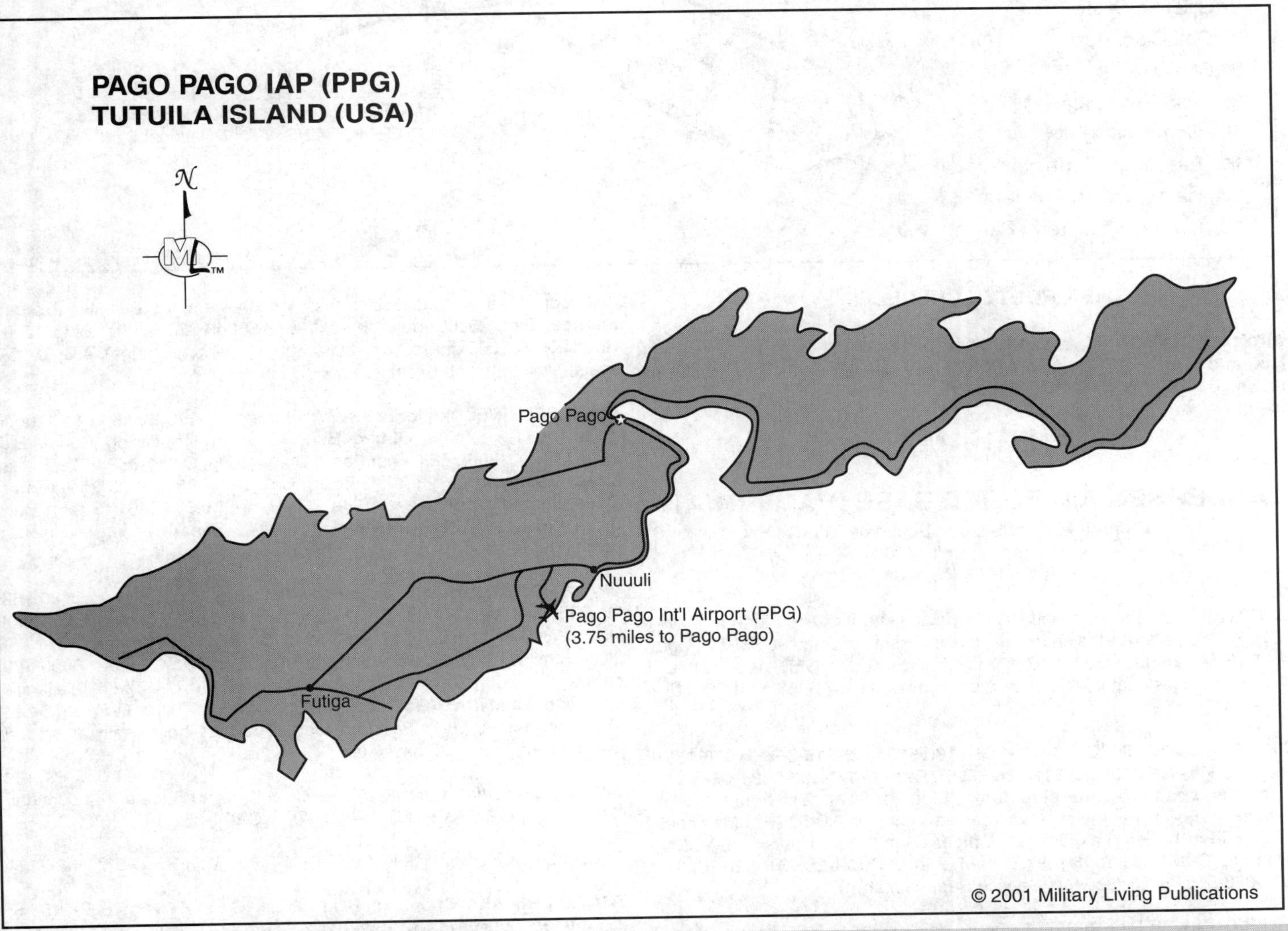

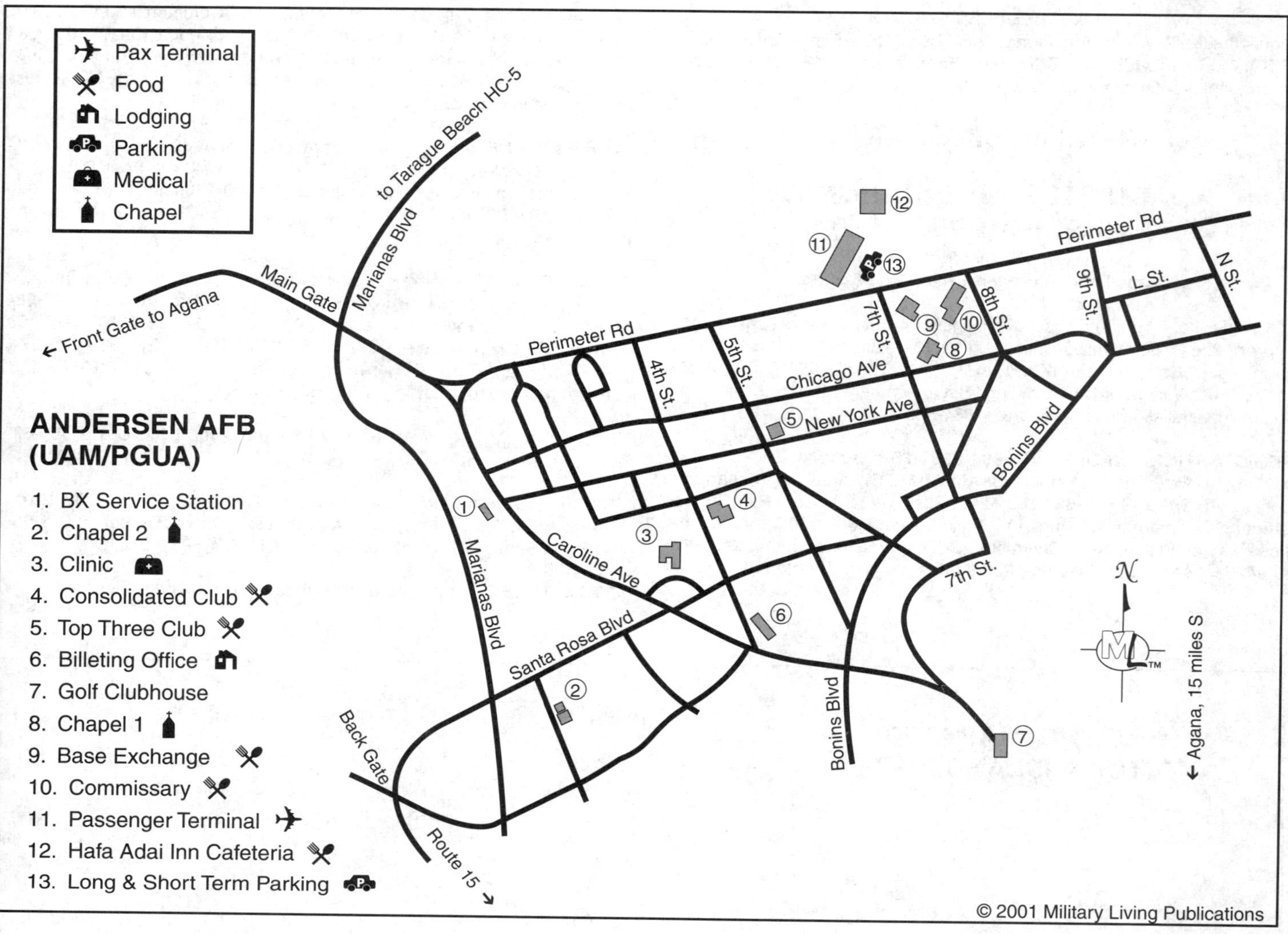


## EN ROUTE SCHEDULES

| AIRPORT/STATION | LI-MISSION (page #) |
| --- | --- |
| McChord AFB | TCM-P6E1P (82) |
| McChord AFB | TCM-P6E7P (82) |

# GUAM

# ANDERSEN AIR FORCE BASE (UAM/PGUA)

634th Air Mobility Support Squadron (AMC)
AMSS/TRP, Unit 14008
APO AP 96543-4008

**LOCATION:** On the north end of the island, access from Marine Drive (GU-1) which extends the entire length of the island of Guam. *USMRA: Page 130 (E,F-1,2). ML-ARM: (13°40'N/144°50'E).* LST: GMT-10:00. NMC: Agana, 15 miles south. Main installation numbers: C-671-366-1110, D-315-366-1110.

**REGISTRATION INFO: C-671-366-5165/5135, D-315-366-5165/5135, Rec: C-671-366-2095, D-312-366-2095, Fax: C-671-366-3984. E-mail: andersen.spacea@andersen.af.mil** Bldg 17002, 24 hours daily. Directions: Follow Perimeter Road from main gate, past B-52 ARC Memorial to Pax Term on left. **Pax Service Office:** Bldg 17002, Hours: 0730-1630 Mon-Fri, C-671-366-2096/2097. **Pax Paging:** C-671-366-5165/5135, D-315-366-5165/5135 (see Pax Service Representative).

**PAX LOUNGES:** Bldg 17002, 24 hours daily (see pax NCO for services). **General:** Bldg 17002, 24 hours daily, C-671-366-5165. A/C, game room, telephone (defense), restrooms, showers, P/C seats. **Special category lounge:** Bldg 17002, Hours: 0600-2000 daily C-671-366-4102 (no hostess).

A/C, coffee/tea served, restrooms, TV, showers, O/S seats. **Protocol Service:** Bldg 23003, duty hours, C-671-366-4228. **Family:** Bldg 17002, Hours: 0600-2000 daily, C-671-366-4102 (off general lounge). A/C, TV, O/S seats, playroom, cribs, refrigerator.

**FOOD SERVICE: Cafeteria:** Hafa Adai Inn, Bldg 17002, 0600-1400 hours daily, C-671-366-8283. **Dining Hall:** Magellan Inn Dining Room, Bldg 25010, C-671-366-3623. **Fast Food:** Burger King, C-671-653-0782, 2 miles away. **Restaurants:** Top of Rock, C-671-653-9810, 1.5 miles away. **Consolidated Open Mess:** Bldg 26006, C-671-366-1201. **Snack Bars:** Plaza Arcade, C-671-653-1396, 1 mile away. Snack Vending available at passenger terminal.

**TRANSPORTATION: Air Tickets:** SATO, Bldg 2202, Hours: 0730-1630 Mon-Fri, C-671-653-8940. **On Base Car Rentals:** National, Bldg 17002, Hours: 0800-1700 daily, C-671-653-6945. **Off Base Car Rental:** C-671-632-0111, 5 miles away. **On Base Shuttle/Bus:** Bldg 17002, Hours: 0600-1800 daily, C-671-366-2239. **Off Base Taxi (Comm):** C-671-477-8620, 15 miles away. **On Base Taxi (Gov):** Bldg 1800, 24 hours daily, C-671-366-2239 (duty passengers only). **Parking:** Bldg 17002, 24 hours daily, short term available; long term, 30 days max.

**TML:** Lodging office, Building 27006, 4th & Caroline Streets, 24 hours daily, C-671-362-4444, D-315-362-4444. DV/VIP C-671-351-4228.

**RVC:** Outdoor Rec, Check-in, 0900-1200 hours Mon-Fri, C-671-366-5204.

**TRAVELERS AID: Chaplain:** Bldg 22024, C-671-366-6139, D-315-366-2981, after hours call C-671-366-8144. **Emergency Relief:** Bldg 21000, C-671-366-4295 (Help Line), after hours call C-671-363-2913. **Lost/Found:** Bldg 17002, 24 hours daily, C-671-366-5135. **Medical:** Bldg 26000, Hours: 0700-1630 daily, Appointments: C-671-366-5273, D-315-366-6548; Urgent

Care: Hours: 1700-2130 daily, C-671-366-4276, D-315-366-4276, 1.5 miles away. **Red Cross:** Bldg 21000, C-671-366-6270, after hours call C-671-366-4267, 1.5 miles away. **Security Police:** Bldg 21000, 24 hours daily, C-671-366-2913, 2 miles away.

**SUPPORT AVAILABLE: Bank/Currency Exchange:** Hours: 0900-1700, C-671-653-8371, 1.5 miles away; Bldg 17002 ATM. Check cashing, AAFES, across from Pax Term. **Credit Union:** Pentagon Federal Credit Union, Bldg 21000, Hours: 0900-1500, C-671-653-6492, 1.5 miles away. **Exchange:** Bldg 22026, Hours: 0900-2000, C-671-362-1136, .25 miles away. **Hair Styles:** Bldg 25005, Hours: 0800-1730 Mon-Fri, 0800-1600 Sat; Barber, C-671-653-8599; Beauty, C-671-653-8598. **Laundry/Dry Cleaning:** Bldg 05005, Hours: 0800-1800, C-671-653-8596, 1 mile away. **Postal Service:** Bldg 21001, Hours: 0730-1700, C-671-366-3243, 1 mile away. **Shoppette:** Hours: 0700-2200, C-671-653-8143.

**OTHER INFORMATION:** Port of Entry and U.S. Customs Service Airport.

**ATTRACTIONS:** U.S. Naval Base, WWII battle areas, beaches.

## EN ROUTE SCHEDULES

| AIRPORT/STATION | LI-MISSION (page #) |
| --- | --- |
| Travis AFB | SUU-P371C (14) |
| Travis AFB | SUU-P371F & G (14) |
| Travis AFB | SUU-P371S & Z (14) |
| Travis AFB | SUU-P379A & B (14) |
| Travis AFB | SUU-P379D (14) |
| McChord AFB | TCM-P6E7P (82) |
| Yokota AB | OKO-ZJ82A (128) |
| Yokota AB | OKO-VH51D (129) |

### UNSCHEDULED FLIGHTS

Frequent flights to Hickam AFB, HI (**HIK**); Kadena AB (Okinawa), JA (**DNA**); Osan AB, KR (**OSN**); Travis AFB, CA (**SUU**) and Yokota AB, JA (**OKO**). Call for destinations, routings and schedules.

# HAWAII

## BARKING SANDS PACIFIC MISSILE RANGE FACILITY (BKH/PHBK)

Air Ops, Bldg 300
Kekaha, Kauai, HI 96752-0128

**LOCATION:** Six miles west of Kekaha on Kaumualii Highway (HI-50 west). *USMRA: Page 129 (B-2). ML-ARM: (22°01'N/159°47'W).* LST: GMT-10:00. NMC: Lihue, 30 miles east. Main installation numbers: C-808-335-4111, D-315-471-6111.

**REGISTRATION INFO: C-808-335-4310, D-315-471-6310.** Air Ops, Bldg 300.

**TRAVELERS AID: Medical:** C-808-335-4203. **Security Police:** C-808-335-4649/4523.

**TML:** Lodging office, Building 1261, Tartar Drive, 0700-1600 daily, C-808-335-4383, D-315-471-6752, Fax: C-808-335-4194; Beach cottages C-808-335-4752. DV/VIP: C-808-335-4752.

**SUPPORT AVAILABLE: Exchange:** C-808-336-4300.

**ATTRACTIONS:** Beaches, hiking and camping; beautiful countryside, views, sunsets, Kalalau lookout. Nicknamed wettest spot on earth and the garden island.

### UNSCHEDULED FLIGHTS

Flights to Hickam AFB, HI (**HIK**) via C-130H aircraft. Call for destinations, routings and schedules.

## HICKAM AIR FORCE BASE (HIK/PHIK)

635th AMSS/TRP
865 O'Malley Blvd
Hickam Air Force Base, HI 96853-5152

**LOCATION:** Adjacent to the Honolulu International Airport. Accessible from H-1 eixt 5 or Nimitz Highway south. Main gate on Vandenberg Blvd. Clearly marked. *USMRA: Page 129 (D-7) and Page 131 (B,C-3,4). ML-ARM: (21°18'N/157°50'W).* LST: GMT-10:00. NMC: Honolulu HI, 6 miles east. Main installation numbers: C-808-449-7110, D-315-449-7110.

**REGISTRATION INFO: C-808-449-1515, D-315-449-1515, Rec: C-808-449-1854/6833, D-315-449-1854/6833, Fax: C-808-448-1503, D-315-448-1503. E-mail: 635amss.prps@hickam.af.mil WEB: www2.hickam.af.mil/spacea.html** (You should receive an automated reply via e-mail after signing up for space-a on this website. Call or fax if there is no e-mail acknowledgment.) Bldg 2028, 24 hours daily. Directions: From main gate straight to Pax Term on left. **Pax Service Office:** Bldg 2028, Hours: 0730-1700 daily, C-808-449-1581, D-315-449-1581. **Pax Paging:** Bldg 2028, 24 hours daily, C-808-449-1515, D-315-449-1515. Also manages departures and arrivals at Honolulu IAP (HNL).

**PAX LOUNGES:** Bldg 2028. USO lounge open 24 hours daily. **General:** Bldg 2028, 24 hours daily, C-808-449-2887. A/C, free TV, restrooms, bag check/lockers, game room, cribs, pay telephones. No food in lounge. **DV/VIP:** Bldg 2028, 24 hours daily, C-808-449-1153. A/C, free TV, restrooms. **Protocol Service:** Bldg 1102, duty hours, C-808-449-1781.

**FOOD SERVICE: Cafeteria:** Bldg 2028, Hours: 0400-2000 Mon, Wed, Thu; 0300-2000 Tue, Fri; 0600-1900 Sat; 0600-1300 Sun; C-808-422-8000. **Dining Hall:** Bldg 1860, Hours: 0530-1800 daily, C-808-449-1666. **NCO Club:** Tradewinds Bldg. 422, Hours: 0630-2100 daily, C-808-449-1188/1092/1292. **O Club:** Bldg 901, Hours: 1115-2100 daily, C-808-449-1998/1592. **Restaurants:** Sea Breeze, Hours: 1100-2100 Tue-Sun, C-808-449-9909. **Snack Bars:** Sub Stop, Bldg.1113, Hours: 0700-2230 daily, C-808-422-5335. **Vending:** Bldg 2028, 24 hours daily, C-808-422-8000 (pay telephone available).

**TRANSPORTATION: Air Tickets:** SATO, Bldg 1113, Hours: 0800-1700 Mon-Fri, C-808-422-0548; Bldg 2028, Hours: 0800-1600 Mon-Sat, C-808-422-2729. **On Base Bus (Comm):** Bldg 2028, Hours: 0600-0100 Mon-Fri (every 20 minutes), C-808-531-1611, Bus #19-HIK, Term, $1.00 (exact amount only); Hours: 0635-2315 weekends (every 30 minutes). *Note: No large luggage.* **On Base Car Rental:** Bldg 2028, Hours: 0700-2000 daily, C-808-422-6915 (EBF/AAFES). **On Base Shuttle/Bus:** Bldg 2028, Hours: 0600-1800 Mon-Fri (every 15 minutes), C-808-449-1742 (key base points). **Taxi (Comm):** 24 hours daily, C-808-422-2222. **Taxi (Gov):** Motor Pool, 24 hours daily, C-808-449-1742 (duty pax only). **Parking:** Northwest of Term, 24 hours daily, 30-day long term parking available, check with passenger agents.

**TML:** Lodging office, Building 1153, 15 G Street, 24 hours daily, C-808-448-5400, D-315-448-5400. Fax: C-808-254-2716. Hale Koa, C-1-800-367-6027, D-315-438-6739.

**TRAVELERS AID: Chaplain:** Bldg 1750, Hours: 0730-1640 daily, C-808-449-1754/6562 (all faiths). **Emergency Relief:** Bldg 1102, 24 hours daily, C-808-449-5987 (Air Force Aid); Bldg 1514, 24 hours daily, C-808-423-1314 (Navy Relief-Pearl Harbor). **Lost/Found:** Bldg 2028, 24 hours daily, C-808-449-5353. **Medical:** Bldg 559, 24 hours daily, C-808-449-5248/9908, D-315-471-5248/9908 (Tripler AMC). **Red Cross:** Pearl Harbor Bldg. 1514, 24 hours daily, C-808-471-3155. **Security Police:** Bldg 1004, 24 hours daily, C-808-449-6372 (Desk Sgt). **USO:** Bldg 2028, 24 hours daily, C-808-449-1850/3351.

**SUPPORT AVAILABLE: Exchange:** Bldg 2028, Hours: 0700-2000 Mon-Fri, 0600-1900 Sat, 0600-1300 Sun, C-808-422-8400 (Main BX); Bldg 1232, C-808-423-1304. **Bank:** First Hawaii Bank, Bldg 1242, Hours: 0800-1500 Mon-Thu, 0800-1800 Fri, C-808-422-2781. **Hair Styles:** Bldg 1232; Barber, Hours: 0930-1800 Mon-Fri, C-808-422-4045; Beauty, Hours: 0930-1700 Mon-Sat, C-808-422-6121. **Laundry/Dry Cleaning:** Bldg 1232, Hours:

Mon-Fri: 0930-1800, Sat: 0930-1700, C-808-422-5821/5555. **Postal Service:** Bldg 2097, Hours: 0830-1500 Mon-Fri, C-808-449-9480, C-808-422-6435.

**OTHER INFORMATION:** Port of Entry and U.S. Customs Service Airport.

**ATTRACTIONS:** Honolulu, Waikiki beach, and Pearl Harbor.

### HICKAM AFB, HI (BKH); REGION: PAC; OPERATOR: AMC; TYPE: CGO W/ PAX; ROUTE: 8H43A; SAMPLE SCHEDULE: 3RD THU; EQUIPMENT: C130H

{HIK *SE* → KWA ⇌ KWA *NW* → HIK}

| LI/ICAO | AIRPORT/STATION | CTRY/STA | DAYS EN ROUTE |
|---|---|---|---|
| HIK/PHIK | Hickam AFB | HI | +0 |
| KWA/PKWA | Bucholz AAF KMR | KA | +1 |
| KWA/PKWA | Bucholz AAF KMR | KA | +1 |
| HIK/PHIK | Hickam AFB | HI | |

### HICKAM AFB, HI (BKH); REGION: PAC; OPERATOR: AMC; TYPE: CGO W/ PAX; ROUTE: 8H45A; SAMPLE SCHEDULE: THU; EQUIPMENT: C130H

{HIK *SE* → JON ⇌ JON *NW* → HIK}

| LI/ICAO | AIRPORT/STATION | CTRY/STA | DAYS EN ROUTE |
|---|---|---|---|
| HIK/PHIK | Hickam AFB | HI | +0 |
| JON/PJON | Johnston Atoll | JO | +1 |
| JON/PJON | Johnston Atoll | JO | +1 |
| HIK/PHIK | Hickam AFB | HI | |

## EN ROUTE SCHEDULES

| AIRPORT/STATION | LI-MISSION (page #) |
|---|---|
| March ARB | RIV-5J43B (10) |
| Travis AFB | SUU-ZJ43A (13) |
| Travis AFB | SUU-P371C (14) |
| Travis AFB | SUU-P371F & G (14) |
| Travis AFB | SUU-P371S & Z (14) |
| Travis AFB | SUU-P379A & B (14) |
| Travis AFB | SUU-P379D (14) |
| McGuire AFB | WRI-TQP5J (50) |
| Memphis IAP | MEM-IDB7B & 7D45A (70) |
| McChord AFB | TCM-T679F (82) |
| McChord AFB | TCM-TU79A (82) |
| McChord AFB | TCM-P6E1P (82) |
| McChord AFB | TCM-P6E7P (82) |
| McChord AFB | TCM-P6PXF (83) |
| McChord AFB | TCM-PUPXE (83) |
| Yokota AB | OKO-ZJ82A (128) |
| Yokota AB | OKO-TQP5V (128) |

## UNSCHEDULED FLIGHTS

Frequent flights to CONUS and Pacific area via C-130H and KC-135R aircraft.

## HICKAM AFB (HIK/PHIK)



1. Officers' Club
2. USAF Clinic
3. Base Chapel
4. Tradewinds Club
5. Class VI
6. Bowling Center and Gym
7. Billeting Office
8. Service Station
9. Commissary
10. Base Exchange
11. Burger King
12. Air Terminal
13. Chapel 2
14. Shoppette
15. Short Term Parking

Pax Terminal
Food
Lodging
Parking
Medical
Chapel

© 2001 Military Living Publications

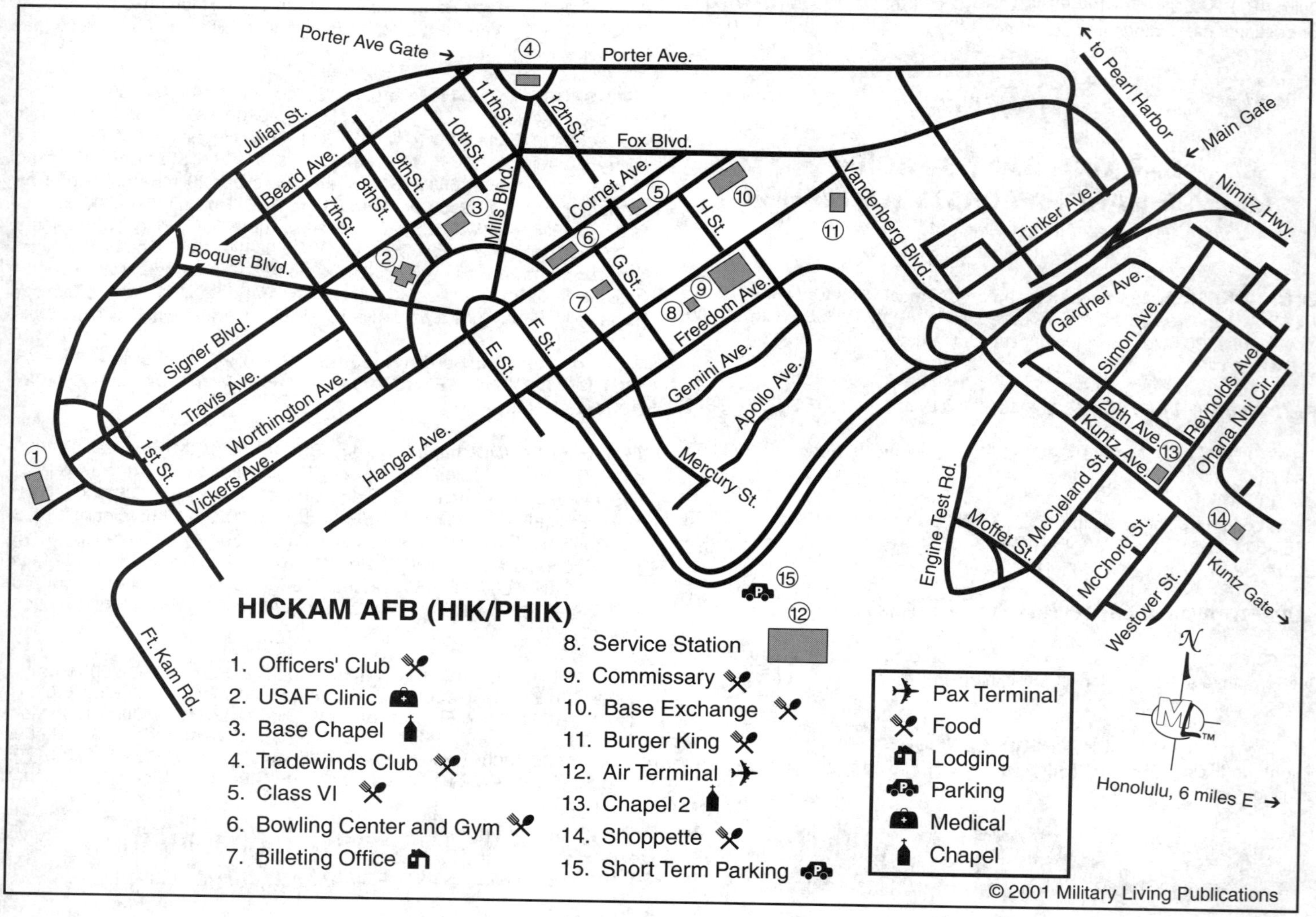

# KANEOHE BAY
## MARINE CORPS BASE (NGF/PHNG)
Commanding Officer
MCAF/MCBH
Attn: OPS/Flight Clearance
P.O. Box 63061
Kaneohe Bay, HI 96863-3061

**LOCATION:** At the end of H-3 on the Windward (east) side of Oahu. From Honolulu IAP: Take H-1 west to H-3 interchange. Take H-3 east to Kaneohe, continue to main gate. Off Mokapu Blvd and Kaneohe Bay Drive. Follow H-3 to Main Gate, left at first intersection (3rd Street), left at next 3-way intersection (1st Street), follow 1st Street past Hangars 1-4, when H105 is reached, park behind Hangar. Locate Flight Clearance next to the Weather Service. *USMRA: Page 129 (E-6). ML-ARM: (21°26'N/157°46'W).* LST: GMT-10:00. NMC: Honolulu, 14 miles southwest. Main installation numbers: C-808-449-7100, D-315-430-0110.

**REGISTRATION INFO: C-808-257-1604, D-315-457-1604. Rec: C-808-257-0777, D-315-457-0777.**

**FOOD SERVICE: Cafeteria:** Anderson Hall, Hours: 0600-0800 Breakfast, 1000-1300 Lunch, 1600-1800 Dinner, C-808-257-1310, D-315-457-1310, 1 mile away. **Fast Food:** McDonald's - C-808-254-4053, Subway - C-808-254-2468, Taco Bell - C-808-254-7090. Hours: 0530-2300 Mon-Sat, 0600-2300 Sun, 0.75 miles away. **Snack Bars:** K-Bay Lanes (Bowling Alley), 1100-2300 daily, C-808-254-7693, 0.5 miles away. **Snack Vending:** Hours: 0730-1630, C-808-254-7682, 0.5 miles away.

**TRANSPORTATION: On Base Car Rental:** Enterprise, C-808-254-0808, 1 mile away. **Off Base Car Rental:** Budget, C-808-537-3600; Enterprise, 808-247-2909; Sears, C-808-599-2205. **Off Base Limo:** Aloha Limousines, C-1-800-345-9344, C-808-955-0055. **On Base Shuttle/Bus:** C-808-848-5555, 1 mile away. **Off Base Shuttle/Bus:** C-808-848-5555, 3-4 miles away. **On Base Taxi:** C-808-257-1431, D-315-457-1431, 1 mile away. **Off Base Taxi:** C-808-422-2222.

**TML:** Lodging office, Building 3038, 0630-1800 Mon-Fri, 0900-1800 Sat-Sun, Holidays, C-808-254-2806; BOQ: 24 hours daily, C-808-257-1317, D-312-457-1317; BEQ: 24 hours daily C-808-257-3470, D-312-457-3470. Beach cottages-C-808-254-2716. DV/VIP: C-808-257-1827.

**RVC:** Special Services, Check-in, Bldg 219 (no Check-in or out on holidays), C-808-254-7667 (campsite), C-808-254-2716 (cottages).

**TRAVELERS AID: Chaplain:** Hours: 0730-1630 Mon-Fri, C-808-257-3552, D-315-457-3552, 1.5 miles away. **Dental:** Hours: 0730-1630, C-808-257-3100, 0.5 miles away. **Medical:** Hours: 0730-1630, C-808-257-3126, 0.5 miles away. **Red Cross:** Hours: 0600-2400, C-808-471-3155. **Security Police:** 24 hours daily, C-808-257-2123, D-315-457-2123, 0.5 miles away. **Travelers Aid:** Hours: 0830-0500, C-808-24-3581.

**SUPPORT AVAILABLE: Bank/Currency Exchange:** Hours: 0900-1500 Mon-Thu, 00900-1600 Fri, C-808-254-1551, 0.5 miles away. **Convenience Store:** Hours: 0600-2200 Mon-Fri, 0730-2200 Sat-Sun, C-808-254-7644, 0.75 miles away. **Credit Union:** Hours: 0930-1700 Mon-Fri, C-808-254-6455, 0.5 miles away. **Dry Cleaner:** Hours: 0800-1800 Mon-Fri, 1000-1700 Sat, C-808-254-3392, 1.5 miles away. **Exchange:** Hours: 1000-2000 Mon-Fri, 1000-1700 Sat-Sun, C-808-254-3890, 1.5 miles away. **Laundry:** Hours: 0800-1800 Mon-Fri, 1000-1700 Sat, C-808-254-3392, 1.5 miles away. **Postal Service:** Hours: 0800-1515 Mon-Fri, C-808-257-2008, D-315-457-2008, 0.5 miles away.

**OTHER INFORMATION:** A Military Port of Entry.

### UNSCHEDULED FLIGHTS
Frequent flights via P-003C, UP-003A and C-20G aircraft to North Island NAS, CA (**NZY**), Miramar MCAS, CA (**NKX**) and other West Coast destinations. Also flights to: Futenma MCAS, JP (**NFO**) and Atsugi NAF, JP (**NJA**). Call for destinations, routings and schedules.

## Other Hawaii Installations with Possible Space-A Air Opportunities

**WHEELER ARMY AIRFIELD (HHI/PHHI),** 25 ID (Light) AVN Support, Wheeler Army Airfield, HI 96854-5000. **LOCATION:** Off H-2 or HI-99 in the center of the island of Oahu. Adjacent to and south of Schofield Barracks. Kunra Gate from HI-750. *USMRA: Page 129 (C-6). ML-ARM: (21°28'N/158°02'W).* LST: GMT-10:00. NMC: Honolulu, 20 miles southeast. Main installation numbers: C-808-449-7110, D-315-471-7110. Support available here and at adjacent Schofield Barracks. **TML:** Nearest TML is at Schofield Barracks. The Inn at Schofield Barracks, 563 Kolekole Avenue, C-808-624-9650, 1-800-490-9638, D-315-624-9650, Fax: C-808-624-5606, E-mail: theinn@aloha.com 24 hours daily. See Military Living's *U.S. Forces Travel Guide to U.S. Military Installations* for more information. Infrequent flights via C-21 to other islands. Call for destinations, routings and schedules.

# PACIFIC ISLANDS

# WAKE ISLAND ARMY AIRFIELD (AWK/PWAK)
Terminal Building
Operation Manager
Wake Island, HI 96898-5000

**LOCATION:** A U.S. island in the Mid-Pacific, 2300 air miles west of Hawaii. *ML-ARM (18°30'N/166°45'E).* LST: GMT-12:00. NMC: Honolulu, 2300 air miles southeast. Main installation numbers: C-808-424-2101, D-315-424-2101.

**REGISTRATION INFO: C-808-424-2210, D-315-424-2210. Fax: C-808-424-2190, D-315-424-2190.** Base Ops, 24 hours daily, ext 101. All arrivals via air. Letter of approval from base commander required for all Active Duty/non-Active Duty visitor. All Space-A pax processed by Base Ops. **Pax Service Office:** Base Ops, Hours: 0800-1700 Mon-Sat, ext 2101.

**PAX LOUNGES:** Terminal Building, 1st Floor, Hours: 0800-1700 Mon-Sat, ext 424-2210. A/C, telephones (commercial), restrooms, P/C seats. General lounge only.

**FOOD SERVICE:** Limited, ext 486. **Bar:** Drifters Reef, Bldg 1109, ext 424-2310.

**TRANSPORTATION: Shuttle/Bus (Gov):** Base Ops, ext 101. Term to support facilities.

**SUPPORT AVAILABLE: Exchange:** ext 310. **Postal Service:** ext 424-2259. Barber and Laundry available.

**TML:** Lodging Office, Building 1502, 0800-1700 Mon-Sat, C-808-424-2210, D-314-424-2210. Very limited.

**ATTRACTIONS:** Tropical climate and nice beaches.

### EN ROUTE SCHEDULES

| AIRPORT/STATION | LI-MISSION (page #) |
| --- | --- |
| McChord AFB | TCM-T679F (82) |
| McChord AFB | TCM-TU79A (82) |

### UNSCHEDULED FLIGHTS
Flights to Hickam AFB, HI (**HIK**) via C-130H aircraft. Call for destinations, routings and schedules.

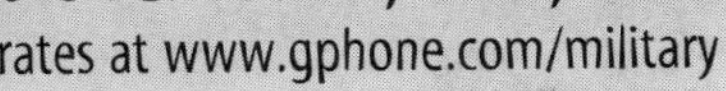

# OTHER UNITED STATES PACIFIC ISLANDS

**BUCHOLZ ARMY AIRFIELD/KMR (KWAJALEIN ATOLL), U.S. Army, KA (KWA/PKWA) (USA), Republic of the Marshall Islands,** Kwajalein Atoll/Kwajalein Missile Range, ATTN: CSSD-KA-IS, P.O. Box 26, APO AP 96555-2526. *ML-ARM: (8°45'N/167°45'E).* LST: GMT-12:00. NMC: Honolulu, HI. NMI: Hickam AFB, HI. For information contact Hickam AFB at **C-808-449-1515, D-315-449-1515, Rec: C-808-449-1854/6833, D-315-449-1854/6833, Fax: C-808-448-1503, D-315-448-1503.** Available: Open air passenger lounge, DV lounge, snack bar, combined club, limited bus service, transient hotel for official visitors only, nice beaches and excellent scuba diving. U.S. Customs Service Airport. ***Note: Permission/official approval required to visit KWA (see Appendix B).***

## EN ROUTE SCHEDULES

| AIRPORT/STATION | LI-MISSION (page #) |
|---|---|
| March ARB | RIV-5J43B (10) |
| Travis AFB | SUU-ZJ43A (13) |
| Hickam AFB | HIK-8H43A (6) |

**JOHNSTON ATOLL, JO (JON/PJON) (USA),** FCDSWA Term Ops JQ/AMC REP, Johnston Atoll, APO AP 96558-5000. *ML-ARM: (16°00'N/160°30'W).* LST: GMT-11:00. **C-808-621-3044 ext 2252. D-314-441-2252, Fax: C-808-621-3044/2343, D-314-441-2343.** ***Note: Permission/official approval required to visit Johnston Atoll (see Appendix B).***

## EN ROUTE SCHEDULES

| AIRPORT/STATION | LI-MISSION (page #) |
|---|---|
| Travis AFB | SUU-ZJ43A (13) |
| Memphis IAP | MEM-IDB7B & 7D45A (70) |
| Hickam AFB | HIK-8H45A (96) |

# PUERTO RICO

## BORINQUEN COAST GUARD AIR STATION (BQN/TJBQ)

CGAS Borinquen
Aquadilla, PR 00604-5000

***Note: Present Commander has suspended Space-A service at press time for an indefinite period.***

**LOCATION:** At the old Ramey Air Force Base, north of Aguadilla. Take PR-22/2 west from San Juan or north from Mayaguez to PR-110 north of CGAS. Main gate is at the end of Wing Road, just past 5th Street. *USMRA: Page 130 (B,C-2). ML-ARM: (18°29'N/67°07'W).* LST: GMT-04:00. NMC: San Juan PR, 65 miles east. Main installation numbers: C-787-890-8400, D-313-831-3385.

**REGISTRATION INFO: C-787-890-8420.** CG hangar, Hours: 0800-1600 Mon-Fri, Station hangar adjacent to main gate. Directions to parking provided by gate guard. Pax gather in training room next to maintenance control in the southeast corner of the hangar. A/C, bag check, restrooms, telephones, TV. **DV/VIP:** Officers' wardroom on second floor in the northeast corner of the hangar. A/C, restrooms, TV. Commuter flights available between San Juan and Mayaguez. Taxi from Mayaguez to Aquadilla. SATO office available.

**TML:** Lodging office, La Plaza, Room 26. 0800-1600 Mon-Fri, C-787-890-8492. Fax: C-787-890-8493. There are 14 guest houses and two VIP cottages. E-mail: mwrbqn@aol.com

**RVC:** Lighthouse reservations, C-787-890-8492, Fax: C-787-890-8493.

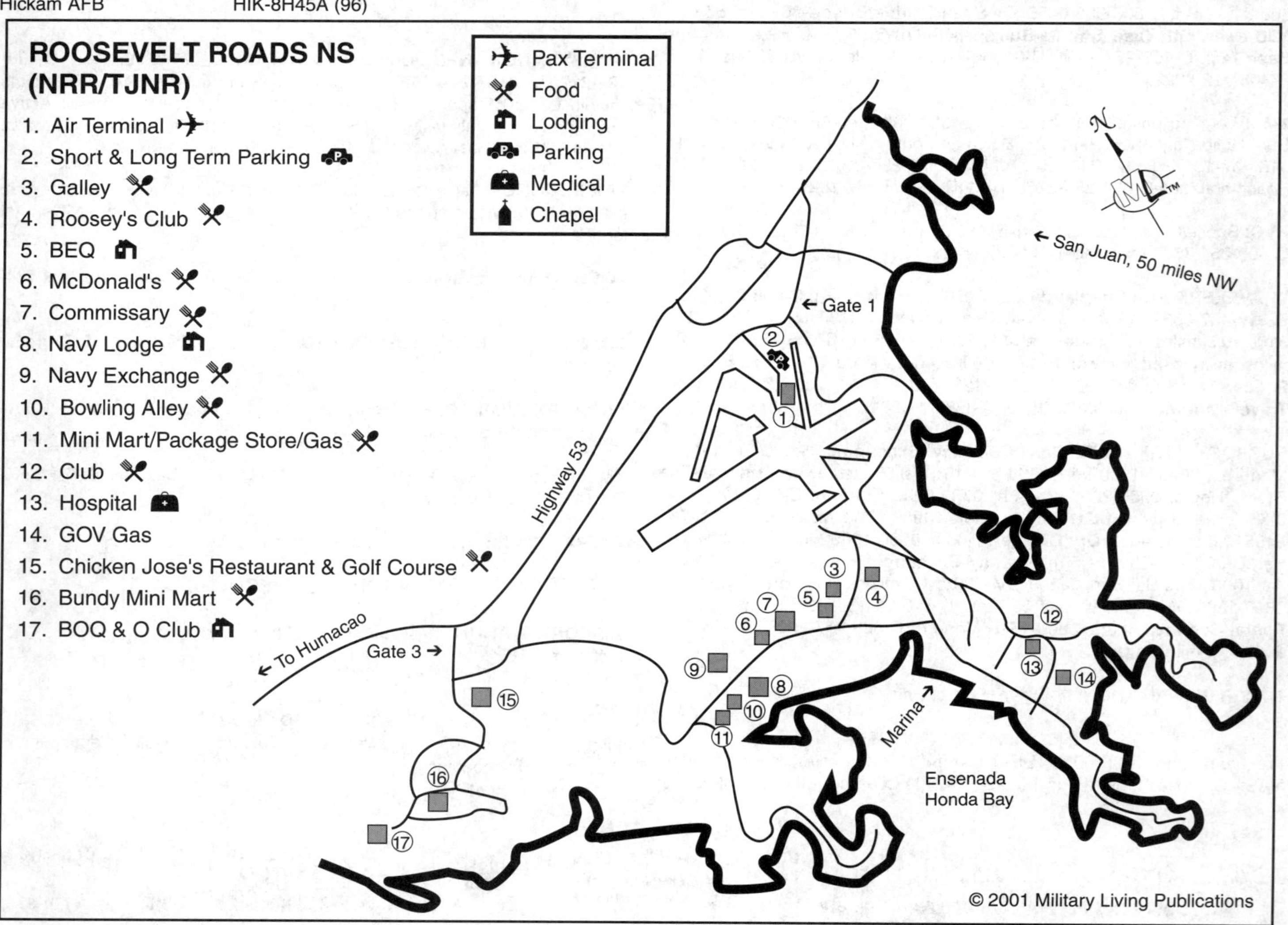

**TRAVELERS AID: Medical:** Housing Area, 24 hours daily, ext 8514. Active Duty only.

**SUPPORT AVAILABLE: Cafeteria:** C-787-882-7109, in airport terminal. **Exchange:** 787-890-3127 ext 3127.

**ATTRACTIONS:** Local beaches (excellent surfing, diving, snorkeling, wind surfing, sailing, flying) and restaurants.

### UNSCHEDULED FLIGHTS

Flights to CONUS and OCONUS locations via C-130H aircraft on logistical and administrative flights. Call for destinations, routings and schedules.

## ROOSEVELT ROADS
## NAVAL STATION (NRR/TJNR)

Air Terminal Division
PSC 1008, Box 3002
FPO AA 34051-3002

**LOCATION:** From Luis Munoz Marin IAP, San Juan left (east) onto PR-3 for 45 miles, sign on right indicating exit to Naval Station. *USMRA: Page 130 (F-2,3).* *ML-ARM: (18°15'N/65°40'W).* LST: GMT-04:00. NMC: San Juan, 50 miles northwest. Main installation numbers: C-787-865-2000, D-313-831-2000.

**REGISTRATION INFO: C-787-865-4383, D-313-831-4388, Rec: C-787-865-3257, D-313-831-3257, Fax: C-787-865-3257, D-313-831-3251. WEB:** www.navstarr.navy.mil (go to AMC Terminal Link). Bldg 426, Hours: 0700-1600 Mon-Fri, 1 hour prior to show time on weekends and holidays. Directions: From main gate straight to first right to Air Ops on left. **Pax Service Office:** C-787-865-4383/4263, D-313-831-4383/4263.

**PAX LOUNGES: General:** Bldg 426, Hours: 0700-1600 daily, C-787-865-4383. A/C, bag check, restrooms, TV, P/C seats. **DV/VIP Lounge:** Bldg 426, Hours: 0700-1600 daily, C-787-865-4383.

**FOOD SERVICE: Cafeteria:** Bldg 426, Hours: 0700-1600 Mon-Fri. **Dining Hall:** Anchor Inn, STOP 5, Hours: 0545-0130 daily, C-787-865-4138/9. **Fast Food:** Chicken Jose, located in the golf course building; McDonald's, near NEX. **Food Court:** STOP 21, NEX. **O Club:** STOP 3, Hours: 1100-2400 daily, C-787-865-3342. **Restaurants:** Woodys, Hours: 1700-2300 Tue-Thu, 1800-0100 Fri-Sat, C-181-865-4142. **Snack Bars:** Bldg 426, Hours: 0700-1400 daily. **Snack Vending:** Bldg 426, 24 hours daily.

**TRANSPORTATION: Air Tickets:** SATO, Hours: 0800-1500 Mon-Fri, C-787-865-1539/1570. **Car Rentals:** Hertz, Hours: 0800-1630 daily, C-787-885-3660/3580 (Drop off at terminal); NEX Car Rental, Hours: 1000-1800 Mon, Tue, Sat, 1000-1900 Thu-Fri, 1000-1600 Sun, C-787-865-3308; World Car Rental and Leasing, Hours: 0800-1700 daily, C-787-865-4495/2655. **On Base Shuttle/Bus:** Bldg 426, every half hour, C-787-865-4013, 1 block away. **Off Base Taxi:** C-787-860-1112. **On Base Taxi:** Bldg 426, 24 hours daily, C-787-865-7444. **Parking:** Air Term, 24 hours daily, C-787-865-4011 (see Security Police).

**TML:** Lodging office, CBQ: C-787-865-4358; Navy Lodge C-787-865-8282, Fax: C-787-865-8283. DV/VIP: C-787-865-3364.

**TRAVELERS AID: Chaplain:** STOP 17, C-787-865-4326/8. **Emergency Relief:** STOP 12, Hours: 0800-1600 Mon-Fri, C-787-865-3210 (Navy Relief). **Lost/Found:** Air Ops Bldg, Hours: 0630-1800 Mon-Sat, C-787-865-4383 (Pax Service NCO). **Medical:** Naval Hospital, 24 hours daily, C-787-865-4144, D-313-831-4144 (emergency); C-787-865-4133 (appointment). **Red Cross:** STOP 19, Hours: 0800-1600 Mon-Fri, C-787-865-5134; after hours, C-787-865-2000. **Security Police:** Gate 1, 24 hours daily, C-787-865-4011 (Desk Sgt). **USO:** STOP 6, Hours: 0800-2300 daily, C-787-865-7350/7275, near Pier 3.

**SUPPORT AVAILABLE: Bank/Currency Exchange:** NFCU: STOP 18, Hours: 0900-1700 Tue-Fri, 0900-1400 Sat, C-787-865-8630. **Exchange:** STOP 21, Hours: 1000-1700 Mon-Fri, 1000-1600 Sat, C-787-865-4365. **Hair Styles:** STOP 21, Hours: 0830-1700 Mon-Fri, 0830-1630 Sat, C-787-865-3465. **Laundry/Dry Cleaning:** STOP 21, Hours: 1000-1700 Mon-Sat, C-787-865-3484. **Postal Service:** STOP 6, Hours: 0900-1500 Mon-Fri, C-787-865-4335.

**ATTRACTIONS:** El Yunque rain forest, Old San Juan, beaches, water sports, waterfalls, hiking, restaurants, 9-hole golf course, malls, cruises, scenic views.

### EN ROUTE SCHEDULES

| AIRPORT/STATION | LI-MISSION (page #) |
| --- | --- |
| Peterson AFB | COS-OPN3B (16) |
| Allen C Thompson (Jackson) | JAN-IKM3A (44) |
| McGuire AFB | WRI-A7N1B (51) |
| Pope AFB | POB-ACN1A (57) |
| Pope AFB | POB-ACN1B (57) |
| Wright-Patterson AFB | FFO-OEM3A (61) |
| Wright-Patterson AFB | FFO-OEM3B (61) |
| Wright-Patterson AFB | FFO-OEN1B (61) |
| Charleston AFB/IAP | CHS-A4M3A (67) |
| Dyess AFB | DYS-A1N1B (73) |
| General Mitchell IAP/ARS | GMF-OTN3C (86) |

### UNSCHEDULED FLIGHTS

Frequent flights to U.S. Virgin Islands, St. Croix and St. Thomas. Also other administrative flights. Call for destinations, routings and schedules.

## Other Puerto Rico Installations with Possible Space-A Air Opportunities

**LUIS MUNOZ MARIN INTERNATIONAL AIRPORT (SJU/TJSJ),** Munoz ANGB, 156th Fighter Wing/ANG, San Juan, PR 00914-5000. **LOCATION:** Leaving main terminal of airport, follow sign for town of Catalina. Pass two exits on right and watch for sign for Base Munoz. Go straight at light at McDonald's to base; about 5-10 minutes from airport. *USMRA: Page 130 (E-2).* *ML-ARM: (18°26'N/66°00'W).* LST: GMT-04:00. **C-787-253-7629, Fax: C-787-253-7437.** Call for destinations, routings and schedules. Flights via C-130H aircraft. **TML:** Nearest TML is at Fort Buchanan, Building 678, 24 hours daily, C-787-792-7977, D-313-740-3633. Fax: C-787-707-3939. DV/VIP C-787-740-5047.

## U.S. VIRGIN ISLANDS

## ALEXANDER HAMILTON AIRPORT (STX/TISX)

Army Aviation Operating Facility
VI National Guard
P.O. Box 2270, Kingshill
St Croix, VI 00851-2270

**LOCATION:** On the south central coast of the island of St Croix. *USMRA: Page 130 (H-4).* *ML-ARM: (17°25'N/64°50'W).* LST: GMT-04:00. NMC: Christiansted, Virgin Island, 8 miles northeast. Main installation numbers: C-340-778-2884.

**REGISTRATION INFO: C-340-778-9261 or 340-712-7890, Fax: C-340-778-2165.** Virgin Islands Army National Guard Hangar, Hours: 0730-1630 Mon-Fri (west end ramp).

**PAX LOUNGES:** General lounge available. Commercial Pax Term. All support facilities can be used. No separate military lounges. All flights handled through Ops Division. Emergency, call office of the Adjutant General, C-340-712-7935. There are no U.S. military facilities, including TML, available for Space-A passengers.

**TRANSPORTATION: Car Rental:** C-340-778-9355/1402/0450. **Taxi:** C-340-778-1088.

**SUPPORT AVAILABLE:** Exchange: C-340-773-6570.

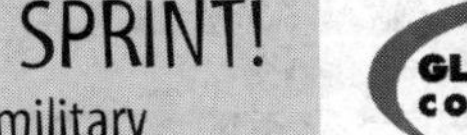

**OTHER INFORMATION:** Port of Entry and U.S. Customs Service Airport.

**ATTRACTIONS:** Fort Christian, Fort Fredrick, Whim Great House, Buc Island National Park, East End Castle, Point Udall and Botanical Garden.

### EN ROUTE SCHEDULES

| AIRPORT/STATION | LI-MISSION (page #) |
|---|---|
| Peterson AFB | COS-OPN3B (16) |
| Allen C Thompson (Jackson) | JAN-IKH5A (44) |
| McGuire AFB | WRI-A7N1B (51) |
| Wright-Patterson AFB | FFO-OEB1D (61) |
| Wright-Patterson AFB | FFO-OEH3B (61) |
| Wright-Patterson AFB | FFO-OEK5C (61) |
| Charleston AFB/IAP | CHS-A4P3A (67) |
| Memphis IAP | MEM-IDB3B (71) |
| Memphis IAP | MEM-IDB5A (71) |
| General Mitchell IAP/ARS | GMF-OTN3C (86) |

### UNSCHEDULED FLIGHTS

Frequent flights to Roosevelt Roads, PR **(NRR/TJNR).** Call for destinations, routings and schedules.

## Other Virgin Island Installations with Possible Space-A Air Opportunities

**CYRIL E. KING AIRPORT (STT/TIST),** Charlotte Amalie, VI. **C-340-774-5100, Fax: C-340-774-0186. LOCATION:** From Jackson Drive, follow signs to airport. *USMRA: Page 130 (H-4). ML-ARM: (18°20'N/64°58'W).* LST: GMT-04:00. Infrequent flights. Call for destinations, routings and schedules.

# FOREIGN COUNTRIES

## AFRICAN CONTINENT

### AFRICA STATIONS
**(Not listed separately in this book)**

The stations listed below have Space-A air opportunities. Base support facilities are provided by United States Embassies and are very limited. Passenger management is accomplished by U.S. Embassy, military or contractor personnel. Procedures for processing passengers at each station are the result of local conditions and services available. Stations in most cases are located at International Airports which have all essential facilities and services for international travelers. Defense telephone service is not available. **See Appendix B for personnel entrance requirements.**

**DAKAR LEOPOLD S. SENGHOR AIRPORT, (Senegal) SN (DKR/GOOY),** USDAO Dakar, Department of State, Washington, D.C. 20521-2130. Dakar, SN. *ML-ARM: (14°45'N/17°30'W).* LST: GMT-01:00. **Location:** On the western most point Africa, opposite the Cape Verde Islands. **REGISTRATION INFO: C-011-221-823-4296/7384, Fax: C: 011-221-822-2991.** Flights coordinated by USDAO, Hours: 0800-1700 daily. **Pax Lounge:** All facilities of local airport available. DV lounge for official visitors only (General Officer and above). **TRANSPORTATION:** Rental cars available at airport, reservations are recommended. Rental cars are also available through most hotels. Taxis are available. Buses are not recommended. **Travelers Aid:** USDAO, C-011-221-823-4296/7384.

#### EN ROUTE SCHEDULES

| AIRPORT/STATION | LI-MISSION (page #) |
| --- | --- |
| Charleston AFB/IAP | CHS-A4P3A (67) |

**JOMO KENYATTA INTERNATIONAL AIRPORT, (Kenya) KE (NBO/HKNA)** Kenya U.S. Liaison Office (KUSLO), Unit 64101, APO AE 09831-4101. **REGISTRATION INFO: C-011-254-2-537-800 ext 3391/2/3/4/5/6/7/8/9, Fax: C-011-254-2-537-810.** U.S. Embassy is located at the corner of Moi Avenue and Haille Sellasic Avenue. Essential services of a local airport available. *ML-ARM: (01°19'S/36°56'E).* LST: GMT+02:00. **Location:** Nairobi, Kenya.

#### EN ROUTE SCHEDULES

| AIRPORT/STATION | LI-MISSION (page #) |
| --- | --- |
| Charleston AFB/IAP | CHS-A4P3A (67) |

**KINSHASA N'DJILI AIRPORT, (Democratic Republic of the Congo) ZR (FIH/FZAA),** Operations Coordinator, USDAO Kinshasa, Unit 31550, APO AE 09828-3900. Kinshasa, Democratic Republic of The Congo (formerly Zaire). *ML-ARM: (04°23'S/15°26'E).* LST: GMT+01:00. **Location:** In central Africa near west coast. Kinshasa is on Zaire river 225 miles northeast of the Atlantic Ocean. Airport is 15 miles southeast of Kinshasa, ZA. **REGISTRATION INFO: C-011-243-12-21804/21807, Fax: C: 011-243-88-46592.** Passengers processed by USDAO/OPSCO. Hours: 0700-1600 Mon-Sat, GMT. No facilities at airport.

**N'DJAMENA INTERNATIONAL AIRPORT, (Chad) TD (NDJ/FTTS),** U.S. Embassy, B.P., 413 Rue Felix Eboue, N'Djamena, Chad. *ML-ARM: (12°07'S/15°02'E).* LST: GMT+01:00. **Location:** in central Africa, 75 miles southeast of Lake Chad. **REGISTRATION INFO: C: 011-235-51-70-09/90-52, Fax: C-011-235-51-56-54.** Pax processed by USDAO personnel. **USDAO N'Djamena, Department of State, State Pouch Room, Washington, D.C. 20521-2410. Pax Lounge:** All facilities of local airport are available but limited.

#### EN ROUTE SCHEDULES

| AIRPORT/STATION | LI-MISSION (page #) |
| --- | --- |
| Charleston AFB/IAP | CHS-A4P3A (67) |

**NIAMEY INTERNATIONAL AIRPORT, (Niger) NE (NIM/DRRN),** USOMC AmEmbassy Niamey, State Department Pouch Room, Washington, D.C. 20521-2420, **Location:** In north central Africa on the Niger River, *ML-ARM: (13°29'N/02°10'E).* LST: GMT+00:00. **REGISTRATION INFO: C-011-227-72-26-61/62/63/64, ext 262 or 245, Fax: C-011-227-73-31-67. Email: usemb@intnet.ne** Hours: 0800-1630 Local Time. **Pax Lounge:** Airport has transit lounge which serves sandwiches and drinks. No lodging at the airport. The AmEmbassy is located on Rue Des Ambassades, B.P. 11201. Space-A travel is managed by the Office of Military Cooperation.

**WATERKLOOF AIR FORCE BASE, (South Africa) ZA (LMB/FAWK),** USDAO Pretoria, Department of State, Washington, D.C. 20521-9300, **Location:** South Africa, south of Pretoria, near town of Lyttleton, next to the highway to Jan Smuts (FAJS), Johannesburg IAP, *ML-ARM: (25°50'S/28°13'E).* LST: GMT+01:00. NMC: Pretoria 10 km NW. **REGISTRATION INFO: C-011-27-12-342-1048 (ask for USDAO), Fax C-011-27-12-342-2244/2090.** Support facilities of a major South Africa Air Force Base.

#### EN ROUTE SCHEDULES

| AIRPORT/STATION | LI-MISSION (page #) |
| --- | --- |
| Charleston AFB/IAP | CHS-A4P3A (67) |

**YAOUNDE/NSIMALEN INTERNATIONAL AIRPORT, (Cameroon) CM (NSI/FKYS),** USDAO, Pouch Address: American Embassy, Department of State, Washington, D.C. 20521-2520. **Location:** Capital of Cameroon. In central west africa on the Gulf of Guinea. *ML-ARM: 03 50'N/11 31'E.* LST: GMT+00:00. NMC: In the city of Yaounde. **REGISTRATION INFO: Tel: C-011-237-22-03-17; Fax: C-011-237-22-51-89. WEB: usembassy@ state.gov/yaounde** Support facilities of an international airport are available.

#### EN ROUTE SCHEDULES

| AIRPORT/STATION | LI-MISSION (page #) |
| --- | --- |
| Charleston AFB/IAP | CHS-A4P3A (67) |

## ANTIGUA & BARBUDA

### V.C. BIRD INTERNATIONAL AIRPORT (ST. JOHN'S) (SJH/TAPA)

Antigua Air Station, Box 4915
Patrick AFB, FL 32925-5000

**LOCATION:** Northeast side of island of Antigua. *ML-ARM: (17°08'N/61°47'W).* LST: GMT-04:00. NMC: St John's, Antigua, 9 miles west. Main installation numbers: C-268-462-0368/3223.

**REGISTRATION INFO: C-268-462-0368, D-313-985-1110 ext 225,** Antigua Term, Hours: 0730-1630 daily. All passenger info and sign up through Patrick AFB, FL, C-321-494-5631/5632, D-312-854-5631/5632, Fax: 321-494-7997, D-312-854-7991 Pax Term 1 mile from V.C. Bird IAP, Antigua. **Note: After sign-up, report to Pax Term at Antigua AS, not V.C. Bird IAP. Must have passport unless Active Duty.**

**PAX LOUNGES:** Limited facilities. **General:** Antigua Term, Hours: 0730-1630 daily, C-268-462-0368. A/C, restrooms, O/S seats.

**FOOD SERVICE: Satellite Club Snack Bar:** Hours: 1700-2200 daily, C-268-462-0368, D-313-985-1110 ext 225. **Note: Food service at Antigua AS is limited to breakfast on morning of departure flight and above snackbar; many choices off base.**

**TRANSPORTATION: Air Tickets:** C-268-462-0950/1 (AA). **Car Rentals:** Avis, C-268-462-2840; Hertz, C-268-462-6450. **Taxi (Comm):** C-268-462-3466.

**SUPPORT AVAILABLE:** Space-A travelers may use the Satellite Club snack bar and Satellite Club bar.

**ATTRACTIONS:** Great beaches, old forts, museums, casino gambling, sailing, and golf course.

## EN ROUTE SCHEDULES

| AIRPORT/STATION | LI-MISSION (page #) |
|---|---|
| Patrick AFB | COF-HJL3A (23) |
| Charleston AFB/IAP | CHS-G8L3A (67) |

### UNSCHEDULED FLIGHTS

Occasional flights from Patrick AFB, Fl (**COF**) and Roosevelt Roads NS, PR (**NRR**) via DC-8, C-17, or C-141. Call for destinations, routings and schedules.

# AUSTRALIA

## ALICE SPRINGS AIRPORT (ASP/YBAS)

Det 421, AMC Representative
APO AP 96548-0007

**LOCATION:** In the northern territory of AU, 1250 air miles northwest of Sydney, AU and 900 air miles south of Darwin, AU. *ML-ARM: (23°46'S/134°00'E)*. LST: GMT+09:30. NMC: Alice Springs, AU, 9.5 miles. Main installation number: C-011-618-8953-0310.

**REGISTRATION INFO: Contact Richmond RAAFB: C-011-61-89-530-570/633, Rec: C-011-61-89-530-570, Fax: C-011-61-89-534-175.** Note: Due to turn around and manifest requirements passengers arriving Alice Springs (ASP) from Raafb Richmond (RMC) may not return on the same mission to RCM. Directions: At the ASP airport. Pax Term, daylight hours daily. Limited support facility available.

**PAX LOUNGES:** Very limited lounge facilities, essentials only. Use ASP Airport terminal.

**FOOD SERVICE:** Restaurants, snack bars, coffee houses, and pubs in Alice Springs.

**TRANSPORTATION: Taxi (Comm):** Pax Term, 24 hours daily, C-011-89-522-201 (9 miles to ASP). ASP has commercial air, train, and motor coach services.

**TML:** No U.S. government billeting. Hotel rates in ASP are AU $20+, Backpacker accommodations. Three and four star accommodations AU $100.

**ATTRACTIONS:** Royal Flying Doctors Base, Ayers Rock (200 air miles southwest).

## EN ROUTE SCHEDULES

| AIRPORT/STATION | LI-MISSION (page #) |
|---|---|
| McChord AFB | TCM-P6E1P (82) |

## RAAFB RICHMOND (RCM/YSRI)

Det I, 635 AMSS/TR
Unit 11028
APO AP 96554-5000

**LOCATION:** Two miles west of Windsor AU and 45 miles northwest of Sydney AU. Gate entrance is located on Percival Road off of Richmond Road, located between the towns of Richmond and Windsor. *ML-ARM: (33°48'S/151°30'E)*. LST: GMT+10:00. NMC: Sydney, 45 miles southeast. Main installation number: C-011-61-245-70-2340, D-none.

**REGISTRATION INFO: C-011-61-2-4587-1651/2, Rec: C-011-61-2-4587-1652, Fax: C-011-61-2-4587-1663, E-mail: space@teamrichmond.org WEB: www.ozemail.com.au/~richmondusaf/spacea.htm** Pax Term, Hours: 0900-1500 Mon-Fri. Directions: From main gate, take first left, then left again and proceed to terminal. $30.00 AUS departure tax (all passengers 12 years +). U.S. passengers services by AMC pax rep personnel ONLY, not RAAFB personnel. Telephone for seat availability. Enter base for sign-up only at above hours or during flight processing. **Pax Service Office:** Bldg 308, Hours: 0900-1500 Mon-Fri, C-011-61-2-4587-3309 (see NCO for flight info).

**PAX LOUNGES:** RAAFB Pax Term building. **General:** Pax Term, Ist floor, Hours: 0800-1700 daily, or as mission dictates. A/C, restrooms, P/C seats, Australian customs.

**FOOD SERVICE:** In-flight meals $3.00 AU, non-refundable. **Cafeteria:** Hours: 0800-2000 Mon-Fri, 1000-2000 Sat-Sun, C-011-61-2-4587-2465, 10 minute walk. **Fast Food:** Many located in Richmond and Windsor, 5 minute drive. **Restaurants:** South Windsor RSL Club, C-011-61-4577-3649; many others located in Richmond and Windsor, 5 minute drive. **Mobile Snack Bars:** Pax

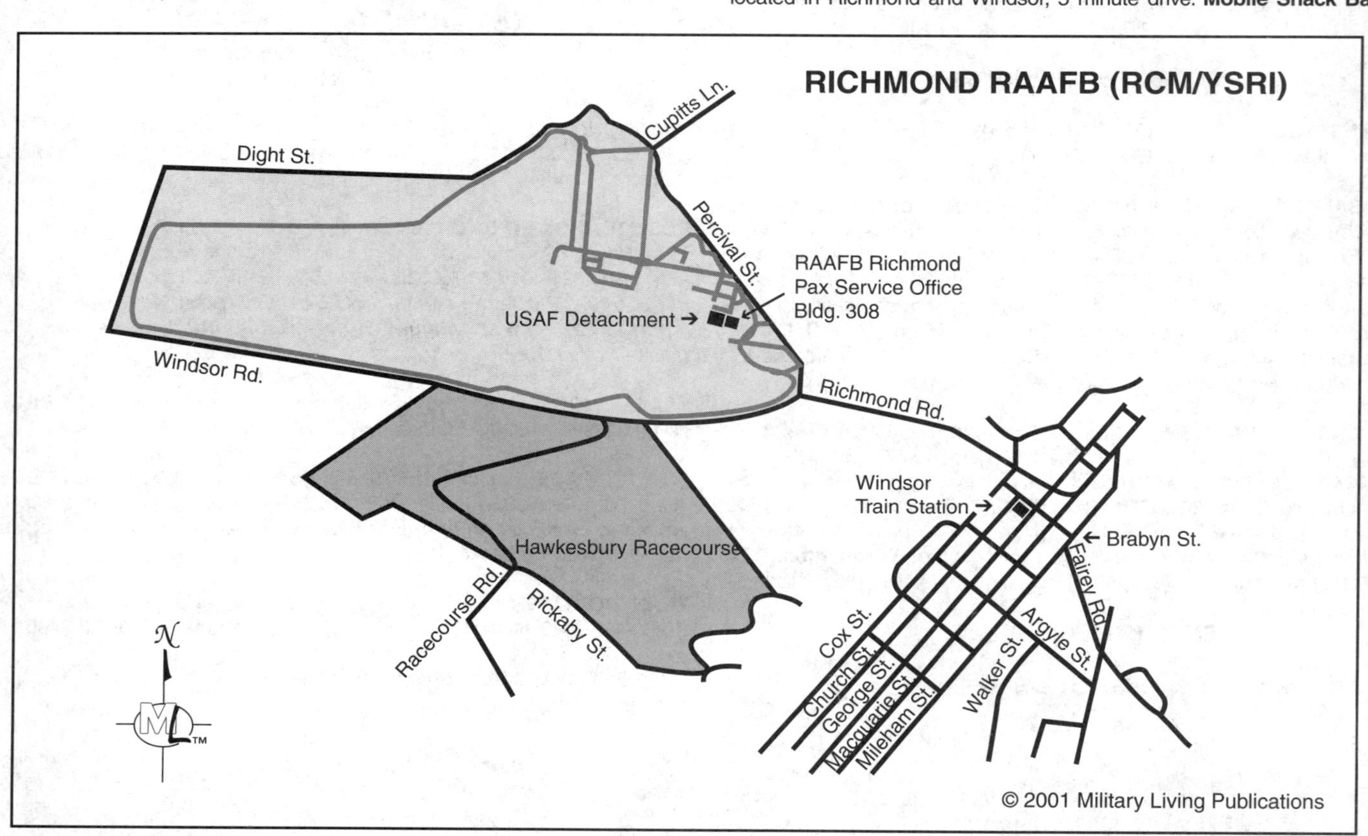


© 2001 Military Living Publications

Term, as required for RAAF flights, comes around morning, noon and evening to cover meal periods. **Snack Vending:** Pax Term, Hours: 0800-1900 daily, (RAAFB facility). Also there are numerous restaurants in Windsor and Richmond including McDonald's, Pizza Hut, and Kentucky Fried Chicken.

**TRANSPORTATION:** Train and commercial taxi only available at RAAFB RCM. **Air Tickets:** Sydney, 24 hours daily, major airlines-Kingsford Smith Apt.(Sydney International) **Off Base Car Rental:** All County Car Rental, C-011-61-245-6868, free courtesy transport; Delta, C-011-61-2-4587-7071, 10 minute drive; Hertz, C-011-61-2-4573-6344, 30 minute drive. **Off Base Shuttle/Bus:** Check with Pax Term, 5 minute walk; South Windsor RSL Club Courtesy Bus, C-011-61-019-397-141. **Off Base Taxi (Comm):** Pax Term, 24 hours daily, C-in AU-011-61-2-4513-1017. Serves local area/Sydney. **Off Base Train Station:** Hours: 0500-2400 daily, C(AU)-011-61-2-4513-1500, 5 minute drive. $8 AU by taxi. **Parking:** Security Police area, 24 hours daily.

**TML:** Several motels in Richmond/Windsor area. Ask at Pax Term for list.

**TRAVELERS AID:** Bldg 308, Hours: 0900-1500 Sun-Fri, C-011-61-2-4587-1652. See AMC personnel.

**SUPPORT AVAILABLE: Bank/Currency Exchange:** Hours: 0930-1600 Mon-Thu, 0930-1700 Fri, C(AU)-800-804-675, 5 minute drive; Richmond or Windsor. Issue Australian dollars only. No U.S. currency is used on base. US currency can be exchanged in Sydney. All passenger charges are taken in Australian currency only. All services available in Sydney.

**OTHER INFORMATION:** Port of Entry, customs and quarantine are very strict. Declare all food, medications and vitamin/workout supplements you are carrying. Climate: Cold months are May through July. Temperatures range from low 40s to 100 degrees F.

**ATTRACTIONS: Sydney (population 4 million) home of the 2000 Olympic Games**, Great Barrier Reef, Ayers Rock, Tasmania Island, Wonderland Theme Park, scenic Blue Mountains, many nice beaches. Continent of Australia is geographically as large as CONUS.

## EN ROUTE SCHEDULES

| AIRPORT/STATION | LI-MISSION (page #) |
|---|---|
| McChord AFB | TCM-P6E1P (82) |
| McChord AFB | TCM-P6E7P (82) |

No scheduled departures Fri-mon, Tue departures to Alice Springs, Wed departures to Pago Pago, Hickam AFB, Travis AFB or McChord AFB. Thu departures to Christchurch, Pago Pago, Hickam AFB, Travis AFB or McChord AFB.

# BAHRAIN

## BAHRAIN INTERNATIONAL AIRPORT (BAH/OBBI)

Administrative Support Unit Southwest Asia
PSC 451
FPO AE 09834-2800

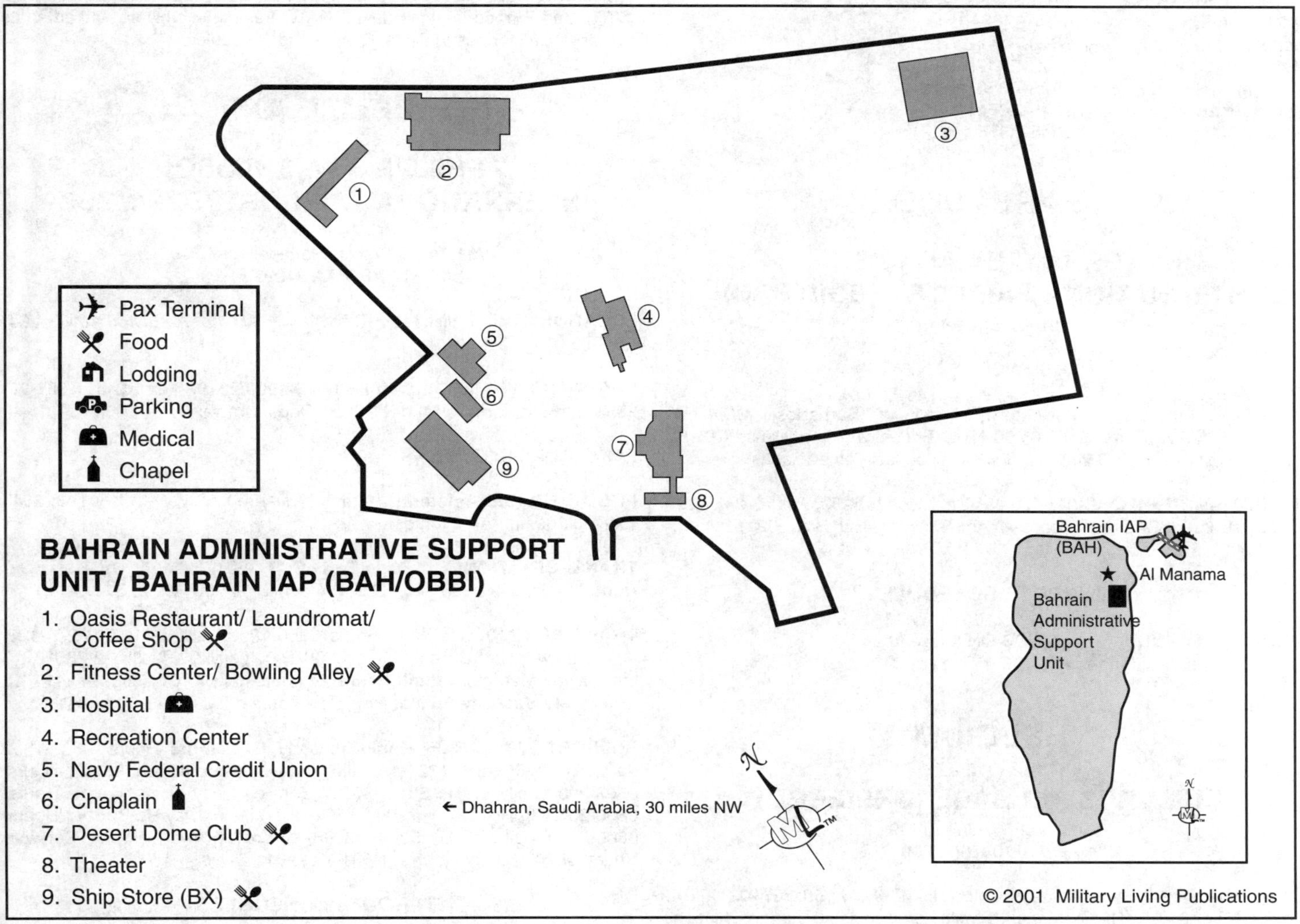

Pax Terminal
Food
Lodging
Parking
Medical
Chapel

## BAHRAIN ADMINISTRATIVE SUPPORT UNIT / BAHRAIN IAP (BAH/OBBI)

1. Oasis Restaurant/ Laundromat/ Coffee Shop
2. Fitness Center/ Bowling Alley
3. Hospital
4. Recreation Center
5. Navy Federal Credit Union
6. Chaplain
7. Desert Dome Club
8. Theater
9. Ship Store (BX)

← Dhahran, Saudi Arabia, 30 miles NW

Bahrain IAP (BAH)
Al Manama
Bahrain Administrative Support Unit

© 2001  Military Living Publications

**LOCATION:** An island nation off the coast of Saudi Arabia in the Persian Gulf. *ML-ARM: (26°16'N/50°38'E)*. Time: GMT+04:00. NMC: Dhahran, Saudi Arabia, 30 miles northwest via causeway. Main installation numbers: C-011-973-724-000, D-318-439-4000.

**REGISTRATION INFO:** C-011-973-743-799, 331-868, 743-224, D-318-439-3799, 439-3321, 439-3224, **Fax: C-011-973-326-246, D-318-439-4000 ext 727-360. For info only E-mail: bahatoc@hotmail.com or s3312@ bahrain.navy.mil WEB: www.cusnc.navy.mil** Pax Term, 0730-1630 Sat-Thu, closed Fri. General pax lounge available. IAP and Aviation Unit located in on Muharraq Island.

**TML:** CBH C-011-973-724-716/762, DSN-318-439-4716, Fax: C-011-973-743-452.

**SUPPORT AVAILABLE:** Support of an International Airport available. Also, admin support unit has cafeteria, restaurants, fast food snack bars, off base car rental, taxi, and shuttle/bus, chaplain, medical/dental, bank/currency exchange, credit union, laundry/dry cleaner, exchange, and postal service. Commercial facilities also available. There is a pax lounge for commercial ticket holders. Restaurants on base include Oasis, Desert Dome, and Parchezzi's. Taxi service 24 hours daily. A/C taxi to city - $5 US.

**ATTRACTIONS:** Bahrain Museum, Gold Souq, Tree of Life, camel farm, Al Dar Island, Dow Trips and desert tours.

## EN ROUTE SCHEDULES

| AIRPORT/STATION | LI-MISSION (page #) |
|---|---|
| McGuire AFB | WRI-A7F3A (51) |
| Norfolk NS | NGU-EX11E (78) |
| Norfolk NAS | NGU-EX17B (78) |
| Ramstein AB | RMS-A8F3A (112) |
| Ramstein AB | RMS-A8F5T (112) |
| Ramstein AB | RMS-A8F5X (112) |

# BARBADOS

## GRANTLEY ADAMS INTERNATIONAL AIRPORT (BGI/TBPB)

USDAO Bridgetown
Box B
FPO AA 34055-5006

**LOCATION:** In the southwestern corner of Barbados. *ML-ARM: (13°04'N/59°29'W)*. Time: GMT -05:00. NMC: Bridgetown, in city limits. C-246-436-4950 ext 272, Fax: C-246-429-5246. Limited facilities available.

**REGISTRATION INFO: C-246-436-4950 ext 272/281/253, Fax: C-246-429-5246.** Ask for USDAO and Space-A. Am Embassy P.O. Box 302, FPO AA 34055-5000. $12.50 Departure Tax.

## EN ROUTE SCHEDULES

| AIRPORT/STATION | LI-MISSION (page #) |
|---|---|
| Wright-Patterson AFB | FFO-OEH3B (61) |

# BELGIUM

## CHIEVRES AIR BASE (CHE/EBCU)

Det 1, 8606, Unit 21409
APO AE 09705-5000

**LOCATION:** Off BE-56 in village of Chievres. *ML-ARM: (50°35'N/03°50'E)*. Time: GMT +01:00. NMC: Mons, 8 miles southeast. Main installation numbers: C-011-32-68-27-5411, D-314-361-5411.

**REGISTRATION INFO: C-011-32-68-27-5411, D-314-361-5411, Fax: C-011-32-68-27-5573.** Bldg 27, Hours: 0800-1700 Mon-Fri.

**PAX LOUNGES: General:** Bldg 27, Hours: 0900-1700 Mon-Fri, D-314-361-5195. Restrooms, showers, telephone. **DV/VIP:** Hangar 1, northeast of Bldg 27, Hours: 0900-1700 Mon-Fri, D-314-361-5195 (notify Base Ops before going to Hangar #1). Coffee/tea served, restrooms, showers, telephone.

**FOOD SERVICE:** Limited. Full club service at SHAPE. **Cafeteria:** D-314-423-4434 (breakfast and lunch only). **Fast Food:** Hours: 1000-1900 Mon-Fri, C-011-326-827-5100, D-314-361-5100, 1 mile away.

**TRANSPORTATION: On Base Shuttle/Bus (Gov):** SHAPE Hq, D-314-423-4514. **On Base Taxi:** C-011-326-827-54276, D-314-361-5476, 300 yards away. Off Base Train station with short term parking also available.

**TML:** Lodging Office: Hotel Maisieres in Mons, SHAPE across from SHAPE Hq Bldg, C-011-32-65-73-00/99, Fax: C-011-32-65-72-42-56.

**TRAVELERS AID: Medical/Dental:** Hours: 0800-1600, C-011-326-544-5820, D-314-423-5820, 8 miles away. **Security Police:** Hours: 24 hours daily, C-011-326-827-5211, D-314-361-5211, 100 yards away.

**SUPPORT AVAILABLE: Bank/Currency Exchange:** C-011-32-65-44-3601, D-314-423-3601 (recording of rates). **Exchange:** Hours: 1000-1800, C-011-32-68-45-5812/5807, D-314-361-5302, 1 mile away. Laundry/Dry Cleaner and Shoppette available within a 1 mile radius.

**ATTRACTIONS:** Beleoil Castle, Pall Pardisio, Brusselette.

### UNSCHEDULED FLIGHTS

To Andrews AFB, MD (**ADW**); Ramstein AB, DE (**RMS**); Stuttgart AAF, DE (**STR**); and Europe stations during NATO training exercises. Limited seats available. Call for destinations, routing and schedules.

# BELIZE (BZ)

## PHILLIP S.W. GOLDSON INTERNATIONAL AIRPORT (BZE/MZBZ)

USMLO Belize,
Attn: AMC Station Manager, Unit 7402,
APO AA 34025

**LOCATION:** NMC: Belize City, 10 south. *ML-ARM: (17°32'N/88°18'W)*. LST: GMT-06:00.

**REGISTRATION INFO: C-011-501-25-2009/2019, Fax: C-011-501-25-2553, E-mail: usmlo@btl.net** $11.25 Departure Tax.

**PAX LOUNGES:** General.

**FOOD SERVICE: Cafeteria:** Hours: 0800-1800 daily, C-011-501-25-2045 Ext 130/200, in PAX lounge.

**TRANSPORTATION: Off Base Taxi:** C-011-501-25-2125. **Off Base Car Rental:** Avis, C-011-501-25-2629; Budget, C-011-501-25-2280.

**TRAVELERS AID: Chaplain:** Hours: 0800-1800 daily, C-011-501-2-72122, 10 miles away.**Red Cross:** Hours: 0800-1800 daily, C-011-501-2-73319, 10 miles away. **Medical/Dental:** Hours: 24 hours daily, C-011-501-2-73415, 10 miles away. **Security Police:** Hours: 24 hours daily, C-011-501-2-72210.

**SUPPORT AVAILABLE: Bank/Currency Exchange:** Hours: 0800-1300 daily, C-011-501-2-77132, 10 miles away. **Convenience Store:** Hours: 0800-2000 daily, C-011-501-2-35587, 6 miles away. **Dry Cleaner:** Hours: 0800-2000 daily, C-011-501-2-73396, 10 miles away. **Laundry:** Hours: 0800-2000 daily, C-011-501-2-73396, 10 miles away. **Postal Service:** Hours: 0800-1600 daily, C-011-501-2-72201.

## EN ROUTE SCHEDULES

| AIRPORT/STATION | LI-MISSION (page #) |
|---|---|
| Maxwell AFB | MXF-OBJ5A (2) |

# CANADA

## GANDER INTERNATIONAL AIRPORT (NEWFOUNDLAND) (YQX/CYQX)

P.O. Box 400
Gander, NF A1V 1W8

**LOCATION:** NMC: St John's, Newfoundland, CN, 100 miles southeast. *ML-ARM: (48°56'N/54°34'W).* LST: GMT-04:00. Main installation numbers: **C-709-256-6666  Fax: C-709-256-6725.  E-mail: Scotta@tc.gc.ca** Limited facilities available. Pax Lounges: International and Domestic. Food Service: Available 24 hours. Transportation: Taxi Service-24 hours.

### EN ROUTE SCHEDULES

| AIRPORT/STATION | LI-MISSION (page #) |
|---|---|
| Charleston AFB/IAP | CHS-A8R1S & A8R1T (67) |

## GOOSE BAY AIR BASE (NEWFOUNDLAND) (YYR/CYYR)

**LOCATION:** In the Canadian Atlantic Providence of Newfoundland on Goose Bay. NMC: Happy Valley, 6 miles southeast. *ML-ARM: (53°20'N/60°20'W).* LST: GMT-04:00. Main installation numbers: **C-709-896-2463.** Limited facilities available.

## ST. JOHN'S AIRPORT (NEWFOUNDLAND) (YYT/CYYT)

USDAO, AmEmbassy
P.O. Box 5000
Ogdensburg, NY 13669-5000

**LOCATION:** NMC: St John, in city limits. *ML-ARM: (47°37'N/52°45'W).* LST: GMT-04:00. Main installation numbers: **C-613-992-6250 or C-613-238-4470 ext 279/360/399, Fax: C-613-238-6485.** Limited facilities available.

*Note: These three above Canadian stations are mainly for refueling and crew change. No overnight facilities except for emergency and transit personnel.*

# CARIBBEAN, CENTRAL & SOUTH AMERICA

The stations listed below have Space-A air opportunities. Base support facilities are provided by United States Embassies in each foreign country and are very limited. Passenger management is accomplished by U.S. Embassy, military or contractor personnel. Procedures for processing passengers at each station are the result of local conditions and services available. Stations in most cases are located at International Airports which have all essential facilities and services for international travelers. Defense telephone service is not available at these stations unless indicated in their listing. Stations are listed in alphabetical order. **See Appendix B for personnel entrance requirements.**

**AUGUSTO C. SANDINO INTERNATIONAL AIRPORT, (Nicaragua) NI (MGA/MNMG),** USDAO, U.S. Embassy (Managua), Unit 2701, Box 13, APO AA 34021-2701. **C-011-505-2-66-2298 ext 4735/4723, Fax: C-011-505-2-66-8022.** *ML-ARM: (12°09'N/86°10'W).* LST: GMT-06:00. $20 Departure Fee

### EN ROUTE SCHEDULES

| AIRPORT/STATION | LI-MISSION (page #) |
|---|---|
| Wright-Patterson AFB | FFO-OEK5C (61) |

**BRASILIA INTERNATIONAL AIRPORT, (Brazil) BR (BSB/SBBR),** USDAO/AIRA Brasilia, AmEmbassy, Unit 3500, APO AA 34030-0008 *OR* USDAO Brasilia, Brazil, State Department Pouch Room, Washington, D.C. 20520-7500. **C-011-55-61-321-7272 ext 2064, C-011-55-61-226-0172, Fax: C-011-55-61-322-4795.** *ML-ARM: (15°52'S/47°55'W).* LST: GMT-03:00. Taxi available. A visa is a must prior to leaving U.S. and cannot be done at an airport. Actual schedule may not be stable due to world events.

### EN ROUTE SCHEDULES

| AIRPORT/STATION | LI-MISSION (page #) |
|---|---|
| Allen C Thompson (Jackson) | JAN-IKH5A (44) |
| Memphis IAP | MEM-IDB3B (71) |
| Memphis IAP | MEM-IDB5A (71) |

**CARRASCO INTERNATIONAL AIRPORT, MONTEVIDEO, (Uruguay) UY (MVD/SUMU),** USDAO, U.S. Embassy (Montevideo), APO AA 34035-0008. **C-011-598-2-408-9085, Fax: C-011-598-2-401-8678.** *ML-ARM: (34°50'S/56°02'W).* LST: GMT-03:00.

### EN ROUTE SCHEDULES

| AIRPORT/STATION | LI-MISSION (page #) |
|---|---|
| Memphis IAP | MEM-IDB5A (71) |

**EL DORADO INTERNATIONAL AIRPORT, (Columbia) CO (BOG/SKBO),** USDAO, U.S. Embassy (Bogota), Unit 5115, APO AA 34038-3030. **C-011-57-1-315-2125, Fax: C-011-57-1-315-2197.** *ML-ARM: (04°42'N/78°09'W).* LST: GMT-05:00.

**EZEIZA AIRPORT, BUENOS AIRES, (Argentina) AR (BUE/SAEZ),** USMILGP, Argentina, Unit 4334, APO AA 34034-0008. **C-011-54-1-777-4533/4534, Fax: C-011-54-1-777-0673/0917.** *ML-ARM: (34°49'S/58°32'W).* LST: GMT-03:00.

### EN ROUTE SCHEDULES

| AIRPORT/STATION | LI-MISSION (page #) |
|---|---|
| Memphis IAP | MEM-IDB5A (71) |

**HATO AIRPORT, CURACAO, (Netherlands Antilles), (CUR/TNCC),** Counsel General, J.B. Gorsiraweg #1, P.O. Box 158, Willemstad, Curacao, **C-011-599-9-461-3066, Fax: C-011-599-9-461-6489.** *ML-ARM: (12°11'N/68°57'W).* LST: GMT-04:00.

### EN ROUTE SCHEDULES

| AIRPORT/STATION | LI-MISSION (page #) |
|---|---|
| Allen C Thompson (Jackson) | JAN-IKB7A (43) |

**J.F. KENNEDY INTERNATIONAL AIRPORT, LA PAZ, (Bolivia) BO (LPB/SLLP),** USDAO, U.S. Embassy (La Paz), Unit 3912, APO AA 34032-0008. **C-011-591-2-430-251/432-253, Fax: C-011-591-2-433-900/431-870.** *ML-ARM: (16°31'S/68°11'W).* LST: GMT-04:00.

### EN ROUTE SCHEDULES

| AIRPORT/STATION | LI-MISSION (page #) |
|---|---|
| Allen C Thompson (Jackson) | JAN-IKB7A (43) |

**JOHAN A. PENGEL INTERNATIONAL AIRPORT, (Suriname) SR (PBM/SMJP),** USDAO Paramaribo, State Department Pouch Room, Washington, D.C. 20521-3390. **C-011-597-4-77881, Fax: C-011-597-4-10565.** *ML-ARM: (05°27'N/55°11'W).* LST: GMT-04:00. Very limited facilities available.

### EN ROUTE SCHEDULES

| AIRPORT/STATION | LI-MISSION (page #) |
|---|---|
| Wright-Patterson AFB | FFO-OEH3B (61) |

**JORGE CHAVEZ INTERNATIONAL AIRPORT, (Peru) PE (LIM/SPIM),** USMAAG, U.S. Embassy (Lima), Unit 3790, APO AA 34031-5000. **C-011-51-1-434-0199, Fax: C-011-51-1-434-0117/3037.** *ML-ARM: (12°01'S/77°07'W).* LST: GMT-04:00.

### EN ROUTE SCHEDULES

| AIRPORT/STATION | LI-MISSION (page #) |
|---|---|
| Wright-Patterson AFB | FFO-OEB1D (61) |

**LA AURORA AIRPORT, (Guatemala) GT (GUA/MGGT),** USDAO, U.S. Embassy (Guatemala City), Unit 3310, APO AA 34024-3190. **C-011-502-331-1541, Fax: C-011-502-334-8477.** *ML-ARM: (14°34'N/90°31'W).* LST: GMT-06:00.

### EN ROUTE SCHEDULES

| AIRPORT/STATION | LI-MISSION (page #) |
|---|---|
| Wright-Patterson AFB | FFO-OEK5C (61) |

**MARISCAL SUCRE AIRPORT, (Ecuador) EC (UIO/SEQU),** USDAO, U.S. Embassy (Quito), Ecuador. Unit 5340, APO AA 34039-5340. **C-011-593-2-503-822, Fax: C-011-593-2-561-344.** *ML-ARM: (00°80'N/78°29'W).* LST: GMT-05:00. **OTHER INFORMATION:** All passengers must submit a country clearance request to the U.S. military group prior to travel C-593-2-232-107. Only one AMC flight to Ecuador monthly from Charleston AFB, stays overnight; returns CONUS.

**NORMAN MANLEY INTERNATIONAL AIRPORT, (Jamaica) JM (KIN/MKJK),** U.S. Military Liaison Office, U.S. Embassy (Kingston), Mutual Life Center, #2 Oxford Road, 3rd Floor, Kingston 5, Jamaica or U.S. State Department Pouch Room, Washington, D.C. 20521-3210. **C-011-876-929-4850, Fax: C-011-876-929-3637.** *ML-ARM: (17°56'N/76°47'W).* LST: GMT-05:00.

### EN ROUTE SCHEDULES

| AIRPORT/STATION | LI-MISSION (page #) |
|---|---|
| Minn-St Paul IAP/ARS | MSP-9QM1B (42) |

**PIARCO INTERNATIONAL AIRPORT (PORT OF SPAIN), (Trinidad/Tobago) TT (POS/TTPP)** USDAO, American Embassy, 15 Queen's Park West, P. O. Box 752, Port-of-Spain, Trinidad and Tobago. **LOCATION:** On Trinidad Island north of Venezuela. *ML-ARM: 10 36'N/61 21'W.* LST: GMT-04:00. **REGISTRATION INFO: Tel: C-011-868-622-6372, Fax: C-011-868-628-5462.** Support facilities of an international airport are available.

### EN ROUTE SCHEDULES

| AIRPORT/STATION | LI-MISSION (page #) |
|---|---|
| Minn-St Paul IAP/ARS | MSP-9QM1B (42) |

**PORT-AU-PRINCE INTERNATIONAL AIRPORT, (Haiti) HT (PAP/MTPP),** USDAO, Port Au Prince, Haiti, State Department - Pouch Room, Washington, D.C. 20521-3400. **C-011-509-223-9697, Fax: C-011-509-223-1641.** *ML-ARM: (18°34'N/72°17'W).* LST: GMT-05:00.

### EN ROUTE SCHEDULES

| AIRPORT/STATION | LI-MISSION (page #) |
|---|---|
| Charleston AFB/IAP | CHS-G4M5A (67) |

**SILVIO PETTIROSSI INTERNATIONAL AIRPORT (Paraguay) PY (ASU/SGAS),** USODC Paraguay, ATTN: ASM, Unit 4742, APO AA 34036-0001. **C-011-595-21-213-715 ext 330/1/2, Fax: C-011-595-21-213-728. E-mail: andresc@highway.com.py** Port of Entry. *ML-ARM: (25°14'S/57°31'W).* LST: GMT-04:00.

### EN ROUTE SCHEDULES

| AIRPORT/STATION | LI-MISSION (page #) |
|---|---|
| Memphis IAP | MEM-IDB3B (71) |

**PUDAHEL AIRPORT/ARTURO MERINO BENITEZ INTERNATIONAL AIRPORT, SANTIAGO (Chile) CL (SCL/SCEL),** USDAO, Unit 4115, APO

AA 34033-4115. **C-011-56-2-330-3413, Fax: C-011-56-2-330-3191.** Commercial transportation available. Tourist must pay a $45 USD reciprocal fee upon arrival. Passport with visa for country being visited will be exempt. *ML-ARM: (33°23'S/70°45'W).* LST: GMT-05:00.

### EN ROUTE SCHEDULES

| AIRPORT/STATION | LI-MISSION (page #) |
|---|---|
| Allen C Thompson (Jackson) | JAN-IKB7A (43) |

**RIO DE JANEIRO INTERNATIONAL AIRPORT, (Brazil) BR (RIO/SBGL),** USDAO/AIRA Brasilia, AmEmbassy, Unit 3500, APO AA 34030-0008. **C-011-55-21-292-7117, Fax: C-011-55-21-220-0439.** *ML-ARM: (22°48'S/43°14'W).* LST: GMT-03:00.

### EN ROUTE SCHEDULES

| AIRPORT/STATION | LI-MISSION (page #) |
|---|---|
| Allen C Thompson (Jackson) | JAN-IKH5A (44) |

**SANGSTER INTERNATIONAL AIRPORT, MONTEGO BAY, (Jamaica) JM (KJS/MKJS),** U.S. State Department Pouch Room, Washington, D.C. 20521-3210. **C-011-876-929-4850, Fax: C-011-876-929-3637.** *ML-ARM: (18°30'N/77°55'W).* LST: GMT-05:00.

**SAN ISIDRO AIR BASE, (Dominican Republic) DO (SDQ/MDSI),** USMAAG, U.S. Embassy (Santo Domingo), Unit 5531, APO AA 34041-5531. **C-809-731-4220, Fax: C-809-687-5222.** *ML-ARM: (18°30'N/69°46'W).* LST: GMT-05:00.

### EN ROUTE SCHEDULES

| AIRPORT/STATION | LI-MISSION (page #) |
|---|---|
| Minn-St Paul IAP/ARS | MSP-9QM1B (42) |

**SIMON BOLIVAR INTERNATIONAL AIRPORT, (Venezuela) VE (MIQ/SVMI),** USMILGP, U.S. Embassy (Caracas), Unit 4934, APO AA 34037-0008. **C-011-58-212-975-6411 Fax: C-011-58-212-975-6542.** *ML-ARM: (10°36'N/66°59'W).* LST: GMT-04:00.

### EN ROUTE SCHEDULES

| AIRPORT/STATION | LI-MISSION (page #) |
|---|---|
| Wright-Patterson AFB | FFO-OEB1D (61) |
| Wright-Patterson AFB | FFO-OEH3B (61) |

**VIRU VIRU INTERNATIONAL AIRPORT, BO (Bolivia) (VVI/SLVR),** USDAO, American Embassy (La Paz), P.O. Box 425, APO AA 34032-5000; **LOCATION:** In Santa Cruz, in south central Bolivia. *ML-ARM: (17 38'S/63 08'W).* LST: GMT-04:00. **REGISTRATION INFO: C-011-591-2-430-251, Fax: C-011-591-2-433-900/431-870.** Support facilities of an international airport are available.

### EN ROUTE SCHEDULES

| AIRPORT/STATION | LI-MISSION (page #) |
|---|---|
| Allen C Thompson (Jackson) | JAN-IKB7A (43) |

# CAYMAN ISLANDS

## OWEN ROBERTS INTERNATIONAL AIRPORT (WCR/MWCR)

U.S. Military Liaison Office
U.S. Embassy (Kingston), Mutual Life Center
#2 Oxford Road, 3rd Floor
Kingston 5, Jamaica

**LOCATION:** Although located in the Cayman Islands on Grand Cayman Island, information may be obtained through the U.S. Embassy in Jamaica. There is no U.S. Embassy in the Cayman Islands. *ML-ARM: (19°17'N/81°21'W).* LST: GMT-05:00.

**REGISTRATION INFO: C-011-809-929-4850, Fax: C-011-809-926-3637** or write to: U.S. Military Liaison Office, U.S. Embassy (Kingston), Mutual Life Center, #2 Oxford Road, 3rd Floor, Kingston 5, Jamaica or U.S. State Department Pouch Room, Washington, D.C. 20521-3210.

# COSTA RICA

## JUAN SANTAMARIA INTERNATIONAL AIRPORT (OCO/MROC)

AMC Station
PSC 20, Box 362
APO AA 34020-0362

**LOCATION:** The Santamaria International Airport in Alajuela, Costa Rica. *ML-ARM: (10°00'N/84°13'W)*. LST: GMT-05:00. NMC: San Jose, 20 miles southeast.

**REGISTRATION INFO: C-011-506-220-2463, Fax: C-011-506-290-0348. E-mail: ciscoamc@sol.racsa.co.cr** Due to hazardous cargo, flights are not always available to travelers, therefore, anyone coming into Costa Rica must have sufficient funds to defray commercial or ground transportation out of the country. Limited flights to Honduras and Puerto Rico.

**TRANSPORTATION:** Buses and taxis are available at the airport. **Car Rental:** Avis, Dollar, Hertz, Thrifty and the like are available at the airport and major cities.

**TRAVELERS AID:** The U.S. Embassy has a small office manned by a Lieutenant Colonel and Sergeant First Class only; help/assistance is extremely limited.

**SUPPORT AVAILABLE:** Surrounding cities and airport facilities only. *Note: Water is drinkable in the entire country, but all supermarkets sell bottled water.*

### EN ROUTE SCHEDULES

| AIRPORT/STATION | LI-MISSION (page #) |
| --- | --- |
| Allen C Thompson (Jackson) | JAN-IKB7A (43) |
| Wright-Patterson AFB | FFO-OEK5C (61) |

### UNSCHEDULED FLIGHTS

Call for destinations, routings and schedules.

# CUBA

## GUANTANAMO BAY NAVAL AIR STATION (NBW/MUGM)

Air Terminal Officer
PSC 1001, Box 35E
FPO AE 09508-0006

**LOCATION:** In the southeast corner of the Republic of Cuba. Accessible only by air. *ML-ARM: (20°10'N/73°10'W)*. LST: GMT-05:00. NMC: Miami, 525 air miles northwest. Main installation numbers: C-011-53-99-6XXX, D-313-723-3960 or 313-564-4063.

**REGISTRATION INFO: C-011-53-99-6204/6408/6397, D-313-564-4063 ext 6204/6408/6397, Fax: C-011-53-99-6170/6398, D-313-564-4063 ext 6204/6408. E-mail: n30atoc@usnbgtmo.navy.mil** Map B/2 Hours during flight processing. All arrivals and departures via air. Prior approval required for non-AD personnel to visit or transfer through station. See Appendix B for personnel entrance requirements. There is no access to Cuba from the Naval Station. All personnel are restricted to the base at all times. **Pax Service Office:** Base Map E/3, C-011-53-99-6-8523 (NCO on duty).

Baggage claim for Winward side is Tropical Aviation and Leeward in hanger Bldg AV600.

**PAX LOUNGES:** Limited, but adequate facilities. Base Map B/2, available during flight processing, C-011-53-99-6204 (see pax NCO). **General:** Cable TV, phones. **Family:** Cable TV. **DV/VIP:** Cable TV, phones.

**FOOD SERVICE:** Extensive facilities operated by clubs and BX. **Cafeteria:** Available at Pax Term. Hours: 0700-1300 Mon, Wed, Thur, 0700-1600 Tues, Fri, closed Sat-Sun. **Enlisted Club:** C-011-53-996-2304. **CPO Club:** C-011-53-99-2501. **O Club:** C-011-53-99-2148.

**TRANSPORTATION: Shuttle/Bus:** On Windward/Leeward. **On Base Taxi (Comm):** Hours: 0930-2100 Sun-Mon, 0700-2100 Tues-Thur, C-011-53-996-2517.

**TML:** Lodging Office: 24 hours daily, C-011-53-99-2400, D-313-564-8877 ext 2400/01, Fax: C-011-53-99-2401. Navy Lodge: C-011-53-99-3103 or 1-800-NAVY INN.

**TRAVELERS AID: Chaplain:** Bldg 762, C-011-53-99-2323/2628. **Medical:** Base Map J/16, 24 hours daily, C-011-53-99-3200/72690. **Red Cross/Navy Marine Corps Relief:** C-011-53-99-4393/4394. **Security Police:** Term, 24 hours daily, C-011-53-99-3720.

**SUPPORT AVAILABLE: Bank/Currency Exchange:** Navy Federal Credit Union, C-011-53-99-4333. **Exchange/Commissary:** C-011-53-99-4355.

**ATTRACTIONS:** Beaches, diving, fishing, and warm climate.

### EN ROUTE SCHEDULES

| AIRPORT/STATION | LI-MISSION (page #) |
| --- | --- |
| Allen C Thompson (Jackson) | JAN-IKM3A (44) |
| McGuire AFB | WRI-A7N1B (51) |
| Pope AFB | POB-ACN1B (57) |
| Wright-Patterson AFB | FFO-OEM3A (61) |
| Wright-Patterson AFB | FFO-OEM3B (61) |
| Wright-Patterson AFB | FFO-OEN1B (61) |
| Charleston AFB/IAP | CHS-A4M3A (67) |
| Dyess AFB | DYS-A1N1B (73) |
| Norfolk NS | NGU-HJM3A & B (79) |

### UNSCHEDULED FLIGHTS

Many flights to Roosevelt Roads, PR (**NRR**) and Patrick AFB, FL (**COF**) and other CONUS locations. Call for destinations, routings and schedules.

# CYPRUS

## RAFB AKROTIRI (AKT/LCRA)

AMC Rep, USDOA Nicosia
PSC 815
FPO AE 09836-5000

**LOCATION:** On Cape Gata, Southern Coast, Island of Cyprus. At UK Akrotiri RAFB. *ML-ARM (35°02'N/32°56'E)*. LST: GMT+02:00. NMC: Limassol, Cyprus, 5 miles northeast. Main installation numbers: at USDAO C-011-357-2-476100 or Defense Attache C-011-357-2-776400.

**REGISTRATION INFO: C-011-357-2-776400,** ask for AMC representative. **Fax: C-011-357-2-780944.** Pax Term. Limited access. See Appendix B for personnel entrance requirements. All major support is in Nicosia, Cyprus, 55 miles northeast.

### EN ROUTE SCHEDULES

| AIRPORT/STATION | LI-MISSION (page #) |
| --- | --- |
| Ramstein AB | RMS-CET1A (111) |

# DENMARK

## THULE AIR BASE (GREENLAND) (THU/BGTL)

12th SWS/CCF, Unit 82501
APO AE 09704-5000

**LOCATION:** Northwest coast of island of Greenland, DK; 800 miles south of North Pole; 800 miles north of Arctic Circle; 2500 miles north of McGuire AFB NJ. Closer to Seattle, WA than New York City, NY by 5 miles. *ML-ARM: (77°35'N/69°50'W)*. LST: GMT-04:30. Main installation numbers: C-011-299-50-636 ext 2711, D-314-268-3840 ext 2711. **Prior written permission from Commander, 12th SWS/CCE, Unit 82501, APO AE 09704-5000 is required to visit Thule AB. Entry into the Thule Defense Area will be approved for official government business only.**

**REGISTRATION INFO:** C-011-299-50-636 ext 2711, D-314-268-3840 ext 2711 Fax: C-011-299-50-636 ext 2314. Bldg 623, Hours: 0800-1700 Mon-Fri, Sat as needed, ext 2711. Access limited. See Appendix B for personnel entrance requirements.

**PAX LOUNGES:** Limited but adequate lounge facilities.

**FOOD SERVICE: Dining Hall:** Bldg 107, ext 2614. **All Ranks Club:** Bldg 236. None off base.

**TRANSPORTATION:** Limited on base. **On Base Shuttle/Bus:** Bus does not service Pax Term. **On Base Taxi (Gov):** Bldg 836, ext 2022.

**TML:** North Star Inn: Bldg 100, 24 hours daily, C-011-299-976-585 ext 3276, D-314-268-1110 ext 3276, Fax: C-011-299-976-585 ext 2270, D-314-268-1110 ext 2270.

**TRAVELERS AID: Chaplain:** ext 2211. **Medical:** ext 2696. **Security Police:** ext 3234.

**SUPPORT AVAILABLE: Exchange:** ext 2732. **Hair Styles:** ext 3127. **Laundry:** ext 2249. **Postal Service:** ext 2615.

**ATTRACTIONS:** Sledge dogs (teams) and glaciers.

**OTHER INFORMATION:** Entry into the Thule Defense Area will be approved for official government business only.

### EN ROUTE SCHEDULES

| AIRPORT/STATION | LI-MISSION (page #) |
| --- | --- |
| McGuire AFB | WRI-HJX1A (49) |
| McGuire AFB | WRI-A7X1A (51) |

# EGYPT
# (ARAB REPUBLIC OF)

## CAIRO INTERNATIONAL AIRPORT/
## CAIRO EAST AIR BASE (CAI/HECA)

OL-B, 621 AMSG/TR (AMC)
Unit 64901, BOX 43
APO AE 09839-4901

**LOCATION:** The Cairo IAP is 9 miles northeast of Cairo on the east side of the Nile River and approximately 75 miles west of the Gulf of Suez. *ML-ARM: (30°07'N/31°24'E)*. LST: GMT+02:00. NMC: Cairo, 9 miles southwest. Main installation numbers: C-011-20-2-357-3212, D-312-725-1456 ext 3212 (Direct Dial from CONUS).

**REGISTRATION INFO:** C-011-20-2-357-3212/2596, D-314-725-1456 ext 3212/2596, Fax: C-011-20-2-357-2273. E-mail:amccairo@omceg. centcom.mil Pax Term, Hours: 0800-1630 Sun-Thu. Directions: The AMC Terminal is located on the opposite side of the main runway from the IAP side of the airport, and is located on Cairo East Air Base, an Egyptian military installation. All flights are managed by U.S. Embassy Cairo, Office of Military Cooperation. There are no U.S. military installations located in the United Arab Republic of Egypt. *Note: Personnel must have authorization to fly into Cairo IAP/Cairo East Air Base. They must also have a sponsor present when they arrive and when they leave the base.* Facilities are extremely limited.

**PAX LOUNGES:** Pax Term, 0800-1630 Sun-Thu, C-011-20-2-357-3212, D-314-725-1456 ext 3212. Seats 15, A/C.

**TRANSPORTATION:** Limited. No transportation available at AMC Terminal. Taxi service is available off base.

**SUPPORT AVAILABLE:** This is a small terminal located on an Egyptian AB. There are no provisions for lodging, food service, car rentals, bank or other normal services. Many hotels provide all services.

**ATTRACTIONS:** Pyramids, museums, bazaars, Nile River.

### EN ROUTE SCHEDULES

| AIRPORT/STATION | LI-MISSION (page #) |
| --- | --- |
| Baltimore/Washington IAP | BWI-LX27A (38) |
| Ramstein AB | RMS-A8Q1A (113) |

**CAIRO WEST INTERNATIONAL AIRPORT/AIR BASE, EG (CIR/HECW)**, Cairo IAP/Cairo East Air Base, EG (CAI/HECA), OL-B, 621 AMSG/TR (AMC), Unit 64901, Box 43, APO AE 09839-4901. **LOCATION:** 30 km and 2 hrs driving time from Cairo East Air Base. *ML-ARM: (30°07'N/31°24'E)*. LST: GMT+02:00. **REGISTRATION INFO:** Contact AMC personnel at Cairo East Air Base as follows: **C-011-20-2-357-3212/2495, D-314-725-1456, ext 3212/2495, Fax: C-011-20-2-279-1290, E-mail: amc_cairo@centcom. dsaa.osd.mil** There are no AMC personnel at Cairo West IAP/AB and space-a passengers are not processed at Cairo West IAP/AB. *No passengers may board or exit the aircraft.*

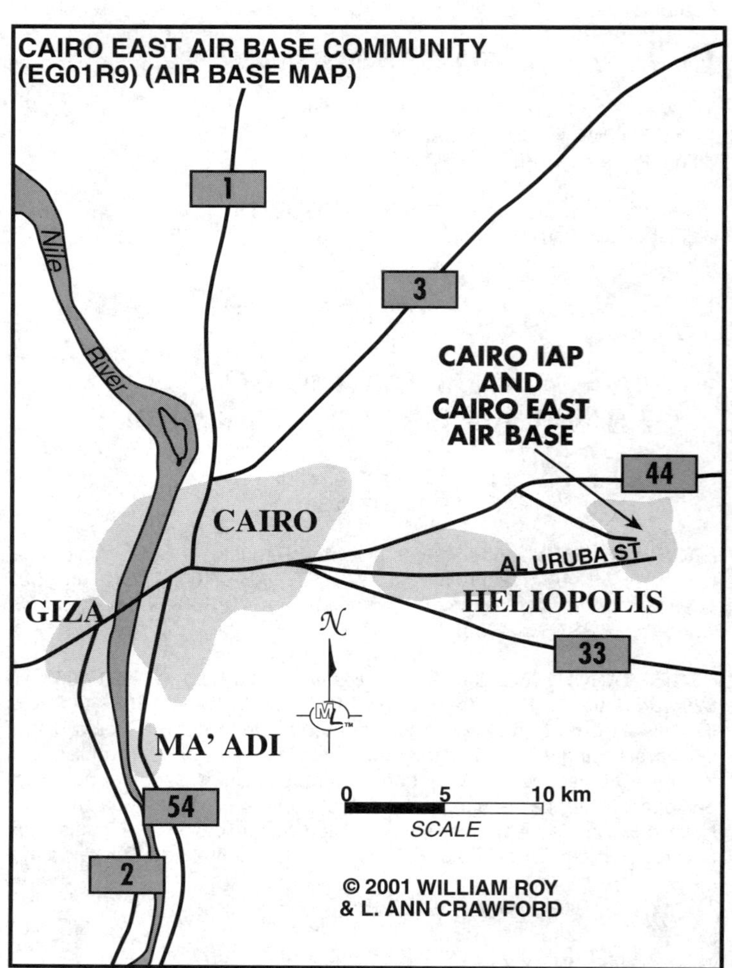

# EL SALVADOR

## ILOPANGO AIR BASE (SAL/MSSS)

USDAO, Unit 3108
APO AA 34023

**LOCATION:** Southeast of San Salvador. *ML-ARM: (13°42'N/89°07'W).* LST: GMT-06:00. NMC: San Salvador, 7 miles northwest.

**REGISTRATION INFO: C-011-503-278-4444, Fax: C-011-503-278-6011.** This is an El Salvadorian military facility located in San Salvador. *Only U.S. military personnel on official orders are authorized on the base with prior USDAO/US MILGROUP approval as it is a restricted area. No personnel are authorized on AMC flights on a Space-A basis without prior USDAO approval due to the nature of the flights arriving and departing Ilopango Air Base.* There are no support facilities.

### EN ROUTE SCHEDULES

| AIRPORT/STATION | LI-MISSION (page #) |
| --- | --- |
| Maxwell AFB | MXF-OBJ5A (2) |

# FIJI

## NANDI INTERNATIONAL AIRPORT (NAN/NFFN)

**LOCATION:** On Viti Nevu island of Fiji, in the South Pacific. *ML-ARM: 17°45'S/177°26'E.* GMT: LST+12:00.

# GERMANY

## GEILENKIRCHEN NATO AIR BASE (GKE/ETNG)

470 ABS/DPF
APO AE 09104-5000

**LOCATION:** Take DE-212 N from Aachen or take 44 (E-39) Autobahn NE exit to DE-56 NW for ten miles. *ML-ARM: (50°57'N/06°2'E).* LST: GMT+01:00. NMC: Aachen, 12 miles east. Main installation numbers: C-011-49-2451-63-113, D-314-452-2715 ext 243/244.

**REGISTRATION INFO: C-011-49-2451-63-4457/4460, Fax: C-011-49-2451-63-4461.** Hangar 4, Hours: 0800-1600. Directions: Ask at gate.

**PAX LOUNGES: General:** Available.

**FOOD SERVICE: Dining Hall:** (available only to those assigned to the E-3A Component commands.) Bldg 70. **All Ranks Club:** (available for visitors) Sentry Club, Hours: Mon-Fri 0730-2030, Bldg 72, C-011-49-2451-63-4998. **NCO Club:** Frisbee Club, Hours: Mon-Thur 0900-2300, Bldg 60, C-011-49-2451-63-4994/4992. **O Club:** Hours: Mon-Fri 1130-1330 Sun 1100-1400, Bldg 50, 011-49-2451-63-4990/4991.

**TRANSPORTATION: Travel Office:** 011-49-2451-63-4088, DER Travel, Bldg 81, C-011-49-2451-63-1256, hours Mon-Fri 0800-1700 Thu 1000-2000 Sat 1000-1400. **Air Tickets:** SATO, C-011-49-2451-63-3414. **On Base Car Rentals:** C-011-49-2451-62-0742. **On/Off Base Taxi:** 011-49-2451-63-2000. **Trains:** Hours: 0600-2200 Mon-Sat, for international travel, C-011-49-2451-63-2413. For travel within Germany C-011-49-1805-99-6633 (Limited English).

**TML:** Billeting: (available only to those assigned to the E-3A Component commands.) Bldg 141, 0815-1600 hours Mon-Thu, 0815-1500 hours Fri, C-

011-49-2451-63-4962. Fax: 011-49-2451-63-4980, All ranks. Payment must be in DM.

**TRAVELERS AID: Chaplain:** Bldg 3, C-011-49-2451-63-2229. **Lost/Found:** Hangar 4, C-011-49-2451-63-4457/4460. **Medical:** Bldg 211, C-011-49-2451-99-3200, D-455-3715 ext 253. **Red Cross:** C-011-49-2451-63-2211. **Security Police:** C-011-49-2451-63-2228.

**SUPPORT AVAILABLE: Bank/Currency Exchange:** C-011-49-2451-68085. Dresdner Bank C-011-49-2451-63-4080. **Commissary:** NATEX C-C-011-49-2451-62-0710. **Credit Union:** Andrews Federal Credit Union C-011-49-3146-443-7507/8. **Exchange:** NATEX C-011-49-2451-62070. **Hair Styles:** C-011-49-2451-63-4087. **Laundry/Dry Cleaning:** C-011-49-2451-63-66365. **Gas Station:** NATEX Hours: Mon-Sat 1000-1800 Sun 1100-1700, Bldg 655, C-011-49-2451-62-0745. **Shoppette:** Getranke Market, Hours: Mon-Sat 1000-1800, Bldg 149, C-011-49-2451-62-0725.

**OTHER INFORMATION:** This is not a U.S. military base, it is an air base of the North Atlantic Treaty Organization (NATO). Many of the support facilities on base are only open to those who are assigned as a part of NATO activities.

**ATTRACTIONS:** Easy access to Netherlands and Belgium.

## RAMSTEIN AIR BASE (RMS/ETAR)

623rd AMSS/TRO-P
Unit 3295, Bldg 2402
APO AE 09094-5000

**LOCATION:** Located near Kaiserslautern, off Autobahn A-6 from Frankfurt, Sembach and Saarbrüken. Take Autobahn A-8 to A-6 from Stuttgart. Located off the Kaiserslautern-Einsiedlerhof exit. *ML-ARM: (49°25'N/07°30'E).* LST: GMT+01:00. NMC: Kaiserslautern, 12 miles east. Main installation numbers: C-011-49-6371-47-1113, D-314-480-1110.

**REGISTRATION INFO: C-011-49-6371-47-2120, D-314-480-2120, Rec: C-011-49-6371-47-5364, D-314-480-5364, Fax: C-011-49-6371-47-2364/ 2433, D-314-480-2364/2433. E-mail: spacea@ramstein.af.mil** Bldg 2402, Hours: 24 hours daily. Get base pass from a Visitor Control Center (on the right, just prior to each gate). Directions: From West Gate straight on Fairchild Ave to Pax Term on left. From East Gate straight on Kisling Memorial Drive to a left on Mitchell Blvd to a right on Fairchild Ave. Pax Term on right. **Pax Paging:** C-011-49-6371-47-5364, D-314-480-5364.

**PAX LOUNGES: General:** Bldg 2402, Hours: 0500-2200 daily, D-480-2433/5364. TV, restrooms with showers, P/C seats, telephones (commercial, defense and base). **DV/VIP:** Bldg 2402, front area, Hours: 0500-2200 daily, D-480-2433/5364. TV, restrooms. **Protocol Service:** Bldg 201, Hours: 0500-2200 daily, D-480-6854, 06+.

**FOOD SERVICE: Cafeteria:** In Pax Term Bldg, 24 hours daily, except U.S. holidays. **Dining Hall:** Bldg 2107, D-480-5750. **Enlisted Club:** Bldg 2411, 24 hours daily, D-480-5637. **Fast Food:** Burger King, Hours: 0600-2200 Bldg 1135, D-480-2555, 25 minutes; Donutland, Bldg 2171, D-480-3163; Popeye's, Bldg 2163, D-480-7000; **NCO Club:** Bldg 2411, 24 hours daily, D-480-2333. **O Club:** Bldg 302, D-480-2848/6066. **Restaurants:** Fred's Lounge, Bldg 2113, D-480-5777; Jawbone Inn, Bldg 2398; Rhineland Inn, Bldg 2107, D-480-5750; Starlight Inn, Bldg 2300; Vesuvio's, Bldg 302, D-480-6200. **Snack Bar:** Hours: 1200-0100, C-011-49-6371-47-6066, D-314-480-6066, 5 minutes away. **Snack Vending:** All located throughout the terminal.

**TRANSPORTATION: Air Tickets:** SATO, Bldg 2320, Hours 0800-1700. C-011-49-6371-44161/42203; Bldg 2402, Hours: 1400-1600 Mon-Fri, C-011-49-6371-43241. **On Base Bus (Comm)** Bldg 2408, D-480-2411 (call for schedule) **Bus (Gov):** (Official travel only) Bldg 2202, D-480-5961 (off base routes) **On Base Car Rentals:** Budget, C-011-49-6371-47-43978; Hertz, C-011-49-6371-47-4420. **Off Base Car Rentals:** Landstuhl, C-011-49-6371-2330; Powell's Auto, C-011-49-6371-52169; Raule, C-011-49-6371-52169;

Avis and Hertz also available. **On Base Shuttle/Bus:** Base Shuttle departs AMC terminal daily at 0615 hours and runs every 30 minutes thereafter until 1845. The bus stop is located across the street from the Pax Term. Schedules are available at the AMC Counter and information center. **On/Off Base Taxi (Comm)/Limo Service:** Bldg 2113, 24 hours daily, C-011-49-6371-50510 or C-011-49-6371-12604. **Trains:** Excellent train service throughout or call train station (Bahnhof) C-011-49-631-19419/66475. **Parking:** Three long term parking lots available by permit only (permits available from Pax Term).

**TML:** Ramstein Inn North + South: Bldg 305, 24 hours daily, C-011-49-6371-45-4940/7345, D-314-480-4920. Fax: C-011-49-6371-42589, DSN-314-480-7627. General Cannon Hotel, Bldg 1013. DV/VIP C-012-48-6371-45-7558, DSN-314-480-7558, Fax: C-011-49-6371-45-7109, DSN-314-450-7109.

**TRAVELERS AID: Chaplain:** Hours: 0800-1700 Mon-Fri, C-011-49-6371-47-6148, D-314-480-6148. **Emergency Relief:** Bldg 2402, D-480-5539. **Lost/Found:** Bldg 2402, D-480-5364. **Medical:** C-011-49-6371-47-5225, D-314-480-5225, 3 minutes away; Emergency 24 hours daily. **Red Cross:** 24 hours daily, C-011-49-6371-47-5464, D-314-480-5464, 2 minutes away. **Security Police:** C-314-480-2050, 2 minutes away. **USO:** Bldg 2402, D-480-6326.

**SUPPORT AVAILABLE: Bank/Currency Exchange:** Hours: 0900-1600 Mon-Fri, 1030-1330 Sat, C-011-49-6371-47-6509, D-314-480-6509, 10 minutes away. **Convenience Store:** 24 hours daily, D-314-480-5300, 10 minutes away. **Credit Union:** Hours: 0900-1700 Mon-Fri, 1000-1300 Sat, D-314-480-5556, 2 minutes away. **Dry Cleaner:** Hours: 1000-1500 Mon-Sat, C-011-49-6371-42069, 5 minutes away. **Exchange:** Hours: 1000-2000 Sat-Sun, C-011-49-6371-42405, D-314-480-7110, 15 minutes away. **Hair Styles:** Barber, Bldg 2162, D-480-5673; Beauty, Bldg 1101, D-480-6040. **Laundry:** C-011-49-6371-58294, 5 minutes away. **Postal Service:** Northside, Hours: 1000-1700, D-314-480-7857, 15 minutes away. **Shoppette:** 24 hours daily, D-314-480-5300, 10 minutes away. **Wire:** Bldg 1101, D-480-7110 (BX).

**OTHER INFORMATION:** Port of Entry.

*Note: Commercially contracted flights are now called Patriot Express.*

**RAMSTEIN AB, DE (RMS); REGION: ATL; OPERATOR: COM; TYPE: MIXED; ROUTE: HJF5A; SAMPLE SCHEDULE: MON; EQUIPMENT: DC862**

{RMS *SE* ➡ AVB *SE* ➡ EKJ ⇌ EKJ *NW* ➡ AVB *NW* ➡ RMS}

| LI/ICAO | AIRPORT/STATION | CTRY/STA | DAYS EN ROUTE |
|---|---|---|---|
| RMS/ETAR | Ramstein AB | DE | +0 |
| AVB/LIPA | Aviano AB | IT | +0 |
| EKJ/OEKJ | Prince Sultan AB | SA | +1 |
| EKJ/OEKJ | Prince Sultan AB | SA | +1 |
| AVB/LIPA | Aviano AB | IT | +1 |
| RMS/ETAR | Ramstein AB | DE | |

**RAMSTEIN AB, DE (RMS); REGION: ATL; OPERATOR: COM; TYPE: MIXED; ROUTE: HJF5B; SAMPLE SCHEDULE: WED; EQUIPMENT: DC863**

{RMS *SE* ➡ AVB *SE* ➡ EKJ ⇌ EKJ *NW* ➡ AVB *NW* ➡ RMS}

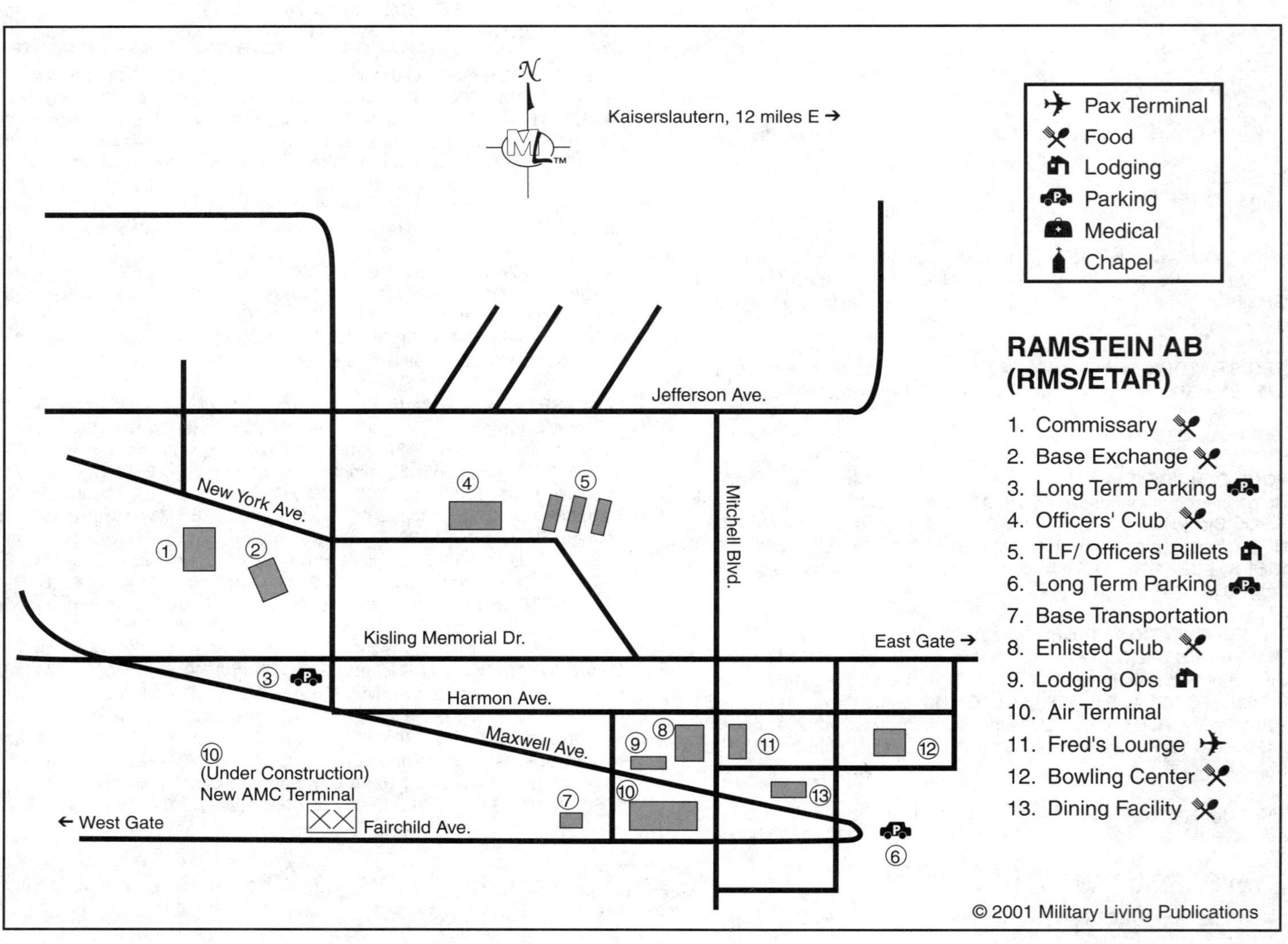

| LI/ICAO | AIRPORT/STATION | CTRY/STA | DAYS EN ROUTE |
|---|---|---|---|
| RMS/ETAR | Ramstein AB | DE | +0 |
| AVB/LIPA | Aviano AB | IT | +0 |
| EKJ/OEKJ | Prince Sultan AB | SA | +1 |
| EKJ/OEKJ | Prince Sultan AB | SA | +1 |
| AVB/LIPA | Aviano AB | IT | +1 |
| RMS/ETAR | Ramstein AB | DE | |

### RAMSTEIN AB, DE (RMS); REGION: ATL; OPERATOR: COM; TYPE: MIXED; ROUTE: HJG5A; SAMPLE SCHEDULE: FRI; EQUIPMENT: DC862

{RMS *SE* ➡ AVB *SE* ➡ KWI ⇌ KWI *NW* ➡ AVB *NW* ➡ RMS}

| LI/ICAO | AIRPORT/STATION | CTRY/STA | DAYS EN ROUTE |
|---|---|---|---|
| RMS/ETAR | Ramstein AB | DE | +0 |
| AVB/LIPA | Aviano AB | IT | +0 |
| KWI/OKBK | Kuwait IAP | KW | +1 |
| KWI/OKBK | Kuwait IAP | KW | +1 |
| AVB/LIPA | Aviano AB | IT | +1 |
| RMS/ETAR | Ramstein AB | DE | |

### RAMSTEIN AB, DE (RMS); REGION: ATL; OPERATOR: COM; TYPE: CGO W PAX; ROUTE: DES1C; SAMPLE SCHEDULE: FRI; EQUIPMENT: L100

{RMS *SE* ➡ SKP *S* ➡ SIZ *N* ➡ SKP *S* ➡ SIZ *N* ➡ SKP ⇌ SKP *NW* ➡ RMS *NW* ➡ MHZ *SE* ➡ RMS}

| LI/ICAO | AIRPORT/STATION | CTRY/STA | DAYS EN ROUTE |
|---|---|---|---|
| RMS/ETAR | Ramstein AB | DE | +0 |
| SKP/LWSK | Skopje* | MK | +0 |
| SIZ/LICZ | Sigonella NAS/APT (Sicily) | IT | +0 |
| SKP/LWSK | Skopje* | MK | +0 |
| SIZ/LICZ | Sigonella NAS/APT (Sicily) | IT | +1 |
| SKP/LWSK | Skopje* | MK | +1 |
| RMS/ETAR | Ramstein AB | DE | +1 |
| MHZ/EGUN | RAF Mildenhall | UK | +1 |
| RMS/ETAR | Ramstein AB | DE | |

* Space-A passengers can not go through Skopje. We list this schedule because many people may wish to use the McGuire to Norfolk to Sigonella & Ramstein to Mildenhall to Ramstein legs of this flight.

### RAMSTEIN AB, DE (RMS); REGION: ATL; OPERATOR: AMC; TYPE: MIXED; ROUTE: G8W5S; SAMPLE SCHEDULE: 1ST & 3RD TUE; EQUIPMENT: C017A

{RMS *SE* ➡ TLV ⇌ TLV *NW* ➡ RMS}

| LI/ICAO | AIRPORT/STATION | CTRY/STA | DAYS EN ROUTE |
|---|---|---|---|
| RMS/ETAR | Ramstein AB | DE | +0 |
| TLV/LLBG | Ben Gurion IAP (Tel Aviv) | IL | +0 |
| TLV/LLBG | Ben Gurion IAP (Tel Aviv) | IL | +0 |
| RMS/ETAR | Ramstein AB | DE | |

### RAMSTEIN AB, DE (RMS); REGION: ATL; OPERATOR: AMC; TYPE: MIXED; ROUTE:CET1A; SAMPLE SCHEDULE: THU; EQUIPMENT: C130E

{RMS *SE* ➡ AVB *SE* ➡ ADA *SW* ➡ AKT *NE* ➡ ADA *W* ➡ ADB *NE* ➡ IST *SE* ➡ ADA ⇌ ADA *NW* ➡ AVB *NW* ➡ RMS}

| LI/ICAO | AIRPORT/STATION | CTRY/STA | DAYS EN ROUTE |
|---|---|---|---|
| RMS/ETAR | Ramstein AB | DE | +0 |
| AVB/LIPA | Aviano AB | IT | +0 |
| ADA/LTAG | Incirlik APT (Adana) | TR | +1 |
| AKT/LCRA | RAF Akrotiri | CY | +1 |
| ADA/LTAG | Incirlik APT (Adana) | TR | +2 |
| ADB/LTBJ | Cumaovasi APT | TR | +2 |
| IST/LTBA | Ataturk/Yesilkoy (Istanbul) | TR | +2 |
| ADA/LTAG | Incirlik APT (Adana) | TR | +3 |
| ADA/LTAG | Incirlik APT (Adana) | TR | +3 |
| AVB/LIPA | Aviano AB | IT | +3 |
| RMS/ETAR | Ramstein AB | DE | |

### RAMSTEIN AB, DE (RMS); REGION: ATL; OPERATOR: AMC; TYPE: MIXED; ROUTE: CET1D; SAMPLE SCHEDULE: FRI & MON; EQUIPMENT: C130E

{RMS *NW* ➡ MHZ *SE* ➡ AVB ⇌ AVB *NW* ➡ RMS}

| LI/ICAO | AIRPORT/STATION | CTRY/STA | DAYS EN ROUTE |
|---|---|---|---|
| RMS/ETAR | Ramstein AB | DE | +0 |
| MHZ/EGUN | RAF Mildenhall | GB | +0 |
| AVB/LIPA | Aviano AB | IT | +0 |
| AVB/LIPA | Aviano AB | IT | +0 |
| RMS/ETAR | Ramstein AB | DE | |

### RAMSTEIN AB, DE (RMS); REGION: ATL; OPERATOR: AMC; TYPE: MIXED; ROUTE:CET1E; SAMPLE SCHEDULE: TUE & THU; EQUIPMENT: C130E

{RMS *SE* ➡ AVB ⇌ AVB *NW* ➡ MHZ *SE* ➡ RMS}

| LI/ICAO | AIRPORT/STATION | CTRY/STA | DAYS EN ROUTE |
|---|---|---|---|
| RMS/ETAR | Ramstein AB | DE | +0 |
| AVB/LIPA | Aviano AB | IT | +0 |
| AVB/LIPA | Aviano AB | IT | +0 |
| MHZ/EGUN | RAF Mildenhall | GB | +0 |
| RMS/ETAR | Ramstein AB | DE | |

### RAMSTEIN AB, DE (RMS); REGION: ATL; OPERATOR: AMC; TYPE: MIXED; ROUTE: CEU1A; SAMPLE SCHEDULE: 2ND & 4TH MON; EQUIPMENT: C130E

{RMS *SE* ➡ SIZ *SE* ➡ CHQ *NW* ➡ SIZ *NW* ➡ NAP *SE* ➡ SIZ *NW* ➡ OLB *SW* ➡ NAP *NE* ➡ OLB *SW* ➡ SIZ *NW* ➡ AVB *SE* ➡ GPA ⇌ GPA *NW* ➡ AVB *NW* ➡ RMS}

| LI/ICAO | AIRPORT/STATION | CTRY/STA | DAYS EN ROUTE |
|---|---|---|---|
| RMS/ETAR | Ramstein AB | DE | +0 |
| SIZ/LICZ | Sigonella NAS/APT (Sicily) | IT | +0 |
| CHQ/LGSA | Souda HAFC (Crete) | GR | +0 |
| SIZ/LICZ | Sigonella NAS/APT (Sicily) | IT | +1 |
| NAP/LIRN | Capodichino APT (Naples) | IT | +1 |
| SIZ/LICZ | Sigonella NAS/APT (Sicily) | IT | +2 |
| OLB/LIEO | Olbia/Costa Smeralda (Sardinia) | IT | +2 |
| NAP/LIRN | Capodichino APT (Naples) | IT | +3 |
| OLB/LIEO | Olbia/Costa Smeralda (Sardinia) | IT | +3 |
| SIZ/LICZ | Sigonella NAS/APT (Sicily) | IT | +3 |
| AVB/LIPA | Aviano AB | IT | +4 |
| GPA/LGRX | GAFB Araxos | GR | +4 |
| GPA/LGRX | GAFB Araxos | GR | +4 |
| AVB/LIPA | Aviano AB | IT | +4 |
| RMS/ETAR | Ramstein AB | DE | |

### RAMSTEIN AB, DE (RMS); REGION: ATL; OPERATOR: AMC; TYPE: MIXED; ROUTE: CEV4B; SAMPLE SCHEDULE: 1ST & 3RD MON; EQUIPMENT: C130E

{RMS *SE* ➡ SIZ *NW* ➡ CHQ *SE* ➡ SIZ *NE* ➡ NAP *SW* ➡ SIZ *NW* ➡ OLB *SE* ➡ NAP *NW* ➡ OLB *SE* ➡ SIZ *SE* ➡ CHQ ⮌ CHQ *NW* ➡ SIZ *N* ➡ NAP *NW* ➡ RMS}

| LI/ICAO | AIRPORT/STATION | CTRY/STA | DAYS EN ROUTE |
|---|---|---|---|
| RMS/ETAR | Ramstein AB | DE | +0 |
| SIZ/LICZ | Sigonella NAS/APT (Sicily) | IT | +0 |
| CHQ/LGSA | Souda HAFC (Crete) | GR | +0 |
| SIZ/LICZ | Sigonella NAS/APT (Sicily) | IT | +1 |
| NAP/LIRN | Capodichino APT (Naples) | IT | +1 |
| SIZ/LICZ | Sigonella NAS/APT (Sicily) | IT | +2 |
| OLB/LIEO | Olbia/Costa Smeralda (Sardinia) | IT | +2 |
| NAP/LIRN | Capodichino APT (Naples) | IT | +3 |
| OLB/LIEO | Olbia/Costa Smeralda (Sardinia) | IT | +3 |
| SIZ/LICZ | Sigonella NAS/APT (Sicily) | IT | +3 |
| CHQ/LGSA | Souda HAFC (Crete) | GR | +4 |
| CHQ/LGSA | Souda HAFC (Crete) | GR | +4 |
| SIZ/LICZ | Sigonella NAS/APT (Sicily) | IT | +4 |
| NAP/LIRN | Capodichino APT (Naples) | IT | +4 |
| RMS/ETAR | Ramstein AB | DE | |

### RAMSTEIN AB, DE (RMS); REGION: ATL; OPERATOR: AMC; TYPE: MIXED; ROUTE: G8F5S; SAMPLE SCHEDULE: SAT; EQUIPMENT: C017A

{RMS *SE* ➡ SIZ *SE* ➡ EKJ ⮌ EKJ *NW* ➡ RMS}

| LI/ICAO | AIRPORT/STATION | CTRY/STA | DAYS EN ROUTE |
|---|---|---|---|
| RMS/ETAR | Ramstein AB | DE | +0 |
| SIZ/LICZ | Sigonella NAS/APT (Sicily) | IT | +1 |
| EKJ/OEKJ | Prince Sultan AB | SA | +1 |
| EKJ/OEKJ | Prince Sultan AB | SA | +1 |
| RMS/ETAR | Ramstein AB | DE | |

### RAMSTEIN AB, DE (RMS); REGION: ATL; OPERATOR: AMC; TYPE: MIXED; ROUTE: G8T1S; SAMPLE SCHEDULE: MON; EQUIPMENT: C017A

{RMS *SE* ➡ ESB *SE* ➡ ADA ⮌ ADA *NW* ➡ RMS}

| LI/ICAO | AIRPORT/STATION | CTRY/STA | DAYS EN ROUTE |
|---|---|---|---|
| RMS/ETAR | Ramstein AB | DE | +0 |
| ESB/LTAC | Esenboga APT (Ankara) | TR | +0 |
| ADA/LTAG | Incirlik APT (Adana) | TR | +1 |
| ADA/LTAG | Incirlik APT (Adana) | TR | +1 |
| RMS/ETAR | Ramstein AB | DE | |

### RAMSTEIN AB, DE (RMS); REGION: ATL; OPERATOR: AMC; TYPE: MIXED; ROUTE: G8T1U; SAMPLE SCHEDULE: 1ST & 3RD WED; EQUIPMENT: C017A

{RMS *SE* ➡ ADA ⮌ ADA *NW* ➡ RMS}

| LI/ICAO | AIRPORT/STATION | CTRY/STA | DAYS EN ROUTE |
|---|---|---|---|
| RMS/ETAR | Ramstein AB | DE | +0 |
| ADA/LTAG | Incirlik APT (Adana) | TR | +1 |
| ADA/LTAG | Incirlik APT (Adana) | TR | +1 |
| RMS/ETAR | Ramstein AB | DE | |

### RAMSTEIN AB, DE (RMS); REGION: ATL; OPERATOR: AMC; TYPE: CGO W/ PAX; ROUTE: A8F1S; SAMPLE SCHEDULE: 2ND & 4TH WED; EQUIPMENT: C017A

{RMS *SE* ➡ ADA *SE* ➡ AMM ⮌ AMM *NW* ➡ RMS}

| LI/ICAO | AIRPORT/STATION | CTRY/STA | DAYS EN ROUTE |
|---|---|---|---|
| RMS/ETAR | Ramstein AB | DE | +0 |
| ADA/LTAG | Incirlik APT (Adana) | TR | +1 |
| AMM/OJAF | King Abdullah AB | JO | +1 |
| AMM/OJAF | King Abdullah AB | JO | +1 |
| RMS/ETAR | Ramstein AB | DE | |

### RAMSTEIN AB, DE (RMS); REGION: ATL; OPERATOR: AMC; TYPE: CGO W/ PAX; ROUTE: A8F3A; SAMPLE SCHEDULE: FRI; EQUIPMENT: C017A

{RMS *SE* ➡ SIZ *SE* ➡ BAH ⮌ BAH *NW* ➡ SIZ *NW* ➡ RMS}

| LI/ICAO | AIRPORT/STATION | CTRY/STA | DAYS EN ROUTE |
|---|---|---|---|
| RMS/ETAR | Ramstein AB | DE | +0 |
| SIZ/LICZ | Sigonella NAS/APT (Sicily) | IT | +1 |
| BAH/OBBI | Bahrain IAP | BH | +1 |
| SIZ/LICZ | Sigonella NAS/APT (Sicily) | IT | +2 |
| RMS/ETAR | Ramstein AB | DE | |

### RAMSTEIN AB, DE (RMS); REGION: ATL; OPERATOR: AMC; TYPE: CGO W/ PAX; ROUTE: A8F5A; SAMPLE SCHEDULE: TUE; EQUIPMENT: C017A

{RMS *SE* ➡ EKJ ⮌ EKJ *NW* ➡ RMS}

| LI/ICAO | AIRPORT/STATION | CTRY/STA | DAYS EN ROUTE |
|---|---|---|---|
| RMS/ETAR | Ramstein AB | DE | +0 |
| EKJ/OEKJ | Prince Sultan AB | SA | +1 |
| RMS/ETAR | Ramstein AB | DE | |

### RAMSTEIN AB, DE (RMS); REGION: ATL; OPERATOR: AMC; TYPE: CGO W/ PAX; ROUTE: A8F5T; SAMPLE SCHEDULE: THU; EQUIPMENT: C017A

{RMS *SE* ➡ BAH ⮌ BAH *SW* ➡ EKJ *NW* ➡ RMS}

| LI/ICAO | AIRPORT/STATION | CTRY/STA | DAYS EN ROUTE |
|---|---|---|---|
| RMS/ETAR | Ramstein AB | DE | +0 |
| BAH/OBBI | Bahrain IAP | BH | +1 |
| BAH/OBBI | Bahrain IAP | BH | +1 |
| EKJ/OEKJ | Prince Sultan AB | SA | +2 |
| RMS/ETAR | Ramstein AB | DE | |

### RAMSTEIN AB, DE (RMS); REGION: ATL; OPERATOR: AMC; TYPE: CGO W/ PAX; ROUTE: A8F5X; SAMPLE SCHEDULE: 2ND & 4TH THU; EQUIPMENT: C017A

{RMS *SE* ➡ BAH *SW* ➡ EKJ *NW* ➡ SIZ *SE* ➡ TTH ⮌ TTH *NW* ➡ SIZ *NW* ➡ RMS}

| LI/ICAO | AIRPORT/STATION | CTRY/STA | DAYS EN ROUTE |
|---|---|---|---|
| RMS/ETAR | Ramstein AB | DE | +0 |
| BAH/OBBI | Bahrain IAP | BH | +1 |
| EKJ/OEKJ | Prince Sultan AB | SA | +1 |
| SIZ/LICZ | Sigonella NAS/APT (Sicily) | IT | +1 |
| TTH/OOTH | OAFB Thumrait | OM | +2 |
| SIZ/LICZ | Sigonella NAS/APT (Sicily) | IT | +1 |
| RMS/ETAR | Ramstein AB | DE | |

**RAMSTEIN AB, DE (RMS); REGION: ATL;
OPERATOR: AMC; TYPE: CGO W/ PAX; ROUTE: A8G5A;
SAMPLE SCHEDULE: WED; EQUIPMENT: C017A**

{RMS *SW* ➡ KWI ⇌ KWI *NW* ➡ RMS}

| LI/ICAO | AIRPORT/STATION | CTRY/STA | DAYS EN ROUTE |
|---|---|---|---|
| RMS/ETAR | Ramstein AB | DE | +0 |
| KWI/OKBK | Kuwait IAP | KW | +1 |
| RMS/ETAR | Ramstein AB | DE | |

**RAMSTEIN AB, DE (RMS); REGION: ATL;
OPERATOR: AMC; TYPE: CGO W/ PAX; ROUTE: A8Q1A;
SAMPLE SCHEDULE: 1ST TUE; EQUIPMENT: C017A**

{RMS *SE* ➡ CAI ⇌ CAI *NW* ➡ RMS}

| LI/ICAO | AIRPORT/STATION | CTRY/STA | DAYS EN ROUTE |
|---|---|---|---|
| RMS/ETAR | Ramstein AB | DE | +0 |
| CAI/HECA | Cairo IAP | EG | +1 |
| RMS/ETAR | Ramstein AB | DE | |

**ATTRACTIONS:** Frankfurt, 78 miles northeast (fairs and retail centers); Kaiserslautern, 10 miles east (wine strasse); and Mannheim, 40 miles east.

## EN ROUTE SCHEDULES

| AIRPORT/STATION | LI-MISSION (page #) |
|---|---|
| Travis AFB | SUU-ATG3A (14) |
| Dover AFB | DOV-A201A & A2F5B (18) |
| Dover AFB | DOV-A2R3D (18) |
| Dover AFB | DOV-A2V1A & B (18) |
| Westover ARB | CEF-OFR3A (41) |
| Westover ARB | CEF-OFV1A (41) |
| Allen C Thompson (Jackson) | JAN-IKX3A (44) |
| McGuire AFB | WRI-A7R1A (51) |
| McGuire AFB | WRI-A7R3A (51) |
| McGuire AFB | WRI-AQ01A (51) |
| Stewart IAP/ANGB | SWF-IFV1A (54) |
| Stewart IAP/ANGB | SWF-IFV3A (54) |
| Wright-Patterson AFB | FFO-OER1A (62) |
| Charleston AFB/IAP | CHS-HJJ7A (69) |
| Charleston AFB/IAP | CHS-A4X3A (67) |
| Charleston AFB/IAP | CHS-A8R1S & A8R1T (67) |
| Charleston AFB/IAP | CHS-A8X5S(68) |
| Norfolk NS | NGU-HJS1G (79) |

### UNSCHEDULED FLIGHTS

There are frequent (daily) inter-theater MEDEVAC, C009A flights. There are also frequent inter-theater flights via C-130E aircraft. Call for destinations, routings and schedules.

# RHEIN-MAIN AIR BASE (FRF/EDDF)

626th AMSS/TRP
Unit 8700, PSC Box 160
APO AE 09050-8770
(Scheduled to close by end of 2005)

**LOCATION:** Adjacent to Frankfurt IAP 10 miles south of Frankfurt DE. Take the Rhein-Main Air Base exit from Autobahn A-5 which runs north to Frankfurt, and Bremerhaven DE, and south to Darmstadt DE, and the Black Forest DE, area. *ML-ARM: (50°10'N/08°35'E)*. LST: GMT+01:00. NMC: Frankfurt, 10 miles north. Main installation numbers: C-011-49-69-699-1110, D-314-330-1110.

**REGISTRATION INFO:** C-011-49-69-699-6567/8, D-314-330-6567/8, **Rec:** C-011-49-69-699-7746, D-314-330-7746, **Fax:** C-011-49-69-699-6309, D-314-330-6309. **E-mail: spacea@rheinmain.af.mil** Bldg 400, Hours: 0700-

1630 daily. From main gate go straight to right on to Vaughn Road, left on Stringer Road. Pax Term on right. **Pax Service Office:** Bldg 400, Hours: 0730-1630 daily.

**PAX LOUNGES: General:** Bldg 400, Hours: 0500-2100 daily. Enter from front of Term. A/C and telephones (commercial and defense). Upper level: TV, restrooms, O/S seats, showers and USO. Luggage lockers available inside front of terminal for $1.00. **DV/VIP:** Bldg 400, Hours: 0500-2100 daily. Center of upper level across from the cafeteria, O6+, GS-15+ eligible. A/C, TV, restrooms, O/S seats. **Protocol Service:** USAFEUR, C-011-49-69-699-6264.

**FOOD SERVICE: Cafeteria:** Bldg 400, Hours: 0600-1300 daily. **Enlisted Club:** Bldg 150, Hours: 1100-2100 daily, C-011-49-69-699-7727. **Snack Vending:** Bldg 400, Hours: 0500-2100 daily.

**TRANSPORTATION: Air Tickets:** SATO, Bldg 400, Hours: 0730-1630 Mon-Fri, C-011-49-69-699-7021. **Bus (Comm):** Bldg 400, schedule available at Info Tree. **On Base Car Rental:** Budget, Bldg 400, 011-49-69-69-59-1624; Hertz, Bldg 400, C-011-49-69-69-2188. **Shuttle/Bus:** Bldg 400, Hours: 0600-0800, 1100-1300, 1700-1900 daily, every 45 minutes. On base and to commercial terminal (FRF). Check with Pax Term for bus to RMS and other Army and AF installations. **Off Base Taxi:** Bldg 400, C-011-49-69-069-23404. **Trains:** Excellent service from Frankfurt to all of Europe. Must have tickets in advance - automatic ticket machines. Schedule available at TMO counter. **Parking:** 12 hour parking is available in front of terminal. If you must leave vehicle on base, limited long term parking is available for eligible. Passengers may leave vehicles for 30 days and must obtain a permit at the pax service counter. Another option is to park at Wiesbaden or Darmstadt and take the bus back to Rhein-Main. This is strongly encouraged during peak season (PCS moves as well as Space-A).

**TML:** Lodging Office: Gateway Inn, Bldg 600, 24 hours daily, C-011-49-69-699-7265/6843, D-314-330-6843/7265, Fax: C-011-49-69-699-7440, Fax: DSN-314-330-7440.

**RVC:** Rhein-Main Rec Area/Campground, Outdoor Rec, 1000-1700 hours Mon-Fri, Check-in campground, self registration, Bldg 705, C-011-49-699-7274, D-314-330-7274.

**TRAVELERS AID: Chaplain:** Bldg 155, duty hours, C-011-49-69-699-7501, D-314-330-7501, 1 mile away. **Lost/Found:** Bldg 400, Hours: 0730-1630 Mon-Fri, C-011-49-69-699-7592. (After normal duty hours contact Passenger Service Shift supervisor for assistance.) **Medical/ Dental:** Duty hours, C-011-49-69-699-7709/7307, D-314-330-7177; Emergency clinic, Bldg 170, C-011-49-69-699-6246 (Ambulance-117). **Red Cross:** Bldg 400, C-011-49-69-699-7514, D-314-330-7514, after hours ext 8742. **Security Police:** Bldg 343, Crime stop, C-011-49-69-699-7177; Emergency C-011-49-69-699-114, D-314-330-7177. **USO:** Bldg 400, 2nd floor, C-011-49-69-699-6424, D-314-330-6424.

**SUPPORT AVAILABLE: Bank/Currency Exchange:** Community Bank, Bldg 153, Hours: 0930-1530 Mon-Sat, C-011-49-69-699-7235/6235, D-314-330-7235, 0.5 miles away. Money exchange at commercial bank, Bldg 153, duty hours. **Convenience Store:** Bldg 400, Hours: 0600-1330. **Credit Union:** Bldg 153, C-011-49-69-699-7380, D-314-330-7380, 0.5 miles away. **Dry Cleaner:** Bldg 150, C-011-49-69-69-704222, 1 mile away. **Exchange:** Mini Exchange, Bldg 400, Hours: 0600-1330; Main Exchange, Bldg 166, Hours: 1000-1900 Tue-Sun, C-011-49-69-69-704123, 1 mile away. **Hair Styles:** Bldg 150; Barber, Hours: 0900-1730 Mon-Fri, 0900-1500 Sat, C-011-49-69-699-2254; Beauty, Hours: 0830-1730 Mon-Fri, 0830-1600 Sat, C-011-49-69-699-1442. **Laundry:** Bldg 349. **Postal Service:** Bldg 166, C-011-49-69-699-7680, D-314-330-7680, 1 mile away. **Shoppette:** Bldg 611, Hours: 0700-2200, C-011-49-69-699-704178, 3 miles away.

**ATTRACTIONS:** Frankfurt, trade fairs, zoo.

**NOTE:** On 23 December 1999 in a ceremony at the base passenger terminal an agreement was signed by officials from the U.S. State Department, U.S. Air Force in Europe, the German government and the German states of Hessen and Rhineland-Palatinate which calls for the complete return of Rhein-Main Air Base by the end of 2005. Negotiations for the return began in May 1998. The return of Rhein-Main's 385 acres will allow the expansion of cargo handling and aircraft parking facilities at Frankfurt IAP. In return, USAFE will receive a total of DM 730 million to relocate Rhein-Main's contingency and airlift operations to Ramstein and Spangdahlem Air Bases, Germany.

***Note: Commercially contracted flights are now called Patriot Express.***

### RHEIN-MAIN AIR BASE, DE (FRF); REGION: ATL; OPERATOR: COM; TYPE: MIXED; ROUTE: HJF5A; SAMPLE SCHEDULE: 2ND MON; EQUIPMENT: DC862

{FRF *SE* ➡ AVB *SE* ➡ EKJ ⇌ EKJ *NW* ➡ AVB *NW* ➡ FRF}

| LI/ICAO | AIRPORT/STATION | CTRY/STA | DAYS EN ROUTE |
|---|---|---|---|
| FRF/EDDF | Rhein-Main AB (Frankfurt) | DE | +0 |
| AVB/LIPA | Aviano AB | IT | +0 |
| EKJ/OEKJ | Prince Sultan AB | SA | +1 |
| AVB/LIPA | Aviano AB | IT | +1 |
| FRF/EDDF | Rhein-Main AB (Frankfurt) | DE | |

### EN ROUTE SCHEDULES

| AIRPORT/STATION | LI-MISSION (page #) |
|---|---|
| WM B Hartsfield IAP (Atlanta) | ATL-EX37A (27) |
| WM B Hartsfield IAP (Atlanta) | ATL-EXR5B (27) |
| Baltimore/Washington IAP | BWI-LZ27A (38) |
| Baltimore/Washington IAP | BWI-LX19A (38) |

### UNSCHEDULED FLIGHTS

There are frequent (daily) inter-theater flights. Call for destinations, routings and schedules.

## Other Germany Installations with Possible Space-A Air Opportunities

**SEMBACH ANNEX (RAMSTEIN AB) (SEX/EDAS)**, APO AE 09094-5000. ***Note: Used as auxiliary landing site. ML-ARM: (49°25'N/08°00'E)***. LST: GMT+01:00. See Ramstein AB, Space-A **C-011-49-6371-47-2120/2433/5364, D-314-480-2120/5364/2433, Fax: C-011-49-6371-47-2364. TML:** 011-49-6371-47-7345/7864/2445/2614, D-314-480-7864, 0730-2000 Mon-Fri. Call for destinations, routings and schedules.

**SPANGDAHLEM AIR BASE (SPM/ETAD)**, APO AE 09123-5000. Limited Space-A opportunities, call 52nd Ops Group at **C-011-49-6565-61-1110/6637, D-314-452-1110/6637.** 52nd Transportation Squadron Combat Readiness and Resources Air Freight Section at **C-011-49-6565-61-7212, D-314-452-7212,** Mon-Fri 0730-1630 hours. *ML-ARM: (49°55'N/06°40'E)*. LST: GMT+01:00. **TML:** Lodging Office: Bldg 3670, **C-011-49-6565-61-6504, D-314-452-6504,** Fax: **C-011-49-6565-95-6530.** DV/VIP Protocol, **C-011-49-6565-61-6057, D-314-452-6057.** O6+. Full base support facilities available. ***Note: Much construction and expansion planned, as Spangdahlem will become a contingency airlift base after Rhein-Main closes at the end of 2005. Obey no passing zones in this area-Entered b Detus Mil High Fines***

### UNSCHEDULED FLIGHTS

Most flights from transient aircraft. Call for destinations, routings and schedules.

**STUTTGART ARMY AIRFIELD (STR/EDDS)**, APO AE 09107-5000, **C-011-49-711-680-1110, D-314-430-1110** (Ask for Army Airfield Operations). *ML-ARM: (48°41'N/09°13'E)*. LST: GMT+01:00. Hours: 0600-2100 Mon-Fri, 0700-1500 Sat-Sun. Located at the Stuttgart IAP. Services U.S. and NATO flights, including heavy lift aircraft such as C-005A/B, C-141B, C-130 and C-009A. Very limited services. ***Note: Flights scheduled to land here are sporadic, and reservations must be organized within the chain of command of a specific flight. No reservations made out of this office.***

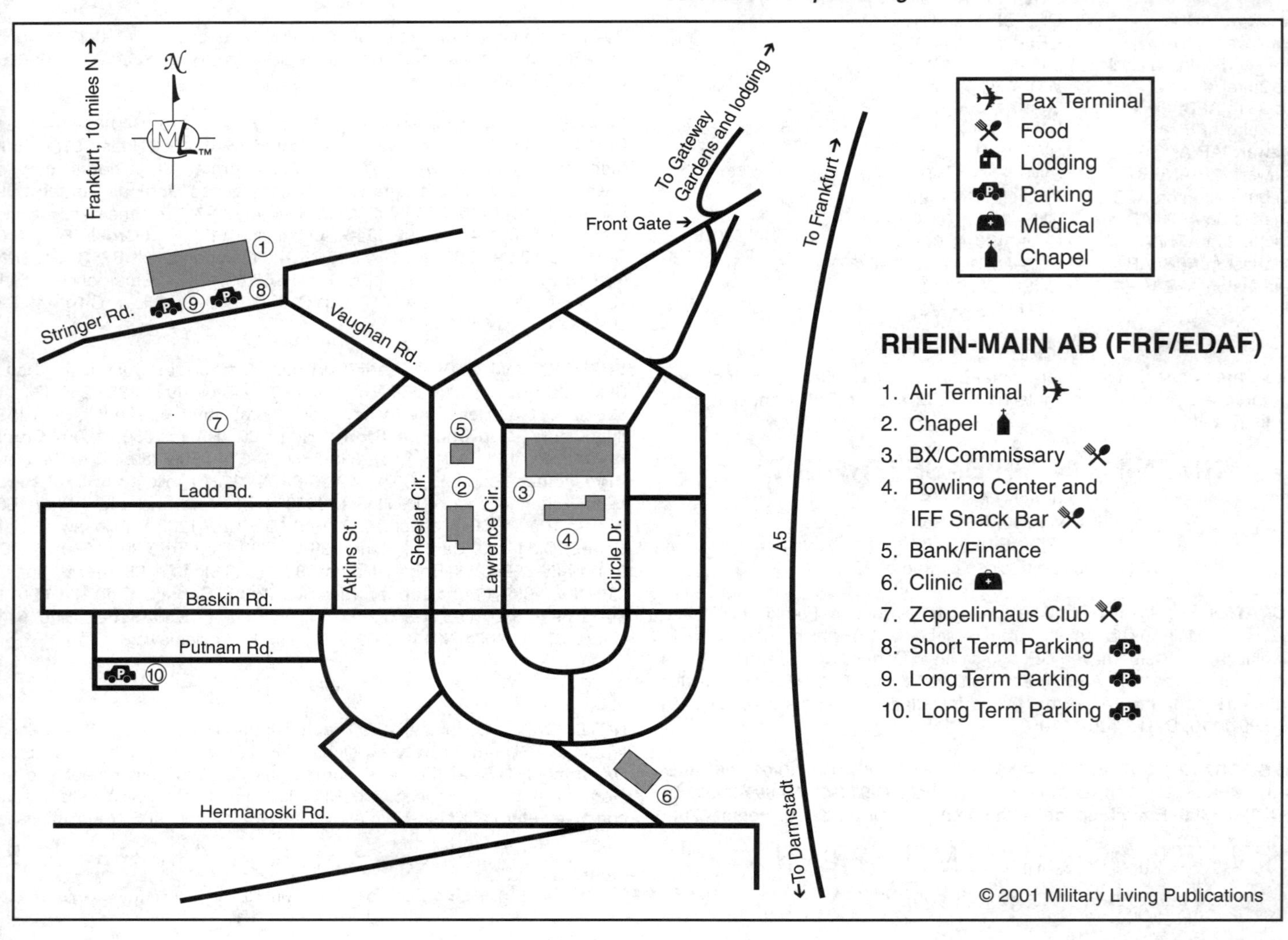


**RHEIN-MAIN AB (FRF/EDAF)**

1. Air Terminal
2. Chapel
3. BX/Commissary
4. Bowling Center and IFF Snack Bar
5. Bank/Finance
6. Clinic
7. Zeppelinhaus Club
8. Short Term Parking
9. Long Term Parking
10. Long Term Parking

# GREECE

## GAFB ARAXOS (GPA/LGRX)

731 MUNSS, LGLO
Bldg 2067
General Delivery ATTN: Passenger Terminal
APO AE 09843-5000

**LOCATION:** A Greek AFB on the Gulf of Araxos, located 125 miles west of Athens, GR and 25 miles southwest of Patrae, GR. *ML-ARM: (38°15'N/21°50'E).* LST: GMT+02:00. **You must have prior approval to land at the installation and must possess Entry Control letter before arrival.**

**REGISTRATION INFO: C-011-30-1-721-2951 ext 212/213, D-314-631-2039, Fax: C-011-30-1-725-0373.** Flights processed by USODA staff or contractor personnel. Make Space-A air applications through the USODA as instructed by that office.

**TRAVELERS AID: Security Police:** D-314-631-2028, 500 yards away.

**SUPPORT AVAILABLE: Exchange:** Hours: 1030-1630, D-314-631-2014, 100 feet away. **Postal Service:** Hours: 0730-1630, D-314-631-2058, 500 yards away.

**OTHER INFORMATION:** Port of entry.

### EN ROUTE SCHEDULES

| AIRPORT/STATION | LI-MISSION (page #) |
| --- | --- |
| Ramstein AB | RMS-CEU1A (111) |

## SOUDA BAY NAVAL SUPPORT ACTIVITY (CRETE) (CHQ/LGSA)

PSC 814, Box 7
FPO AE 09865-0032

**LOCATION:** On the northwest end of the island of Crete on Souda Bay. City of Chania located 10 miles west. The NATO Missile Firing Installation (NAMFI) is 5 miles north of Souda, Greece. *ML-ARM: (35°30'N/24°10'E).* LST: GMT+01:00. NMC: Chania, GR, 10 miles west. Main installation numbers: C-011-30-821-66200-5, D-314-266-1110.

**REGISTRATION INFO: C-011-30-821-66200 ext 1275/1383, D-314-266-1275/1383, Fax: C-011-30-821-66200 ext 1525, D-314-266-1525.** Air Terminal processes all Space-A passengers. Chania, Greece Airport co-located with Souda Bay NSA.

**PAX LOUNGES:** Pax Term currently under construction. Temporary trailer located next to hangar functions as Air Term. Available: TV.

**FOOD SERVICE:** All Hands Dining Facility, Bldg 2, ext 266. All Hands Club (Graffitis), ext 289. Bowling Center and Stars and Stripes, ext 1343, offer limited fast food. Many local fast food establishments.

**TRANSPORTATION: Air Tickets:** MWR Tours agency, Chania term, Olympic Airlines. **Taxi (Comm):** C-011-30-821-98700/98701. Car Rental available on base. Taxis available outside main gate. No taxis allowed on base. Ten minute walk from terminal to main gate. Base shuttle bus to the downtown and peninsula area available at regular schedule daily intervals.

**TML:** For official duty only: C-011-30-821-66200 ext 1601/1602. No billeting.

**TRAVELERS AID: Medical:** ext 591 (limited).

**SUPPORT AVAILABLE:** MWR, NEX, ext 432. **Postal Service:** ext 339. Laundry available.

**OTHER INFORMATION:** Port of Entry.
**ATTRACTIONS:** Museums, historical sights and great beaches. In winter many archeological sights and museums on the island may be closed.

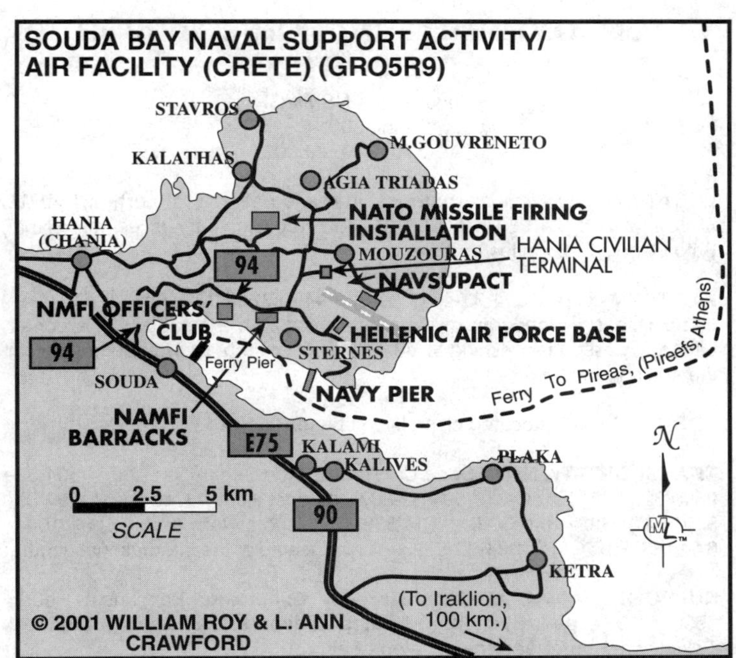


### EN ROUTE SCHEDULES

| AIRPORT/STATION | LI-MISSION (page #) |
| --- | --- |
| Ramstein AB | RMS-CEU1A (111) |
| Ramstein AB | RMS-CEV4B (112) |

# HONDURAS

## SOTO CANO AIR BASE (PLA/MHSC)

Pacific Architects and Engineers, Inc.
Air Transportation Manager
PSC 42, Unit 5720
APO AA 34042-5000

**LOCATION:** In southeast Honduras. From Tegucigalpa take the highway northwest to Comayagua, after about 24 miles you will see the signs for Soto Cano Air Base. Comayagua is 8 miles farther northwest. The elevation in this area is about 3000 feet above sea level. *ML-ARM: (14°08'N/87°12'W).* LST: GMT-06:00. NMC: Tegucigalpa, 30 miles southeast. Main installation numbers: C-011-504-234-4634, D-313-449-4000/4634.

**REGISTRATION INFO: C-011-504-234-4634 ext 6630/6629, D-313-449-4000/4634 ext 6630/6629, Fax: C-011-504-234-4634 ext 6629, D-313-449-4000/4634 ext 6629.** Air Transportation Manager, C-011-504-234-4634, ext 4491, D-313-449-4491. Ask at the main gate for directions to the Air Passenger/Ops Bldg. All passengers departing on commercial airlines must pay a 95.00 lempira (approximately $12.00) exit tax.

**PAX LOUNGES:** Very limited area for passenger processing.

**FOOD SERVICE:** Three clubs and several dining facilities on base.

**TML:** BQs. substandard conditions. Emergency lodging only. No charge.

**TRANSPORTATION:** Commercial Bus and Taxi service to Tegucigalpa. Lodging only. No charge

### EN ROUTE SCHEDULES

| AIRPORT/STATION | LI-MISSION (page #) |
| --- | --- |
| Charleston AFB/IAP | CHS-HJJ7A (69) |

# TONCONTIN INTERNATIONAL AIRPORT (TGU/MHTG)

Tegucigalpa USMILGP
Unit 3001
APO AA 34022-5000

**LOCATION:** Two miles south of the international airport. *ML-ARM: (14°04'N/87°13'W)*. LST: GMT-06:00. NMC: Tegucigalpa, 5 miles north. NMI: Soto Cano AB, 30 miles northwest.

**PAX TERM: C-011-504-33-4618, D-313-449-5328/5329, Fax: D-313-449-5330.** This is a Honduran military installation with a small UH1 helicopter pad; any passenger wishing to enter has to make prior arrangements with the station manager.

**FOOD SERVICE:** Located close by, off base.

**TRANSPORTATION: Off Base Car Rental:** Avis Rent A Car, C-011-504-33-9548/32-2510, Fax: C-011-504-32-8871; Budget Rent A Car, C-011-504-33-5161/5171/6927, Fax: C-011-504-33-5170; Toyota Rent A Car, C-011-504-34-3183, Fax: C-011-504-33-5790. All are located at the international airport.

**SUPPORT AVAILABLE: Bank/Currency Exchange:** Bancahsa, Hours: 0900-1700, airport. **Exchange:** located at airport. **Laundry/Dry Cleaner:** Downtown. **Postal Service:** located at airport.

## EN ROUTE SCHEDULES

| AIRPORT/STATION | LI-MISSION (page #) |
| --- | --- |
| Maxwell AFB | MXF-OBJ5A (2) |

# ICELAND

## KEFLAVIK AIRPORT (KEF/BIKF)

Air Terminal Officer
PSC 1003, Box 27
Keflavik Naval Station
FPO AE 09728-0327

**LOCATION:** In North Atlantic, 2300 miles northeast of New York City and 1000 miles northwest of Oslo, NO. On the southwest coast of the island. *ML-ARM: (63°59'N/22°36'W)*. LST: GMT+00:00. NMC: Reykjavik, 45 miles northeast. Main installation numbers: C-011-354-425-2000, D-EUR-312-228-2000, D-CONUS-312-450-2000. Switchboard Ops: Hours: 0800-1700 Mon-Fri.

**REGISTRATION INFO: C-011-354-425-6139, D-312-450-6139/7564, Fax: C-011-354-425-4649, D-312-450-4649. E-mail: air.terminal@ naskef.navy.mil** Bldg 782, Hours: 0800-1700 Mon-Fri. Directions: Main gate straight to dead end at Pax Term, white building to the right of the Navy Lodge. **Pax Service Office:** C-011-354-425-6139, D-312-450-6139/7564. **Pax Paging:** C-011-354-425-6139, D-312-450-6139/7564.

**PAX LOUNGES:** Bldg 782, 24 hours daily, next to arrival/departure area. **General:** Bldg 782, ext 6139. Restrooms, TV, P/C seats. **Family:** nursery. **DV/VIP:** Bldg 782, 24 hours daily, ext 6139. Private area, coffee/tea service, restrooms. Host as required. **Protocol Service:** Bldg 782, duty hours, ext 4494.

**FOOD SERVICE: Dining Hall:** Bldg 743, Hours: 0600-2330 daily, ext 2220/4459 (4th meal 2230-0030). **Fast Food:** Wendy's, Bldg 771, Hours: 0700-2130 Mon-Fri, 0830-2100 Sat, 1200-2100 Sun. **Marine Enlisted Club:** Bldg 741, Hours: 1100-2300 Sun-Thu, 1100-0100 Fri-Sat, ext 7083. **Restaurants:** Parcheezi's, Bldg 749, Hours: 1100-2200 Sun-Thu, 1100-2300

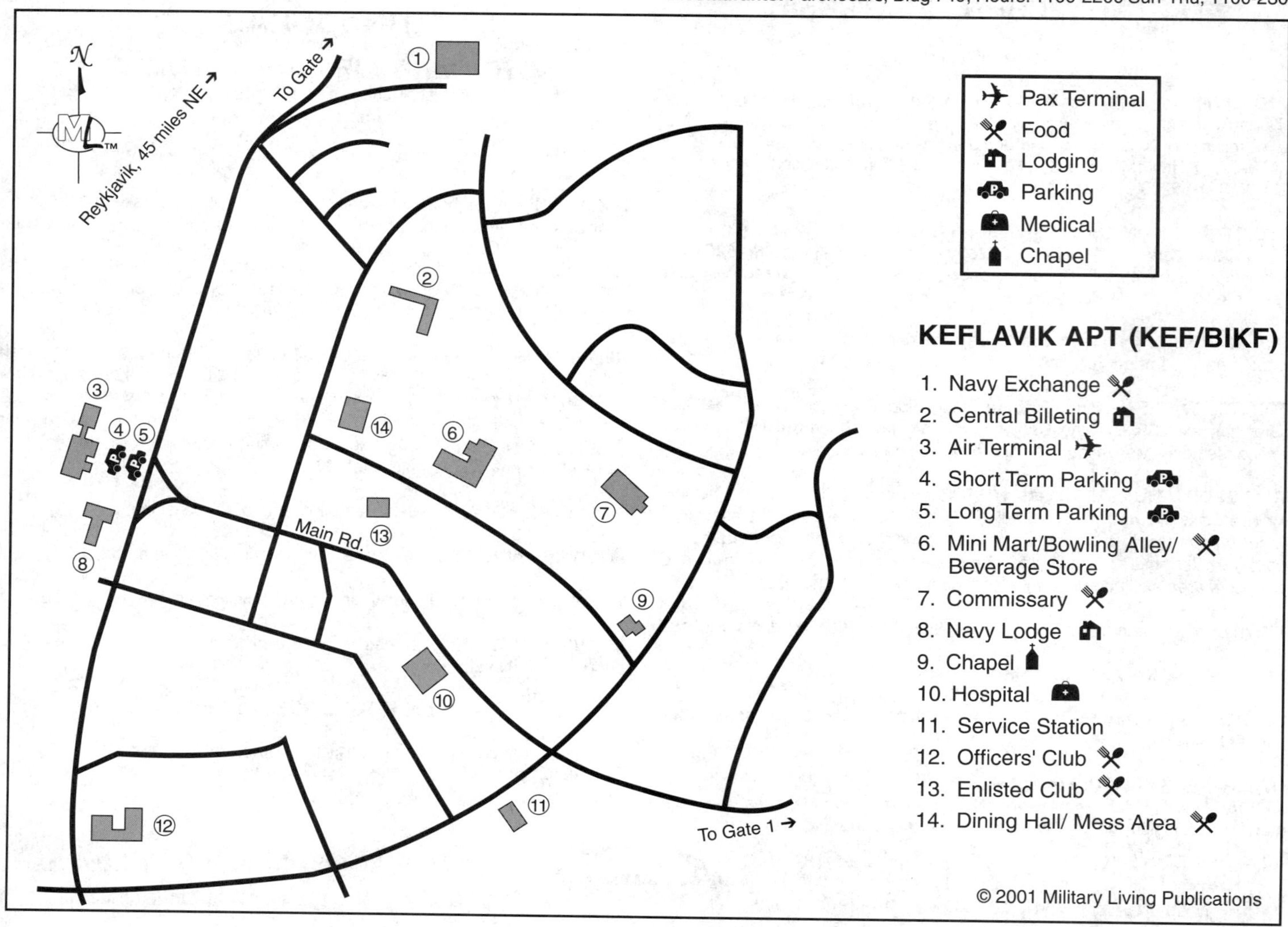


### KEFLAVIK APT (KEF/BIKF)

1. Navy Exchange
2. Central Billeting
3. Air Terminal
4. Short Term Parking
5. Long Term Parking
6. Mini Mart/Bowling Alley/ Beverage Store
7. Commissary
8. Navy Lodge
9. Chapel
10. Hospital
11. Service Station
12. Officers' Club
13. Enlisted Club
14. Dining Hall/ Mess Area

Fri-Sat, ext 6126; Three Flags O Club, Bldg 691; Hours: 1100-1300 Tue-Fri Lunch, 1800-2100 Tue-Sat Dinner, 1100-1400 Sun Brunch, ext 7004.

**TRANSPORTATION: Tour Office:** Bldg 771, Hours: 0900-1645 Mon-Fri. **Air Tickets:** Iceland Air, IAP Term, 24 hours daily, ext 9-50200. **On Base Car Rentals:** Navy Lodge, Bldg 786, 24 hours daily, C-011-354-425-2210, D-314-450-2210; Bldg 755, C-011-354-425-4200, D-314-450-4200. **On Base Shuttle/Bus:** Bldg 782 (Stop #34), Hours: 0700-2140 Mon-Fri (Bus #1); 1400-1700 Mon-Fri (Bus #2). All on base locations. **Off Base Shuttle/Bus (Comm):** Keflavik, Hours: 0645-2300 Mon-Fri (Keflavik to Reykjavik). Proceed out main gate, left to bus station. Also at IAP Terminal ($4 for 45 minute ride to Reykjavik hotels). **On/Off Base Taxi:** Adalston, 24 hours daily, ext 2525; Okuleidir, ext 4141. Any place on base: $5.00. **Parking:** Bldg 782, 24 hours daily (limited spaces, no restrictions).

**TML:** Lodging Office: Bldg 761, 24 hours daily; BOQ/BEQ, C-011-354-425-4333, D-314-450-4333. All ranks. Fax: C-001-354-425-511. Navy Lodge: Bldg 786, 24 hours daily, 011-354-425-2210 or 1-800-NAVY-INN. DV/VIP: 011-354-425-4414.

**TRAVELERS AID: Chaplain:** Bldg 775 (Chapel), Hours: 0800-1700, C-011-354-425-4111, D-314-450-4111. **Emergency Relief:** Bldg 782, Hours: 0900-1400 Mon-Fri, ext 4923. **Lost/Found:** Bldg 782, 24 hours daily, ext 2280. **Medical/Dental:** Bldg 710, 24 hours daily, C-011-354-425-3300/3301, D-314-450-3300/3301. **Red Cross:** Bldg 782, Hours: 0800-1600, C-011-354-425-6210, D-314-450-6210. **Security Police:** Bldg 810, 24 hours daily, C-011-354-425-2211, D-314-450-2211. **USO:** Bldg 758, Hours: 0800-2100 Mon-Thu, 0800-2200 Fri-Sun, ext 6113/7980/6124. Full service including grill and free coffee.

**SUPPORT AVAILABLE: Bank/Currency Exchange:** Bldg 645, Hours: 0900-1600, C-011-354-425-4625, D-314-450-4625. **Credit Union:** Bldg 771, Hours: 0900-1630, C-011-354-425-6441, D-314-450-6441. **Exchange:** Bldg 869B, Hours: 1000-1800, C-011-354-425-2141, D-314-450-2141. **Hair Styles:** Barber, Hours: 0900-1800 Mon-Fri, 0900-1600 Sat, 1300-1800 Sun; Beauty, Bldg 771, Hours: 0900-1900 Mon-Thu, 0900-1700 Fri-Sat, ext 6211. **Laundry/Dry Cleaning:** Bldg 632, Hours: 0800-1700 Mon-Fri, 1000-1300 Sat, C-011-654-425-4163, D-314-450-4163. **Postal Service:** Bldg 771, Hours: 1000-1730, C-011-354-425-2203, D-314-450-2203. **Shoppette:** Bldg 771, Hours: 1000-2200, C-011-354-425-6519, D-314-450-6519.

**OTHER INFORMATION:** Port of Entry and U.S. Customs Service Airport.

**ATTRACTIONS:** Wildlife, glaciers, and ice-caps.

### EN ROUTE SCHEDULES

| AIRPORT/STATION | LI-MISSION (page #) |
| --- | --- |
| Allen C Thompson (Jackson) | JAN-IKX3A (44) |
| McGuire AFB | WRI-A7X3C (51) |
| Charleston AFB/IAP | CHS-A4X3A (67) |
| Norfolk NS | NGU-EX13DM & EX23A (78) |
| Norfolk NS | NGU-HJS1G (79) |

# INDONESIA

## HALIM PERDANAKUSUMA AIR BASE (HLP/WIIH)

OMADP
Attn: AMC Rep
Box 2, Unit 8133
APO AP 96520-8133

**LOCATION:** On northwest end of the island of Java. *ML-ARM: (06°16'S/106°53'E).* LST: GMT+07:00. NMC: Jakarta, 45 miles east. Main installation number (US Embassy): C-011-62-21-344-2211 ext 2621 or 2631, D-none.

**REGISTRATION INFO: C-011-62-21-344-2211 ext 2621 or 2631, Fax: C-011-62-21-386-2259.** Contact the AMC representative at the U.S. Embassy in advance or upon arrival into Indonesia as entrance to base is restricted. Pax Term, Hours: 0730-1530 Mon-Fri. No U.S. base support facilities. Cab from HLP to Jakarta approximately $8 US.

**PAX LOUNGES: General:** telephones (local), restrooms, wooden seats. Located next to aircraft parking area.

### EN ROUTE SCHEDULES

| AIRPORT/STATION | LI-MISSION (page #) |
| --- | --- |
| Yokota AB | OKO-T8F7E (128) |

# IRELAND

## SHANNON AIRPORT (SNN/EINN)

**LOCATION:** *ML-ARM: (52°42'N/08°55'W).* LST: GMT+00:00. ***Note: AMC flights transit this airport only for the purpose of refueling and crew change. No passengers may board or exit the aircraft, therefore, no Space-A to Ireland is permitted.***

### EN ROUTE SCHEDULES

| AIRPORT/STATION | LI-MISSION (page #) |
| --- | --- |
| Baltimore/Washington IAP | BWI-LX27A (38) |

# ISRAEL

## BEN GURION INTERNATIONAL AIRPORT (TEL AVIV) (TLV/LLBG)

OL-A, 621 AMSG (AMC)
Unit 7228, Box 7
APO AE 09830-7228

**LOCATION:** In the Eastern Mediterranean. The airport is 9 miles east of the city. *ML-ARM: (32°01'N/34°53'E).* LST: GMT+02:00. NMC: Tel Aviv Yafo, 9 miles west. Main installation numbers: C-011-972-3-971-2018.

**REGISTRATION INFO: C-011-972-3-971-4333, Fax: C-011-972-3-972-1989.** Pax Term. Near Gate 3. Pax processed by contractor, Laufer Aviation. Full services of IAP. No U.S. military facilities available.

**TRANSPORTATION: On Base Bus:** Pax Term, Hours: 0400-2400 daily (United Tours #222, TLV to city, $3 US). **Taxi:** Pax Term, 24 hours daily (TLV to city, $25 US, 15-20 minute ride).

**ATTRACTIONS:** Jerusalem.

### UNSCHEDULED FLIGHTS
Flights to: Ramstein AB, DE (**RMS**); Rhein-Main AB, DE (**FRF**); and Sigonella NAS/Airport, IT (**SIZ**). Call for destinations, routings and schedules.

### EN ROUTE SCHEDULES

| AIRPORT/STATION | LI-MISSION (page #) |
| --- | --- |
| Ramstein AB | RMS-G8W5S (111) |

# ITALY

## AVIANO AIR BASE (AVB/LIPA)

Det 3, 621st AMSG/TROP
Unit 6165, Box 215, Bldg 933
APO AE 09601-5215

**LOCATION:** From A-28 N exit Pordenone to IT-159 N for 8 miles to Aviano AB. *ML-ARM (46°05'N/09°35'E)*. LST: GMT+01:00. NMC: Pordenone, 6 miles south. Main installation numbers: C-011-39-0434-66-113, D-314-632-1110.

**REGISTRATION INFO:** C-011-39-0434-66-7680, D-314-632-7680. **Rec:** C-011-39-0434-66-7520, D-314-632-7520, **Fax:** C-011-39-0434-66-7782, D-314-632-7782. **E-mail: spacea@aviano.af.mil WEB: www.aviano.af.mil** Bldg 933, Hours: 0600-2200 Sun-Fri, 24 hours Sat. Directions: In area F, south of Aviano on the right of Pordenone. **Pax Service Office:** C-011-39-0434-66-7680, D-314-632-7680 (NCO on duty). **Pax Paging:** C-011-39-0434-66-7680, D-314-632-7680.

**PAX LOUNGES:** Bldg 933, family lounges available. **General:** Bldg 933, Hours: 0600-2100 Mon-Fri, 0800-1700 Sat-Sun. C-011-39-0434-66-7730. A/C, restrooms, TV, O/S seats. **Family Lounge:** Small dependents' lounge located within main lounge. Microwave, refrigerator, sink. **Protocol Service:** Hq 40th TACG, Hours: 0800-1700 Mon-Fri, C-011-39-0434-66-7604 (ask for Chief of Staff). AT&T and U.S. direct phones are available for use in the pax lounge.

**FOOD SERVICE: Cafeteria:** Bldg 1133, Hours: 0600-0800 Breakfast, 1100-1300 Lunch, 1600-1800 Dinner Mon-Fri, C-011-39-0434-66-7297, D-314-632-7297, Flightline, 1.5 miles away. **Combined Club:** Bldg 147, Hours: 1100-0200 daily, C-011-39-0434-66-7483. **Dining Hall:** Bldg 244, C-011-39-04034-66-7297; Bldg 250, C-011-39-0434-66-7463. **Fast Food:** Burger King, Hours: 0600-2100 Mon-Fri, 0700-2100 Sat-Sun, C-011-39-0434-66-7840, D-314-632-7840, Area 1, 0.5 miles away. **Snack Bars:** Bldg 914, Flightline, 100 yards away. Hours: 0600-2000 Mon-Fri, 0600-1400 Sat, C-011-39-0434-66-7736, D-314-632-7736. **Snack Vending:** Bldg 179 AAFES Food Mall, Area 1, 24 hours daily.

**TRANSPORTATION: Air Tickets:** SATO, Bldg 224, Hours: 0800-1700 Mon-Fri, C-011-39-0434-66-7791. **On Base Car Rentals:** In Terminal, C-011-39-0434-66-8719, D-314-632-8719 (Eurocar). **Off Base Car Rentals:** Beritich, 3 miles away, C-011-39-0434-65-2911; Hertz, 5 miles away, C-011-39-0434-52-0200. **On/Off Base Shuttle/Bus (Comm):** Runs hourly to all areas, C-011-39-0434-66-7666, D-314-632-7666. **On Base Taxi (Gov):** Bldg 1004, 24 hours daily, C-011-39-0434-66-7666. **Off Base Taxi (Comm):** Not allowed on base; meet at gate. C-011-39-0434-65-1073. **Off Base Trains:** Aviano, 3 miles away, and Pordenone, 5 miles away, 24 hours daily. **Parking:** Short and long term, Bldg 1020, 24 hours daily, C-011-39-0434-66-7200. Check with Security Police.

**TML:** Lodging Office: Bldg 256, 24 hours daily, C-011-39-0434-66-5722/5041, D-314-632-5722/5041, Fax: C-011-39-0434-66-5581. DV/VIP: C-011-39-0434-66-0598, O6+.

**TRAVELERS AID: Chaplain:** Bldg 172, Hours: 0800-1700 Mon-Fri, C-011-39-0434-66-7211, Area 1, 5 miles away. **Emergency Relief:** Bldg 600, Hours: 0800-1700 Mon-Fri, C-011-39-0434-66-7216. **Lost/Found:** Bldg 933, Hours: 0600-2100 Mon-Fri, 0800-1700 Sat-Sun, C-011-39-0434-66-7680. **Medical/Dental:** Bldg 121, 24 hours daily, C-011-39-0434-66-8150, D-314-637-8150, Area 1. **Red Cross:** Bldg 118, Hours: 0800-1630 Mon-Fri, C-011-39-0434-66-7576, D-314-632-7576, Area 1. **Security Police:** Bldg 1019, 24 hours daily, C-011-39-0434-66-7200, D-314-632-7200, 50 yards away.

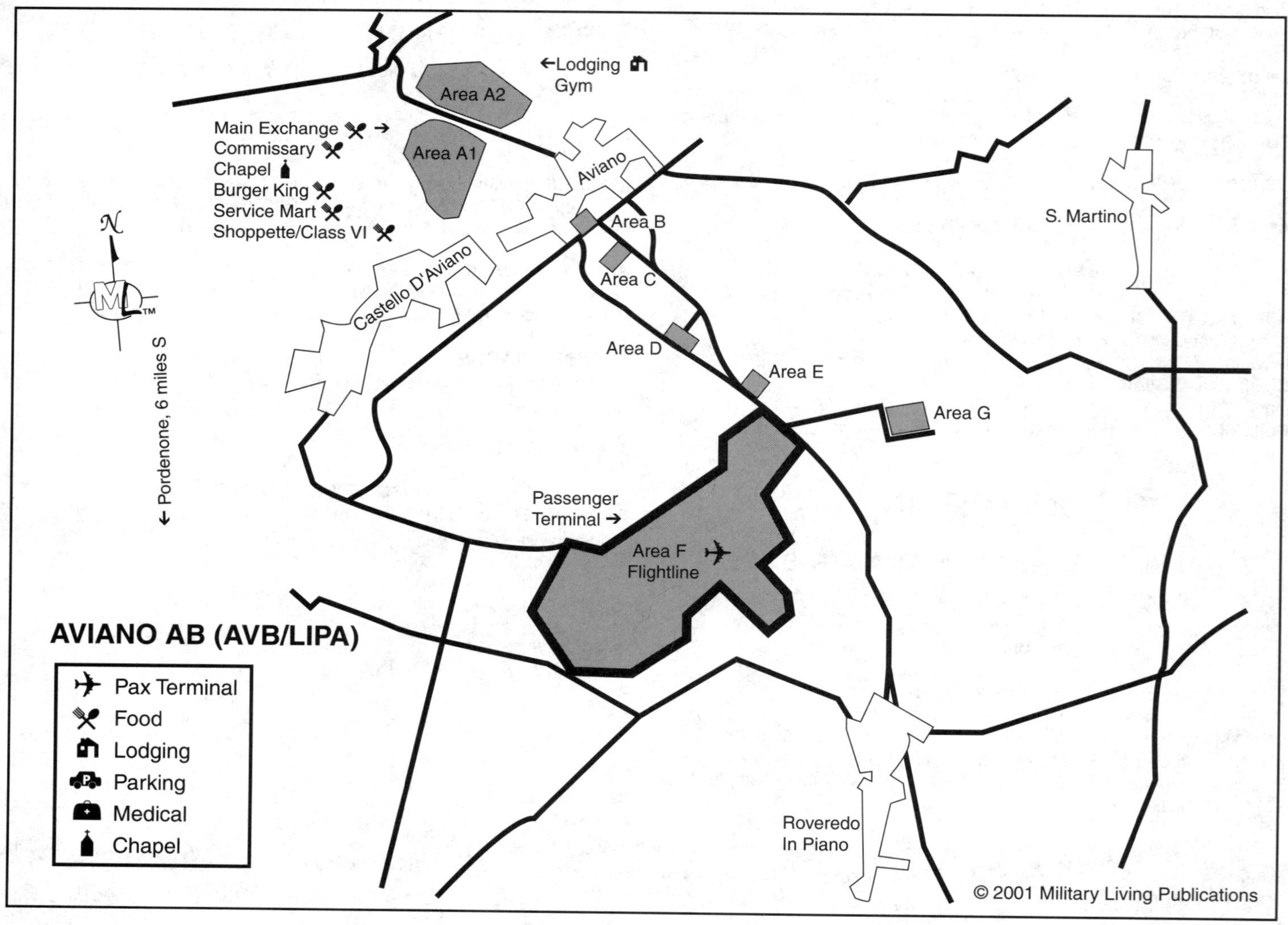

**SUPPORT AVAILABLE: Bank/Currency Exchange:** Bldg 140, Hours: 0900-1430 Mon-Fri, C-011-39-0434-66-7637, D-314-632-7637, Area 1, 5 miles away. Currency exchange at Combined Club and billeting. **Credit Union:** Hours: 0900-1600 Mon-Fri, 0900-1200 Sat, C-011-39-0434-66-7288, D-314-632-7288, Area 1, 5 miles away. **Exchange:** Bldg 179, Hours: 0900-1900 Mon-Sat, 0900-1700 Sun, C-011-39-0434-66-7571, D-314-632-7551, Area 1, 5 miles away. **Hair Styles:** Bldg 179, Hours: 0900-1800 Mon-Fri, 0900-1600 Sat; Barber, C-011-39-0434-66-7539; Beauty, C-011-39-0434-66-7539. **Laundry:** Bldg 257, 24 hours daily (coin operated). **Postal Service:** Bldg 142, Hours: 1100-1730 Mon-Fri, 1100-1300 Sat, C-011-39-0434-66-7735, D-314-632-7735. **Shoppette:** Hours: 0900-2300 Mon-Thu, 0900-2400 Fri-Sun, C-011-39-0434-66-7876, D-314-632-7876, Area 1, 5 miles away. **Valet/Dry Cleaning:** Bldg 256, Hours: 1000-1700 Mon-Sat, C-011-39-0434-66-7737, D-314-632-7737.

**ATTRACTIONS:** Excellent snow skiing in nearby Piancavallo, wine, beaches, Venice 1 hour. ***Note: Massive plan to renovate Aviano AFB to include new mall at Zappala Barracks and new roadways by the year 2000.***

### EN ROUTE SCHEDULES

| AIRPORT/STATION | LI-MISSION (page #) |
|---|---|
| Dover AFB | DOV-A2V1A & B (18) |
| Baltimore/Washington IAP | BWI-EXG5A (37) |
| Baltimore/Washington IAP | BWI-LX19A (38) |
| Westover ARB | CEF-OFV1A (41) |
| Stewart IAP/ANGB | SWF-IFV1A (54) |
| Ramstein AB | RMS-HJF5A (110) |
| Ramstein AB | RMS-HJF5B (110) |
| Ramstein AB | RMS-HJG5A (111) |
| Ramstein AB | RMS-CET1A (111) |
| Ramstein AB | RMS-CET1D (111) |
| Ramstein AB | RMS-CET1E (111) |
| Ramstein AB | RMS-CEU1A (111) |
| Rhein-Main AB (Frankfurt) | FRF-HJF5A (114) |

# CAPODICHINO AIRPORT (NAPLES) (NAP/LIRN)

U.S. Naval Support Activity
Air Terminal Division
PSC 817, Box 3
FPO AE 09622-1200

**LOCATION:** On the Gulf of Naples. Take Capodichino exit off Naples Tangenziale (local highway bypassing city). Route to airport is marked. *ML-ARM: (40°53'N/14°17'E)*. LST: GMT+01:00. NMC: Naples, 3 miles southeast. Main installation numbers: C-011-39-81-724-1110, D-314-625-1110.

**REGISTRATION INFO: C(USA)-011-39-081-568-5283/5247, C(EUR)-039-081-568-5283, D-314-626-5283/5247, Rec: C-011-39-081-568-5336, Fax: C(USA)-011-39-081-568-5259/5499, C(EUR)-039-081-568-5259, D-314-626-5259/5499. WEB: www.naples.navy.mil/airops E-mail: spacea@ naples.navy.mil** Bldg 405, Hours: 0600-2200 Mon-Sat, closed Sun. **Pax Paging:** C(USA)-011-39-081-568-5283, C(EUR)-039-081-568-5283, D-314-626-5283.

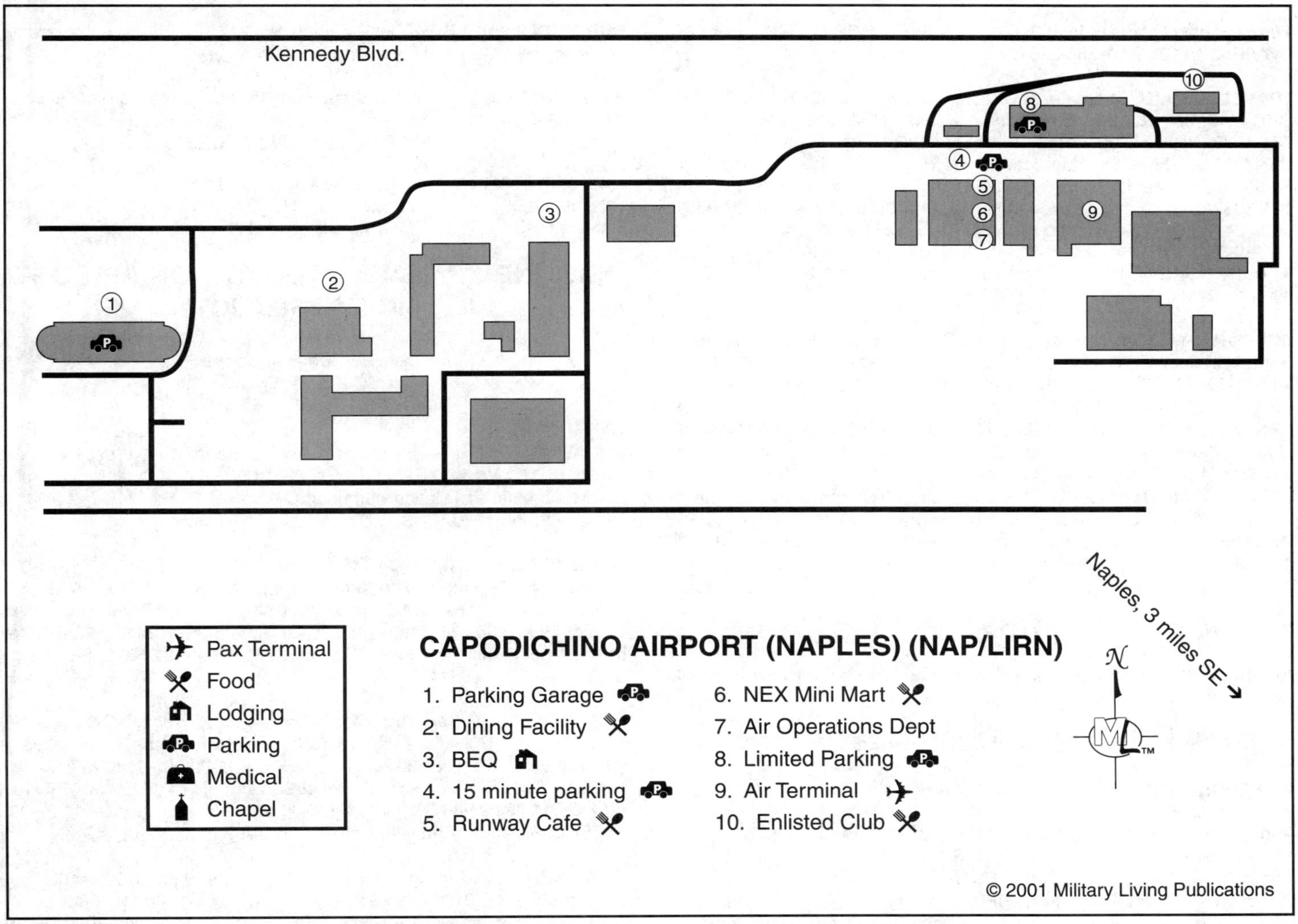

**PAX LOUNGES:** No family lounge. **General:** Bldg 405, Hours: 0600-2200 Mon-Sat, C-011-39-081-568-5283. A/C, nursery, restrooms, TV, P/C seats. **DV/VIP:** Across from Bldg 405, Hours: 0600-2200 Mon-Sat, C-011-39-081-568-5283. A/C, restrooms, TV, O/S seats. No host. **Protocol Service:** Map #8, Hours: 0700-1900 Mon-Sat, C-011-39-081-724-5224/6. *Note: A new passenger terminal is scheduled to open September 2000, and will include new lounges, restaurant, bookstore, convenience store, currency exchange and ATMs.*

**FOOD SERVICE: Dining Hall:** AFSOUTH Bldg D, Hours: 0615-1800 daily, C-011-39-081-721-2792. **Restaurants:** Nato Club, AFSOUTH, C-011-39-081-721-2760 or C-011-39-081-230-3317; Ciao Hall Capo, Hours: 0615-800/1100-1300/1645-1800 Mon-Fri, 0700-0815/1030-1300/1645-1800 Sat-Sun, C-011-39-081-568-5502. **Fast Food:** Burger King, Hours: 0500-1800 Mon-Fri, 1000-1700 Sat, C-011-39-081-568-5228. **Snack Bar:** Sports Bar, Hours: 1100-2200 daily, C-011-39-081-568-5384.

**TRANSPORTATION: Air Tickets:** SATO, Capo Bldg 1, Hours: 0900-1545 Mon-Fri, C-011-39-081-599-2671/2616. **Bus (Comm):** NAP, 24 hours daily. Ask for schedule (500 lire per ride), one mile. **Shuttle/Bus:** Bldg 405, Hours: 0600-0105 daily. Every 90 minutes NAP-NSA-HOSP-AFSOUTH to fleet landing. Every 30 minutes when fleet is in, 20 yards away. **Car Rentals:** NAP Apt, 24 hours daily; Avis, C-011-39-081-780-5790, 1 mile away; Eurocar, C-011-39-081-626-5298, inside terminal; Hertz, C-011-39-081-780-2971, 1 mile away; Italy-By-Car, C-011-39-081-780-5702. **Taxi (Comm):** Commercial airport, 24 hours daily, C-011-39-081-560-6060, 600 yards away. **Taxi (Gov):** GAETA, 24 hours daily, C-011-39-081-724-4797 (duty passengers only). **Trains:** Naples Central Station, 24 hours daily, 3 miles away. **Parking:** Bldg 405, 24 hours daily, 100 yards away. Check with Security Police.

**TML:** Lodging Office: Bldg 453, C-011-39-081-568-5250, D-314-568-5250. DV/VIP: C-011-39-081-568-3161.

**TRAVELERS AID: Chaplain:** NSA #30, 24 hours daily, C-011-39-081-568-5291, ADMIN 1CAPO. **Emergency Relief:** NSA #30, C-011-39-081-724-4139 (Navy Relief). **Lost/Found:** Bldg 405, Hours: 0600-2200 Mon-Fri, C-011-39-081-568-5283. **Medical:** Naval Hospital, 24 hours daily, C-011-39-081-724-4110/4300, D-314-625-4110 (ambulance), C-011-39-081-724-3333, D-314-625-3333 (emergency). **Red Cross:** NSA #30, C-011-39-081-724-4788/9; 24 hours daily. **Security Police:** NSA #9, 24 hours daily, C-011-39-081-724-3114. **USO:** NSA #10, Hours: 0800-1630 Mon-Fri, C-011-39-081-724-4664. Also, near fleet landing, Hours: 0815-2200 daily, C-011-39-081-724-4142.

**SUPPORT AVAILABLE:** Services at NSA, AFSOUTH Post, and GAETA. **Bank/Currency Exchange:** ADMIN 1, Hours: 0900-1500 Mon-Fri, C-011-39-081-568-5818. **Credit Union:** C-011-39-081-568-4145/4481. **Dry Cleaner:** 0800-1800 Mon-Fri, 0800-1600 Sat, C-011-39-081-724-4386 **Exchange:** NSA #2, Hours: 1000-1730 Tue-Fri, 1000-1600 Sat, C-011-39-081-568-5261 **Hair Styles:** Barber, Hours: 0800-1600 Mon-Fri, C-011-39-081-568-5298 inside the Air Terminal; Beauty, Hours: 0830-1730 Tue-Fri, 0830-1530 Sat, C-011-39-081-724-4349. **Laundry/Dry Cleaning:** NSA #2, Hours: 0800-1800 Tue-Fri, 0800-1600 Sat, C-011-39-081-724-4386. **Personnel Services Detachment CAPO:** Hours: 0900-1500, C-011-39-081-568-5818. **Postal Service:** NSA #4, Hours: 0900-1600 Mon-Fri, C-011-39-081-724-1110.

**OTHER INFORMATION:** Port of Entry.

**ATTRACTIONS:** Flea markets, Pompei, Island of Capri, Ischia, Sorrento, Ravello Positano, Amalfi, archeological sites.

### EN ROUTE SCHEDULES

| AIRPORT/STATION | LI-MISSION (page #) |
| --- | --- |
| Westover ARB | CEF-OFR3A (41) |
| Norfolk NS | NGU-EX11E (78) |
| Norfolk NS | NGU-EX17B (78) |
| Ramstein AB | RMS-CEU1A (111) |
| Ramstein AB | RMS-CEV4B (112) |

# www.MilitaryLiving.com

# OLBIA/COSTA SMERALDA AIRPORT (SARDINIA) (OLB/LIEO)

USNSO, Supply Office
PSC 816, Box 1795
FPO AE 09612-0051

**LOCATION:** The airport is located on the northeastern coast of the island of Sardinia. To reach the Naval Support Activity, from the airport follow highway SS-125 to Palau. At Palau, buy ticket for ferry (Palau Pier) and take ferry to La Maddalena. The installation is located next to the Italian Navy Hq approximately 3 blocks east of the ferry landing. *ML-ARM: (40°54'N/09°31'E).* LST: GMT+01:00. NMC: Olbia, 27 miles southeast. Main installation numbers: C-011-39-0789-798-254, D-314-623-8254/324.

**REGISTRATION INFO: C-011-39-0789-69516 (limited), Fax: C-011-39-0789-68874.** GEASAR/US Navy Office at Airport Terminal, Hours: 0800-1600 Mon-Fri.

**PAX LOUNGES:** Regular passengers terminal lounge and VIP lounge.

**FOOD SERVICE:** Snack bar available at the main airport close to the U.S. Navy office. Staff canteen also available near the airport.

**TRANSPORTATION:** Bus, Rental Cars and Taxi service available. City Bus to and from Olbia (tickets available from the bar cashier). Guarded car parking in front of the airport. Free parking in the airport area.

**TRAVELERS AID:** Customs, Medical assistance, Red Cross, Security Police.

**SUPPORT AVAILABLE:** Bank automatic desk (exchange not available). Tobacco, magazine and gift shops.

**ATTRACTIONS:** "Citta Mercato" shopping mall 0.5 miles from the airport.

### EN ROUTE SCHEDULES

| AIRPORT/STATION | LI-MISSION (page #) |
| --- | --- |
| Ramstein AB | RMS-CEU1A (111) |
| Ramstein AB | RMS-CEV4B (112) |

# SIGONELLA NAVAL AIR STATION/AIRPORT (SICILY) (SIZ/LICZ)

Commanding Officer
Attn: Air Terminal Officer
PSC 812, Box 3160
FPO AE 09627-3030

**LOCATION:** On the island of Sicily. Accessible from A-19 or IT-417. *ML-ARM: (37°20'N/15°00'E).* LST: GMT+01:00. NMC: Catania, 10 miles northeast. Main installation numbers: C-011-39-095-86-1110 (NAS II), C-011-39-095-56-1110 (NAS I), D-314-624-1110.

**REGISTRATION INFO: C-011-39-095-86-6725/6726/5576, D-314-624-6725/6726/5576, Fax: C-011-39-095-86-5211/6729, D-314-624-6729/1547.** Bldg 436, 24 hours daily. Main gate NAS II straight to Pax Term. **Pax Service Office:** Bldg 436, 24 hours daily, C-011-39-95-86-6725/6726/5576. **Fleet Info:** 24 hours daily, C-011-39-095-86-5575, D-314-624-5575, Fax: C-011-39-095-86-5211, D-314-624-5211.

**PAX LOUNGES: General:** Bldg 436, 24 hours daily, C-011-39-095-86-6725/6726/5576. A/C, telephones (commercial and defense), TV, restrooms, P/C seats. **DV/VIP:** Bldg 436, 24 hours daily, C-011-39-095-86-5575 (06+). A/C and other facilities in Pax Term. **Protocol Service:** Bldg 476, Hours: 0730-1600 daily, C-011-39-095-86-5313. **Family:** Bldg 436, 24 hours daily, C-011-39-095-86-5575. A/C, nursery, and other facilities in Pax Term.

**FOOD SERVICE: Dining Hall:** Bldg 533, Hours: 0530-0730, 1100-1300, 1600-1800, 2300-0100 Mon-Sat, 0700-0900, 1000-1200, 1600-1800 Sun, C-011-39-095-86-5738. **Enlisted Club:** (City Beat), Bldg 151, Hours: 1100-2330 Sun-Thu, 1900-0200 Fri-Sat, C-011-39-095-56-4264. **Fast Food:** Wendy's, Bldg 436, Hours: 0600-1900 Mon-Fri, 0700-1700 Sat-Sun, C-011-39-095-86-5469. **Restaurants:** Khaki Club, NAS I, (Philo Mcgiffin's) Closed for renovations; will re-open in February 1998; Jox Sports Bar, NAS

II, Hours: 1100-2330 Sun-Thu, 1100-0100 Fri-Sat, C-011-39-095-86-5603; Khaki Club (Fly Trap), Hours: 1630-2330 Tue-Thu, 1600-2300 Fri, 1630-2300 Sun, closed Mon, C-011-39-095-56-2222; Da Michele's, (BOQ) NAS II, Hours: 0730-0900 Mon-Fri (doughnuts and coffee), 1100-1400 Mon-Sat Lunch, 1700-1930 Mon-Fri Dinner, 1630-1900 Sat, closed Sun, C-011-39-095-86-5927. **Snack Bars:** Bowling Alley, Hours: 0700-2130 Mon-Sat, 1000-2130 Sun, C-011-39-095-56-4302. **Snack Vending:** Bldg 436, 24 hours daily, C-011-39-095-86-5576.

**TRANSPORTATION: Air Tickets:** SATO (Official Travel only), Bldg 436, Hours: 0900-1500 Mon-Fri, C-011-39-095-86-5428; Angie's Travel (Leisure Travel), Hours: 1000-1730 Mon-Fri, C-011-39-095-56-4388; ITT (Tours and Travel), Hours: 1000-1730 Mon-Fri, C-011-39-095-56-4396/4215, D-314-624-4396/4215, Fax: C-011-39-095-713-0147. **On Base Bus (Comm):** Bldg 200, Hours: 0600-2400 Sun-Thu, 0600-0200 Fri-Sat, C-011-39-095-56-4201/2. **On Base Shuttle/Bus:** Bldg 476, 24 hours daily, C-011-39-095-86-5248/5255. **Car Rentals:** Eurocar, Hours: 0830-1700 Mon-Fri, 0830-1230 Sat, closed Sun, C-011-39-095-86-5468/5982. **On Base Taxi (Comm):** Bldg 200, 24 hours daily, C-011-39-095-56-4201/2 (to Catania $25-35). **Parking:** Bldg 436, 24 hours daily, C-011-39-095-56-4201/2 (see Security Police).

**TML:** BOQ/BEQ: 24 hours daily, C-011-39-095-86-2300/6830. Navy Lodge: 24 hours daily, C-011-39-095-56-4082 or 1-800-NAVY-INN , D-314-624-4082. Fax: C-011-39-095-56-7130.

**TRAVELERS AID: Chaplain:** Bldg 180, C-011-39-095-56-4295/6. **Dental:** NAS II, Hours: 0700-1600, C-011-39-095-86-5447, after hours C-011-39-095-86-3848. **Emergency Relief:** NAS I, Hours: 0900-1300 Mon-Fri, C-011-39-095-56-4490. **Lost/Found:** Bldg 436, C-011-39-095-86-5576 (Pax Service NCO). **Medical:** Bldg 201, 24 hours daily, C-011-39-095-56-3842. **Red Cross:** NAS I, Hours: 0800-1300 Mon-Fri, C-011-39-095-56-5446; after hours, C-011-39-095-56-5248. **Security Police:** Bldg 200, 24 hours daily, C-011-39-095-56-4201/2 (Desk Sgt). **USO:** NAS II (MWR), Hours: 0730-1600 Mon-Fri, C-011-39-095-86-5271.

**SUPPORT AVAILABLE: Dry Cleaning:** NAS I mini mall, Hours: 1000-1800 Tue-Thu, 1000-1900 Fri, 0930-1700 Sat, 1200-1700 Sun. **Exchange:** Bldg 192, Hours: 1000-1800 Tue-Thu, 1000-1900 Fri, 0930-1700 Sat, 1200-1700 Sun, C-011-39-095-56-4326/79. **Laundry:** Bldg 174, 24 hours daily, C-011-39-095-56-4346 (coin operated). **Postal Service:** Bldg 189, Hours: 1000-1700 Mon-Fri , 1100-1300 Sun (package pick-up only), C-011-39-095-86-5242.

**ATTRACTIONS:** Mount Etna (popular ski resort) - 20 miles north; Taromina (popular beach) - 40 miles. Year round golf at il Piccilo golf club. Castiglione di Sicilia (CT) C-011-39-042-986-252.

## EN ROUTE SCHEDULES

| AIRPORT/STATION | LI-MISSION (page #) |
| --- | --- |
| Travis AFB | SUU-GTA7B (13) |
| Travis AFB | SUU-ATG3A (14) |
| Dover AFB | DOV-A2F3R (18) |
| Westover ARB | CEF-OFF3A (41) |
| McGuire AFB | WRI-A7W7B (50) |
| McGuire AFB | WRI-A7F3A (51) |
| Norfolk NS | NGU-EX11E (78) |
| Norfolk NS | NGU-EX17B (78) |
| Ramstein AB | RMS-CEU1A (111) |
| Ramstein AB | RMS-CEV4B (112) |
| Ramstein AB | RMS-G8F5S (112) |
| Ramstein AB | RMS-A8F3A (112) |
| Ramstein AB | RMS-A8F5X (112) |

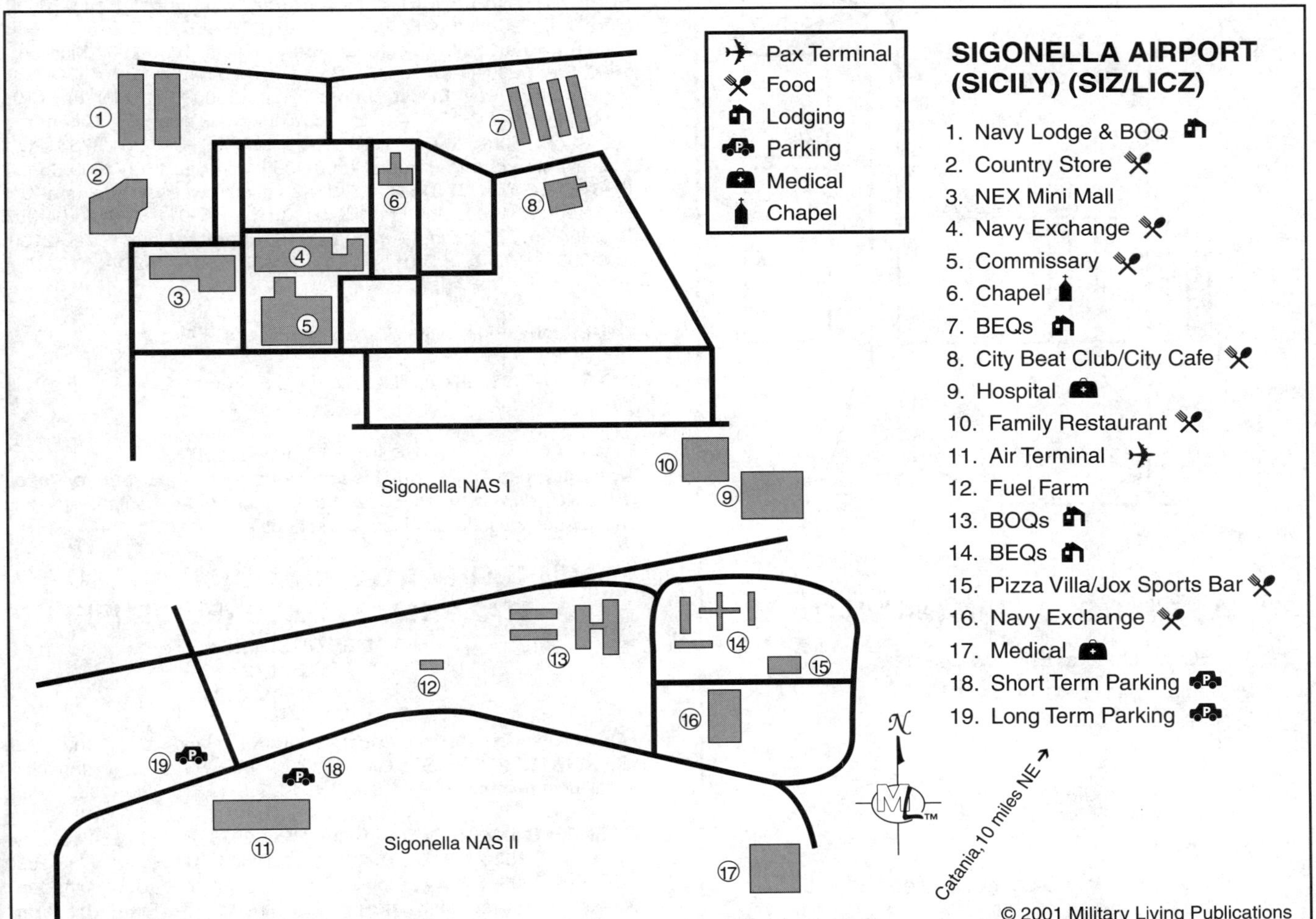

## SIGONELLA AIRPORT (SICILY) (SIZ/LICZ)

Legend:
- ✈ Pax Terminal
- 🍴 Food
- 🏠 Lodging
- 🅿 Parking
- Medical
- ⛪ Chapel

1. Navy Lodge & BOQ 🏠
2. Country Store 🍴
3. NEX Mini Mall
4. Navy Exchange 🍴
5. Commissary 🍴
6. Chapel ⛪
7. BEQs 🏠
8. City Beat Club/City Cafe 🍴
9. Hospital
10. Family Restaurant 🍴
11. Air Terminal ✈
12. Fuel Farm
13. BOQs 🏠
14. BEQs 🏠
15. Pizza Villa/Jox Sports Bar 🍴
16. Navy Exchange 🍴
17. Medical
18. Short Term Parking 🅿
19. Long Term Parking 🅿

Sigonella NAS I

Sigonella NAS II

Catania, 10 miles NE

© 2001 Military Living Publications

# JAPAN

## ATSUGI NAVAL AIR FACILITY (NJA/RJTA)

Air Operations, Box 13, PCS 477
FPO AP 96306-1213

**LOCATION:** In Central Japan off Tokyo Bay. Yokohama is 15 miles east and Tokyo is 28 miles northeast. Camp Zama is 5 miles north. *ML-ARM: (35°25'N/139°20'E)*. LST: GMT+09:00. NMC: Tokyo, 28 miles northeast. Main installation numbers: C-011-81-6160-64-1110, D-315-264-1110.

**REGISTRATION INFO:** C-011-81-6160-64-3118/3803, D-315-264-3118/3803, **Fax:** C-011-81-6160-64-3149, D-315-264-3149. Bldg 206, Hours: 0600-2200 daily. Directions: Main gate to traffic circle, turn left, 4 blocks turn left, 0.25 miles on right, Pax Term on left. No immigration facilities. Persons not assigned in Japan must acquire entry and exit stamps on passports at Yokohama within 24 hours. **Pax Service Office:** Bldg 206, Hours: 0600-2200 daily, C-011-81-6160-64-3118/3803. **Pax Paging:** Bldg 206, Hours: 0600-2200 daily, C-011-81-6160-64-3118/3803.

**PAX LOUNGES: General:** Bldg 202-206. **DV/VIP:** Bldg 202. **Protocol Service:** Bldg 66, Hours: 24 hours daily, C-011-81-6160-64-3111.

**FOOD SERVICE: Cafeteria:** Hours: 0600-0745 Breakfast, 1030-1230 Lunch, 1600-1800 Dinner Mon-Fri; 0700-0900 Breakfast, 1000-1230 Lunch, 1600-1800 Dinner Sun. (CVW-5 is in 0545-1745.) **Restaurants/Fast Food:** American Eatery, at Air Terminal; McDonald's, 25 minute walk away; 19th Hole, closed Tue, 5 minute walk away; The Oasis, 25 minute walk away; O Club, closed Mon, 25 minute walk away; Parcheeze's, 25 minute walk away; CPO Club, Skymasters, 25 minute walk away; Smokey's, 25 minute walk away; The Wall, closed Mon, 20 minute walk away.

**TRANSPORTATION: Air Tickets:** Bldg 77, C-011-81-6160-64-3786 (tours office). **On Base Car Rental:** C-011-81-6160-64-6230, D-315-264-6230, 20 minute walk away. **On Base Shuttle/Bus:** C-011-81-6160-64-3562, D-315-264-3562, 10 minute walk away. **Off Base Taxi:** C-0462770100, 25 minute walk away.

**TML:** Lodging Office: BEQ, Bldg 1290, 24 hours daily, C-011-81-6160-64-3698, D-315-264-3698, Fax: C-011-81-6160-64-3256; BOQ, Bldg 482, 24 hours daily, C-011-81-6160-64-3696, D-315-264-3696, Fax: C-011-81-6160-64-3256. Navy Lodge: 24 hours daily, C-011-81-6160-64-6880, D-315-264-6880, 25 minute walk away. DV/VIP: 24 hours daily, C-011-81-6160-64-3104, D-315-264-3104, O6+.

**TRAVELERS AID: Chaplain:** Hours: 0800-1430 Mon-Fri, C-011-81-6160-64-3202, D-315-264-3202, 25 minute walk away. **Dental:** Hours: 0715-1600 Mon-Fri, closed Thurs after 1430, C-011-81-6160-64-3612, D-315-264-2612, 20 minute walk away. **Medical:** Hours: 0730-1130, 1300-1600 Mon-Fri, closed Thurs 1300-1600, C-011-81-6160-64-3611, D-315-264-3611, 20 minute walk away. **Red Cross:** C-011-81-6160-64-6794 (Recording), D-315-264-6794, 15 minute walk away. **Security Police:** 24 hours daily, C-011-81-6160-64-3200, D-315-264-3200, 15 minute walk away. **Travelers Aid:** Hours: 0800-1600 Mon-Fri, C-011-81-6160-64-6291, D-315-264-6291, 15 minute walk away.

**SUPPORT AVAILABLE: Bank/Currency Exchange:** Hours: 0900-1500 Mon-Thu, 0900-1700 Fri, C-011-81-6160-64-6500, D-315-264-6500, 20 minute walk away. **Convenience Store:** Hours: 1000-1800 Mon-Fri, 0900-1800 Sat, 0900-1700 Sun, C-011-81-6160-64-3653, D-315-364-3653, 20 minute walk away. **Credit Union:** Hours: 0900-1530 Mon-Fri, C-011-81-6160-64-6601, D-315-264-6601, 15 minute walk away. **Dry Cleaner:** Hours: 0800-1730 Mon-Sat, C-011-81-6160-64-3733, D-315-264-3733, 20 minute walk away. **Exchange:** Hours: 1000-2000 Mon-Sat, 1100-1700 Sun, C-011-81-6160-64-3721, D-315-264-3721, 20 minute walk away. **Postal Service:** Hours: 1000-1600 Mon-Fri, 1000-1400 Sat, C-011-81-6160-64-3570, D-315-264-3570, 20 minute walk away. **Shoppette:** Hours: 0700-2100 Mon-Sat, 0900-2100 Sun, C-011-81-6160-64-3715, D-315-264-3715, 20 minute walk away.

**OTHER INFORMATION:** U.S. Customs Service Airport.

**ATTRACTIONS:** Tokyo, New Sanno U.S. Forces Center, Tama Hills Rec area, Yokohama.

### UNSCHEDULED FLIGHTS
*Note: Atsugi NAF JP (NJA) is used as alternate location for Yokota AB, JP (OKO) during runway downtime.* Flight info 24 hours in advance only. Call for destinations, routings and schedules.

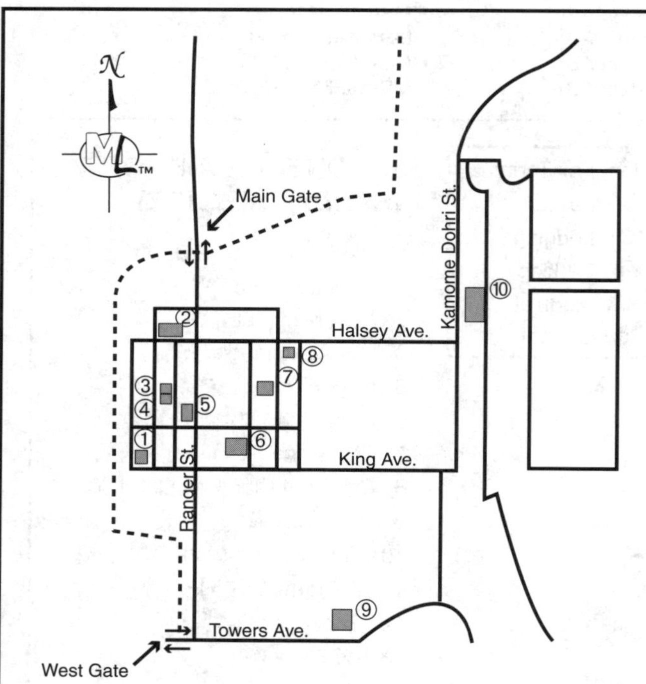



## NAF ATSUGI, JAPAN (NJA/RJTA)

1. BEQ (Bachelors Enlisted Quarters)
2. Medical Clinic, Atsugi Branch
3. Bank
4. Enlisted Club
5. Navy Exchange, Main Store
6. Navy Lodge
7. CPO Club
8. BOQ (Bachelors Officers Quarters)
9. Commissary
10. Passenger Terminal

© 2001 Military Living Publications

## FUKUOKA INTERNATIONAL AIRPORT/ ITAZUKE AIR BASE (FUK/RJFF)

630 AMSS/OL-B, Itazuke/TR
PSC Box 12
FPO AP 96322-0006

**LOCATION:** On the northwest corner of Island of Kyushu. *ML-ARM: (33°35'N/130°27'E)*. LST: GMT+09:00. NMC: Fukuoka, in the city. Main installation numbers: C-011-81-92-451-2558, D-315-225-2438.

**REGISTRATION INFO:** C-011-81-92-451-2558, D-315-225-2438., **Fax:** C-011-81-611-752-2421, D-315-252-2421. Bldg 2518, Hours: 0730-1630 Tue-Fri, 1200-2000 Sat (All hours subject to change depending on flight schedule). Ask at west gate for directions to Pax Term. The terminal is located on what remains of Itazuke AB. The base was closed and returned to the Japanese government in 1971. The U.S. maintains only one building and a small parking area for POVs. The terminal has a soda machine only. There are no other facilities here. The nearest military base is U.S. Fleet Activities, Sasebo, about 115 kilometers away (2 hour drive depending on traffic). Although a small facility, Sasebo NB offers the usual services available on larger military bases.

## EN ROUTE SCHEDULES

| AIRPORT/STATION | LI-MISSION (page #) |
|---|---|
| Yokota AB | OKO-VH79A (129) |
| Yokota AB | OKO-VH79C (130) |

## FUTENMA MARINE CORPS AIR STATION (NFO/ROTM)

Air Freight & Passenger Terminal
Air Operations Division
FPO AP 96372-0618

**LOCATION:** On southern part of Okinawa Island off JA-58. *ML-ARM: (26°50'S/127°40'E).* LST: GMT+09:00. NMC: Naha, 10 miles southwest. Main installation numbers: C-011-81-98-892-5111 (enter ext at dial tone or hold for operator), D-315-640-1110.

**REGISTRATION INFO:** C-011-81-98-636-3064, D-315-636-3064. Bldg 541, Duty Hours. From main gate to a right at runway. Follow Perimeter Road to Bldg 541 on the left. All flights processed by Base Ops.

**PAX LOUNGES:** Each lounge has essential facilities. **General:** Bldg 541, Duty Hours. **DV/VIP:** Bldg 510, C-011-81-98-636-3064, D-315-636-3064.

**TRANSPORTATION: Off Base Bus:** C-011-81-98-863-3636. **On Base Car Rental:** AAFES, C-ext 633-0007. **Off Base Car Rental:** Papasan, C-011-81-98-939-7930. **Off Base Taxi:** C-011-81-98-937-2467. Free inter-camp shuttle available, Hours: 0500-2000 daily.

**TML:** Lodging Office: Camp S.D. Butler, C-011-81-98-892-2455, D-315-635-2191, Fax: C-011-81-6117-45-7549, D-315-645-7549.

**TRAVELERS AID: Chaplain:** C-011-81-611-736-3844/3907. **Medical:** C-011-81-611-736-3105. **Red Cross:** C-011-81-611-736-3235. **USO:** C-011-81-611-736-5202.

**SUPPORT AVAILABLE: Credit Union:** C-011-81-611-736-4200/4201. **Exchange:** C-011-81-6117-736-4156.

### UNSCHEDULED FLIGHTS

Frequent flights to: Iwakuni MCAS, JP (**IWA**); Misawa AB, JP (**MSJ**); and Osan AB, KR (**OSN**); and Yokota AB, JP (**OKO**). Call for destinations, routings and schedules.

## IWAKUNI MARINE CORPS AIR STATION (IWA/RJOI)

Logistics Department, 4th Air Transportation Division
PSC 561, Box 1872
FPO AP 96310-0029

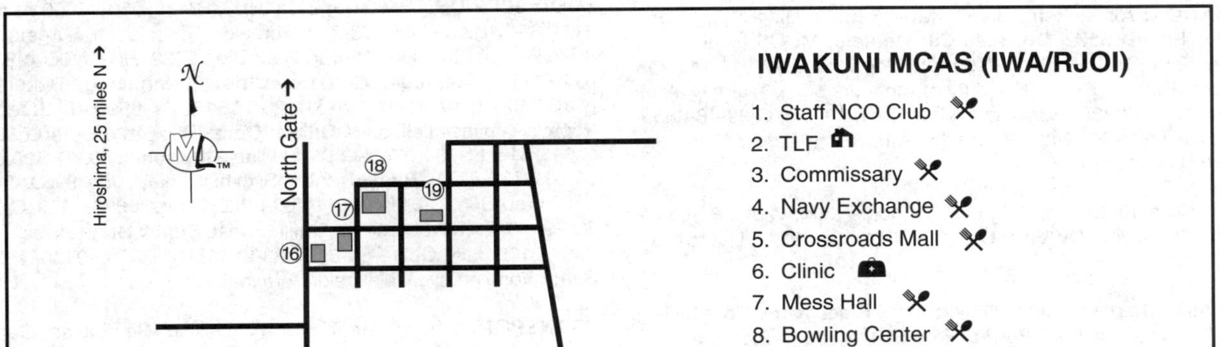

### IWAKUNI MCAS (IWA/RJOI)

1. Staff NCO Club
2. TLF
3. Commissary
4. Navy Exchange
5. Crossroads Mall
6. Clinic
7. Mess Hall
8. Bowling Center
9. Tomadachi Club
10. Officers' Club
11. Iwakuni House
12. Long & Short Term Parking
13. Air Terminal
14. Chapel
15. TLF
16. Skating Rink/Bowling Center
17. Service Station/Mini Mart
18. Club End Zone
19. Mess Hall

Legend:
- Pax Terminal
- Food
- Lodging
- Parking
- Medical
- Chapel

© 2001 Military Living Publications

**LOCATION:** Facing the Inland Sea on the south portion of the island of Honshu, 450 miles southwest of Tokyo, 0.5 miles off JA-188 on JA-189. *ML-ARM: (34°15'N/132°15'E).* LST: GMT+09:00. NMC: Hiroshima, 25 miles north. Main installation numbers: C-011-81-6117-53-1110, D-315-253-1110.

**REGISTRATION INFO:** C-011-81-6117-53-5509/3947, D-315-253-5509/3977, Fax: C-011-81-6117-53-4294, D-315-253-3301. Bldg 779, Hours: 0600-2200 Mon-Fri, 0700-1600 Sat, 1100-2000 Sun (1700-2000 first Sunday of every month). Directions: Main gate left to 2nd intersection, right to next intersection, left to flight line and Pax Term. **Pax Service Office:** C-011-81-827-21-4171 ext 3818 (NCO on duty). **Pax Paging:** C-011-81-827-21-4171 ext 5509 (see Pax Service NCO).

**PAX LOUNGES:** No family lounge. **General:** Bldg 779, Hours: 0600-2200 Mon-Fri, 0700-1600 Sat, 1100-2000 Sun (1700-2000 first Sunday of every month), C-011-81-827-21-4171 ext 5509. A/C, bag check, telephone (local, long distance and defense), TV, restrooms. **DV/VIP:** Bldg 779, Hours: 0600-2200 Mon-Fri, 0700-1600 Sat, 1100-2000 Sun (1700-2000 first Sunday of every month), C-011-81-827-21-4171 ext 5509 (06+). A/C, bag check, restrooms, TV, O/S seats. **Protocol Service:** Bldg 360, Hours: 0800-1630 Mon-Fri, C-011-81-827-21-4171 ext 4211 (06+).

**FOOD SERVICE: Combined Club:** End Zone, Bldg 1470, 253-5798. **O Club:** Bldg 601, ext 6625. **Staff NCO Club:** Bldg 443, 253-3363. **Restaurants:** Pizza Inn, Bldg 410, ext 4444; Eagle's Nest, Bldg 702, ext 3407/4778. **Snack Bar:** Miss T's, Bldg 779, during flight operations, ext 3801. **Snack Vending:** Bldg 779, ext 3570.

**TRANSPORTATION: Air Tickets:** SATO Travel Bureau, Bldg 163, Hours: 0800-1630 Mon-Fri, ext 3572. **On Base Car Rentals:** MCCS Rent-A-Car, Bldg 1353, ext 4245. **On Base Taxi (Comm):** Bldg 779, C-99-21-1111. **On Base Taxi (Gov):** Bldg 170, ext 3063 (duty passengers only). **Train:** Iwakuni train station, C-99-21-3933/3935; Shin Iwakuni Train station, C-99-46-0655. **Trains:** IWA, See Travel Bureau for schedules. **Parking:** Bldg 779, across from Term. See Security Police.

**TML:** Lodging Office: Kintai Inn, Bldg 606, 24 hours daily, C-011-81-6117-53-3181/3221. All ranks. DV/VIP: C-011-81-6117-53-4211, D-315-258-4211, 06+.

**TRAVELERS AID: Chaplain:** Bldg 360, ext 3414. **Emergency Relief:** Bldg 360, ext 5311 (Navy Relief). **Lost/Found:** Bldg 610, ext 3247. **Medical:** Bldg 125, 24 hours daily, C-011-81-827-21-4171 ext 3300/5941, D-315-253-3300/5941. **Red Cross:** Bldg 360, ext 4525; after hours, ext 4211. **Security Police:** Bldg 610, C-011-81-827-21-4171 ext 3222/119 (Desk Sgt).

**SUPPORT AVAILABLE: Bank/Currency Exchange:** NFCU, Bldg 410, ext 4794; Community Bank, Bldg 410, Hours: 0900-1500 Mon-Fri, ext 4777. **Exchange:** Bldg 446, ext 5673/5641. **Hair Styles:** Barber, Bldg 446, ext 4728; Beauty, Bldg 446 ext 4708. **Laundry/Dry Cleaning:** Bldg 348, ext 4710. **Postal Service:** Bldg 405, ext 4542, D-315-253-4542. **Valet/Dry Cleaning:** Bldg 408, ext 4744.

**ATTRACTIONS:** Kintai Bridge, Miyajima, Hiroshima (Peace Memorial Park, A-Bomb Dome, 25 miles north).

## EN ROUTE SCHEDULES

| AIRPORT/STATION | LI-MISSION (page #) |
|---|---|
| Los Angeles IAP | LAX-2X87A (8) |
| Yokota AB | OKO-VH79A (129) |

### UNSCHEDULED FLIGHTS

There is a C-009A, MEDEVAC flight each Mon and Thu. The route is: Yokota AB, JP (**OKO**), Atsugi NAF, JP (**NJA**), Misawa AB, JP (**MSJ**), Iwakuni MCAS, JP (**IWA**), Atsugi NAF, JP (**NJA**) and Yokota AB, JP (**OKO**). Flights to Beaufort MCAS, SC (**NBC**), Cherry Point MCAS, NC (**NKT**), and Miramar MCAS (**NKX**). Call for destinations, routings and schedules.



# KADENA AIR BASE (OKINAWA) (DNA/RODN)

633 AMSS/TRP
Unit 5145
APO AP 96368-5145

**LOCATION:** On central Okinawa, adjacent to JA-58, 27 and 16. *ML-ARM: (27°00'N/127°45'E).* LST: GMT+09:00. NMC: Naha JP, 15 miles south. Main installation numbers: C-011-81-98938-1111, D-315-634-1110.

**REGISTRATION INFO:** C-011-81-6117-34-1281, D-315-634-2159, Rec: C-011-81-611-734-2159, Fax: C-011-81-611-734-4221, D-315-634-4221. E-mail: spacea@kadena.af.mil WEB: www.kadena.af.mil/current/spacea/ Bldg 3409, Hours: 0600-2200 daily, after hours as needed. Directions: From gate 1 on Douglas Blvd to a left on W Perimeter Road to Pax Term on the right. **Pax Service Office:** Bldg 3409, Hours: 0700-1630 Mon-Fri, C-011-81-611-734-4495/1273 (Space-A counter). **Pax Paging:** C-011-81-611-734-2159, D-315-634-2159. Space-A calls now three hours prior to flight.

**PAX LOUNGES:** No separate family lounge. **General:** Bldg 3409, Hours: 0600-2300 daily, C-011-81-611-733-3183 (center building). A/C, bag lockers, game room, restrooms, TV, video movies, O/S seats, nursery. No food or sleeping overnight. **DV/VIP:** Bldg 3409, Hours: 0600-2200 daily, C-011-81-611-734-2159 (at Gate 2). A/C, bag check, restrooms, showers, TV, separate read/write rooms, coffee/tea service, O/S seats. Staffed as required (06+). **Protocol Service:** Bldg 3409, Hours: 0600-2200 daily, C-011-81-611-734-1808.

**FOOD SERVICE: Cafeteria:** Bldg 3409, Hours: 0600-2000 daily, C-011-81-611-733-3183, D-315-633-3183, breakfast and lunch, burgers and chicken (Flag Room), 2nd floor. **Dining Hall:** Bldg 3522, Hours: 0600-2300 daily, C-011-81-611-734-1684. **Enlisted Club:** Bayan Tree, Bldg 431, Hours: 0600-2400 daily, C-011-81-611-734-0644. **Fast Food:** Burger King and Popeye's on installation. **NCO/CPO Club:** Bldg 621, Hours: 0630-2400 daily, C-011-81-611-734-0740. **O Club:** Bldg 313, Hours: 0630-2400 daily, C-011-81-611-734-6071. **Restaurants:** Skoshi Room, Bldg 9950, Hours: 1700-2200 Wed-Sun, C-011-81-611-733-3220; Hours: 0630-2400, C-011-81-611-734-0470, D-315-634-0470, 2 miles west. **Snack Bars:** Vincent Ave, Hours: 0900-2100 daily, C-011-81-611-733-9150, D-315-633-9150, 1.5 miles west. Snack Vending available inside terminal.

**TRANSPORTATION: Air Tickets:** Schilling Recreation Center, Hours: 0900-1715 Mon-Fri, 0900-1500 Sat, C-011-81-611-733-0411. **On Base Car Rentals:** Bldg 219, Hours: 0800-1730 daily, C-011-81-611-733-0007, D-315-633-0007, 1 mile northwest. **On Base Shuttle/Bus:** Bldg 3409, Hours: 0530-0030 daily, every 30 minutes, C-011-81-611-634-4462 (base area). **On Base Taxi (Gov):** 24 hours daily, C-011-81-611-734-3345. **On Base Taxi (Comm):** 24 hours daily, C-011-81-98-939-1660. **Parking:** Bldg 3409, 24 hours daily, C-011-81-611-634-2475 (short term, 2 hours in front of Pax Term; long term, on hill above Pax Term).

**TML:** Lodging Office: Shogun Inn, Bldg 332, Beeson Avenue, 24 hours daily, C-011-81-611-732-11001101/1010/1050, D-315-632-1100/1101/1010/1050, Fax: C-011-81-611-732-1740, D-315-632-1740. DV/VIP: Protocol Office, D-315-634-0106/18, 06+.

**TRAVELERS AID: Chaplain:** Bldg 9800, duty hours, C-011-81-611-734-1288, D-315-634-1288, after hours C-011-81-611-734-4274. **Emergency Relief:** Bldg 99, Hours: 0730-1630 Mon-Fri , C-011-81-611-734-7521 (Air Force Aid Society). **Lost/Found:** Bldg 3409, Hours: 0730-1630 Mon-Fri, C-011-81-611-734-3851. **Medical/Dental:** Bldg 703, Hours: 0700-1800 Mon-Fri, 1000-1200 Sat, C-011-81-611-734-1922, D-315-634-1922 (emergency care). **Red Cross:** Bldg 910, Hours: 0730-1630 Mon-Fri, C-011-81-611-734-1294, D-315-634-1294, after hours C-011-81-611-734-4611. **Security Police:** Main gate, 24 hours daily, C-011-81-611-733-2475, D-315-633-2475 (Desk Sgt). **Travelers Aid:** Bldg 99, Hours: 0730-1630, C-011-81-611-734-7521, D-315-634-7521. **USO:** Bldg 337, Hours: 0730-2100 daily, C-011-81-611-734-0473/0438.

**SUPPORT AVAILABLE: Bank/Currency Exchange:** Community Bank, Bldg 409, Hours: 0900-1500 Mon-Thu, 0900-1700 Fri, C-011-81-611-734-2208, D-315-634-2208. **Exchange:** Bldg 3409, Hours: 0600-2200, C-011-81-611-733-4570; Main BX, Bldg 413, 1000-2000 Mon-Sun, C-011-81-611-733-4570, D-315-633-4570. **Hair Styles:** Barber, Bldg 409, Hours: 1000-1700 Mon-Sat, C-011-81-611-734-4927; Beauty, Bldg 409, Hours:

1000-1800 daily, C-011-81-611-733-4176. **Laundry/Dry Cleaning:** Bldg 97, Hours: 1000-1800 daily, C-011-81-611-733-8090, D-315-633-8090 (Service Mall). **Postal Service:** Bldg 160, Hours: 0900-1700 Tue-Fri, 0900-1500 Sat, C-011-81-611-734-2237, D-315-634-2237.

**OTHER INFORMATION:** Port of Entry and U.S. Customs Service Airport.

**ATTRACTIONS:** Naha JP, Okuma Rec Center, White Beach Rec Center.

### EN ROUTE SCHEDULES

| AIRPORT/STATION | LI-MISSION (page #) |
| --- | --- |
| Los Angeles IAP | LAX-2W71B (8) |
| Los Angeles IAP | LAX-2W79A (8) |
| Travis AFB | SUU-P371C (14) |
| Travis AFB | SUU-P371S & Z (14) |
| Travis AFB | SUU-P379A & B (14) |
| Travis AFB | SUU-P379D (14) |
| McChord AFB | TCM-T679F (82) |
| McChord AFB | TCM-TU79A (82) |
| Yokota AB | OKO-VH71F (129) |
| Yokota AB | OKO-VH79A (129) |
| Yokota AB | OKO-VH79C (130) |
| Yokota AB | OKO-VHC7D/E (130) |

## MISAWA AIR BASE (MSJ/RJSM)

Contract Air Terminal Operation
AMC/CATO
Unit 5008, Bldg 944
APO AP 96319-5008

**LOCATION:** On the northeast portion of the Island of Honshu, 400 miles north of Tokyo. *ML-ARM: (40°45'N/141°30'E).* LST: GMT+09:00. NMC: Hachinohe City, 17 miles southeast. Main installation numbers: C-011-81-3117-66-111 or switchboard C-011-81-176-53-5181, D-315-226-1110.

**REGISTRATION INFO:** C-011-81-3117-66-2370/71 or 011-81-3117-626141, D-315-226-2370/71, **Rec:** C-011-81-3117-66-2852/2444, D-315-226-2852/2444, **Fax:** C-011-81-3117-66-4455, D-315-226-4455. Bldg 943, Hours: 0500-1900 daily. Directions: From main gate drive down Friendship Blvd. At the intersection turn left on W Falcon Drive and go approximately 0.75 miles until you come to a passenger terminal direction sign. At that intersection turn right and drive 0.25 miles to the Pax Term. Bldg 943 is on the right. **Pax Info (other services):** Bldg 961, Hours: 0800-1630 Mon-Fri, ext 226-4004 (Navy Operations). **Pax Paging:** C-011-81-3117-66-4004, D-315-226-4004.

**PAX LOUNGES:** Small **DV/VIP** lounge and family lounge. **General:** Bldg 943, Hours: 0500-2100 daily, ext 226-2444. A/C, bag check, game room, telephones (local and defense), TV, restrooms. **Protocol Service:** Bldg 504, Hours: 0730-1630 daily, D-315-226-4804.

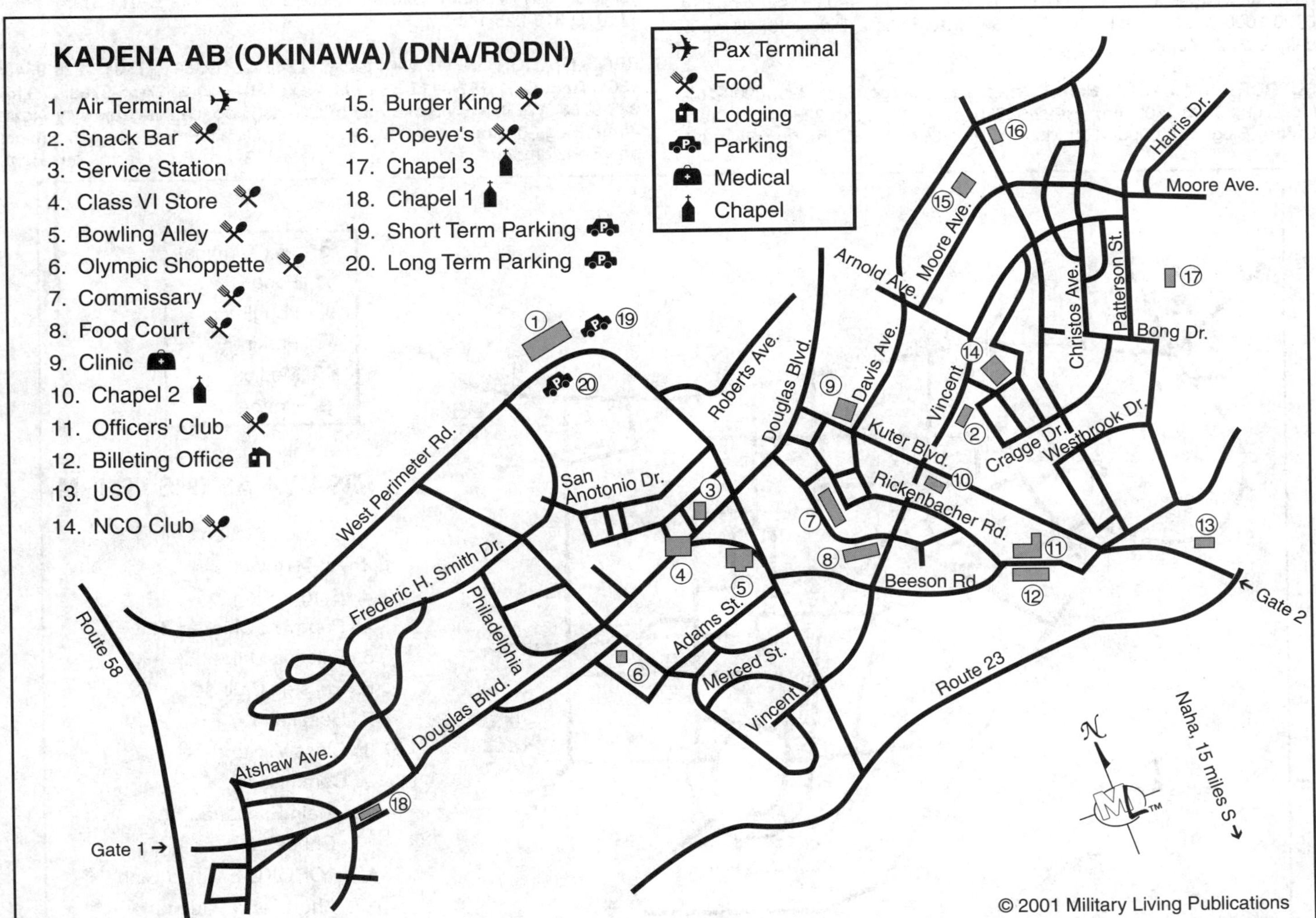

## KADENA AB (OKINAWA) (DNA/RODN)

1. Air Terminal
2. Snack Bar
3. Service Station
4. Class VI Store
5. Bowling Alley
6. Olympic Shoppette
7. Commissary
8. Food Court
9. Clinic
10. Chapel 2
11. Officers' Club
12. Billeting Office
13. USO
14. NCO Club
15. Burger King
16. Popeye's
17. Chapel 3
18. Chapel 1
19. Short Term Parking
20. Long Term Parking

Pax Terminal
Food
Lodging
Parking
Medical
Chapel

© 2001 Military Living Publications

**FOOD SERVICE: Cafeteria:** Bldg 1044, Hours: 0630-1300 Mon-Fri, 0730-1300 Sat, ext 222-5671. **Dining Hall:** Bldg 624, 0500-0800 Breakfast Mon-Fri, 0500-1000 Sat-Sun, 1030-1300 Lunch daily, 1500-1930 Dinner, 2115-2400 Midnight meal, ext 226-4463. **Enlisted Club:** Hours: 0800-1700 Mon-Fri, ext 222-9513. **Fast Food:** Burger King, Bldg 526, Hours: 0630-2100 Mon-Thu, 0630-2200 Fri, 0800-2200 Sat, 0800-2100 Sun, ext 226-5905; Popeye's, Bldg 528, 1000-2100 Mon-Fri, 1030-2100 Sat-Sun, 1000-1900 holidays, ext 222-7772. **Food Court:** Bldg 325, Hours: 1100-1930 Sun-Thu, 1100-2000 Fri-Sat, ext 222-6129. **In-flight Meals:** Bldg 624, 24 hours daily, ext 226-3889 (24 hours notification). **O Club:** Bldg 22, Hours: 0800-1600 Mon-Fri, ext 222-9516. **Snack Bar:** Bldg 961, Hours: 0700-1300 Mon-Fri, ext 226-5619. **Snack Vending:** Bldg 431, Hours: 0800-1700 Mon-Fri, ext 226-5491.

**TRANSPORTATION: Air Tickets:** Bldg 670, Hours: 0730-1600 Mon-Fri, ext 226-5555. **Bus (Gov):** Bldg 1310, 24 hours daily, ext 226-4062. **Car Rentals:** Bldg 325, Hours: 0800-1630 Mon-Fri, ext 222-6722. **On Base Shuttle/Bus:** Bldg 1310, 24 hours daily, ext 226-4062. **Taxi (Comm):** Bldg 14, 24 hours daily, ext 222-5438/9. **Taxi (Gov):** Bldg 1310, 24 hours daily, ext 226-4062. **Parking:** Front of the Pax Term, ext 226-2370/71 no overnight/reserved parking. Long term close to Pax Term.

**TML:** Lodging Office: Misawa Inn, C-011-81-176-53-5181 ext 3526, D-315-226-2165, 24 hours daily, Fax: C-011-81-3117-66-2165. DV/VIP: C-011-81-3117-66-4804, 06+.

**TRAVELERS AID: Chaplain:** Bldg 358, 0730-1630 Mon-Fri, ext 226-4630. **Dental:** Bldg 99, 0730-1630 Mon-Fri, ext 226-6700. **Emergency Relief (CBPO):** Bldg 961, ext 226-3721. **Lost/Found:** Bldg 943, ext 226-2444/45. **Medical:** Bldg 99, 0730-1630 Mon-Fri, ext 226-6111. **Red Cross:** Bldg 674, 0700-1600 Mon-Fri, ext 226-3772. **Security Police:** Bldg 646, 24 hours daily, ext 226-4358.

**SUPPORT AVAILABLE: Bank/Currency Exchange:** Bldg 320, 0900-1500 Mon-Thu, 0900-1700 Fri, ext-226-3880; Bldg 470, ext 226-5412. **Credit Union:** Bldg 320, 0900-1600 Mon-Fri, ext 226-5412. **Exchange:** Bldg 325, 1000-2000 Mon-Sat, 1200-1700 Sun, ext 222-6049. **Hair Styles:** Barber, Bldg 325, ext 226-6186; Beauty, Bldg 325, ext 226-5755. **Laundry/Dry Cleaning:** Bldg 1017, 1000-1800 Mon Sat, 1200-1700 Sun, ext 226-5521. **Postal Service:** Bldg 519, 0800-1200 Mon & Sat, 1000-1700 Tue-Fri, ext 226-3492. **Shoppette:** Bldg 552, 0700-2300 daily, ext 222-5750. **Valet/Dry Cleaning:** Bldg 325, ext 226-5521 (main Exchange). **Wire:** Bldg 320, ext 226-3880/5412.

**OTHER INFORMATION:** Port of Entry and U.S. Customs Service Airport.

**ATTRACTIONS:** Ski area, lodge on base. Skeet shooting, deep sea fishing trips.

## EN ROUTE SCHEDULES

| AIRPORT/STATION | LI-MISSION (page #) |
| --- | --- |
| Los Angeles IAP | LAX-2X87A (8) |
| Yokota AB | OKO-VH71C (129) |
| Yokota AB | OKO-VH71F (129) |
| Yokota AB | OKO-VH79A (129) |
| Yokota AB | OKO-VH79C (129) |

# YOKOTA AIR BASE (OKO/RJTY)

630th AMSS/TRP
Unit 5093, Bldg 80
APO AP 96328-5093

**LOCATION:** Take Route-16 S from Tokyo. AB is 1 mile west of Fussa JP. Clearly marked. *ML-ARM: (35°25'N/139°45'E).* LST: GMT+09:00. NMC: Tokyo JP, 35 miles northeast. Main installation numbers: C-011-81-3117-55-1110, D-315-225-1110.

**REGISTRATION INFO: C-011-81-3117-55-9540/5661, D-315-225-9540/5661, Rec: C-011-81-3117-55-7111, Fax: C-011-81-3117-55-9768, D-315-225-9768. WEB: www.yokota.af.mil E-mail: space.available@ yokota.af.mil** Bldg 80, Hours: 0300-2200 daily. Directions: From Gate #15 straight on Bobzien Ave to a left at Gate 12 to Pax Term on right.

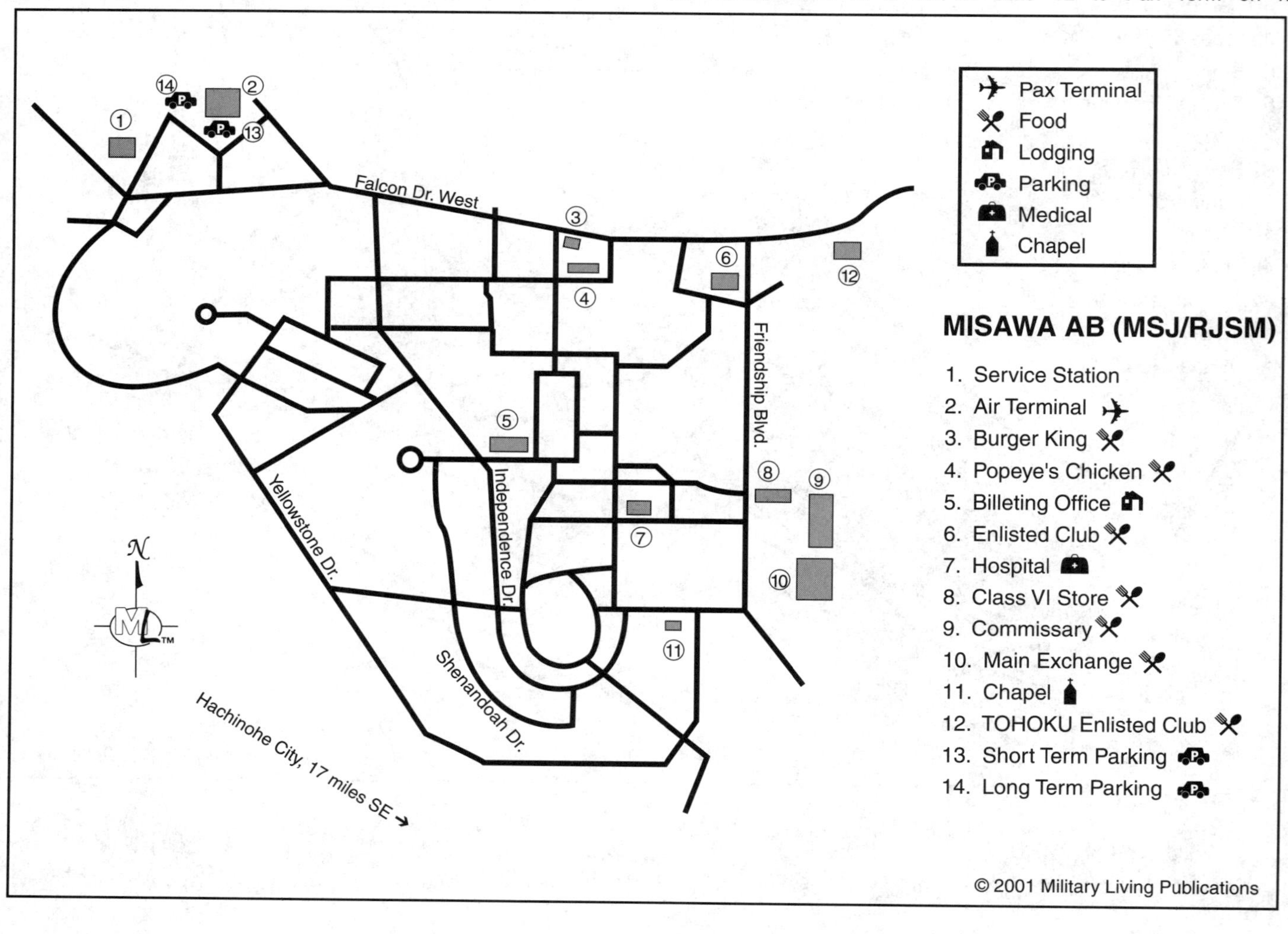


## MISAWA AB (MSJ/RJSM)

1. Service Station
2. Air Terminal
3. Burger King
4. Popeye's Chicken
5. Billeting Office
6. Enlisted Club
7. Hospital
8. Class VI Store
9. Commissary
10. Main Exchange
11. Chapel
12. TOHOKU Enlisted Club
13. Short Term Parking
14. Long Term Parking

**Pax Service Information:** Bldg 80, Hours: 0400-2200 daily, C-011-81-3117-55-7119/9540, D-315-225-7119/9540, 2200-0400 Rec: C-011-81-3117-55-7111, D-315-225-7111. **Pax Paging:** Bldg 80, 24 hours daily, C-011-81-3117-55-7119, D-315-225-7119.

**PAX LOUNGES:** Bldg 80, 0400-2130 hours daily. USO provides both accompanied and unaccompanied lounges. **General:** Bldg 80, 24 hours daily, C-011-81-3117-55-9540. A/C, bag check, coffee/tea served, game room, restrooms, showers, TV, P/C seats. No sleeping in the Terminal overnight. **DV/VIP:** Bldg 80, Hours: 0300-2200, no sleeping overnight, C-011-81-3117-55-9540 (06+), A/C, restrooms, read/write rooms, TV, O/S seats. Not staffed. Protocol Service: Bldg 714, 24 hours daily, C-011-81-3117-55-4141.

**FOOD SERVICE: Cafeteria:** Bldg 80, 0400-2130 hours daily, D-315-225-6430. **Dining Hall:** Bldg 427, D-315-225-8870. **Enlisted Club:** Bldg 2066, D-315-227-8820, O Club: Bldg 31, D-315-225-8341. Restaurants: Bldg 442 Charlie T's, D-315-225-8837. Fast food available 0600-2100, 0.75 miles away. Snack vending available in terminal.

**TRANSPORTATION: Air Tickets:** Yujo Community Center, D-315-225-6430. **On Base Shuttle/Bus:** Hours: 0600-2130, D-315-225-9121. **Off Base Shuttle/Bus:** Bldg 80, D-315-225-7720. **(Gov):** Bldg 80, D-315-225-7750/0519. Service to New Sanno 0930 daily, free. Service to Narita 0900, 1100 and 1300 daily, $24 adults/$12 children. **Trains:** 3 miles west of terminal. **Parking:** Bldg 80, short-term at Pax Term; long term - across Route 16.

**TML:** Lodging Office: Kanto Lodge, Bldg 10 at Airlifter Ave and 1st Street, 24 hours daily. C-011-81-3117-55-7712, D-315-224-2002. Fax: C-011-81-3117-55-3499. All ranks. DV/VIP: C-011-81-3117-55-4141 06+, 0.5 miles away.

**TRAVELERS AID: Chaplain:** Bldg 345, 0730-1630, D-315-225-7009, 1 mile away. **Emergency Relief:** Bldg 535, D-315-225-8725 (Air Force Aid). **Lost/Found:** Bldg 80, Hours: 0400-2200 daily, D-315-225-9543 (Pax Service NCOIC). **Medical:** Bldg 4408, 24 hours daily, C-011-81-0425-225-7740, D-315-225-7740 (emergency), 3 miles away. **Red Cross:** Bldg 4018, 0800-1630, D-315-225-7522; after hours, ext 9901, 3 miles away. **Security Police:** Bldg 555, 24 hours daily, 911. **USO:** Bldg 4018, 24 hours daily, D-315-225-2087/2093.

**SUPPORT AVAILABLE: Bank/Currency Exchange:** Bldg 4018, Hours: 0900-1500, D-315-225-7147, 0.75 miles away. **Convenience Store:** Hours: 0700-2200, D-315-225-2341, 0.75 miles away. **Credit Union:** Hours: 0900-1600, D-315-225-4886, 0.75 miles away. **Dry Cleaning:** Bldg 436, Hours: 1000-1800, D-315-225-9878, 0.5 miles away. **Exchange:** Bldg 4018, Hours: 1000-2000, D-315-225-8656, 0.5 miles away. **Hair Styles:** Bldg 416, D-315-225-8379. **Postal Service:** Bldg 538, Hours: 0900-1800, D-315-225-8511, 1 mile away. **Shoppette:** Hours: 0700-0900, D-315-225-9192, 1 mile away.

**OTHER INFORMATION:** Port of Entry and U.S. Customs Service Airport.

**ATTRACTIONS:** Tokyo, Mount Fuji, New Sanno U.S. Forces Center, Hakone National Park, Central Alps, Toshimien Water Park, Ueno Zoo, Disneyland, Seibu Lions Professional Baseball Stadium, Imperial Palace, The Ginza, Akihabara Electronic Districk, Tokyo Tower, The Ski Dome, Tama Lodge and Golf Course, Tama Tech amusement park, Tama Zoo, Tokyo Dome, Yokohama Indoor water park, Roppangi.

*Note: Commercially contracted flights are now called Patriot Express.*

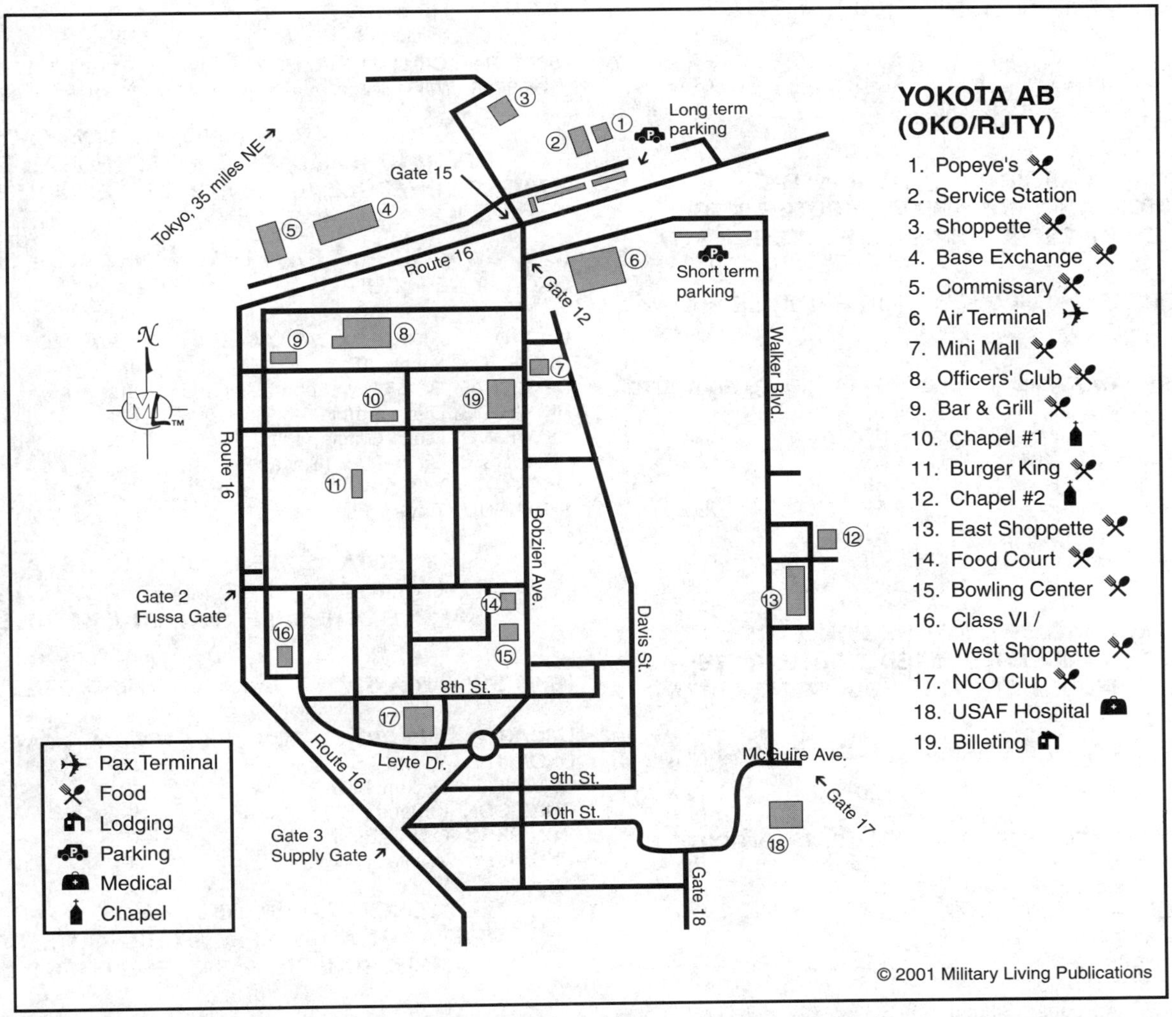

© 2001 Military Living Publications

### YOKOTA AB, JP (OKO); REGION: PAC;
### OPERATOR: COM; TYPE: MIXED; ROUTE: ZJ82A;
### SAMPLE SCHEDULE: FRI; EQUIPMENT: DC862

{OKO *SE* ➡ UAM *NE* ➡ HIK *NE* ➡ SUU (★) ⇌ SUU *SW* ➡ HIK *SW* ➡ UAM *NW* ➡ OKO}

| LI/ICAO | AIRPORT/STATION | CTRY/STA | DAYS EN ROUTE |
|---|---|---|---|
| OKO/RJTY | Yokota AB | JP | +0 |
| UAM/PGUA | Andersen AFB | GU | +0 |
| HIK/PHIK | Hickam AFB | HI | +0 |
| SUU/KSUU | Travis AFB | CA | +1 |
| SUU/KSUU | Travis AFB | CA | +1 |
| HIK/PHIK | Hickam AFB | HI | +1 |
| UAM/PGUA | Andersen AFB | GU | +2 |
| OKO/RJTY | Yokota AB | JP | |

### YOKOTA AB, JP (OKO); REGION: PAC;
### OPERATOR: COM; TYPE: MIXED; ROUTE: ZJF7A;
### SAMPLE SCHEDULE: SUN; EQUIPMENT: DC862

{OKO *SW* ➡ QPG *SW* ➡ NKW *NW* ➡ FJR ⇌ FJR *SE* ➡ NKW *NE* ➡ QPG *NE* ➡ OKO}

| LI/ICAO | AIRPORT/STATION | CTRY/STA | DAYS EN ROUTE |
|---|---|---|---|
| OKO/RJTY | Yokota AB | JP | +0 |
| QPG/WSAP | RSAF Paya Lebar (Singapore) | SG | +1 |
| NKW/FJDG | Diego Garcia Atoll | GB | +2 |
| FJR/OMFJ | Al Fujayrah IAP | AE | +2 |
| FJR/OMFJ | Al Fujayrah IAP | AE | +2 |
| NKW/FJDG | Diego Garcia Atoll | GB | +3 |
| QPG/WSAP | RSAF Paya Lebar (Singapore) | SG | +4 |
| OKO/RJTY | Yokota AB | JP | |

### YOKOTA AB, JP (OKO); REGION: PAC;
### OPERATOR: AMC; TYPE: MIXED; ROUTE: T8F7C;
### SCHEDULE: 1ST, 2ND & 4TH THU; EQUIPMENT: C017A

{OKO *SW* ➡ QPG *SW* ➡ NKW *NW* ➡ FJR ⇌ FJR *SE* ➡ NKW *NE* ➡ QPG *NE* ➡ OKO}

| LI/ICAO | AIRPORT/STATION | CTRY/STA | DAYS EN ROUTE |
|---|---|---|---|
| OKO/RJTY | Yokota AB | JP | +0 |
| QPG/WSAP | RSAF Paya Lebar (Singapore) | SG | +1 |
| NKW/FJDG | Diego Garcia Atoll | GB | +2 |
| FJR/OMFJ | Al Fujayrah IAP | AE | +2 |
| FJR/OMFJ | Al Fujayrah IAP | AE | +2 |
| NKW/FJDG | Diego Garcia Atoll | GB | +3 |
| QPG/WSAP | RSAF Paya Lebar (Singapore) | SG | +4 |
| OKO/RJTY | Yokota AB | JP | |

### YOKOTA AB, JP (OKO); REGION: PAC;
### OPERATOR: AMC; TYPE: MIXED; ROUTE: T8F7E;
### SAMPLE SCHEDULE: 3RD THU; EQUIPMENT: C017A

{OKO *SW* ➡ HLP *SW* ➡ NKW *NW* ➡ FJR ⇌ FJR *SE* ➡ NKW *NE* ➡ QPG *NE* ➡ OKO}

| LI/ICAO | AIRPORT/STATION | CTRY/STA | DAYS EN ROUTE |
|---|---|---|---|
| OKO/RJTY | Yokota AB | JP | +0 |
| HLP/WIIH | Halim Perdanakusuma | ID | +1 |
| NKW/FJDG | Diego Garcia Atoll | GB | +2 |
| FJR/OMFJ | Al Fujayrah IAP | AE | +2 |
| FJR/OMFJ | Al Fujayrah IAP | AE | +2 |
| NKW/FJDG | Diego Garcia Atoll | GB | +3 |
| QPG/WSAP | RSAF Paya Lebar (Singapore) | SG | +4 |
| OKO/RJTY | Yokota AB | JP | |

### YOKOTA AB, JP (OKO); REGION: PAC;
### OPERATOR: AMC; TYPE: MIXED; ROUTE: T8P5A;
### SAMPLE SCHEDULE: MON; EQUIPMENT: C017A

{OKO *SW* ➡ QPG *SW* ➡ NKW ⇌ NKW *NE* ➡ QPG *NE* ➡ OKO}

| LI/ICAO | AIRPORT/STATION | CTRY/STA | DAYS EN ROUTE |
|---|---|---|---|
| OKO/RJTY | Yokota AB | JP | +0 |
| QPG/WSAP | RSAF Paya Lebar (Singapore) | SG | +1 |
| NKW/FJDG | Diego Garcia Atoll | GB | +2 |
| NKW/FJDG | Diego Garcia Atoll | GB | +2 |
| QPG/WSAP | RSAF Paya Lebar (Singapore) | SG | +3 |
| OKO/RJTY | Yokota AB | JP | |

### YOKOTA AB, JP (OKO); REGION: PAC;
### OPERATOR: AMC; TYPE: MIXED; ROUTE: TQP5V;
### SAMPLE SCHEDULE: 2ND WED; EQUIPMENT: KC010A

{OKO *SW* ➡ QPG *SW* ➡ NKW ⇌ NKW *NE* ➡ SIN *NE* ➡ OKO *SE* ➡ HIK (★) *NE* ➡ SUU (★) *NE* ➡ WRI}

| LI/ICAO | AIRPORT/STATION | CTRY/STA | DAYS EN ROUTE |
|---|---|---|---|
| OKO/RJTY | Yokota AB | JP | +0 |
| QPG/WSAP | RSAF Paya Lebar (Singapore) | SG | +1 |
| NKW/FJDG | Diego Garcia Atoll | GB | +2 |
| NKW/FJDG | Diego Garcia Atoll | GB | +2 |
| SIN/WSSS | Changi IAP (Singapore) | SG | +3 |
| OKO/RJTY | Yokota AB | JP | +4 |
| HIK/PHIK | Hickam AFB | HI | +5 |
| SUU/KSUU | Travis AFB | CA | +5 |
| WRI/KWRI | McGuire AFB | NJ | |

### YOKOTA AB, JP (OKO); REGION: PAC;
### OPERATOR: AMC; TYPE: MIXED; ROUTE: TTP5V;
### SAMPLE SCHEDULE: 3RD & 4TH WED; EQUIPMENT: KC010A

{OKO *SW* ➡ QPG (★) *SW* ➡ NKW ⇌ NKW *NE* ➡ SIN *NE* ➡ OKO (★) *NE* ➡ SUU}

| LI/ICAO | AIRPORT/STATION | CTRY/STA | DAYS EN ROUTE |
|---|---|---|---|
| OKO/RJTY | Yokota AB | JP | +0 |
| QPG/WSAP | RSAF Paya Lebar (Singapore) | SG | +1 |
| NKW/FJDG | Diego Garcia Atoll | GB | +2 |
| NKW/FJDG | Diego Garcia Atoll | GB | +2 |
| SIN/WSSS | Changi IAP (Singapore) | SG | +3 |
| OKO/RJTY | Yokota AB | JP | +4 |
| SUU/KSUU | Travis AFB | CA | |

### YOKOTA AB, JP (OKO); REGION: PAC;
### OPERATOR: AMC; TYPE: MIXED; ROUTE: UE07A;
### SAMPLE SCHEDULE: SUN; EQUIPMENT: L100

{OKO *SW* ➡ IWA *SW* ➡ DNA *NW* ➡ OSN ⇌ OSN *SE* ➡ OKO}

| LI/ICAO | AIRPORT/STATION | CTRY/STA | DAYS EN ROUTE |
|---|---|---|---|
| OKO/RJTY | Yokota AB | JP | +0 |
| IWA/RJOI | Iwakuni MCAS | JP | +1 |
| DNA/RODN | Kadena AB | JP | +1 |
| OSN/RKSO | Osan ABI | KR | +1 |
| OKO/RJTY | Yokota AB | JP | |

### YOKOTA AB, JP (OKO); REGION: PAC;
### OPERATOR: AMC; TYPE: MIXED; ROUTE: UE07B;
### SAMPLE SCHEDULE: SAT; EQUIPMENT: L100

{OKO *NW* ➡ OSN ⇌ OSN *SE* ➡ DNA *NE* ➡ OKO}

| LI/ICAO | AIRPORT/STATION | CTRY/STA | DAYS EN ROUTE |
|---|---|---|---|
| OKO/RJTY | Yokota AB | JP | +0 |
| OSN/RKSO | Osan ABI | KR | +1 |
| DNA/RODN | Kadena AB | JP | +1 |
| OKO/RJTY | Yokota AB | JP | |

### YOKOTA AB, JP (OKO); REGION: PAC; OPERATOR: AMC; TYPE: MIXED; ROUTE: UE07C; SAMPLE SCHEDULE: MON; EQUIPMENT: L100

{OKO *W* ➡ KUZ ⇌ KUZ *NE* ➡ MSJ *S* ➡ OKO}

| LI/ICAO | AIRPORT/STATION | CTRY/STA | DAYS EN ROUTE |
|---|---|---|---|
| OKO/RJTY | Yokota AB | JP | +0 |
| KUZ/RKJK | Kunsan AB | KR | +1 |
| MSJ/RJSM | Misawa AB | JP | +1 |
| OKO/RJTY | Yokota AB | JP | |

### YOKOTA AB, JP (OKO); REGION: PAC; OPERATOR: AMC; TYPE: MIXED; ROUTE: UE07D; SAMPLE SCHEDULE: WED; EQUIPMENT: L100

{OKO *SW* ➡ DNA *NW* ➡ OSN ⇌ OSN *SE* ➡ OKO}

| LI/ICAO | AIRPORT/STATION | CTRY/STA | DAYS EN ROUTE |
|---|---|---|---|
| OKO/RJTY | Yokota AB | JP | +0 |
| DNA/RODN | Kadena AB | JP | +1 |
| OSN/RKSO | Osan ABI | KR | +1 |
| OKO/RJTY | Yokota AB | JP | |

### YOKOTA AB, JP (OKO); REGION: PAC; OPERATOR: AMC; TYPE: MIXED; ROUTE: UE07E; SAMPLE SCHEDULE: 1ST & 3RD FRI; EQUIPMENT: L100

{OKO *N* ➡ MSJ *SW* ➡ OSN ⇌ OSN *SE* ➡ OKO}

| LI/ICAO | AIRPORT/STATION | CTRY/STA | DAYS EN ROUTE |
|---|---|---|---|
| OKO/RJTY | Yokota AB | JP | +0 |
| MSJ/RJSM | Misawa AB | JP | +1 |
| OSN/RKSO | Osan ABI | KR | +1 |
| OKO/RJTY | Yokota AB | JP | |

### YOKOTA AB, JP (OKO); REGION: PAC; OPERATOR: AMC; TYPE: MIXED; ROUTE: UE07F; SAMPLE SCHEDULE: 2ND & 4TH FRI; EQUIPMENT: L100

{OKO *N* ➡ MSJ *SW* ➡ DNA ⇌ DNA *NE* ➡ OKO}

| LI/ICAO | AIRPORT/STATION | CTRY/STA | DAYS EN ROUTE |
|---|---|---|---|
| OKO/RJTY | Yokota AB | JP | +0 |
| MSJ/RJSM | Misawa AB | JP | +1 |
| DNA/RODN | Kadena AB | JP | +1 |
| OKO/RJTY | Yokota AB | JP | |

### YOKOTA AB, JP (OKO); REGION: PAC; OPERATOR: AMC; TYPE: MIXED; ROUTE: VH51D; SAMPLE SCHEDULE: SUN; EQUIPMENT: C130E

{OKO *SE* ➡ UAM ⇌ UAM *NW* ➡ OKO}

| LI/ICAO | AIRPORT/STATION | CTRY/STA | DAYS EN ROUTE |
|---|---|---|---|
| OKO/RJTY | Yokota AB | JP | +0 |
| UAM/PGUA | Andersen AFB | GU | +2 |
| UAM/PGUA | Andersen AFB | GU | +2 |
| OKO/RJTY | Yokota AB | JP | |

### YOKOTA AB, JP (OKO); REGION: PAC; OPERATOR: AMC; TYPE: MIXED; ROUTE: VH71C; SAMPLE SCHEDULE: TUE; EQUIPMENT: C130E

{OKO *NE* ➡ MSJ *SW* ➡ KUZ ⇌ KUZ *E* ➡ OKO}

| LI/ICAO | AIRPORT/STATION | CTRY/STA | DAYS EN ROUTE |
|---|---|---|---|
| OKO/RJTY | Yokota AB | JP | +0 |
| MSJ/RJSM | Misawa AB | JP | +1 |
| KUZ/RKJK | Kunsan AB | KR | +1 |
| KUZ/RKJK | Kunsan AB | KR | +1 |
| OKO/RJTY | Yokota AB | JP | |

### YOKOTA AB, JP (OKO); REGION: PAC; OPERATOR: AMC; TYPE: MIXED; ROUTE: VH71D; SCHEDULE: 1ST, 3RD & 4TH THU; EQUIPMENT: C130E

{OKO *SW* ➡ OSN ⇌ OSN *S* ➡ KUZ *NE* ➡ OKO}

| LI/ICAO | AIRPORT/STATION | CTRY/STA | DAYS EN ROUTE |
|---|---|---|---|
| OKO/RJTY | Yokota AB | JP | +0 |
| OSN/RKSO | Osan AB | KR | +1 |
| OSN/RKSO | Osan AB | KR | +1 |
| KUZ/RKJK | Kunsan AB | KR | +1 |
| OKO/RJTY | Yokota AB | JP | |

### YOKOTA AB, JP (OKO); REGION: PAC; OPERATOR: AMC; TYPE: MIXED; ROUTE: VH71D/J; SAMPLE SCHEDULE: THU; EQUIPMENT: C130E

{OKO *NE* ➡ OSN ⇌ OSN *S* ➡ KUZ *SE* ➡ OKO}

| LI/ICAO | AIRPORT/STATION | CTRY/STA | DAYS EN ROUTE |
|---|---|---|---|
| OKO/RJTY | Yokota AB | JP | +0 |
| OSN/RKSO | Osan AB | KR | +1 |
| OSN/RKSO | Osan AB | KR | +1 |
| KUZ/RKJK | Kunsan AB | KR | +1 |
| OKO/RJTY | Yokota AB | JP | |

### YOKOTA AB, JP (OKO); REGION: PAC; OPERATOR: AMC; TYPE: MIXED; ROUTE: VH71F; SAMPLE SCHEDULE: TUE; EQUIPMENT: C130E

{OKO *SW* ➡ DNA *NE* ➡ KHE *NW* ➡ OSN ⇌ OSN *S* ➡ KUZ *NE* ➡ MSJ *SW* ➡ OKO}

| LI/ICAO | AIRPORT/STATION | CTRY/STA | DAYS EN ROUTE |
|---|---|---|---|
| OKO/RJTY | Yokota AB | JP | +0 |
| DNA/RODN | Kadena AB | JP | +1 |
| KHE/RKPK | Kimhae IAP/AB | KR | +1 |
| OSN/RKSO | Osan AB | KR | +2 |
| OSN/RKSO | Osan AB | KR | +2 |
| KUZ/RKJK | Kunsan AB | KR | +2 |
| MSJ/RJSM | Misawa AB | JP | +2 |
| OKO/RJTY | Yokota AB | JP | |

### YOKOTA AB, JP (OKO); REGION: PAC; OPERATOR: AMC; TYPE: MIXED; ROUTE: VH79A; SAMPLE SCHEDULE: WED; EQUIPMENT: C130E

{OKO *SW* ➡ FUK *NE* ➡ IWA *SW* ➡ DNA (★) ➡ FUK *NE* ➡ MSJ ⇌ MSJ *S* ➡ OKO}

| LI/ICAO | AIRPORT/STATION | CTRY/STA | DAYS EN ROUTE |
|---|---|---|---|
| OKO/RJTY | Yokota AB | JP | +0 |

| FUK/RJFF | Fukuoka IAP/Itazuke AB | JP | +1 |
| IWA/RJOI | Iwakuni MCAS | JP | +1 |
| DNA/RODN | Kadena AB | JP | +2 |
| FUK/RJFF | Fukuoka IAP/Itazuke AB | JP | +2 |
| MSJ/RJSM | Misawa AB | JP | +2 |
| MSJ/RJSM | Misawa AB | JP | +2 |
| OKO/RJTY | Yokota AB | JP | |

## YOKOTA AB, JP (OKO); REGION: PAC; OPERATOR: AMC; TYPE: MIXED; ROUTE: VH79C; SAMPLE SCHEDULE: SUN; EQUIPMENT: C130E

{OKO *NE* ➡ MSJ *SW* ➡ KUZ ⇋ KUZ *S* ➡ DNA *NE* ➡ FUK (★) *NE* ➡ MSJ *SW* ➡ OKO}

| LI/ICAO | AIRPORT/STATION | CTRY/STA | DAYS EN ROUTE |
|---|---|---|---|
| OKO/RJTY | Yokota AB | JP | +0 |
| MSJ/RJSM | Misawa AB | JP | +1 |
| KUZ/RKJK | Kunsan AB | KR | +1 |
| KUZ/RKJK | Kunsan AB | KR | +1 |
| DNA/RODN | Kadena AB | JP | +2 |
| FUK/RJFF | Fukuoka IAP/Itazuke AB | JP | +2 |
| MSJ/RJSM | Misawa AB | JP | +2 |
| OKO/RJTY | Yokota AB | JP | |

## YOKOTA AB, JP (OKO); REGION: PAC; OPERATOR: AMC; TYPE: MIXED; ROUTE: VHC7D/E; SAMPLE SCHEDULE: 1ST & 3RD MON, 4TH SUN, 2ND WED; EQUIPMENT: C130E

{OKO *SW* ➡ DNA *SW* ➡ BKK *SE* ➡ UTP *NW* ➡ BKK ⇋ BKK *NE* ➡ DNA *NE* ➡ OKO}

| LI/ICAO | AIRPORT/STATION | CTRY/STA | DAYS EN ROUTE |
|---|---|---|---|
| OKO/RJTY | Yokota AB | JP | +0 |
| DNA/RODN | Kadena AB | JP | +0 |
| BKK/VTBD | Don Muang APT (Bangkok) | TH | +1 |
| UTP/VTBU | U-Tapao RTN | TH | +16 |
| BKK/VTBD | Don Muang APT (Bangkok) | TH | +16 |
| BKK/VTBD | Don Muang APT (Bangkok) | TH | +16 |
| DNA/RODN | Kadena AB | JP | +17 |
| OKO/RJTY | Yokota AB | JP | |

## YOKOTA AB, JP (OKO); REGION: PAC; OPERATOR: AMC; TYPE: CGO W/ PAX; ROUTE: P8F7C; SAMPLE SCHEDULE: TUE; EQUIPMENT: C017A

{OKO *SW* ➡ QPG *SW* ➡ NKW *NE* ➡ FJR ⇋ FJR *SE* ➡ NKW *NE* ➡ UTP *NE* ➡ OKO}

| LI/ICAO | AIRPORT/STATION | CTRY/STA | DAYS EN ROUTE |
|---|---|---|---|
| OKO/RJTY | Yokota AB | JP | +0 |
| QPG/WSAP | RSAF Paya Lebar (Singapore) | SG | +1 |
| NKW/FJDG | Diego Garcia Atoll | GB | +2 |
| FJR/OMFJ | Al Fujayrah IAP | AE | +2 |
| FJR/OMFJ | Al Fujayrah IAP | AE | +2 |
| NKW/FJDG | Diego Garcia Atoll | GB | +3 |
| UTP/VTBU | U-Tapao RTN | TH | +4 |
| OKO/RJTY | Yokota AB | JP | |

## EN ROUTE SCHEDULES

| AIRPORT/STATION | LI-MISSION (page #) |
|---|---|
| Los Angeles IAP | LAX-2W79A (8) |
| Los Angeles IAP | LAX-2X87A (8) |
| Travis AFB | SUU-TTP5J (13) |
| Travis AFB | SUU-P371C (14) |
| Travis AFB | SUU-P371F & G (14) |
| Travis AFB | SUU-P371S & Z (14) |
| Travis AFB | SUU-P379A & B (14) |
| Travis AFB | SUU-P379D (14) |
| Travis AFB | SUU-PT03A (14) |
| McGuire AFB | WRI-TQP5J (50) |
| Charleston AFB/IAP | CHS-P803R (68) |
| Charleston AFB/IAP | CHS-P803S (68) |
| McChord AFB | TCM-P6PXF (83) |
| McChord AFB | TCM-PUPXE (83) |
| Yokota AB | OKO-TQP5V (128) |

# JAPAN AIR BASES & AIRPORTS

(Not listed separately in this book)

The bases listed below have Space-A air opportunities. Base support facilities are very limited.

**CHITOSE AIRPORT - JP (CTS/RJCJ),** c/o Yokota AB, 630th AMSS/TRP, Unit 5093, Bldg 80, APO AP 96328-5093. **REGISTRATION INFO: C-011-81-3117-55-7119/9526/9520, D-315-225-7119/9526/9520, Fax: C-011-81-3117-55-6768/9526, D-315-225-9768/9526. WEB: www.yokota.af.mil** *ML-ARM: (42°50'N/141°40'E).* LST: GMT+09:00. Very limited support facilities available. No Government TML.

## UNSCHEDULED FLIGHTS

Flights to Japan Air Bases. Call for destinations, routings and schedules.

**OBIHIRO AIRPORT - JP (OBO/RJCB),** c/o Yokota AB, 630th AMSS/TRP, Unit 5093, Bldg 80, APO AP 96328-5093. **REGISTRATION INFO: C-011-81-3117-55-7119/9526/9520, D-315-225-7119/9526/9520, Fax: C-011-81-3117-55-6768/9526, D-315-225-9768/9526. WEB: www.yokota.af.mil** *ML-ARM: (42°50'N/143°10'E).* LST: GMT+09:00. Very limited support facilities available. No Government TML.

## UNSCHEDULED FLIGHTS

Flights to Misawa AB, JP (**MSJ**); Yokota AB, JP (**OKO**); and other JP bases. Call for destinations, routings and schedules.

# JORDAN

## KING ABDULLAH AIR BASE (AMM/OJAF)

American Embassy MAP, Unit 70207
APO AE 09892-0207

**LOCATION:** In Amman, Jordan, capital city of Hashemite Kingdom of Jordan. *ML-ARM: (30°10'N/35°55'E).* LST: GMT+02:00. NMC: Amman, 3 miles west. Main installation numbers: C-011-962-6-820-101 ext 2537. Secondary - American Embassy 011-962-6-592-0101.

**REGISTRATION INFO: C-011-962-6-592-0101; Fax: C-011-962-6-592-0163. E-mail: wrahhal@san.osd.mil or sflowers@san.osd.mil** Pax Term, Hours: During flight processing. Contact AMC/AmEmbassy personnel for passenger processing. No U.S. base support facilities. $15 departure tax for out-bound pax through civilian airport. *Visa for entry into country must be obtained before arrival. Note: Active Duty personnel on leave require Country clearance from USDAO Amman upon arrival and prior to departure. Consult Appendix B - Personnel Entrance Requirements.*

**OTHER INFORMATION:** The MAP Amman Air Terminal Facility at King Abdullah AB is staffed only during arrival and departure of AMC aircraft. An AMC Cargo Channel flight is normally scheduled twice monthly from Ramstein, Germany. It will normally depart the same day back to Germany. There are no other DoD scheduled flights in/out of Jordan. Military personnel on leave require Country clearance from USDAO Amman and must contact USDAO upon arrival and prior to departure.

## EN ROUTE SCHEDULES

| AIRPORT/STATION | LI-MISSION (page #) |
|---|---|
| Ramstein AB | RMS-A8F1S (112) |

# KOREA (REPUBLIC OF)

## KIMHAE AIR BASE (KHE/RKPK)

CATO-Kimhae, Bldg 2005, Unit #2004
APO AP 96214-0006

**Location:** On the southern coast, southeast sector of South Korea. *ML-ARM: (35°00N/129°00'E).* LST: GMT+09:00. NMC: Pusan, 15 miles southeast. Main installation numbers: C-011-82-51-801-1110, D-315-763-1110.

**REGISTRATION: C-011-82-51-801-3584, D-315-763-3584, Fax: D-315-787-4102.** Bldg 2005, Hours: 0730-1630 Mon-Fri. Directions: Approximately 1.5 miles from main gate on main Blvd. USAF compound located on left side of road prior to T on main Blvd. No food service available at Kimhae AB. Commercial snack bar and restaurants available at Kimhae IAP.

**FOOD SERVICE:** Camp Hileah, Pusan: Restaurants: Haven Club, C-011-82-51-763-3685; Harbor Lights (AAFES), C-011-82-51-763-3704; Anthony's Pizza, C-011-82-51-763-3753.

**TRANSPORTATION:** Bus, Rental Cars, and Taxi service are available at commercial airport (approximately 1 mile southeast of Kimhae AB main gate). Train station (Pusan) destinations include Seoul, Pyongtaek (Osan), Taegu, Taejon, and Kunsan.

**TML:** Lodging Office: Camp Hialeah, Pusan, C-011-82-51-801-3668, D-315-763-3668.

**TRAVELERS AID:** Camp Hialeah, Pusan: **Chapel:** C-011-82-51-801-3131, D-315-763-3131. **Dental:** C-011-82-51-801-3366, D-315-763-3366. **Medical:** C-011-82-51-801-3625, D-315-763-3625. **Red Cross:** C-011-84-51-801-7410, D-315-763-7410.

**SUPPORT AVAILABLE:** Camp Hialeah, Pusan: Bank, Dispensary, Exchange, Gym, Laundry/Dry Cleaning and Postal Service.

**ATTRACTIONS:** Pusan: U.N. Memorial Cemetery, Children's Park, Pomosa Temple, Chungyolsa Shrine, Haeundae Beach, Kwananli Beach, Casino (Paradise Beach Hotel), Tongdo Fantasia (amusement park), international market (specializing in leather goods, athletic wear, etc.).

### EN ROUTE SCHEDULES

| AIRPORT/STATION | LI-MISSION (page #) |
| --- | --- |
| Yokota AB | OKO-VH71F (129) |

### UNSCHEDULED FLIGHTS

Frequent flights to Osan AB, KR (**OSN**), via C-12 aircraft. Call for destinations, routings and schedules.

## KUNSAN AIR BASE (KUZ/RKJK)

Contract Air Terminal Ops
Unit 2106
APO AP 96264-2106

**LOCATION:** On the southwest coast of the Korean peninsula at the terminus of RK-26 pipeline. *ML-ARM: (35°59'N/126°45'E).* LST: GMT+09:00. NMC: Kunsan, 10 miles west. Main installation numbers: C-011-82-63-470-1110, D-315-782-1110.

**REGISTRATION INFO: C-011-82-63-470-4666/5403, D-315-782-4666/5403, Fax: C-011-82-63-470-7550, D-315-782-7550. E-mail: spacea@kunsan.af.mil** Bldg 2858, Hours: 0730-1630 Mon-Fri. Directions: 3 miles from main gate on Ave B, west. Adjacent to Base Ops and weather tower. **Pax Service Office:** C-011-82-63-470-4666/5403, D-315-782-4666/5403 (also Pax Paging/lost and found).

**PAX LOUNGES: General:** Bldg 2858, Hours: 0730-1630 Mon-Fri. 44 seat capacity, TV, telephones (local and defense), restrooms, A/C, no smoking. **Family and DV/VIP:** None. **Protocol Service:** Hq 8 FW ext 5270. No USO lounge.

**FOOD SERVICE: Jet Stream Snack Bar:** Bldg 1004, C-011-82-63-470-4736, includes cafeteria, Burger King, Anthony's Pizza, Chicken Loft, and Baskin Robbins. **Dining Hall:** O'Malley Inn, Bldg 550, C-011-82-63-470-5160. C-PAD: Bldg 2850, C-011-82-63-470-4951. **NCO/CPO Club:** Loring Club: Bldg 1025, C-011-82-63-470-4575. **O Club:** Bldg 387, C-011-82-63-470-4494. **Restaurants:** Oriental House: Bldg 565, C-011-82-63-470-4100. **Snack Bars:** Bldg 2858, Hours: 0730-1500 Mon-Fri, 0800-1400 Sat, closed Sunday, C-011-82-63-470-4350.

**TRANSPORTATION: Air Tickets:** Bldg 1027, C-011-82-63-470-7653. **On Base Shuttle/Bus:** Hours: 0600-1800 Mon-Fri. **On Base Taxi:** AAFES Taxi, Bldg 712, C-011-82-63-470-4318; **(Gov):** Bldg 960, 24 hours daily, C-011-82-63-470-4597. **Parking:** Long term parking at BX parking lot. Ground transportation to Osan and Seoul consists of commercial bus and/or train. One MWR bus leaves Kunsan for Osan at 0800 daily and returns to Kunsan leaving Osan at 1600 daily (tickets sold at recreation center Bldg 1027 C-011-82-63-470-4679). Commercial transportation requires Korean money. Osan is approximately 3.5 hours north by bus or train. Seoul is four and a half hours by bus or train.

**TML:** Lodging Office: Bldg 391, C-011-82-63-470-4604, D-315-782-4604, Fax C-011-82-63-472-5275, 24 hours daily.

**TRAVELERS AID: Chaplain:** Bldg 501, C-011-82-63-470-4300. **Lost/Found:** Bldg 2858, C-011-82-63-470-4666. **Medical:** Bldg 405, C-011-82-63-470-4323, D-315-782-4323. **Red Cross:** Bldg 755, C-011-82-63-470-4601. **Security Police:** Bldg 590, C-011-82-63-470-4944.

**SUPPORT AVAILABLE: Bank:** Bldg 1006, C-011-82-63-470-4633. **Credit Union:** Bldg 1001, C-011-82-63-470-4801. **Exchange:** Bldg 1102, C-011-82-63-470-4520. **Hair Styles:** Barber Shop, Bldg 1009, C-011-82-63-470-4328; Beauty, Bldg 1008, C-011-82-63-470-4329. **Laundry:** Bldg 1360, C-011-82-63-470-4429. **Postal Service:** Bldg 1058, C-011-82-63-470-5514.

**ATTRACTIONS:** Yellow Western Sea.

### EN ROUTE SCHEDULES

| AIRPORT/STATION | LI-MISSION (page #) |
| --- | --- |
| Seattle/Tacoma IAP | SEA-3W77A (83) |
| Yokota AB | OKO-VH71C (129) |
| Yokota AB | OKO-VH71D (129) |
| Yokota AB | OKO-VH71D/J (129) |
| Yokota AB | OKO-VH71F (129) |
| Yokota AB | OKO-VH79C (130) |

## OSAN AIR BASE (OSN/RKSO)

631st AMSS/TRP
Unit 2073
APO AP 96278-2073

**LOCATION:** At Song Tan city, 6 miles west of Seoul-Pusan North/South Expressway. Directions to AB from expressway are marked. *ML-ARM: (37°10'N/127°00'E).* LST: GMT+09:00. NMC: Seoul KR, 38 miles north. Main installation numbers: C-011-82-31-661-1110, D-315-784-4110.

**REGISTRATION INFO: C-011-82-31-661-1854, D-315-784-1854, Fax: C-011-82-31-661-4897, D-315-784-4897. E-mail: spacea@osan.af.mil WEB: www.osan.af.mil** AFKN broadcast next day's schedule at 1815 hours daily. Bldg 884, Hours: 0630-2100 daily. Directions: From main gate straight on Headquarters Road to a right on Broadway to a left on Texas Road. Pax Term ahead. **Pax Service Office:** C-011-82-31-661-1854, D-315-784-1854/6883. **Pax Paging:** C-011-82-31-661-1854, D-315-784-1854/6883.

**PAX LOUNGES:** Bldg 884. No family lounge. **General:** Bldg 884, Hours: 0630-2100 daily, C-011-82-31-661-1854/6809. A/C, bag check, telephones (local and defense), TV, restrooms, O/S seats, flight monitors. No smoking. **USO Lounge:** Hours: 0800-1700 daily, C-011-82-31-661-3491, D-315-784-3491. Limited dependent care items. Free beverages and movies. **DV/VIP:** Bldg 884, Hours: 0630-2100 daily, C-011-82-332-284-1854/6809. A/C, telephones (local and defense), TV, restrooms, O/S seats. **Protocol Service:** 7th AF, duty hours, C-011-82-31-661-5669, D-315-784-5669 (see Pax Service NCO).

**FOOD SERVICE: Dining Facilities:** Bldgs: 773 and 1343, Hours: 0600-2100 daily. **NCO Club:** Bldg 342, Hours: 0600-2100 daily. Bldg 1313, Hours: 1100-2400 daily. **O Club:** Bldg 910, Hours: 1100-2100 daily. **Snack Bars:** AMC Terminal, Hours: 0630-1800; Rec Center, Bldg 948, 24 hours daily; Bowling Center, Bldg 977, Hours: 1100-2230 daily; Burger Bar, Bldg 920, Hours: 0630-2130 daily.

**TRANSPORTATION: Air Tickets:** Bldg 955, Hours: 1000-1800 Mon-Fri, C-011-82-31-661-3043/3236. **On Base Bus (Comm):** Bldg 980, Hours: 0700-2100 daily, OSN-Yongsan $1.50, Kunsan 1600 daily $3. **On Base Shuttle/Bus:** Bldg 884, 24 hours daily, C-011-82-31-661-1843 (OSN Base); 0600-2300 daily (OSN main gate). **Off Base Car Rentals:** Kimpo IAP arrival lobby. Major rent-a-car companies. **On Base Taxi (Comm):** Bldg 884, 24 hours daily, C-011-82-31-661-4121/2/3, D-315-784-4121/22/23 (AAFES). **On Base Taxi (Gov):** Bldg 1310, 24 hours daily, C-011-82-31-661-5841 (duty passengers only). **Trains:** TMO Bldg, duty hours, C-011-82-31-661-4997. **Parking:** Bldg 884, 24 hours daily, C-011-82-332-284-5515, short term, on overnight. Long term-72 hours at main gate (notify Security Police).

**TML:** Lodging Office: Bldg 771, 24 hours daily, C-011-82-331-661-1844/4597, D-315-784-1844/4597, Fax C-011-82-331-661-4872, D-315-784-4872. DV/VIP: Protocol Office, C-011-82-31-661-6020.

**TRAVELERS AID: Chaplain:** Bldg 779, 24 hours daily, C-011-82-31-661-4184. **Emergency Relief:** Bldg 936, duty hours, C-011-82-31-661-5826 (AF Aid). **Lost/Found:** Bldg 884, Hours: 0700-1700 daily, C-011-82-31-661-5191 (Pax Service NCO). **Medical:** Bldg 76B, 24 hours daily, C-011-82-31-661-4732, D-315-784-4732. **Red Cross:** Bldg 944, Hours: 0730-1630 Mon-Fri, C-011-82-31-661-4140/1855. **Security Police:** Bldg 363, 24 hours daily, C-011-82-31-661-5515. **USO:** Yongsan, Hours: 0800-2200 daily, C-011-82-31-793-3478.

**SUPPORT AVAILABLE: Bank/Currency Exchange:** Merchants National, Bldg 952, Hours: 0930-1730 Tue-Fri, 0930-1500 Sat, C-011-82-31-661-4185. **Exchange:** Bldg 920, Hours: 1000-2000 daily, C-011-82-31-661-3371. **Hair Styles:** Barber, Bldg 954, Hours: 1000-1700 daily, C-011-82-31-661-3133; Beauty, Bldg 957, 1000-1800 Mon-Sat, C-011-82-31-661-3285. **Laundry/Dry Cleaning:** Bldg 958, Hours: 1030-1700 Tue-Sun, C-011-82-31-661-3144. **Postal Service:** Bldg 959, Hours: 1000-1800 Tue-Sat, C-011-82-31-661-4394/4658.

**ATTRACTIONS:** DMZ, Korean customs and culture, Seoul, Inchon.

## EN ROUTE SCHEDULES

| AIRPORT/STATION | LI-MISSION (page #) |
| --- | --- |
| Los Angeles IAP | LAX-2W71B (8) |
| Travis AFB | SUU-P371C (14) |
| Travis AFB | SUU-P371F & G (14) |
| Travis AFB | SUU-P371S & Z (14) |
| Seattle/Tacoma IAP | SEA-3W77A (83) |
| Yokota AB | OKO-VH71D/J (129) |
| Yokota AB | OKO-VH71F (130) |

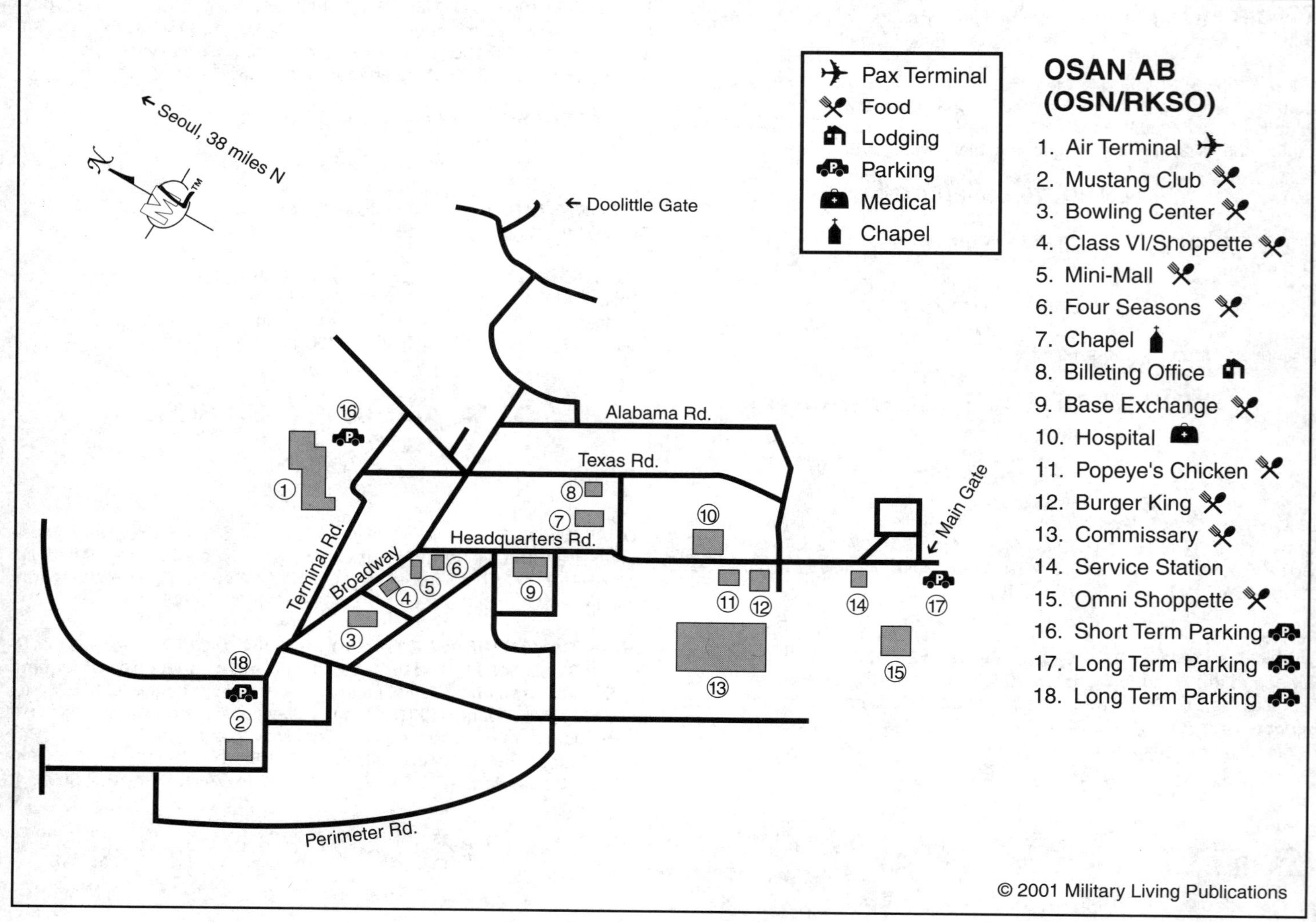

## Other Korea Installations with Possible Space-A Air Opportunities

**CHEJU INTERNATIONAL AIRPORT (CJU/RKPC)**, Liaison MWR, 2nd ID, APO AP 96220-5000. *ML-ARM: (33°20'N/126°15'E).* LST: GMT+09:00. **REGISTRATION INFO: C-011-82-64-792-5698, D-315-763-3330.** AMC Desk, Hours: During flight processing. **Location:** Cheju IAP is 15 miles southwest of Cheju City, on the subtropical island of Cheju Do, which is 50 miles south of the South Korean Peninsula. 2nd Infantry Division, Camp Casey operates an R&R facility here, C-011-82-53-470-4003.

**ROKAB KWANG JU (KWJ/RKJJ), KR.** 631 AMSS/TRP, Bldg 884, Unit 2073, APO AP 96278-2073. *ML-ARM: (35°00'N/127°00'E).* LST: GMT+09:00. **Location:** In southwest Korea, 80 miles south of Taejon and 120 miles west of Pusan. Arrange Space-A applications and processing through Osan AB, KR. **C-011-82-31-661-1854/6883, D-315-754-1854/6883, Fax: C-011-82-31-661-4897, D-315-784-4897.**

### UNSCHEDULED FLIGHTS

Flights to Korean and Japanese bases. Call for destinations, routings and schedules.

# KUWAIT

## KUWAIT INTERNATIONAL AIRPORT (KWI/OKBK)

US Forces Passenger/Cargo Terminal
Unit 69905
CDR USAG-K
ATTN: APOE/D
APO AE 09889-9000

**LOCATION:** Kuwait IAP is 5 miles southwest of Kuwait City, which is located on the northwest corner of the Persian Gulf. *ML-ARM: (29°30'E/48°00'N).* LST: GMT+03:00. NMC: Kuwait City, 5 miles northwest. Also 95 miles south of Basra, Iraq.

**REGISTRATION INFO: C-011-965-539-5307/8, D-318-438-5307/8, Fax: C-011-965-538-0282,** Bldg 325, Hours: 0400-1200 daily or until departure of last scheduled aircraft.

*Note: Space-A passengers are discouraged from traveling through Kuwait. There are no services available to accommodate passenger in case of aircraft failure.*

### EN ROUTE SCHEDULES

| AIRPORT/STATION | LI-MISSION (page #) |
| --- | --- |
| Baltimore/Washington IAP | BWI-EXG5A (37) |
| Baltimore/Washington IAP | BWI-LX27A (37) |
| Ramstein AB | RMS-HJG5A (111) |
| Ramstein AB | RMS-A8G5A (113) |

# MACEDONIA
# (FORMER YUGOSLAV REPUBLIC OF)

## SKOPJE AIRPORT (SKP/LWSK)

**LOCATION:** *ML-ARM: (41°58'N/21°38'E).* LST: GMT+01:00. *Note: Only military personnel on official orders may travel to and from Macedonian airfields by AMC aircraft. Therefore, there is no Space-A travel to Macedonia.*

# MICRONESIA
# (FEDERATED STATES OF)

## KOSRAE INTERNATIONAL AIRPORT (KSA/PTSA)

USCINCPAC REP GUAM
AmEmbassy Kolonia, P.O. Box 1286
Kolonia, Pohnpei
Federated States of Micronesia 96941

**LOCATION:** On the Northwest corner of Kosrae Island. *ML-ARM: (04°50'N/163°00'E).* LST: GMT+10:00. NMC: Tafonsak, 3 miles northeast. Main installation numbers: C-011-691-320-2187, D-None, Fax: C-011-691-320-2186.

**REGISTRATION INFO: C-011-691-320-2187-ext-ask for CINCPAC REP Office, Fax: C-011-691-320-2186.** All of the services of a regional airport.

## POHNPEI INTERNATIONAL AIRPORT (PNI/PTPN)

**LOCATION:** On Pohnpei Island. *ML-ARM: (07°00'N/158°20'E).* LST: GMT+10:00. NMC: Kolonia, FM in the city. Main installation numbers: Same as KSA above.

**REGISTRATION INFO: Same as KSA above.**

## TRUK INTERNATIONAL AIRPORT (TKK/PTKK)

**LOCATION:** On Moen Island, in the Truk Islands group. *ML-ARM: (07°00'N/151°50'E).* LST: GMT+10:00. NMC: Truk, FM in the city. Main installation numbers: Same as KSA above.

**REGISTRATION INFO: Same as KSA above.**

# NEW ZEALAND

## CHRISTCHURCH INTERNATIONAL AIRPORT (CHC/NZCH)

Det 2, 615th AMSG/TRO
PSC 467, Box 214
FPO AP 96531-2000

**LOCATION:** Near Yaldhurst. *ML-ARM: (43°29'S/172°32'E).* LST: GMT+12:00. NMC: Christchurch, 5 miles southeast. NMI: Burnhasrm New Zealand Army Camp, 8 miles west. Main installation numbers: C-011-64-3-358-1422.

**REGISTRATION INFO: C-011-64-3-358-1455, Rec: C-011-64-3-358-1457 (updated daily at 1700), Fax: C-011-64-3-358-1458. E-mail: chc.amcops @iac.org.nz** Pax Term, Hours: 0900-1200 and 1300-1600 Mon-Fri. Sign-up by fax only. **Pax Service Office:** Gate 3 Orchard Road. C-011-64-3-358-1457. **Pax Paging:** Gate 3 Orchard Road or Gate 9 IAP Term, C-011-64-3-358-1457.

**PAX LOUNGES:** CHC IAP. No DV/VIP or family lounges. **General:** Pax Term, Hours: 0600-2300 daily. A/C, bag check/lockers, game room, TV, telephones (local and long distance), restrooms, O/S seats. Pax Term has support facilities: bank, restaurant, cafeteria, rent-a-car, barber/beauty, book/gift shops.

**TRANSPORTATION: Bus (Comm):** Pax Term, CHC IAP to CHC and return. **Taxi (Comm):** Pax Term, C-011-64-3-795-795/799-799.

**SUPPORT AVAILABLE: Postal Service:** USAF, C-011-64-3-358-1475. Letters and post cards only.

**OTHER INFORMATION:** Port of Entry and NZ Customs Service Airport.

**ATTRACTIONS:** Christchurch, sheep ranches, snow skiing, diving, hiking, fishing, wineries, restaurants, bungee jumping, jet boats, rafting, and Mount Cook.

## EN ROUTE SCHEDULES

| AIRPORT/STATION | LI-MISSION (page #) |
| --- | --- |
| McChord AFB | TCM-P6E7P (82) |

# NORTHERN MARIANAS (COMMONWEALTH OF THE)

## SAIPAN INTERNATIONAL AIRPORT (SPN/PGSN)

USCINCPAC Rep, Guam
Commonwealth Ports Authority
Saipan, Northern Marianas

**LOCATION:** Located on the southern tip of the island of Saipan. *ML-ARM: (15°00'N/145°30'E).* LST: GMT+10:00. The Saipan International Airport is relatively small. The Pax Terminal is just inside the open air main gate area. Very limited facilities.

**REGISTRATION INFO: C-670-664-3500, Fax: C-670-234-3962. E-mail for sign-up site: cpa.admin@saipan.com**

**PAX LOUNGES:** North West World Perks Club.

**FOOD SERVICE:** Food Court - LSG concession.

**TRANSPORTATION:** Taxi Cab, Rental Cars.

**SUPPORT AVAILABLE:** Marianas Visitors Authority. C-670-664-3200.

# NORWAY

## STAVANGER SOLA AIR BASE (SVG/ENZV)

426 Air Base Squadron (MS)
Unit 6655
APO AE 09706-5000

**LOCATION:** *ML-ARM: (58°52'N/5°38'E).* LST: GMT+01:00. NMC: Oslo, 480 km northeast. Main installation numbers: C-011-47-51-64-1110/113, DSN-314-224-1110/113.

**REGISTRATION INFO: C-011-47-51-64-1512, DSN-314-224-1512.** Pax services limited.

**FOOD SERVICE: Restaurants:** Pizza Pub, Bldg 33, C-011-47-51-64-1562.

**UNSCHEDULED FLIGHTS**
Limited, bi-monthly C-12 aircraft to RAF Mildenhall, GB.

# OMAN

## OAFB THUMRAIT (TTH/OOTH)

AmEmbassy Muscat
PO Box 202, Code No. 115
Medinat Qaboos, Muscat, Oman

**LOCATION:** Midway Oman. In southeast area of Oman, 85 miles north of the Yemen border. Approximately 500 miles southwest of Muscat, OM. *ML-ARM: (17°32'N/54°00'E).* LST: GMT+04:00.

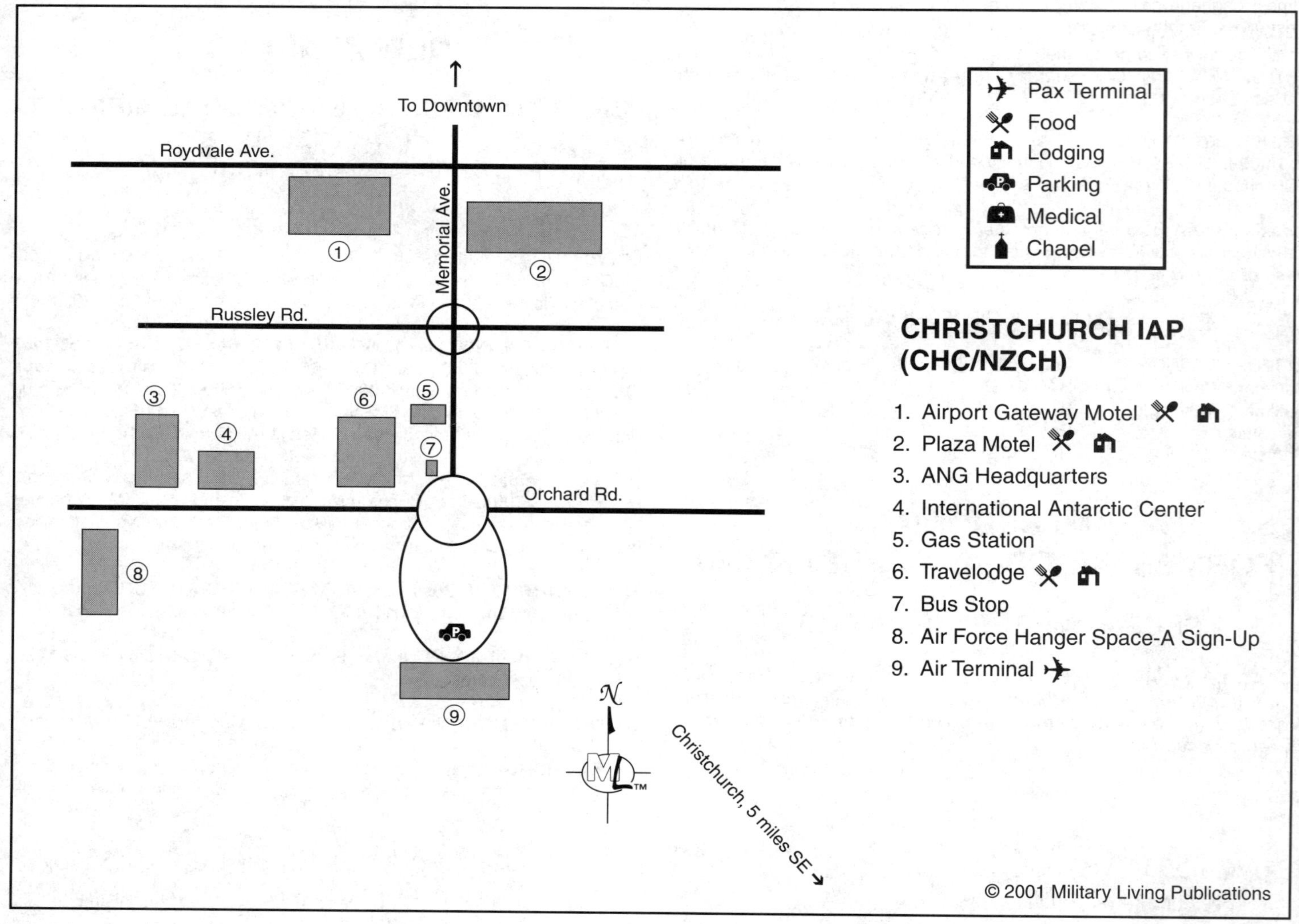


## CHRISTCHURCH IAP (CHC/NZCH)

1. Airport Gateway Motel
2. Plaza Motel
3. ANG Headquarters
4. International Antarctic Center
5. Gas Station
6. Travelodge
7. Bus Stop
8. Air Force Hanger Space-A Sign-Up
9. Air Terminal

REGISTRATION INFO: C-011-968-698-989, **after hours C-011-968-699-049, Fax: C-011-968-699-779.** AMC Desk, Hours: During flight processing, pax processed by AmEmbassy or contractor personnel. No U.S. base support. Facilities of IAP available. Individuals cannot leave or enter base without prior permission. Visa required to exit country via commercial air, and visas are not obtainable from AmEmbassy except in extreme emergencies.

### EN ROUTE SCHEDULES

| AIRPORT/STATION | LI-MISSION (page #) |
| --- | --- |
| Travis AFB | SUU-ATG3A (14) |
| Ramstein AB | RMS-A8F5X (112) |

# PALAU (REPUBLIC OF)

## BABELTHUAP INTERNATIONAL AIRPORT (ROR/PTRO)

US Embassy Koror
P.O. Box 6028
Koror, Republic of Palau 96940-5000

**LOCATION:** Topside, Koror State about 10-15 minutes ride from the airport. *ML-ARM: (08°00'N/134°30'E).* LST: GMT+09:00. NMC: Airai (where airport is located). Main installation numbers: C-011-680-488-2920/2990.

**REGISTRATION INFO: C-011-680-488-2920/2990, Fax: C-011-680-488-2911.** Civic Action team located on the other side of the airport. Palau has one airport for all commercial and non-commercial planes.

**PAX LOUNGES: General:** First floor of the terminal, open only during flight times, baggage check. **DV/VIP:** Same as General, A/C, baggage check, restrooms. **Family Lounge:** Same as General, baggage check. **Protocol Service:** Koror, 0730-1630, C-011-680-488-2408, eligibility: VIP.

**FOOD SERVICE: Cafeteria:** Terminal, Hours: flight times, C-011-680-587-3509. **Snack Bar:** First floor terminal, Hours: flight times.

**TRANSPORTATION: Bus (Comm):** Outside terminal, by reservations. **Car Rentals:** Terminal, during flight hours. **Taxi (Comm):** Terminal. **Parking:** Security annexed to terminal building.

**TRAVELERS AID: Chaplain:** Koror. **Emergency Medical:** Meyuns, Koror, 24 hours daily, 911/488-2558. **Security Police:** Koror, 24 hours daily, C-011-680-488-1422. **USO:** Koror, 0730-1630, C-011-680-488-2920.

**SUPPORT AVAILABLE: Hair Styles:** Koror; Barber, Hours: 0730-2000; Beauty Shop, Hours: 0730-2000. **Laundry:** Koror, Hours: 0600-2100. **Postal Service:** Koror, Hours: 0730-1630. No Government TML.

### UNSCHEDULED FLIGHTS
Infrequent flights to: Anderson AFB, GU (**UAM**) and Hickam AFB, HI (**HIK**).

# PANAMA (REPUBLIC OF)

## TOCUMEN INTERNATIONAL AIRPORT (PTY/MPTO)

**LOCATION:** Tocumen IAP is 17 miles northeast of Panama City, Republic of Panama. *ML-ARM: (79°23'W/09°04'N).* LST: GMT-05:00. NMC: Panama City, 17 miles southwest. Main installation numbers: C-011-507-207-7000.

**REGISTRATION INFO: C-011-507-207-7000, Fax: C-011-507-227-1964,** ask for USDAO office and space-a, write to U.S. Embassy, USDAO, Unit 0945, APO AA 34002-5000. Civic Action team located on the other side of the airport. Palau has one airport for all commercial and non-commercial aircraft.

# PHILIPPINES (REPUBLIC OF THE)

## NINOY AQUINO INTERNATIONAL AIRPORT (MANILA) (MNL/RPLL)

**LOCATION:** *ML-ARM: (14°31'N/121°01'E).* LST: GMT+08:00. *Note: AMC flights transit the Philippines only for the purpose of refueling and crew change. No passengers may board or exit the aircraft, therefore, no Space-A to the Philippines is permitted.*

## CLARK INTERNATIONAL AIRPORT (CRK/RPLC)

**LOCATION:** Pampanga, Philippines. *ML-ARM: (15°11'N/120°33'E).* LST: GMT+08:00. PSC 517, Box RC, FPO AP 96517-1000. **Manila: C-011-63-2-551-2551/891-6113, Fax: C-011-63-2-831-5283. AMC: C-917-924-7284, Fax: C-011-63-2-888-5079/2748. Email: clrkmilasstgrp@hotmail.com WEB: www.2.mozcom.com/~rao-cabr** Limited flights, no passenger facilities at departure location. Up to $25 USD Airport Fees.

### EN ROUTE SCHEDULES

| AIRPORT/STATION | LI-MISSION (page #) |
| --- | --- |
| Norfolk NS | NGU-EX11E (78) |

# PORTUGAL

## LAJES FIELD AIR BASE (AZORES) (LGS/LPLA)

629th AMSS/TRO
Unit 7795
APO AE 09720-8010

**LOCATION:** On Terceira Island (Azores PO) 20 miles long and 12 miles wide. Lajes AB is 2 miles west of Praia da Vitoria PO, on Mason Highway. *ML-ARM: (38°10'N/27°05'W).* LST: GMT-01:00. NMC: Lisbon, 850 miles east. Main installation numbers: C-011-351-295-540-100, C-EUR-351-95-540100, D-312-535-1110, D-314-245-1110.

**REGISTRATION INFO: C(US)-011-351-295-57-3227/3582, D(US)-312-535-3227, D-314-245-3227, Fax: C-011-351-295-57-5110, D(US)-312-535-5110, D314-245-5110. E-mail: spacea.questions@lajes.af.mil (for info only), spacea@lajes.af.mil (sign up only)** When in Portugal, the area code for Terceira island is (95) then 540100 (on base operator). Bldg T-612, 24 hours daily. Directions: From main gate straight for one quarter mile. Pax Term on the right. **Pax Service Office: C(US)011-351-295-57-3227/3582,**

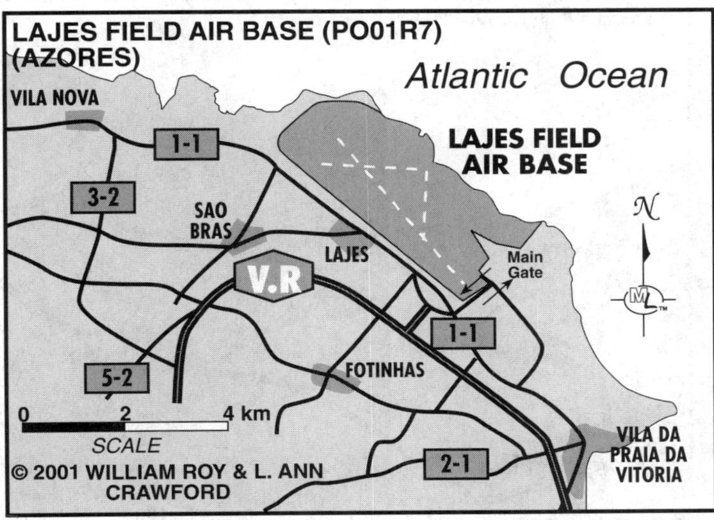

D-312-535-3227, D-314-245-3227. **Pax Paging:** C(US)-011-351-295-57-3227/3582, D-312-535-3227, D-314-245-3227.

**PAX LOUNGES:** Bldg T-612. **General:** Bldg T-612, 24 hours daily, ext 23227/23582, 1st floor. Telephones (local and defense), TV, restrooms, P/C seats. **Protocol Service:** Base Ops, 24 hours daily, ext 24106 (06+). **Family:** Bldg T-612, 24 hours daily, ext 23227/23582. To the right inside main door is the nursery. Same facility as above and nursery.

**FOOD SERVICE: Tradewinds Dining Facility:** Bldg T-415, 0600-0830 Breakfast, 1100-1330 Lunch, 1600-1830 Dinner, 2300-0100 Midnight Meal, Mon-Fri; 0700-1300 Brunch, 1500-1800 Dinner, weekends and holidays, ext 24156. **Combined Club:** Bldg T-112, 0600-0930 Breakfast, 1100-1330 Lunch, 1630-2200 Dinner daily, ext 23202. **Snack Bars:** Bldg T-169, 24 hours daily, ext 23849, T-612, 24 hours daily ext 25123.

**TRANSPORTATION: Air Tickets:** Commercial Term, Hours: 0700-1900 daily, TAP/SATA Info: C-011-351-95-52011/12, Res C-011-351-95-53013. **Bus (Comm):** Main gate, 0700-1900, every hour daily. **Shuttle/Bus:** Bldg T-612, Hours: 0715-0815; 1115-1315; 1615-1715, every half hour daily, C-011-351-95-540100-23151. **Car Rentals:** Commercial Term, Hours: 0800-1600 daily, C-011-351-95-52969. **Taxi (Comm):** Bldg T-612, 24 hours daily, call operator-ask for taxi or 23488. **Taxi (Gov):** Bldg T-220, 24 hours daily, ext 23151 (duty passengers only). **Parking:** Short term, across from Bldg T-612 at the Portuguese Terminal, 24 hours daily. Long Term, behind Bldg T-612 (10 spaces).

**TML:** Lodging Office: Mid-Atlantic Lodge, Bldg T-166, 24 hours daily, C-011-351-295-57-4138/24/46, D-314-535-4138, Fax: C-011-351-295-57-3436, D-314-535-3426.

**TRAVELERS AID: Chaplain:** Bldg T-305, Hours: 0800-1700 Mon-Fri, ext 24211 (other hours-operator). **Lost/Found:** Bldg T-815, 24 hours daily, ext 23222. **Red Cross:** Bldg T-615, Hours: 0800-1600 Mon-Fri, ext 23516 (other hours ext 26252). **Security Police:** Bldg T-815, 24 hours daily, ext 23222 (Desk Sgt).

**SUPPORT AVAILABLE: Bank/Currency Exchange:** Near Bldg T-612, BCA Bank, Hours: 0830-1500 Mon-Fri, ext 23271, and NCO/O Clubs. **Exchange:** Bldg T-323, Hours: 1000-1800 Mon-Sat, ext 23288/23280. **Hair Styles:** Barber, Bldg T-112, Hours: 0800-1700 Tue-Sat, ext 23386; Beauty, Bldg T-400, Hours: 0800-1700 Tue-Sat, ext 24124. **Laundry/Dry Cleaning:** Bldg T-331, Hours: 0800-1430 Mon-Sat, ext 23630. **Medical:** Bldg T-241, 24 hours daily, ext 23237, D-314-245/535-1110 ext 23237. **Postal Service:** Bldg T-324, Hours: 0800-1700 Mon-Fri, ext 23625/23338. **Wire:** PO Term, Hours: 0900-1230 Mon-Fri, across the street from the AMC terminal.

**ATTRACTIONS:** Bull fights, caves, cliffs. CAUTION: DO NOT export scrimshaw (whale ivory) or elephant ivory to the U.S.

## EN ROUTE SCHEDULES

| AIRPORT/STATION | LI-MISSION (page #) |
| --- | --- |
| Baltimore/Washington IAP | BWI-EXG5A (37) |
| McGuire AFB | WRI-HJX5A (50) |
| McGuire AFB | WRI-A7R3A (51) |
| McGuire AFB | WRI-A7X3C (51) |
| McGuire AFB | WRI-G7X5A (51) |
| Charleston AFB/IAP | CHS-A8X5S (68) |
| Norfolk NS | NGU-EX11E (78) |
| Norfolk NS | NGU-EX17B (78) |

## LISBON INTERNATIONAL AIRPORT (LIS/LPPT)

US Embassy
Avenida das Forcas Armadas, 1600 Lisbon
PSC APO AE 09726

**LOCATION:** Lisbon IAP is four miles north of the center of Lisbon. *ML-ARM: (38°46'N/09°08'W).* LST: GMT-01:00.

**REGISTRATION INFO: C-011-351-21-770-2232.** Contact the Defense Attache Office for information at **C-011-351-1-727-3300.**

**SUPPORT AVAILABLE:** Small Navy Exchange located on embassy compound. Authorized patrons restricted to active duty military personnel. C-011-351-21-770-2381.

**UNSCHEDULED FLIGHTS**
Infrequent flights from Rota Naval Station, ES (**RTA**) via C-12 aircraft.

# SAUDI ARABIA

## PRINCE SULTAN AIR BASE (AL KHARJ) (EKJ/OEKJ)

USDAO, Unit 61307
APO AE 09803-1307

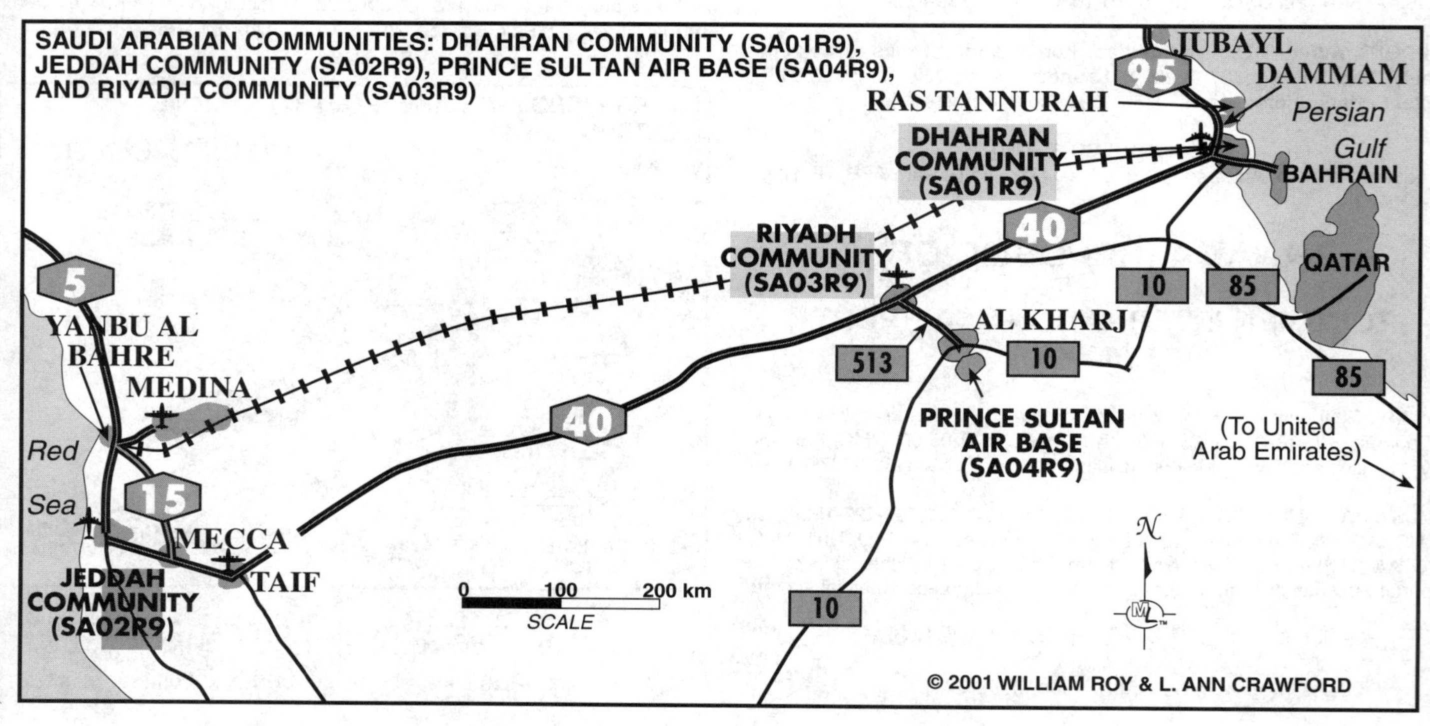

**LOCATION:** Base is 50 miles southeast of Riyadh. *ML-ARM: (24°20'N/47°30'E)*. LST: GMT+03:00. NMC: Riyadh, 50 miles northwest.

**REGISTRATION INFO:** C-011-966-1-488-3800 ext 1275, D-318-435-2560 ext 1275, Fax: C-011-966-1-488-7809. *Note: To enter/exit Saudi Arabia, you must obtain a visa before you travel. To receive a visa, you must have a sponsor within Saudi Arabia or travel on an organized commercial tour.* The airfield is controlled by The Royal Saudi Air Force (RSAF). All ground transportation should be pre-arranged prior to arrival. No commercial transportation is available from the Pax Term.

## EN ROUTE SCHEDULES

| AIRPORT/STATION | LI-MISSION (page #) |
| --- | --- |
| Baltimore/Washington IAP | BWI-EXG5A (37) |
| Baltimore/Washington IAP | BWI-LX27A (38) |
| Ramstein AB | RMS-HJF5A (110) |
| Ramstein AB | RMS-HJF5B (110) |
| Ramstein AB | RMS-G8F5S (112) |
| Ramstein AB | RMS-A8F5A (112) |
| Ramstein AB | RMS-A8F5T (112) |
| Ramstein AB | RMS-A8F5X (112) |
| Rhein-Main AB (Frankfurt) | FRF-HJF5A (114) |

# SINGAPORE

## RSAF PAYA LEBAR (QPG/WSAP)

AMC Terminal Singapore
PSC 470, Box 2450
FPO AP 96534-2450

**LOCATION:** Tip of Malay Peninsula. Off Airport Road. *ML-ARM: (01°15'N/103°30'E)*. LST: GMT+07:30. NMC: Singapore, 5 miles southwest. Main installation numbers: C-011-65-280-0624, D-None.

**REGISTRATION INFO: C-011-65-381-3653, Fax: C-011-65-382-3614.** Bldg 30, Hours: 0800-1600 Mon-Fri. AMC Terminal Office is located next to the Air Movements Center. Turn right off Airport Road upon seeing sign indicating Air Movements Center. Follow signs leading to AMC Terminal Office at Bldg 30. Extremely limited facility. No photos at RSAF Paya Lebar. **Pax Service Office:** Bldg 30, Hours: 0800-1600 Mon-Fri, C-011-65-280-0624. General pax lounge available. No money changing available.

**FOOD SERVICE: Cafeteria:** Airport Road (breakfast, fast food). **Snack Bar:** Hours: 0730-1600 Mon-Fri, 0730-1000 Sat, 5 minute walk away.

**TRANSPORTATION: Off Base Shuttle/Bus:** 10 minute walk to bus at Airport Road, (to downtown). **Off Base Taxi:** Airport Road. (Getting a taxi to downtown hotels can take as long as 2 hours.) C-011-65-552-2255, C-011-

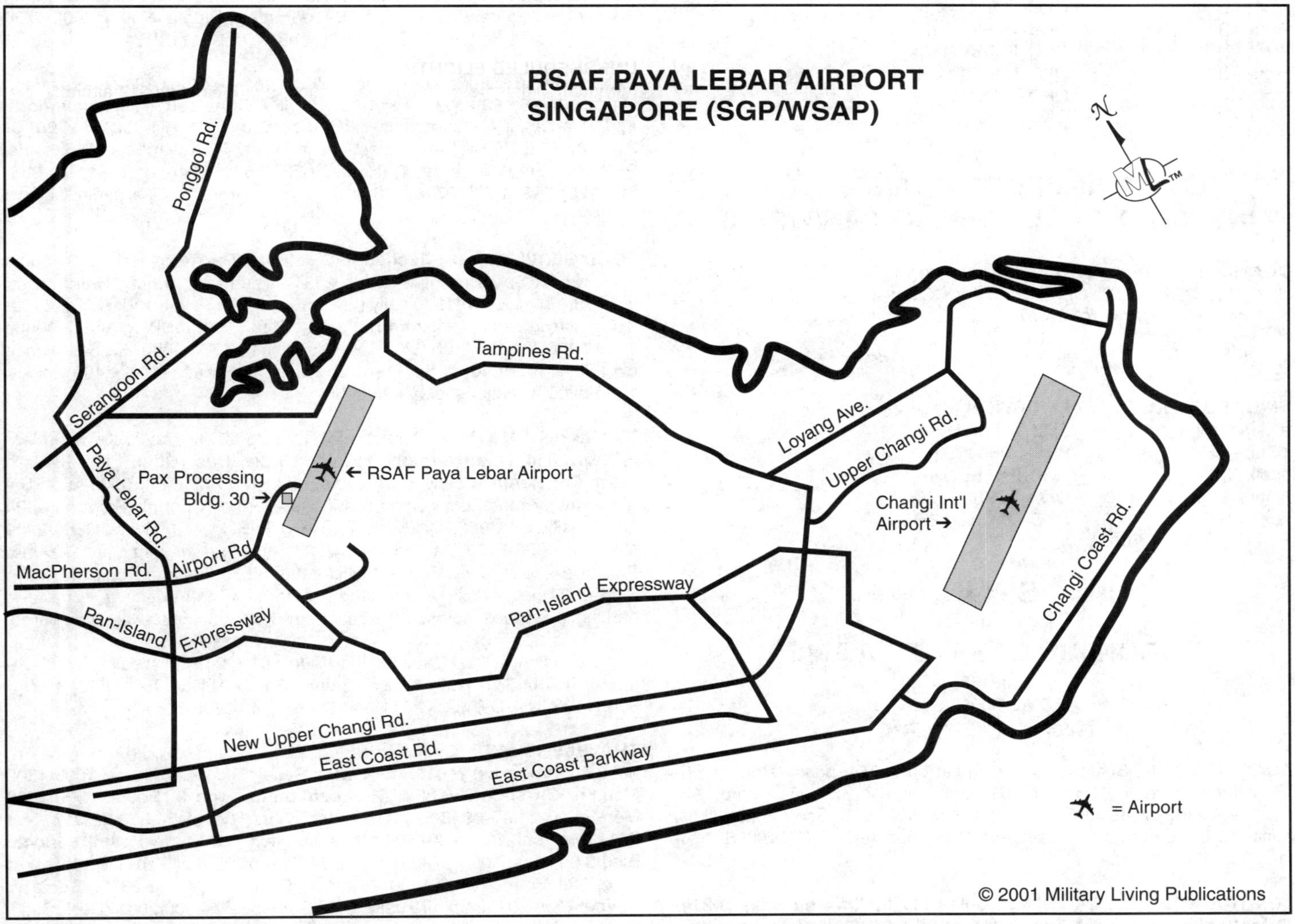

552-1111, C-011-65-6696. **Parking:** No parking for Space-A or other travelers, C-011-65-280-0624.

**TML:** Lodging Office: Sling Inn, 247 Bermuda Road, C-011-65-257-0256, Fax C-011-65-257-9597, 24 hours daily. Distance: 30 minutes by taxi.

**TRAVELERS AID:** Consulate secretary. **Chaplain:** 011-65-350-2361, PSA Sembawang Terminal, 30 minutes by taxi. **Emergency Relief:** American Embassy, 30 Hill Street, Hours: 0730-1615 Mon-Fri, C-011-65-338-0251. **Medical:** American Embassy, 30 Hill Street, 24 hours daily, C-011-65-338-0251 (very limited). **Red Cross:** 24 hours daily, C-011-65-995. **Security Police:** Bldg 30, 24 hours daily, C-011-65-999. **Travelers Aid:** Hours: 1130-2015 Mon-Fri, C-011-65-476-9100.

**SUPPORT AVAILABLE:** Limited at SGP. Many in Singapore. **Credit Union:** Hours: 1200-1830 Mon-Fri, C-011-65-750-2350, PSA Sembawang Terminal, 30 minutes by taxi. **Exchange:** Hours: 1330-2030 Mon-Fri, C-011-65-750-0407, PSA Sembawang Terminal, 30 minutes by taxi. **Postal Service:** Hours: 1200-2030 Mon-Fri, 1400-1600 Sat, C-011-65-750-2570/71, PSA Sembawang Terminal, 30 minutes by taxi.

**OTHER INFORMATION:** Port of Entry.

## EN ROUTE SCHEDULES

| AIRPORT/STATION | LI-MISSION (page #) |
| --- | --- |
| Travis AFB | SUU-TTP5J (13) |
| McGuire AFB | WRI-TQP5J (50) |
| Yokota AB | OKO-ZJF7A (128) |
| Yokota AB | OKO-T8F7C (128) |
| Yokota AB | OKO-T8F7E (128) |
| Yokota AB | OKO-T8P5A (128) |
| Yokota AB | OKO-TQP5V (128) |
| Yokota AB | OKO-TTP5V (128) |
| Yokota AB | OKO-P8F7C (130) |

# SINGAPORE CHANGI INTERNATIONAL AIRPORT (SIN/WSSS)

**LOCATION:** International airport for Singapore. *ML-ARM: (01°22'N/103°59'E).* LST: GMT+07:30. NMC: Singapore, in city limits. ***Note: See Paya Lebar above for information.***

## EN ROUTE SCHEDULES

| AIRPORT/STATION | LI-MISSION (page #) |
| --- | --- |
| Travis AFB | SUU-TTP5J (13) |
| McGuire AFB | WRI-TQP5J (50) |
| Norfolk NS | NGU-EX11E (78) |
| Yokota AB | OKO-TQP5V (128) |
| Yokota AB | OKO-TTP5V (128) |

# SPAIN

# MORON AIR BASE (OZP/LEMO)

Unit 6585
APO AE 09643-5000
*This is a contingency base.*

**LOCATION:** Sevilla, Spain to Alcala, Spain on N-334, pass Alcala to SE-333. At intersection of SE-342 and B-333 proceed on SE-342 to Moron AB. Base well marked. *ML-ARM: (37°10'N/05°25'W).* LST: GMT-00:00. NMC: Sevilla, 40 miles northwest. Main installation numbers: C-011-34-95-5-84-8111, D-314-722-1110.

**REGISTRATION INFO: C-011-34-95-5-84-8111 (ask for air ops), D-314-722-1110 (ask for air ops), Fax: C-011-34-95-5-84-8008.** Limited support, medical emergency: ext 8069.

**FOOD SERVICE: Dining Facility:** Very limited hours, Bowling alley snack bar, hours limited.

**TML:** Lodging Office: Hotel Frontera, Bldg P-303, 1st Street, C-011-34-955-84-8098, D-314-722-8098, Fax C-011-34-95-584-8009, D-314-722-1110, 24 hours daily. DV/VIP: C-011-34-55-84-2798. Very limited. Nearest off-base lodging is located in Seville (60 Km).

**ATTRACTIONS:** City of Sevilla, beaches 2-3 hours away.

### UNSCHEDULED FLIGHTS

This is a contingency base with no scheduled service. It is very busy during inclement weather in Northern Europe. Flights to Europe, Middle East and CONUS. Call for destinations, routings and schedules.

# ROTA NAVAL STATION (RTA/LERT)

Air Terminal Office
PSC 819, Box 7
FPO AE 09645-1500

**LOCATION:** On Spain's South Atlantic Coast. Accessible from A4/E5/N IV South and SP-342 West. *ML-ARM: (36°35'N/06°25'W).* LST: GMT-00:00. NMC: Cadiz, 22 miles south. Main installation numbers: C-011-34-956-82-1110, D-314-727-1110.

**REGISTRATION INFO: C-011-34-956-82-2171/2411, D-314-727-2171/2411, Fax: C-011-34-956-82-1734, D-314-727-1734. E-mail: spacea@ navsta.rota.navy.mil** Bldg 580, main floor, 24 hours daily. Directions: From main gate, straight on 3rd Street to Pax Term on right. Get base pass from Security or at gate. **Pax Service Office/Paging:** Bldg 2, Hours: 0800-1700 Mon-Fri, C-011-34-956-82-2411/2171, D-314-727-2411/2171.

**PAX LOUNGES:** In Pax Term, main floor. **General:** Bldg 580, 24 hours daily, C-011-334-956-82-2411, D-314-727-2411. A/C, nursery, telephones (local and defense), TV, restroom. **DV/VIP:** Bldg 580, C-011-34-956-82-2725, D-314-727-2725 (O6+), A/C, telephones (local), TV, restrooms, O/S seats. **Protocol Service:** Bldg 1, Hours: 0730-1630 Mon-Fri, C-011-34-956-82-2725, D-314-727-2725 (O6+); after hours contact Quarterdeck at ext 2222.

**FOOD SERVICE: Navy Exchange Cafeteria:** (Pax Term) Bldg 2, 24 hours daily except Spanish holidays, ext 2331, in terminal. **Dining Hall:** Galley, Bldg 38, Hours: 0600-1830 daily (varies), ext 2317. **Fast Food:** Hours: 0700-2200, 1 mile away. **Reflections Family Steak House:** Bldg 1631, Hours: 1100-1400 Lunch, 1700-2200 Tue-Thu Dinner, 1700-2300, Fri-Sat Dinner, ext 2851. **Champion's Sports Club:** Bldg 49, Hours: 1100- 2400 weekly, 1100-0200 weekends, ext 2433/2066.

**TRANSPORTATION: Air Tickets:** SATO, Bldg 52, Hours: 0830-1600 Mon-Fri, ext 2034. **Bus (Comm):** Downtown Rota. **Bus (Gov):** Bldg 197, ext 2720. **Car Rentals:** Bldg 580, Hours: 0830-1900 Mon-Fri, 0900-1500 Sat (other major rental car companies in Rota). **Taxi (Comm):** Front gate, 24 hours daily, ext 2929, **On Base Taxi (Gov):** Bldg 149, Hours: 0600-2400 Mon-Fri, 0600-1400 Sat-Sun, ext 2403 (duty passengers only). **Trains:** Puerto, 24 hours daily, Puerto-Sevilla-Madrid Express and Rapid. **Parking:** Bldg 2, 24 hours daily, 2 hour time limit for short term parking. Long term parking is available across the street from Bldg 583, contact security police.

**TML:** Lodging Office: Gateway Inn, Bldg 1610, 24 hours daily, C-011-34-956-82-1871/1751. Navy Lodge: Bldg 1674, C-011-34-956-82-2643 or 1-800-NAVY-INN. DV/VIP: C-011-34-956-82-2440/2795, O6+.

**TRAVELERS AID: Chaplain:** Bldg 204, Hours: 0800-1700 Mon-Fri, 0900-1400 Sun, ext 2161. **Emergency Relief:** Bldg 268, Hours: 1000-1500 Mon-Fri, C-011-34-956-82-2805. **Lost/Found:** Bldg 2, Hours: 0600-1600 Mon-Fri, C-011-34-956-82-2816; after hours, C-011-34-956-82-2171 ext 2411. **Medical:** Bldg 1802, 24 hours daily, ext 2225/4601. **Postal Service:** Bldg 37, Hours: 1000-1730 Mon-Fri, 1100-1400 Sat, ext 3105. **Red Cross:** Bldg 52, Hours: 0800-1630 Mon-Fri, C-011-34-956-82-2333. **Security Police:** Bldg 207, 24 hours daily, C-011-34-956-82-2000/2001 (Desk Sgt).

**SUPPORT AVAILABLE: Bank/Currency Exchange:** Bldg 52, Hours: 0900-1700 Mon-Fri, ext 2913. Currency exchange also available at clubs and NEX. Cambio machines located at PSD (Bldg 52) and Pax Term - best rates. **Exchange:** Bldg 40, Hours: 1000-1800 Tue-Sat, ext 2616/2162. Retirees, DVs, and unaccompanied dependents are only authorized use of post office, banks, clubs, hospital, air terminal, and rec facility due to SOFA. **Hair Styles:** Barber, Bldg 40, Hours: 1000-1730 Tue-Sat, ext 2507; Beauty, Bldg 134, Hours: 0930-1700 Tue-Sat, ext 4034. **Laundry/Dry Cleaning:** Bldg 41, Hours: 1000-1700 Mon-Fri, 1000-1400, 1500-1700 Sat, ext 2559; Bldg 183, 24 hours daily, ext 2275.

**OTHER INFORMATION:** Port of Entry.

**ATTRACTIONS:** Andalucia area, sherry, flamenco dancing, bull fighting.

### EN ROUTE SCHEDULES

| AIRPORT/STATION | LI-MISSION (page #) |
|---|---|
| Travis AFB | SUU-GTA7B (13) |
| Travis AFB | SUU-ATG3A (14) |
| Dover AFB | DOV-A2F3R (18) |
| Westover ARB | CEF-OFF3A (41) |
| Westover ARB | CEF-OFR3A (41) |
| McGuire AFB | WRI-A7F3A (51) |
| Norfolk NS | NGU-EX11E (78) |
| Norfolk NS | NGU-EX17B (78) |

### UNSCHEDULED FLIGHTS

Infrequent flights to Lisbon IAP, PT (**LIS**) via C-12 aircraft.

# THAILAND

## DON MUANG AIRPORT (BKK/VTBD)

AMC Passenger Services
CHJUSMAGTHAI/MAGTAF-LGXT
APO AP 96546-5000

**LOCATION:** Bangkok is on the Chao Phraya River, 20 miles north of the gulf of Thailand. Airport is 20 miles northeast of Bangkok. *ML-ARM: (13°55'N/100°36'E).* LST: GMT+07:00. NMC: Bangkok, 20 miles southwest. Main installation numbers: C-011-66-2-287-1036 ext 333, D-None.

**REGISTRATION INFO:** C-011-66-2-287-1036 ext 166 or ext 333, Fax: C-011-66-2-287-1036 ext 167. E-mail: ppookpanich@san.osd.mil CHJUSMAGTHAI, Bldg D, Room 114, 7 Sathorntai Road, Tungmahamek, Yannawa, Bangkok. Hours: 0700-1600 Mon-Fri. Check-in here, transfer by Thai Airways bus directly to Military Air Terminal, Royal Thai Air Force Base, Don Muang. No commercial taxi at airport. Limited U.S. facilities.

**PAX LOUNGES: General**, Bldg D, Room 114, Hours: 0700-1600 daily., closed on American and Thai holidays, restrooms.

**FOOD SERVICE: Cafeteria:** Hours: 0600-1600, C-011-66-2-287-1036 ext 150, in compound. **Snack Bar:** Hours: 1100-1900, C-011-66-2-287-1036 ext 150, in compound.

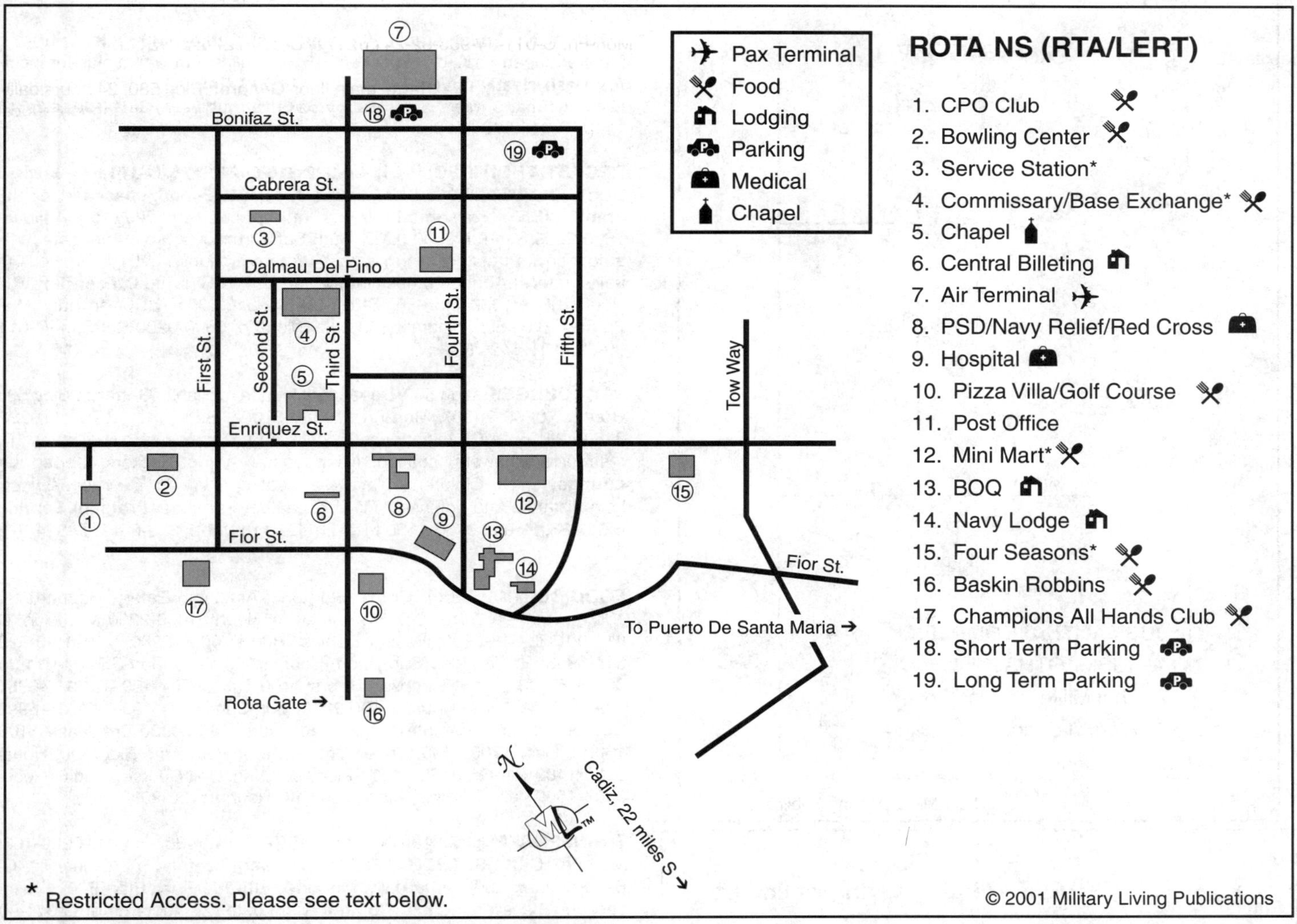

---

**Legend:**
- ✈ Pax Terminal
- ✖ Food
- 🏠 Lodging
- Ⓟ Parking
- 🧰 Medical
- ⛪ Chapel

## ROTA NS (RTA/LERT)

1. CPO Club ✖
2. Bowling Center ✖
3. Service Station*
4. Commissary/Base Exchange* ✖
5. Chapel ⛪
6. Central Billeting 🏠
7. Air Terminal ✈
8. PSD/Navy Relief/Red Cross 🧰
9. Hospital 🧰
10. Pizza Villa/Golf Course ✖
11. Post Office
12. Mini Mart* ✖
13. BOQ 🏠
14. Navy Lodge 🏠
15. Four Seasons* ✖
16. Baskin Robbins ✖
17. Champions All Hands Club ✖
18. Short Term Parking Ⓟ
19. Long Term Parking Ⓟ



* Restricted Access. Please see text below.

© 2001 Military Living Publications

**TRANSPORTATION:** No commercial taxi. There is transportation available for outbound passengers provided by Thai Airways.

**SUPPORT AVAILABLE: Hair Styles:** Barber, Bldg C-129. No Government TML.

### EN ROUTE SCHEDULES

| AIRPORT/STATION | LI-MISSION (page #) |
|---|---|
| Yokota AB | OKO-VHC7D/E (130) |

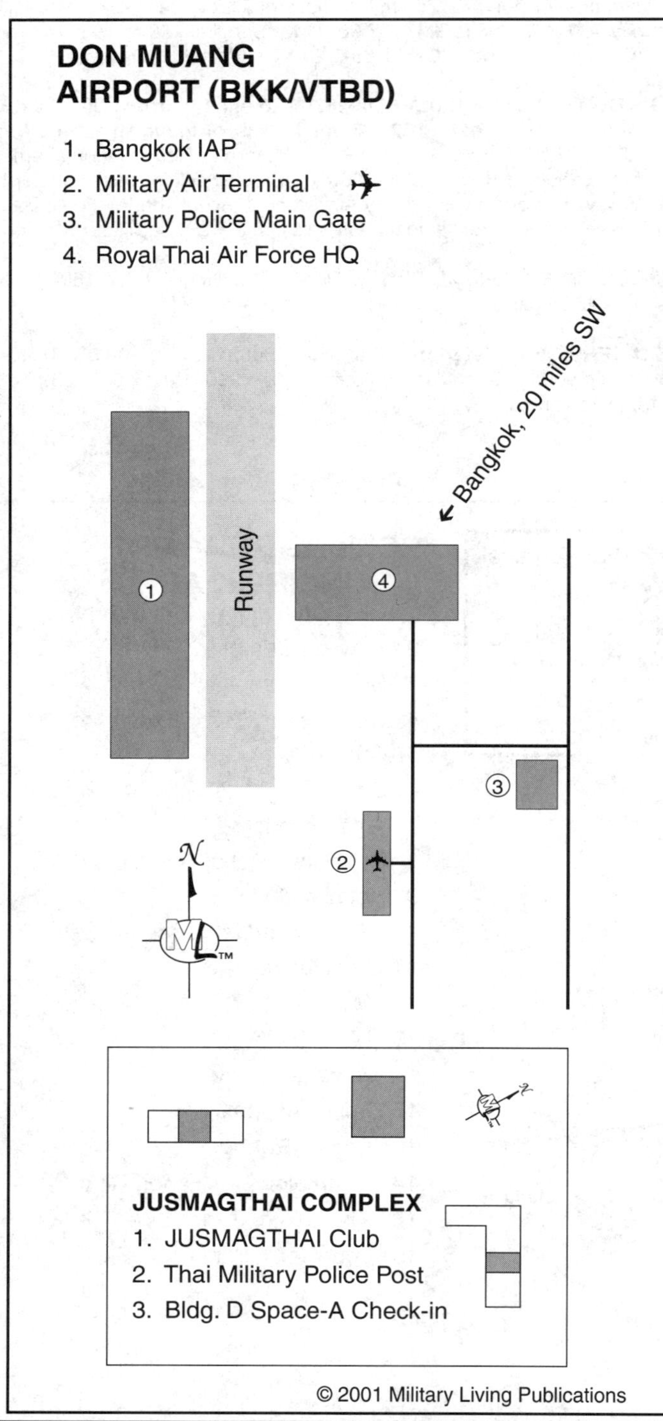

## RTN U-TAPAO (VBU/VTBU)

CHJUSMAGTHAI
MAGTAF-LGXT
AMC Passenger Services
APO AP 96546-5000

**LOCATION:** On the Gulf of Thailand; Royal Thai Navy Base, Rayong, Thailand. *ML-ARM: (12°41'N/101°00'E).* LST: GMT+07:00. NMC: Bangkok, 75 miles northwest. ***Note: Don Muang IAP is the only airport for entry, exit or transit of Space-A passengers in Thailand.***

### EN ROUTE SCHEDULES

| AIRPORT/STATION | LI-MISSION (page #) |
|---|---|
| Yokota AB | OKO-VHC7D/E (130) |
| Yokota AB | OKO-P8F7C (130) |

# TURKEY

*Note: At press time there was still a restriction on all Space-A travel to Turkey and only those stationed in the country on official duty orders were allowed to travel there.*

## INCIRLIK AIR BASE (ADANA) (ADA/LTAG)

628th AMSS/TRO, Unit 7100
PSC 94, Box 190
APO AE 09824-0190

**LOCATION:** From Adana (in southeast Turkey, 30 miles north of Mediterranean Sea), drive east on E-5 for 3 miles, turn left at sign for Incirlik AB. Base clearly marked. *ML-ARM: (36°59'N/34°50'E).* LST: GMT+02:00. NMC: Adana, 3 miles west. Main installation numbers: C-011-90-322-316-1110, D-314-676-1110.

**REGISTRATION INFO:** C-011-90-322-316-6424/6425, D-314-676-6424/25, **Fax:** C-011-90-322-316-3420, D-314-676-3420. **E-mail: spacea@ incirlik. af.mil WEB: www.amc.incirlik.af.mil/spacea.htm** Bldg 500, Hours: 0600-2000 Sun-Fri, 0600-0200 (Sun) Sat. Directions: From front gate make a right on E Street, Pax term is past 4th Street on the right. Recording 0700 daily on local Armed Forces Network radio. **Pax Service Office:** Bldg 500, Hours: 0730-1630 Mon-Fri, C-011-90-322-316-6001 (NCO on duty). **Pax Paging:** Bldg 500, Hours: 0600-2000 Mon-Fri, 0600-0200 Sat-Sun, C-011-90-322-316-6424/5.

**PAX LOUNGES:** Bldg 500. Dependent lounge available. **General:** Bldg 500, Hours: 0600-2000 Mon-Fri, 0600-0200 Sat-Sun, C-011-90-322-316-6424/25. A/C, telephones (local, long distance and defense), TV, restrooms, showers, seating. No baggage storage lockers. **Dependent Lounge:** Cribs, Children's play area, seating. **DV/VIP:** Telephones (local, long distance and defense), TV, O/S Leather Furniture. **Protocol Service:** Bldg 833, Hours: 0730-1630 Mon-Fri, C-011-90-322-316-6347, D-314-676-8352.

**FOOD SERVICE: Food Court:** Bldg 957; American Eatery, Hours: 0630-1900, C-011-90-322-316-6981; Anthony's, Hours: 1000-2200 Mon-Sun, C-011-90-322-316-6993; Baskin Robins, Hours: 0630-2200, C-011-90-322-316-6993; Robin Hood Sub Shop, Hours 1000-1900 Mon-Sun, C-011-90-322-316-6981; Royal Chopstix, Hours: 1100-1900, C-011-90-322-316-6981; Sweet Reflections, Hours: 0630-2200 Mon-Sun, C-011-90-322-316-6993. **Combined Club Complex:** Bldg 878, Hours: 0630-0830 Breakfast, 1100-1300 Lunch, 1700-2100 Dinner. **Snack Bars:** Pax Term: Bldg 500, Hours: 0630-1400 Tue-Fri, 0630-1400 Sat, closed Sun. Golf Course: Bldg 6, Hours: 0900-1500 daily. Bowling Alley: Bldg 914, Hours: 1100-2030 daily.

**TRANSPORTATION: Air Tickets:** DELTA, Bldg 833, Hours: 0900-1630 Mon-Fri, C-011-90-322-316-6520/6763. **Car Rentals:** AJAX-Incirlik: Off Base, Hours: 0800-1900 daily. **On Base Shuttle/Bus:** Bldg 500, Limited service - base area. **Taxi (Comm):** Main gate, 24 hours daily, C-011-90-322-316-6461 (give your location). **Taxi:** Bldg 492, 24 hours daily, C-011-90-322-316-6756/6284 (duty passengers only). **Parking:** Bldg 500, 24 hours daily, C-011-90-322-316-6424. Short term, front of Pax Term; long term, in commissary parking lot. No restrictions.

**TML:** Lodging Office: Hodja Inn, Bldg 1081, 7th Street, 24 hours daily, C-011-90-322-316-6786/9357, D-314-676-6786/9357, Fax: 001-90-322-316-9393/9341. DV/VIP: C-011-90-322-316-8352, O6/GS-15+.

**TRAVELERS AID: Chaplain:** Bldg 945, Hours: 0730-1630 Mon-Fri, C-011-90-322-316-6441. **Emergency Relief:** Bldg 924, Hours: 0730-1630 daily, C-011-90-322-316-6201 (Air Force Aid). **Lost/Found:** Bldg 500, Hours: 0600-2000 daily, C-011-90-322-316-6424/5. **Red Cross:** Bldg 978, Hours: 0730-1630 Mon-Fri, C-011-90-322-316-6927; after hours, C-011-90-322-316-6376. **Security Police:** Bldg 649, 24 hours daily, C-011-90-322-316-6826 (Desk Sgt).

**SUPPORT AVAILABLE: Bank/Currency Exchange:** Bldg 480, Hours: 0800-1530 Mon-Fri, C-011-90-322-316-63204 (finance office). **Exchange:** Bldg 912, Hours: 1000-2000 Tue-Sat, 1100-1800 Sun, C-011-90-322-316-6764/37. **Hair Styles:** Barber, Bldg 958, Hours: 0730-1800 Mon-Sat, 1200-1700 Sun, C-011-90-322-316-3087; Beauty, Bldg 957, Hours: 0830-1730 Mon-Thu & Sat, 1000-1930 Fri, C-011-90-322-316-6093. **Laundry:** Bldg 958, 24 hours daily (self-serve), C-011-90-322-316-3955. **Medical:** Bldg 3850, 24 hours daily, C-011-90-322-316-6666, D-314-676-6666. **Postal Service:** Bldg 977, Hours: 1000-1700 daily, C-011-90-322-316-6301. **Shoppette:** Bldg 912, Hours: 0800-2300 daily, C-011-90-322-316-6053.

**ATTRACTIONS:** Snow skiing, beaches, mountain climbing and fishing.

## EN ROUTE SCHEDULES

| AIRPORT/STATION | LI-MISSION (page #) |
|---|---|
| Baltimore/Washington IAP | BWI-LX19A (38) |
| Ramstein AB | RMS-CET1A (111) |
| Ramstein AB | RMS-G8T1S (112) |
| Ramstein AB | RMS-G8T1U (112) |
| Ramstein AB | RMS-A8F1S (112) |

## IZMIR AIR STATION (IGL/LTBL)

Cigli Air Base
425 ABS/LGTA
Unit 6870, Box 105
APO AE 09821-0130

**LOCATION:** In Western Turkey on the Aegean Sea. From Izmir take E-24 N for 12 miles to W exit for Camalti and Air Base on the right. *ML-ARM: (38°18'N/27°10'E).* LST: GMT+02:00. NMC: Izmir, 15 miles southeast. Main installation numbers: C-011-90-232-484-5360/1110, D-314-675-1110.

**REGISTRATION INFO: C-011-90-232-484-5360 ext 3442, D-314-675-1110 ext 3442/3248, Fax: C-011-90-232-441-7044, D-314-675-3232. E-mail: spacea@izmir.af.mil** Pax Term, Hours: 0730-1630 Mon-Fri, (Sat-Sun: 0830-1030 passenger sign up only). General, family, and DV/VIP lounges available. Access to Air Base is restricted to passengers only. No U.S.

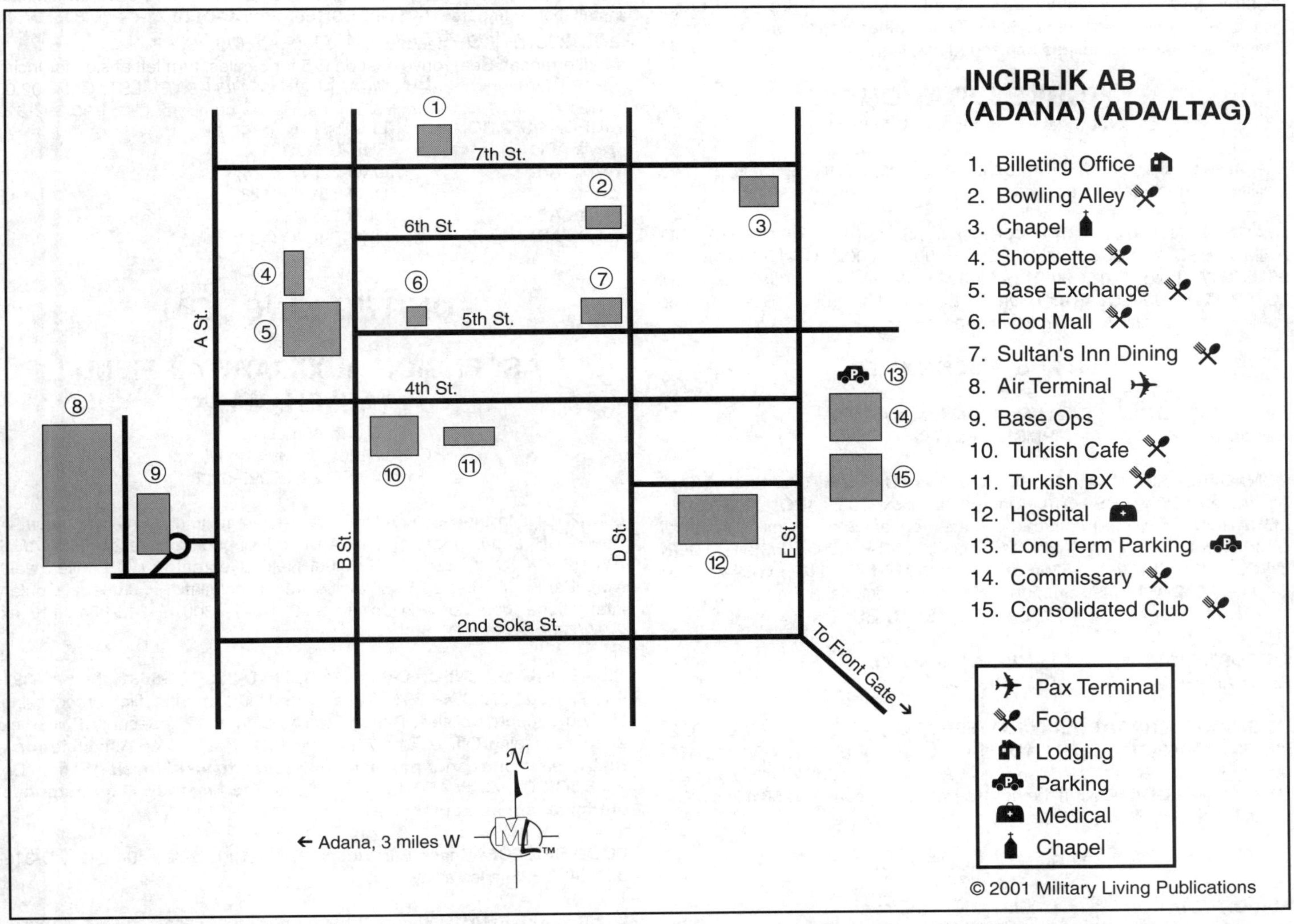
INCIRLIK AB
(ADANA) (ADA/LTAG)
1. Billeting Office
2. Bowling Alley
3. Chapel
4. Shoppette
5. Base Exchange
6. Food Mall
7. Sultan's Inn Dining
8. Air Terminal
9. Base Ops
10. Turkish Cafe
11. Turkish BX
12. Hospital
13. Long Term Parking
14. Commissary
15. Consolidated Club
7th St.
6th St.
5th St.
4th St.
2nd Soka St.
A St.
B St.
D St.
E St.
To Front Gate
← Adana, 3 miles W
Pax Terminal
Food
Lodging
Parking
Medical
Chapel
© 2001 Military Living Publications

facilities at AB. U.S. AMC rep meets all flights with bus transport directly to Pax Term located at FAC 46, Downtown Izmir.

**FOOD SERVICE: Restaurant:** Hours: 0530-2200 daily, Map #13, located in Akin Bldg. AAFES Snack Bar and Baskin Robbins available.

**TRANSPORTATION:** Generous and cheap public transportation: taxi, buses, and horse carriages. Most U.S. support facilities easy walk from each other. Limited shuttle bus service to rec areas only, i.e. swimming, arts and crafts and tennis and racquetball courts.

**TML:** Lodging Office: Grand Hotel Mercure, Facility 77, Lobby, C-011-90-232-489-4090, D-314-675-3379, Fax: C-011-90-232-489-4089, D-314-675-3368. DV/VIP: D-314-675-1110 ext 3341, O6+/E9.

**TRAVELERS AID: USAF Clinic:** Hours: 0730-1630 daily, C-011-90-232-484-5360. Map #12 - Chaplain's office.

**SUPPORT AVAILABLE: Exchange/Shoppette/Commissary:** C-011-90-232-484-5360 ext 3469. Use of Exchange and commissary restricted to Active Duty stationed in Turkey or TDY personnel. **Security Police:** C-011-90-232-484-5360 ext 3222; AAFES Bookstore, Barber/Beauty Shops, Class VI Store, Family Services, Rec Center available.

**OTHER INFORMATION:** Port of Entry.

**ATTRACTIONS:** Ancient biblical and historic sites, Aegean Sea.

### UNSCHEDULED FLIGHTS
C-009A MEDEVAC flights: Sun, Wed, Thu, Fri, Sat to Europe locations/stations. Frequent flights to TU and other Mediterranean stations. Call for destinations, routings and schedules.

# TURKEY STATIONS
### (Not listed separately in this book)

The bases listed below have Space-A air opportunities. Base support facilities at most stations are very limited.

**ATATURK INTERNATIONAL AIRPORT (ISTANBUL) (IST/LTBA)**, OL-A/TMO, PSC 97, Box 0003, APO AE 09827-0002. **C-011-90-212-663-0925/0917, Fax: C-011-90-212-663-0925.** *ML-ARM: (40°59'N/28°45'E).* LST: GMT+02:00. **LOCATION:** On the European side of the Bosporus and the Marmara Denizi. No US military support.

### EN ROUTE SCHEDULES

| AIRPORT/STATION | LI-MISSION (page #) |
| --- | --- |
| Ramstein AB | RMS-CET1A (111) |

**CUMAOVASI AIRPORT (IZMIR), TR (ADB/LTBJ)**, IZMIR Air Station, Cigli Air Base, 425th ABS/LGTA, Unit 6870, Box 105, APO 09821-0130. **LOCATION:** In western Turkey near the Aegean Sea, 15 miles south of Izmir. *ML-ARM: (38 18'N/27 10'E).* LST: GMT+02:00. **REGISTRATION INFO: C-011-90-232-484-5360 ext 3442, D-314-675-1110, ext 3442, Fax: C-011-90-232-441-7044.** Support facilities of a regional airport.

### EN ROUTE SCHEDULES

| AIRPORT/STATION | LI-MISSION (page #) |
| --- | --- |
| Ramstein AB | RMS-CET1A (111) |

**ESENBOGA AIRPORT (ANKARA) (ESB/LTAC)**, APO AE 09823-5000. **C-011-90-312-468-6110/6111/6112/6113 ext 2300, Fax: C-011-90-312-467-0019.** Hours: 0830-1730 Mon-Fri. *ML-ARM: (40°07'N/33°00'E).* LST: GMT+02:00. **LOCATION:** In the north center of the country, 250 miles south of the Black Sea. NMC: Ankara, 16 miles southwest.

### EN ROUTE SCHEDULES

| AIRPORT/STATION | LI-MISSION (page #) |
| --- | --- |
| Ramstein AB | RMS-G8T1S (112) |

# UNITED ARAB EMIRATES

## AL DHAFRA AIRFIELD (DHF/OMAM)

| USDAO AmEmbassy | | USDAO Abu Dhabi |
| --- | --- | --- |
| P.O. Box 4009 | **OR** | State Department Pouch Room |
| Abu Dhabi, AE | | Washington, D.C. 20521-6010 |

**LOCATION:** Al Dhafra Airfield, UAE, located 110 miles southwest of Abu Dhabi. *ML-ARM: (23°30'N/53°20'E).* LST: GMT+04:00.

**REGISTRATION INFO: C-011-971-2-443-6691, after hours: C-011-971-2-443-4457, Fax: C-011-971-2-434-771.** AMC Desk, Hours: During flight processing. All the facilities of a regional airport are available. No military support facilities, including TML.

### EN ROUTE SCHEDULES

| AIRPORT/STATION | LI-MISSION (page #) |
| --- | --- |
| Travis AFB | SUU-GTA7B (13) |
| Travis AFB | SUU-ATG3A (14) |

## AL FUJAYRAH INTERNATIONAL AIRPORT (FJR/OMFJ)

**LOCATION:** Al Fujayrah IAP is located on the northwest corner of the Gulf of Oman. *ML-ARM: (25°30'N/56°20'E).* LST: GMT+04:00. NMC: Dubay, 75 miles west and Abu Dhabi, the capital of UAE, is 125 miles southwest. Main installation numbers: **C-011-971-9-165, Fax: C-011-971-9-229-045.** *Note: See above listing, Al Dhafra, for more information.*

### EN ROUTE SCHEDULES

| AIRPORT/STATION | LI-MISSION (page #) |
| --- | --- |
| Travis AFB | SUU-GTA7B (13) |
| Yokota AB | OKO-ZJF7A (128) |
| Yokota AB | OKO-T8F7C (128) |
| Yokota AB | OKO-T8F7E (128) |
| Yokota AB | OKO-P8F7C (130) |

# UNITED KINGDOM

## ASCENSION AUXILIARY AIRFIELD (ASI/FHAW)

Det 2, 45 LG/CC
P.O. Box 4235, Ascension Island
Patrick AFB, FL 32925-0235

**LOCATION:** In the South Atlantic Ocean approximately halfway between Recife, BR, and Luanda, Angola. A United Kingdom possession. *ML-ARM: (08°10'S/14°30'W).* LST: GMT-00:00. NMC: Georgetown, 0.5 miles west. NMI: Patrick AFB, FL, 5,065 miles. Main installation numbers: Contact international operator and ask for C-011-247-2200, D-312-854-1110 ext 2219/2200.

**REGISTRATION INFO: C-321-494-5631, D-312-854-5631, Fax: C-321-494-7991, D-312-854-7991.** Base Ops, Hours: during flight processing. Limited support facilities. Dining Facility: Bldg 12120, Security Police: ext 2222/3, Lodging Office: Bldg Adm II: ext 2487, all ranks. **Ascension is a restricted island; prior permission required to visit/transit ASI** from Det 2, 45 LG/CC, Patrick AFB, FL 32925-0235. **See Appendix B for personnel entrance requirements.**

**FOOD SERVICE:** Snack Bar: Hours: 1700-2130, C-321-494-2429, D-312-854-2429, .25 miles away.

**OTHER INFORMATION:** Port of Entry and U.S. Customs Service Airport.

## EN ROUTE SCHEDULES

| AIRPORT/STATION | LI-MISSION (page #) |
| --- | --- |
| Patrick AFB | COF-HJL3A (23) |
| Charleston AFB/IAP | CHS-G8L3A (67) |
| Charleston AFB/IAP | CHS-A4P3A (67) |

# DIEGO GARCIA ATOLL (CHAGOS ARCHIPELAGO) (NKW/FJDG)

Det 1, 630 AMSS/TRO
PSC 466, Box 27
FPO AP 96595-0027

**LOCATION:** In the Chagos Archipelago, approximately 1000 miles off the southern tip of India in the Indian Ocean. *ML-ARM: (07°10'S/72°00'E).* LST: GMT+06:00. NMC: Colombo, Sri Lanka, 900 air miles northeast. Main installation numbers: C-011-246-370-2000, D-315-370-2000.

**REGISTRATION INFO:** C-011-246-370-2745, D-315-370-2745, Fax: C-011-246-370-2787, D-315-370-2787. WEB: www.diego.af.mil Bldg 341, Hours: 0730-2330 daily, Center of island near main pier. **Space-A passengers must be stationed at or employed at Diego Garcia in order to fly into, out of or through Diego Garcia; no families are permitted on the island - No exceptions. See Appendix B for personnel entrance requirements. Pax Service Office:** C-011-246-370-2745, D-315-370-2745.

**PAX LOUNGES:** Bldg 360, Hours: 24 hours daily. Also, **DV/VIP** lounge. **Protocol Service:** Bldg 136, Hours: 0800-1600 daily, C-011-246-370-4002, D-315-370-4002, other hours contact Quarter Deck at ext 4120/4121.

**FOOD SERVICE: Dining Hall:** Bldg 140, hours vary, ext 2737. **Enlisted Club:** Bldg 110, ext 2810. **NCO/CPO Club:** Bldg 114, ext 2897/2807. **O Club:** Bldg 127, ext 4737. **Restaurants:** Peacekeeper Inn, ext 2810; Diego Burger II, ext 2816. **Seaman's Club:** ext 2878.

**TRANSPORTATION: On Base Shuttle/Bus:** ext 2770. **On Base Taxi:** ext 2770. Official bus and taxi for duty pax only. *Note: No commercial transportation.*

**TML:** Lodging Office: C-011-246-370-4830, D-315-370-4830. Three miles north of island airport, across from base swimming pool.

**TRAVELERS AID: Chaplain:** Bldg 141, Hours: 0200-1000 daily, ext 4601. **Medical:** Bldg 151, 24 hours daily, ext 4211/4220. **Police:** Bldg 208, 24 hours daily, ext 4600. **Red Cross:** Bldg 141, Hours: 0200-1000 daily, ext 4603.

**SUPPORT AVAILABLE: Bank/Currency Exchange:** Bldg 132, Tue-Sun, ext 2966. **Exchange:** Bldg 133, Hours: 1100-2100, ext 2717. **Hair Styles:** Barber, Bldg 132, Hours: 0800-1900 daily, ext 2720; BEQ 12, ext 2721 (appointments necessary). **Laundry:** Bldg 157, Hours: 0800-2200 Tue-Sat, ext 2926. **Post Office:** Bldg 132, Hours: Mon-Fri 0900-1800, Sat 0900-1200 ext 4119.

## EN ROUTE SCHEDULES

| AIRPORT/STATION | LI-MISSION (page #) |
| --- | --- |
| Travis AFB | SUU-TTP5J (13) |
| McGuire AFB | WRI-TQP5J (50) |
| Norfolk NS | NGU-EX11E (78) |
| Yokota AB | OKO-ZJF7A (128) |
| Yokota AB | OKO-T8F7C (128) |
| Yokota AB | OKO-T8F7E (128) |
| Yokota AB | OKO-T8P5A (128) |
| Yokota AB | OKO-TQP5V (128) |
| Yokota AB | OKO-TTP5V (128) |
| Yokota AB | OKO-P8F7C (130) |

# RAF LAKENHEATH (LKZ/EGUL)

United Kingdom
Unit 5200, Box 105
APO AE 09464-0105

**LOCATION:** Located in the northwest corner of the county of Suffolk, approximately 25 miles northeast of Cambridge. Take the M 11 north to the 11, then take the 11 to the Five-ways Roundabout. Change to the 1065 to RAF Lakenheath. Follow the road signs. *ML-ARM: (52°20'N/00°29'E).* LST: GMT-00:00. NMC: Cambridge 25 miles southwest. Main installation numbers: **C-011-44-1638-52-3000, D-314-226-1110.** Ask for U.S. Flight Operations. **TML:** Liberty Lodge, Building 955, 24 hours daily, C-011-44-1038-52-6700/6713, D-314-226-6700/6713. Fax: C-011-44-1638-52-6717.

### UNSCHEDULED FLIGHTS

Flights to European stations. Call for destinations, routings and schedules.

# RAF MILDENHALL (MHZ/EGUN)

627th AMSS/TRP
Unit 8965, Box 430
APO AE 09459-8965

**LOCATION:** Twenty-seven miles from Cambridge in eastern UK. Follow the A-11 (M) to Newmarket, then to Barton Mills. Take the A-1101 for 2.5 miles through Mildenhall Town to Beck Row Village to RAF Mildenhall. *ML-ARM: (52°18'N/00°29'E).* LST: GMT-00:00. NMC: Cambridge, 24 miles southwest and London is 55 miles southwest. Main installation numbers: C-011-44-1638-54-3000, D-314-238-3000.

**REGISTRATION INFO:** C-011-44-1638-54-2248/2526, D-314-238-2248/2526, Rec: C-011-44-1638-54-5951/5948, D-314-238-5951/5948, Fax: C-011-44-1638-54-2250, D-314-238-2250. E-mail: spacea@mildenhall.af.mil Bldg 598, Hours: 0500-2230 Mon-Sat, 0600-2230 Sun. Directions: From front gate make a left. Pax Term is 0.25 miles ahead. **Pax Service Office:** Bldg 598, Hours: 0800-1630 Mon-Fri, C-011-44-1638-54-2526/2861. **Pax Paging:** C-011-44-1638-54-1854.

**PAX LOUNGES:** Lounges for all categories of travelers. **General:** Bldg 598, Hours: 0500-2230 Mon-Sat, 0600-2230 Sun, C-011-44-1638-54-1854. TV, restrooms, lockers, P/C seats, telephones (commercial and defense). **Special Category:** Bldg 598, Hours: 0500-2230 Mon-Sat, 0600-2230 Sun, (ground floor to the left of Gate 1). Lockers, TV, telephones (commercial and defense), restrooms, O/S seats. Not staffed. **Protocol Service:** Bldg 239, Hours: 0800-1700 Mon-Fri, C-011-44-1638-54-2132, O7+. **Family:** Bldg 598, Hours: 0500-2230 Mon-Sat, 0600-2230 Sun, C-011-44-1638-54-2248 (upstairs to the left - no restrictions). Lockers, telephones, TV, restrooms, O/S seats, playroom, nursery.

**FOOD SERVICE: Cafeteria:** Woody's, Bldg 423, C-011-44-1638-54-2488. **Dining Hall:** Bldg 436, (4th meal and officers' breakfast), C-011-44-1638-54-2689. **Enlisted Club:** Bldg 449, C-011-44-1638-54-2683. **NCO/CPO Club:** Galaxy, Bldg 291, C-011-44-1638-54-2633/2683. **O Club:** Bldg 464, C-011-44-1638-54-2606. **Restaurants:** Pizza Cove, Bldg 433, C-011-44-1638-54-2795; Marauder Sports Lounge, Bldg 291, C-011-44-1638-54-2323. **Snack Bars:** Bldg 423, C-011-44-1638-54-2488; Bowling Center: Bldg 598, C-011-44-1638-54-2248/2526.

**TRANSPORTATION: Air Tickets:** SATO, Bldg 598, Hours: 0800-1630 Mon-Fri, C-011-44-1638-54-2968/2766, D-314-238-2766. **Off Base Bus (Comm):** To London Lakenheath and London Gatwick, Daily. Bury St Edmonds (on base) C-98-66171 and Cambridge (on base) C-92-34-3418. To London - near Gate 2, schedule in Bldg 598. **Off Base Bus (Gov):** Lakenheath-Mildenhall-Gatwick-Mildenhall-Lakenheath (2 routes daily) and Lakenheath-Mildenhall-Heathrow-Mildenhall-Lakenheath (2 routes daily), Traffic Management Office Mildenhall, C(UK)-0638-54-2929, D-314-238-2929, after 1630 (UK) C-0638-54-2339. Space-A passengers are Space-A on these buses. **Car Rentals:** Autorent, (on base) C-717717; Budget, (on base) C-717474; Car Hire, AAFES Concession, Bldg 598, (on base) C-712455, Hours: 1000-1700 Mon-Sat; Mildenhire, (on base) C-717835;

Hertz, (on base) C-717354; Willhire, (on base) C-717452. **On Base Shuttle/Bus:** Bldg 598, Hours: 0630-1730 daily. MHZ to LKZ, hourly, (UK) C-0638-542929. **On Base Taxi (Comm):** Bldg 461, 24 hours daily, C-1638-54-2984 (Base Cab Stand). **On Base Taxi (Gov):** Bldg 611, 24 hours daily, C-011-44-1-638-54-2339. **Trains:** Bury St Edmonds, Hours: 0745-2138 Mon-Sat, 0924-0256 Sun, (on base) C-983947; Cambridge, (on base) C-01223-311999. Schedule available, Bldg 598, London, etc. **Parking:** Short term in front of Bldg 598, 12 hour limit; long term near AAFES Gas Station, Bldg 645, 24 hours daily, C-011-44-1638-54-2667.

**TML:** Lodging Office: Gateway Inn, Bldg 459, 24 hours daily, reservations: C-011-44-1638-54-2655/3093/6001, D-314-238-2655/3093/6001, Fax: C-011-44-1638-54-3688. DV/VIP: C-011-44-1638-54-2777/5432, D-314-238-2777/5432.

**TRAVELERS AID: Chaplain:** Bldg 474, C-011-44-1638-54-2822. **Emergency Relief:** Bldg 436, C-011-44-1638-54-2084 (Air Force Aid Society). **Lost/Found:** Bldg 598, (weekends, ask Shift Supervisor). **Medical:** RAF Lakenheath Hospital, 24 hours daily, D-314-226-2226. **Red Cross:** Bldg 460, C-011-44-1638-54-2113; after hours, C-011-44-1638-54-2107. **Retiree's Activities:** Bldg 598, C-011-44-1638-54-2039. **Security Police:** Bldg 645, 24 hours daily, C-011-44-1638-54-2667.

**SUPPORT AVAILABLE: Bank/Currency Exchange:** Merchants, Bldg 436, C-011-44-1638-54-2850; Kessler FCU, C-011-44-1638-54-2686; ATM, Bldg 598. **Exchange:** Bldg 998, C-011-44-1638-54-2996. (Main BX at RAF Lakenheath). **Hair Styles:** Bldg 178; Barber; C-011-44-1638-54-2676; Beauty; C-011-44-1638-54-2977. **Laundry/Dry Cleaning:** Bldg 123, (on base) C-717906. **Postal Service:** Bldg 442, C-011-44-1638-54-2151.

**ATTRACTIONS:** Newmarket, 13 miles south; Cambridge, 24 miles southwest; London; Bury St Edmunds, 12 miles east.

## EN ROUTE SCHEDULES

| AIRPORT/STATION | LI-MISSION (page #) |
|---|---|
| Dover AFB | DOV-A2R3D (18) |
| Dover AFB | DOV-A2V1A & B (18) |
| Westover ARB | CEF-OFV1A (41) |
| McGuire AFB | WRI-A7W7B (50) |
| Stewart IAP/ANGB | SWF-IFV1A (54) |
| Stewart IAP/ANGB | SWF-IFV3A (54) |
| Norfolk NS | NGU-EX13DM & EX23A (78) |
| Ramstein AB | RMS-CET1D (111) |
| Ramstein AB | RMS-CET1E (111) |



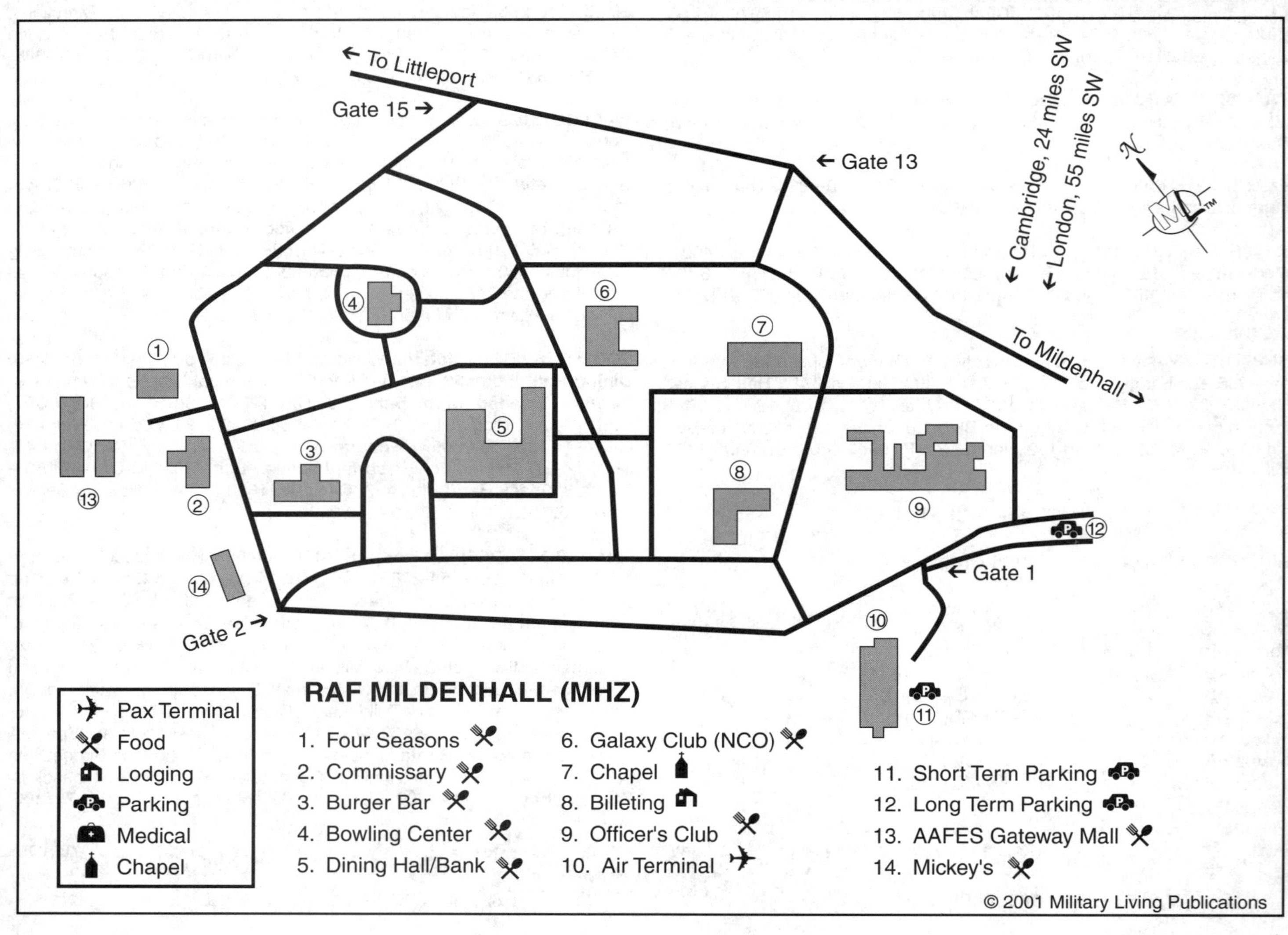


### RAF MILDENHALL (MHZ)

| | | |
|---|---|---|
| ✈ Pax Terminal | 1. Four Seasons 🍴 | 6. Galaxy Club (NCO) 🍴 |
| 🍴 Food | 2. Commissary 🍴 | 7. Chapel ⛪ |
| 🏠 Lodging | 3. Burger Bar 🍴 | 8. Billeting 🏠 |
| 🚗 Parking | 4. Bowling Center 🍴 | 9. Officer's Club 🍴 |
| 🏥 Medical | 5. Dining Hall/Bank 🍴 | 10. Air Terminal ✈ |
| ⛪ Chapel | | |

11. Short Term Parking 🚗
12. Long Term Parking 🚗
13. AAFES Gateway Mall 🍴
14. Mickey's 🍴

© 2001 Military Living Publications

# APPENDIX A
## SPACE-A PASSENGER REGULATIONS
### DOD 4515.13-R AIR TRANSPORTATION ELIGIBILITY

### CHAPTER 6: SPACE-AVAILABLE TRAVEL

A.  GENERAL POLICY

1. <u>Definition and Scope.</u> Space-available travel is the specific program of travel authorized by this Chapter allowing authorized passengers to occupy DoD aircraft seats which are surplus after all space-required passengers have been accommodated. Space-available travel is allowed on a nonmission interference basis only. DoD aircraft shall not be scheduled to accommodate space-available passengers. No (or negligible) additional funds shall be expended and no additional flying hours shall be scheduled to support this program. In order to maintain the equity and integrity of the space-available system, seats may not be reserved or "blocked" for use at en route stops along mission routes.

2. <u>Purpose of the Space-Available Program.</u> Space-available travel is a privilege (not an entitlement) which accrues to Uniformed Services members as an avenue of respite from the rigors of Uniformed Services duty. Retired Uniformed Services members are given the privilege in recognition of a career of such rigorous duty and because they are eligible for recall to active duty. The underlying criteria for extending the privilege to other categories of passengers is their support to the mission being performed by Uniformed Services members and to the enhancement of active duty Service members' quality of life.

3. <u>Leave Status for Travel.</u> Uniformed Services members on active duty must be in a leave or pass status to register for space-available travel, remain in a leave or pass status while awaiting travel, and be in a leave or pass status the entire period of travel. DoD civilian employees, when afforded space-available privileges listed in table 6-1, below, must be in a leave or nonduty (i.e., weekend or holiday) status to register for space-available travel. If in a nonduty status, leave must have been approved for the first normal working day following the nonduty period. A leave status must then be maintained while awaiting travel and for the entire period of travel. Those members in appellate leave status are not authorized space-available travel privileges.

4. <u>In Conjunction with Space-Required Travel or to Restricted Tour Areas.</u> Space-available travel may not be used instead of space-required travel for such movement as TDY, TAD, or PCS travel. Space-available travel may be used in conjunction with space-required travel as long as space-available travel does not substitute for any single leg for which the traveler has a space-required entitlement. For example, a Uniformed Services member may take leave with a TDY or TAD, as allowed by Service regulations, and may travel space-available while on leave. Travel from the PDS to the TDY or TAD location shall be space-required with the traveler in a duty status; any space-available travel from the TDY or TAD duty location shall return to the TDY or TAD location, with the traveler in a leave status; and the final leg shall be space-required from the TDY or TAD location to the PDS with the traveler in a duty status. Dependents may not use space-available travel options in this Regulation to accompany their sponsor on space-required travel or to travel to or from a sponsor's restricted or all others (unaccompanied) tour location.

5. <u>Registers and Sign-Up Procedures</u>
    a. Each base, installation or post from which space-available travel is accomplished shall maintain a single space-available register and all space-available passengers accepted for airlift from that location must have been selected from the register's roll. The maintenance of such a roster shall be the responsibility of the AMC passenger activity, where established. Where no AMC passenger activity is established, it shall be the responsibility of the base, installation, or post commander to designate the Agency responsible for maintaining the space-available roster.

    b. To compete for space-available travel, eligible personnel must sign up on the space-available roster in person and present all required documentation (see subsection A.6., below). The DoD Components and the USTRANSCOM may also accept sign up information in writing from eligible space-available travelers (through mail, fax transmission, or courier). When adopted, the DoD Components and the USTRANSCOM shall provide detailed guidance outlining procedures for using "remote sign up" services. Passengers shall declare their final destination when they sign up for space-available travel. The original date and time of sign-up shall be documented and stay with the traveler until his or her destination is reached. On reaching the destination, the traveler may again sign up for space-available travel to return to home station. Those registered are not required to accept any seat offered, and failure to accept an offered seat shall not jeopardize a passenger's position on the space-available register. All but Category VI passengers (see table 6-1, below) are automatically removed from the space-available register on expiration of leave, pass or after 45 days, whichever is sooner. Category VI passengers are removed from the list after 45 days. All space-available passengers dropped from the register may sign up again in their respective categories (see table 6-1, below) with a new date and time of sign-up.

    c. Reservations shall not be made for any space-available passenger. Travel opportunity shall be afforded on an equitable basis to officers, enlisted personnel, civilian employees, and their accompanying dependents without regard to rank or grade, military or civilian, or branch of Uniformed Service.

6. <u>Required Documentation.</u> Unique documentation required for specific types of individuals (e.g., Medal of Honor recipients) is cited in table 6-1, below, on a case-by-case basis. Additionally, the following types of travelers shall present the documentation listed below to air terminal personnel, and shall have all the documentation in their possession during travel:

    a. <u>Active Duty Uniformed Services Members</u> (includes National Guard, Reserve members on active duty in excess of 30 days, and cadets and midshipmen of the U.S. Service academies).

    (1) DD Form 2 (Green) U.S. Armed Forces Identification Card (Active), or Form 2 NOAA (Green) Uniformed Services Identification and Privilege Card (Active), or PHS Form 1866-3 (Green) United States Public Health Service Identification Card (Active).

    (2) A valid leave authorization or evidence of pass status as required by the Service concerned.

    b. <u>Retired Uniformed Services Members.</u> DD Form 2 (Blue) U.S. Armed Forces Identification Card (Retired), or DD Form 2 (Blue) NOAA Uniformed Services Identification Card (Retired), or PHS Form 1866-3 (Blue) United States Public Health Service Identification Card (Retired).

    c. <u>National Guard and Reserve Members</u>

    (1) <u>Authorized Reserve Component Members (National Guard and Reserve) of the Ready Reserve, and members of the Standby Reserve who are on the Active Status List;</u> On presentation of the following valid:
    (a) DD Form 2 (Red), "Armed Forces of the United States Identification Card (Reserve).
    (b) DD Form 1853, "Verification of Reserve Status for Travel Eligibility."

    (2) <u>Retired Reservists Entitled to Retired Pay at Age 60;</u> On presentation of the following valid:
    (a) DD Form 2 (Red).
    (b) A notice of retirement eligibility as described in DoD Directive 1200.15, (reference (kk)). If the automated DD Form 2 (Red) has been issued, the member is registered in his or her Service personnel system as a Reserve retiree entitled to retired pay at age 60, and a notice of retirement eligibility is not required.

    (3) <u>Retired Reservists Qualified for Retired Pay;</u> Documentation, as prescribed in subsection A.6.b., above. For space-available travel eligibility, no distinction is made between members retired from the Reserves and members retired from active duty.

    (4) <u>On Active Duty for 30 Days or Less;</u> On presentation of the following valid:
    (a) DD Form 2 (Red).
    (b) Orders placing the Reservist on active duty.
    (c) A valid leave authorization or evidence of pass status as required by the Service concerned.

    (5) <u>ROTC, Nuclear Power Officer Candidate (NUPOC), and Civil Engineer Corps (CEC) Members;</u> When enrolled in an advanced ROTC, NUPOC, or CEC course or enrolled under the financial assistance program, on presentation of the following valid:

(a) DD Form 2 (Red).
    (b) DD Form 1853.

d. <u>Dependents of Uniformed Services Members</u>. DD Form 1173, "United States Uniformed Services Identification and Privilege Card."

e. <u>EML Travelers.</u> Besides any documentation required by paragraphs A.6.a. through A.6.d., above, EML orders issued in accordance with Unified Command procedures (see paragraph B.4.a., below).

7. <u>Categories of Travel and Priorities of Movement</u>

a. <u>Categories</u>. The numerical order of space-available categories indicates the precedence of movement between categories; e.g., travelers in Category III move before travelers in Category IV. The order in which travelers are listed in a particular category in table 6-1, below, does not indicate priority of movement in that category. In each category, transportation is furnished on a first-in, first-out basis.

b. <u>Priority of Movement</u>. The numerical order of space-available categories indicates the precedence of movement between categories; e.g., travelers in Category III move before travelers in Category IV. The order in which travelers are listed in a particular category in table 6-l, below, does not indicate priority of movement in that category. In each category, transportation is furnished on a first-in, first-out basis.

c. <u>Changes to Movement Priorities</u>. Wherever the issue may arise, the local installation commander may change the priority of movement of any space-available traveler for emergency or extreme humanitarian reasons when the facts provided fully support such an exception. The installation commander may delegate the authority to make such changes to no lower than the Chief of the Passenger Service Center or its equivalent. When a movement priority is changed, the passenger shall be moved no higher than the bottom of the Category I space-available list. Where AMC units are tenants, the senior local AMC authority shall advise the installation commander of this authority and offer technical assistance, as needed.

8. <u>Destinations and international Restrictions</u>

a. If authorized by this Chapter for a particular traveler's status and situation (see table 6-1, below), transportation may be between overseas stations, between CONUS stations, and between overseas and CONUS stations where adequate border clearance facilities exist or can be made readily available. Theater or international restrictions shall be observed and all requirements pertaining to passports, visas, foreign customs, and immunizations shall be met.

b. Individuals traveling to or from the CONUS, and who are not otherwise eligible to travel space-available in the CONUS, may travel on any CONUS leg segment (i.e., on a flight with enroute stops) when no change of aircraft or mission is involved.

9. <u>Conditions of Travel</u>. There is no guaranteed space for any traveler. The Department of Defense is not obligated to continue an individual's travel or return him or her to point of origin, or any other point. Travelers shall have sufficient personal funds to pay for commercial transportation to return to their residence or duty station if space-available transportation is not available. Space-available travel shall not be used for personal gain, for a business enterprise or outside employment, when theater or international restrictions prohibit such travel, or to establish a home overseas or in the CONUS (except for permissive TDY house hunting trips as authorized in table 6-1, below).

10. <u>Dependent Travel</u>. Except where specifically noted in this chapter, dependents may travel space-available only when accompanied by their sponsor.

B.   <u>EML TRAVEL</u>

Except as noted, unfunded EML travel is subject to the space-available travel program rules and guidance outlined in this section A., above, and table 6-l, below. Funded EML travel is discussed in Chapter 2, sections B.l.e. B.3.a.(14).

1. <u>Definition</u>. EML is leave granted with an EML program, as prescribed in DoD Directive 1327.5 (reference (d)), established at an overseas installation where adverse environmental conditions require special arrangements for leave in more desirable places at periodic intervals.

2. <u>Program Description</u> For a complete description of the EML program, see reference (d).

a. <u>EML Locations and Destinations</u>. Specified locations where adverse environmental conditions exist and at which EML is authorized, are called "EML locations" The Under Secretary of Defense (Personnel and Readiness) designates Funded EML (FEML) locations and relief destinations. Unified commanders designate locations under the unfunded EML program. Under the EML program, not more than two relief destinations shall be designated unless additional destinations are needed to provide a reasonable prospect of relief. The CONUS shall not be designated an "EML destination" except when such designation is necessary to provide a realistic opportunity for relief.

b. <u>Priority, Timing, and Frequency</u>. Passengers traveling space-available under the EML program are given a higher priority than those traveling on ordinary leave (see table 6-1, below). The timing and the frequency of EML is limited by DoD Directive 1327.5 (reference (d)). Transportation officials are not responsible for monitoring this timing and frequency, but rather are responsive to EML documentation issued by the commanders concerned.

3. <u>Responsibilities</u>. Unified commanders shall ensure that administrative controls are in place to ensure that all eligible travelers are able to participate in the EML space-available travel program on a fair and equitable basis. The unified commanders concerned shall forward two copies of each implementing directive, and of any modifications to such directive, to The Department of the Army (DAPE-MBB-C), the Commandant of the U.S. Marine Corps (LFT), the Chief of Naval Operations (N4l), HQ USAF/LGTT, NOAA Corps (NC), and the USTRANSCOM (TCJ3/J4).

4. <u>Policy and Procedures</u>
a. Unified command procedures shall include the issuance of a separate set of EML orders each time an individual is approved for EML.

b. Unfunded EML travelers may travel in Category II status (See table 6-1, below) to only one EML destination for each set of EML orders. This does not preclude several approved EML destinations being included in a single set of EML orders as long as procedures are in effect to ensure that the individual is provided Category II status only for travel to and from the first authorized EML destination actually reached. Subsequent space-available travel; e.g., from the EML destination to a third location and return, or from the third location to another EML location, may only be provided in Category III status (table 6-1, below).

c. When traveling under EML orders, dependents who are 18-years of age or older may travel unaccompanied by their sponsor. Dependents who are under 18-years of age traveling under EML orders must be accompanied by an EML eligible parent or legal guardian who is traveling in an EML status.

C. <u>ELIGIBILITY</u>
The travelers listed in table 6-1, below, are eligible to travel space-available in the categories and over the geographical segments cited, subject to any limitations cited in table 6-1, below, under "Traveler's Status and Situation," or elsewhere in this Regulation.

<u>ELIGIBLE SPACE-AVAILABLE TRAVELERS, PRIORITIES, AND APPROVED GEOGRAPHICAL TRAVEL SEGMENTS</u>

This table lists travelers who are eligible to travel on DoD aircraft according to the space-available program outlined in paragraphs A. and B., above. "Item" is a sequential numbering and is for reference purposes only. "Cat" is the category of travel as explained in section A.7.a., above. These are used to determine priority of movement as explained in section A.7.b., above. "Traveler's Status and Situation" lists specific travelers and conditions under which space-available travel may be authorized. The approved geographical travel segments, i.e. origin and destination combinations, are C-C (CONUS to CONUS), O-O (overseas to overseas), C-O (CONUS to overseas) and O-C (overseas to CONUS) (reference section A.8.). A "yes" in the column headed by one of these abbreviations indicates that travel is authorized in that particular geographical travel segment for the particular type traveler cited in that item number, and subject to any limitations cited. Lack of a "yes" indicates travel is not authorized in that particular geographical travel segment. "Uniformed Services" and "Uniformed Services members," as used in the chart, refer to Active Duty Uniformed Services and members, unless otherwise specified (Category VI).

| Item | Category | Traveler's Status and Situation Table 6.1 | C-C | O-O | C-O and O-C |
|---|---|---|---|---|---|
| 1 | | **Category I - Emergency Leave**<br>**Unfunded Travel** | | | |
| 2 | | Transportation by the most expeditious routing only for bona fide immediate family emergencies, as determined by DoD Directive 1327.5 (reference(d)) and Service regulations, for the following travelers: (This travel privilege shall not be used in lieu of a funded travel entitlement.) | | | |
| 3 | I | Uniformed Services members with emergency status indicated in leave orders (for space-required option see Chapter 2, sections B.1.A. and B.1.b., above). | yes | | |
| 4 | I | Civilians, U.S. citizens, stationed overseas, employees of: (1) Uniformed Services; or (2) NAF activities and whose travel from the CONUS, Alaska or Hawaii was incident to a PCS assignment at NAF expense (for space-required option see Chapter 2, sections B.2.a. and B.4.a., above | | yes | yes |
| 5 | I | Dependents of members of the Uniformed Services accompanied by their sponsor. | yes | | |
| 6 | I | Dependents, accompanied or unaccompanied, of members of the Uniformed Services who are assigned and domociled in the CONUS. | | | yes |
| 7 | I | Dependents of members of the Uniformed Services, noncommand sponsored, residing overseas with the sponsor, one-way only to emergency destination (for space-required option see Chapter 2 sections.3.b.(1) and B.3.b.(2), above. | | yes | C-O no<br>O-C yes |
| 8 | I | Dependents, command sponsored, of: (1) U.S. citizen civilian employees of the Uniformed Services stationed overseas;(2) U.S. citizen civilian employees of the DoD stationed overseas and paid from NAF; or (3) American Red Cross full-time, paid personnel, serving with a DoD Component overseas (for space-required option see Chapter 2, section B.3.a. (2) above). | | yes | yes |
| 9 | I | Professional Scout leaders, and American Red Cross full-time, paid personnel, serving with a DoD Component overseas (for space-required option see Chapter 2 section B.6., above). | | yes | yes |
| 10 | I | Dependents of retired Uniformed Services members who die overseas. Travel is authorized for the purpose of accompanying the remains of the deceased retired member from overseas to the CONUS. Return travel is authorized if accomplished within one year of arrival in the CONUS. Documentation certified by DoD mortuary affairs personnel, and shall be in the dependents' possession during travel. | | | yes |
| 11 | | **Category II - EML** | | | |
| 12 | II | Sponsors in an EML status and their dependents traveling with them, also in an EML status. "Sponsors" includes: (1) Uniformed Services members. (2) U.S. citizen civilian employees of the Armed Forces who are eligible for Government-funded transportation to the United States at tour completion (including NAF employees). (3) American Red Cross full-time, paid personnel on duty with a DoD Component overseas. (4) USO professional staff personnel on duty with the Uniformed Services.5) DoDDS teachers during the school year and for Employer-approved training during recess periods. | | yes | yes |
| 13 | | **Category III - Ordinary Leave, Close Blood or Affinitive Relatives, House Hunting Permissive TDY, Medal of Honor Holders, Foreign Military, and Others** | | | |
| 14 | III | Uniformed Services members in a leave or pass status other than emergency leave (use Category I), environmental and morale leave (use Category II), or excess appellate leave, for which space-available travel is not authorized. This includes members of the Reserve components on active duty, in a leave or pass status. | yes | yes | yes |
| 15 | III | Dependents of a member of the Uniformed Services accompanied by their sponsor in a leave status other than emergency leave (use Category I), environmental and morale leave (use Category II), or excess appellate leave, for which space-available travel is not authorized. | | yes | yes |
| 16 | III | Close blood or affinitive relatives who are permanent members of the household and dependent upon a Military Service member, a DoD civilian employee, or American Red Cross employee serving with a DoD Component overseas, when the sponsor is authorized transportation of dependents at Government expense. Travel must be with the sponsor's, or his or her dependent's, PCS move. | | yes | yes |

| Item | Category | Traveler's Status and Situation Table 6.1 | C-C | O-O | C-O and O-C |
|---|---|---|---|---|---|
| 17 | III | Dependent spouses of military personnel officially reported in a missing status under 37 U.S.C.551 (reference (11)), and accompanying dependent children and parents, when traveling for humanitarian reasons and on approval on a case-by-case basis by the Head of the Service concerned (Chief of Staff of the Army, the Chief of Naval Operations, the Chief of Staff of the Air Force, and the Commandant of the Marine Corps) or their designated representative. Travelers shall present an approval document from the Service concerned. | yes | yes | yes |
| 18 | III | Uniformed Services members traveling under permissive TDY orders for house hunting incident to a pending PCS. | yes | yes | yes |
| 19 | III | One dependent when accompanying a Uniformed Services member traveling under permissive TDY orders for househunting incident to a pending PCS | yes | yes | yes |
| 20 | III | Medal of Honor recipients. Except for active duty, traveler shall present a copy of the Medal of Honor award certificate. | yes | yes | yes |
| 21 | III | Dependents of Medal of Honor recipients when accompanied by their sponsor. | | yes | yes |
| 22 | III | Command sponsored dependents of Uniformed Services members accompanying their sponsor on approved circuitous travel. Commanders authorized to publish circuitous travel orders for members under current policy of their Uniformed Service, where extenuating circumstances prevail, may approve requests for space-available travel of their dependents within and between overseas areas and the CONUS, incident to approved circuitous travel of the member. (For space-required option see Chapter 2, section B.3.a.(7), above). | | yes | yes |
| 23 | III | Foreign Cadets and midshipmen of the U.S. Service academies in a leave status. Foreign cadets' and midshipmen's native countries must be identified in the leave authorization. | | | yes |
| 24 | III | Civilian U.S. Armed Forces patients who have recovered after treatment in medical facilities and their accompanying nonmedical attendants. Travel is permitted by the most expeditious routing to return the recovered patient and nonmedical attendant to the overseas post of assignment. (During the death or extended hospitalization of the patient, the nonmedical attendant retains the space-available travel authority to return to the patient's overseas post of assignment.) | | yes | C-O yes<br>O-C no |
| 25 | III | Foreign exchange service members on permanent duty with the Department of Defense, when in a leave status. | yes | yes | yes |
| 26 | III | Dependents of foreign exchange service members on permanent duty with the Department of Defense, when accompanying their sponsor. | | yes | yes |
| 27 | | **Category IV - Unaccompanied Dependents on EML and DoDDS Teachers on EML During Summer** | | | |
| 28 | IV | Dependents traveling under the EML Program, unaccompanied by their sponsor, traveling under subsection B.4.c., above ("Sponsor" as defined in item 10, above). | | yes | yes |
| 29 | IV | DoDDS teachers or dependents (accompanied or unaccompanied) traveling under the EML Program. | | yes | yes |
| 30 | | **Category V - Permissive TDY (Non-househunting), Students,** | | | |
| 31 | V | Military personnel traveling on permissive TDY orders other than for house hunting. | yes | yes | yes |
| 32 | V | Dependents (children) who are college students attending in residence an overseas branch of an American (U.S.) university located in the same overseas area in which they reside, command sponsored, stationed overseas with their sponsor who is: (1) A member of the Uniformed Services; (2) A U.S. citizen civilian employee of the Department of Defense (paid from either appropriated funds or NAF); or (3) An American Red Cross full-time, paid employee serving with the Department of Defense. Unaccompanied travel is permitted from the overseas military passenger terminal nearest their sponsor's permanent duty station to the overseas military passenger terminal nearest the university, and to return during school breaks. Students must present written authorization from an approving authority and only one round trip each year is authorized. Unused trips may not be accumulated from school year to school year. | | yes | |

| Item | Category | Traveler's Status and Situation Table 6.1 | C-C | O-O | C-O and O-C |
|---|---|---|---|---|---|
| 33 | V | Dependents, command sponsored, stationed overseas with their sponsor who is: (1) A member of the Uniformed Services; (2) A U.S. citizen civilian employee of the Department of Defense (paid from either appropriated funds or NAF); or (3) An American Red Cross full-time, paid employee serving with the Department of Defense. Unaccompanied travel is permitted to and from the nearest overseas military academy testing site to take scheduled entrance examinations for entry into any of the U.S. service academies. | | yes | |
| 34 | V | Dependents of active duty U.S. military personnel stationed overseas who, at the time of PCS, were not entitled to transportation at Government expense. Travel is to accompany or join their sponsor at his or her duty station. Travel may be unaccompanied and is limited to travel from the APOE in the CONUS, Alaska, or Hawaii to the overseas APOD serving the sponsor's duty station. Before travel, approval of the overseas major commander is required. (For space-required option see Chapter 2, section B.3. a. (8), above.) | | | C-O yes<br>O-C no |
| 35 | V | Noncommand sponsored dependents, acquired in an overseas area during a military member's current tour of assigned duty, not otherwise entitled to transportation at Government expense. Travel must be with the member's PCS, may be unaccompanied, and is limited to travel from the overseas APOE to the APOD in the CONUS, Alaska, or Hawaii. Member's PCS orders are required for travel. Command regulations pertaining to the acquisition of dependents must have been followed. (For space-required option see Chapter 2, section B.3.b. (2) above.) | | | C-O no<br>O-C yes |
| 36 | V | Unaccompanied spouses of Uniformed Services members stationed in overseas areas in response to written requests from school officials, when deemed essential, authorized, and directed in writing by the sponsor's commander for personal consultation on matters about the needs of family members attending school at an overseas location away from the Uniformed Service member's PDS. | | yes | |
| 37 | V | Command sponsored dependents of Uniformed Services members, accompanied or unaccompanied, who are stationed overseas. Travel restrictions may apply to certain overseas destinations as determined by the appropriate unified commander. Documentation signed by the sponsor's commander verifying command sponsorship shall be presented to air terminal personnel and shall be in the dependent's possession during travel. This documentation is valid for one round trip from sponsor's PCS duty location. Dependents under 18 years of age must be accompanied by an eligible parent or legal guardian. | | yes | yes |
| 38 | | **Category VI - Retired, Dependents, Reserve, ROTC, NUPOC, and CEC** | | | |
| 39 | VI | Retired Uniformed Services members. | yes | yes | yes |
| 40 | VI | Dependents of retired Uniformed Services members, when accompanying their sponsor. | | yes | yes |
| 41 | VI | Dependents, command sponsored, stationed overseas with their sponsor who is: (1) A member of the Uniformed Services; (2) A U.S. citizen civilian employee of the Department of Defense (paid from either appropriated funds or NAF); or (3) An American Red Cross full-time, paid employee serving with the Department of Defense. Unaccompanied travel is permitted to the U.S. for enlisting in one of the Armed Forces when local enlistment in the overseas area is not authorized. If an applicant for Military Service is rejected, return travel to the overseas area may be provided under this eligibility. | | yes | yes |
| 42 | VI | Authorized Reserve component members and authorized Reserve component members entitled to retired pay at age 60, (gray area retiress) traveling in the CONUS and directly between the CONUS and Alaska, Hawaii, Puerto Rico, the U.S. Virgin Islands, Guam, and American Samoa (Guam and American Samoa travelers may transit Hawaii or Alaska); or traveling within Alaska, Hawaii, Puerto Rico or the U.S. Virgin Islands. | yes | | |
| 43 | VI | NUPOC, CEC, and ROTC students of the Army, Navy, or Air Force, receiving financial assistance or enrolled in advanced training, in uniform, during authorized absences from the school. Travel is authorized within and between the CONUS, Alaska, Hawaii, and the U.S. territories. | yes | | |
| 44 | VI | Newly commisioned ROTC officers who are awaiting call to extended active duty. Travel is authorized within and betweeen the CONUS, Alaska, Hawaii, and the U.S. territories. | yes | | |

**ADDITIONAL SPACE-A INFORMATION FROM CHAPTER 1**

### C. USE OF MILITARY AIRCRAFT. INELIGIBLE TRAFFIC. AND RESTRICTIONS

1. Commanders' Responsibility. The commanders at all levels shall exercise prudent judgment to ensure that only authorized traffic is transported and that they do not misuse the authority delegated to them by this Regulation. The commanders and other officials responding to requests for transportation not specifically authorized by this Regulation shall make no commitments concerning prospective travelers or cargo until they receive all required approvals.

2. Ineligible Traffic Procedures

a. When an order or authorization for movement of traffic (passenger or cargo) which is neither authorized by this Regulation nor approved according to the procedures in this Regulation is presented, transportation shall be denied. The station making the determination shall document the case and forward it through channels to USTRANSCOM TCJ3/J4-LP, 508 SCOTT DRIVE, SCOTT AFB IL 62225-5357 for necessary action.

b. Any traffic transported by DoD aircraft which is ineligible, even though documentation may have been issued, is liable for reimbursement at the non-U.S. Government rate tariff according to APR 76-28 (reference (f)) for all transportation furnished. If any passenger or cargo is challenged for eligibility or authority, every effort shall be made to provide assistance short of delaying a scheduled aircraft.

3. Restrictions on Use of Unit or Operational Support Aircraft. Unless requested and authorized under DoD Directive 4500.43 (reference (t)), unit aircraft shall not be utilized to transport DoD passengers and cargo. Similarly, the use of unit or operational support airlift aircraft to provide PCS transportation for DoD members or their dependents is not authorized.

4. Pregnant and Post-Partum Mothers and Newborn Infants

a. Pregnant women up to the 34th week of gestation may be accepted for air transportation unless medically inadvisable.

b. Women who are 6 weeks, or more, postpartum and infants at least 6 weeks old may be accepted for air transportation unless medically inadvisable. Infants under 6 weeks old and women who are less than 6 weeks post partum may be accepted if considered medically sound and so certified in writing by a responsible medical officer or civilian physician.

5. Unaccompanied Minors. Restrictions on travel by unaccompanied minors vary with types of travel (see Chapters 2, 5, 6, and 7).

6. Passengers on "Non-Transport-Type" Aircraft. Aircraft not designed or normally configured for passenger (nonaircrew personnel) carrying capability, such as, but not limited to, fighter aircraft, are not to be used for passenger travel. This does not restrict use of these type aircraft for orientation flights, as prescribed in Chapter 4 below.

7. Disabled Passenger. Every effort shall be made to transport passengers with disabilities who are otherwise eligible to travel. Passenger service personnel and crew members shall provide assistance in loading, seating, and unloading the disabled passenger. Travel may be disapproved by the chief of the passenger travel section or the aircraft commander if there is an unacceptable risk to the safety of the disabled passenger, other passengers or the crew, or if operational necessity or equipment or manpower limitations preclude accepting disabled passengers. Such disapprovals shall be rare. In such cases, air terminal personnel must ensure that the passenger understands why air transport is not possible on the mission in question. When a disabled passenger is denied transportation for the above reasons, and when his or her sponsor or dependent, who is otherwise eligible to travel, accompanies the disabled passenger to assist in his or her needs, travel shall be approved if such assistance will eliminate the reasons for denying travel.

### D. BAGGAGE

1. Timeliness. Baggage must arrive at the APOE either with the traveler or sufficiently in advance to permit the owner to document and offer it for movement as "accompanied baggage."

2. Allowances

a. Normal Free Checkable Baggage Allowance. Duty and space-available passengers are authorized two pieces of checked baggage and one carry-on piece. Checked baggage may not exceed 62 linear inches (length plus width plus height) or 70 pounds for each piece. Carry-on baggage must fit under the seat and may not exceed 45 linear inches (length plus width plus height). For duty passengers only, a duffel bag, sea bag, B-4 bag, flyer's kit bag, or diver's traveling bag, any of which exceeds 62 linear inches, may be substituted for one of the 62 linear inch items.

b. Excess Baggage Allowance. When authorized by service regulations or directives, an excess baggage allowance may be included in an individual's orders. Excess baggage shall be stated in terms of number of pieces, not by weight. Use the formula of 70 pounds for each piece and round to the next highest whole piece to determine the number of pieces necessary. For example, if 100-pounds excess is needed, then two pieces of excess baggage are authorized. Excess baggage is not authorized for space-available passengers.

c. Unauthorized Excess Baggage. Baggage which exceeds the normal baggage allowance without proper authorization may be accepted for shipment at the discretion of air terminal representatives. Passengers owning such baggage will be charged the appropriate excess baggage fee. Air terminal representatives are authorized to refuse to accept baggage in excess of that authorized. Disposition of unauthorized baggage not accepted for shipment shall be the personal responsibility of the owner. Shipment may be made at personal expense through postal facilities or commercial transportation companies. If shipment is otherwise authorized to be made at Government expense,arrangements for forwarding may be made with the APOE transportation office.

d. Patients. Patients are limited to two pieces of baggage not to exceed 70-pounds each.

e. Baggage Allowance Restriction. To maximize seat availability, terminal personnel may further restrict passenger baggage allowances when air transportation services are provided by an activity not financed through the DBOF-T.

f. Other Modes. This Regulation limits only the baggage that may be carried by passengers traveling on DoD aircraft. It does not restrict or increase the baggage allowance that may be prescribed by other directives for shipment by other modes.

3. Firearms and Ammunition. Unloaded personal firearms and small arms ammunition may be carried as checked baggage within the authorized weight allowance as long as they are in compliance with the laws and regulations of the United States, foreign governments, the Department of Defense, and the Military Departments. The Military Departments shall establish procedures which require the passenger to identify the items to passenger service personnel or their equivalent at the time of processing for flight and which ensure that the items are in checked baggage, or otherwise adequately secured, so as to be inaccessible to passengers while they are aboard the aircraft.

### E. DRESS. CONDUCT. AND STANDARD OF SERVICE

1. Dress. The wearing of the uniform on DoD aircraft by members of the Uniformed Services on active duty, members of the Reserve components not on active duty, and authorized foreign military personnel shall be governed by the directives of the Service concerned and by DoD 4500.54-6, "Foreign Clearance Guide" (reference (u)). When civilian clothing is worn, it shall be in good taste and not in conflict with accepted attire in the overseas country of departure, transit, or destination.

2. <u>Conduct</u>. Under no circumstances shall a passenger be accepted for transportation or be permitted to board an aircraft if he or she is unruly, under the influence of alcohol or narcotic, may create a hazard to the safety of the aircraft or passengers, or is a disruptive influence.

3. <u>Standard of Service</u>. The DoD Components shall establish and maintain standards of appearance, conduct, and service for flight and ground personnel who come in contact with customers of the airlift system which shall ensure professional, courteous, and responsive service.

F. <u>ANIMALS</u>

1. <u>Seeing Eye Dogs</u>

a. Transportation of a dog properly trained to lead the blind, and officially identified by a bona fide organization which trains or registers such dogs, is authorized without charge when accompanying its blind owner who is otherwise authorized transportation under this Regulation.

b. The dog must be properly harnessed to lead a blind person, muzzled to safeguard other passengers and crew members, remain at the blind person's feet, and not create a safety hazard to others by being in the aisle. The dog shall be permitted to accompany the owner in the cabin, but may not occupy a seat or be in the galley area. Sanitation must be maintained at all times.

c. Transportation of seeing eye dogs shall be subject to country quarantine procedures. When it is necessary to detain the animal pending determination of its admissibility, the owner shall provide detention facilities satisfactory to the cognizant quarantine officer. The owner shall bear the expense of such detention, including necessary examinations and vaccinations, and other expenses incurred due to the dog's accompanying the owner.

2. <u>Pets</u>. Passengers traveling under PCS orders may be allowed to ship their pets at their own personal expense. For this privilege, pets are defined as "dogs and cats only," and are limited to two for each family. Requests to deviate from this policy, i.e. number, type, or weight of pets, will be submitted through Service Headquarters to AMC for consideration.

a. <u>Owner Responsibilities.</u> The owner of the pet(s) is responsible for the preparation and care of the animal and for all documentation, immunization, and border clearance requirements including quarantine. The owner shall provide a pet shipment container approved by the International Air Transport Association of sufficient size to allow the animal to stand up, turn around, and lie down with normal posture and body movements.

b. <u>Aircraft Operator Responsibility</u>. The DoD Component operating the aircraft shall ascertain that the means and facilities exist at origin and destination to permit the owner to accomplish his or her responsibilities before accepting the animal for shipment. The operator of the aircraft shall establish procedures to ensure that the pets accepted for movement are stowed in areas heated and pressurized adequately to sustain health and comfort according to accepted commercial industry practice.

3. <u>Other Animals</u>. There is no restriction on shipping other animals aboard DoD aircraft for official purposes if they meet all criteria for shipment of official cargo established by this Regulation. Animals shall be housed, caged, and shipped in a humane fashion consistent with law and industry standards.

G. <u>FORMS</u>

1. <u>DD Form 1381. "Air Transportation Agreement."</u> Before travel aboard aircraft operated by an activity not financed through DBOF-T, the DD Form 1381 shall be executed by the non-DoD personnel specified in Chapters 2, 3, 4,5, 8, and 10, below, when their flight originates in a foreign country. NATO member national personnel traveling in the performance of official duties are exempt from this requirement. The completed DD Form 1381 shall be attached to the passenger manifest and filed at the point of origin. Sponsors will execute DD Form 1381 for minor dependents or individuals incapable of signing for themselves.

2. <u>DD Form 1839. "Baggage Identification."</u> All checked and carry-on baggage shall be identified with required data clearly annotated on the DD Form 1839. When the DD Form is unavailable, substitute tags, such as those used in the commercial aviation industry, may be used.

3. <u>DD Form 1853. "Verification of Reserve Status for Travel Eligibility."</u> Members of the Reserve components traveling under the provisions of Chapter 6, below, shall have a completed DD Form 1853 in their possession at all times.

4. <u>Boy Scouts of America. "Parent/Guardian Consent Form for Aviation Flights."</u> Explorer Scouts participating in an orientation flight under the provisions of Chapter 4, below, shall present a completed Parent/Guardian Consent Form for Aviation Flights before the flight.

5. <u>Supply of Forms</u>. DD Forms 1381, 1839, and 1853 shall be made available to users by forms management officers of the DoD Components. To ensure availability to users, forms management officers are encouraged to permit local reproduction of these forms. The Parent/Guardian Consent Form for Aviation Flights shall be obtained from the individual's Scout Troop.

**AUTHOR'S NOTE:** This Appendix (chapter 6, SPACE AVAILABLE TRAVEL, of DoD 4515.13-R and related) contains references to other related documents which are independent of DoD 4515.13-R and other chapters in DoD 4515.13-R all of which are not published here because of space limitations. In most cases, this documentation amplifies, provides background information and further explains chapter 6 of DoD 4515.13-R. Although not completely essential to the understanding of the Space Available Travel directive, persons wishing to view the entire DoD 4515.13-R and related documents may do so upon request and presentation of appropriate entitlement identification at military Space-A departure locations and Uniformed Services Personnel Offices. The following chapter 6, SPACE AVAILABLE TRAVEL and part of chapter 1, DoD 4515.13-R was released to Military Living Publications by the Office of The Under Secretary of Defense, Jan 1995.

## TRAVEL ON AMC FLIGHTS BY NON U.S. CITIZENS

Non U.S. citizens are not authorized to travel on AMC flights unless they are in possession of a valid visa of the country being visited (if required). For those traveling to the U.S., passengers must have an immigration visa, green card or a tourist visa. This prohibition for travel to the U.S. has taken place within the past year.

## INFANTS AND INFANT/CAR SEATS ABOARD AIRCRAFT

1. When traveling on an AMC (CAT B) flight, children under the age of 2, below the weight of 40 pounds, and under the height of 40 inches are accepted as passengers, **the parent or guardian must provide their own FAA-approved infant/car seat (ICS).** This requirement does not preclude a passenger from temporarily holding an infant during the cruise portion of a flight when safety considerations are not violated.

2. The approved infant/car seat must bear one or more labels as follows:
    a. Seats manufactured to U.S. standards between 1 Jan 81 and 25 Feb 85 must bear the label: "this child restraint system conforms to all applicable federal motor vehicle safety standards."
    b. Seats manufactured to U.S. standards on or after 26 Feb 85 must bear two labels:
        (1) "this child restraint system conforms to all applicable federal motor vehicle safety standards."
        (2) "this restraint is certified for use in motor vehicles and aircraft" (printed in red lettering).

3. Infant/car seats that do not qualify under paragraph 2 above must bear either a label showing approval of a foreign government or a label showing the seat was manufactured under the standards of the United Nations. Booster-type child restraint systems (as defined in federal motor vehicle standard no. 213 (49 CFR 571.213)), vest- and harness-type child restraint systems, and lap-held child restraints are not approved for use in aircraft.

## AIR MOBILITY COMMAND (AMC) PASSENGER RESERVATION PROCEDURES

1. Public law (14CFR Part 243) requires emergency next of kin information for all international airline passengers. As such, AMC is modifying their procedures for making passenger reservations on AMC aircraft to comply with

this law. AMC has announced that effective immediately, AMC passenger reservations will require the names and social security numbers (SSAN) of all passengers including dependents. While dependent SSANs are not required by public law, inclusion of this information at the time reservations are made will help expedite passenger processing for travelers at AMC aerial ports and commercial gateways. The dependent SSAN will be used as a link to Defense Eligibility Enrollment Report System (DEERS) to positively identify the travelers and obtain next of kin notification information in the event of an emergency.

2. To assist AMC with their efforts, we are requesting that the MPF be the collection point for this vital information. Please provide the full name and SSAN in the remarks portion of section VI on the AF Form 1546 for all dependents requesting international travel prior to submitting the request to the traffic management office (TMO).

3. Failure to comply with this requirement could result in departure delays while TMO attempts to obtain the required information. All personal information collected is subject to the Privacy Act of 1974 and will be protected as required under the act.

## EXCERPTS FROM THE COAST GUARD MILITARY SPACE AVAILABLE TRAVEL PROGRAM REGULATIONS RELEVANT TO 100% DAV PASSENGERS

5. USCG Military Space Available Travel Program. Title l0 USC §4744 authorizes a Military Space Available Travel Program . . .

b. Military Space Available Travel Program Categories.

(1) Category A: Transportation of Military Space Available Passengers Between the CONUS and Overseas Areas by Coast Guard Aircraft.

(d) Priority 4.

1/ Retired military members and veterans rated totally disabled by the Department of Veteran Affairs.

(2) Category B: Transportation of Military Space Available Passengers Within CONUS by Coast Guard Aircraft.

(d) Priority 4.

1/ Unaccompanied retired military members and veterans rated totally disabled by the Department of Veteran Affairs.

(3) Category C: Transportation of Military Space Available Passengers Within and Between Overseas Areas by Coast Guard Aircraft.

(d) Priority 4.

1/ Unaccompanied retired military members and veterans rated as totally disabled by the Department of Veteran Affairs (VA).

Last modified: Sat Mar 9 22:35:41 1996

*Passengers board a Navy C-009B.*

## SPACE-A AIR TRAVEL UPGRADES FOR RETIREES

Readers are often confused regarding the policy governing upgrading the space-available priority category for military retirees traveling in Department of Defense aircraft who may have to return home in an emergency. Some retirees believe that their space-available priority (Category 6) may be upgraded in an emergency by base commanders along their travel route on request.

The Air Force Directorate of Transportation advised that before retirees may ask for a base commander's travel priority upgrade, they must be notified by the American Red Cross, in writing, that immediate return to their home address is required. Further, while category upgrading may facilitate earlier movement, approval does not guarantee seats aboard a particular aircraft, nor does the upgrade extend to a military retiree's accompanying spouse and/or other family members.

The directive governing transportation in military aircraft is DoD 4515.13-5. Air Transportation Eligibility dated November 1994 as ammended.

## SPACE-A PROCESSING

Space-A flights in the Pacific should soon be more customer-friendly. A new system to speed boarding time and better inform travelers of seat availability is expected to hit all Pacific Air Mobility Command passenger terminals before the end of the summer, officials said.

Yokota air terminal employees already use the new procedure on some flights for training purposes. It will be extended to all flights Tuesday.
"It takes the mystery out of Space-A (travel), that uneasy feeling of whether they're going to be on," said Captain Randy Koram, officer in charge at Yokota's AMC terminal.

Active-duty military personnel, their dependents and military retirees may fly for free on flights that have available space after those on official military business or on emergency leave are serviced.

As it stands now, travelers don't know if they're booked on a Space-A flight until just prior to boarding. When the flight is announced three hours prior to departure, passengers check in with their travel documents. They are then ranked based on travel category and time of initial sign-up. Then they wait to see if they'll get on a flight.

Retiree Al Stembridge has sometimes waited up to two hours after the Space-A call, only to be bumped from a flight. "Anything must be an improvement from my experience," he said last week while waiting for a return flight home to California.

The drawn-out process of checking in for a flight was a sore point with Space-A travelers, said Master Sergeant Bob Tura, superintendent of passenger operations at Yokota's terminal. Under the new system, passengers will be able to check in and get their documents processed up to 24 hours before flight time. Then, 30 minutes before the Space-A call, a computer printout will be posted of registered passengers in order of priority.

Prior to boarding, the list will be used for a roll call. "We're just trying to streamline the whole process," said Master Sergeant Kurt Music, passenger operations manager at the terminal. During a test run last week, "We had 32 passengers at the counter going on a flight; it took us five minutes to do a roll call."

The new procedure was first implemented earlier this year at Travis Air Force Base in California on a 90-day trial period, Music said. After "it proved that it improved the process, headquarters said make it happen," he said.

The system is expected to eventually be in place at all military passenger terminals worldwide.

(Courtesy of Stars and Stripes)

# EXCEPTION TO POLICY FOR SPACE-AVAILABLE TRAVEL UPGRADE FOR UNACCOMPANIED FAMILY MEMBERS OF DEPLOYED USEUCOM SERVICE MEMBERS

Effective 19 Nov 1998 some unaccompanied family members may be eligible for Space Available Upgrade from Category V to Category III. Requirements of DoD 4515.13R, *Air Transportation Availability,* for unaccompanied travel are still valid but with additional documentation the unaccompanied family member may travel at a higher priority. The following are requirements for the travel:

1. Military Sponsor must be on a USEUCOM Command Sponsored tour.

2. This entitlement is good for one round trip during the sponsors 120 day or longer TDY.

3. Unaccompanied dependents must present a letter signed by the sponsor's commander verifying command sponsorship and sponsor's TDY status. The letter must include:

    a. Sponsor's name, social security number, date assigned unit, statement to the effect that the military member has been deployed and that 120 days has lapsed since the last use of the Cat III entitlement by the family member

    b. Statement of understanding from family member

    c. List all command sponsored traveling dependents by name

    d. Commander's signature

4. Other documentation required for travel by each dependent include a military ID (for all dependents 10 years and older) and passport with appropriate Visa(s) if required.

5. Dependents must have documentation signed by sponsor's commander in their possession during the entire travel period.

6. Dependents are allowed upgraded travel within USEUCOM or to and from CONUS to the USEUCOM area of responsibility.

7. Family members are eligible for this entitlement effective the first day of the deployment as indicated on the member's deployment orders and will remain on the Space Available List for 30 days only.

---

## USEUCOM DEPENDENT UPGRADE SAMPLE LETTER

**Department of the (your Service)**
**Unit or Command**

Memorandum for AMC Terminal

From (Unit ID) Example HHC 3/25th Armor

Subject: Authorization for Command Sponsored Dependents and USEUCOM Upgrade

1. The following individuals are command-sponsored dependents of Doe, John A, USA (branch of service), Sgt 123-45-6789:

    a. Jane Doe      SSN: 012-34-5678            German Passport
    b. John Doe Jr   SSN: 098-76-5432     DOB 2/12/96    US Passport
    c. Jeff Doe       SSN: 345-67-8910     DOB 3/16/97    US Passport

2. Sgt Doe has been assigned to this unit since 3 Nov 96. On 6 Dec 98, he deployed to __(Location)__ to support __(name of deployment)__.

3. Sgt Doe will be deployed 120 days (or more) and his/her command sponsored family member(s) understand that this is a one time entitlement per 120 day or more deployment.

Signature _________________________________________________Date____________________.

4. This upgrade entitlement has not been used in the last 120 days.

5. Please direct any questions to Maj. Help at DSN: XXX-XXXX

                                    I.L. Help, Maj, USA
                                    Commander*
                                      Or Acting Commander
                                      Or By Direction (US Navy)

Notes:
* Commanders whose name is typed on the form must sign the form. Having someone sign in lieu of the commander is NOT authorized.
-Please include all above information on all requests for dependent travel.
-Please make sure you include the SSN of each dependent and Date of Birth for children.
-Include the nationality of dependents. Those without U.S. passports may encounter difficulties when traveling to certain countries without their sponsor.
-Traveling dependents must keep original copy of the letter on their person at all times during travel.

---

**Visit Military Living online at** **www.militaryliving.com**

## UNACCOMPANIED DEPENDENT TRAVEL

Change to DOD 4515.13R, Air Transportation Eligibility

Command sponsored dependents of uniformed members who are stationed overseas are now eligible for unaccompanied travel aboard any DoD-owned or controlled aircraft. This includes travel within the overseas area as well as between the overseas and the Continental United States (CONUS). The following are requirements and details regarding unaccompanied dependent travel.

1. Military Sponsor must be stationed overseas and serving a command sponsored tour.
2. Unaccompanied dependents must present a letter signed by their sponsor's commander verifying command sponsorship. This letter will be used to sign up for space available travel, as well as signing up for the return flight. This letter from the sponsor's commander must:
a. list the military Sponsor's name and social security number
b. list all eligible command sponsored traveling dependents by name
c. have the commander's signature.
3 Other documentation required for travel includes a military ID card and passport, with appropriate Visa(s) if required, for each dependent.
4. In order to sign up, dependent (s) must show documentation signed by Sponsor's commander and they must have this letter with them during the entire travel period. Each authorization is good for one (1) round trip.
5. Dependents are not allowed military travel within the CONUS.
6. There is no restriction on the number of trips that eligible dependents can take. However, a new authorization letter is required for each separate trip.
7. Dependents may remain on the space available register for sixty (60) days.
8. Unaccompanied dependents will travel as Category five (5).
9. Dependents under 18 years of age must be accompanied by an eligible parent or legal guardian who is the child's sponsor.
10. Travelers should be prepared to make commercial travel arrangements in the event Space-A military travel is not available.

For more information concerning unaccompanied travel, please call the Ramstein Passenger Terminal at DSN-314-480-2433/5364, Civilian 011-49-6371-47-2433/5364.

## NON-COMMAND SPONSORED FAMILIES CAN NOW FLY SPACE-A TO KOREA

Accompanied and unaccompanied dependents of non-command sponsored families are now allowed to fly Space-A to Korea. Accompanied dependents fly Space-A in Cat III; unaccompanied dependents in Cat V.

The new policy is in addition to the existing benefits and allow for one 30-day visit per year. Dependents cannot travel to Korea with their sponsor for initial reporting to the new station.

Each dependent family member must carry an authorization letter from the unit and group commander of his or her sponsor. Dependents must also prove sufficient resources to purchase a return ticket in case Space-A is unavailable for their return.

Families must fly in and out of the Republic of Korea through Kunsan Air Base or Osan Air Base. Visiting dependents are also authorized to stay in base housing.

More information on dependent visits to Korea may be found on the web at www.korea.army.mil/pao/

*This Space-A traveler is "travel-ready!"*

---

## UNACCOMPANIED DEPENDENT TRAVEL SAMPLE LETTER

Department of the (your service) Unit or Major Command

Memorandum for AMC Terminal

FROM (unit ID): Example HHC 3/25th Armor

SUBJECT: Dependent Travel Authorization

1. The following individual (s) are the command sponsored dependents of Doe, Joe A., SGT 123-45-6789

| | | |
|---|---|---|
| Jane B. Doe | SSN: 012-34-5678 | German passport |
| Josh C. Doe | SSN: 901-23-4567  DOB: 12 Mar 82 | U.S. Passport |
| Julie V. Doe | SSN: 890-12-3456  DOB: 27 Apr 89 | U.S. Passport |

2. Please direct any questions to Maj Havoc at DSN 999-1111

Signed_________________________________________ Date____________________________
      John J. Havoc, Major, USA
      Commander
      or Acting Commander

Notes:   Please include all the above information on all requests for dependent travel.
         Please make sure to include the dependent's Social Security Number.
         Be sure to include the nationality of all dependents in the letter.
         Include the date of birth for all children. Children must be at least 18 years of age to travel along with the letter.
         Traveling dependents should remember to keep the original letter, with the original signature, throughout the period of sign-up and travel.
         Each letter of authorization is good for one (1) round trip.
         Dependents may remain on the Space Available register for sixty (60) days.

# STATUS OF SPACE-AVAILABLE TRAVEL FOR 100 PERCENT DISABLED VETERANS AND WIDOW/ERS

**Statement on Transportation Policy by the Office of the Assistant Deputy Under Secretary of Defense for Logistics regarding space-available travel for 100 Percent Disabled Veterans**

The Department of Defense (DoD) greatly values the contributions of every veteran, especially those who have sacrificed their health in the service of their country. However, the primary purpose of the Department of Defense (DoD) space-available travel program is to provide active duty service members a respite from the rigors of military service. This travel privilege is becoming increasingly critical to our active duty personnel, who are experiencing more frequent family separations due to the DoD's high operational tempo. The privilege is extended to retired members at a lower priority, in recognition of the fact that they may still be recalled to active duty, and as a reward for their many years of military service. The underlying criteria for extending the travel privilege to other categories of passengers is their support to the mission being performed by active duty military personnel, and to the enhancement of active duty Service members' quality of life. In either case, veterans who are not on active duty or retired are not authorized space-available travel. The reference to paragraph 8.1 in Air Force Instruction 36-3026 deals with pay entitlements and does not pertain to space-available privileges. Categories of eligible space-available travelers are defined in DoD Regulation 4515.13-R, Air Transportation Eligibility, and contrary to your statement, the space-available privilege has never been specifically extended to 100 percent disabled veterans.

The Department receives numerous requests to extend space-available travel to additional categories of people. The entire space-available program, including seats on aircraft and air terminal functions necessary to support travel, is resource constrained. If the privilege were extended to the over 164,000 totally disabled veterans or other categories of personnel, the increases in numbers of people seeking space-available travel could overtax present resources and diminish the limited benefit currently available to active duty personnel. Already those currently authorized space-available travel are often disillusioned by the contrast between the promise of space-available travel as a benefit of military service, and the reality of the arduous conditions often encountered when they use the system.

**Statement on Transportation Policy by the Office of the Assistant Deputy Under Secretary of Defense for Logistics Regarding Space-Available Travel for Widow/ers**

Space-available travel is a privilege which accrues to active duty military members as an avenue of respite from the rigors of military duty. Although travel is available to other categories of travelers at a lower priority, the principle objective of the privilege is the morale and welfare of those currently serving on active duty.

The entire space-available program, including both seats on aircraft and air terminal functions necessary to support travel, is resource constrained. Extending space-available travel privileges to the over 314,000 widows of military veterans could overtax present resources and diminish the limited benefit currently available to active duty personnel and their families.

Already, those currently authorized space-available travel are often disillusioned by the contrast between the promise of space-available travel as a benefit of military service and the reality of the arduous conditions often encountered when they use the system. Any increase in the number of eligible people who seek space-available travel would impact the DoD's ability to effectively accomplish airlift mission support activities. To expand this list would not be prudent in today's resource constrained environment, considering the heavy operational demands that are being placed on our air mobility forces.

The DoD receives numerous requests to extend space-available travel to additional categories of people, including Service-connected disabled veterans, Federal civil service employees, and Peace Corps volunteers. In each case, our review of present and future air travel requirements has precluded the Department from expanding the privilege. As a matter of DoD policy, the space-available travel privilege has not been extended to persons or groups beyond those currently authorized. This policy is primarily based on mission requirements and resource constraints.

While the Department recognizes and appreciates the contributions of widows of military veterans, the space-available travel privilege cannot be extended to them for the above reasons. I regret I cannot provide a more positive response to your request.

---

Editor's Note: Bills are introduced in almost every Congress to permit 100% Disabled Veterans and Widow/ers to fly Space-A, none have passed. Military Living Publications is not organized or staffed to lobby on such political issues but we do recommend that persons interested in Space-A privileges for these groups contact the National Association for Uniformed Services, 5535 Hempstead Way, Springfield, VA 22151-4049, 1(800)842-3451, www.haus.org

---

# APPENDIX B
## PERSONNEL ENTRANCE REQUIREMENTS

The information contained in this appendix has been extracted from the Department of Defense (DoD) FOREIGN CLEARANCE GUIDE(S): NORTH AND SOUTH AMERICA; EUROPE; AFRICA AND SOUTHWEST ASIA; PACIFIC, SOUTH ASIA AND INDIAN OCEAN, DoD 4500.54-G. The information extracted is largely from SECTION II, Personnel Entrance Requirements, and SECTION III, General Information. Some data from other sections which we believe meets the needs of Space-A travelers has also been included in this appendix. Note: Only Countries/Areas with regular space-available passenger traffic are listed in this appendix.

All Space-A passengers departing on commercial contract mission (Patriot Flights) inbound to the United States must pay a $5 immigration inspection fee, a $5 customs inspection fee and a $2 agriculture inspection fee. **Some foreign departure terminals may also collect a departure tax, which have been noted in the respective country listings.**

Because currency exchange rates fluctuate frequently, limited information about rates has been included. Space-A travelers are advised to check recent newspaper listings, i.e., "New York Times" and "USA Today," for current exchange rates.

It should be noted that immunization requirements are established by and listed in each service's directives and are not listed in the Foreign Clearance Guide(s). The only immunization requirements listed in the attached pages are in addition to those required by individual services. U.S. Armed Forces immunization requirements are based on decisions by the World Health Organization (WHO). U.S. requirements are stated in AR 40-562, BUMED-COMINST 6230.15, AFJI 48-110, CG COMDTINST M6230.4E, Immunization Requirements & Procedures. Additional information may be obtained from the Centers for Disease Control, International Travelers Hotline at C: 404-332-4559, or 888-232-3229 in Atlanta, GA, or via the CDC web page on the internet at www.cdc.gov. Additional requirements are posted on individual country listings. Also, additional immunization requirements may be levied based on the requirements of local foreign governments.

The data in this appendix is subject to change without notice as political situations change and new developments occur in foreign countries. When in doubt about Personnel Entrance Requirements, Space-A travelers should call or write to the anticipated departure location or military personnel office (which issues official duty orders) for the latest information on Personnel Entrance Requirements to the countries which you plan to visit.

**Please note abbreviations below: ID/C: Identification Credentials, ICQI: Immigration/Customs/Quarantine Inspections, IR: Immunization Requirements, IAFIA: If arriving from an infected area.**

IDENTIFICATION CREDENTIALS: NOTE: When U.S. citizens travel to a country where a valid passport is not required, they must possess documentary evidence of both their U.S. citizenship and personal identity. Proof of U.S. citizenship includes valid U.S. passport, expired U.S. passport, a certificate of Naturalization, Certificate of Citizenship, or Report of Birth Abroad of a Citizen of the United States. Proof of identity includes a valid driver's license or government identification card provided they identify you by physical description or photograph. Travelers must prove both citizenship and identity.

### AMERICAN (EASTERN) SAMOA (AS) (U. S. TERRITORY)
**ID/C:** *AD:* ID Card, Leave orders. *Ret/Civ:* ID Card.
**ICQI:** Normal U.S.
**IR:** None except Yellow Fever vaccination IAFIA.
**Other:** *All:* Samoa Air Services handles in-transit AMC aircraft at Pago Pago IAP, AS is U.S. Territory & includes Manua, Tutuila (location of IAP), & Swains Islands. No U.S. Gov lodging or messing.

### ANTIGUA & BARBUDA (AG & BD)
**ID/C:** *AD:* ID Card, Leave orders. *Ret/Civ:* ID Card or Passport. Passport & visa stays over six months.
**ICQI:** Embark/Debark Card if arriving on a civilian aircraft.
**IR:** Service.
**Other:** *All:* Proof of return/onward ticket and/or proof of sufficient funds for stay up to six months. No currency restrictions. Declare all currency. Currency export requires license. TML at Antigua AS for duty personnel only.

### ARGENTINA (AR)
**ID/C:** *All:* ID Cards, Passport, No visa up to 3 months. *AD:* Leave orders.
**ICQI:** None
**IR:** Cholera affected area, take precautions.
**Other:** *AD:* Civilian clothing and notify USDAO of travel plans, name, rank, Service, and dates and points of arrival/departure, C-011-54-114-4511-4978. *All:* Declare all currency. No limit on currency imports. Exports limited to imported amount less expenses. Check local photographic restrictions. Photography of military installations and infrastructure strictly prohibited and carefully enforced. Avoid cream pastries. Select seafood and shellfish with care. Firearms prohibited.

### ASCENSION ISLAND (United Kingdom) (AI)
**ID/C:** *AD:* ID Card, Leave orders. *Ret/Civ:* ID, Passport or documentary of U.S. citizenship and personal identity.
**ICQI:** Yes
**IR:** Service
**Other:** *AD:* No data available on uniform restrictions. *All:* Transient passengers must confirm availability of quarters prior to travel from ASCENSION/AAF/CC; info copy ESMC Patrick AFB/FL/FA. **Space-A travel is not authorized except when approved in writing by the Ascension AAF commander.** Sterling imports limited 10 pounds. Exports limited to 10 pounds sterling or equivalent. Mess and extremely limited lodging available on base only. Firearms prohibited. Swimming discouraged due to sharks and heavy undertow.

### AUSTRALIA (AU)
**ID/C:** *AD:* ID Card, Passport, visa or ETA (Electronic Travel Authority) and Leave orders. *Ret/Civ:* ID Card, Passport, visa or ETA. Visa or ETA must be obtained before arrival. All travelers receiving an ETA and intending to travel via Military Space-A Air must ensure that the Australian Embassy or consulate issuing the ETA provide written confirmation to the traveler that an ETA was issued or places a visa stamp in the passport. The cost of a visa stamp is $33.00 U.S. The ETA can be obtained free through the Australia Embassy, Washington, D.C. 20036-5000, C-202-797-3000/3145/3161.
**ICQI:** Yes
**IR:** Service. Yellow Fever vaccination required IAFIA.
**Other:** *AD:* Uniforms OK, except to and from Woomera AS & Alice Springs. No import of animals, animal products and germinal vegetables. *All:* Do not use cameras in prohibited areas. Boil water in rural areas. No currency import restrictions. Export limit $100 AU. **There is a $30 AU passenger movement charge for Space-A passengers (except age 12 or under).**

### AZORES (Also see Portugal) (PT)
**ID/C:** *AD:* ID Card, Leave orders. *Ret/Civ:* ID Card, Passport. Visa required after 90 days.
**ICQI:** Yes, if aircraft 24 hours delay. Personnel in transit not permitted to leave base.
**IR:** Yellow Fever IAFIA.
**Other:** *AD:* No uniforms off base except to and from quarters and base. *All:* Passport valid for three months beyond stay. Cliff area of Terceira Island off limits. Do not participate in bullfights. Use bottled or boiled water.

### BAHRAIN (BH)
**ID/C:** *All:* ID Cards, Passport, visa (Three and seven day visas may be obtained upon arrival at the airport, obtaining visas before arrival is recommended).
**ICQI:** Yes. Possession of video tapes will cause delays.
**IR:** Yellow Fever IAFIA.
**Other:** *All:* No uniforms. Note: Area has experienced some terrorist incidents. Host country is committed to controlling them, but take special precautions. No evidence of entry into Israel admitted. No currency restrictions. No liquor, no weapons. Check American Embassy for other restricted items. No photography of local women or religious acts. Do not enter mosques or other Arab places of worship. Use purified water for drinking or cooking. Raw fruits and vegetables require special cleaning procedures. Summer temperatures can reach 130 degrees.

### BARBADOS (BB)
**ID/C:** *AD:* ID cards and orders. *All:* Proof of U.S. citizenship and onward/return ticket required. Passport required for visits over 28 days.
**ICQI:** Yes.
**IR:** Yellow Fever, IAFIA.

**Other:** *AD:* No restrictions on uniforms. *All:* **Departure tax $12.50 if staying over 24 hours.** No limit on foreign currency imports; local imports limited to 250 Barbados dollars. U.S. currency accepted island-wide when making purchases or paying bills.

BELGIUM (BE)
**ID/C:** *AD:* ID Card, Leave orders. *Ret/Civ:* ID Card, Passport, visa after three months (all Schengen territory countries).
**ICQI:** No
**IR:** Service
**Other:** *AD:* Civilian clothing recommended. *All:* If not registered in a hotel, register with local "police entrangers" within eight days of arrival. Declare all currency. No limit on imports. Export limit 50,000 BF. Photography of canals, bridges, and military installations is restricted.

BELIZE (BZ)
**ID/C:** *All:* Passport, ID Cards, return/onward ticket and sufficient funds required. Permit from immigration authorities required for visit over one month; visa required for stay over three months.
**ICQI:** Yes.
**IR:** Yellow Fever, IAFIA; malaria precautions advised.
**Other:** *AD:* Civilian clothing unless conducting business at USMLO. Notify USMLO of in-country location, phone 011-501-2-52009/52019. No currency restrictions, no exchange facilities at airport. **Airport departure tax U.S. $11.25.** Boil water for drinking; avoid uncooked and unpeeled fruits and vegetables. No firearms.

BOLIVIA (BO)
**ID/C:** *AD:* ID Card, Passport, Clearance required from USMILGP, C-011-591-2-430-251-EX-2671/2672, Leave orders (except Ret/Civ), Passport stamped by immigration at airport on entry, with tourist entry permit, for 30 days. Visa not approved if passport expires within six months. *Ret/Civ:* ID Card, Passport. tourist entry permit same as AD above.
**ICQI:** Required
**IR:** Yellow Fever infected area, vaccination required IAFIA. Gamma globulin and typhoid vaccine recommended for adults.
**Other:** *AD:* Civilian clothing worn on arriving military or commercial aircraft. No uniforms in public places. *All:* Declare all currency. No limit on imports, exports limited to amount imported. Due to altitude, limit physical activity for first 48 hours. Cholera present almost all parts of country. Use bottled water & beverages. Vegetables and shellfish should be well cooked & eaten while hot. All fruits should be peeled in presence of customer. The altitude of La Paz (13,400 feet) can have a deleterious effect on persons with medical problems and/or respiratory infections. Limit physical activity for first 36-48 hours after arrival.

BRAZIL (BR)
**ID/C:** *All:* ID Card, Passport, visa. *AD:* Leave orders.
**ICQI:** Yes
**IR:** Yellow Fever infected area, vaccination required IAFIA.
**Other:** *AD:* Civilian clothing required. *All:* Visas required prior to arrival, not issued at airport. Travel notification should be sent to USDAO Brasilia (C-011-55-61-321-7272 . No currency restrictions on imports. Exports limited to 50% of imports and on conversions. Minors under 18 need both parents' written authorization in Portuguese and authenticated. Use bottled water. AIDS is prevalent. Crime is high in Rio de Janeiro. Keep cameras in luggage until leaving airport.

CAMEROON (CM)
**ID/C:** ALL: ID Card, Passport, visa. *AD:* Leave Orders.
**ICQI:** Yes
**IR:** Cholera-infected area. Gamma Globulin recommended. Yellow fever vaccination required over one year of age.
**Other:** *AD:* No uniform restrictions, Civilian clothing is preferred. Notify USDAO on arrival, C-011-237-23-40-14. *All:* Declare currency, keep records for departure. Credit cards and checks rarely accepted. Cash in local currency ius usually the only form of payment. Boil and filter water, wash vegetables and soak in a bleach solution for 20 minutes, and peel fruit. Antimalarial drugs and mosquito nets are recommended. Carry passports at all times.

CANADA (CA)
**ID/C:** *All:* ID Card. *AD:* Leave orders.
**ICQI:** Yes.
**IR:** Service.
**Other:** Civilian clothing. Limited military accommodations available at Canadian Armed Forces and USAF installations; prior arrangements required for facilities in Arctic Canada.

CAYMAN ISLANDS (GB)
**ID/C:** *AD:* ID Card and Leave orders. *Ret/Civ:* Passport or proof of citizenship, photo ID, onward/return ticket and proof of sufficient funds. Visa required for stays over three months.
**ICQI:** No information available.
**IR:** Service.
**Other:** *AD:* Civilian clothing. There is no American Embassy in the Cayman Islands. The Amembassy in Kingston, Jamaica is responsible for U.S. interests in the Cayman Islands, There are no U.S. defense attaches or diplomatic officials stationed here. USDAO Kingston, Jamaica C-011-876-935-6021. ALL: No firearms.

CHAD (TD)
**ID/C:** *All:* ID Card, Passport, visa (immunization record showing vaccination against yellow fever must be provided when applying for visa).
**ICQI:** Yes, if leaving airport.
**IR:** Yellow Fever over one year old & Gamma Globulin recommended.
**Other:** *AD:* Notify USDAO N'djamena upon arrival, C-011-235-51-70-09/90-52. *All:* Visas valid for single entry (multiple entries on request) and must be obtained prior to arrival in Chad. No photography allowed without a permit from the government of Chad. No limit on foreign currency imports. Boil water. Eat at recommended places. Check with national police and obtain a registration stamp within 72 hours of arrival.

CHILE (CL)
**ID/C:** *AD:* ID Card, Passport, Leave orders. *Ret/Civ:* ID Card, Passport, onward/return ticket. *All:* A tourist card obtained in the airport for $20.00 U.S., exact change only, is required, and good for 90 days.
**ICQI:** Yes, inbound and outbound.
**IR:** Yellow Fever
**Other:** *AD:* No data available on uniform restrictions. *All:* U.S. citizens should register with Amembassy upon arrival, phone 011-56-2-330-3302. Visas required after 90 days. No currency restrictions. **Airport departure tax $18 U.S.** Gold exports other than jewelry are prohibited. Use bottled water. Eat only cooked seafood, cooked or disinfected fruits and vegetables. No firearms. Hotels charge large surcharges for international phone calls. Transient personnel may call (collect, credit card or reimbursed only) from Amembassy.

COLOMBIA (CO)
**ID/C:** *AD:* Passport, ID card, Leave orders (visa not required for visits of less than 30 days). *Ret/Civ:* Passport and proof of onward/return ticket. Visa required for visits over 30 days, must be obtained in advance.
**ICQI:** Yes.
**IR:** Yellow Fever infected area; malaria precautions advised.
**Other:** Designated a High Physical Threat Country. *AD:* Civilian clothing. Personnel on leave require clearance from USDAO, strongly encouraged to contact USDAO upon arrival for security briefing, phone 011-57-1-315-2125. Retired military personnel traveling via Space-A must contact USDAO Bogota via Fax C-011-57-1-315-2197 to obtain the latest security information prior to travel to Columbia. Country clearance not required. Minors under 18 need both parents' written authorization and copy of birth certificate translated into Spanish and authenticated. **Departure tax $35 U.S.** Use bottled water; shellfish and vegetables should be well-cooked, fruit should be peeled. No photographs on or near airports and defense installations. Avoid dress/actions identifying traveler as foreigner. Currency exchange illegal except at officially designated facilities, banks and hotels.

CONGO (Democratic Republic of) (ZR) (Formerly Zaire)
**ID/C:** *AD:* ID Card, Passport, visa, Leave orders. *Ret/Civ:* ID Card, Passport, visa. ALL: Immunization records.
**ICQI:** Yes
**IR:** Immunization records required arriving and departing. Cholera & Yellow Fever area. Yellow fever vaccination for all travelers over one year of age.
**Other:** Designated a Potential Physical Threat Country. *All:* All Space-A travel is highly discouraged and must be approved in advance in writing by USDAO, 30 days prior to travel. *AD:* Civilian clothing. *All:* Visa (three month) must be obtained before arrival. Register with Amembassy in Kinshasa upon arrival and obtain information on travel and security, C-011-243-12-21804 EX-21807. Declare all currency. Keep records. Do not show dollars or other foreign currency except at legal exchange agency. Drink boiled or treated water. Photography prohibited of airport or infrastructure; consult with USDAO prior to taking photos. No travel in some areas without government authorization.

COSTA RICA (CR)
**ID/C:** *All:* ID card, Passport, onward/return ticket. Dependents under 18 years of age who remain in Costa Rica more than 30 days fall under the

authority of the National Child Welfare Agency, which requires signed and authenticated permission of parents for child to leave country alone or with one parent. Exit permits required, available at airport. Exit tax $6 U.S.
**ICQI:** Yes.
**IR:** Service, Reemergence of Dengue fever in recent years; Dengue is transmitted by mosquito bite and there is no vaccine.
**Other:** *AD:* Without passport may purchase tourist card for $2 U.S. at airport but must show proof of citizenship on departure. Civilian clothing. Leave personnel should contact CHODR, American Embassy, San Jose, within two working days of arrival; phone, 011-506-220-3939. Military groups of 5 or more must notify CHODR 10 days prior to arrival. Declare all currency imports, exports limited to amount imported. It is illegal to spend U.S. dollars in country or to exchange dollars for colones at any location except banks and hotels. Boil water outside of large cities.

### CRETE (GR). See Greece.

### CUBA (CU) (U.S. Guantanamo Bay)
**ID/C:** *AD:* ID Card, Leave orders. *Ret/Civ:* ID Card.
**ICQI:** Yes
**IR:** Service
**Other:** *AD:* Class "A" uniform worn on arrival and departure. *All:* U.S. Guantanamo Bay is not considered part of the special area of Cuba. Only individuals personally hosted by base residents may take leave on the base. To receive required written authorization, submit request 30 days in advance to commander, U.S. Naval Base (ATTN: Ops), PSC 1005, Box 25, FPO AE 09593-1000. Personnel traveling to Kingston, Jamaica, on regularly scheduled AMC flight may transit USNB upon written request. No overnight lodging.

### CYPRUS (CY)
**ID/C:** *All:* ID Card, Passport, *AD:* Leave orders, ALL: Visas are issued at the port of entry for a stay of up to three months (extendable).
**ICQI:** Yes
**IR:** Service, Yellow fever IAFIA.
**Other:** *AD:* No uniforms except in transient at departure ramp area. AD on leave require country clearance from USDAO Nicosia. Inform USDAO of arrival, duration of stay, address, phone 011-357-2-776400. *All:* Export of foreign currency limited to amount imported less expenditures. Imports and exports of local currency limited to ten pounds sterling. No firearms.

### DENMARK (DK) (Greenland)
**ID/C:** *AD:* ID Card, Passport, Leave orders. Passport if landing at non-U.S. base. *Ret/Civ:* ID Card. Passport if landing at non-U.S. base.
**ICQI:** U.S. aircraft exempt from inspection.
**IR:** Service.
**Other:** *AD:* Civilian clothes. Visa required for stays over three months. *All:* Off-base visits require permission from Danish liaison officer through base commander. Clearance to visit air base itself required. Quarters confirmation required prior to arrival.

### DIEGO GARCIA (Chagos Archipelago) (IO) (United Kingdom, UK)
**ID/C:** *All:* ID Card, Leave orders or PCS orders. Civilians: Passports.
**ICQI:** Not Applicable.
**IR:** Service
**Other:** *AD:* Uniforms, USN-Tropical dress and summer khaki/white are authorized year round, USA-BDU, USAF-BDU, USMC-Camouflage Utility is authorized year round. Clearance required for TAD/TDY entry to Diego Garcia. *All:* Leave travel and Space-A travel (including circuitous travel for persons on official orders) are not authorized to or through Diego Garcia. Access to Diego Garcia is limited to mission-essential personnel. U.S. dollar standard currency, credit cards not accepted, limited travelers checks cashing facilities.

### DOMINICAN REPUBLIC (DO)
**ID/C:** *All:* ID Card, Passport, visa or Purchase Tourist Card ($10 U.S.) upon arrival.
**ICQI:** Yes, exempt at San Isidro AB.
**IR:** Gamma Globulin recommended
**Other:** *All:* Civilian clothing. All Space-A travelers must notify USDAO 48 hours before arrival, C-011-809-221-2171. Convert all dollar instruments at banks and hotel, export limit is $5,000 U.S. CAUTION- water is not potable. Medical care limited. HIV poses a significant health risk and is prevalent in tourist areas.

### ECUADOR (EC)
**ID/C:** *All:* ID card, Passports, and return/onward ticket, tourist card (valid for 90 days) issued on arrival. *AD:* Leave orders.

**ICQI:** Yes.
**IR:** Chloroquine resistant malaria has reached epidemic proportions on west coast below 1,500 feet elevation. Individuals who expect to visit this area should begin pre-exposure treatment prior to arriving in Ecuador. Yellow Fever, IAFIA.
**Other:** Civilian clothing. **Airport departure tax $25 U.S. per person.** Visas required for cumulative stay more than 90 days, must be obtained in advance. No restrictions on import of currency; once exchanged, cannot be re-exchanged for foreign currency. No photography on or near airports and defense installations. Boil water, wash fruits, wash and cook vegetables.

### EGYPT (Arab Republic of) (EG)
**ID/C:** *AD:* Leave orders. *All:* ID Card, Passport, visa.
**ICQI:** Customs processing may take up to three hours, and be further delayed if traveler is carrying video camera, computer or other electrical equipment. Not co-located with AMC terminal.
**IR:** Yellow Fever IAFIA. Beware of bilharzia parasite when swimming or walking barefoot. Meningococcal meningitis "A" vaccination recommended.
**Other:** *All:* Civilian clothing. Visas (valid for six months) obtainable at airport banks for $15 U.S. Local currency 1,000 EG Pounds can be taken outside country. Declare currency and other valuables on arrival. Only typical tourist-type photography is allowed. The penalty in Egypt for conviction of smuggling or selling drugs may be death. Space-A travel to and from Egypt is limited to: a) those eligible persons stationed in or assigned TDY to Egypt; b) those persons personally sponsored by U.S. agencies or official U.S. persons in country. Cairo East is an Egyptian military base with strict-controlled access, no food service, and no transportation. AMC representatives cannot furnish sponsorship or transportation to and from Cairo East AB. Space-A passengers must have written permission from Chief OMC (Officer of Military Cooperation, American Embassy Cairo, Box 29, FPO New York, NY 09527-5000) prior to travel. Requests for permission (sponsorship) should be submitted to OMC by sponsoring in-country agency or individual. Requests should include names, passport numbers; type passport; expiration dates of visas; proposed arrival & departure dates; and local sponsor's name, address, & phone number. Request must also include a statement that: 1) Sponsor will be responsible for traveler's transportation and base access to and from Cairo East passenger terminal; 2) Sponsor will be available at Cairo East AB until aircraft is airborne. Uniforms will not be worn for Space-A travel to and from Egypt due to GOE (Government of Egypt) regulations. 3) Because of heavy workload, it is impossible for OMC Cairo and USDAO Cairo to honor individual requests for sponsorship. Personnel arriving in Cairo by other than AMC travel will not be authorized to depart by AMC travel. A letter of permission is required for individuals to sign up for AMC Space-A travel into and out of Egypt.

### EL SALVADOR (SV)
**ID/C:** *AD:* ID cards and Leave orders. *All:* Passport and visa required. Tourist cards available at airport for $10 U.S. *AD:* Contact USDAO on arrival and departure at: C-011-503-228-2017.
**ICQI:** Yes.
**IR:** Service. Yellow Fever IAFIA.
**Other:** El Salvador is designated a Potential Physical Threat Country. *AD:* Personnel are not authorized to visit El Salvador on ordinary leave for tourist purposes without a U.S. sponsor who resides in and is present in El Salvador. Travelers should arrive by air rather than by road. **Airport departure tax $26 U.S., if departing commercial airport.** Do not photograph airports or military installations or discuss local politics. Use bottled or boiled water; wash and peel fruits; wash and cook vegetables.

### FIJI (FJ)
**ID/C:** *AD:* ID Cards, Passport, Leave Orders, Proof of sufficient funds, and an onward/return ticket. Visa is issued upon arrival for an initial stay of up to four months. *Ret/Civ:* ID Cards, Passport. Visas not required; visitor permits, valid for up to one month, are issued on arrival.
**ICQI:** Yes
**IR:** Services, Yellow fever IAFIA.
**Other:** Civilian clothes, No currency restrictions, exchange at local banks. A license is required for firearms.

### GERMANY (DE)
**ID/C:** *AD:* ID Card, Leave orders. *Ret/Civ:* ID Card, Passport, visa after 90 days.
**ICQI:** Yes
**IR:** Service
**Other:** *AD:* Civilian clothing in non-duty status. *All:* Visas for stays in excess of 90 days. No currency restrictions.

## GREECE (GR) (Includes all Greek Islands in the Aegean Sea)
**ID/C: *AD:*** ID Card, Leave orders, or Passport. ***Ret/Civ:*** ID Card, Passport.
***All:*** Visa required after 90 days.
**ICQI:** Yes
**IR:** Yellow Fever IAFIA. Smallpox if arriving from Israel.
**Other: *AD:*** Civilian clothing advisable and required on arrival and departure. ***All:*** Visa required for visits over 90 days and resident permit or police ID card. Declare $500 or more of non-Greek currency. Boil and filter water. Cameras prohibited on military installations; no photos of military installations.

## GUAM (GU) (U.S. TERRITORY)
**ID/C: *AD:*** ID Card, Leave orders. ***Ret/Civ:*** ID Card.
**ICQI:** Yes
**IR:** Service
**Other: *AD:*** Summer uniform. ***All:*** No currency restrictions. Check with military authorities prior to any recreational water activity. Lodging limited at Andersen AFB and Agana NAS. Ground transportation limited. Local hotels near capacity.

## GUATEMALA (GT)
**ID/C: *AD:*** ID card, Passport and Leave orders. ***All:*** Passport and visa or tourist card (good for 30 days) $5 U.S. purchased in advance. Must carry identification credentials with them at all times.
**ICQI:** Yes.
**IR:** Yellow Fever. Gamma globulin or havrix vaccination recommended.
**Other:** Designated a Potential Physical Threat Country. ***AD:*** Civilian clothing. ***All:*** Contact USDAO for country clearance and travel and security information, phone, C-011-502-331-1541. Avoid traveling alone and contact with Guatemalan children. **Airport departure tax 145 quetzales (approximately $20 U.S.).** Photography of military installations is prohibited. Request permission before photographing Indians. Use of rental cars for any purpose requires prior approval by USMILGP or USDAO. Use bottled beverages; wash and disinfect all fruits and vegetables; cook vegetables.

## HAITI (HT)
**ID/C: *AD:*** ID Card, Passport. ***Ret/Civ:*** ID Card, Passport.
**ICQI:** Yes
**IR:** Yellow Fever IAFIA.
**Other:** Haiti is designated a Potential Physical Threat Country; exercise vigilance. ***AD:*** Civilian clothing. Report to USDAO, C-011-509-222-0354 within 24 hours of arrival in Haiti. ***All:* If departing via commercial airline, a departure tax of $25 U.S.** Haitian citizens in U.S. military require Passport and Exit Permit. No currency restrictions. Avoid water, ice and milk if source is unknown. Firearms prohibited.

## HONDURAS (HN)
**ID/C: *All:*** ID Card, Passport (valid six months), onward/return ticket.
**ICQI:** Yes
**IR:** Yellow Fever IAFIA & Gamma Globulin
**Other: *AD:*** Civilian clothing. Road travel between Honduras and Nicaragua is dangerous; air travel recommended between Honduras, Nicaragua and El Salvador. Register with USDAO, in person or phone C-011-504-238-5114 or 236-9320. ***All:* If departing via commercial airline, an Exit fee of 95 lempira, (approximately $12 U.S.) is charged.** Embassy has extremely limited check cashing facilities. Use boiled or bottled water, eat at recommended restaurants. No weapons. No photography of military installations.

## ICELAND (IS)
**ID/C: *AD:*** ID Card, Leave orders. ***Ret/Civ:*** ID Card, Passport
**ICQI:** Yes
**IR:** Services.
**Other: *AD:*** Civilian clothing off base. ***All:*** No currency restrictions except reconversion of kroner to U.S. $ limited to $250 U.S. visas required for 90 or more days; period begins when entering the Scandinavian area (Denmark, Finland, Norway and Sweden). No pets.

## INDONESIA (ID)
**ID/C: *AD:*** ID Card, Leave orders, Passport and onward/return tickets.
***Ret/Civ:*** ID Card, Passport and onward/return tickets.
**ICQI:** Yes
**IR:** Cholera and Yellow Fever IAFIA.
**Other: *AD:*** Civilian clothing, and advise USDAO Jakarta, C-011-62-21-3435-9000, Fax: C-011-62-21-386-2259. ***All:*** Visa required after 60 days. Declare currency. Indonesian rupiah imports prohibited. Use only bottled water. Antimalarial drugs recommended outside Jakarta. Photography of military installations, airports, terminals prohibited. No AD travel to Irian Jaya and Timor without permission. Declare currency. Imports of Indonesian rupiah are prohibited. No firearms.

## ISRAEL (IL)
**ID/C: *All:*** ID Card, Leave Orders, Passport, visa. (Valid 90 days, can be obtained at Ben Gurion IAP, and can be renewed)
**ICQI:** Yes
**IR:** Meningococcal Vaccine (Type A/C) prior to arrival
**Other: *AD:*** Civilian clothing. ***All:*** Onward/return ticket and proof of sufficient funds required. Visa at Ben Gurion airport for Tourist Passport (90 days). Israeli currency may not be imported or exported. Exit reconvert up to $300 U.S. Do not photograph military installations or persons. Use bottled water. Check with Amembassy on local travel restrictions.

## ITALY (IT)
**ID/C: *AD:*** ID Card, Leave orders (Passport highly recommended). ***Ret/Civ:*** ID Card, Passport. Visa required for stays longer than 90 days.
**ICQI:** Yes
**IR:** Service
**Other: *AD:*** Civilian clothing. ***All:*** Tourist Passport highly recommended. Non-U.S. and non-European Union citizens require visa. Import and export restrictions to 350,000 lire per border crossing. Bottled water in rural areas. No raw fish. In rural areas, use canned or dried milk products.

## JAMAICA (JM)
**ID/C: *AD:*** ID Card, Leave orders. ***Ret/Civ:*** ID Card, Proof of citizenship.
**ICQI:** Yes
**IR:** Yellow Fever IAFIA.
**Other: *AD:*** Civilian clothing. ***All:*** Onward/return ticket and proof of sufficient funds required. **Departure fee $26 U.S. each passenger at commercial airport.** No import and export of Jamaican currency. Exchange currency only at designated money exchanges. No firearms imported or used. Strict drug laws.

## JAPAN (JP)
**ID/C: *AD:*** ID Card, Leave orders (Japan as destination). ***Ret/Civ:*** ID Card, Passport.(Onward/return tickets are required for passengers arriving at commercial ports; AMC passengers are exempt).
**ICQI:** Yes
**IR:** Service
**Other: *AD:*** Military uniform. ***All:*** Visa for stay over 90 days. Reconversion of Yen to U.S. currency 500,000 Yen per day. It is illegal to bring over-the-counter medicines containing trace amounts of amphetamine-like drugs (i.e., Vicks inhaler, Sudafed) into Japan. Very limited Space-A billeting at Yokota AB. No firearms.

## JOHNSTON ATOLL (JO) (U.S.) (U.S. TERRITORY)
**ID/C: *AD:*** ID Card, Leave orders, Entrance approval. ***Ret/Civ:*** ID Card, Entrance approval.
**ICQI:** No
**IR:** Service
**Other: *AD:*** Summer uniform. ***All:*** Passengers not permitted to RON without approval of Commander. No persons allowed to RON with beards or facial hair which preclude the proper wearing and sealing of a M17A1 protective mask or its equivalent. Facilities available at terminal to remove excess hair. Accommodations are very limited.

## JORDAN (JO)
**ID/C: *AD:*** ID Card, Leave orders, Passport, visa. ***Ret/Civ:*** ID Card, Passport, visa.
**ICQI:** Yes
**IR:** Yellow Fever IAFIA
**Other:** Designated a High Physical Threat Country. ***AD:*** Civilian clothing. Military personnel on leave require country clearance from USDAO Amman and must contact USDAO on arrival and prior to departure, C-011-962-6-592-0101-EX-2647, Fax: C-011-962-6-592-0163. ***All:*** The stated policy does not prohibit travelers whose passports contain Israeli stamps or markings. However, implementation of this change from previous policy has been inconsistent. **Exit fee of ten dinar (approximately $15 U.S.) if departing** from civilian airport. Boil and filter water. Persons traveling via King Hussein/Allen Bridge between Israel and Jordan can cross bridge one way in either direction, but travel must commence in Jordan to make a round-trip. Commence travel in the Moslem countries. Photographing military installations or objects prohibited. Declare currency. Import of dinars limited to 20; exports same less expenses.

KENYA (KE)
**ID/C:** *All:* ID Card, Passport, visa.
**ICQI:** Yes
**IR:** Yellow Fever IAFIA, Malaria prophylaxis preferred, Immunization records should be carried by all travelers.
**Other:** *AD:* Contact KUSLO, C-011-254-2-537-800-EX-3391/2/3/4/5/8/9, Fax C-011-254-2-537-810 and provide leave address, phone number and duration of stay in Kenya. Civilian clothing, casual slacks, shirt with collar (coat and tie evenings). *All:* Transit visas are available for limited stays up to seven days. Tourist passport visas are $50 U.S. Up to 100,000 Kenyan shillings may be exported. No limits on U.S. currency; British bank notes are limited to ten pounds. Check source of water. AIDS is high-risk in Kenya. Kenya license or import permit is required for all firearms brought into Kenya. **$20 U.S. departure tax paid in U.S. dollars.**

KOREA (Republic of) (RK)
**ID/C:** *AD:* ID Card, Leave orders. *Ret/Civ:* ID Card, Passport, visa, (for 15 or more days visit).
**ICQI:** Yes
**IR:** Service, (military personnel) update to include anthrax vaccination series.
**Other:** *AD:* Military and Civilian clothing (off duty). *All:* No import of Korean won. No restrictions on the export of U.S. and foreign currency. Use bottled water. Clearance required to visit Panmunjom. **Airport departure tax of 6,000 won or approximately $4.50 U.S., except EML leave, funded emergency leave and overseas tour leave.**

KOSRAE (FM) (SEE FEDERATED STATES OF MICRONESIA)

KUWAIT (KW)
**ID/C:** AD/DoD Civ: ID card, Passport, Visa, Leave orders, country clearance approval message. *Ret/Civ:* ID card, Passport, Visa.
**ICQI:** Yes
**IR:** Service
**Other:** AD/DoD Civ: Obtain country clearance from OMC-K at Amembassy, C-011-965-539-5307/8, No currency restrictions. Importation of pork, alcoholic beverages, pornography or sexually explicit material prohibited. No photographs that reflect unfavorably on country or local people; do not photograph women. Respect local religious beliefs and local customs.

KWAJALEIN ATOLL (KA) (U.S. ARMY KA, (USAKA))
(REPUBLIC OF THE MARSHALL ISLANDS)
**ID/C:** *AD:* ID Card, Leave orders, Entry approval. *Ret/Civ:* ID Card, Entry approval.
**ICQI:** No
**IR:** Service
**Other:** *AD:* Uniforms, Command restrictions, if any govern. *All:* Immediate first aid recommended for all burns, bites, etc., U.S. currency used. See FCG for detailed Clearance Requirements.

MARSHALL ISLANDS (Republic of) (MH)
[Includes Ailinglapalap Atoll, Arno Atoll, Bikini Atoll, Ebon Atoll, Enewetak Atoll, Jaluit Atoll, Kili Island, Kwajalein Atoll (except U.S. Army Kwajalein Atoll), Majuro Atoll, Maloelap Atoll, Mili Atoll, Namorik Atoll, Ralik Chain, Ratak Chain, Rongelap Atoll, Taongi Atoll, Ujelang Atoll, Utirik Atoll, Wotje Atoll]
**ID/C:** *AD:* ID Card, Leave orders. *Ret/Civ:* ID Card, Passport.

**ICQI:** No
**IR:** Service
**Other:** *All:* Command restrictions, if any, apply. No currency restrictions. Sufficient funds for stay of 30 days and onward/return ticket. Water outside major hotels and restaurants not potable. Immediate first aid recommended for all burns, bites, etc.

MICRONESIA, (FEDERATED STATES OF) (FM)
[Includes Eauripik Atoll, Fais Island, Faraulep Atoll, Gaferut Island, Kapingamarangi Atoll, Kosrae State, Mortlock Islands, Hall Islands, Ifalik Atoll, Namonuito Atoll, Oroluk Atoll, Pingelap Atoll, Pohnpei State, Pulap Atoll, Pulusak Island, Puluwat Atoll, Chuuk State, Ulithi Atoll, West Fayu Atoll, Woleai Atoll, Yap State.]
**ID/C:** *AD:* ID Card, Leave orders. *All:* ID Card, Proof of citizenship.
**ICQI:** Yes
**IR:** Service
**Other:** Onward/return ticket and sufficient funds required. **Departure tax of $5 U.S. for all persons.** No import/export restrictions on U.S. dollars which are legal tender in FM. No USDAO personnel, see USCINCPAC Rep Guam who acts as DoD Rep to FM. Uniforms, Command restrictions if any apply. Water outside major hotels and restaurants not potable. Immediate first aid recommended for all burns, bites, etc.

NETHERLANDS ANTILLES (AN)
**ID/C:** *AD:* ID Cards and Leave orders. *Ret/Civ:* ID Cards and Proof of U.S. Citizenship.
**ICQI:** Yes
**IR:** Services, Yellow fever over age 6 months, IAFIA.
**Other:** *All:* Personnel staying over 24 hours must have orders authorizing travel outside AN, ID cards and POC, documents necessary to continue journey or return to country of origin, and means of support during stay. A visa is required for stays of more than 90 days. Tourist may be asked to show onward/return ticket or proof of sufficient funds for their stay. No currency restriction, declare ony paper money over $500 U.S. or CN, import/export up to 500 florins. Wash and peel fruits and vegetables. Firearms are prohibited.

NEW ZEALAND (NZ)
**ID/C:** *AD:* ID Card, Passport (valid for six months), Leave orders. *Ret/Civ:* ID Card, Passport.
**ICQI:** Yes
**IR:** Service
**Other:** *AD:* No uniform restrictions. *All:* Onward/return ticket and visa for next destination; proof of sufficient funds. Visa required when stay exceeds 90 days. Military ID Card is accepted in lieu of usual outward ticket requirement for Space-A traveler. Maximum currency export is $100 NZ. No U.S.-NZ SOFA. Drug offenders receive sentences up to life imprisonment. No handguns, other firearms require permit.

NICARAGUA (NI)
**ID/C:** *All:* Passport (valid at least six months), Tourist card in lieu of visa (paid), onward/return ticket and sufficient funds ($500 minimum).
**ICQI:** Yes.
**IR:** Yellow Fever, IAFIA.
**Other:** *AD:* Civilian clothing. Military and DoD personnel require country clearance from USDAO Managua prior to visiting Nicaragua in leave status, phone, 011-505-2-66-2298/6010, Fax: C-011-505-2-66-8022. Travel by road between Nicaragua and Honduras, even on main roads, is potentially dangerous. Road travel after dark is hazardous in all areas of country. Photography of military installations or airports prohibited. Use bottled water; eat at recommended places. **There is a $20 U.S. departure fee for all except diplomats.**

NIGER (NE)
**ID/C:** *AD:* Passport, visa, ID Card and Leave orders. *Ret/Civ:* Passport, visa and ID card.
**ICQI:** Yes. Video cassettes will be impounded for review by officials; normally returned if no questionable contents.
**IR:** Yellow Fever, Malaria Prophylactic Treatment (begin one week before arrival), Meningitis. Cholera IAFIA, prior cholera should be annotated "cholera vaccination not received for medical reasons."
**Other:** Designated a High Physical Threat Country. *All:* Civilian clothing outside airport. Register with U.S. Embassy. Declare currency, no limits. Boil water. Wash all fruits and vegetables. No firearms. No photographs near military installations, radio, TV stations, Presidency building and airport. All U.S. citizens register with American Embassy in Niamey, C-011-227-72-26-61 thru 64, EX-262 or 245. No limit on foreign currency or travel checks. CFA Francs limited to 4,000 import and 50,000 export.

NORTHERN MARIANAS (COMMONWEALTH OF THE) (MP)
**ID/C:** *AD:* ID cards and orders. *Ret/Civ:* ID Cards and Passport, DOD Civilians: Orders and personal identification card with name, status, date of birth and photo.
**ICQI:** Yes.
**IR:** Service.
**Other:** U.S. currency is legal tender. Use bottled or boiled water outside of major hotels and restaurants; wash fruits thoroughly. Immediate first aid recommended for all wounds, burns, abrasions, insect bites, and stings from marine animals.

OMAN (OM)
**ID/C:** *All:* ID Card, Passport, visa.
**ICQI:** Yes
**IR:** Yellow Fever IAFIA. Antimalarial drugs recommended.
**Other:** *All:* Civilian clothing. Visa (validation for 7-90 days) not available at airport. Advise USDAO of travel plans, phone 011-968-698-989. Travelers may transit Oman without FCG compliance provided they do not disembark the aircraft. Liquor and adult-only literature are prohibited. Video tapes may be confiscated for up to six weeks for censorship review. No currency restrictions. Boil water. Photography of ports and airports prohibited. No firearms or ammunition.

PALAU (REPUBLIC OF) (PW)
**ID/C: *AD:*** ID Card, Leave orders. ***All:*** ID Card, Proof of citizenship, onward/return ticket for stay of up to 30 days. Visa for stays longer than 30 days, fee of $50 U. S.
**ICQI:** Yes
**IR:** Service
**Other: *AD:*** Uniforms, Command restrictions if any govern, No currency restrictions. U.S. currency is legal tender in PW. No firearms. Water outside major hotels and restaurants not potable. Immediate first aid recommended for all wounds, bites, etc.

PANAMA (REPUBLIC of) (PA)
**ID/C: *AD:*** ID Card, Leave orders. ***Ret/Civ:*** ID Card, Passport (valid for six months), visa before arrival or purchase within first 3 days of visit to Panama ($10 for a 30-day stay), onward/return ticket.
**ICQI:** Yes
**IR:** Service
**Other: *AD:*** Civilian clothing. ***All:*** Contact USDAO, C-011-507-207-7000. No currency restrictions. Use bottled water, wash fruits and vegetables.

PARAGUAY (PY)
**ID/C: *AD:*** ID Card, Passport, visa for stay longer than 90 days, Leave orders, Immunization record. ***Ret/Civ:*** ID Card, Passport, visa for stay longer than 90 days.
**ICQI:** Yes
**IR:** Yellow Fever
**Other: *AD:*** Military uniforms. Contact USDAO on arrival, phone C-011-595-21-213-715 ext 330, Fax: C-011-595-21-213-728. ***All:*** No currency restrictions. Outside Asuncion, use bottled water. Rabies is a problem in Paraguay. Visits less than 90 days require Tourist Card ($3 U.S.) at airport. Minors (under 20) need both parents' written authorization in Spanish and authenticated. No currency restrictions. No firearms. Burglaries, larcenies and car thefts are common.

PERU (PE)
**ID/C: *AD:*** ID Card, Passport, Leave orders, tourist card. ***Ret/Civ:*** ID Card, Passport, onward/return ticket.
**ICQI:** Yes
**IR:** Yellow Fever and cholera IAFIA.
**Other:** Designated a High Physical Threat Country. ***AD:*** Summer uniforms. Consult with USDAO, APO AA 34031. ***All:*** Contact USDAO to arrange security briefing. C-011-51-1-434-3000. Visa for stay longer than 90 days. **Exit Tax at Lima airport $18 U.S.** No currency restrictions. Use bottled water. Photography of infrastructure and military installations is prohibited.

PHILIPPINES, REPUBLIC OF THE (PH)
**ID/C: *All:*** Passport and visa if staying over 21 days, round-trip ticket and sufficient funds.
**ICQI:** Yes.
**IR:** Yellow Fever IAFIA. Immunization for Typhoid and Hepatitis A and B are recommended.
**Other: *AD:*** Personnel in a leave status do not have legal protection under the Visiting forces Agreement. Personnel on leave must submit country clearance requests to CHIEF JUSMAG MANILA RP//. Currency restrictions; Maximum 500 pesos entering or departing. Exchange dollars only at authorized agencies; use of U.S. dollars on Philippine economy prohibited. ATM's are unreliable and should not be used. Use boiled water. No firearms.

POHNPEI (See FEDERATED STATES OF MICRONESIA)

PORTUGAL (PT)
**ID/C: *AD:*** ID Card, Leave orders. ***Ret/Civ:*** ID Card, Passport.
**ICQI:** Yes
**IR:** Service
**Other: *AD:*** Civilian clothing. No uniforms off base. ***All:*** Visa after 90 days. No currency restrictions. Water in Lisbon unsafe to drink. Persons stationed in Azores may visit without Passport and visa up to 60 days. Permission from Portuguese government required to import firearms. Most US ATM cards are accepted at MultiBanco Machines throughout Portugal. Operating instructions are available in English.

PUERTO RICO (PR) (U.S. TERRITORY)
**ID/C: *AD:*** ID Card, Leave orders. ***Ret/Civ:*** ID Card. Proof of citizenship if entering from other than North, South or Central America.
**ICQI:** No
**IR:** Service
**Other: *AD:*** Uniforms allowed. Wash or peel fruits and vegetables.

SAUDI ARABIA (SA) (KINGDOM OF)
**ID/C: *AD:*** ID Card, Passport, visa, Leave orders. ***Ret/Civ:*** ID Card, Passport, visa.
**ICQI:** Yes
**IR:** Yellow Fever IAFIA.
**Other:** Designated a High Physical Threat Country. ***AD:*** Civilian clothing. Country clearance is required for all leave travel to Saudi Arabia, including the Hajj pilgrimage. Submit request to CHUSMTM RIYADH SA//CC/MR// and USDAO RIYADH SA using the Content of Personnel Clearance Request format in this FCG. Passport and visa are required. The Kingdom does not issue airport/plane-side visas. Saudi Arabia does not grant visas to personnel desiring leave unless they are sponsored by family members within the Kingdom or attending the Hajj. Space-A air travel to Prince Sultan Air Base, Al Kharj is limited to DoD personnel, DoD sponsored personnel, and dependents/immediate family members of personnel permanently assigned to DoD activities in Saudi Arabia. Space available air to/from or transit of Prince Sultan Air Base, Al Kharj by individuals not directly assigned or attached to DoD activities in Saudi Arabia is prohibited. This limitation is based on lack of accommodations and force protection issues. Use bottled water. No photography of women, military installations, or ports. The following are some of the items prohibited:
a. Alcoholic beverages and liquor or liquor by-products of any type.
b. Arabian music records
c. Weapons, firearms, ammunition, swords, knives, etc.
d. Pornographic materials.
e. Pork products.
f. Chewing tobacco.
g. Videotapes.
h. Fireworks.
i. Global Positioning Systems (GPS).
See Foreign Clearance Guides for a more detailed list.

SENEGAL (SN)
**ID/C: *AD:*** Passport, ID Card, Leave orders, except if arriving by Navy ships -ID card, ***Ret/Civ:*** Passport, ID Card.
**ICQI:** Yes.
**IR:** Yellow Fever vaccination required for all travelers over one year of age, malaria prophylaxis recommended.
**Other: *All:*** No uniform restrictions. Visa required if staying over 90 days. No limit on currency import. Exports limited to amount imported less expenses. Imports or exports of CFA francs are limited to 10,000. Use bottled water. Wash fruits and vegetables with disinfectant. Eat only at recommended places. Firearms must be registered, no automatic or semi-automatic long guns permitted.

SINGAPORE (SG)
**ID/C: *AD:*** ID Card, Leave orders, Passport. ***Ret/Civ:*** ID Card, Passport.
**ICQI:** Yes
**IR:** Yellow Fever, IAFIA. ***All:*** Valid immunization records required.
**Other: *AD:*** Emergency leave do not require Passport. Personnel on EML orders may transit with EML orders and ID card, no Passport. ***All:*** Entry valid for 30 days. Visa after 30 days required. Physician must sign and authenticate with stamp International Certificate of Vaccination. Currency declared. No adult literature. No cameras exhibited or used on military installations. Coordinate taxi with AMC terminal manager. No chewing gum, littering, spitting or jaywalking.

SOUTH AFRICA (ZA)
**ID/C: *AD:*** ID Cards, Passport (valid for 6 months), Leave orders, and immunization record. ***Ret/Civ:*** ID Cards, Passport, Visa before arrival.
**ICQI:** Yes
**IR:** Service, Yellow fever IAFIA, malaria prophylaxis.
**Other: *AD:*** Notify USDAO of arrival, travel plans, and departure date and point of contact for emergencies, C-011-27-12-342-1048, ask for USDAO. Civilian clothes, No limits on currency. Bank of England notes, limited to 10 pounds sterling. Boil water in rural areas. Wash fruits and vegetables. Register firearms with local police. Photographs of military installations are prohibited.

## SPAIN (ES)
**ID/C: *AD:*** ID Card, Leave orders, Passport (except if stationed in Europe).
***Ret/Civ:*** ID Card, Passport.
**ICQI:** Yes
**IR:** Service
**Other: *AD:*** Civilian clothing. ***All:*** Visa required after three months. AD and Retired military personnel on leave who are not permanently assigned within Spain are not authorized Base Exchange, Commissary, or Class VI privileges. Declare currency. Import of Bank of Spain notes limited to 500,000 pesetas and export of 100,000 pesetas. Recommend transients use ATM machines, which are widely available. Wash fruits and vegetables well.

## SURINAME (SR)
**ID/C: *AD:*** ID Card, Passports, visas and return airline ticket. ***Ret/Civ:*** Passport, Visa, ID card.
**ICQI:** Yes
**IR:** Yellow Fever, IAFIA.
**Other: *All:*** Civilian clothing is mandatory at all times. After eight days in Suriname, all foreigners are required to report to the Office of Foreign Affairs (VREEMDELINGENDIENST) for an extension-of-stay stamp. Due to continuing and growing insurgent activities, Americans should use caution while traveling to areas outside Paramaribo and Nieuw Nickerie. Register with Defense Attache, C-011-597-4-72900/77881. Plane-side visas not available except in extreme emergency. Permission required to use personal cameras or carry firearms. Photography of "military terrain" prohibited. Urban water is safe for use. **There is an airport departure tax of $10 U.S. and a terminal fee of $5 U.S.**

## THAILAND (TH)
**ID/C: *All:*** ID Card, Passport, visa, onward/return ticket.
**ICQI:** No
**IR:** Cholera infected area, Yellow Fever IAFIA.
**Other: *AD:*** Civilian clothing. ***All:*** Stamp (good for 30 days) given at airport or border. Tourist visa (valid up to 60 days) or non-immigration visa (good for 90 days) must be obtained in advance. Exchange money only at licensed money changers (10% loss). No photography at military airports. Persons desiring follow-on U.S. military air transportation contact AMC Rep, Bangkok, phone C-011-66-2-287-1036 ext 333 at JUSMAGTHAI Compound, 7 South Sathorn Rd (1 mile south of Amembassy). Only APO & snack bar available. U.S. Embassy, Bangkok C-011-66-2-205-4000.

## TRINIDAD AND TOBAGO (TT)
**ID/C: *AD:*** ID Cards, Passport, Leave orders, ***Ret/Civ:*** ID Cards, Passport.
**ICQI:** Yes
**IR:** Services, Yellow fever IAFIA.
**Other: *All:* Departure tax of 75 TTD (approx $18 U. S.).** Civilian clothes. Visa required after 3 months or pay a visa waiver fee of TTD 100 (approx $23.50 U.S.), Declare U.S. currency over $10,000 U.S. upon entry. No more than TTD 200 imported or exported. Tap water is potable; know the water source.

## TURKEY (TR)
**ID/C: *AD:*** ID Card, Passport, Leave orders, visa. ***Ret/Civ:*** ID Card, Passport, visa. Holders of tourist passports can purchase a sticker visa at the port of entry for $45 U.S.
**ICQI:** Yes
**IR:** Service, yellow fever IAFIA.
**Other:** Designated a High Physical Threat Country. ***AD:*** Civilian clothing. Travelers should inform USDAO Ankara (C-011-90-312-468-6110/1/2/3 ext 2300), and info to CJUSMMAT/TDAI of arrival and place of residence. ***All:*** Visa for visit of 90 days available in advance at border crossing points. Declare currency and valuables. Import/export limit is 5,000 TL. Boil or chlorinate water, avoid ice cubes. No photography of Turkish military installations. Check with American Embassy on special travel restrictions. No firearms.

## UNITED ARAB EMIRATES (AE)
**ID/C: *All:*** Passport and visa (obtained in advance).
**ICQI:** Yes
**IR:** Service
**Other: *AD:*** Country clearance is required for U.S. military personnel in leave status. Contact: USDAO, C-011-971-2-443-6691/6692. Civilian clothing. Personnel arriving at a military airfield must depart thru a military airfield. Alcohol and "adult" literature prohibited. No photography at airports, near military installations. Obtain advance permission before taking an individual's photograph. Crimes of fraud are regarded seriously. Penalties for possession, use or trafficking in illegal drugs are strict. Drink bottled water. Serious risk of heat prostration from high temperatures and humidity. No currency restrictions. Firearms are prohibited.

## UNITED KINGDOM (GB)
[England, Northern Ireland, Scotland, & Wales]
**ID/C: *AD:*** ID Card, Leave orders. ***Ret/Civ:*** ID Card, Passport, visa (not required for six months).
**ICQI:** Yes
**IR:** Service
**Other: *AD:*** Civilian clothing. Uniform is appropriate for visits to U.S. and British military installations outside London. No currency restrictions. No U.S. government transportation available in London.

## URUGUAY (UY)
**ID/C: *AD:*** ID Card, Passport, Leave orders. ***Ret/Civ:*** ID Card, Passport.
**ICQI:** Yes
**IR:** Service
**Other: *AD:*** Civilian clothing. ***All:*** Visa required after three months. Photography of military installations or equipment prohibited. All gold and jewels over $500 U.S. must be declare to customs officers at port of entry. Carrying of firearms is prohibited.

## VENEZUELA (VE)
**ID/C: *All:*** ID Cards, Passport and tourist card (issued by commercial airlines).
**ICQI:** Yes
**IR:** Service
**Other:** Visas required if remaining over 72 hours, not available plane side. **Departure tax of $15 U.S. will be charged to all DoD travelers and crew arriving via military air and remaining over 72 hours in country.** Exchange currency at commercial banks and exchange houses. Photography of airports, oil installations, or port and coastal areas prohibited. Use bottled water, eat at recommended places. Firearms require special approval.

## U.S. VIRGIN ISLANDS (VI) (U.S. TERRITORY)
**ID/C: *AD:*** ID Cards, Leave orders. ***Ret/Civ:*** ID Card.
**ICQI:** Yes
**IR:** Service
**Other: *All:*** Boil water unless sure of source. Fruits and vegetables should be washed and peeled or cooked.

## WAKE ISLAND (WK) (U.S. TERRITORY)
**ID/C: *AD:*** ID Card, Leave orders. ***Ret/Civ:*** ID Card.
**ICQI:** Normal U.S. Customs
**IR:** None
**Other: *All:*** Personal clearance required from CMDR, U.S. Army Space and Strategic Defense Command, ATTN: CSSD-EN-F, P. O. Box 1500, Huntsville, AL 35807-3801, FAX: C-205-955-5074. Enter and depart Wake Island Airfield. Limited billeting for RON persons. Billeting, food service, ground transportation, and medical services are austere and severely limited. No off base quarters.

PROOF OF U.S. CITIZENSHIP (POC)

The following documents are considered valid proof of U.S. citizenship:

a)  United States of America Passport
b)  Birth or Baptismal Certificate
c)  State ID Card
d)  Naturalization Certificate
e)  Voter ID Card
f)  U.S. Military ID Card
    (regardless of true citizenship of military member)
g)  U.S. Military Dependent ID Card
    (regardless of true citizenship of military member)

*How's this for Space-A travel?  Ellen Hart waits to board the C-21 to Stuttgart, Germany, from Rota Naval Station.*

# APPENDIX C
## MEDEVAC SCHEDULES

**SUNDAY**

**EVAC 1626**
*Departure Time: 0800*
BLV Scott AFB, IL (O)
ADW Andrews AFB, MD
NGU Norfolk NS, VA
POB Pope AFB, NC
AGS Bush Field Apt, GA
BIX Keesler AFB, MS
SKF Kelly AFB, TX
BLV Scott AFB, IL (T)

**EVAC 1456**
SUU Travis AFB, CA (O)
NKX Miramar MCAS, CA
LUF Luke AFB, AZ
DMA Davis-Monthan AFB, AZ
IKR Kirtland AFB, NM
CVS Cannon AFB, NM
BIF Biggs AAF, TX
SKF Kelly AFB, TX
BLV Scott AFB, IL (T)

**MONDAY**

**EVAC 1614**
*Departure Time: 0800*
BLV Scott AFB, IL (O)
ADW Andrews AFB, MD
SKF Kelly AFB, TX
NKX Miramar MCAS, CA
SUU Travis AFB, CA (T)

**EVAC 1652**
*Departure Time: 0830*
BLV Scott AFB, IL (O)
LRF Little Rock AFB, AR
AEX Alexandria, LA
BAD Barksdale AFB, LA
TIK Tinker AFB, OK
LAW Lawton/Fort Sill Reg Apt, GA
HLR Fort Hood, TX
SKF Kelly AFB, TX
BIX Keesler AFB, MS (T)

**TUESDAY**

**EVAC 1635**
*Departure: 0800*
BLV Scott AFB, IL (O)
RCA Ellsworth AFB, SD
CYS Cheyenne Mun Apt, WY
COS Peterson AFB, CO
MHK Marshall AAF/Manhattan Mun Apt, KS
MCI Kansas City, MO
IAB McConnell AFB, KS
SKF Kelly AFB, TX (T)

**EVAC 1226**
BIX Keesler AFB, MS (O)
MCF MacDill AFB, FL
NQX Key West NAS, FL
COF Patrick AFB, FL
NIP Jacksonville NAS, FL
AGS Bush Field Apt, GA
VPS Eglin AFB, FL
BIX Keesler AFB, MS
BLV Scott AFB, IL (T)

**TUESDAY**, *continued*

**EVAC 1436**
SUU Travis AFB, CA (O)
MUO Mountain Home AFB, ID
TEM McChord AFB, WA
SKA Fairchild AFB, WA
GTF Great Falls IAP/ANGB, MT
MIB Minot AFB, ND
RDR Grand Forks AFB, ND
BLV Scott AFB, IL (T)

**WEDNESDAY**

**EVAC 1666**
*Departure Time: 0800*
BLV Scott AFB, IL (O)
TBN Waynesville Reg Apt/Forney AAF, MO
SZL Whiteman AFB, MO
OFF Offutt AFB, NE
MKE General Mitchell IAP/ARS, WI
HOP Campbell AAF, KY
SDF Louisville IAP/Kentucky ANGB, KY
FFO Wright-Patterson AFB, OH
BLV Scott AFB, IL (T)

**EVAC 1616**
*Departure Time: 0830*
BLV Scott AFB, IL (O)
SKF Kelly AFB, TX
AEX Alexandria, LA
BIX Keesler AFB, MS
NGU Norfolk NS, VA
ADW Andrews AFB, MD
BLV Scott AFB, IL (T)

**EVAC 1546**
SKF Kelly AFB, TX (O)
BIF Biggs AAF, TX
SUU Travis AFB, CA
NKX Miramar MCAS, CA
BLV Scott AFB, IL (T)

**THURSDAY**

**EVAC 1621**
*Departure Time: 0800*
BLV Scott AFB, IL (O)
LSF Lawson AAF, GA
AGS Bush Field Apt, SC
CHS Charleston AFB, SC
SSC Shaw AFB, SC
POB Pope AFB, NC
NKT Cherry Point MCAS, NC
NGU Norfolk NS, VA
ADW Andrews AFB, MD (T)

**EVAC 1656**
*Departure Time: 0830*
BLV Scott AFB, IL (O)
SKF Kelly AFB, TX
LAW Lawton/Fort Sill Reg Apt, OK
TIK Tinker AFB, OK
COS Colorado Springs, CO
MHK Marshall AAF/Manhattan Mun Apt, KS
MCI Kansas City, MO
BLV Scott AFB, IL (T)

**THURSDAY**, *continued*

**EVAC 1626**
*Departure Time: 0900*
BLV Scott AFB, IL (O)
BIX Keesler AFB, MS
UPS Eglin AFB, FL
AGS Bush Field Apt, GA
NIP Jacksonville NAS, FL
NQX Key West NAS, FL
MCF MacDill AFB, FL
BLV Scott AFB, IL (T)

**FRIDAY**

**EVAC 1666**
*Departure Time: 0800*
BLV Scott AFB, IL (O)
FFO Wright-Patterson AFB, OH
SDF Louisville IAP/Kentucky ANGB, KY
HOP Campbell AAF, KY
MKE General Mitchell IAP/ARS, WI
OFF Offutt AFB, NE
SZL Whiteman AFB, MO
TBN Waynesville Reg Apt/Forney AAF, MO
BLV Scott AFB, IL (T)

**EVAC 1116**
ADW Andrews AFB, MD (O)
WRI McGuire AFB, NJ
SWF Stewart IAP, NY
PVD Providence, RI
BED Hanscom Field, MA
BGR Bangor, ME
GIB Fort Drum, NY
ADW Andrews AFB, MD
BLV Scott AFB, IL (T)

**SATURDAY**

**EVAC 1634**
*Departure Time: 0800*
BLV Scott AFB, IL (O)
RDR Grand Forks AFB, ND
MIB Minot AFB, ND
GTF Great Falls IAP/ANGB, MT
SKA Fairchild AAFB, WA
TEM McChord AFB, WA
MUO Mountain Home AFB, ID
SUU Travis AFB, CA (T)

**NOTES:**

O = Originating Station
T = Terminating Station
Read top to bottom for routing --
i.e., Sunday, EVAC 1626, Scott AFB, I
to Andrews AFB, MD to Norfolk NS, VA,
etc.

Showtime for all flights is two hours prior
to departure

All flight schedules/routes are completed
(flown) in a 24-hour day.

# APPENDIX D
## INTERNATIONAL CERTIFICATES OF VACCINATION AND PERSONAL HEALTH HISTORY
### (PHS Form 731)

This document provides for the recording of international certificates of vaccination and revaccination in both the English and French languages and the personal health history of international travelers. This document, with current health entries, is required as a Personnel Entrance Requirement for many foreign countries.

### I. INTERNATIONAL CERTIFICATES OF VACCINATION
### AS APPROVED BY THE WORLD HEALTH ORGANIZATION
#### (EXCEPT FOR ADDRESS OF VACCINATOR)

CERTIFICATS INTERNATIONAUX DE VACCINATION APPROUVES PAR L'ORGANISA-
TION MONDIALE DE LA SANTE
(SAUF L'ADRESSE DU VACCINATEUR)

### II. PERSONAL HEALTH HISTORY

Traveler's Name—Nom du voyageur

Address—Adresse  (Number—Numéro)                         (Street—Rue)

(City—Ville)

(Country—Départment)                                      (State—Etat)

### U.S. DEPARTMENT OF HEALTH, EDUCATION, AND WELFARE
### PUBLIC HEALTH SERVICE

PHS—731, Rev. 9-66 READ INSTRUCTIONS CAREFULLY

### INTERNATIONAL CERTIFICATES OF VACCINATION AND PERSONAL HEALTH HISTORY (PHS FORM 731)

### INTERNATIONAL CERTIFICATE OF VACCINATION OR REVACCINA-TION AGAINST SMALLPOX
CERTIFICAT INTERNATIONAL DE VACCINATION OU
DE REVACCINATION CONTRE LA VARIOLE

This is to certify that . . . . . . . . . . . . . . . . . . . . . . . . . . . . . . . . . . . . . .sex
Je soussigné(e) certifie que . . . . . . . . . . . . . . . . . . . . . . . . . . . . . . . . . . . . . sexe
whose signature follows . . . . . . . . . . . . . . . . . . . . . . . . . . . . . . . . . date of birth
dant la signature suit . . . . . . . . . . . . . . . . . . . . . . . . . . . . . . . . . . . . . né(e) le
has on the date indicated been vaccinated or revaccinated against smallpox with a freeze-dried liquid vaccine certified to fulfill the recommended requirements of the World Health Organization.
a été vacciné(e) ou revacciné(e) contre la variole à la date indiquée ci-dessous avec un vaccin iyophilisé ou liquide certifié conforme aux normes recommandée par L'Organisation mondiale de la Santé.

### INTERNATIONAL CERTIFICATE OF VACCINATION OR REVACCINA-TION AGAINST YELLOW FEVER
CERTIFICAT INTERNATIONAL DE VACCINATION OU
DE REVACCINATION CONTRE LA FIEVRE JAUNE

This is to certify that . . . . . . . . . . . . . . . . . . . . . . . . . . . . . . . . . . . . . .sex
Je soussigné(e) certifie que . . . . . . . . . . . . . . . . . . . . . . . . . . . . . . . . . . . . . sexe
whose signature follows . . . . . . . . . . . . . . . . . . . . . . . . . . . . . . . . . date of birth
dant la signature suit . . . . . . . . . . . . . . . . . . . . . . . . . . . . . . . . . . . . . né(e) le
has on the date indicated been vaccinated or revaccinated against yellow fever.
a été vacciné(e) ou revacciné(e) contre la fievre jaune à la date indiquée.

### INTERNATIONAL CERTIFICATE OF VACCINATION OR REVACCINA-TION AGAINST CHOLERA
CERTIFICAT INTERNATIONAL DE VACCINATION OU
DE REVACCINATION CONTRE LE CHOLERA

This is to certify that . . . . . . . . . . . . . . . . . . . . . . . . . . . . . . . . . . . . . .sex
Je soussigné(e) certifie que . . . . . . . . . . . . . . . . . . . . . . . . . . . . . . . . . . . . . sexe
whose signature follows . . . . . . . . . . . . . . . . . . . . . . . . . . . . . . . . . date of birth
dant la signature suit . . . . . . . . . . . . . . . . . . . . . . . . . . . . . . . . . . . . . né(e) le
has on the date indicated been vaccinated or revaccinated against cholera.
a été vacciné(e) ou revacciné(e) contre la choléra à la date indiquée.

# APPENDIX E
## STANDARD TIME CONVERSION TABLE

The world is divided into 24 time zones or areas. The zero time zone is known as Greenwich Mean Time (GMT), also referred to as Zulu Time, which is physically located at Greenwich, England (UK), near London. Other areas in this time zone include Iceland, Ascension Island, England and Scotland. The following table shows major areas and their respective time zones in + or - hours from Greenwich Mean Time (GMT). Across the top row of the table, each area (zone) to the right of GMT is a plus (+), meaning an hour ahead. Each zone to the left of GMT is a minus (-), meaning an hour behind. The columns down the page are simply the next 24 hours from the baseline at the top. For example, if you are in Germany, Italy or Spain (GMT +1), the local time is 0800 hours. If you want to know the local time in San Francisco, CA, USA, you read down the GMT +1 column to 0800 hours and left to GMT -8 (Pacific TIme U.S., San Francisco, CA, USA) where it is 2300 hours. Practice with this table until you are proficient.

| Kwajalien | Midway/Pago Pago/ Canton | Hawaii/Shemya | Elmendorf | Pacific Time U.S. | Mountain Time U.S. | Central Time U.S. | Eastern Time U.S. | Bermuda/Puerto Rico/ Greenland | Azores | Iceland/Ascension/ England/Scotland | Germany/Italy/ Spain | Greece/Egypt/ Johannesburg/Turkey | Dhahran/Bahrain | Diego Garcia | Thailand/Singapore | Philippines/Taiwan/ S Vietnam/ Perth (AU) | Okinawa/Japan/ Korea | Alice Springs (AU)/ Woomera (AU) | Guam/Richmond (AU) | Wake Island/ New Zealand |
|---|---|---|---|---|---|---|---|---|---|---|---|---|---|---|---|---|---|---|---|---|
| -12 | -11 | -10 | -9 | -8 | -7 | -6 | -5 | -4 | -1 | GMT | +1 | +2 | +3 | +6 | +7 | +8 | +9 | +9:30 | +10 | +12 |
| 0600 | 0700 | 0800 | 0900 | 1000 | 1100 | 1200 | 1300 | 1400 | 1700 | 1800 | 1900 | 2000 | 2100 | 2330 | 0100 | 0200 | 0300 | 0330 | 0400 | 0600 |
| 0700 | 0800 | 0900 | 1000 | 1100 | 1200 | 1300 | 1400 | 1500 | 1800 | 1900 | 2000 | 2100 | 2200 | 0030 | 0200 | 0300 | 0400 | 0430 | 0500 | 0700 |
| 0800 | 0900 | 1000 | 1100 | 1200 | 1300 | 1400 | 1500 | 1600 | 1900 | 2000 | 2100 | 2200 | 2300 | 0130 | 0300 | 0400 | 0500 | 0530 | 0600 | 0800 |
| 0900 | 1000 | 1100 | 1200 | 1300 | 1400 | 1500 | 1600 | 1700 | 2000 | 2100 | 2200 | 2300 | 2400 | 0230 | 0400 | 0500 | 0600 | 0630 | 0700 | 0900 |
| 1000 | 1100 | 1200 | 1300 | 1400 | 1500 | 1600 | 1700 | 1800 | 2100 | 2200 | 2300 | 2400 | 0100 | 0330 | 0500 | 0600 | 0700 | 0730 | 0800 | 1000 |
| 1100 | 1200 | 1300 | 1400 | 1500 | 1600 | 1700 | 1800 | 1900 | 2200 | 2300 | 2400 | 0100 | 0200 | 0430 | 0600 | 0700 | 0800 | 0830 | 0900 | 1100 |
| 1200 | 1300 | 1400 | 1500 | 1600 | 1700 | 1800 | 1900 | 2000 | 2300 | 2400 | 0100 | 0200 | 0300 | 0530 | 0700 | 0800 | 0900 | 0930 | 1000 | 1200 |
| 1300 | 1400 | 1500 | 1600 | 1700 | 1800 | 1900 | 2000 | 2100 | 2400 | 0100 | 0200 | 0300 | 0400 | 0630 | 0800 | 0900 | 1000 | 0130 | 1100 | 1300 |
| 1400 | 1500 | 1600 | 1700 | 1800 | 1900 | 2000 | 2100 | 2200 | 0100 | 0200 | 0300 | 0400 | 0500 | 0730 | 0900 | 1000 | 1100 | 1130 | 1200 | 1400 |
| 1500 | 1600 | 1700 | 1800 | 1900 | 2000 | 2100 | 2200 | 2300 | 0200 | 0300 | 0400 | 0500 | 0600 | 0830 | 1000 | 1100 | 1200 | 1230 | 1300 | 1500 |
| 1600 | 1700 | 1800 | 1900 | 2000 | 2100 | 2200 | 2300 | 2400 | 0300 | 0400 | 0500 | 0600 | 0700 | 0930 | 1100 | 1200 | 1300 | 1330 | 1400 | 1600 |
| 1700 | 1800 | 1900 | 2000 | 2100 | 2200 | 2300 | 2400 | 0100 | 0400 | 0500 | 0600 | 0700 | 0800 | 1030 | 1200 | 1300 | 1400 | 1430 | 1500 | 1700 |
| 1800 | 1900 | 2000 | 2100 | 2200 | 2300 | 2400 | 0100 | 0200 | 0500 | 0600 | 0700 | 0800 | 0900 | 1130 | 1300 | 1400 | 1500 | 1530 | 1600 | 1800 |
| 1900 | 2000 | 2100 | 2200 | 2300 | 2400 | 0100 | 0200 | 0300 | 0600 | 0700 | 0800 | 0900 | 1000 | 1230 | 1400 | 1500 | 1600 | 1630 | 1700 | 1900 |
| 2000 | 2100 | 2200 | 2300 | 2400 | 0100 | 0200 | 0300 | 0400 | 0700 | 0800 | 0900 | 1000 | 1100 | 1330 | 1500 | 1600 | 1700 | 1730 | 1800 | 2000 |
| 2100 | 2200 | 2300 | 2400 | 0100 | 0200 | 0300 | 0400 | 0500 | 0800 | 0900 | 1000 | 1100 | 1200 | 1430 | 1600 | 1700 | 1800 | 1830 | 1900 | 2100 |
| 2200 | 2300 | 2400 | 0100 | 0200 | 0300 | 0400 | 0500 | 0600 | 0900 | 1000 | 1100 | 1200 | 1300 | 1530 | 1700 | 1800 | 1900 | 1930 | 2000 | 2200 |
| 2300 | 2400 | 0100 | 0200 | 0300 | 0400 | 0500 | 0600 | 0700 | 1000 | 1100 | 1200 | 1300 | 1400 | 1630 | 1800 | 1900 | 2000 | 2030 | 2100 | 2300 |
| 2400 | 0100 | 0200 | 0300 | 0400 | 0500 | 0600 | 0700 | 0800 | 1100 | 1200 | 1300 | 1400 | 1500 | 1730 | 1900 | 2000 | 2100 | 2130 | 2200 | 2400 |
| 0100 | 0200 | 0300 | 0400 | 0500 | 0600 | 0700 | 0800 | 0900 | 1200 | 1300 | 1400 | 1500 | 1600 | 1830 | 2000 | 2100 | 2200 | 2230 | 2300 | 0100 |
| 0200 | 0300 | 0400 | 0500 | 0600 | 0700 | 0800 | 0900 | 1000 | 1300 | 1400 | 1500 | 1600 | 1700 | 1930 | 2100 | 2200 | 2300 | 2330 | 2400 | 0200 |
| 0300 | 0400 | 0500 | 0600 | 0700 | 0800 | 0900 | 1000 | 1100 | 1400 | 1500 | 1600 | 1700 | 1800 | 2030 | 2200 | 2300 | 2400 | 0030 | 0100 | 0300 |
| 0400 | 0500 | 0600 | 0700 | 0800 | 0900 | 1000 | 1100 | 1200 | 1500 | 1600 | 1700 | 1800 | 1900 | 2130 | 2300 | 2400 | 0100 | 0130 | 0200 | 0400 |
| 0500 | 0600 | 0700 | 0800 | 0900 | 1000 | 1100 | 1200 | 1300 | 1600 | 1700 | 1800 | 1900 | 2000 | 2230 | 2400 | 0100 | 0200 | 0230 | 0300 | 0500 |

Note: This chart is for planning purposes only, as local times may vary from the above due to local conditions, such as Daylight Savings Time, etc. For exact local times, consult DoD Foreign Clearance Guide, DoT Flight Information Publication or Air Almanac.

# APPENDIX F
# JULIAN DATE CALENDARS AND MILITARY (24-HOUR) CLOCK

**Julian Date Calendar:** The following tables will be used to convert the Gregorian (official United States Commerce Calendar) calendar dates to a three numerical digit Julian Date. The first Julian Date Calendar table is a perpetual calendar for all years except leap years. The second Julian Date Calendar table is a perpetual calendar for leap years only, such as 2000, 2004, 2008, etc.

**How to use Julian Date Calendars:** The calendars are constructed in a matrix with the days of the month in the left hand column from 1 through 31. The months are displayed in rows from left to right starting with January and continuing through each month to December on the extreme right.

**Example:** If you made an application for space available travel on 15 April 2000 (a leap year), go to the lower table for leap years and read down the date column to 15 and across to the right to April where you find the number 106, or the 106th day in the Julian Date Calendar. If this were not a leap year, i.e. 15 April 2001, check the number in the non-leap year calendar—it would be the 105th day. Please try to convert some sample dates (birthdays, holidays, etc.) until you are comfortable using this system.

The entire Julian Date is constructed using the last two digits of the calendar year, i.e., 2000 is 00, 105 for 15 April. The last four digits of the Julian date are taken from the twenty-four hour clock, frequently known as the military clock, or time when the hour is a period of time equal to one twenty-fourth of a mean solar or civil day and equivalent to sixty minutes. The Julian Day is divided into a series of twenty-four hours from midnight to midnight. See the table on the next page.

Using the tables on the prior pages, along with the table below, if you are applying for Space-A air travel at 2:45pm on April 15, 2000, your complete Julian Date and time would be 00 106 1444 or the year 2000, 106th day 14th hour and 45th minute.(Note that 2000 is a leap year.)

## JULIAN DATE CALENDAR ENCODE/DECODE TABLE

| DAY | JAN | FEB | MAR | APR | MAY | JUN | JUL | AUG | SEP | OCT | NOV | DEC |
|---|---|---|---|---|---|---|---|---|---|---|---|---|
| 1 | 001 | 032 | 060 | 091 | 121 | 152 | 182 | 213 | 244 | 274 | 305 | 335 |
| 2 | 002 | 033 | 061 | 092 | 122 | 153 | 183 | 214 | 245 | 275 | 306 | 336 |
| 3 | 003 | 034 | 062 | 093 | 123 | 154 | 184 | 215 | 246 | 276 | 307 | 337 |
| 4 | 004 | 035 | 063 | 094 | 124 | 155 | 185 | 216 | 247 | 277 | 308 | 338 |
| 5 | 005 | 036 | 064 | 095 | 125 | 156 | 186 | 217 | 248 | 278 | 309 | 339 |
| 6 | 006 | 037 | 065 | 096 | 126 | 157 | 187 | 218 | 249 | 279 | 310 | 340 |
| 7 | 007 | 038 | 066 | 097 | 127 | 158 | 188 | 219 | 250 | 280 | 311 | 341 |
| 8 | 008 | 039 | 067 | 098 | 128 | 159 | 189 | 220 | 251 | 281 | 312 | 342 |
| 9 | 009 | 040 | 068 | 099 | 129 | 160 | 190 | 221 | 252 | 282 | 313 | 343 |
| 10 | 010 | 041 | 069 | 100 | 130 | 161 | 191 | 222 | 253 | 283 | 314 | 344 |
| 11 | 011 | 042 | 070 | 101 | 131 | 162 | 192 | 223 | 254 | 284 | 315 | 345 |
| 12 | 012 | 043 | 071 | 102 | 132 | 163 | 193 | 224 | 255 | 285 | 316 | 346 |
| 13 | 013 | 044 | 072 | 103 | 133 | 164 | 194 | 225 | 256 | 286 | 317 | 347 |
| 14 | 014 | 045 | 073 | 104 | 134 | 165 | 195 | 226 | 257 | 287 | 318 | 348 |
| 15 | 015 | 046 | 074 | 105 | 135 | 166 | 196 | 227 | 258 | 288 | 319 | 349 |
| 16 | 016 | 047 | 075 | 106 | 136 | 167 | 197 | 228 | 259 | 289 | 320 | 350 |
| 17 | 017 | 048 | 076 | 107 | 137 | 168 | 198 | 229 | 260 | 290 | 321 | 351 |
| 18 | 018 | 049 | 077 | 108 | 138 | 169 | 199 | 230 | 261 | 291 | 322 | 352 |
| 19 | 019 | 050 | 078 | 109 | 139 | 170 | 200 | 231 | 262 | 292 | 323 | 353 |
| 20 | 020 | 051 | 079 | 110 | 140 | 171 | 201 | 232 | 263 | 293 | 324 | 354 |
| 21 | 021 | 052 | 080 | 111 | 141 | 172 | 202 | 233 | 264 | 294 | 325 | 355 |
| 22 | 022 | 053 | 081 | 112 | 142 | 173 | 203 | 234 | 265 | 295 | 326 | 356 |
| 23 | 023 | 054 | 082 | 113 | 143 | 174 | 204 | 235 | 266 | 296 | 327 | 357 |
| 24 | 024 | 055 | 083 | 114 | 144 | 175 | 205 | 236 | 267 | 297 | 328 | 358 |
| 25 | 025 | 056 | 084 | 115 | 145 | 176 | 206 | 237 | 268 | 298 | 329 | 359 |
| 26 | 026 | 057 | 085 | 116 | 146 | 177 | 207 | 238 | 269 | 299 | 330 | 360 |
| 27 | 027 | 058 | 086 | 117 | 147 | 178 | 208 | 239 | 270 | 300 | 331 | 361 |
| 28 | 028 | 059 | 087 | 118 | 148 | 179 | 209 | 240 | 271 | 301 | 332 | 362 |
| 29 | 029 | | 088 | 119 | 149 | 180 | 210 | 241 | 272 | 302 | 333 | 363 |
| 30 | 030 | | 089 | 120 | 150 | 181 | 211 | 242 | 273 | 303 | 334 | 364 |
| 31 | 031 | | 090 | | 151 | | 212 | 243 | | 304 | | 365 |

## TWENTY-FOUR HOUR CLOCK/ MILITARY TIME

| Conventional Clock | Military Clock |
|---|---|
| midnight 12am | 2400 hours |
| 1am | 0100 hours |
| 2am | 0200 hours |
| 3am | 0300 hours |
| 4am | 0400 hours |
| 5am | 0500 hours |
| 6am | 0600 hours |
| 7am | 0700 hours |
| 8am | 0800 hours |
| 9am | 0900 hours |
| 10am | 1000 hours |
| 11am | 1100 hours |
| noon 12pm | 1200 hours |
| 1pm | 1300 hours |
| 2pm | 1400 hours |
| 3pm | 1500 hours |
| 4pm | 1600 hours |
| 5pm | 1700 hours |
| 6pm | 1800 hours |
| 7pm | 1900 hours |
| 8pm | 2000 hours |
| 9pm | 2100 hours |
| 10pm | 2200 hours |
| 11pm | 2300 hours |

## JULIAN DATE LEAP YEAR CALENDAR ENCODE/DECODE TABLE

| DAY | JAN | FEB | MAR | APR | MAY | JUN | JUL | AUG | SEP | OCT | NOV | DEC |
|---|---|---|---|---|---|---|---|---|---|---|---|---|
| 1 | 001 | 032 | 061 | 092 | 122 | 153 | 183 | 214 | 245 | 275 | 306 | 336 |
| 2 | 002 | 033 | 062 | 093 | 123 | 154 | 184 | 215 | 246 | 276 | 307 | 337 |
| 3 | 003 | 034 | 063 | 094 | 124 | 155 | 185 | 216 | 247 | 277 | 308 | 338 |
| 4 | 004 | 035 | 064 | 095 | 125 | 156 | 186 | 217 | 248 | 278 | 309 | 339 |
| 5 | 005 | 036 | 065 | 096 | 126 | 157 | 187 | 218 | 249 | 279 | 310 | 340 |
| 6 | 006 | 037 | 066 | 097 | 127 | 158 | 188 | 219 | 250 | 280 | 311 | 341 |
| 7 | 007 | 038 | 067 | 098 | 128 | 159 | 189 | 220 | 251 | 281 | 312 | 342 |
| 8 | 008 | 039 | 068 | 099 | 129 | 160 | 190 | 221 | 252 | 282 | 313 | 343 |
| 9 | 009 | 040 | 069 | 100 | 130 | 161 | 191 | 222 | 253 | 283 | 314 | 344 |
| 10 | 010 | 041 | 070 | 101 | 131 | 162 | 192 | 223 | 254 | 284 | 315 | 345 |
| 11 | 011 | 042 | 071 | 102 | 132 | 163 | 193 | 224 | 255 | 285 | 316 | 346 |
| 12 | 012 | 043 | 072 | 103 | 133 | 164 | 194 | 225 | 256 | 286 | 317 | 347 |
| 13 | 013 | 044 | 073 | 104 | 134 | 165 | 195 | 226 | 257 | 287 | 318 | 348 |
| 14 | 014 | 045 | 074 | 105 | 135 | 166 | 196 | 227 | 258 | 288 | 319 | 349 |
| 15 | 015 | 046 | 075 | 106 | 136 | 167 | 197 | 228 | 259 | 289 | 320 | 350 |
| 16 | 016 | 047 | 076 | 107 | 137 | 168 | 198 | 229 | 260 | 290 | 321 | 351 |
| 17 | 017 | 048 | 077 | 108 | 138 | 169 | 199 | 230 | 261 | 291 | 322 | 352 |
| 18 | 018 | 049 | 078 | 109 | 139 | 170 | 200 | 231 | 262 | 292 | 323 | 353 |
| 19 | 019 | 050 | 079 | 110 | 140 | 171 | 201 | 232 | 263 | 293 | 324 | 354 |
| 20 | 020 | 051 | 080 | 111 | 141 | 172 | 202 | 233 | 264 | 294 | 325 | 355 |
| 21 | 021 | 052 | 081 | 112 | 142 | 173 | 203 | 234 | 265 | 295 | 326 | 356 |
| 22 | 022 | 053 | 082 | 113 | 143 | 174 | 204 | 235 | 266 | 296 | 327 | 357 |
| 23 | 023 | 054 | 083 | 114 | 144 | 175 | 205 | 236 | 267 | 297 | 328 | 358 |
| 24 | 024 | 055 | 084 | 115 | 145 | 176 | 206 | 237 | 268 | 298 | 329 | 359 |
| 25 | 025 | 056 | 085 | 116 | 146 | 177 | 207 | 238 | 269 | 299 | 330 | 360 |
| 26 | 026 | 057 | 086 | 117 | 147 | 178 | 208 | 239 | 270 | 300 | 331 | 361 |
| 27 | 027 | 058 | 087 | 118 | 148 | 179 | 209 | 240 | 271 | 301 | 332 | 362 |
| 28 | 028 | 059 | 088 | 119 | 149 | 180 | 210 | 241 | 272 | 302 | 333 | 363 |
| 29 | 029 | 060 | 089 | 120 | 150 | 181 | 211 | 242 | 273 | 303 | 334 | 364 |
| 30 | 030 | | 090 | 121 | 151 | 182 | 212 | 243 | 274 | 304 | 335 | 365 |
| 31 | 031 | | 091 | | 152 | | 213 | 244 | | 305 | | 366 |

# APPENDIX G
## PROCEDURES FOR REMOTE SPACE-A TRAVEL SIGN-UP AND ONE-TIME SIGN-UP
### (USE AMC FORM 140, FEB 95 APPENDIX H)

The Assistant Secretary of Defense (OSDUSD-TP), gave approval to USCINCTRANS on 30 March 1994 to implement remote sign-up for Space-available (Space-A) travel and sought service headquarters planned implementation instructions/guidelines. The following (summarized) procedures for this initiative became effective 1 July 1994.

**1. ACTIVE DUTY MEMBERS OF THE SEVEN UNIFORMED SERVICES:**

A. Fax a copy of the applicable service leave (or pass) **(OF Form 988, DA Form 31, NAVCOMP 3065 and NAVMC 3) and other service leave (or pass) forms from USCG, USPH and NOAA or use AMC Form 140, Feb 95 (Appendix H).**

B. A statement that required border clearance documents are current, i.e., I.D. cards for sponsor and eligible dependents (family members); passports for sponsor (if required) and dependents (family members); visas for sponsor and dependents (family members) and immunizations (PHS-731, I. International Certificates of Vaccination and II. Personal Health History), as required for all travelers.

C. A list of five desired country destinations (5th may be "ALL" to take advantage of opportune airlift).

D. The fax should be sent on the effective date of leave (or pass): **Therefore, the fax header will establish the basis for date/time of sign-up.**

E. Members will remain on the Space-A travel register for a period of 60 days or upon expiration of leave (or pass), whichever is sooner. As an option the Services (USA, USN, USMC, USCG, USAF, USPH, NOAA) may designate a central point of contact to assist members by answering basic questions and ensuring information is correct to minimize delayed sign-up. (NOTE: none have been so designated.)

F. Mail (United States Postal Service) and Courier (Base/Installation official distribution) entries will be permitted. The Air Mobility Command (AMC) has indicated that commercial courier/delivery services such as United Parcel Service (UPS), Federal Express (FEDEX), and e-mail on the worldwide web (where available) are acceptable media for filing your application for Space-A air travel. Upon receipt, the service leave (or pass) form can then be stamped with the current date/time (please keep in mind that mail on military installations goes through distribution channels and may take longer than normal mail). NOTE: Active duty members on pass may utilize this enhancement. Fax a request indicating desired destination, name, rank and inclusive dates of pass.

**2. ACTIVE STATUS MEMBERS OF THE RESERVE COMPONENTS:**

A. Fax a current copy of their DD Form 1853, **"Authentication of Reserve Status For Travel Eligibility" and use AMC Form 140, Feb 95.**

B. A statement that border clearance documents are current, if applicable for United States possessions.

C. A list of five desired destinations (no foreign country destinations; 5th destination may be "ALL" to take advantage of opportune airlift).

D. Active Status members will remain on the Space-A register for a period of 60 days. NOTE: Active Status members of the Reserve components may only register for travel to/from the CONUS and Alaska, Hawaii, Puerto Rico, the U.S. Virgin Islands, American Samoa and Guam. **Dependents (family members) of an Active Status Reservist do not have a Space-Available travel eligibility.**

E. Mail and Courier entries will be permitted. Upon receipt the DD Form 1853 can then be stamped with the current date/time (please keep in mind, mail on military installations goes through distribution channels and may take longer than normal mail).

**3. ELIGIBLE RETIRED MEMBERS OF THE SEVEN UNIFORMED SERVICES:**

A. Fax a request to the desired aerial port(s) (station) of departure giving five desired destinations (5th destination may be "ALL" to take advantage of opportune airlift). **The fax data/time header will be the basis for the date/time of Space-A travel sign-up, or use AMC Form 140, Feb 95.**

B. Retirees may remain on the Space-A travel register for a period of 60 days.

C. Mail, e-mail and courier entries will be permitted. Upon receipt the request can be stamped with the current date/time (please keep in mind that mail on military bases goes through distribution channels and may take longer than normal mail).

**4. MEMBERS OF THE RESERVE COMPONENTS (GRAY AREA RETIREES) WHO HAVE RECEIVED NOTIFICATION OF RETIREMENT ELIGIBILITY BUT HAVE NOT YET REACHED AGE 60:**

A. These members are limited to the same travel destinations as Active Status Reserve Members. Dependents (family members) of these Reservists do not have a Space-Available travel eligibility. Use AMC Form 140, Feb 95.

5. This Book has a list of AMC Terminals (Stations) having the best capability of providing Space-A travel. Units listed in USAF, AMCP 76-4 will also provide remote Space-A travel sign-up. The Services (other than USAF/AMC, USA, USN, USMC, USCG and other USAF) are requested to augment this listing with their Base/Installation manifesting agencies capable of providing this service. **NOTE: Remote Space-A travel sign-up is the sole responsibility of each member unless a (Uniformed) Service designates a single Point of Contact (POC) for a specific installation. Uniformed Services have not designated single POCs.**

6. Please note that **worldwide Space-A sign-up in person and at self-service counters remains available at Services terminals and stations which operate Space-A registers.** Times available for registration in person are based on local operating hours.

**ONE-TIME SIGN-UP FOR SPACE-AVAILABLE PASSENGERS**

Passengers traveling Space-A on military and contract charter aircraft **now can retain their initial date/time (Julian date) of sign-up when traveling through more than one destination/station (traveling in the same general direction, i.e., east to west, north to south) to reach their final destination.** The new procedure is the result of a recommendation made by the U.S. Air Force's Air Mobility Command (AMC) and approved by the Assistant Under Secretary of Defense.

In the past, travelers received a new sign-up date at each stop on their way to their final destination, which caused some to say that those stationed or living at or in the vicinity of the en route location had an unfair advantage. **Under the new rules, passengers still are required to sign up at all en route stops, but they keep their date and time of sign-up from their originating location.** For example a passenger who originates his/her travel at Incirlik AB (ADA), TR to Rhein-Main AB (FRF), DE, and plans to continue straight through to CONUS, will get priority over people starting their flights at Rhein-Main AB, DE.

The process is not automatic. Passengers must still sign up at all stops to continue their Space-A flights and retain their original sign-up date. However, passengers receive an "in transit" stamp on their travel order or boarding pass indicating date, time and location where they entered the system. This stamp identifies en route travelers to terminal personnel and gives the travelers priority on subsequent flights.

*Ed's Note: Message from HQ AMC Scott AFB, FL//DOJP//, R 51515Z Aug 96- -paragraph 1-D "One-time Space-Available sign-up. We continue to receive inquiries on this subject. Apparently, some passenger terminals have procedures to honor other terminals' date/time of sign-up for passengers who do not arrive in-transit on DoD aircraft. This is a misapplication of the one-time sign-up rules. Unless arriving your station via DoD aircraft, passengers desiring Space-Available transportation must sign up with a new date/time of sign-up in person or use established remote means, i.e,. fax or e-mail. **We are exploring future implementation of a one-time/round-trip Space-A sign-up. We will be soliciting your input in the near future. Until then, all passenger terminals must consistently follow current guidance."***

There are restrictions. **Passengers traveling (hopping) by Space-A air through terminals/bases for extended visits will lose their transient status.** For example, if the above passenger gets to Rhein-Main, AB, DE and takes six days of leave/pass/vacation there, he/she will get a new date and time for his next Space-A flight.

# APPENDIX H
## SPACE-A TRAVEL REQUEST

<table>
<tr><td colspan="2">

## SPACE AVAILABLE TRAVEL REQUEST
*(This form is affected by the Privacy Act of 1974-See below)*

</td><td>

*INSERT HERE*

</td></tr>
<tr><td colspan="2">

This information is required for space available travel registration. Upon completion, place the upper right corner of this form, and the back of your leave form into the Date/Time validator. Be sure to deposit one copy of this request into the box; retain carbon copy for the Space Available roll call. Space A sign-up is good for a 60-day period, or when your leave expires, whichever comes first. For facsimile (fax) requests, telefax header will establish date/time of sign-up.

### PLEASE PRINT CLEARLY

**1. NAME** *(Last, First, MI)*

</td><td></td></tr>
</table>

**2. RANK/GRADE**

**3. SSN**

**4. SEATS REQUIRED**

**5. TRAVEL STATUS** *(Type of Leave)*

CATEGORY I -- Civ or Mil Dependent on Emergency Leave

CATEGORY II -- Environmental Morale Leave (EML)

CATEGORY III -- Active Duty on Ordinary Leave / House Hunting

CATEGORY IV -- (EML) Unaccompanied Dependents

CATEGORY V -- Permissive TDY or TAD / Student Travel

CATEGORY VI -- Retired Military / Reserves

FOR OVERSEAS TRAVEL:

Border Clearance Documents Current?

[ ] YES   [ ] NO

(See Appendix B)

**6. SERVICE:** | ARMY | NAVY | AF | MARINES | OTHER

**7. DATE LEAVE BEGINS** *(Active Duty Only)*

**8. DATE LEAVE ENDS** *(if extended, you must notify us before this date)*

**9. COUNTRY CHOICES** *(List up to 5; one choice may be all)*

**10. LIST NAMES OF DEPENDENTS TRAVELING AND TYPE OF PASSPORT** *(US or Foreign)*

**11. I CERTIFY THAT I AM ON LEAVE OR PASS STATUS AT THE TIME I REGISTER FOR SPACE AVAILABLE TRAVEL AND WILL REMAIN IN SUCH STATUS WHEN AWAITING AND/OR HAVE BEEN ACCEPTED FOR SPACE AVAILABLE TRAVEL. IF ACCOMPANIED BY DEPENDENTS, I FURTHER CERTIFY THAT MY TRAVEL IS NOT IN CONJUNCTION WITH TDY/TAD AND THAT I AM NOT USING SPACE AVAILABLE TRAVEL TO TRANSPORT MY DEPENDENTS TO OR FROM MY RESTRICTED DUTY STATION OF ALL OTHERS (UNACCOMPANIED) TOUR LOCATION STATION. I CERTIFY THAT MY REQUEST FOR, AND ACCEPTANCE OF, TRANSPORTATION VIA DOD-OWNED OR CONTROLLED AIRCRAFT IS NOT FOR PERSONAL GAIN, NOR FOR, OR IN CONNECTION WITH BUSINESS OF ANY NATURE AND THAT THIS TRIP WILL NOT RESULT IN ANY FORM OF RENUMERATION TO MYSELF OR TO MY FAMILY. I UNDERSTAND VIOLATION OF ANY OF THE ABOVE COULD RESULT IN BILLING AND/OR PUNITIVE ACTION.**

**12. DATE**

**13. SIGNATURE**

### PRIVACY ACT STATEMENT

AUTHORITY:  10 U.S.C. 8013; EO 9397, 22 November 1943.

PRINCIPAL PURPOSE:  To apply for air travel.  SSN is needed for positive ID.

ROUTINE USE(S):  Records from this system of records may be disclosed for any of the blanket routine uses published by the Air Force.

DISCLOSURE IS VOLUNTARY:  Failure to proved the information may result in member not being accepted for travel on military aircraft.  Disclosure of SSN is voluntary.

**AMC FORM 140, FEB 95** *(EF) (PerFORM PRO)*                    **PASSENGER COPY**

# APPENDIX I
# RESERVIST SPACE-A TRAVEL/
## VERIFICATION OF RESERVE STATUS FOR TRAVEL ELIGIBILITY (DD FORM 1853)

### RESERVISTS NOW AUTHORIZED TO TRAVEL IN A SPACE-REQUIRED STATUS
### FOR INACTIVE DUTY TRAINING WORLDWIDE

SCOTT AIR FORCE BASE, III–U.S. Transportation Command announced here today an expansion of space-required travel options for reservists traveling for inactive duty training (IDT) worldwide.

Based on the recently enacted Public law 106-65, in the Department of Defense Authorization act, members can now travel on DOD aircraft worldwide in a space required status from their home to their authorized IDT assembly, when performing IDT training.

The travel eligibility is nonchargeable if the member moves on DOD aircraft. This change will be incorporated in the next update of DOD 4515.13-R (Air Transportation Eligibility).

Seat reservations can be made 30 days in advance of travel for certain destinations. Reserve members must provide written authorization for travel. All charges above and beyond the seat tariff rate are the responsibility of the member (head tax, excess baggage, federal inspection fees, meal charges, etc.).

Individuals cannot use this travel in conjuction with man-days and annual tours.

For more information, members should contact their local reserve unit advisor. The USTRANSCOM point of contact is Patti Hutt, (618)229-1985 or DSN 779-1985. The Air Mobility Command point of contact is Cindy Rothenbach, (618) 229-4592 or DSN 779-4592.

| **VERIFICATION OF RESERVE STATUS FOR TRAVEL ELIGIBILITY**<br>(Part B may be completed by the requester's commander, First Sergeant, or a DoD personnel official with access to the Personnel Data System.) | 1. Date Prepared<br>(YYMMMDD)<br>94 Nov 10 |
|---|---|

**PRIVACY ACT STATEMENT**

AUTHORITY:  10 USC 8102, 44 USC 3101 and EO 9397.
PRINCIPAL PURPOSE: Use of your SSN is necessary to positively identify you.
ROUTINE USE: Used by Reserve personnel to verify eligibility for space available transportation on DoD-owned or controlled aircraft.
DISCLOSURE: Voluntary; however, failure to disclose will prevent the applicant from traveling on a DoD-owned or controlled aircraft.

**PART A - TO BE COMPLETED BY APPLICANT**

| 2. NAME (*Last, First, Middle Initial*)<br>Smith, John C. | 3. PAY GRADE<br>E-3 | 4. BRANCH OF SERVICE<br>USAFR | 5. SSN<br>123-45-6789 |
|---|---|---|---|
| 6. UNIT/COMMAND NAME<br>459 APS | | 7. UNIT COMMAND ADDRESS<br>Andrews AFB, MD 20331 | |
| 8. SIGNATURE | | 9. DATE SIGNED (YYMMMDD) | |

**PART B - TO BE COMPLETED BY VERIFYING OFFICIAL**

The Reservist named above is an active reserve component member and is eligible for space available transportation on DoD-owned or controlled aircraft in accordance with DoD Regulation 4515.13-R, and is authorized to so travel (*not to exceed six months*).

| 10. FROM (*YYMMMDD*)　　95 NOV 10 | 11. TO (*YYMMMDD*)　　96 JAN 10 | |
|---|---|---|
| 12. NAME OF VERIFYING OFFICIAL<br>Jones, Jane M. | 13. PAY GRADE<br>0-5 | 14. TITLE<br>Commander |
| 15. ORGANIZATION<br>459 APS | 16. SIGNATURE | 17. DATE SIGNED (*YYMMMDD*)<br>95 NOV 10 |

DD FORM 1853, AUG 94　　　　　　PREVIOUS EDITIONS MAY BE USED.

## Travel Notes

# APPENDIX J
## SAMPLE WEB SIGN-UP FORM
## MacDill Air Force Base
## Tampa Bay, Florida
## Online Travel Request Sample

You may be able to sign up for Space-A via the Web. Here is a typical Web signup form.

---

### *Important Notes*

YOUR LEAVE MUST HAVE ALREADY STARTED WHEN THIS FORM IS SENT OR YOU WILL NOT BE SIGNED UP FOR SPACE-A TRAVEL. WE CANNOT HOLD REQUESTS.

**Keep the PRINTED automated reply as your proof of sign-up.**

---

***All fields are required***

Last Name:　　　　　　　First Name:　　　　　　　SSN:

***Please provide the following in case we need to contact you.***

Email Address:　　　　　　Home Phone:　　　　　　Duty Phone:

Travel Category:　　　　　　　　　　　　Branch of Service:　　Rank:

1 - Civilian or Military Dependent on Emergency leave ▼　　　Marines ▼　　E1 ▼

Date Leave begins *(Active Duty only)*:　　　Date Leave ends *(Active Duty only)*:

Country Choices *(up to five choices; one may be all)*:　　　Seats required:

1 One ▼

List full names of dependents traveling and their passport types *(e.g. US, UK)*:

Additional Notes or Comments:

**By submitting this form you certify that you are on leave or pass status at the time you register for space-available travel and remain in such status when awaiting and/or have been accepted for space-available travel. If accompanied by dependents, you further certify that your travel is not in conjunction with TDY/TAD and that you are not using space-available travel to transport dependents to or from a restricted duty station or all others (unaccompanied) tour location station. You certify that your request for, and acceptance of, transportation via DoD-owned or controlled aircraft is not for personal gain, nor for, or in connection with business of any nature and that this trip will not result in any form of renumeration to oneself or one's family. Understand violation of any of the above could result in billing and/or punitive action.**

**PRIVACY ACT STATEMENT AUTHORITY 10 U.S.C.**
B013; EO 8397, 22 November 1943.
PRINCIPAL PURPOSE: To apply for air travel, SSN is needed for positive ID.
ROUTINE USE(S): Records from this system of records may be disclosed for any of the blanket routine uses published by the airforce.
DISCLOSURE IS VOLUNTARY: Failure to provide the information may result in not being accepted for travel on military aircraft. Disclosure of SSN is voluntary.

SUBMIT

# APPENDIX K
## BAGGAGE ID, AIR PASSENGER COMMENT AND BOARDING PASS/TICKET RECEIPT STANDARD FORMS

### BAGGAGE IDENTIFICATION
**(DD Form 1839, AMC Form 20-ID, and USAF Form 94)**

This baggage identification tag, and others, are used to identify checked and cabin luggage.

| BAGGAGE IDENTIFICATION |
| --- |
| NAME *(Last, First, M.I.)* |
| STREET ADDRESS *(Home or Unit / APO)* |
| CITY, STATE AND ZIP CODE |
| DD    FORM    1839    USE PREVIOUS EDITION. 80 SEP |

| FOLD HERE    AND TUCK UNDER FLAP | |
| --- | --- |
| PRINT NAME *(Last, First, Middle Initial)* | ADDRESS *(Unit / New Station)* |
| CITY/BASE | STATE |
| ZIP CODE | TELEPHONE NUMBER (COMMERCIAL/AUTOVON) |

AMC FORM 20-ID, DEC 92

### AIR PASSENGER COMMENTS
**(AMC Form 253)**

As a Space-A passenger you are encouraged to use this (or similar) form to report positive and negative information to managers of the system who are in a position to correct deficiencies and/or reward outstanding performance of duty. You may also be requested to participate in AMC Passengers Surveys from time to time (AMC Form 22 APR 96). (Form size adjusted to fit on this page; actual size is larger.) *Please send a courtesy copy of your comments to: Military Living's **R&R Travel News®**, PO Box 2347, Falls Church, VA 22042-0347.*

**AIR PASSENGER COMMENTS**

Please provide a copy to terminal management by placing in the slot marked for Squadron/Port Operations Officer. Terminal addresses are listed on the reverse in case you desire to mail your comments to a terminal you have passed through. Your comments to Squadron/Port Operations Officers will let them take immediate action. If you feel we need to know about a particular item, send a copy of your comments to us:

HQ Air Mobility Command/DOJP
402 Scott Drive Unit 3A1
Scott AFB, IL 62225-5302

**COMMENTS**

To assist us, please provide the following information when applicable.

| NAME *(Last, First, M.I.)* *(Optional)* | GRADE *(Optional)* | DUTY ADDRESS *(Optional)* | DUTY PHONE *(Optional)* |
| --- | --- | --- | --- |
| FLIGHT NUMBER | DEPARTING FROM | DESTINATION | DATE FORM PREPARED *(Day, Month, Year)* |

**AMC FORM 253, MAR 95 (EF) (PerFORM PRO)**    PREVIOUS EDITION IS OBSOLETE

## BOARDING PASS/TICKET RECEIPT
### (AMC FORM 148/2)

This or similar form will be used to record boarding, baggage, meals and other charges.

| AMC- | BOARDING PASS/TICKET | | | | | AMC- |
| --- | --- | --- | --- | --- | --- | --- |
| NAME *(Last, First, Middle)* | FLIGHT NO | GATE | BOARDING TIME | SEAT NO. | TAX/INSP FEE | FLIGHT CODE/DATE |
| DESTINATION | DEPARTURE DATE | | MEAL *(Kind / Type / Quantity)* | | MEAL COST | SEAT NO |
| VIA | BAG WGT/PIECES | | EXCESS WEIGHT | | BAGGAGE COST | AGENT NUMBER |
| ORIGIN | REMARKS | | | | OTHER COSTS | CASH COLLECTED |
| CARRIER | REASON/DATE OF REFUND | | | | TOTAL | FROM |
| AGENT | SIGNATURE | PASSENGER SIGNATURE | | | FINAL DEST | TO |

AMC FORM 148, JUN 96    PREVIOUS EDITIONS ARE OBSOLETE

# APPENDIX L
## IN-FLIGHT FOOD SERVICE, AIR MOBILITY COMMAND (AMC)

No matter where you travel throughout the Air Mobility Command (AMC), you will find totally different, greatly improved flight meals. Flight menus have traditionally lacked variety, quality and overall customer appeal. An exciting new in-flight food services program has been developed by the AMC Food Services Branch. The program was established to improve the quality, nutritional content, packaging and presentation of flight meals within AMC.

Improvements to the food service program include the addition of "Healthy Heart" and breakfast menus, the exclusive use of deli meats, fresh fruits and vegetables, pasta salads, fruit cups, one-percent milk, cholesterol-free snacks, and whole wheat bread. "Junk food" items high in fats and sodium, such as candies and cream-filled pastries, are no longer served.

This food service and the in-flight kitchens that produce it are positioned throughout the world. All passengers ordering in-flight meals, even from Space-A terminals in exotic locales, will experience the same high-quality and nutritious food AMC now provides.

Following are some sample menus available on AMC flights. In-flight menu prices are established at the beginning of each fiscal year (1 October) and may vary at different locations.

The following are the FY2001 charges for flight meals and snacks: For all Space-A passengers (except dependents of enlisted personnel in the pay grades of E-1 through E-4); $3.20 for lunch and/or dinner; $1.30 for breakfast, and $1.65 for snacks. Space-A travelers who are dependents of enlisted personnel in the pay grades of E-1 through E-4 and all duty passengers: $2.65 for lunch/dinner; $1.30 for breakfast, and $1.65 for snacks.

### COMPONENTS OF CORE FLIGHT MEALS

| ITEM | CALORIES | FAT GRAMS |
| --- | --- | --- |
| Grilled Chicken Sandwich | 225 | 07.07 |
| Yogurt, Non Fat, Fruited | 100 | 00.00 |
| Banana, One Medium | 080 | 00.60 |
| Grapes, Fresh, One Cup | 058 | 00.30 |
| Gingersnaps, Five Cookies | 100 | 03.00 |
| Juice, Orange, 6 Ounces | 060 | 00.00 |
| Soda, Diet | 000 | 00.00 |
| Vegetable Tray, Carrot Sticks, Celery Sticks, Radishes (3), Spring Onion (2) | 025 | 00.27 |
| Chewing Gum, sugar Free | 000 | 00.00 |
| Hard Candy Mint, 1 Piece | 006 | 00.00 |
| Total: | 654 | 11.24 (15%) |

### ALTERNATIVE SANDWICHES
1. Three ounces of deli meat (1 gram of fat or less) sandwich on submarine, hamburger, wheat bread.
2. Three ounce tuna salad with fat free salad dressing on wheat, rye, or roll.
3. Three ounce tuna packed in water with two packages saltine crackers, vegetarian pita bread sandwich.

### ALTERNATIVES FOR THE MILK GROUP
1. One percent white milk    2. One percent chocolate milk 3. Skim milk

### ALTERNATIVES FOR THE FRUIT GROUP
1. Apple, pear, orange    2. One cup of cut fruit such as watermelon, cantaloupe, honeydew melon
3. One half cup of canned fruit such as peaches, fruit cocktail.

### ALTERNATIVES FOR THE DESSERT GROUP
1. Fig Newtons, 2 bars    2. Raisins, 1.5 ounce container
3. Pretzels, 1 ounce bag.

### ALTERNATIVES FOR THE JUICE GROUP
1. Orange    2. Apple    3.Cranapple    4. Tomato

### ALTERNATIVES FOR THE BEVERAGE GROUP
1. Diet Sodas    2. Carbonated Water    3. Noncarbonated Water

### OTHER ALTERNATIVES FOR MEAL COMPONENTS
1. Sugar-Free Gum
2. Salad with Fat-Free Dressing in place of the Vegetable Tray
3. Sugar-Free Hard Candy in place of the Candy Mint

### RECIPES FOR MANDATORY FLIGHT SANDWICHES

**MENU 1:** Flight Deli Turkey Sandwich, NSN 8905-01-388-1166. Turkey, 3 ounce; shaved deli style, one gram of fat or less per ounce. Lettuce leaves, fresh trimmed, tomato sliced onion, thinly sliced bread, white or whole wheat, salad dressing, fat-free, individual packet, one ounce condiments & accessory pack. Variation: Jalapeno jelly in place of salad dressing, alfalfa sprouts in addition to lettuce for variation.

**MENU 2:** Flight Deli Ham Sandwich, NSN 8905-01-388-1668. Ham, 3 ounces, shaved deli style, one gram of fat or less per ounce. Lettuce leaves, fresh trimmed, tomato sliced onion, thinly sliced bread, dark, rye, white or whole wheat, honey mustard, two individual packs condiments & accessory pack. Variation: Jalapeno jelly or fat-free salad dressing. Alfalfa sprouts in addition to lettuce for variation.

**MENU 3:** Flight Deli Roast Beef Sandwich, NSN 8905-01-388-1668. Roast beef, 3 ounces, shaved deli style, one gram of fat or less per ounce. Lettuce leaves, fresh trimmed tomato sliced onion, thinly sliced bread, white or whole wheat, horseradish, individual packet condiments & accessory pack. Variation: Mustard in place of horseradish and/or fat-free salad dressing. Alfalfa sprouts in addition to lettuce for variation.

**MENU 4:** Flight Boneless Skinless Chicken Breast Sandwich, NSN 8905-01-388-1360. Broiled, boneless, skinless, chicken breast, 3 ounce. Lettuce leaves, fresh trimmed tomato sliced onion, thinly sliced. Salad dressing, fat free, individual packet, one ounce mustard, individual packet, 5/16 ounce roll, hamburger, whole wheat condiments & accessory pack. Variation: 1000 Island salad dressing, fat-free, in place of salad dressing, fat-free and mustard.

**MENU 5:** Flight Tuna Salad Sandwich, NSN 8905-00-267-0040. Tuna, water-packed, 3 ounce. Onions chopped, celery, diced relish, pickle, sweet juice, lemon salad dressing, fat-free. Lettuce, fresh trimmed, bread, whole wheat or rye. Variation: NSN 8915-01-392-8285 Tuna, water-packed, canned, 3 ounce. Fat-free salad dressing, individual packet, one ounce relish, sweet pickle, individual packet, 5/16 ounce disposable bowl, disposable spoon. Saltine crackers, 4 individual packet, one ounce condiments & accessory pack.

**MENU 6:** Flight Vegetarian Pita Sandwich, 8905-01-069-6664. Cheese, cheddar, reduced fat, two ounce alfalfa sprouts, carrots, shredded cucumbers, sliced mushrooms, peppers, green, sliced, Italian dressing, fat free, individual packet, one ounce condiments & accessory pack.

**The following optional components are provided to develop the flight feeding menu:**

**SANDWICH MEALS AT 65% OF THE BASIC DAILY FOOD ALLOWANCE (BDFA)**

Turkey and American Cheese Hoagie
Turkey, Ham and Swiss Cheese Hoagie
Ham and Roast Beef Hoagie
Ham and American Cheese Hoagie
Roast Beef and Swiss on Whole Wheat
Ham, Corned Beef and American Cheese on Whole Wheat
Ham and Swiss Cheese on Rye
Turkey, Ham and American Cheese on whole Wheat
Ham and Provolone Cheese on a Croissant
Corned Beef and Swiss Cheese on Rye
Turkey on Whole Wheat
Roast Beef, Corned Beef and Provolone Cheese on Wheat
Ham, Roast Beef and American Cheese on a Kaiser Roll
Roast Beef, Pastrami and Provolone Cheese On Rye
Pastrami and Swiss cheese on a Kaiser Roll
Peanut Butter and Jelly on White or Wheat (2)
Tuna (unprepared) and Tomato with Wheat Pita Bread
Baked Turkey Fillet with a Dinner Roll
Baked Chicken and a Dinner Roll
Fried Chicken and a Dinner Roll
Turkey and Low Fat Cheese Hoagie on a Whole Wheat Bun
Baked Chicken on a Whole Wheat Bun

## SUPPLEMENT PACK OPTIONS

**A**
Fresh Fruit Cup
Vegetable Tray
Assorted Snack Items (low fat)
Elfin Loaf
Soft Drink and Juice
Condiments & Accessory Pack

**B**
Fresh Fruit/Fruit Cup
Marinated Vegetable Mix
Raisins
Apple Cinnamon Cookies
Soft Drink and Fruit Juice
Condiments & Accessory Pack

**C**
Cut Fruit, Fresh
Seashells &Vegetables
Assorted Snack Items (low fat)
Fruited Gelatin
1% Skim Milk and Juice
Condiments & Accessory Pack

**D**
Fresh Fruit/Fruit Cup
Tossed Salad with Crackers
Applesauce
Blueberry Muffin
1% Skim Milk, Fruit Juice (2)
Condiments & Accessory Pack

**E**
Fresh Fruit/Fruit Cup
Italian Vegetable Pasta
Raisins
Pudding Cup
Soft Drink and Fruit Juice
Condiments & Accessory Pack

**F**
Fresh Fruit/Fruit Cup
Rotini with Vegetables
Assorted Snack Items (low fat)
Orange Parfait Cup
1% Skim Milk, Fruit Juice (2)
Condiments & Accessory Pack

## HEALTHY SELECTION SNACK MEALS AT 30% OF THE BASIC DAILY FOOD ALLOWANCE (BDFA)

**A**
Chef Salad (Note 1)
Low-Fat Dressing
Fresh Fruit Cup
1% Skim Milk
Condiments & Accessory Pack

**B**
Baked chicken
Fresh Fruit Cup
Vegetable Tray
Vegetable Juice
Condiments & Accessory Pack

**C**
Turkey on Whole Wheat
Vegetable Tray
Applesauce
1% Skim Milk
Condiments & Accessory Pack

**D**
Tuna Unprepared and Tomato with Wheat Pita Bread
Salad Dressing
Vegetable Tray
Fruited Jello
Fruit Juice

**E**
Baked Turkey Breast
Fresh Fruit Cup
Crackers
Low-Fat Dressing
Fruit Juice

Note 1: Make chef Salad with turkey, chicken, and mozzarella cheese only! No Boiled egg or ham.

## SANDWICH MEAL BREAKFAST MENU

**A**
Ham and Swiss Cheese on a Croissant
Half Grapefruit, quartered
Raisins
Breakfast Cereal (2)
2 1/4 ounce Bran Muffin (2)
Yogurt
1% Skim Milk
Fruit Juice (2)
Condiments & Accessory Pack

**B**
Ham and Cheese on English Muffin
Small Orange quartered
Raisins
Breakfast Cereal (2)
2 1/4 ounce Bran Muffin
Yogurt
1% Skim Milk
Fruit Juice (2)
Condiments & Accessory Pack

## BREAKFAST SNACK MEALS AT 30% OF THE BASIC DAILY FOOD ALLOWANCE (BDFA)

**A**
Ham and American Cheese on a Croissant
Fruit Cup
1% Skim Milk
Condiments & Accessory Pack

**B**
Breakfast Cereal

Fruit Cup
Danish/Fruit Muffin
1% Skim Milk
Condiments & Accessory Pack

**C**
Ham & Swiss Cheese on a Bagel
Fruit Cup
1% Skim Milk
Condiments & Accessory Pack

## SNACK MEALS AT 30% OF THE BASIC DAILY FOOD ALLOWANCE (BDFA)

**A**
Fried or Baked Chicken
Vegetable Tray
Fresh Fruit Cup
1% Skim Milk
Condiments & Accessory Pack

**B**
Ham and Cheese on Wheat
Marinated Vegetables
Fruited Jello
Fruit Juice
Condiments & Accessory Pack

**C**
Turkey, Ham, Swiss on Whole Wheat
Rotini with Vegetables
Fresh Fruit Cup
1% Skim Milk
Condiments & Accessory Pack

**D**
Corned Beef and Swiss on Whole Wheat
Italian Vegetable Pasta Salad
Fresh Fruit Cup
1% Skim Milk
Condiments & Accessory Pack

**E**
Pastrami and Swiss on Kaiser Roll
Seashells with Vegetables
Fresh Fruit Cup
Soft Drink
Condiments & Accessory Pack

**F**
Roast Beef Hoagie
Marinated Vegetables
Fresh Fruit Cup
Fruit Juice
Condiments & Accessory Pack

## FROZEN MEALS

| NSN | ITEM | AVAILABLE FROM |
|---|---|---|
| 8970-01-316-1976 | Chicken Ala King | ConAgra Frozen Food |
| 8970-01-316-1974 | Salisbury Steak | Night Hawk Foods |
| 9870-01-316-1978 | Chicken Parmesan | ConAgra Frozen Food |
| 8970-01-316-1973 | Chopped, Formed Steak | Night Hawk Foods |
| 9870-01-316-1972 | Fillet of Chicken Breast (Healthy) | Night Hawk Foods |
| 9870-01-316-2295 | Glazed Chicken Breast (Healthy) | Night Hawk Foods |
| 9870-01-316-1979 | Pepper Steak | ConAgra Frozen Food |
| 8970-01-316-1975 | Sirloin Steak | Night Hawk Foods |
| 8970-01-316-4451 | Sirloin Tips | ConAgra Frozen Food |
| 9870-01-316-1977 | Sweet & Sour Chicken (Healthy) | ConAgra Frozen Food |

When selecting your meal (sandwich), please indicate the supplement packages you would like to compliment your meal. Diet soft drinks may be substituted upon request. Menus subject to change due to non-availability.

**NOTE:** If Healthy Heart Lunch/Dinner Menus are not available, a hot TV-Dinner with soft drink, juice or milk and snacks will be served.

Meals served to Space-A passengers on commercial contract flights (Patriot Flights) are standard airline food and are free.

# APPENDIX M
## A BRIEF DESCRIPTION OF AIRCRAFT ON WHICH MOST SPACE-A TRAVEL OCCURS

The following transport, tanker, and special mission aircraft are used by the military services (USPHS and NOAA do not have aircraft which are suitable for Space-A travel) for missions having Space-A air opportunities. **Only the major channel and support aircraft are listed.** We have not listed minor, some special mission, and helicopter (rotary wing) aircraft due to space limitations. **We have provided for you a brief description of each aircraft with emphasis on performance and passenger accommodations.** The total number of each aircraft changes in the inventory due to acquisitions, conversions, reconfiguration, and attrition. **Our best estimate of current specific aircraft inventories are listed below.**

**C-005A/B GALAXY**

The C-005A/B is a long-range, air-refuelable, heavy logistics transport which is capable of airlifting loads up to 291,000 pounds. This aircraft was developed, designed and configured to meet a wide range of military airlift missions. This is the "Free World's" largest aircraft.
**PROGRAM/PROJECT CONTRACTOR:** Lockheed Aeronautical Systems Company.
**POWER SOURCE:** Four General Electric TF39-GE-1C turbofan engines. Each engine has 43,000 lbs of thrust.
**DIMENSIONS:** Wing span is 222 ft, 8.5 in. Length is 247 ft, 10 in. Height is 65 ft, 1.5 in.
**WEIGHTS:** Empty weight is 374,000 lbs. Maximum payload is 261,000 lbs. Gross weight is 837,000 lbs.
**PERFORMANCE:** Maximum speed at 25,000 ft is 571 mph. Service ceiling with 615,000 lbs gross weight is 35,750 ft. Range with maximum payload is 3,434 miles and range with maximum fuel is 6,469 miles. Between 1982-1987 the 77 C-005As were upgraded to C-005B capabilities. From 1985-1989, 50 C-005Bs were acquired.
**FACILITIES:** Aircraft crew of six. Relief crew/rest area of 15. **Seating for 75 passengers, 2nd deck airline type seats facing to the rear of the aircraft for safety purposes.** Cargo, 1st deck, 36 standard 463L pallets or mounted weapons and vehicles or a maximum of 340 passengers in a wide-body jet configuration. There is a program to repaint all USAF C-005A/Bs flat grey. AMC has control of all C-005A/Bs.
**INVENTORY: Total USAF 126.**

**C-009A/E NIGHTINGALE**

This aircraft was designed as a commercial airliner. The DC-9 Series 30 commercial aircraft was reconfigured, modified and equipped to perform aeromedical (air ambulance) airlift transport missions. The C-009A/C performs aeromedical missions in CONUS, and in the European and Pacific Theaters.
**PROGRAM/PROJECT CONTRACTOR:** Douglas Aircraft Company. Division of McDonnell Douglas Corporation.
**POWER SOURCE:** Two Pratt & Whitney JT8D-9 turbofan engines. Each engine produces 14,500 lbs of thrust.
**DIMENSIONS:** Wing span is 93 ft, 3 in. Length is 119 ft, 3 in. Height is 27 ft, 6 in.
**WEIGHT:** Gross weight 108,000 lbs.
**PERFORMANCE:** The maximum cruising speed at 25,000 ft is 565 mph. Ceiling is 35,000 ft. Range is in excess of 2,000 miles.
**FACILITIES:** Aircraft crew of three (includes flight mechanic and spare parts) and five medical staff. There can be a combination of 40 litter (stretcher) or 40 ambulatory patients. Most MEDEVAC patients are ambulatory, that is, they can walk but may be

put in a litter for comfort. The ambulatory seats are spacious airline type seats. These are the seats used by Space-A passengers.
**INVENTORY:** Twenty-one in CONUS, four in Europe, three in Pacific, for a total inventory of 28 aircraft configured for aeromedical missions. Three are specifically configured C-9Cs which are assigned for Presidential and related missions. **The USN has 29 each C-9B SKYTRAIN II aircraft procured in FY 1985 to meet major Navy logistics requirements. This aircraft is configured for cargo and passenger (airline type seats, up to approximately 100). Total 52.**

**C-017A GLOBEMASTER III**

This aircraft will be capable of using unimproved landing facilities (runways - 90 ft wide x 3,000 ft long). The planned total acquisition is 120 aircraft.
**PROGRAM/PROJECT CONTRACTOR:** McDonnell Douglas Aerospace Transport Aircraft Division of McDonnell Douglas Aerospace.
**POWER SOURCE:** Four Pratt & Whitney F117-PW 100 turbofans; each 40,000 lbs of thrust on each aircraft.
**DIMENSIONS:** Wing span is 169 ft 10 in. Length is 174 ft. Height is 55 ft 1 in.
**WEIGHT:** Payload 172,000 lbs, Gross weight 585,000 lbs.
**PERFORMANCE:** Cruising speed (estimated) 518 mph, range with 160,000 lbs payload is 2,765 miles.
**FACILITIES:** Up to 102 passengers or paratroops, or 48 litters.
**INVENTORY: Total USAF 67.**

**C-21A EXECUTIVE AIRCRAFT**

There is a group of executive type aircraft in use in all of the Military Services. The C-21A is typical of these aircraft. **We will list the data for the C-21A and then list the inventory and passenger capacity of executive type aircraft in the Military Services.**
**PROGRAM/PROJECT CONTRACTOR:** Learjet Corporation.

**POWER SOURCE:** Two Garrett TFE731-2 turbojet engines. Each engine has 3,500 lbs thrust.
**DIMENSIONS:** Wing span is 39 ft, 6 in. Length is 48 ft, 8 in. Height is 12 ft, 3 in.
**WEIGHT:** Gross 18,300 lbs.
**PERFORMANCE:** Cruising speed is Mach 0.81. Service ceiling is 45,000 ft. Range with maximum passengers is 2,420 miles and with maximum cargo load is 1,653 miles.
**FACILITIES:** Aircraft crew of two. **Eight passengers in airline type seats,** or cargo of 3,153 lbs. Also convertible to aeromedical (MEDEVAC) configuration.
**INVENTORY: Total 556.**

C-12A-J HURON (8 Pax): USAF-33, USN-100. Total-133.
HU-25A GUARDIAN (APPROXIMATELY 12 Pax): USCG-41.
C-20A/B GULFSTREAM III/IV (14-18 Pax): USAF-13, USCG-1, USN-5. Total-19.
C-21A EXECUTIVE AIRCRAFT (8 Pax): USAF-76.
C-22B (BOEING 727 (APPROXIMATELY 100 Pax): USAF-3, CV-22, OSPREY USAF-50 (planned).
C-23A SHERPA (APPROXIMATELY 8 Pax): USAF-13.
C-26-A/B FAIRCHILD METRO III (19-20 Pax): USAF -16, USN-7. Total:23. (53 ON ORDER)
C-27A STOL (53 Pax): USAF-5
C-29A (125-800 BUSINESS JET, APPROXIMATELY 8 Pax): USAF-6.

The U.S. Army operates a fleet of C-12, RC-12 Fixed-Wing Aircraft of approximately 200 in number. Each aircraft can seat approximately 8 passengers.

**C-40A CLIPPER**

The C-40A Clipper provides logistics support to the Navy. Its flight deck features a flight management computer system with an integrated Global Positioning Satellite (GPS) systeam. It is RVSM capable. It has the Traffic Alert and Collision Avoidance System II on board. It also has an enhanced ground proximity warning system, predictive wind shear, head-up display and TACAN/UHF/Iff functions. It is the latest generation of the Boeing 737, configured for carrying cargo or passengers.

**PROGRAM/PROJECT CONTRACTOR:** Boeing Company.
**POWER SOURCE:** Two CFM56-7 SLST engines.
**DIMENSIONS:** Wing span is 112 ft, 7 in. Length is 110 ft, 4 in. Height is 41 ft, 2 in.
**PERFORMANCE:** The maximum cruising speed is 615 mph. The service ceiling for 130,000 lbs is 33,000 ft. The range with 121 passengers or 40,000 lbs of cargo is 3,452 miles.
**FACILITIES:** Aircraft crew of 4, carries **121 passengers,** 3 cargo pallets, or combination of pallets and up to 70 passengers.
**INVENTORY:** USN-6.

**C130A-H HERCULES**

The C-130 Hercules is a very versatile aircraft which is used to perform a wide range of missions for all of the military services. The aircraft has been used mainly in a cargo and passenger role. It has also been used in specialized combat, electronic warfare, Arctic ice cap resupply, aerial spray, aeromedical MEDEVAC, and aerial refueling among many similar missions. This aircraft is found in the inventory of all the military (Armed) services.

**PROGRAM/PROJECT CONTRACTOR:** Lockheed Aeronautical Systems Company.
**POWER SOURCE:** Four Allison T-56-A-15 turboprop engines. Each engine has 4,508 ehp.
**DIMENSIONS:** Wing span is 132 ft, 7 in. Length is 97 ft, 9 in. Height is 38 ft, 3 in.
**PERFORMANCE:** The maximum cruising speed at 20,000 ft is 374 mph. The service ceiling for 130,000 lbs is 33,000 ft. The range with maximum payload is 2,356 miles.
**FACILITIES:** Aircraft crew of five, **92 passengers in commercial airline type seats,** 74 litter patients, five 463L standard pallets, and assorted mounted weapons and vehicles. Seating ranges from side "bucket" seats along the sides of the aircraft to airline type seating with aisles and facing to the rear. The noise level is extremely high in this aircraft. Ear plugs are highly recommended for all passengers and crew.
**INVENTORY: Total 822.** C-130A-H and HC-130H/N/P: USAF-APPROXIMATELY 696. USN-24, USMC-76 (KC-130), USCG-30 (HC-130), USA-1 (EW MISSIONS).

**KC-135A-R STRATOTANKER**

This stratotanker was designed to military specifications. The aircraft is similar in size and design appearance to the commercial 707 aircraft but there the similarity ends. The KC-135 has different internal structural designs and materials which stress the ability to operate at high gross weights. The fuel carried in this tanker is located in the "wet wings" and in the fuel tanks below the floor in the fuselage. Passengers traveling on this aircraft are allowed, subject to mission restraints, to observe the Air to Air Refueling Operations which usually take place over the world's oceans.

**PROGRAM/PROJECT CONTRACTOR:** Boeing Military Airplanes.
**POWER SOURCE:** Four CFM international F108-CF-100 turbofan engines. Each engine has 22,224 lbs of thrust.
**DIMENSIONS:** Wing span is 130 ft, 10 in. Length is 136 ft, 3 in. Height is 38 ft, 4 in.
**WEIGHT:** Empty weight is 119,231 lbs. Gross 322,500 lbs.
**PERFORMANCE:** The maximum speed at 30,000 ft is 610 mph. Service ceiling 50,000 ft. Range with 12,000 lbs of transfer fuel is 11,192 miles.
**FACILITIES:** Aircraft crew of 4 or 5. **Maximum of 80 passengers in airline type seats facing to the rear of the aircraft.**
**INVENTORY: USAF 579.**

**C-135B STRATOLIFTER**

This aircraft is similar to the KC-135 Stratotanker without the refueling equipment. These aircraft were initially purchased as an interim cargo/passenger aircraft placed in service before delivery of the C-141s. The appearance of this aircraft is similar to the KC-135.

**PROGRAM/PROJECT CONTRACTOR:** Boeing Military Airplanes.
**POWER SOURCE:** Four CFM international F108-CF-100 turbofan engines. Each engine has 22,224 lbs of thrust.
**DIMENSIONS:** Wing span is 130 ft, 10 in. Length is 134 ft, 6 in. Height is 38 ft, 4 in.
**WEIGHT:** Empty 102,300 lbs. Gross 275,000 lbs.
**PERFORMANCE:** Maximum speed 600 mph. Range with 54,000 lb payload is 4,625 miles.
**INVENTORY: USAF 6.**

## Travel Notes

### VC-137B/C STRATOLINER

This is a special mission aircraft which has been modified from the commercial Boeing 707 transport. Two of these aircraft were the original "Air Force One" aircraft used by past United States Presidents.
**PROGRAM/PROJECT CONTRACTOR:** The Boeing Company.
**POWER SOURCE:** Four Pratt & Whitney JT3D-3 turbofan engines. Each engine has a 17,200 lb thrust.
**DIMENSIONS:** VC-137B: Wing span is 130 ft, 10 in. Length 144 ft, 6 in. Height 42 ft, 10 in. VC137-C: Wing span is 145 ft, 9 in. Length is 152 ft, 11 in. Height is 42 ft, 5 in.
**WEIGHT:** VC-137B: Gross 258,000 lbs. VC-137C: Gross 322,000 lbs.
**PERFORMANCE:** VC-137C: Maximum speed 627 mph. Service ceiling 42,000 ft. Range 5,150 miles.
**FACILITIES:** This is a special mission aircraft with a variety of configurations. There are full-service galleys, dining, sleeping berths, and airline type seating.
**INVENTORY:** USAF 2.

### C-141A/B STARLIFTER

The C-141A/B STARLIFTER transport has undergone extensive modification to extend the airframe and modernization to all aspects of the aircraft. The result is a modern air transport which is fully capable of performing many missions from routine cargo and passengers to intertheater MEDEVAC and humanitarian missions around the world. All of the C-141A/B fleet are scheduled for repainting to a flat grey.
**PROGRAM/PROJECT CONTRACTOR:** Lockheed-Georgia Company.
**POWER SOURCE:** Four Pratt & Whitney TF33-P-7 turbofan engines. Each engine has 21,000 lbs of thrust.
**DIMENSIONS:** Wing span is 159 ft, 11 in. Length is 168 ft, 3.5 in. Height is 39 ft, 3 in.
**WEIGHT:** Operating 149,000 lbs. Maximum payload 89,000 lbs. Gross 343,000 lbs.
**PERFORMANCE:** Maximum cruising speed is 566 mph. Range with maximum payload is 2,293 miles without air refueling.
**FACILITIES:** Air crew of five. **200 passengers in commercial airline seats facing to the rear of the aircraft.** 103 litter patients plus attendants. Cargo on 13 standard 463L pallets or alternate mounted weapons, vehicles or other cargo.
**INVENTORY:** USAF 130.

### KC-010A EXTENDER

This advanced tanker/cargo aircraft is based on the commercial DC-10 Series, 30 CF. It has been modified to include fuselage fuel cells, aerial refueling operator station and boom. Military avionics have been added. The aircraft is fit to perform a role of extending and enhancing worldwide military mobility. The latest modifications to this aircraft are wing-mounted air-refueling pods designed to supplement the basic system and increase capability.
**PROGRAM/PROJECT CONTRACTOR:** Douglas Aircraft Company, Division of McDonnell Douglas Corporation.
**POWER SOURCE:** Three General Electric CF-6-50C2 turbofan engines. Each engine has 52,500 lbs of thrust.
**DIMENSIONS:** Wing span is 165 ft, 4.5 in. Length is 181 ft, 7 in. Height is 58 ft, 1 in.
**WEIGHT:** Gross 590,000 lbs.
**PERFORMANCE:** Cruising speed Mach 0.825. Service ceiling 42,000 ft range with maximum cargo 4,370 miles.
**FACILITIES:** Aircraft crew of four. **75 passengers in commercial airline seats facing to the rear of the aircraft.** 27 standard 463L pallets. Maximum cargo payload 169,409 lbs.
**INVENTORY:** USAF 59.

### P-3C-ORION

This is a propeller-driven aircraft which has been used by the U.S. Navy since 1958 in an Anti-Submarine Warfare (ASW) role. Many improvements have been incorporated in the basic airframe over the years. The latest improvements allow the aircraft to detect, track and attack quieter new generation submarines. **The replacement P-7A program, with Lockheed as the contractor, was terminated in July 1990. The USN is investigating alternative programs.**

**PROGRAM/PROJECT CONTRACTOR:** Lockheed.
**POWER SOURCE:** Four Allison T-56-A-14 turboprop engines. Each engine has 4,900 ehp.
**DIMENSIONS:** Wing span is 100 ft. Length is 117 ft. Height is 34 ft.
**WEIGHT:** Gross weight is 139,760 lbs.
**PERFORMANCE:** Maximum speed 473 mph. Cruise speed 377 mph. Ceiling 28,300 ft.
**FACILITIES:** Aircraft crew of 10. **18 passengers in airline seats.**
**INVENTORY:** USN-256.

Visit Military Living online at

# www.militaryliving.com

and click on Space-A
Travel/Hops for the best
Space-A links on the Internet!

## Commercial Aircraft Used by Contractors

| | |
|---|---|
| **B-727** | Boeing, twin engine aicraft |
| **B-747** | Boeing, wide-bodied transport |
| **B-757** | Boeing, twin engine aircraft |
| **DC-862** | Boeing, carries up to 258 passengers |
| **DC-863** | Boeing, carries up to 259 passengers and baggage 4,500 miles, built for aerodynamics and long range |
| **L-100** | Lockhead Martin, commercial version of C-130 |
| **L-1011** | Lockhead Martin, wide-bodied tri-jet engine, carries up to 400 passengers |
| **MD-011** | McDonald Douglas, wide-bodied tri engine jet |

# APPENDIX N
## LOCATION/STATIONING OF ARMED FORCES HEAVY-LIFT (PAX/CGO) AIRCRAFT

The heavy-lift passenger and cargo aircraft of the Armed Forces [United States Army (None), United States Navy, United States Marine Corps, United States Coast Guard and United States Air Force] are assigned to both the active and reserve forces. The majority of these aircraft are stationed in the CONUS and U.S. Possessions overseas. Very few of these aircraft are stationed at U.S. Bases in foreign countries.

Examining the home base (stationing) of military aircraft is one approach to understanding Space-A Air Opportunities. Following are the stationing locations and the types of aircraft assigned to units at these locations. We have not included the number of aircraft at each location, as this is constantly changing.

| LI/ICAO | Base/Station | Aircraft |
|---|---|---|
| **UNITED STATES AIR FORCE** | | |
| **Air Combat Command** | | |
| DMA/KDMA | Davis-Monthan AFB, AZ | C-130E/H |
| VAD/KVAD | Moody AFB, GA | C-130H |
| MUO/KMUO | Mountain Home AFB, ID | KC-135R |
| OFF/KOFF | Offutt AFB, NE | KC-135E |
| **Air Education & Training Command** | | |
| LTS/KLTS | Altus AFB, OK | C-005A/B |
| | | C-017A |
| | | C141B |
| | | KC-135R |
| IKR/KIKR | Kirtland AFB, NM | C-130H |
| LRF/KLRF | Little Rock AFB, AR | C-130A/H |
| **Air Force Material Command** | | |
| FFO/KFFO | Wright-Patterson AFB, OH | C-017A |
| | And other Air Force Material Bases | C-130H |
| | | C-135 |
| | | NC-130 |
| | | KC-135R |
| **Air Force Special Operations Command** | | |
| HRT/KHRT | Hurlburt Field, FL | C-130E |
| DNA/RODN | Kadena AB, JP | C-130H |
| MHZ/EGUN | RAF Mildenhall, GB | C-130H |
| **Air Mobility Command** | | |
| ADW/KADW | Andrews AFB, MD | C-009B |
| | | C-32 |
| | | C-37A |
| | | C-135 |
| | | C-137 |
| CHS/KCHS | Charleston AFB/IAP, SC | C-017A |
| DOV/KDOV | Dover AFB, DE | C005A/B |
| DYS/KDYS | Dyess AFB, TX | C-130H |
| SKA/KSKA | Fairchild AFB, WA | KC-135R |
| RDR/KRDR | Grand Forks AFB, ND | KC-135R |
| LRF/KLRF | Little Rock AFB, AR | C-130H |
| MCF/KMCF | MacDill AFB, FL | KC-135R |
| TCM/KTCM | McChord AFB, WA | C-017A |
| | | C-141B |
| IAB/KIAB | McConnell AFB, KS | KC-135R |
| WRI/KWRI | McGuire AFB, NJ | C-141B |
| | | KC-010A |
| POB/KPOB | Pope AFB, NC | C-130A/H |
| WRB/KWRB | Robins AFB, GA | KC-135R |
| BLV/KBLV | Scott AFB, IL | C-009A |
| SUU/KSUU | Travis AFB, CA | C005A/B |
| | | KC-010A |
| **Pacific Air Forces** | | |
| EDF/PAED | Elmendorf AFB, AK | C-130H |
| HIK/PHIK | Hickam AFB, HI | C-135E |
| DNA/RODN | Kadena AB, JP | KC-135R |
| OKO/RJTY | Yokota AFB, JP | C-009A |
| | | C-130E/H |
| **United States Air Forces In Europe** | | |
| MHZ/EGUN | RAF Mildenhall, GB | KC-135R |
| RMS/ETAR | Ramstein AB, DE | C-009A |
| | | C-130E |
| **Air Force Reserve Commands** | | |
| **4th Air Force (AMC)** | | |
| BAB/KBAB | Beale AFB, CA | KC-135E |
| GUS/KGUS | Grissom ARB, IN | KC-135R |
| SKF/KSKF | Kelly AFB, TX | C-005A/B |
| RIV/KRIV | March ARB, CA | C-141C |
| | | KC-135R |
| TCM/KTCM | McChord AFB, WA | C-017A |
| | | C-141B |
| IAB/KIAB | McConnell AFB, KS | KC-135R |
| BLV/KBLV | Scott AFB, IL | C-009A |
| GSB/KGSB | Seymour Johnson AFB, NC | KC-135R |
| MTC/KMTC | Selfridge ANGB, MI | KC-135R |
| TIK/KTIK | Tinker AFB, OK | KC-135R |
| SUU/KSUU | Travis AFB, CA | C-005A/B |
| | | KC-010A |
| FFO/KFFO | Wright-Patterson AFB, OH | C-141C |

| LI/ICAO | Base/Station | Aircraft |
|---|---|---|
| **10th Air Force (AMC)** | | |
| VPS/KVPS | Eglin AFB, FL (Duke Field) | MC-130E/P |
| PDX/KPDX | Portland IAP, OR | HC-130N/P |
| **22nd Air Force (AMC)** | | |
| ADW/KADW | Andrews AFB, MD | C-141B/C |
| CHS/KCHS | Charleston AFB/IAP, SC | C-017A |
| | | C-141B |
| MGE/KMGE | Dobbins ARB, GA | C-130H |
| DOV/KDOV | Dover AFB, DE | C-005A/B |
| GMF/KMKE | General Mitchell IAP/ARS, WI | C-130H |
| BIX/KBIX | Keesler AFB, MS | C-130E |
| MXF/KMXF | Maxwell AFB, AL | C-130H |
| WRI/KWRI | McGuire AFB, NJ | C-141B |
| | | KC-010A |
| MSP/KMSP | Minneapolis-St.Paul AP/ARS, MN | C-130E |
| IAG/KIAG | Niagara Falls IAP/ARS, NY | C-130H |
| COS/KCOS | Peterson AFB, CO | C-130H |
| PIT/KPIT | Pittsburgh IAP/ARS, PA | C-130H |
| CEF/KCEF | Westover ARB, MA | C-005A/B |
| NXX/KNXX | Willow Grove NAS/JRB, PA | C-130E |
| YNG/KYNG | Youngstown-Warren Regional Airport/ARS, OH | C-130H |
| **Air National Guard** | | |
| JAN/KJAN | Allen C.Thompson Field, MS | C-141C |
| BGR/KBGR | Bangor IAP, ME | KC-135R |
| BHM/KBHM | Birmingham IAP/ANG, AL | KC-135R |
| NTD/KNTD | Channel Island ANGB, CA | C-130A/H |
| CLT/KCLT | Charlotte/Douglas IAP, NC | C-130A/H |
| CYS/KCYS | Cheyenne Municipal Airport, WY | C-130A/H |
| MRB/KMRB | Eastern West Virginia Regional Airport, WV | C-130A/H |
| EIL/PAEI | Eielson AFB, AK | KC-135R |
| SKA/KSKA | Fairchild AFB, WA | KC-135R |
| FOE/KFOE | Forbes Field IAP/ANGB, KS | KC-135R |
| NFW/KNFW | Fort Worth NAS/JRB, TX | C-130A/H |
| GMF/KMKE | General Mitchell IAP/ARS, WI | KC-135R |
| PIA/KPIA | Greater Peoria Regional Airport, IL | C-130A/H |
| HIK/PHIK | Hickam AFB, HI | C-130A/H |
| | | KC-135R |
| MEI/KMEI | Key Field Airport, MS | KC-135R |
| ANC/PANC | Kulis ANGB/Anchorage IAP, AK | C-130A/H |
| LNK/KLNK | Lincoln Municipal Apt, NE | KC-135R |
| LRF/KLRF | Little Rock AFB, AR | C-130A/H |
| SDF/KSDF | Louisville IAP/KANGB, KY | C-130A/H |
| SJU/TJSJ | Luis Munoz Marin IAP | C-130A/H |
| MFD/KMFD | Mansfield Lahm Apt, OH | C-130A/H |
| RIV/KRIV | March ARB, CA | KC-135R |
| MEM/KMEM | Memphis IAP, TN | C-141C |
| TYS/KTYS | McGhee Tyson ANGB, TN | KC-135R |
| WRI/KWRI | McGuire AFB, NY | KC-135R |
| MSP/KMSP | Minneapolis-St. Paul IAP/ARS, MN | C-130A/H |
| BNA/KBNA | Nashville IAP/TANGB, TN | C-130A/H |
| ILG/KILG | New Castle County Apt, DE | C-130A/H |
| IAG/KIAG | Niagara Falls IAP/ARS, NY | KC-135R |
| PSM/KPSM | Pease ANGB, NH | KC-135R |
| PIT/KPIT | Pittsburgh IAP/ARS, PA | KC-135R |
| OQU/KOQU | Quonset Point Sta Apt, RI | C-130A/H |
| RNO/KRNO | Reno/Tahoe IAP, NV | C-130A/H |
| LCK/KLCK | Rickenbacker ANGB, OH | KC-135R |
| STJ/KSTJ | Rosecrans Memorial Airport, MO | C-130A/H |
| SLC/KSLC | Salt Lake City IAP, UT | KC-135R |
| SAV/KSAV | Savannah IAP, GA | C-130A/H |
| BLV/KBLV | Scott AFB, IL | KC-135R |
| PHX/KPHX | Sky Harbor IAP, AZ | KC-135R |
| SWF/KSWF | Stewart IAP/ANGB, NY | C-005A |
| SCH/KSCH | Stratton ANGB, NY | C-130A/H |
| OKC/KOKC | Will Rogers World Airport/ANGB, OK | C-130A/H |
| CRW/KCRW | Yeager Airport, WV | C-130A/H |

**UNITED STATES NAVY**
Active and Reserve Component Forces

| | | |
|---|---|---|
| USN and Reserve (247 Acf) | | P-3C |
| USN and Reserve (97 Acf) | | C-130A/H |
| USN and Reserve (29 Acf) | | C-009B |
| USN and Reserve (6 Acf) | | C-40 |

**UNITED STATES MARINE CORPS**
Active and Reserve Component Forces

| | | |
|---|---|---|
| USMC and Reserve (42) | | KC-130 |

**UNITED STATES COAST GUARD**
Active and Reserve Component Forces

| | | |
|---|---|---|
| USCG and Reserve (30 Acf) | | HC-130 |

**Note:** There is a very large number of lightweight executive type aircraft on which there are Space-A Air Opportunities. The limited range of these aircraft restricts their flights to CONUS and local areas in OCONUS. For more information on this type of aircraft, please see Appendix M in this book.

# APPENDIX O
## OTHER SPACE-A AIR OPPORTUNITY AIRLIFT SYSTEMS

In addition to the major airlift systems operated worldwide by the Air Mobility Command (AMC) of the United States Air Force, there are several other minor airlift systems operated by the USAF (including AMC) and the other military services (USA, USN, USMC, USCG). These minor airlift systems are best known as Operational Support Airlift (OSA). There are Space-A Air Opportunities on each of these systems. The departure locations, with contact information, for most of these systems, are listed in the body of the text of this book.

This appendix is designed to amplify and explain the minor airlift systems. The additional information contained in this appendix will strengthen the Space-A customer's knowledge and understanding of these alternative Space-A airlift systems, which will improve the customer's total Space-A system utilization.

Most of these Operational Support Airlift (OSA) aircraft are scheduled centrally by the Joint Operational Support Airlift Center (JOSAC) at Scott AFB, IL, approximately three to five days before originating flights. (See below: Finding Space-A Information on the World Wide Web.) Since there are frequent changes in schedules, due to changes in missions and related matters, it is best for Space-A travelers to contact each base from which they plan to depart in order to obtain Space-A seat availability, schedules and routing information. The departure locations with telephone, recording and telefax numbers are located in each listing in the body of the text of this book. Also, typical mission profiles are listed when known in the departure base listings.

Below is a chart showing the types of Operational Support Airlift (OSA) Aircraft.

## OPERATIONAL SUPPORT AIRLIFT (OSA) SPACE-A AIR OPPORTUNITIES

The access for OSA daily/current flights and the OSA Searchable OSA flight system is as follows: 1. Go to www.militaryliving.com (Military Living Home Page), 2. Click on SPACE-A AIR TRAVEL (HOPS) (button on left side of screen). Once on that page, 3. Click on SPACE-A LINKS & FORMS. Once on that page, 4. Click on Links to OSA.

This page allows you to quickly find scheduled OSA flights which are of interest to you. You can search for flights which only match specific criteria such as date range, departure airport, and arrival airport. Then, only the flights which are of interest to you are returned. Or, you can display all scheduled OSA flights for a date range by simply hitting "Clear Form," setting the date, and pressing "Submit."

The OSA flight schedules returned are "live," so any changes to flight schedules are immediately available to you. Just hit "Submit" again to get the latest information.

All Arrival and Departure times are in Greenwich Mean Time (5 hours ahead of Eastern Standard Time, when it is 12:00 GMT it is 07:00 EST), or "ZULU" time. The OSA flights returned are sorted by mission number.

START DATE: Set this to the date you are interested in traveling. If you are looking for flights starting over a range of dates, set the "plus days" menu to the number of days you desire from the start date. You can search for dates from 0 to 5 days out from the start date. For example: if the start date is set to March 5, 2000 plus 3 days, only OSA flights starting March 5 through March 8, 2000 will be returned.

**WHAT IS AN ICAO?**: An ICAO (International Civil Aviation Organization) is a 4-letter designator for an airport. For example, "Los Angeles IAP" is "KLAX." You must use the ICAO's to search for flights going through an airport you're interested in. To find the ICAO for an airport, use the "Lookup an ICAO" window, described below or look up the airport in the text of this book where the ICAO will be listed for each airport in the book.

**LOOK UP AN ICAO CODE:** Hitting this link will bring up a smaller window to allow you to find out the ICAO code for an airport. Just enter all or part of the airport name and hit "Submit." You can enter upper or lower case letters/numbers. For example: entering "Chicago" will return "Chicago Midway, IL-"KMDW" and "Chicago O'Hare IAP, IL-"KORD."

**DEPARTURE ICAO:** Enter the ICAO for the airport you are interested in leaving from, and only OSA flights leaving from that airport will be displayed. If both Departure and Arrival ICAO's are entered, then the OSA flight must pass through both ICAO's to be displayed. This field is optional.

**ARRIVAL ICAO:** Enter the ICAO of the airport you are interested in going to, and only OSA flights going to that airport will be displayed. If both Departure and Arrival ICAO's are entered, then the OSA flight must pass through both ICAO's to be displayed. This field is optional.

**HELP:** Displays this help page.

**SUBMIT:** Starts the search of the OSA scheduled flights.

**CLEAR FORM:** Returns the form to its original state.

**ARRANGING FOR SPACE-A AIR TRAVEL:** Space-A arrangements (application for Space-A Air Travel, AMC Form 140) are made through airfield passenger terminals or base operations. The contact telephones, telefax and e-mail addresses and numbers are listed in this book, *Military Space-A Air Opportunities Around the World,* at each departure/arrival location. By exception, arrangements may be made with the flying unit, or directly with the pilot where base operations/passenger terminal facilities do not exist. The JOSAC schedules may be accessed on the web as above. The JOSAC telephone numbers are: C-618-256-6639 or C-800-256-7609, D-312-576-6639.

## Note: This Web-based information is subject to frequent changes.

---

### TYPES OF OSA AIRCRAFT*

| AIRCRAFT | MANUFACTURER | TYPE | MAX SEATS | AIRSPEED (knots) | RANGE (nm) |
|---|---|---|---|---|---|
| C-9 | McDonnell/Douglas DC9 | Jet | 90 | 440 | 2000 |
| C-20 | Gulfstream III | Jet | 26 | 450 | 3500 |
| C-21 | Learjet LJ35 | Jet | 7 | 440 | 1700 |
| C-22 | Boeing 727 | Jet | 77 | 460 | 1800 |
| UC-35 | Cessna Citation II | Jet | 7 | 420 | 1300 |
| C-38 | Astra SPX | Jet | 7 | 483 | 2100 |
| CT-39 | Rockwell Saberliner | Jet | 6 | 440 | 1300 |
| C-12 | Beechcraft King Air 200 | Prop | 8 | 240 | 1200 |
| C-23 | Shorts Sherpa | Prop | 18 | 180 | 600 |
| C-26 | Fairchild Metroliner | Prop | 14 | 265 | 1100 |

* Note: These aircraft are owned by the military department which provides the aircraft and crews to the OSA to fly missions scheduled by the JOSAC. The aircraft are stationed or located at military department bases in CONUS and OCONUS.

# APPENDIX P
## MAJOR WORLDWIDE SPACE-A ROUTES

Most of the major worldwide passenger and cargo routes were established during and immediately after World War II. The routes have remained in full time operation utilizing Military Services organic and contractor aircraft since that time. Major air routes are changed or reoriented when the need to support an area with intra-theater airlift changes, i.e. when the U.S. Forces withdrew from South Vietnam. Also the number and frequency of missions flown on these major routes change as the requirements for inter-theater airlift change.

The missions that are flown on these major worldwide routes are on a scheduled and a non-scheduled basis to meet the operational needs of the Military Services and the Unified and Specified commands overseas. These missions are performed by organic units of the Active USAF, USAFRES, USANG and contractors assigned to the Air Force, Air Mobility Command (AMC).

Missions on these major worldwide routes are largely manned by crews and aircraft that are assigned in the CONUS and fly overseas to one or more countries or U.S. possessions and then return to their home station. There are some theater airlift assets which are stationed overseas and fly local theater missions.

We will identify and explain the details about major routing on which Space-A Air Opportunities are available each month of the year. We have divided these routes into regions of the world where these routes exist. Complete sample details regarding routing/stations, schedules, days en route and equipment are contained in (this book) Military Living's ***Military Space-A Air Opportunities Around The World***. Also, you may find a graphic presentation of these data and much more in Military Living's ***Military Space-A Air Opportunities Air Route Map. Note: Originating stations for some routes change often; however, the missions are flown from other stations.***

### NORTH ATLANTIC ROUTE

Missions on this route originate at McGuire AFB, NJ (WRI/KWRI), Baltimore/Washington IAP, MD (BWI/KBWI, Norfolk NAS, VA (NGU/KNGU), Charleston IAP\AFB, SC (CHS/KCHS), Jackson IAP/Allen C. Thompson Field, MS (JAN/KJAN) and are routed direct to Keflavik Airport/Naval Base, IS (KEF/BIKF). These flights continue on to the European mainland at Ramstein AB, DE (RMS/ETAR) and Lajes Field AB (Azores), PT (LGS/LPLA). Most of these flights return to their CONUS bases via Keflavik Airport or Lajes Field AB. There are also missions from McGuire AFB to Thule AB (Greenland), DK (THU/BGTL) and return. Most of these routes require 2 to 3 days of flying and en-route time using heavy lift (C-005A/C, KC-10A, C-17A, KC-135A-R, C-141A/B) Air Force and contractor (DC010, B757, L1011, etc) aircraft.

### MIDDLE ATLANTIC ROUTE

This is the most densely traveled route in the Air Mobility Command System (AMC). Missions on this route originate at Westover ARB, MA (CEF/KCEF), Stewart IAP/ANGB, NY (SWF/KSWF), McGuire AFB, NJ (WRI/KWRI), Baltimore/Washington IAP, MD (BWI/KBWI), Wright-Patterson AFB, OH (FFO/KFFO), Dover AFB, DE (DOV/KDOV), Charleston AFB/IAP, SC (CHS/KCHS), Wm B. Hartsfield Atlanta IAP, GA (ATL/KATL), and Jackson IAP/Allen C. Thompson Field (Jackson), MS (JAN/KJAN). Most of the originating stations stage through the primary East Coast stations of McGuire AFB, Baltimore/Washington IAP, Andrews AFB, Dover AFB, Norfolk NAS and Charleston AFB/IAP. Staging means that flights which originate at inland and West Coast stations stop for crew rest, cargo and passengers at these primary (staging) East Coast stations for approximately 3 to 15 hours depending upon the mission requirements. These flights continue on to the Primary Middle Atlantic Stations in Europe: Lajes Field AB, PT (LGS/LPLA), RAF Mildenhall, GB (MHZ/EGUN), Rota NS, ES (RTA/LERT), Ramstein AB, DE (RMS/ETAR), and Rhein-Main AB, DE (FRF/EDDF). Many of these flights continue into the Mediterranean area and the Middle East before they turn around and return to CONUS through the Primary European Middle Atlantic Stations and to their assigned (home) stations. These complete missions require two to seven or more days of flying and en-route time, utilizing Air Force and commercial heavy lift aircraft.

### SOUTH ATLANTIC ROUTE

Missions on this route originate at many of the same stations as the Middle Atlantic Route. The primary originating stations on the East Coast of CONUS are Dover AFB, DE (DOV/KDOV), McGuire AFB, NJ (WRI/KWRI), Baltimore/Washington IAP, MD (BWI/KBWI), Norfolk NAS, VA (NGU/KNGU), and Charleston AFB/IAP, SC (CHS). One flight originate on the West Coast at Travis AFB, CA (SUU/KSUU). These missions fly through the Primary Middle Atlantic (Staging) Stations to the Primary European Stations (as listed above in the Middle Atlantic Route) before continuing on to their mission stations in the Mediterranean and Middle East. These stations west to east are Lajes Field AB (Azores), PT, (LGS/LPLA), Rota NS, ES (RTA/LERT), Aviano AB, IT (AVB/LIPA), Capodichino Airport (Naples), IT (NAP/LIRN), Sigonella Airport (Sicily), IT (SIZ/LICZ), Cairo IAP, EG, (CAI/HECA), Incirlik Airport (Adana), TR (ADA/LTAG) (turnaround point), Bahrain IAP/NSA, BH (BAH/OBBI) (turnaround point), Kuwait IAP, KW (KWI/OKBK), Prince Sultan AB, SA (EKJ/OEKJ) (turnaround point), (limited entry to SA), OAFB Thumrait, OM (TTH/OOTH), Al Dhafra Airfield, AE (DHF/OMAM) (limited entry), Al Fujayrah IAP, AE (FJR/OMFJ), and Diego Garcia Atoll, GB (NKW/FJDG) (turnaround point, and NO ACCESS TO SPACE-A PASSENGERS). Most of these flights turn around and return through the Primary Middle Atlantic Stations in Europe and then continue on to the East Coast of CONUS and their home stations. These complete missions require two to nine days or more of flying and en-route time, utilizing Air Force and commercial heavy lift aircraft.

### ATLANTIC THEATER ROUTE

The missions in the Atlantic Theater originate at Ramstein AB, DE (RMS/ETAR). These missions are accomplished by theater assigned aircraft and crews. The missions from Ramstein AB fly to the following destinations and return to Ramstein AB: Aviano AB, IT (AVB/LIPA), Capodichino APT (Naples), IT (NAP/LIRN), Olbia Costa Smeralda (Sardinia), IT (OLB/LIEO), Sigonella NAS/APT (Sicily), IT (SIZ/LICZ), GAFB Araxos, GR (GPA/LGRX), RAFB Akrotiri, CY, (AKT/LCRA), Ataturk/Yesilkoy Airport (Istanbul), TR (IST/LTBA), Izmir AS, TR (IGL/LTBL), Incirlik Airport (Adana), TR (ADA/LTAG), (turnaround), Esenboga Airport (Ankara), TR (ESB/LTAC), Souda Bay HAFC (Crete), GR (CHQ/LGSA), Cairo IAP, EG (CAI/HECA), (turnaround) Ben Gurion IAP, IL (TLV/LLBG), (turnaround) Prince Sultan AB, SA (EKJ/OEKJ), (turnaround), King Abdullah AB, JO (AMM/OJAF), (turnaround), Bahrain IAP, BH (BAH/OBBI), (turnaround), OAFB Thumrait, OM (TTH/OOTH), (turnaround), and RAF Mildenhall, GB (MHZ/EGUN) (turnaround). There are numerous missions flown on the routes each month.

### ATLANTIC/AFRICA ROUTE

Missions on this route originate at Charleston AFB/IAP, SC (CHS/KCHS). Stations visited from west to east are Dakar Yoff Airport, SE (DKR/GOOY), N'Djamena IAP, TD (NDJ/FTTJ), Yaounde/Nsimalen IAP, CM (NSI/FKYS), Jomo Kenyatta IAP, KE (NBO/HKJK) (turnaround), Waterkloof AB, ZA (LMB/FAWK), Ascension AUX AF, GB (ASI/FHAW), Alexander Hamilton APT (St Croix), VI (STX/TISX) and return to Charleston AFB, SC. These flights turnaround in West Africa and return to CONUS and their home stations. As a footnote to African travel, most stations on this route require that U.S. personnel, including Space-A passengers, notify the Office of the U.S. Defense Attache (ODA) of their arrival and plans for travel in the country.

### CARIBBEAN, CENTRAL AND SOUTH AMERICA ROUTES

There are many missions which cover the Caribbean area, Central America area and South America area. However, similar to the European area these three areas are interconnected in terms of missions. Please note that the destinations in South America are south of the equator and thus have reverse seasons from North America.

### CARIBBEAN ROUTE

Missions on the Caribbean route originate at the following stations: Minneapolis-St Paul IAP/ARS, MN (MSP/KMSP), Niagara Falls IAP/ARS, NY (IAG/KIAG), General Mitchell IAP/ARS, WI (MKE/FMKE), McGuire AFB, NJ (WRI/KWRI), Peterson AFB, CO (COS/KCOS), Wright-Patterson AFB, OH (FFO/KFFO), Memphis IAP/ANGB, TN (MEM/KMEM), Norfolk NAS, VA

(NGU/KNGU), Pope AFB, NC (POB/KPOB), Charleston AFB/IAP, SC (CHS/KCHS), Dyess AFB, TX (DYS/KDYS), Jackson IAP/Allen C. Thompson Field, MS (JAN/KJAN) and Patrick AFB, FL (COF/KCOF). From these originating stations there are missions to: Roosevelt Roads NAS, PR (NRR/TJNR), Alexander Hamilton Airport, VI (STX/TISX), Grantley Adams IAP (Bridgetown), BB (BGI/TBPB), Port-au-Prince IAP, HT (PAP/MTPP), San Isidro AB, DO (SDQ/MDSI), Guantanamo Bay NAS, CU (NBW/MUGM), Norman Manley IAP, JM (KIN/MKPG), V.C. Bird IAP, AG (SJH/TAPA), Piarco APT (Port-of-Spain), TT (POS/TTPP), Ascension Auxiliary AF, GB (ASI/FHAW). Most of the above flights stage through Norfolk NAS, VA and return through Norfolk NAS en route to their originating (home) stations.

### CENTRAL AMERICA ROUTE

Missions on the Central America route originate at the following stations: Wright-Patterson AFB, OH (FFO/KFFO), Jackson IAP/Allen C. Thompson Field, MS (JAN/KJAN) and Maxwell AFB, AL (MXF/KMXF). From these originating stations there are missions to: Belize IAP, BZ (BZE/MZBZ), La Aurora APT (Guatemala City), GT (GUA/MGGT), El Salvador IAP, SV (SAL/MSLP), Toncontin IAP, HN (TGU/MHTG), Augusto C Sandino IAP (Managua), NI (MGA/MNMG), and Juan Santamaria IAP (San Jose), CR (SJO/MROC).

### SOUTH AMERICA ROUTE

Missions on the South America route originate at the following stations: Wright-Patterson AFB, OH (FFO/KFFO), Memphis IAP/ANGB, TN (MEM/KMEM), Jackson IAP/Allen C. Thompson Field, MS (JAN/KJAN) and March ARB, CA (RIV/KRIV). From these originating stations missions fly to: Simon Bolivar IAP (Carasco), VE (MIQ/SEGU), Johan A Pengel IAP (Paramaribo), SR (PBM/SMJP), El Dorado IAP (Bogota), CO (BOG/SKBO), Mariscal Sucre Apt (Quito), EC (UIO/SEQU), Jorge Chavez IAP (Lima), PE (LIM/SPIM), Arturo Merino Benitez IAP (Santiago), CH (SCL/SCEL), JF Kennedy IAP (La Paz), BO (LPB/SLLP), Viru Viru IAP (Santa Cruz), BO (VIU/SLVR), Silvio Pettirossi IAP (Asuncion), PY (ASU/SGAS) Brasilia Airport, BR (BSB/SBBR), Rio De Janeiro IAP, BR (RIO/SBGL), Carrasco IAP (Montevideo), UY (MVD/SUMU), and Ezeiza IAP (Buenos Aires), AR (BUE/SAEZ). These missions are known as the "Capitol Run" because of the capital cities in South America which they serve.

### NORTH PACIFIC ROUTE

Missions on the North Pacific route originate at the following stations: Elmendorf AFB, AK (EDF/PAED). Travis AFB, CA (SUU/KSUU), Los Angeles IAP, CA (LAX/KLAX), March ARB, CA (RIV/KRIV), and Charleston IAP/AFB, SC (CHS/KCHS). From these originating stations missions fly to: McChord AFB, WA (TCM/KTCM), Seattle/Tacoma IAP, WA (SEA/KSEA), Elmendorf AFB, AK (EDF/PAED), Eielson AFB, AK (EIL/PAEI), King Salmon APT, AK (AKN/PAKN), Eareckson AS, AK (SYA/PASY), Yokota AB, JP (OKO/RJTY), Misawa AB, JP (MSJ/RJSM), Iwakuni MCAS, JP (IWA/RJOI), Osan AB, KR (OSN/RKSO), Kadena AB, JP (DNA/RODN), RSAF Paya Lebar (Singapore), SG (QPG/WSAP), Diego Garcia Atoll, GB (NKW/FJDG), Andersen AFB, GU (UAM/PGUA). These missions turnaround at Osan AB, Yokota AB and Kadena AB and return through Alaska to their home stations.

### CENTRAL PACIFIC ROUTE

Missions on the Central Pacific route originate at the following stations: McChord AFB, WA (TCM/KTCM), Travis AFB, CA (SUU), March ARB, CA (RIV/KRIV) and Hickam AFB, HI (HIK/PHIK). From these originating stations missions fly to: Hickam AFB, HI (HIK/PHIK), Wake IS AAF, WK (AWK/PWAK), Bucholz AAF/KMR (Kwajalein Atoll), KA (KWA/PKWA), Johnson Atoll, JO (JON/PJON), Andersen AFB, GU (UAM/PGUA), Yokota AB, JP (OKO/RJTY), Kadena AB, JP (DNA/PGUA), Osan AB, KR (OSN/RKSO), RSAF Paya Lebar (Singapore), SG (QPG/WSAP), Diego Garcia Atoll, GB (NKW/FJDG). Most of these missions transient through Hickam AFB, HI and Andersen AFB, GU turnaround at Yokota AB and Osan AB and return through Hickam AFB and Travis AFB en route their home stations. This route is very rich in flights each month of the year. Yokota AB is the business station in the AMC system.

### PACIFIC THEATER ROUTE

These missions, like the European Theater Route, originate outside the CONUS in the overseas theater. Missions on the Pacific Theater Route originate at the following station: Yokota AB, JP (OKO/RJTY). From these originating stations missions fly to: Halim Perdanakusum, ID (HLP/WIIH), Fukuoka IAP/Itazuke AB, JP (FUK/RJFF), Misawa AB, JP (MSJ/RJSM), Kadena AB, JP (DNA/RODN), Kunsan AB, KR (KUZ/RKJK), RSAF Paya Lebar (Singapore), SG (SGP/WSAP), Changi IAP (Singapore), SG (SIN/WSSS), Diego Garcia Atoll, GB (NKW/FJDG), Al Fujayrah IAP, AE (FJR/OMFJ), Iwakuni MCAS, JP (IWA/RJOI), Don Muang Airport (Bangkok) TH, (BKK/VTBD), U-Tapao RTN, TH (UTP/VTBU), Andersen AFB, GU (UAM/PGUA), Hickam AFB, HI (HIK/PHIK), Travis AFB, CA (SUU/KSUU), Osan AB, KR (OSN/RKSO), and Kimhae IAP/AB, KR (KHE/RKPK).

### SOUTH PACIFIC ROUTE

These missions originate at: McChord AFB, WA (TCM/KTCM) The missions fly the following routes, over a seven day period including en-route stops: (first & third Friday): McChord AFB, WA (TCM/KTCM), Travis AFB, CA (SUU/KSUU), Hickam AFB, HI (HIK/PHIK), Pago Pago IAP, AS (PPG/NSTU), RAAFB Richmond, AU (RDM/YSRI), Alice Springs APT, AU (ASP/YBAS), RAAFB Richmond, AU, Pago Pago IAP, AS, Hickam AFB, HI, Travis AFB, CA, McChord AFB, WA.
(Sunday, over a seven day period): McChord AFB, WA, Travis AFB, CA, Hickam AFB, HI, Andersen AFB, GU, RAAFB Richmond, AU, Andersen AFB, GU, Hickam AFB, HI, McChord AFB, WA.
(First & third Sunday over an eight day period): McChord AFB, WA, Travis AFB, CA, Hickam AFB, HI, Andersen AFB, GU, RAAFB Richmond, AU, Christchurch IAP, NZ, Pago Pago IAP, AS, Hickam AFB, HI, McChord AFB, WA.

# APPENDIX Q
## APPROACHES TO THE STUDY OF SPACE-A AIR OPPORTUNITIES

Space-A Air Opportunities appear on the surface to be very complicated and difficult to use. A brief study of the Space-A Air Opportunity systems using one or more approaches will significantly improve your success with and understanding of the Space-A systems. The knowledge possessed by users of the Space-A systems range from first-time users to seasoned Space-A users. Many persons have experience in two or more priority of use categories, i.e., Active Duty and Retired or Active Reservist/Gray Area Retirees and Retired.

There are four basic approaches to the study and understanding of Space-A Air Opportunities. The Space-A user can use one, two, three or all four of these basic approaches to gain knowledge, and therefore better understand and use the Space-A Air Opportunity Systems. These four basic approaches are

I. Space-A, DoD 4515.13R Air Transportation Eligibility, and Service Department Implementing Instructions. **"WHAT ARE THE SPACE-A RULES AND PROCEDURES?"**

II. Routes, Scheduling, Type Missions and Aircraft Equipment. **"WHERE DO THE AIRCRAFT GO, WHEN, WHY AND HOW?"**

III. Organizations/Commands-Stations (Airports/Bases) of Assignment of Aircraft, Air Crews and Support Facilities in CONUS, OCONUS and Foreign Countries. **"WHERE ARE THE AIRCRAFT?"**

IV. Aircraft type, Number, Performance, Passenger Capability Owned or Operated (Leased) by the Military Department (U.S. Army, U.S. Navy, U.S. Marine Corps, U.S. Coast Guard and U.S. Air Force) which are Passenger Capable Aircraft. **"WHO HAS THE AIRCRAFT (MEANS OF TRANS-PORTATION)?"**

The Space-A student can start the study of Space-A Air Opportunities at any level, I through IV, or from the top down or bottom up, IV through I. Most people start where they have the most expertise, experience or knowledge of the Space-A systems. This arrangement of study levels or areas can be viewed conceptually as: **"THE PYRAMID OF SPACE-A KNOWLEDGE."**

The books *Military Space-A Air Basic Training and Reader Trip Reports* and *Military Space-A Air Opportunities Around the World* provide the information needed to study the Space-A systems.

I: Both titles contain the complete Space-A regulations with all approved changes. The detailed information on how the system works or Services implementing instructions are contained in the sample Space-A trip and trip reports contained in the text portion of *Military Space-A Air Basic Training and Reader Trip Reports.* Thorough and in-depth knowledge of the Space-A rules and implementing procedures are essential to successful Space-A travel.

II. The Military Space-A Air Opportunities book contains detailed routes, scheduling, mission and equipment information for AMC scheduled international flights and domestic (CONUS) MEDEVAC flights around the world. Also, the *Military Space-A Air Opportunities Air Route Map* shows the details of worldwide Space-A routes and is a wonderful planning tool. These scheduled flights move the predominance of the Space-A flights (trips) made by authorized persons each year. These along with the Location Identifier and Cross Reference Index are indispensable tools for planning Space-A trips. Routes, scheduling, mission and equipment are the center-pieces of successful Space-A air travel.

III. The Military Space-A Air Opportunities book shows where each type of aircraft is stationed in CONUS, OCONUS and Foreign Country by station or location. Also, the crews and essential support for these aircraft are in most cases located with the aircraft at each station. Good Space-A Air Opportunities include the use of aircraft which are capable of executing missions to your desired destinations.

IV. The Military Space-A Air Opportunities book lists at each station the types of aircraft stationed at that location, also Appendix N lists the stationing of aircraft by each military department around the world. Appendix M lists a description and performance characteristics of aircraft on which most Space-A travel occurs and the recent inventory of each type of aircraft by military departments.

This approach can be used on a top down basis as described above or on a bottom up basis to obtain a clearer understanding of Space-A systems. In addition to the above, the *Military Space-A Air Opportunities Air Route Map* clearly shows the major overseas/international routes and the CONUS MEDEVAC routes. Traveling to your desired Space-A destination may not always be in a straight line. In fact, sometimes it is beneficial to travel east in order to eventually go west to your desired destination, i.e., you may want to go east from Germany to stations in the Near East in order to turn around and return through Germany to CONUS. This and many other useful tips are contained in the Military Space-A Air Basic Training book.

## APPROACHES TO THE STUDY OF SPACE-A AIR OPPORTUNITIES
### (TOP DOWN OR BOTTOM UP)

**I** **"WHAT ARE THE SPACE-A RULES AND PROCEDURES?"**
DoD Directive 4515.13R AIR TRANSPORTATION ELIGIBILITY with changes and Military Departments Implementing Instructions

**II** **"WHERE DO THE AIRCRAFT GO, WHEN, WHY AND HOW?"**
Space-A Routes, Schedules, Missions and Equipment

**III** **"WHERE ARE THE AIRCRAFT?"**
Organizations/Commands, Stations of Assignment in CONUS, OCONUS and Foreign Countries (Tail codes indicate wing/group and base)

**IV** **"WHO HAS THE AIRCRAFT (MEANS OF TRANSPORTATION)?"**
Aircraft Type, Number(Inventory), Performance, Passenger Capability; Military Department Passenger Capable Aircraft U.S. Army; U.S. Navy; U.S. Marine Corps; U.S. Coast Guard and U.S. Air Force

**IV** **"WHO HAS THE AIRCRAFT (MEANS OF TRANSPORTATION)?"**
Aircraft Type, Number(Inventory), Performance, Passenger Capability; Military Department Passenger Capable Aircraft U.S. Army; U.S. Navy; U.S. Marine Corps; U.S. Coast Guard and U.S. Air Force

**III** **"WHERE ARE THE AIRCRAFT?"**
Organizations/Commands, Stations of Assignment in CONUS, OCONUS and Foreign Countries (Tail codes indicate wing/group and base)

**II** **"WHERE DO THE AIRCRAFT GO, WHEN, WHY AND HOW?"**
Space-A Routes, Schedules, Missions and Equipment

**I** **"WHAT ARE THE SPACE-A RULES AND PROCEDURES?"**
DoD Directive 4515.13R AIR TRANSPORTATION ELIGIBILITY with changes and Military Departments Implementing Instructions

# APPENDIX R
# TEN ESSENTIAL STEPS FOR TRAVELING BY SPACE-A AIR

We have listed below the ten essential steps or functions which are required for all Space-A Air Opportunity travel. These ten steps must be executed or performed for each and every Space-A Air Opportunity travel or trip. Due to space limitations, we have not included here all of the details about each step. However, the details are contained in other text or appendices of *Military Space-A Air Basic Training and Reader Trip Reports.*

**Step 1. Destination Planning and Selection:** What is your destination? In your Space Available Travel Request (AMC Form 140 or equivalent) you can designate (in order of priority) five foreign countries (including CONUS and U.S. Possessions overseas), or four countries, U.S. Possessions overseas and "all" to take advantage of opportune airlift. The "all" designation means that you will accept transportation to CONUS, U.S. Possessions or any foreign country. This system gives you a wide range of destinations.

**Step 2. Travel Identification and Documentation:**
A. All Space-A travelers must have been issued a Uniformed Services Identification Card (from one of the seven Uniformed Services).
B. All Active Duty personnel must have a Leave or Pass Authorization (approved by their Service).
C. Depending upon your category of travel (I-VI) and Personnel Entrance Requirements to Foreign Countries and Areas, the following identification and authorization documentation are required: 1. Passports; 2. Visas; 3. International Certificates of Vaccination and Personal Health History, PHS Form 1839; 4. Authentication of Reserve Status For Travel Eligibility, DD Form 1853; 5. Medal of Honor Award Certificate; 6. Active Duty Environmental & Morale Leave (EML) Orders; 7. House Hunting Orders; 8. Permissive TDY/TAD Orders; 9. Students and Unaccompanied Dependents Orders/Letters and; 10. Special Entry Authorization Letters. All documentation will be reviewed by Passenger Service Personnel at the "Show Time" of your flight.

**Step 3. Space Available Travel Request (AMC Form 140 or Equivalent):**
You can apply for Space-A travel one of four ways:
A. Report to any terminal, complete AMC Form 140 and present your identification/documentation as in 2 above.
B. Apply to any terminal for Space-A Travel by mail/package service with completed AMC Form 140 and statement that all Personnel Entrance Requirements as appropriate for your travel have been met.
C. Fax to any terminal a completed AMC Form 140 and statement that all Personnel Entrance Requirements as appropriate for your travel have been met.
D. E-mail any terminal with the information required in the AMC Form 140 and statement that all Personnel Entrance Requirements as appropriate for your travel have been met. Carry with you copies of all correspondence with the terminals. A few days after you make your application, it is prudent to confirm/verify your application with the terminals and obtain the "Julian Date" which has been assigned to your application. You may apply at more than one terminal for Space-A Air Travel (some areas, i.e., Mid-Atlantic have terminals which are located in the same or nearby areas). Applications are deleted when you fly or at the end of 60 days or the end of your leave, whichever is earlier. Note: All terminals may not have fax and/or e-mail sign-up capability.

**Step 4. Space Available Travel Request for Return Trip:** You may also apply for return transportation at one or more overseas terminals via mail/package service, fax and e-mail at anytime. The timing of this application should fit with your expected departure, duration overseas and expected return. Caution: If you have your return application positioned at a terminal for return to CONUS from that terminal, and you fly from that terminal to other locations, your application for CONUS travel will be deleted from the system. Pick another terminal for local travel or you will lose your priority return to CONUS.

**Step 5. Reporting To The Terminal and "Travel Ready":** When to report to the terminal is an important decision that may well determine the success of your trip. Determine via telephone, fax or e-mail that your application is at the departure terminal. Verify that flights are departing for your desired destinations and your category and priority status on the Space-A waiting list. These factors: Your priority category for travel, position on the Space-A waiting list, available flights/seats to your destinations and other Space-A travelers competing for these seats, will determine your chances for travel. You should be "Travel Ready" which means that you (and all your party) have all required documentation, baggage and essential funds (including emergency commercial backup travel ticket or funds. Also if over 65 years old, you need medical insurance, as MEDICARE is not valid in foreign countries. Rental cars should be turned in. Personal cars should be parked in long-term parking. You should be checked out of hotels. Frequently there is not enough time to accomplish these essential items before "Show Time" and you may miss a flight.

**Step 6. Space-A Flight Call/Selection Process:** A. Space-A seats are normally identified as early as two or three hours or as late as 30 minutes prior to flight departure. The standard Space-A Show Time (Space-A Flight Call) for international/overseas flights is two hours. Due to increased security this time could be three hours. This is the same standard for international flights on commercial airlines. Always check with the passenger service center for the Space-A Show Time. It may be posted on monitors or status boards in the passenger terminal waiting and processing areas.
B. Space-A "Show Time" is important because it is the time at which selection of registered Space-A prospective passengers begins and you must be present to answer when your (sponsor's) name (family/travel group) is called in your travel category (I-VI).
C. The Space-A Flight Call---example, "Anyone desiring Space-A air transportation to a series of stations i.e., Ramstein, DE please assemble at the Space-A desk or other location."
D. All registered Space-A passengers will be offered air transportation on a "first-in, first-out" basis (regardless of rank or service), based on established Space-A categories. The flight processing team knows the number of seats available and will select a sign up or Julian Date near the middle of the register. They will ask if anyone has that date and time, or an earlier date and time, then work forward or move back on the list as appropriate. Each category is processed separately, starting with Category I and moving through to Category VI (there is a roster for each category which is combined into one roster at each terminal). It is important to remember that the number of seats your party requires is a factor in your selection. There must be sufficient seats for your party or the processor will move on and select someone with a later sign-up date. Space-A passengers arriving at the flight information counter after a specific Space-A call has begun must wait until all other Space-A passengers at the Space-A Call have been afforded an opportunity for available seats.

**Step 7. Flight Processing:** After selection for a flight the following processing is required.
A. Payment of Fees and Document Review: There are no fees for departure or arrival at U.S. Military Airports on U.S. military aircraft. The following fees apply to each passenger departing or arriving at U.S. Commercial airports on Category B, "Patriot" flights. These fees are as follows: 1. U.S. Airport Departure (Head) tax-$12.40; 2. Arrivals Fees: Immigration Inspection fee, Customs Inspection fee, and Agriculture Inspection fee $11.00, total fees $23.40  Please note that all commercial airline passengers pay these taxes and fees in the price of their airline tickets. Payment for these fees must be in United States Dollar Currency or via personal check in U.S. dollars.
B. Documents Processing: All documents are inspected for authenticity, dates, and compliance with regulations. Active Duty leave/pass orders must cover sign-up to end of flight. At some point the processing team will want to observe each passenger directly and verify their identity against their travel documents.
C. Baggage Processing: Each person is authorized two pieces of checked baggage, and each piece must not exceed 62 linear inches (length + height + width =62 inches) and not more than 70 pounds for a total of 140 pounds for both pieces. Groups/families may pool their baggage allowances. All hand carried items must fit under the seat or in the overhead bins or other approved storage areas and may not exceed 45 linear inches. There is a 30 pound, one piece limit on small executive aircraft and a 45 pound, one piece limit on C-9 MEDEVAC aircraft. Space-A passengers may not pay for baggage in excess of the allowed weight limit.
D. Ordering and Payment for In-Flight Meals: Current meal cost are as follows: Breakfast=$1.30; Snack Meal=$1.65; Dinner=$3.20. Meals include milk or a soft drink of your choice. Meal prices change are made on 1 October. Each Space-A passenger orders and pays for the meals of their choice. Food and soft drinks are free on AMC "Patriot Flights" (Commercial Contract). You may purchase wine or beer on these flights. No specialized meals are available for Space-A passengers. If you require special food, suggest that you bring your own. No alcoholic beverages for consumption on military aircraft are allowed.
E. Boarding Pass/Ticket Receipt, AMC Form 148/2 or similar: This document assigns seats, verifies and documents payment of fees, if appropriate, payment for meals and most importantly shows your one-time sign-up Julian Date. You now wait for your flight number and destination to be called for boarding.

F. Passenger Security Screening and Boarding Gates: Passengers and carry on items are screened through electronic gates into a secure boarding area. Some passenger terminals perform this screening for everyone entering the passenger terminal. Body searches may also be required. Boarding is as instructed, often in this order: families with small children, passengers needing assistance, DV/VIP and others. The boarding will be through a bus to the aircraft and then up a courtesy/mobile stairs, cargo ramp, or passenger stairs. Some terminals may have the conventional commercial boarding ramp direct from the terminal to the aircraft.

**Step 8. In-Flight:** A. Seating: Most seats will be comfortable padded commercial airline seats mounted facing to the rear of the aircraft for safety. Some aircraft will have plastic formed seating or even web seating along the sides of the aircraft. There will be pillows and blankets and other comfort items. Bring your own reading materials and non-electronic games, as these items along with in-flight movies and music are not available on military aircraft.
B. Clothing: Your clothing should be loose fitting and in layers. Wear comfortable walking shoes. Women should wear slacks and a blouse or sweater. Take a light jacket depending upon the climate. The layers of clothing will be handy on MEDEVAC flights, which are keep warm for patient comfort.
C. Rest Rooms: Restrooms are similar to commercial airlines—plentiful and unisex. Passengers are expected to keep the restrooms clean.
D. Climate Control: The climate is maintained at a comfortable temperature. However there are cold and hot spots on some aircraft. The cabin personnel may be able to adjust the temperature.
E. Noise: You may experience some higher than normal levels of noise during takeoff, landings, special maneuvers and turns. There is no need for earplugs on most aircraft. You will most definitely want earplugs on flights on the C-130 aircraft. Bring your own or ask the cabin crew for wax self-forming earplugs.
F. Safety: Use safety belts when instructed to do so. Only walk about the aircraft when allowed to do so. Never tamper with controls, doors or equipment within the aircraft. Listen very carefully to the in-flight safety lecture given by the cabin crew. Locate the exit nearest to your seating. Know where the emergency oxygen and your life preserver are located.
G. Electronic Devices: The use of computers, electronic games, radios, recorders, TVs, and other devices which may interfere with the aircraft navigation, radar and communication systems is prohibited.
H. Refreshments: There is always fresh water, coffee and tea available in the galley. Meals which were ordered will be served at the appropriate time given, flight conditions.

**Step 9. Post-Flight:** A. Arrival and Aircraft Clearance: After landing, the flight attendants will spray fumigation/insect repellent throughout the cabin as required by international health rules. The manifest and declaration of the health of the crew and passengers will be handed over to local authorities or United States authorities acting on their behalf. After clearance is obtained from the local authority, deplaning of passengers and crew can begin.
B. Deplaning. Passengers are required to complete immigration and customs forms prior to deplaning. The crew will give instructions regarding post-flight processing such as deplaning, immigration, baggage claims and customs. Physical deplaning will be through a passenger chute, stairs or ramp into the terminal or to a bus which will take passengers to the terminal.
C. Immigration: All passengers must report to the immigration processing station with their documentation (Service ID Cards, Passports, Visas, and others as required). Documents are examined carefully and may be checked against persons barred entry to that country.
D. Baggage Claim and Customs: After you have all of your baggage, report to the customs inspection with your customs form and baggage. If you do not have items on which duties are due, entry will quick and easy.

**Step 10. Return Flight to CONUS:** Registration and Return Space-A Air Opportunities: A. Pre-Registration: We recommend that you apply for Space-A travel from one or more overseas departure stations back to CONUS before arriving overseas. This can be done via mail/package delivery, fax or e-mail up to 60 days before you plan to return to CONUS. Note: All travel applications from a station are deleted at that location when you fly or travel from that location to another location overseas. If you have not applied for return travel prior to arriving overseas, the application for return travel should be an item of urgency.
B. Circuitous Routing: You may not find an immediate direct return to your home station when you plan to return to CONUS. You may want to consider taking a less than direct route to CONUS depending upon the availability of flights, i.e., you may want to travel farther east, turn around at some point and go back CONUS.
C. Return Flight: Same general process as flight from CONUS. With luck—"welcome home."

# APPENDIX S
# PASSPORTS & VISAS

Q. Other Than at Passport Agencies, Where Can I Apply for a Passport?

A. You can apply for a passport at many Federal and state courts, probate courts, some county/municipal offices, and some post offices. Over 2500 courts and 1100 post offices in the United States accept passport applications. Court, county/municipal offices and post offices are usually more convenient because they are near your home or your place of business. You save time and money by not having to travel to one of the 13 major U.S. cities where passport agencies are located.

Q. When Do I Have to Apply in Person?

A. You must always apply in person if you are 13 or older, and if you do not meet the requirements for applying by mail. (See "May I Apply for a Passport by Mail?") Usually, for children under 13, only a parent or legal guardian need appear to execute a passport application.

Q. What Do I Need to Do to Apply for a Passport at a Courthouse or Post Office?

A. Go to a courthouse, county/municipal office, or post office authorized to accept passport applications and complete the DSP-11 application form, but do not sign it until instructed to do so. You must present:

　　1. **PROOF OF U.S. CITIZENSHIP**—That is—a previous U.S. Passport or, if you were born in the U.S., a certified copy of your birth certificate issued by the state, city, or county of your birth (a certified copy will have a registrar's raised, embossed, impressed, or multicolored seal and the date the certificate was filed with the registrar's office).

If you have neither a U.S. passport nor a certified birth certificate issued in the U.S.—bring a notice from the registrar of the state where you were born that indicates no birth record exists; also, bring as many as possible of the following: a baptismal certificate, hospital birth record, early Census, early school record, or family Bible record. (To be considered, these documents must show your full name and date and place of birth.) Also, bring a notarized affidavit completed by an older blood relative who has personal knowledge of your birth.

If you were born abroad, bring a Certificate of Naturalization, Certificate of Citizenship, Report of Birth Abroad of a U.S. Citizen, or a Certificate of Birth (Form FS-545 or DS-1350). If you do not have these documents, check with the passport acceptance agent for documents that can be used in their place.

　　2. **TWO PHOTOGRAPHS:** Photographs must be recent (taken within the past six months), identical, 2 X 2 inches, and either color or black/white; they must show a front view, full face, on a plain, light (white or off-white) background. (Vending machine photographs are not acceptable.)

　　3. **PROOF OF IDENTITY:** That is—a previous U.S. passport, a Certificate of Naturalization or Citizenship, a valid driver's license, government or military ID.

　　4. **FEES:** $60.00 for a ten-year passport (age 16 or older); $40.00 for a five-year passport (under 16). These amounts include a $15.00 execution fee. Make your check or money order payable to **Passport Service.** Post offices (and passport agencies) accept cash, but courts are not required to do so. If you must have your passport in less than 25 business days, you will need to pay an additional $35.00 expedite fee to ensure urgent handling. (See "What If I Need a Passport in a Hurry?")

　　5. **SOCIAL SECURITY NUMBER:** Although a Social Security number is not required for issuance of a passport, Section 6039E of the Internal Revenue Code of 1986 requires that passport applicants provide this information. Passport Services gives this information to the Internal Revenue Service (IRS) routinely. Any applicant who fails to provide the information is subject to a $500.00 penalty enforced by the IRS. Questions on this matter should be referred to the nearest IRS office.

Q. Where Can I Get Passport Forms?

A. Passport forms are available from passport agencies, many post offices, and travel agencies or by calling the National Passport Information Center at 1-900-225-5674 (See **"Passport Agencies"** section for more information). They can also be downloaded via the internet at this website: travel.state.gov.

Q. May I Apply for a Passport by Mail?

A. Yes, if you already have a passport and that passport is your most recent one, and it was issued within the past 12 years, and if you were over age 16 when it was issued.

Obtain DSP-82 "Application For Passport By Mail." Fill it out, sign, and date it. **Attach to it:** Your most recent passport; two identical passport photographs (see previous section on passport photographs); and a $40.00 fee, and if applicable, a $35.00 expedite fee for urgent service. (See **"What If I Need a Passport in a Hurry?"**) Make your check or money order payable to **Passport Services.** (The $15.00 execution fee is waived for those eligible to apply by mail.)

If your name changed, enclose a certified copy of the Court Order, Adoption Decree, Marriage Certificate, or Divorce Decree, specifying another name for you to use. (Photocopies will not be accepted.) If your name has changed by any other means, you must apply in person.

Mail (if possible, in a padded envelope) the completed DSP-82 application and attachments to: National Passport Center, P.O. Box 371971, Pittsburgh, PA 15250-7971. Include the appropriate fee for overnight return of your passport. Please note that overnight service will not speed up processing time unless payment for expedited service is also included. (See **"What If I Need a Passport in a Hurry?"**)

Note: *If your passport has been **mutilated, altered or damaged,** you cannot apply by mail. You must **apply in person** using Form DSP-11, present evidence of U.S. citizenship, and acceptable identification. (If you mutilate or alter your U.S. passport, you may render it invalid and expose yourself to possible prosecution under the law [Section 1543 of Title 22 of the U.S. Code]).

Q. When Should I Apply for a Passport?

A. Apply several months in advance of your planned departure. If you will need visas from foreign embassies, allow more time.

Q. What Happens to My Passport Application After I Submit It?

A. If you apply at a passport acceptance facility, the day that you apply, your application will be sent to Passport Services for processing. Your passport will be issued within 25 business days after receipt of complete applications by Passport Services. Your passport will be sent to you by mail at the address you provided on your application.

Q. What Should I Do if My Passport Is Lost or Stolen?

A. If your passport is lost or stolen report the loss on form DSP-64, when you apply, in person, for your new passport. If you are abroad, report the loss immediately to local police authorities and the nearest U.S. embassy or consulate. Remember to write your current address in the space provided in your passport, so that, if it is found, it can be returned to you.

Q. What Else Should I know About Passports?

A. All persons, including newborn infants, are required to obtain passports in their own name. If you need to get a valid passport amended due to a name change, use form DSP-19. (See "May I Apply for a Passport by Mail" for the documentation required.)

Before traveling abroad, make a copy of the identification page so it is easier to get a new passport, should it be necessary. It is also a good idea to carry two extra passport size photos with you. If you run out of pages before your passport expires, submit Form DSP-19, along with your passport to one of the passport agencies listed below. (Please allow time for the processing of the request.) If you travel abroad frequently, you may request a 48-page passport at the time of application.

Some countries require that your passport be valid at least 6 months beyond the dates of your trip. Check with the nearest embassy or consulate of the countries you plan to visit to find out their entry requirements.

In addition to foreign entry requirements, U.S. law must be considered. With certain exceptions, it is against U.S. law to enter or leave the country without a valid passport. Generally for tourists, the exceptions refer to direct travel within U.S. territories or between North, South or Central America (except Cuba).

Q. What If I Need a Passport in a Hurry?

A. If you are leaving on an emergency trip within five working days, apply in person at the nearest passport agency and present your tickets or itinerary from an airline, as well as the other required items. Or, apply at a courthouse, county or municipal office, or post office and have the application sent to the passport agency through an overnight delivery service of your choice (include a self-addressed, prepaid envelope for the overnight return of the passport). Be sure to include dates of departure and travel plans on your application and all fees (including the $35.00 expedite fee).

For more information, contact the National Passport Information Center (NPIC). The NPIC is the only public telephone number for passport information. Callers can dial 1-900-225-5674* to receive passport applications, information on applying for a U.S. passport, or to check on the status of a passport application, or emergency passport procedures. Automated information is available 24 hours/day, 7 days/week. Operators can be reached Monday-Friday, excluding Federal holidays, 0800 to 2000 hours Eastern Standard time. Services are provided in English, Spanish, and by TDD (1-900-225-7778*).

*The cost per minute for 1-900 services is $.35 for recorded information and $1.05 for operator assisted calls. This service also includes an optional number, 1-888-362-8668 (TDD 1-888-498-3648), for those calling from telephones with blocked 1-900 service. These calls require a credit card for payment of a flat rate of $4.95 per call.

## Do you need immediate passport assistance, passport information or the status on your pending passport application?

**If so, you may call the**

### National Passport Information Center

Passport Services has committed itself to responding to the needs of its customers and established the National Passport Information Center (NPIC).

**You may reach the center by calling 1-900-225-5674 (1-900-CALL-NPI) or TDD: 1-900-225-7778 (for the hearing impaired).**

Live operators will be available 8am-8pm, Eastern Time, Monday-Friday, excluding Federal holidays. Automated Voice Response Unit (VRU) service is available 24 hours a day, seven days a week.

Live operator service is $1.05 per minute and is available from 8am to 8pm, Eastern Time, Monday through Friday, excluding Federal Holidays. If your 900 service is blocked, you may use a credit card to call 1-888-362-8668 or TDD: 1-888-498-3648 at $4.95 per call. Callers must be over 18 years old to use this service.

Information provided by the U.S. Department of State, Washington, DC.

# PASSPORT AGENCIES

**Boston Passport Agency**
Thomas P. O'Neill Federal Building
Room 247
10 Causeway Street
Boston, MA 02222-1094

**Chicago Passport Agency**
Suite 380, Kluczynski Federal Office Building
230 South Dearborn Street
Chicago, IL 60604-1564

**Honolulu Passport Agency**
First Hawaii Tower
1132 Bishop Street, Suite 500
Honolulu, HI 96813-2809

**Houston Passport Agency**
Mickey Leland Federal Building, Suite 1100
1919 Smith Street
Houston, TX 77002-8049

**Los Angeles Passport Agency**
Room 1000
11000 Wilshire Boulevard
Los Angeles, CA 90024-3615

**Miami Passport Agency**
3rd Floor, Claude Pepper
Federal Office Building
51 Southwest First Avenue
Miami, FL 33130-1680

**New Orleans Passport Agency**
Postal Service Building
701 Loyola Avenue, Room T-12005
New Orleans, LA 70113-1931

**New York Passport Agency**
Greater Manhattan Federal Building
376 Hudson Street
New York, NY 10014-5000
Appointment line: 212-206-3500
(this line is only for individuals in
the New York City area who are
traveling in less than 14 days.)

**Philadelphia Passport Agency**
U.S. Customs House
200 Chestnut Street, Room 103
Philadelphia, PA 19106-2970

**San Francisco Passport Agency**
95 Hawthorne Street, 5th Floor
San Francisco, CA 94105-3901

**Seattle Passport Agency**
Room 992, Federal Office Building
915 Second Avenue
Seattle, WA 98174-1091

**Stamford Passport Agency**
One Landmark Square
Broad and Atlantic Streets
Stamford, CT 06901-2667

**Washington Passport Agency**
1111 19th Street, N. W.
Washington, D.C. 20524-5000

# VISAS

## OBTAINING A FOREIGN VISA

A visa is a permit to enter and leave the country to be visited. It is a stamp of endorsement placed in a passport by a consular official of the country to which entry is requested. Many countries require visitors from other nations to have in their possession a valid visa obtained before departing from their home country. A visa may be obtained from foreign embassies or consulates located in the U.S. (Visas are not always obtainable at the airport of entry of the foreign location and verification of visa issuance must be made in advance of departure.) Various types of visas are issued depending upon the nature of the visit and the intended length of stay. **Passport services of the Department of State cannot help you obtain visas.**

**A valid passport must be submitted when applying for a visa of any type.** Because the visa is usually stamped directly onto one of the blank pages in your passport, you will need to fill out a form and give your passport to an official of each foreign embassy or consulate. The process may take several weeks for each visa, so apply well in advance. The visa requirements of each country will differ.

**Some visas require a fee.** You may need one or more photographs when submitting your visa applications. They should be full-faced, on white background and should not be larger than 3" x 3" nor smaller than 2.5" x 2.5."

**Several countries do not require U.S. citizens to obtain passports and visas for certain types of travel, mostly tourist.** Instead, they issue a simple tourist card which can be obtained from the nearest consulate of the country in question (presentation of a birth certificate or similar documentary proof of citizenship may be required.) In some countries, the transportation company is authorized to grant tourist cards. A fee is required for some tourist cards.

Some Arab or African countries will not issue visas or allow entry if your passport indicates travel to Israel or South Africa. Consult the nearest U.S. Passport Agency for guidance if this applies to you.

The official institutions (embassies or consulates) representing foreign governments in the U.S. are located in Washington, D.C. (see below) and major U.S. cities and have the most up-to-date information. They are, therefore, your best source. Double check visa requirements before you leave. (*The Congressional Directory,* **available at most public libraries, lists their addresses and phone numbers.) The names, addresses, phone numbers, website and e-mail addresses of embassies in the countries where stations are frequently used by DoD-owned or controlled aircraft can be found on the Internet at http://travel.state.gov/foreignentryreqs.html. A booklet with this information is available at the Passport Agencies listed to the left.**

U.S. Trust territories and possessions overseas have the same requirements as the U.S. has for U.S. citzens upon return from a foreign country. If you wish to travel to a country not listed below, visa and other personnel entry requirements can be obtained from the "DoD Foreign Clearance Guides" available at most AMC (USAF) and other passenger service counters or at many military personnel offices.

NOTE: Embassies may close on their respective national holidays. Call before going to be sure they are open.

*Active duty members on a PCS may take pets on commercial contract Patriot Flights. Space-A passengers, however, may NOT take pets by Space-A air travel. Sorry, Fido.*

# APPENDIX T
# CUSTOMS AND DUTY

**DECLARATIONS:** You must declare all articles acquired during your trip and in your possession at the time you return. This includes: 1) Articles you purchased; 2) Articles given to you while abroad, such as gifts or inherited items; 3) Articles purchased in the duty-free shops or on board carrier; 4) Repairs or alterations made to any articles taken abroad and returned, whether they were performed free of charge or not; 5) Items you have been requested to bring home for another person; 6)All articles you intend to sell or use in your business (Promotional items and samples for Customs purposes are only those items valued at $1.00 or less.) Any articles acquired in the U.S. Virgin Islands, American Samoa, Guam or a country of the Caribbean Basin Economic Recovery Act and not accompanying you when you return. The price actually paid for each article must be stated on your declaration in U.S. currency or its equivalent in the country of acquisition. The stated price must include any value-added tax (VAT) unless it was refunded prior to your arrival in the U.S. If the article was given to you, obtain an estimate of its fair retail value in the country in which it was acquired. *Note: Wearing or using an article acquired abroad does not exempt it from duty. It must be declared at the price you paid for it.*

**Oral Declarations:** A Customs declarations form will be distributed on your plane on the return trip. Fill it out before your arrival so that you can give it to Immigration and Customs inspectors when you disembark. You may make an oral declaration of the articles you acquired abroad if they accompany you and if you have not exceeded the duty-free exemption. A Customs officer may, however, ask you to prepare a written list of the articles.

**Written Declaration:** A written declaration will be necessary when: 1) The total fair retail value of articles acquired abroad exceeds your personal exemption; 2) More than 1 liter (33.8 fl oz) of alcoholic beverages, 200 cigarettes (one carton), and 100 cigars are included; 3) Some of the items are not intended for your personal or household use, like commercial samples, items for sale or use in your business, or articles you brought home for another person; 4) Articles acquired in the U.S. Virgin Islands, American Samoa, Guam or a Caribbean Basin Economic Recovery Act country are being shipped to the United States; 5) A Customs duty or Internal Revenue tax is collectible on any article in your possession; 6) You have used your exemption within the last 30 days.

**Family Declaration:** The head of a family may make a joint declaration for all members residing in the same household as long as they return to the United States together. Family members making a joint declaration may combine their personal exemptions; for example, if Mrs. Smith bought $600.00 worth of merchandise but Mr. Smith only purchased $200.00 worth, Mr. and Mrs. Smith may combine their $400.00 exemptions and will not have to pay any duty on their purchases. **Infants and children** returning to the United States are entitled to the same exemptions as adults, except for alcoholic beverages. Children born abroad, who have never lived in the United States, are entitled to the customs exemptions granted nonresidents.

**Visitors** to the United States should obtain the leaflet **Visiting the U.S.: Customs Requirements for Non-Residents.**

**Military and civilian personnel of the U.S. government** should obtain the leaflet **Customs Highlights for Government Personnel** for information about their customs exemptions when returning from an extended duty assignment abroad.

**WARNING!** If you understate the value of an article you declare, or if you otherwise misrepresent an article in your declaration, you may have to pay a penalty in addition to payment of duty. That article may also be subject to seizure and forfeited if the penalty is not paid. You may find that some merchants abroad offer travelers invoices or bills of sale showing false or understated values. The Customs Service is well-aware of this practice, which can not only delay your Customs examination, but could also result in civil or even criminal penalties. If you fail to declare an article acquired abroad, not only is it subject to seizure or forfeiture, but you will also be liable for a personal penalty in an amount equal to the article's value in the United States. You may also be liable for criminal prosecution. Be very careful about advice given by individuals outside the Customs Service. It could be misleading, and could even cause you to violate Customs laws and incur costly penalties. Please direct any questions to the Customs office nearest you before your departure or upon entry into the United States. If you're uncertain about whether to declare a particular article, always declare it first and then direct your questions to the Customs inspector. If in doubt about an article's value, declare the article at the price actually paid, known as the transaction value. Customs inspectors routinely handle tourist items and are knowledgeable about for-

eign prices. Moreover, current commercial prices of foreign items are available at all times, so on-the-spot comparisons of these values can be made when you return.

Be especially wary of anyone who asks you to carry an item back to the United States. You are responsible for anything in your possession when you clear Customs. Packages from other individuals have been known to contain contraband or currency, and in such a case, you would be responsible for any penalties that may be assessed. **Play it safe—Declare it All.**

**YOUR EXEMPTIONS:** In clearing U.S. Customs, a traveler is considered either a "returning U.S. resident" or a "nonresident." Generally speaking, if you leave the United States for purposes of traveling, working or studying abroad, and then return to resume residency in the United States, Customs considers you a returning resident. American citizens who reside in American Samoa, Guam, or the U.S. Virgin Islands are also classified as returning U.S. residents. Articles acquired abroad and brought into the United States are subject to applicable duty and Internal Revenue tax, but as a returning resident you are allowed certain exemptions from the payment of duty on items obtained while abroad. U.S. residents living abroad temporarily, however, are entitled to be classified as nonresidents, and thus receive more liberal Customs exemptions, on short visits to the United States, provided they export any foreign-acquired items at the completion of their visit.

**Exemptions:** $400.00, $600.00, or $1,200.00. Articles totaling $400.00, $600.00, or $1,200.00, depending on your trip destinations, may be entered free of duty, subject to the limitations on alcoholic beverages, cigarettes, and cigars, If: 1. The articles were acquired during your trip for your personal or household use. 2. The articles accompany you at the time of your return to the United States and they are properly declared to U.S. Customs. Articles purchased abroad and shipped to follow at a later date cannot be applied to your $400.00 exemption. This includes purchases made abroad and left for repairs, alterations, or for other reasons. The flat rate of duty does not apply to mailed articles, but Customs will pass mailed articles worth up to $200.00 duty-free. If the package is valued at more than $200.00, duty will be assessed on the entire amount. Duty is assessed when received and cannot be prepaid. 3. You are returning from a stay abroad of at least 48 hours. Example: A resident who leaves United States territory at 1:30 p.m. on June 1st would complete the required 48 hour period at 1:30 p.m. on June 3rd. This time limitation does not apply if you are returning from Mexico or the U.S. Virgin Islands. 4. You have not used the $400.00, $600.00 or $1,200.00 exemption, or any part of it, within the preceding 30 day period. Also, your exemption is not cumulative. If you use a portion of your exemption on entering the United States, you must wait another 30 days before you are entitled to another exemption, other than a $200.00 exemption. 5. Articles are not prohibited or restricted.

**$400.00 Exemption:** Residents of the U.S. who meet the above conditions are entitled to a $400.00 exemption from paying duty on goods that would otherwise be dutiable. This means that articles acquired abroad with a total value of up to $400.00 will be admitted duty-free as long as they accompany you. Articles you mail home have a different exemption; see the sections on Gifts and Customs Pointers for more information.

Articles beyond the $400.00 duty-free limit may still qualify for duty-free treatment under other exemptions authorities, such as the Generalized System of Preferences, which awards duty-free treatment to many goods from developing countries. Fine art (not handicrafts) and antiques, defined as at least 100 years old, are also duty-free.

This means that a resident could spend more than $400.00 and still not be charged duty when reentering the U.S. For instance, a traveler buys a $300.00 gold bracelet, a $40.00 hat, a $60.00 purse, and a $200.00 unframed painting. Duty would not be charged on these items. The first three items qualify for the $400.00 exemption, and, because fine art is not subject to duty, the traveler can bring in $600.00 worth of goods duty-free. If the painting were framed, however, duty would be charged on the value of the frame.

**$1,200.00 Exemption:** If you return directly or indirectly from a U.S. insular possession—American Samoa, Guam or the U.S. Virgin Islands—your customs exemption is $1,200.00. You may also bring in 1,000 cigarettes, but only 200 of them may have been acquired elsewhere.

**$600.00 Exemption:** If you are returning directly from any of the following 24 beneficiary countries, your customs exemption is $600.00:

| | | |
|---|---|---|
| Antigua & Barbuda | El Salvador | Nicaragua |
| Aruba | Grenada | Panama |
| Bahamas | Guyana | Saint Kitts |
| Barbados | Haiti | and Nevis |
| Belize | Honduras | Saint Lucia |
| Costa Rica | Jamaica | Saint Vincent |
| Dominica | Montserrat | and the |
| Dominican Republic | Netherlands | Grenadines |
| British Virgin | Antilles | Trinidad and |
| Islands | | Tobago |

If you are returning from any of the three U.S. insular possessions, up to $600.00 worth of the merchandise may have been obtained in any of the beneficiary countries, listed above, or up to $400.00 in any other country. For example, if you travel to the U.S. Virgin Islands and Jamaica and then return home, you would be entitled to bring in $1,200.00 worth of merchandise duty-free. Of this amount, $600.00 worth may have been acquired in Jamaica. In the case of the $600.00 exemption for Caribbean Basin Economic Recovery Act countries, up to $400.00 worth of merchandise may have been acquired in other foreign countries. For instance, if you travel to England and the Bahamas, and then return home, your exemption is $600.00, no more than $400.00 of which may have been acquired in England.

**$200.00 Exemption:** If you cannot claim the $400.00, $600.00 or $1,200.00 exemption because of the 30-day or 48-hour minimum limitations, you may bring in free of duty up to $200.00 worth of articles for your personal or household use. This is an individual exemption only; it may not be grouped with other family members on a single customs declaration.

Your $200.00 exemption may include any of the following: 50 cigarettes, 10 cigars, 150 milliliters (4 fl. oz.) of alcoholic beverages, or 150 milliliters (4 fl oz) of perfume containing alcohol. If any article brought with you is subject to duty or tax, or if the total value of all dutiable articles exceeds $200.00, no article may be exempted from duty or tax.

**Cigars and Cigarettes:** Up to 100 cigars and 200 cigarettes (one carton) may be included in your $400.00 exemption. (See other exemption levels for exceptions.) Tobacco products of Cuban origin are generally prohibited. This exemption is available to each person. Cigarettes, however, may be subject to a tax imposed by state and local authorities. For more information on Cuban products, please visit the following Web site: www.ustreas.gov/treas-ury/services/fac/fac.html.

**Liquor:** One liter (33.8 fl. oz.) of alcoholic beverages may be included in the $400.00 exemption if: You are at least 21 years of age; It is for your own use or for a gift; It is not in violation of the laws of the state in which you arrive. (See other exemption levels for exceptions.)

**Note:** Duty on alcoholic beverages is assessed according to alcoholic content; beer and wine will have a lower rate of duty than liqueurs or hard liquor. Also, most states restrict the amount of alcoholic beverages you may import. If the state in which you arrive permits less liquor than you have legally brought into the United States, that state's laws prevail. Information about state restrictions and taxes should be obtained from the state government because laws vary from state to state. Alcoholic beverages beyond the one-liter limitation are subject to duty and Internal Revenue tax. Shipping alcoholic beverages by mail is prohibited by United States postal laws. Alcoholic beverages include wine, beer, and distilled spirits.

**GIFTS:** Gifts accompanying you are considered to be for your personal use and may be included in your exemption. This includes gifts given to you by others after you return. Gifts intended for business, promotional or other commercial purposes may not be included. **Bona fide gifts** of up to $100.00 in fair retail value may be shipped and received by friends and relatives in the United States free of duty and tax as long as the same person does not receive more than $100.00 in gift shipments in one day. The "day" in reference is the day in which the parcel(s) are received for customs processing. Gifts intended for more than one person may be shipped in a single, consolidated package provided they are individually wrapped and labeled with the recipients' names. A consolidated gift package's outer wrapper should bear the words **consolidated gift package** and should list the recipients' names and the value of each gift. The exemption for gifts is increased to $200.00 if they are shipped from the U.S. Virgin Islands, American Samoa, or Guam. Gifts sent by mail need not be declared when you return to the United States. Perfume containing alcohol and valued at more than $5.00 retail, tobacco products, and alcoholic beverages are excluded from the gift provision. Be sure all gift packages are marked on the outer wrapping: 1) "unsolicited gift," 2) nature of the gift—shoes, sweater, toy truck, etc., and 3) its fair retail value. This will facilitate Customs clearance of your package. If any article imported in a gift parcel is subject to duty and tax, or should any single gift within a consolidated package exceed the bona fide gift allowance, then that gift will be dutiable.

**You, as a traveler, cannot send a "gift" to yourself, nor can persons traveling together send "gifts" to each other. Gifts ordered by mail from the United States do not qualify under this duty-free gift provision and are subject to duty.** If a parcel is subject to duty, the United States Postal Service will collect it along with any handling charges. Duty cannot be pre-paid.

**OTHER ARTICLES FREE OF DUTY OR DUTIABLE: Duty preferences** are granted to certain developing countries under the Generalized System of Preferences (GSP). Some products that would otherwise be dutiable if imported from any other country have been exempted from duty when imported from GSP countries. For details, obtain the leaflet **GSP & The Traveler** from the nearest Customs office.

**The North American Free Trade Agreement (NAFTA)** was implemented on 1 January 1994. U.S. residents returning directly or indirectly from Canada or Mexico are eligible for free or reduced duty rates on goods originating, as defined by NAFTA, in either country. Travelers can support a claim of NAFTA origination with either an oral or written statement or with an invoice that contains a valid NAFTA declaration.

**Personal belongings** taken abroad are entitled to duty-free entry on your return provided they are of U.S. origin. Items such as worn clothing or other American-made belongings may be sent home by mail before you return and receive free entry as long as they have not been altered or repaired while abroad. These packages should be marked "American Goods Returned." When a claim of United States origin is made, marking on the article to so indicate facilitates Customs processing.

**Foreign-made personal articles taken abroad** are dutiable each time they are brought into our country unless you have acceptable proof of prior possession. Documents that fully describe the article, like bills of sale, insurance policies, jeweler's or other appraisals, or purchase receipts may be considered reasonable proof of prior possession. Items like watches, cameras, tape recorders, or other articles that can be readily identified by serial numbers or permanently affixed markings may be taken to the Customs office nearest you and registered before your departure. You'll get a Certificate of Registration (CF 4457) that will expedite free entry of these items when you return. Keep the certificate, since it remains valid for any future trips as long as the information on it is legible. The Customs officer must actually see the item(s) you wish to register, so it cannot be done by phone, nor can blank forms be given or mailed to you to be filled out at a later time.

**Vehicles, boats, and planes** taken abroad for non-commercial use may be returned duty-free by proving to the Customs officer that you took them out of the United States. This proof may be a state registration card for an automobile, an FAA certificate for an aircraft, a yacht license or motorboat identification certificate for a pleasure boat, or a Customs certificate of registration (CF-4457) filled out and certified before departure. Repairs performed or accessories acquired abroad for articles taken out of the United States are dutiable and must be declared on your return. **Warning:** Catalytic converter-equipped vehicles (models manufactured in or after 1976) driven outside North America will, in most cases, not meet EPA standards when brought back to the United States.

**Household effects and tools of trade or occupation** taken out of the United States are duty-free at the time you return if properly declared and entered. All furniture, carpets, paintings, tableware, linens, stereos, and similar household furnishings acquired abroad may be imported free of duty, if: They are not imported for another person or for sale. You have used them abroad for at least one year, or they were available for use in a household in which you resided for one year. **Articles imported in excess** of your Customs exemption will be subject to duty unless the items are entitled to free entry or are prohibited. The Customs inspector will place items with the highest rate of duty under your exemption, and duty will be assessed on the lower-rated items. After deducting your exemptions and the value of any duty-free articles, a flat 10 percent rate of duty will be applied to the next $1,000.00 (fair retail value) of merchandise, except for NAFTA-originating goods. Any dollar amount more than $1,000.00 will be dutiable at the various rates of duty applicable to the articles, as provided for in the Harmonized Tariff schedule. Articles to which the flat 10 percent rate is applied must be for your personal use or for use as gifts. You cannot receive this flat-rate provision more than once every 30 days, excluding the day of your last arrival. The flat rate of duty for articles purchased in the U.S. Virgin Islands, American Samoa, or Guam is five percent, whether the articles accompany you or are shipped.

*Customs and Duty, continued*

**Payment of duty** on articles accompanying you is required at the time of your arrival and may be made by any of the following ways: U.S. currency (foreign currency is not acceptable). Personal check in the exact amount of duty, drawn on a national or state bank or trust company of the United States, made payable to the "U.S. Customs Service." Government checks, money orders or traveler's checks are acceptable as long as they don't exceed the duty owed by more than $50.00. Second endorsement on checks are not acceptable, and identification—passport, driver's license or other picture ID—must be presented. In some locations you may pay duty with credit cards from MasterCard or VISA.

**PROHIBITED AND RESTRICTED ARTICLES:** Certain articles considered injurious or detrimental to the general welfare of the United States are prohibited entry by law. Among these are: Lottery tickets, narcotics and dangerous drugs, obscene articles and publications, seditious and treasonable materials, hazardous articles (e.g., fireworks, dangerous toys, toxic or poisonous substances) and switchblade knives. Other items must meet special requirements before they can be released. You will be given a receipt for any articles retained by Customs.

**Artifacts/Cultural Property:** U.S. law prohibits the importation of pre-Columbian monumental and architectural sculpture and murals from certain countries in Central and South America without proper export permits. Federal law and international treaties prohibit the importation of any pieces of cultural property stolen from museums or from religious or secular public monuments.

**Automobiles:** Automobiles imported into the United States must conform to Environmental Protection Agency emission requirements and Department of Transportation safety, bumper, and theft-prevention standards. Information on importing vehicles can be obtained from the EPA, Attn: 6405J, Washington, D.C. 20460, Tel: C-202-233-9660, and from DOT's National Highway Traffic Safety Administration, www.nhtsa.dot.gov/cars/rules/import>, Office of Vehicle Safety Compliance (NSA-32), Washington, D.C. 20590 or C-1-800-424-9393.

**Biological Materials:** Biological materials of public health or veterinary importance (disease organisms and vectors for research and educational purposes) require import permits. Write to the Foreign Quarantine Program, U.S. Public Health Service, Centers for Disease Control, Atlanta, GA 30333.

**Books, Computer Programs, Cassettes, Video Tapes:** Pirated copies of copyrighted articles—that is, unlawfully made articles produced without the authorization of the copyright's owner—are prohibited from importation into the United States. Pirated copies will be seized and destroyed.

**Copyright and Trademark-Protected Articles:** Customs separates foreign-made products bearing American-registered trademarks into two categories: 1. **counterfeit,** which are illegal products manufactured without the authorization of the company or person who owns the trademark, commonly known as "knock-offs," and 2. **parallel imports,** which are products manufactured under the trademark owner's authorization, but are imported into the U.S. by an unauthorized person or company. Parallel imports are commonly known as "gray-market goods." Returning travelers are allowed an exemption, usually one article of each type bearing a protected trademark.

**Ceramic Tableware:** Some ceramic tableware sold abroad contains dangerous levels of lead in the glaze that can leach into certain foods and beverages served in them. The FDA recommends that ceramic tableware, especially when purchased in Mexico, China, Hong Kong or India, be tested for lead release on your return or be used for decorative purposes only.

**Drug Paraphernalia:** The importation, exportation, manufacture, sale, and transportation of drug paraphernalia are prohibited.

**Firearms and Ammunition:** Firearms and ammunition are subject to restrictions and import permits approved by the Bureau of Alcohol, Tobacco and Firearms (ATF). Applications to import may only be made by or through a licensed importer, dealer, or manufacturer. No import permit is required when it can be demonstrated that the firearm or ammunition were previously taken out of the United States by the same person who is returning with them.

**Fish, Wildlife, Hunting Trophies:** Fish and wildlife are subject to certain import and export restrictions, prohibitions, permits or certificates, and quarantine requirements. These requirements pertain to: 1. Wild birds, mammals including marine mammals, reptiles, crustaceans, fish, mollusks, and invertebrates. 2. Any part or product, such as skins, feathers, eggs. 3. Products and articles manufactured from wildlife and fish.

**Hunting Trophies:** If you plan to import a hunting trophy or game, check with the Fish and Wildlife Service first.

**Food Products:** Bakery items and all cured cheeses are admissible.

**Fruits and Vegetables:** Most fruits and vegetables are either prohibited from entering the country or require an import permit. Most canned or processed items are admissible.

**Meats, Livestock, Poultry:** Meats, livestock, poultry, and their by-products are either prohibited or restricted from entering the United States, depending on the animal disease condition in the country of origin. Canned meat is permitted if the inspector can determine that it is commercially canned, cooked in the container, hermetically sealed, and can be kept without refrigeration.

**Plants:** Plants, cuttings, seeds, unprocessed plant products, and certain endangered species either require an import permit or are prohibited from entering the United States.

**Gold:** Gold coins, medals, and bullion, formerly prohibited, may be brought into the United States. Gold items originating in or brought from Cuba, Iran, Iraq, Libya and North Korea are prohibited entry.

**Medicine/Narcotics:** Narcotics and dangerous drugs, including anabolic steroids, are prohibited: A traveler requiring medicines containing habit-forming drugs or narcotics (e.g., cough medicines, diuretics, heart medications, tranquilizers, sleeping pills, antidepressants, stimulants, etc. 1. Have all drugs, medicinal and similar products properly identified; 2. Carry only such quantity as might normally be carried by an individual having that health problem. 3. Have a prescription or written statement from your physician that the medications are being used under a doctor's direction and that they are necessary for your physical well-being while traveling.

**Merchandise from Embargoed Countries:** The importation of goods from the following countries is generally prohibited under regulations administered by the Office of Foreign Assets Control: Cuba, Iran, Iraq, Libya and North Korea.

**Money and Other Monetary Instruments:** There is no limit or restriction on the total amount of monetary instruments that may be brought into or taken out of the United States, nor is it illegal to do so. However, if you transport or cause to be transported, including by mail or other means, more than $10,000.00 in monetary instruments on any occasion into or out of the United States, or if you receive more than that amount, you must file a report, Customs Form 4790, with U.S. Customs (Currency & Foreign Transactions Reporting Act, 31 U.S. C. 1101, et seq). Failure to comply can result in civil, criminal and/or forfeiture penalties.

**Pets:** There are controls, restrictions, and prohibitions on the entry of animals, birds, turtles, wildlife, and endangered species. 1. **Cats** must be free of evidence of diseases communicable to man when examined at the port of entry. 2. **Dogs** must be free of evidence of diseases communicable to man. Dogs older than three months must be vaccinated against rabies at least 30 days prior to arrival, and a valid rabies vaccination certificate must accompany the animal. 3. **Personally-owned pet birds** may be entered (limit of two if of the psittacine family), but APHIS and Public Health Service requirements must be met, including quarantine at an APHIS facility at specified locations at the owner's expense. Advance reservations are required. **Non-human primates** such as monkeys, apes and similar animals may not be imported.

**Textiles:** Textiles and clothing that accompany you and that you have acquired abroad for personal use or as gifts are generally not subjected to restrictions on the amount. However, unaccompanied textiles and clothing may be subject to certain quantity restrictions, called quotas.

## CUSTOMS POINTERS

**Traveling Back and Forth Across Borders.** If your travel plans include trips back and forth across the Canadian or Mexican border, don't risk losing your Customs exemption because of the 48-hour rule. If you make a swing-back inquire at the nearest Customs office about these requirements.

# APPENDIX U
## SPACE-A QUESTIONS AND ANSWERS

One of the biggest fringe benefits, dollar-wise, for uniformed services personnel and their family members is Space-A air travel on U.S. military owned and operated aircraft. While there are some old pros who know all the ropes, having learned the hard way by flying Space-A, there are those who are a bit afraid to jump into the unknown. This appendix is for those who want to know as much as they can about Space-A air travel. Answers are based on information available to us at press time. Because policies can change or be interpreted differently, these general answers must be regarded only as guides - not rules. Specific questions, particularly those dealing with changes in policy, should be directed to military officials who are the final authority on the subject. We have divided the questions and answers into general functional categories. We hope that this appendix will aid readers in locating questions and answers in which they have a special interest.

### GENERAL INFORMATION

01. Is Space-A travel a reasonable substitute for travel on a commercial airline? The answer depends on you! If your travel schedule is flexible and your finances permit for a stay (sometimes in a "high-cost" area), while awaiting movement, space-available travel is a good travel choice. While some travelers sign up and travel the same day, many factors could come together to make buying a commercial ticket your best or only option. Remember, Space-A travel success depends on flexibility, patience and good timing.

02. What facilities are available at AMC terminals (nursery, BX, snack bar)? Facilities at most military terminals are generally the same as commercial facilities. Facilities include exchanges, barber shops, snack bars, pay television (free television lounge in some military terminals), traveler assistance, baggage lockers or rooms, United Service Organization (USO) lounges, and nurseries (at major terminals). The type of facility available will vary according to the terminal size, passenger volume, location and military mission.

03. What documents are required for traveling Space-A? All travelers require a uniformed services ID card. Dependent family members and Retirees require a passport in most cases. Visas or visitor cards may be required for passport holders traveling to some destinations. In some cases immunization records are required. See Appendix B: Personnel Entrance Requirements for detailed requirements.

04. Will Space-A travel cost much? In general, no. Some terminals must collect a federal departure tax and/or a federal inspection fee from Space-A passengers on commercial contract missions. Meals may be purchased at a nominal fee out of most air terminals while traveling on military aircraft. Meal service on AMC Category B "Patriot Flights" full plane load charters is complimentary.

05. What fees will Space-A passengers be required to pay? All passengers departing CONUS, Alaska or Hawaii on a commercial aircraft from a commercial airport must pay a $6 Airport Departure Tax that goes toward airport improvements. Also, all Space-A passengers departing on commercial contract mission inbound to the United States must pay a $12.40 Head Tax and an $11.00 Federal Inspection Fee. Some foreign departure terminals may also collect a departure tax, e.g., $30 AU when leaving Australia.

06. What are the trends in the availability of Space-A travel? Does it seem as if there will be more or less Space-A travel in the coming years? Although AMC has lead efforts to improve Space-A travel in the past few years, movement still remains a result of unused seats. Present DoD personnel and budget trends are effecting Space-A movement opportunity. AMC is dedicated to putting a passenger in every available seat.

07. How can I find where my name is on the Space-A register? Each terminal maintains a Space-A register (organized by priority and the date and time of registration for travel) that is updated daily. The register is conveniently located in the terminal and directly accessible to you. Travelers may call the terminal directly to find where they stand travelwise.

08. As a Reservist, where can I fly? Reserve members with DD Form 2 (Red) identification and DD Form 1853 may fly to, from, and between Alaska, Hawaii, Puerto Rico, the U.S. Virgin Islands, Guam, American Samoa, and CONUS. Additionally, when on active duty (for 30 days or more), members may fly anywhere overseas that AMC has flights operating.

09. As a Retiree, where can I fly? Retired members with DD Form 2 (Blue; the old form is gray) identification card may fly anywhere AMC has flights operating including CONUS, with the exception of occasional restricted areas such as Vietnam and Diego Garcia which have been restricted for many years. Some areas require special permission to enter, such as Kenya.

10. Can I have family members travel with another military member if given power of attorney, other releases, or authority? No, with the exception of Category IV EML Leave and Category V, command-sponsored dependents may only travel when accompanied by their sponsor.

11. Who determines eligibility to fly Space-A? The four services jointly establish Space-A eligibility which is published in DoD 4515.13-R "Air Transportation Eligibility." AMC's first responsibility is airlifting official DoD traffic. Space-A passengers are accommodated only after official duty passengers and cargo.

12. How long does my name stay on the Space-A list? All travelers remain on the register for 60 days after registration, for the duration of their travel orders authorization, or until they are selected for travel, whichever occurs first. Revalidation has been eliminated.

13. What is country sign-up and how does it affect me? Under this program, you may sign up for five different countries rather than five different destinations. You are also eligible for the "ALL" sign-up which makes you eligible for all other destinations served. The applicant can sign up for four countries and "ALL" as the fifth destination. This gives you a greater selection of destinations from which to choose.

14. What is remote sign-up? Remote sign-up allows passengers to enter the backlog by telefaxing copies of proper service documentation along with desired country destinations and family members' first names to the aerial port of departure. The telefax data header will establish date/time of sign-up; therefore, Active Duty personnel must ensure the telefax is sent no earlier than the effective date of leave. Mail entries will also be permitted. The original date and time of sign-up shall be documented and stay with the passenger until his or her destination is reached. Also at any time the passenger may sign up for space-available travel to return to home station. NOTE: If applicable, a statement that all required border clearance documents are current is required.

15. What is self sign-up? Self sign-up is a program that allows passengers to sign up at a terminal without waiting in line. Most locations now provide self sign-up counters with easy to follow instructions for registration.

### BAGGAGE

16. How much baggage can Space-A passengers check? Each Space-A passenger (regardless of age) can check two pieces of baggage totaling 140 pounds. Air Mobility Command (AMC) limits the size of each item to 62 linear inches. This measurement is obtained by adding together the item's length, width and height. The rules permit some exceptions to the 62 linear inches size limitation. For Active Duty personnel, all duffel bags, sea bags, Air Force issue B-4 bags and civilian-origin versions that have the same approximate dimensions can be checked. Similarly, the size restrictions do not apply to golf bags with golf clubs, snow skis, folding bicycles, fishing equipment, musical instruments and rucksacks. Any one of these oversized items listed above may be checked if it is the only piece checked and meets weight requirements of 140 pounds total.

17. We have heard that families and other groups can "pool" their baggage authorization. What's the story? Space-A passengers traveling together as a group (that is, listed on a single Military Transportation Authorization or AMC Form 140 (Space Available Travel Request)) may pool their baggage authorization so long as the total number of checked pieces does not exceed the number of travelers times 140 pounds, i.e., a five person family travel group could not exceed 700 pounds (5 x 140 pounds = 700 pounds) and 10 pieces (5x2=10).

18. How much baggage can I carry with me into the passenger cabins? All passengers boarding the aircraft can carry on one or more pieces so long as they fit under the passenger's seat, in the overhead compartment or

**Space-A Questions and Answers, continued**

other approved storage area, e.g., closets for hang-up garment bags. If available storage space is important to your baggage carrying needs, inquire at the terminal regarding storage areas for carry-on baggage before checking your baggage for a particular flight. As a guideline carry-on bags should not exceed 45 linear inches (length + width + height = 45 inches). Passengers traveling with infants can also carry on any Federal Aviation Administration (FAA) approved infant car seat regardless of any other baggage. Each AMC facility has a list of the FAA approved car seats. Passengers can call the FAA at tel: (202) 426-3800 to determine if new seats have been added to the list of approved seats.

19. Is the baggage limit the same for all aircraft? No. The baggage limit for smaller executive aircraft and the C-009A/E Nightingale is considerably less. On small two-engine executive and operational support aircraft, the baggage limit for Space-A passengers is 30 pounds. Also, on the C-009A/E aircraft the size limit for carry-on baggage is 18" long, 5" wide and 19" high or 42" overall.

20. As a Space-A passenger, may I pay for excess checked baggage over 140 pound or two pieces? No. Only duty status passengers may pay for excess baggage.

NOTE: See APPENDIX V: Space-A Travel Tips for more information on baggage.

## ELIGIBILITY

21. May all Active Duty and Retired members of all the Uniformed Services fly Space-A? Yes. All Active Duty and Retired members (as well as their eligible family members) of all seven uniformed services (U.S. Army, U.S. Navy, U.S. Marine Corps, U.S. Coast Guard, U.S. Public Health Service Officer Corps, National Oceanic and Atmospheric Administration Officer Corps and U.S. Air Force) may fly Space-A as provided for in DoDD 4515.13-R as revised. Dependent family members may only accompany their sponsor on flights going overseas and in overseas areas. Dependents may not fly point to point in CONUS unless the same mission/flight continues overseas. As the result of a recent change in the regulation, one adult Active Duty dependent may accompany the sponsor on CONUS point-to-point flights when the sponsor is on "emergency leave" and when the sponsor is on an approved house hunting trip prior to a PCS.

22. May National Guard and Reservists fly Space-A? National Guard members and Reservists in an Active paid status may fly anywhere in CONUS, Alaska, Hawaii, Puerto Rico, Guam, American Samoa and the U.S. Virgin Islands. Guard and Reserve members cannot fly Space-A to a foreign country. Congressman Tom Campbell of California (Tel: C-202-225-2631) has introduced a bill H. R. 3267, Fairness for the Military Reserve Act of 1999, which among other things, would extend Space-A air travel to selected Reservists, including National Guard to outside the United States and its possessions, to foreign countries--the same as retired military, and would give Reservists the same priority status as Active Duty personnel when traveling for their monthly drills. Caution: This is not law at press time. Guard and Reserve members must have the ID Card, DD Form 2 (Red), and DD Form 1853, Authentication of Reserve Status for Travel Eligibility (authenticated by the Unit Commander within the last six months). The same is true of Guard and Reserve personnel who have received official notification of retirement eligibility but have not reached retirement age (60). This "gray area" retirement eligible group must present their ID cards (Red) and retirement eligibility notices (letters) or possess a red DD Form 2 which has been generated from the DEERS database.

23. When may National Guard and Reservist eligible family members fly Space-A? When the sponsor retires and receives retired pay and full benefits at age 60, eligible family members may then fly Space-A. Family members must be accompanied by their sponsor when flying Space-A and may only fly on flights going overseas and in the overseas area, except CONUS legs of overseas flights.

24. Is there any difference in Space-A rules regarding eligibility for Active Duty versus Retired service members? Yes. First of all, Active Duty sponsors

personnel have priority (Categories I Emergency Leave (retirees may be added to this category when approved under special circumstances), II

EML, III Ordinary Leave, IV Unaccompanied Dependents on EML and V Permissive TDY) on Space-A flights at all times. Other differences include the fact that Active Duty personnel may take their "dependent" mothers and fathers (who have ID Cards DD Form 1173), with them on Space-A trips. Dependent in-laws are NOT included in this privilege. Retired members do not have this privilege, and Retired members and their families travel in Category VI.

25. I am a 100% disabled American veteran (DAV). I've heard that some of us can fly Space-A and some can't. Could you give me more information on 100% DAVs and Space-A? Disabled American veterans must be RETIRED from a uniformed service to qualify for Space-A travel. Those members who were separated in lieu of being retired are not eligible. Here's an easy way to check your eligibility. If your monthly retired check is paid by a uniformed services finance center, e.g., Defense Finance and Accounting Service, Cleveland Center, and your ID card is DD Form 2 (old cards are gray in color; new cards are blue), you can fly Space-A. If you are paid by the Veterans Administration and your ID card is a DD Form 1173 (butterscotch in color) or the more recently issued DD Form 2765, you cannot fly Space-A. The color of ID cards and their form numbers are the key to being allowed to sign up for a Space-A flight. The DD Form 1173 is the same ID form used by dependents. In any case, dependents are not generally allowed to fly Space-A without their sponsors, so this butterscotch color card is a red flag alerting the officials at the Space-A desk that the carrier of the DD Form 1173 is not eligible to fly Space-A unaccompanied.

26. I am Retired military and disabled and carry a blue ID card. Can I have a brother, sister, or friend accompany me to help me? The only persons permitted to accompany you are your dependents (not in the CONUS) or other persons eligible for Space-A travel. Every effort shall be made to transport passengers with disabilities who are otherwise eligible to travel. Passenger service personnel and crew members shall provide assistance in boarding, seating, and deplaning passengers with special needs.

27. May a Retired service member, who relies on a guide dog because of vision deficiency, travel with the animal aboard military aircraft Space-A? Yes. This is allowed when the dog is properly harnessed and muzzled and the animal does not obstruct the aisle. Also, the dog may not occupy a seat in the aircraft, it must sit at the feet of the service member.

28. Who may fly on National Guard and Reserve flights of the Military Services? All uniformed services personnel and their eligible dependents may fly on most National Guard and Reserve flights depending upon the mission. The National Guard and Reserve have some of the best flights available. The catch is that many are not scheduled flights. Many different types of flight missions are given to National Guard and Reserve units; therefore, one can often find some very special flights to places not normally seen on flight schedules. Most National Guard and Reserve departure locations are listed in Military Living's *Military Space-A Air Opportunities Around The World* book.

29. Are Active Duty personnel in a leave or pass status traveling Space-A, always required to wear the service uniform? No. All Active Duty members (except USMC flying on USMC Marine aircraft) in a leave or pass status traveling Space-A on military department owned and operated aircraft are not required to wear the class A or B uniform of their service.

30. May an Active Duty service member use Space-A to take dependents to his/her unaccompanied duty station overseas or back from overseas to CONUS after the unaccompanied duty tour is completed? No. Family members may use Space-A only when they are with the sponsor on an accompanied tour (on service orders) overseas. The Space-A privilege is intended only for a visit to an overseas or CONUS area on a round-trip basis with the sponsor. Space-A cannot be used to establish a home for dependents overseas or in CONUS.

31. May an Active Duty service member sign out on leave, sign up (register) for Space-A and if there is a wait for the flight, go back to work to avoid loss of leave time? When registering for Space-A travel, either by fax, mail/courier or in person, the member must have an approved leave or pass authorization effective on or before the date of registration for Space-A travel. You must show your approved leave with an effective date on or before your sign-up date. If a member registers for Space-A travel but voluntarily returns

to work during the intervening days before the actual flight departure, leave will be charged for those days. You must be on leave throughout your entire Space-A leave travel period.

32. What does it mean to be "bumped?" The mission needs of space required passengers or cargo may require the removal of Space-A passengers at any point. If removed after being manifested (approved for this particular flight) on a flight or en route, you may re-register with the date and time adjusted to reflect the date and time of registration at the point of origin. The Space-A passengers will be placed no higher than the bottom of the category I on the Space-A register. Space-A passengers cannot be bumped by other Space-A passengers.

33. What can service families do if they become extremely ill while overseas and need to return to the United States? Air medical evacuation (MEDEVAC) through AMC is available to Active Duty, Retired and their eligible family members. Space-A travelers should get in touch with a U.S. military medical facility, preferably a hospital, or the American Embassy or Consulate to be considered for this service. In a change of military regulations, the remains of a retiree who died overseas may be returned on AMC aircraft to the U.S. for burial. Watch our *R&R Travel News*™ for more info.

34. What is "show time?" "Show time" is the time when a roll call of prospective Space-required and Space-A passengers, who are waiting for a specific flight, is made. The total available seats are allocated to travelers based on priority category and date/time of sign-up. See Section I for details. Failure to make "show time" will result in not making the flight and "show times" can be changed without notice depending on operational requirements.

35. Why can't passengers arriving at the terminal after "show time" for a flight be processed for that flight? Passengers should realize that many tasks are performed before a flight departs. Every possible effort will be made to process passengers arriving after "show time" if it doesn't jeopardize the aircraft's departure time or mission safety.

36. Are there special eligibility requirements for pregnant women and infants? Yes. Children must be older than six weeks to fly on military aircraft. If the infant is younger than six weeks old, there must be written permission from a physician to fly for mother and child. Pregnant women may fly without approval until their 34th week of pregnancy. In a medical emergency, a pregnant woman of more than 34 weeks or a child younger than six weeks and the mother will be flown on a medical evacuation (MEDEVAC) flight as patients.

37. What is the scope of the DoD student travel program? Dependent students who attend school in the United States are authorized one round-trip travel per fiscal year from the school location to the parents' duty station overseas, including U.S. possessions. The student travel program began in 1984 as a quality of life initiative for service members stationed overseas who had children attending secondary or undergraduate school in the United States. The plan has fluctuated over the years. The rule for the travel program applies to service members permanently assigned outside CONUS authorized to have family members reside with them. The student dependent must be unmarried, under age 23, pursuing a secondary or undergraduate education and possess a valid DD Form 1173 ID card.

38. What is the Environmental and Morale Leave (EML) Program? This program is designed to provide environmental relief from a duty station which has some "drawbacks" and to offer a source of affordable recreation otherwise not available. In simple terms, it boils down to allowing Active Duty military personnel and their dependents to fly Space-A on military aircraft. There are, however, a couple of big differences in EML leave and regular Space-A leave. First, dependents are permitted to travel accompanied or UNACCOMPANIED by their sponsor. They may utilize "suitably equipped DoD logistic-type aircraft" as well as AMC channel and contract aircraft. Secondly, EML has a Category II classification (for sponsors and their dependents traveling together) which is higher than regular Active Duty, Category III and Retired Space-A classification (Category VI). Dependents traveling on EML leave orders alone are in category IV. Military sponsors and/or dependents on EML revert to ordinary leave status when they arrive in CONUS. They regain their EML status only when they depart CONUS for their EML program area. A good bit of EML travel is utilized in the Middle and Far East areas. This means that fewer flights may be available from this area for lower category personnel. The EML program is a tremendous morale booster to those assigned in far-off places and is very popular in these areas.

39. My husband was killed in Vietnam and is buried in the Punch Bowl (National Memorial Cemetery of the Pacific) in Hawaii. The children and I would like to take a trip to Hawaii to visit his grave. Can we fly in a Space-A status? No. Sorry, but widow/ers are not afforded the privilege of Space-A air travel. The rules state that family members must be accompanied by their military sponsor, so naturally this is impossible. There have been proposals advanced, namely by the National Association of Uniformed Services/Society of Military Widows (NAUS/SMW) and others, to support a change to the DoD Space-A Directive which does not provide for widow/ers of uniformed personnel from using overseas (and any other) Space-A travel.

40. May I register (sign-up) by fax, e-mail, letter/courier or in person at the same departure terminal more than one time for five different foreign countries in order to improve my chances for selection to a particular country? Space-A passengers may have only one registration (sign-up) record at a passenger terminal specifying a maximum of five countries (the fifth country may be "ALL" in order to allow the widest opportunity for Space-A air travel). This record may be changed at any time to include adding or deleting countries to which a passenger wants to travel, but the Julian date and time will be adjusted to the date of the latest change. No passenger may have two or more records with separate information; however, you may sign-up at several departure terminals in order to improve your chances for selection for air travel. This may change in the near future if "round-trip sign-up or one-time sign up" is approved. For example, in the Mid-Atlantic States Area you can sign up at McGuire AFB, Baltimore/Washington IAP, Andrews AFB and Dover AFB for air travel to Central Europe and the Near East Area.

41. What happens to your sign-up records at a departure location when you fly from that station? Note carefully that once passengers are selected for a flight, their name will be removed from the station standby register for all destinations.

42. May pets be transported Space-A? Not by Space-A passengers. Active Duty personnel may move pets Space-A on military contract flights when the sponsor is traveling on a permanent change of station.

43. I am retired. When I was on active duty, my personnel officer issued me travel and leave orders which specified travel documents and other requirements for visiting foreign countries. Where can I now get that information? Appendix B: Personnel Entrance Requirements. You may also check the personnel entrance requirements to foriegn countries and the latest changes to the DoD Foreign Clearance Guides at local personnel offices, AMC Space-A counters or most other air departure locations.

44. As a Space-A passenger, will I be subjected to security screening prior to boarding a flight? Yes. In most cases you and your baggage will receive electronic and/or personal security screening prior to boarding the flight or entering a secure area for aircraft boarding.

45. May adult family members who are dependent children because of a handicap or a permanent disability, and who have a valid DD Form 1173 military ID card, travel with their sponsor regardless of age? Yes. They may travel on the same basis as any other dependent on flights going overseas and in the overseas theater. Documentation of the dependent's permanent disability may be required.

## FOOD AND BEVERAGE SERVICES

46. Is food served to Space-A passengers on the flight? Food and soft drinks are free on AMC contract "Patriot Flights". Space-A passengers, like duty passengers, may purchase beer and wine on AMC contract Patriot Flights. There is a charge if Space-A passengers want to eat on other (military) flights. You can purchase healthy heart menus from the in-flight kitchen. The snack menu, at $1.65, includes sandwich, salad or vegetables, fruit and milk or soft drink. The breakfast menu, at $1.30, includes cereal or bagel, fruit, danish and milk or juice. The sandwich meal, at $3.20, includes sandwich, fruit, vegetable or salad, snack or dessert, milk, juice or soft drink. These meals are served at the appropriate time in the flight. Reservations for meals are made at the time of seat assignment or other times in the flight processing. You may bring your own snacks (food) aboard (no alcohlic beverages). New meal prices are established on 1 October each year.

*Space-A Questions and Answers, continued*

47. Are specialized meals available to Space-A passengers? Specialized meals are made available for duty passengers only for medical or religious reasons. If you need special food, we suggest you bring your own to maintain flexibility. Check with the Air Passenger Terminals regarding any restrictions on carrying food aboard as this can differ from place to place. While you can make your requirements known to passenger processing personnel at the time of flight processing, the chance of having additional specialized meals available at the last minute for passengers might be slim.

48. How are alcoholic beverages handled? Alcoholic beverages are not served on military aircraft. All open (seals broken) containers of alcoholic beverages will be confiscated if on your person or in your carry-on baggage. In many cases, sealed alcoholic containers may be checked. Check with the Air Passenger Terminal for more information. You may not consume alcoholic beverages from your own supply on a military aircraft. The AMC commercial contract Patriot Flights, which frequently carry Space-A passengers, offer alcoholic beverages to everyone of legal age. Beer and wine are $3.00 and mixed drinks are $4.00.

49. How is food service handled on USN, USMC, USCG, USAF (USAFR, USAG) and other non-AMC flights? Most departure terminals have food service for crews and passengers. If the flight duration is more than approximately four hours, you will be notified in time to obtain your own box of food and drinks. Most flights have coffee and tea and all flights have drinking water on board.

### CHANCES OF FLYING SPACE-A

50. How about Space-A availability? Space-A air opportunities change daily and, in fact, even hourly. There are more than 325 very active locations at which uniformed personnel, their eligible family members, and others may fly Space-A. There are also many other less active locations which offer some Space-A air opportunities. We estimate that more than 800,000 Space-A flights (all services) are taken every year. Availability is subject to time of the year, air mission, needs of the military services, quantity of flights, frequency of flights and the number of people attempting to fly Space-A. This large number of interactive variables which impact Space-A Air Opportunities makes it very difficult to precisely predict the availability of Space-A seats to a particular destination at a precise time.

51. What is the best time of the year to travel Space-A? The best time is a function of departure locations, arrival locations, space-required needs and the number of people waiting for Space-A transportation. Generally the best times to travel Space-A are autumn, late winter, early spring and after 15 July. It is best to avoid travel between 1-5 January, 15 May-15 July, 15-30 November and 15-25 December when traffic is heaviest.

52. Who flies Space-A the most - enlisted personnel, officers, Retired members or dependents? Enlisted members travel Space-A more than all other groups (of course there are more Active Duty enlisted members than any other group).

53. Which uniformed service uses Space-A more than the others? Air Force members travel Space-A more than members from any other service followed by the U.S. Army, U.S. Navy and U.S. Marine Corps.

### PRIORITY FOR SPACE-A TRAVEL

54. Who has priority on Space-A flights? The DoD has established a priority system for allocating Space-A air travel. This system is described in detail in Appendix A, which is taken from Chapter 6, Space Available Travel, DoD 4515.13-R. The general categories and their travel priorities are as follows:

Category I: Emergency Leave, Unfunded Travel.

Category II: Environmental and Morale Leave (EML).

Category III: Ordinary Leave, Close Blood or Affinitive Relatives, House Hunting Permissive TDY, Medal of Honor Holders, Cadets and Midshipmen of the U.S. Service Academies and Others.
Category IV: Unaccompanied Dependents on EML and DoDDS Teachers on EML During Summer.

Category V: Permissive TDY (Non-House Hunting), Foreign Military, Students, Dependents and Others.
Category VI: Retired, Dependents, Reserve, ROTC, NUPOC and CEC.
Note: More details concerning each category is available in  Chapter VI, DoDD 4515.13-R in this book.

55. May any eligible passenger make reservations for Space-A travel? No. Space-A passengers may not make reservations and are not guaranteed seats. The application for Space-A travel is not a reservation. The DoD is not obligated to continue Space-A passengers travel or to return them to their point of origin.

56. Does rank/grade have anything to do with who gets a Space-A flight? No. Travel opportunities are available on a first-in first-out basis within DoD established categories. Travel is afforded on an equitable basis to officers, enlisted personnel, DoD/other civilian employees and their dependents without regard to rank or grade, military or civilian or branch of service.

57. Are there any circumstances under which a Retired service member in Category VI may be upgraded to a higher category? You bet there are. If you are traveling Space-A overseas and an emergency occurs at home, you may be upgraded to Category I, Emergency Leave, Unfunded Travel, by the installation commander or his representative under par 7-C, Chapter 6, DoDD 4515.13-R. However, you should have the emergency verified, in writing, by the Red Cross before attempting to obtain an upgrade.

### TEMPORARY DUTY AND SPACE-A TRAVEL

58. May uniformed services personnel on official temporary duty orders (TDY) elect to travel Space-A to the TDY point (station)? No. Uniformed services personnel on official TDY orders must travel in a duty status from their permanent duty station to the TDY point and return to their permanent duty station.

59. Is there any way family members can travel Space-A to their sponsor's TDY point? No. Family members are not authorized Space-A to and from a sponsor's TDY point. TDY personnel may not travel Space-A between their duty station and TDY point as a means to have their dependents travel with them.

60. Can the service member take leave and travel Space-A from the TDY point? Upon arrival at the TDY point, personnel must conduct their business in a TDY status. They may then take ordinary leave while at the TDY point and travel Space-A from the TDY point to another location, but leave must be terminated prior to return travel from the TDY point of origin to the service member's duty station or next TDY location.

61. May family members travel Space-A when the sponsor takes leave at the TDY point? Family members may join the sponsor at the TDY point (at their own expense) in order to travel Space-A with the sponsor while the sponsor is on leave.

62. May the service member and dependents travel Space-A between CONUS and overseas? When the service member's permanent duty station and TDY location are within CONUS, Space-A travel to an overseas area and return is authorized. Also, when the service member's duty station and TDY location are overseas, Space-A travel to CONUS and return is authorized. (NOTE: Dependents may not travel point to point Space-A within CONUS except on the CONUS legs of overseas flights, emergency leave and PCS house hunting.)

63. When the service member's duty station and TDY location are in different countries overseas, and the service member travels Space-A to CONUS, may they return Space-A to their duty station? No. The service member must return Space-A from CONUS to the overseas TDY point or to a location other than the permanent duty station. He must return to the TDY point (at personal expense, if necessary, if Space-A travel is not possible to the TDY point) in order to complete travel to the permanent duty station in TDY status.

64. What is a simple summary of the above complex guidelines? The bottom line is that service members must always travel between their permanent duty station and a TDY point or between two TDY points in a TDY status.

## OTHER

65. May Space-A eligible passengers take Space-A air transportation around the world? No. There are insufficient Space-A flights to circumnavigate the earth north to south or south to north. There are adequate flights to travel around the earth east to west or west to east. However, there is one choke point, Diego Garcia Atoll (NKW/KJDG), Chagos Archipelago, GB, through which you are not authorized to travel Space-A. The Secretary of Defense (SECDEF) has limited access to Diego Garcia to mission-essential personnel. Space-A travel through Diego Garcia, including circuitous travel for personnel on official orders, is not authorized. This prohibition is found in SECDEF message 250439Z JAN 1986 and the DoD Foreign Clearance Guides. Commercial facilities at this UK territory in the Indian Ocean are extremely limited to nonexistent. The Diego Garcia Naval Base does not have lodging, messing and other support facilities essential for non-mission essential travelers.

66. Should I expect to find more than one Space-A roster on a base? No. Only one Space-A roster shall be maintained on a base, installation or post. The maintenance of such a roster is the responsibility of the AMC passenger or terminal service activity. If there is no AMC transportation activity, then the base, installation or post commander designates the agency responsible for maintaining the Space-A roster. You may find an exception at locations where a second service has a separate facility such as Andrews AFB and the Washington NAF.

67. Can people travel Space-A to Alaska or South America? Yes. Travelers may obtain Space-A travel to Alaska, South America, and other interesting locations; i.e., Australia, New Zealand, etc. Travel to Alaska is relatively easy when departing from the West Coast (Travis AFB, California, and McChord AFB, Washington). Travel to South America and other remote areas is more difficult. Infrequent flights to remote areas are primarily cargo missions and have few seats available for passenger movement. Expect long waiting periods for movement.

68. I am retired and am traveling on a passport and my flight originated overseas. Where in the CONUS can I fly into? When traveling on a passport, (family members, Retired Uniform Service, Reserve, etc.,) you may return to CONUS only through authorized ports of entry where customs and immigration clearance is available. While you may depart CONUS literally from any military airfield, reentry locations for passport holders are limited. Active Duty passengers who do not require immigration clearance have more reentry options open.

69. Is it easier to go to some destinations? Space available travel occurs year round. However, travelers will find it is much more difficult to travel during the summer months (June-August) and the November-December holiday periods. It is particularly important that passengers be prepared to make alternate arrangements if they are not able to travel during these times.

70. Q. Some very big people cannot buckle their seatbelts in many of the military aircraft with conventional airline seats, such as the C-005, C-017, C-141 and most of the smaller executive military aircraft. Can these passengers bring their own seatbelt extenders?
A. If a person is too large to fit the seat belt supplied on the C-005, C-017, C-141 they may have to try to obtain travel on another military aircraft i. e. C-130, C-141 and C-17 and utilize the web seats (side seats), which have a little longer seat belt. Travelers are not authorized to supply their own "extenders" and no such extender has yet been certified for use on the C-005 or any other military aircraft..

71. Q. Are alcoholic drinks available on Space-A flights? How much do they cost?
A. Beer and Wine are offered on all Patriot Express (commercial contract) missions. For the Patriot Express flights that land in Saudi Arabia, alcoholic drinks are generally not served once the aircraft enters Saudi Arabia airspace, or sooner as determined by the contracted air carrier. The current charge for beer and wine is $3.00 and mixed drinks are $4.00.

72. Q. What can you tell me about Airport Head Tax and Federal Inspection Fees?
A. The current Airport Head Tax is $12.40 and the Federal Inspection Fee (FIS) is $11.00. If the passenger is originating at a commercial airport overseas en route to the CONUS, or originating at a military port overseas en route to the CONUS, the Airport Head Tax and Federal Inspection Fee are both charged. If you are originating at a commercial airport in the CONUS en route to overseas, or if you are originating at a military port in the CONUS en route to overseas, only the Airport Head Tax is charged.

# APPENDIX V
## SPACE-A TRAVEL TIPS

### DOCUMENTS

Carry passports, military IDs and travelers checks with you and not in your luggage. Make photo copies of your ID cards, credit/debit cards, title page of passports, immunization records, title page of international driver's permit, list of travelers' checks, list of baggage contents and other important documents. Take one copy with you (not in your luggage) and leave one copy at home or at the office where it is accessible from overseas.

### MEDICATIONS

Take all medications (prescriptions and over-the-counter) in their original (labeled) containers, and take any essential medications with you on the plane/train, not in your baggage. If you require prescription refills overseas, take an original physician's prescription for each drug.

If possible, and when necessary, it is recommended by physicians and travelers that you do not take Dramamine until the plane has been in the air for a while.

### CLOTHING

If you are planning to launder clothes, pack a well wrapped (plastic bag) liquid laundry soap as opposed to a powder soap. Woolite works well for hand as well as machine washing and comes in both liquid and powder form. Note that laundromats overseas may not have a "permanent-press" cycle on the washer/dryer. They also have a much smaller capacity than U.S. laundry machines.

Know the climate at your destination. Travel light. In most cases you will be carrying your own bags. Wear wash-and-wear type clothes. Travel in casual clothes that are loose-fitting and comfortable. Plan your wardrobe such that you can take off or add clothes in layers. Always wear a jacket, lightweight or heavy depending on the weather at your destination. Include a light raincoat or all-purpose coat in lieu of the jacket. Always wear comfortable shoes with low heels or no heels. Pack/roll socks, underwear, etc., and place in plastic bags.

### BAGGAGE

Folding luggage carriers do not count as weight against your checked baggage.

Because of security problems and other reasons, many U.S. bases may no longer have lockers available for storing your luggage. If lockers are available, they will most likely be located outside the terminal. So locations may have lockers located in the secure passenger area to which you may not have access unless you are awaiting departure.

Consider using soft-sided luggage to get more into each suitcase. Allow space for items you purchase overseas, or take a collapsible suitcase to bring gifts home.

There are very few porters at European and Far Eastern airports and train stations, and there are limited to no porters at Space-A terminals. Pack only what you can carry or roll comfortably. Can you carry your bags for one mile (15-20 minutes) without setting them down? If not, your bags are too heavy. Get a shoulder bag with small outer compartments. The bag must fit under your seat in the aircraft, and it should be stain resistant and waterproof. Never carry one large bag but split travel articles into two bags for ease in carrying. Bring less clothing and more money. As a general rule, pack a first time, and then cut your original amount of clothes in half and repack.

Always put your name and address in the inside of your bags as well as on the outside tag of each bag. If the outside tag is lost, your bag can still be returned to you. Put identifying marks (e.g., 1" wide masking tape) in bright colored tape on the outside of your bags for easy identification. (We have a large "C" on each side of our bags.) Lock your bags to protect against partial loss or to at least slow down the would-be thief. Officials (hotel bell stand and porters) have keys for different types of bags to be used in an emergency.

As said earlier, always lock and strap, if available, every bag (place straps from luggage inside before locking). Never pack cash, jewelry, medicine or other valuables or hard to get items in your bags. After you have packed your bags, never leave them unattended, anywhere, for any reason, at any time, until they are checked for travel.

### CUSTOMS

Keep receipts for Value Added Tax refunds and for proof of purchase at U.S. Customs. Keep all of your dutiable items in one bag or area for ease in locating during customs inspections.

### AMC PLANES AND FLIGHTS

In a C-005A/B/C, your seats are above the cargo area, and the seats are airline seats. In a C-141B, your seats are in lieu of cargo. There may be regular seats or red fabric/canvas fold down seats. Avoid seats 1A and 1B in a C-005A/B/C. They are against the bulkhead and do not recline, as well as being opposite the restroom(s).

Boarding may be quite different from commercial airlines. There may be ladders to climb, or passengers might be boarded from the open flight line rather than through an enclosed passenger gate. For these reasons slacks are better than skirts for women.

Climate in the plane may not be standard. In each type of plane there are hot spots and cold spots. Try to dress in layers for comfort and convenience. The flight crew will supply a small pillow, a blanket and earplugs (on some flights).

Planes are usually boarded and deplaned with DV/VIPs or families first. (May not be followed at all stations/locations.)

Bring something to eat, to read or games to play on the plane. You can also buy a meal to be served on the flight. The food is good, and it also gives you something to do during the seven to nine hour flight to Europe.

Usually there is a DV/VIP lounge in the AMC airport terminal available to O-6 and above of the Uniformed Services and to E-9s of the Armed Services.

### MONEY

Exchange some U.S. currency for the currency of at least your first destination country before you go overseas. Exchange at least $25 for local transportation and tips.

Distribute travelers' checks among those traveling in your group. Consider travelers' checks in various U.S. denominations ($20, $50 or $100) as well as in foreign currency denominations (French francs, Italian lire, German marks, British pounds sterling, Japanese yen and other Asian currencies). Travelers checks are now available in the new Euro. The Euro currency will soon be available for the European Market Countries (less the United Kingdom).

If possible, bring foreign coins with you for telephones, tips, etc. Bring along U.S. change to use in the vending machines on U.S. bases/installations. Bring a personal check or two to cash at an Officers' Club/NCO Club overseas. (You will need a U.S. military club card to cash a check in overseas clubs.) When dealing with foreign coinage, watch for non-money coins, e.g., telephone tokens in Italy and UK.

Bring a pocket calculator to convert local prices into U.S. dollars.

Border towns will usually accept either country's money.

Bring along U.S. dollars for the flight home ($23.40 per person for head tax and federal inspection when departing on a contract mission (Patriot Flight); $3.20 per person for a dinner meal on military aircraft). Be prepared to take a commercial flight home, and have enough money or credit/debit card for that type of flight.

Be aware that foreign banks may close early on some days; usually the exchanges at major airports and train stations are open 24 hours a day. Exchange your travelers' checks at banks or exchanges rather than in stores or restaurants. Hotels and stores tend to charge expensive exchange commissions.

MasterCard and Visa are widely accepted in Europe, as is American Express. Internationally accepted credit cards can be used for cash advances (execute/use with care for security reasons). Also, carry one or two airline credit cards in case of an emergency. Arrange to have funds sent to you via wire to a local bank. For tips and payment for services, carry some foreign currency and coins if available, or carry new U.S. one dollar bills which are readily accepted by service personnel in foreign countries (strongly recommended). You know how much the tip is worth and the dollar is readily accepted by service personnel in foreign countries.

## BILLETING

Check for hotel/motel accommodations at post offices (AU, NZ and GB), the tourist offices at main train stations and airports. There are also computer matching services at these locations that will provide a list of accommodations, base or location, price range, length of stay and your needed accommodation.

Your room rate will most often include a continental breakfast.
The room rate will vary according to the following:
Class of hotel (Deluxe, First Class, Second Class, etc.);
Type of accommodations (Double bed, King-size bed);
With or without toilet (W/C) in room;
With or without bath/shower in room;
Whether or not the hotel has a restaurant;
Whether or not the hotel has a parking lot;
Whether or not the hotel has an elevator (lift).

In Great Britain, area libraries and post offices usually have a list of local Bed and Breakfast ("B&B") establishments.

In France and its overseas territories, check with the French Armed Forces for lodging and meals/bar service in their Officer and NCO clubs. Also check with Canadian military forces for billeting and mess facilities.

Consider traveling before or after the tourist season in a country; when "in season" rates are no longer in effect. Watch out for trade or other seasonal fares/events, Book Fair in Frankfurt and Oktoberfest in Munich, that will tie up a large number of hotel rooms.

Address and telephone numbers (800) can be obtained from the research section of your local library.

Write the foreign country's tourist office; in the U.S., most are located in New York City and other gateway cities. Addresses and telephone numbers are available in base and public libraries. They will send various kinds of tourist information as well as hotel/motel price lists.

Look for different types of accommodations such as a "Bed and Breakfast" or a "Pension."

## TRANSPORTATION

European and most Asian transportation runs on time!

Use the local public transportation system whenever and wherever possible. Note that there is usually a "smoking" and "non-smoking" section on public transportation.

Public transportation (buses/subways) usually accepts exact change only. You may have to buy a ticket before boarding, but frequently no one collects bus or tram tickets from you (i.e., the Frankfurt, DE light rail system). NOTE: Do not fail to buy and retain your ticket. The fine for not buying a ticket is extremely high.

Look for special tourist rates or tourist passes offered by your hotel or the local tourist office. Ask about special transportation rates for round-trip travel or time-limited travel, i.e., weekend, five, seven, or fifteen-day passes. Most European train stations and airports are open 24 hours a day.

Note the difference between first class and second class on trains. Trains in Europe and Asia are heavily utilized, and second class may be jammed with students and vacationers during holiday times (Easter, Christmas, New Year's, school breaks, etc.). Pay for a reserved seat if you want to insure that you have a seat. The ticket is for transportation only, not a seat.

Note that in most cases you can reserve a seat on a train, etc., especially if you want a window seat or a seat facing in the same direction in which the train is traveling (many seats are reversible).

As in the U.S., food and drink aboard a train or boat is expensive. You may want to bring your own snack, drink or lunch on board.

Be aware of the different fare structures, e.g., a special rate for children (may not be based on age but height), military and animals.

A few points on rental cars: (1) Check the base MWR office for rentals, (2) rent away from the airport to save money and use low rental agencies, (3) return the car full of gas, (4) your insurance may cover the rental car, (5) consider drive-aways, (6) you pay a refundable deposit, (7) they put in the first tank of gas and you put in the rest, (8) rental car reservations are essential in most foreign countries, (9) you can make reservations from the U.S. for major car rental companies, (10) check any car damage very carefully before renting, and make sure that damages are documented on the rental agreement.

## LOCAL CUSTOMS

Know if a visa is necessary for your entry into or exit from the country. See Appendix B or the DoD Foreign Clearance Guide(s) at AMC Space-A counters or military personnel offices which issue worldwide travel orders.

Know what language is spoken in the part of the country you are visiting, e.g., Switzerland has no official language of its own; rather, the Swiss speak a Swiss-German in the north, French near Geneva, Italian in the south and English everywhere.

Bring an English (foreign language) dictionary with you. Try to learn the basics in the appropriate foreign language, e.g., "Hello," "Goodbye," "Please," "Thank You," "Good Morning," "Good Evening," "Yes," "No," "One," "Two," "Toilet," "Train Station," "Restaurant," etc.

Study the local customs and manners in the country you plan to visit. For example, know when to shake hands, how to greet a guest and when to ask for the menu.

Restaurant menus are often available in English; ask the waiter or hostess for an English-language menu.

Know when the local and national holidays are in the country you are visiting. Know the stores that are open late. Get a local map and mark the location of your hotel on it, and memorize or write down the address where you are staying.

Look for an English-speaking tour. You'll get more out of it if the guide does not have to translate into multiple languages.

Plan to visit the countryside, not just the big cities.

Note the time differences between where you are and the East Coast of the U.S., especially in late April and October when our time changes. Typically, there are a telephone, telegraph and post office located in one central and several other locations.

Be sure to send postcards and other mail to the U.S. via air mail.

## TOP TEN TIPS FOR TRAVELERS
(from Dept of State Publication 10541)

1. Make sure you have a signed, valid passport (and visas, if required). Also, before you go, fill in the emergency information page of your passport.

2. Read the Consular Information Sheets (and Public Announcements or Travel Warnings, if applicable) for the countries you plan to visit.

3. Familiarize yourself with local laws and customs of the countries to which you are traveling. Remember, the U.S. Constitution does not follow you. While in a foreign country, you are subject to its laws.

4. Make two copies of your passport identification page. This will facilitate replacement if your passport is lost or stolen. Leave one copy at home with friends or relatives. Carry the other with you in a separate place from your passport.

5. Leave a copy of your itinerary with family or friends at home so that you can be contacted in case of emergency.

6. Do not leave your luggage unattended in public areas. Do not accept packages from strangers.

7. Notify by phone or register in person with the U.S. embassy or consulate upon arrival.

8. To avoid being a target, try not to wear conspicuous clothing and expensive jewelry and do not carry excessive amounts of money or unnecessary credit cards.

9. In order to avoid violating local laws, deal only with authorized agents when you exchange money or purchase art or antiques.

10. If you get into trouble, contact the U.S. consul.

## OTHER TIPS

Travel Preparation Time Schedule - Ninety (90) days before departure: Documents: Health, language training, guide books and maps, money requirements, travelers' checks. Sixty (60) days before departure: Documents: ID, passport, visas, international driver's permit, immunizations. Thirty (30) days before departure: Health insurance, money. Seven (7) days before departure: Clothes, insurance, luggage, medicines, glasses, film, audio/video tape.

The successful Space-A traveler has time, patience, funds and is flexible in all aspects of travel.

Have a map of your destination area for orientation purposes and to avoid becoming lost. It is also useful for measuring local travel distances and paying fares.

Be flexible in selecting your Space-A route. A direct line to your desired destination may not be the only route to your destination. If possible, select a place with frequently scheduled departures to your planned destination.

When leaving your car at a departure location, be aware that you may not be able to return via Space-A to your car's location.

Some bases are more fun than others; try to pick a fun and inexpensive base if you expect to wait for a few days before obtaining a flight.

Get information from libraries, book and map stores, tourist offices (state, regional and national), travel agents, uniformed services personnel and their families and friends about your destination. See Military Living's ***European U.S. Military Road Atlas Plus Near East Areas***, ISBN 0-914862-73-1, an excellent guide to U.S. installations in Europe and Near East Countries and much, much more. See the appendices which are indispensible to overseas travel. See coupon in the back of this book.

## FINDING SPACE-A INFORMATION ON THE INTERNET

Here's an easy way to find Space-A information as you surf the Internet. You can reach many of these destinations through Military Living's Web site, located at **www.militaryliving.com**

Once at our site, click on **Space-A Air Travel (HOPS).** When you reach that page, take a look at **Space-A Links and Forms**. Under that title, you will find some very helpful Space-A information. For instance, you can sign up for many worldwide Space-A flights under Worldwide Sign-up. There, with a click of your mouse you may visit many AMC bases' Web sites as well.

The Operational Support Aircraft (OSA) schedules are listed along with seats available. Here you can check over a week of current schedules day-by-day on these small aircraft traversing the U.S. on military business. Unique opportunities are sometimes available to get you where you want to go Space-A including many small cities in the U.S.

In addition, we post some Space-A Web sites of others. You will be surprised to see some of the goodies in those locations which are usually managed by volunteers.

While you are at Military Living's Web site, take a look around. If you are interested in the Vietnam War, you will enjoy this special section. Have a pet? Get them to write to Tootie, a military dependent dog!

All of Military Living's publications are described at our Web site as well. You can order directly from our Web site or you may print out an order form and mail or fax it to us with your order. You may also call the numbers listed and order with your Visa, Master Card, American Express or Discover Card.

# APPENDIX W

## STATE ABBREVIATIONS

AK-Alaska
AL-Alabama
AR-Arkansas
AZ-Arizona
CA-California
CO-Colorado
CT-Connecticut
DC-District of Columbia
DE-Delaware
FL-Florida
GA-Georgia
HI-Hawaii
IA-Iowa
ID-Idaho
IL-Illinois
IN-Indiana
KS-Kansas

KY-Kentucky
LA-Louisiana
MA-Massachusetts
MD-Maryland
ME -Maine
MI-Michigan
MN-Minnesota
MO-Missouri
MS-Mississippi
MT-Montana
NE-Nebraska
NC-North Carolina
ND-North Dakota
NH-New Hampshire
NJ-New Jersey
NM-New Mexico
NY-New York

NV-Nevada
OH-Ohio
OK-Oklahoma
OR-Oregon
PA-Pennsylvania
RI-Rhode Island
SC-South Carolina
SD-South Dakota
TN-Tennessee
TX-Texas
UT-Utah
VA-Virginia
VT-Vermont
WA-Washington
WI-Wisconsin
WV-West Virginia
WY-Wyoming

## POSSESSION ABBREVIATIONS

AS-American Samoa
GU-Guam
JO-Johnston Atoll

KA-Kwajalein Atoll
MW-Midway Island
PR-Puerto Rico

VI-US Virgin Islands
WK-Wake Island

## COUNTRY ABBREVIATIONS

Foreign Country two letter abbreviations are taken from ISO 3166, prepared by the International Organization for Standardization.

AE-United Arab Emirates
AG-Antigua
AN-Netherlands Antilles
AR-Argentina
AU-Australia
BB-Barbados
BE-Belgium
BZ-Belize
BH-Bahrain
BM-Bermuda
BO-Bolivia
BR-Brazil
BS-Bahamas
BZ-Belize
CA-Canada
CL-Chile
CM-Cameroon
CO-Columbia
CR-Costa Rica
CU-Cuba
CY-Cyprus
DE-Germany
DJ-Djibouti
DK-Denmark
DO-Dominican Republic
EC-Ecuador
EG-Arab Republic of Egypt
ER-Eritrea
ES-Spain
ET-Ethiopia

FJ-Fiji
FM-Federated States of Micronesia
FR-France
GB-United Kingdom
GL-Greenland
GR-Greece
GT-Guatemala
GY-Guyana
HK-Hong Kong
HN-Honduras
HR-Croatia
HT-Haiti
ID-Indonesia
IE-Ireland
IL-Israel
IS-Iceland
IT-Italy
JM-Jamaica
JO-Jordan
JP-Japan
KE-Kenya
KR-Republic of Korea
KW-Kuwait
KY-Cayman Islands
LR-Liberia
MH-Marshall Islands
MK-Macedonia
MP-Northern Marianas,
Commonwealth of
MY-Malaysia

NE-Niger
NI-Nicaragua
NL-Netherlands
NO-Norway
NZ-New Zealand
OM-Oman
PA-Republic of Panama
PE-Peru
PH-Republic of the Philippines
PT-Portugal
PW-Republic of Palau
PY-Paraguay
SA-Saudi Arabia
SD-Sudan
SG-Singapore
SH-Ascension Island
SN-Senegal
SO-Somalia
SR-Suriname
SV-El Salvador
TD-Chad
TH-Thailand
TR-Turkey
TT-Trinidad and Tobago
US-United States
UY-Uruguay
VE-Venezuela
ZA-South Africa
ZR-Democratic Republic of the Congo

# APPENDIX X
# GENERAL ABBREVIATIONS USED IN THIS BOOK

This appendix contains general abbreviations used in this book. Commonly understood abbreviations and standard abbreviations found in addresses have not been included in order to save space.

Days of the week:  Mon, Tue, Wed, Thu, Fri, Sat, Sun
1st/Mon - i.e., First Monday of the month.
1st/2nd/3rd/Tue - i.e., First, second and third Tuesdays of the month.
2 Monthly - Two flights monthly, call for dates.
3 Weekly - Three flights weekly, call for days.

**A**
AAF-Army Airfield
AAFES-Army Air Force Exchange System
AB-Air Base
A/C-Air Conditioning
AD-Active Duty
AE-Army Europe
AF-Air Force
AFB-Air Force Base
AFRC-Armed Forces Reserve Center
AFRC-Armed Forces Recreation Center
AFRES-Air Force Reserve
AMC-Air Mobility Command
ANG-Air National Guard
ANGB-Air National Guard Base
AP-Army Pacific
APT-Airport
APO-Army Post Office
ARB-Air Reserve Base
ARS-Air Reserve Station
AS-Air Station
ATC-Air Traffic Control
ATL-Atlantic
ATM-Automatic Teller Machine

**B**
BEQ-Bachelor Enlisted Quarters
BOQ-Bachelor Officers' Quarters
BX-Base Exchange

**C**
C-Commercial Telephone System
CG-Coast Guard
CGAS-Coast Guard Air Station
CGO-Cargo
CO-Commanding Officer
Comm-Commercial
CONUS-Continental United States
CPO-Chief Petty Officer

**D**
D-Defense Switched Network
DoD-Department of Defense
DV-Distinguished Visitor

**E**
EM-Enlisted Members
ext-Telephone Extension

**F**
FCU-Federal Credit Union
FPO-Fleet Post Office

**G**
GAFB-Greek Air Force Base
GMT-Greenwich Mean Time
Gov-Government

**H**
HP-Home Page
Hq-Headquarters

**I**
IAP-International Airport
ICAO-International Civil Aviation Organization
ITT-Information, Ticket and Tours

**J**
JRB-Joint Reserve Base

**L**
LI-Location Identifier
LST-Local Standard Time

**M**
MCAF-Marine Corps Air Facility
MCAS-Marine Corps Air Station
MCB-Marine Corps Base
MEDEVAC-Aeromedical Evacuation
MWR-Morale, Welfare and Recreation

**N**
NAF-Naval Air Facility
NAF-Non-appropriated Funds
NARS-Naval Air Reserve Station
NAS-Naval Air Station
NASA-National Aeronautics & Space Administration
NATO-North Atlantic Treaty Organization
NAWC-Naval Air Warfare Center
NAWS-Naval Air Weapons Station
NCO-Non-commissioned Officer
NEX-Navy Exchange
NFCU-Navy Federal Credit Union
NMC-Nearest Major City
NMI-Nearest Military Installation
NS-Naval Station
NSA-Naval Support Activity
NWC-Naval Weapons Center

**O**
OAFB-Oman Air Force Base
O Club-Officers' Club
OCONUS-Outside Continental US
OIC-Officer in Charge
OOD-Officer of the Day
Ops-Operations
O/S-Over-Stuffed

**P**
PAC-Pacific
PAO-Public Affairs Officer
PAX-Passenger
P/C-Plastic/Contour
PCS-Permanent Change of Station
POV-Privately Owned Vehicle
PX-Post Exchange

**R**
RAAFB-Royal Australia Air Force Base
RAF-Royal Air Force
RAFB-Royal Air Force Base
Rec-Recording
Rec-Recreation
RON-Remain over night
RSAF-Royal Singapore Air Force
RV-Recreational Vehicle

**S**
SAC-Strategic Air Command
SATO-Scheduled Airline Ticket Office
SDO-Staff Duty Officer
SES-Senior Executive Service
Sgt-Sergeant
SHAPE-Supreme Headquarter Allied Powers Europe
SNCO-Senior Non-commissioned Officer
SP-Security Police
Space-A-Space available

**T**
TAD-Temporary Attached Duty
TDY-Temporary Duty
Term-Terminal
TML-Temporary Military Lodging

**U**
USA-United States Army
USAF-United States Air Force
USCG-United States Coast Guard
USDAO-United States Defense Attache Office
USEUCOM-United States European Command
USMRA-United States Military Road Atlas
USMC-United States Marine Corps
USN-United States Navy
USPS-United States Postal Service
USO-United Service Organization

**V**
VAQ-Visiting Airmen's Quarters
VIP-Very Important Person
VOQ-Visiting Officer Quarters

# APPENDIX Y
# CAR RENTAL Q&A/GUIDE

## CAN I BE TOO OLD TO RENT A CAR ABROAD?

**(Q:)** I've heard some car companies have upper age limits for renters—especially in other countries. Can you tell me where and why?

**(A:)** Rental companies don't impose upper age limits for people driving cars in the United States. For people driving cars abroad, however, restrictions sometimes apply to drivers over 65. Sometimes foreign governments impose these restrictions; several countries prohibit even their own citizens from driving after a specified age. More often, companies cite "fleet insurance costs" as the basis for age limitations, claiming it's more expensive to insure abroad.

The result is a hodgepodge of regulations throughout the world. Even within one country the limits can differ. For example, in Greece Hertz and Auto Europe have no upper age limit, while National restricts drivers to those 75 and under, Budget to those 65 and under. In Europe, Alamo and Renault Eurodrive impose no age limits in the countries where they have rental locations, with no exception: Alamo has a maximun age of 70 in Ireland. Auto Europe and Hertz have restrictions in Ireland and Malta, Hertz in Gibraltar. Avis, Budget, National, and Thrifty also impose various restrictions, depending upon locale. With very few exceptions Dollar (Eurodollar in Europe) and Kemwel, and Eurorent with no exceptions, require all drivers to be 70 or under.

Before making a reservation, follow these guidelines:
Comparison-shop for price and age restrictions.
If you are over 65, tell the reservation clerk your age and ask if there are any restrictions. It's better to learn about age
limits before you leave on your trip.
If there are age restrictions, ask if you can pay a surcharge to avoid them. Although rarely offered, it is worth an inquiry.
Consider alternatives, including hiring a driver or traveling with someone under the age limit who can do the driving.

The issue of age restrictions is not the only one you need to investigate when renting a car abroad. For an excellent discussion of additional questions to consider before renting a car as well as when you arrive at the rental location, while on the road, and before returning the car, take a look at *Autorental Europe: A guide to Choosing And Driving a Rental Car in Europe* by Mill Meier (Lansing Publications, 1993, $12.95); in bookstores or by mail (add $2 S&H) from Lansing Publications, PO Box 1887, Pleasanton CA 94566.
(Courtesy AARP Modern Maturity Sep/Oct 95)

## QUICK GUIDE TO COMMERCIAL CAR RENTAL COMPANIES

**Alamo Rent-A-Car**
800-327-9633
www.goalamo.com

**Auto Europe**
888-223-5555
www.autoeurope.com

**Avis**
800-331-1212
www.avis.com

**Budget Rent a Car**
800-527-0700
www.budgetrentacar.com

**Dollar Rent A Car**
800-800-6000
www.dollar.com

**Enterprise Rent-A-Car**
800-736-8222
www.enterprise.com

**Europcar/Eurocar**
877-940-6900
www.europcar.com or
www.eurocar.com

**Hertz**
800-654-3131
www.hertz.com

**National Car Rental**
800-227-7368
www.nationalcarrental.com

**Payless Car Rental**
800-729-5377
www.paylesscarrental.com

**Thrifty**
800-THRIFTY (800-847-4389)
www.thrifty.com

**Other Helpful Car Rental Sites**
www.autorentalguide.com
www.rentalcars.com

Visit Military Living online at

# www.militaryliving.com

# APPENDIX Z
## GROUND TRANSPORTATION FOR EUROPEAN INTERNATIONAL AIRPORTS AND MILITARY INSTALLATIONS

## GERMANY

### FRANKFURT INTERNATIONAL AIRPORT (FRF)

Most International arrivals are in Terminal #2. Take the "Sky Line" tram over to Terminal #1 and the Immigration/Customs area. You will exit this area into Hall "B" or "C" of the arrival deck. There is a manned military information booth in the middle of Hall "B". In Hall "C" there is a United Service Organization (USO) lounge. The USO has coffee, papers, telephones and personnel to assist new arrivals.

There is taxi service from the front of Terminal #1. Taxi ride from the terminal to Frankfurt city center (main train station ) is DM 40.00/EUR 20.45. If traveling by Commercial bus, the bus station is directly opposite the Terminal #1 exit. Frankfurt Airport has two railway stations, both are directly connected to Terminal #1. The Regional station for local area trains is platforms 1-3. The long distance trains for Germany and neighboring countries use platforms 4-7. All major rental car companies are represented in the arrival area.

There is local military shuttle bus service from the front of Terminal #1 to Rhein-Main AB, building 400, military passenger terminal, which operates 0600-0800 hrs, 1100-1300 hrs and 1700-1900 hrs, daily, every 45 minutes, info C-011-49-69-669-6009. Also, Markl "white Swan" Shuttle Bus Service to regional U.S. air bases is available, please see routes, schedules and cost below. Check with USO for additional details.

### RHEIN-MAIN AIR BASE (FRF)

On base shuttle and to Frankfurt IAP, see above. Schedules posted inside/outside military passenger terminal. Regional trains and long distance trains are available from Terminal #1 at Frankfurt IAP. Commercial Off Base Taxi: C-011-49-69-69-250001. Rental Cars, military passenger terminal, bldg 400, Budget: C-011-49-69-69-59-1624; Hertz: C-011-49-69-69-2188.

The 64th Replacement Detachment at Rhein-Main AB operates a duty bus which goes to the major U.S. Army bases in Germany. This bus can be used with ID on Space-A basis. Contact: C-011-49-69-699-6006.

### RAMSTEIN AIR BASE (RMS)

There are a large variety of ground transportation available to travelers at RAMSTEIN Air Base. On Base Shuttle/Bus departs the military passenger terminal starting at 0615 hours Mon-Fri, week-ends and holidays bus operates on restricted hours and operates every 30 minutes thereafter until 1845 hours. The bus stop is located across the street from the Pax Terminal. Schedules are available at the AMC counter and information center. Contact information: D-314-480-5961.

There is also a Shuttle/Bus which operates between Ramstein Air Base and the Sembach Annex. Hours of operation are Mon-Fri 0530-1715. Contact information: D-314-480-5961. In the local area there is a Ramstein Triangle Shuttle which serves Ramstein, Landstuhl and the Vogelweh area. There are two routes which operate seven day per week from. Route 1 operates from 0605 to 1835 hours and Route 2 operates from 0520 to1945 hours. There is also the Markl "White Swan" Commercial Shuttle/Bus which serves Ramstein Air Base, for details, please see the schedule below. German buses operate on base and to the outlying communities off base. Schedules and routes are posted at German bus stops.

Commercial taxi service is available from taxi stands on base or from C-011-49-6371-50510/12604. The Kaiserslautern City Train Station/Bus Info: C-011-49-631-19419/631-66475; Landstuhl Train: C-011-49-6371-2330; Taxi Van Service: C-011-49-161-1637314.

On Base Car Rentals: Budget: C-011-49-6371-47-43978; Hertz: C-011-49-6371-47-44202. Off Base Car Rental: Ramstein Village: Avis: C-011-49-6371-51705; Hertz: C-011-49-6371-5419; Powell's: C-011-49-6371-52169; Roland's: C-011-49-6371-70182.

### SPANGDAHLEM AIR BASE (SPM)

There is a Shuttle/Bus which operates Mon-Fri, 0600-2158 hours, between Spangdahlem Air Base and the Bitburg Annex. Copies of the schedules are available at Vehicle Operations, Bldg 170 or the Family Support Center, Bldg 2001, Bitburg Annex , and at bus stops. **Contact: D-314-452-6661.** The Markl "White Swan" Commercial Shuttle Bus also serves Spangdahlem Air Base. See below for details.

Commercial taxi service is available: C-011-49-6565-951010 or C-011-49-6561-17066

You can also reach Spangdahlem AB via train but it is a bit complicated and involves two changes of trains.

### MARKL "WHITE SWAN" SHUTTLE BUS SERVICE

**Routing:** Ramstein ➤ Rhein-Main ➤ Sembach ➤ Vogelweh ➤ Frankfurt IAP

**Contact Information:** C-011-49-6385-246, D-314-480-5373/4.

Passengers on official orders have priority. All other passengers may ride on a space-available basis.

**Hours of Operation:** Seven days per week including holidays, with the exception of Christmas and New Years Day.

**Rates:**

| | |
|---|---|
| Ramstein/Vogelweh/Sembach to Frankfurt IAP | $20 or 35,-DM |
| Frankfurt IAP- Ramstein, Sembach, Vogelweh | $20 or 35,-DM |
| Rhein-Main AMC Pax Terminal- Frankfurt IAP | $5 or 10,-DM |
| Frankfurt IAP- Rhein-Main AMC Pax Terminal | $5 or 10,-DM |
| Ramstein-Vogelweh, Sembach | $5 or 10,-DM |

**Bus #1**

| Location | Building | Arrive | Depart |
|---|---|---|---|
| Ramstein AMC Pax Term | 2402 | 0450 | 0510 |
| Ramstein TLF Billeting | 908 | 0520 | 0525 |
| Ramstein Billeting | 305 | 0530 | 0535 |
| Ramstein AMC Pax Term | 2402 | 0540 | 0545 |
| Vogelweh Billeting | 1002 | 0555 | 0600 |
| Sembach Billeting | 216 | 0615 | 0620 |
| Rhein-Main AMC Pax Term | 400 | 0730 | 0735 |
| Frankfurt IAP | Gate 1-C | 0745 | END |
| Frankfurt IAP | Gate 1-C | 1030 | 1100 |
| Rhein-Main AMC Pax Term | 400 | 1110 | 1115 |
| Rhein-Main Billeting | 600 | 1120 | 1125 |
| Sembach Billeting | 216 | 1235 | 1240 |
| Vogelweh Billeting | 1002 | 1300 | 1305 |
| Ramstein Billeting | 305 | 1315 | 1320 |
| Ramstein AMC Pax Term | 2402 | 1325 | END |

**Bus #2**

| Location | Building | Arrive | Depart |
|---|---|---|---|
| Ramstein TLF Billeting | 908 | 1205 | 1210 |
| Ramstein Billeting | 305 | 1215 | 1217 |
| Ramstein AMC Pax Term | 2402 | 1220 | 1225 |
| Vogelweh Billeting | 1002 | 1235 | 1240 |
| Sembach Billeting | 216 | 1255 | 1300 |
| Frankfurt IAP | Gate 1-C | 1405 | 1410 |
| Rhein-Main AMC Pax Term | 400 | 1415 | 1420 |
| Rhein-Main Billeting | 600 | 1422 | 1425 |
| Sembach Billeting | 216 | 1525 | 1530 |
| Vogelweh Billeting | 1002 | 1545 | 1550 |
| Ramstein Billeting | 305 | 1600 | 1605 |
| Ramstein AMC Pax Term | 2402 | 1610 | END |

**Bus #3**

| Location | Building | Arrive | Depart |
|---|---|---|---|
| Ramstein Billeting | 305 | 1755 | 1800 |
| Ramstein AMC Pax Term | 2402 | 1805 | 1810 |
| Vogelweh Billeting | 1002 | 1830 | 1825 |
| Sembach Billeting | 216 | 1845 | 1850 |
| Rhein-Main AMC Pax Term | 400 | 2000 | 2005 |
| Rhein-Main Billeting | 600 | 2010 | 2015 |
| Sembach Billeting | 216 | 2125 | 2130 |
| Vogelweh Billeting | 1002 | 2150 | 2155 |
| Ramstein Billeting | 305 | 2205 | 2210 |
| Ramstein AMC Pax Term | 2402 | 2215 | END |

# UNITED KINGDOM

### RAF MILDENHALL (MHZ)

The RAF Mildenhall/RAF Lakenheath Shuttle/Bus service is daily, inclusive of holidays. Pick-up point at RAF Mildenhall is behind the Bob Hope Community Center, and next to the Billeting Office. (Bldg 404/459). There is also Shuttle/Bus service from RAF Lakenheath to RAF Feltwell. Pick up points for this shuttle service are at RAF Lakenheath near the gas station, at Bldg 956 the Billeting Office and near the BX. Base Shuttle services are free. A current schedule can be obtained at the Billeting Office. Contact: C-011-44-1638-544349, D-314-238-4349.

The Airport Shuttle Bus Service is listed below. Contact: C-011-44-1638-542929, D-314-238-2929. Note: There is no shuttle bus service provided from Stansted Airport to RAF Mildenhall.

On Base Commercial Taxi: Bldg 611, 24 hours daily, C-011-44-1638-54-2984 (Base Cab Stand).

Trains: British Rail: Stations near by: Bury St. Edmonds, Cambridge, Ely and Thetford.; Call for schedules and fares: C-011-44-345-484950. Bus Station: Contact: C-011-44-1284-766171. There is local bus service to Mildenhall Village, Brandon, Cambridge, bury St. Edmunds, London and Norwich. Schedules at Community Activity center.

The following Rental Cars are on base: Autorent: C-717717; Budget: C-717474; Car Hire (AAFES concession): C-712455; Mildenhire: C-717835; Hertz: C-717354 and Willhire: C-717452.

## LONDON HEATHROW AND GATWICK SHUTTLE SERVICE

RAF Mildenhall and RAF Lakenheath have two daily shuttles that depart to and from Heathrow and Gatwick International Airports. The bus service is primarily for PCS or TDY personnel arriving and departing at these two airports. Space-available travel is authorized for those personnel wishing to ride the bus to the airports or for those who wish to take a trip to London to spend the day sight-seeing. You MUST have a valid Department of Defense identification card to ride the bus. Here are the times and places that the buses depart and arrive:

### HEATHROW SCHEDULE

| | Bus #1 | Bus#2 |
|---|---|---|
| Depart Long-Term Parking RAF Lakenheath | 0430 | 0700 |
| Depart Billeting, Bldg 995, RAF Lakenheath | 0445 | 0715 |
| Depart Passenger Terminal RAF Mildenhall | 0515 | 0745 |
| Depart RAF Mildenhall Long-Term Parking | 0530 | 0800 |
| Arrive Heathrow IAP Terminal 3 | 0730 | 1000 |
| Depart Heathrow IAP Terminal 3 Arrivals | 1000 | 1230 |
| Arrive RAF Mildenhall | 1200 | 1430 |
| Arrive RAF Lakenheath | 1230 | 1500 |

### GATWICK SCHEDULE

| | Bus #1 | Bus#2 |
|---|---|---|
| Depart Long-Term Parking RAF Lakenheath | 0430 | 0700 |
| Depart Billeting, Bldg 955, RAF Lakenheath | 0445 | 0715 |
| Depart Passenger Terminal RAF Mildenhall | 0515 | 0745 |
| Depart RAF Mildenhall Long-Term Parking | 0530 | 0800 |
| Arrive South Terminal Gatwick IAP | 0800 | 1030 |
| Arrive North Terminal Gatwick IAP | 0815 | 1045 |
| Depart North Terminal Gatwick IAP, Coach Road | 0930 | 1200 |
| Depart South Terminal Gatwick IAP, Bus Bay "D" | 1000 | 1230 |
| Arrive RAF Mildenhall | 1230 | 1500 |
| Arrive RAF Lakenheath | 1300 | 1530 |

If you have any questions or if you encounter problems concerning the shuttle bus service please contact the Passenger Services Element at RAF Mildenhall on C-011-44-1-638-54-2929/2061 (UK 01-638-54-2929/2061). After 1630 hours contact vehicle operation at RAF Mildenhall on C-011-44-1-638-54-2339 (UK 01-638-54-2339).

*Commercial airline seating.*

*Inside the 2nd deck, passenger seating of a C005B is similar to commercial airline seating (shown right).*

# INDEX TO FOUR-LETTER LOCATION IDENTIFIERS (ICAO)

BGTL/THU = Thule AB (Greenland), DK

BIKF/KEF = Keflavik Apt, IS

CYQX/YQX = Gander IAP (Newfoundland), CA

CYYR/YYR = Goose Bay AB (Newfoundland), CA

CYYT/YYT = St. John's Apt, (Newfoundland), CA

DRRN/NIM = Niamey IAP, NE

EBCU/CHE = Chievres AB, BE

EDAF/FRF = Rhein-Main AB, DE

EDAS/SEX = Sembach Annex (Ramstein AB), DE

EDDS/STR = Stuttgart AAF, DE

EGUL/LKZ = RAF Lakenheath, GB

EGUN/MHZ = RAF Mildenhall, GB

EINN/SNN = Shannon Apt, IE

ENZV/SVG = Stavanger Sola AB, NO

ETAD/SPM = Spangdahlem AB, DE

ETAR/RMS = Ramstein AB, DE

ETNG/GKE = Geilenkirchen NATO AB, DE

FAWK/LMB = Waterkloof AFB, ZA

FHAW/ASI = Ascension Auxiliary Airfield, GB

FJDG/NKW = Diego Garcia Atoll
(Chagos Archipelago), GB

FKYS/NSI = Yaounde/Nsimalen IAP, CM

FTTJ/NDJ = N'Djamena IAP, TD

FZAA/FIH = Kinshasa N'Djili Apt, ZR

GOOY/DKR = Dakar Leopold S. Senghor Apt, SN

HECA/CAI = Cairo IAP, Cairo East AB, EG

HECW/CIR = Cairo West IAP, EG

HKNA/NBO = Jomo Kenyatta IAP, KE

KADW/ADW = Andrews AFB, MD

KAEX/AEX = Alexandria IAP, LA

KAGS/AGS = Bush Field Apt, GA

KAPN/APN = Alpena Combat Readiness
Training Center/Alpena County
Regional Apt, MI

KATL/ATL = The William B. Hartsfield
Atlanta IAP, GA

KBAB/BAB = Beale AFB, CA

KBAD/BAD = Barksdale AFB, LA

KBED/BED = Hanscom AFB, MA

KBGR/BGR = Bangor IAP/ANGB, ME

KBHM/BHM = Birmingham IAP/ANG, AL

KBIF/BIF = Biggs AAF, TX

KBIX/BIX = Keesler AFB, MS

KBKF/BKF = Buckley AFB, CO

KBKT/BKT = Blackstone AAF, VA

KBLV/BLV = Scott AFB, IL

KBNA/BNA = Nashville IAP/Tennessee ANGB, TN

KBOI/BOI = Boise Air Terminal/Gowen
Field Apt, ID

KBWI/BWI = Baltimore/Washington IAP, MD

KBYS/BYS = Bicycle Lake AAF, CA

KCBM/CBM = Columbus AFB, MS

KCEF/CEF = Westover ARB, MA

KCHS/CHS = Charleston AFB/IAP, SC

KCLT/CLT = Charlotte/Douglas IAP, NC

KCMY/CMY = Fort McCoy Aviation
Support Facility, WI

KCOF/COF = Patrick AFB, FL

KCOS/COS = Peterson AFB, CO

KCRW/CRW = Yeager Apt, WV

KCUB/CUB = Columbia Owens
Downtown Apt, SC

KCVS/CVS = Cannon AFB, NM

KCYS/CYS = Cheyenne Municipal Apt, WY

KDAA/DAA = Davison AAF, VA

KDLF/DLF = Laughlin AFB, TX

KDMA/DMA = Davis-Monthan AFB, AZ

KDOV/DOV = Dover AFB, DE

KDPG/DPG = Michael AAF, UT

KDYS/DYS = Dyess AFB, TX

KECG/ECG = Elizabeth City CGAS, NC

KEDW/EDW = Edwards AFB, CA

KEFD/EFD = Texas ANG/Ellington Field, TX

KEND/END = Vance AFB, OK

KFAF/FAF = Felker AAF, VA

KFBG/FBG = Simmons AAF, NC

KFCS/FCS = Butts AAF, CO

KFEW/FEW = F.E. Warren AFB, WY

KFFO/FFO = Wright-Patterson AFB, OH

KFHU/FHU = Libby AAF, AZ

KFLV/FLV = Sherman AAF, KS

KFMH/FMH = Otis ANGB, MA

KFOE/FOE = Forbes Field IAP/ANGB, KS

KFOK/FOK = Francis S. Gabreski IAP/ANG, NY

KFRI/FRI = Marshall AAF, KS

KFSI/FSI = Henry Post AAF, OK

KFTK/FTK = Godman AAF, KY

KFTY/FTY = Atlanta Regional Flight Center, GA

KGRF/GRF = Gray AAF, WA

KGRK/GRK = Robert Gray AAF, TX

KGSB/GSB = Seymour Johnson AFB, NC

KGTB/GTB = Wheeler-Sack Army Airfield
(Fort Drum), NY

KGTF/GTF = Great Falls IAP/Montana ANGB, MT

KGUS/GUS = Grissom ARB, IN

KHGT/HGT = Fort Hunter Liggett, CA

KHIF/HIF = Hill AFB, UT

KHLR/HLR = Fort Hood, TX

KHMN/HMN = Holloman AFB, NM

KHOP/HOP = Campbell AAF, KY

KHRT/HRT = Hurlburt Field, FL

KHST/HST = Homestead ARS, FL

KHUA/HUA = Redstone Arsenal AAF, AL

KIAB/IAB = McConnell AFB, KS

KIAG/IAG = Niagara Falls IAP, NY

KIKR/IKR = Kirtland AFB, NM

KILG/ILG = New Castle County Apt, DE

KJAN/JAN = Jackson IAP/
Allen C. Thompson Field, MS

KLAW/LAW = Lawton/Fort Sill Regional Apt, OK

KLAX/LAX = Los Angeles IAP, CA

KLCK/LCK = Rickenbacker ANGB, OH

KLFI/LFI = Langley AFB, VA

KLHW/LHW = Wright AAF, GA

KLMT/LMT = Kingsley Field, OR

KLNK/LNK = Lincoln Municipal Apt/
Nebraska ANGB, NE

KLRF/LRF = Little Rock AFB, AR

KLSF/LSF = Lawton/Fort Sill Regional Apt, GA

KLSV/LSV = Nellis AFB, NV

KLTS/LTS = Altus AFB, OK

KLUF/LUF = Luke AFB, AZ

KMCC/MCC = Sacramento CGAS, CA

KMCF/MCF = MacDill AFB, FL

KMCI/MCI = Kansas City IAP, KS

KMEI/MEI = Key Field Apt, MS

KMEM/MEM = Memphis IAP/ANGB, TN

KMFD/MFD = Mansfield Lahm Apt, OH

KMGE/MGE = Dobbins ARB, GA

KMHK/MHK = Marshall AAF/
Manhattan Municipal Apt, KS

KMIB/MIB = Minot AFB, ND

KMKE/GMF = General Mitchell IAP/ARS, WI

KMMT/MMT = McEntire ANG Station, SC

KMOB/MOB = Mobile CG Aviation Training
Center, AL

KMRB/MRB = Eastern West Virginia
Regional Apt, WV

KMSP/MSP = Minneapolis-St. Paul IAP/ARS, MN

KMTC/MTC = Selfridge ANGB, MI

KMTN/MTN = Martin State Apt, MD

KMUI/MUI = Muir AAF, PA

KMUO/MUO = Mountain Home AFB, ID

KMXF/MXF = Maxwell AFB, AL

KNBC/NBC = Beaufort MCAS, SC

KNBG/NBG = New Orleans NAS/JRB, LA

KNCA/NCA = New River MCAS, NC

KNCQ/NCQ = Atlanta NAS, GA

KNEL/NEL = Lakehurst NAWC, NJ

KNFL/NFL = Fallon NAS, NV

KNFW/NFW = Fort Worth NAS/JRB, TX

KNGP/NGP = Corpus Christi NAS, TX

KNGU/NGU = Norfolk NS, VA

KNHK/NHK = Patuxent River NAWC, MD

KNHZ/NHZ = Brunswick NAS, ME

KNID/NID = China Lake NWC, CA

KNIP/NIP = Jacksonville NAS, FL

KNJK/NJK = El Centro NAF, CA

KNKT/NKT = Cherry Point MCAS, NC

KNKX/NKX = Miramar MCAS, CA

KNLC/NLC = Lemoore NAS, CA

KNMM/NMM = Meridian NAS, MS

KNOM/NOM = Miami CGAS, Opa Locka Apt, FL

KNPA/NPA = Pensacola NAS, FL

KNQA/NQA = Millington Municipal Apt/
Mid-South NSA, TN

KNQI/NQI = Kingsville NAS, TX

KNQX/NQX = Key West NAS, FL

KNRB/NRB = Mayport NS, FL

KNSF/NSF = Washington NAF, DC

KNTD/NTD = Point Mugu NAS, CA

KNTU/NTU = Oceana NAS, VA

KNUW/NUW = Whidbey Island NAS, WA

KNXX/NXX = Willow Grove NAS/JRB, PA

KNYG/NYG = Quantico MCB, VA

KNYZ/YUM = Yuma MCAS, AZ

# INDEX TO FOUR-LETTER LOCATION IDENTIFIERS (ICAO)

# LOCATION IDENTIFIERS AND
# CROSS-REFERENCE INDEX

The Location Identifiers (LIs) used in this book are the Federal Aviation Administration coordinated **three letter** LIs for the United States, its possessions and Canada. Foreign Country LIs have been coordinated by the Department of Defense. An LI represents the name/location of an airport/airbase. They are considered permanent (changes are made for air safety only) and cannot be transferred. The original LI remains in effect even if it becomes necessary to change the name of a given facility.

The International Civil Aviation Organization (ICAO) has established an international indicator which is a **four letter** code used in international aviation and telecommunications. The ICAO/LIs listed below are primarily used to identify military stations/locations around the world.

This index has been cross-referenced so that each LI is followed by the page numbers on which the LI appears as the destination of a scheduled or unscheduled flight possibility. The number in bold face indicates the page number of the main base listing for the given LI. The four stars (****) indicates that ICAO have not been assigned.

# STATION (ARRIVAL/DEPARTURE) INDEX

# WANT TO TRAVEL? WANT TO HAVE FUN AND SAVE MONEY?

## We have the Prescription for You.

**PRESCRIPTION FOR FUN & SAVINGS**

FOR *(Full name, address & phone number.) (If under 12 years, give age.)*

**RETIREES**
**Active Duty**
**Guard and Reserve**
**Family Members**

MEDICAL FACILITY | DATE

℞

Take 6 times yearly
and
digest well!

Subscribe to the
R&R Travel News™

MFGR: | EXP DATE:
LOT NO: | FILLED BY:

℞ NUMBER | SIGNATURE

## New Lodging at Novato USCG Near San Francisco

**Message from Ann Crawford:**

After covering military recreation and temporary military lodging for 33 years, it takes a lot to surprise me! This new lodging not only surprised me, it also delighted me. The reason for my excitment is that practically all temporary military lodging in San Francisco has been closed because of base closures.

Even though Novato is about a 25-minute drive from San Francisco, it is close enough to make this a very attractive option for military ID card holders who find themselves needing lower cost temporary lodging.

San Francisco, a popular vacation option, has been too expensive for some military folks to enjoy. Now, there's another option, and we suspect that you are hearing it first in Military Living's R&R Travel News. Another $aver - Shop at the military exchange and commissary near the waterfront at the "closed" Presidio of San Francisco. Novato is on the site of the old Hamilton Air Force Base.

These bases, Novato and the exchange and commissary stores at the Presidio, are just a couple of examples of never believing a base is closed completely until you see the locks on the front gate!

The information that follows was furnished to R&R Travel News by U.S. Coast Guard MWR. We thank them!

**New Lodging at Novato**

MWR at ISC Alameda, CA has ten

Novato Continued to Pg. 14

**IT'S HERE!**

Save hundreds by staying at military facilities throughout the U.S. and the world.

This guide gives you all the vital information you need to travel more and spend less.

See Pg. 16 for ordering information.

### New Little Creek Navy Lodge Offers Modern Conveniences

Guests staying at Navy Lodge Little Creek have always had excellent service, a clean, comfortable room and a convenient location near area attractions. Now guests will find it even bigger and better with the grand opening of the new two-story Navy Lodge on March 26, 2001. Located on the original site of Seal Team 2 and the Seal Underwater Demolition Team, the new Navy Lodge is more modern than the Navy Lodge it replaces, which was built in 1971.

"Probably the biggest change our guests will notice is the new Navy Lodge has interior hallways, which means the rooms don't open to the outside," said Margaret Massie, Little Creek's Navy Lodge manager. "I think our guests will feel more comfortable entering their rooms through the lodge's hallway rather than from the outside."

The new Navy Lodge has 100 rooms, including 4 handicapped rooms, 16 Business Class rooms, which feature one queen-size bed, a "living room" area with a desk, and 80 standard rooms, all of which have two queen-size beds. Each room has a kitchenette, complete with stove, microwave, refrigerator, utensils and cookware as well as iron, ironing board, hair dryer and coffee maker. The Navy Lodge itself has a guest laundry facility, vending machines, playground, video rental service and complimentary coffee in the lobby every day. To make guests feel like they're at home, compli-

Continued to Pg. 15

### In This Issue

Report #178 May-June 2001 Volume 31, No. 3

- Surprise! New TML Near San Francisco
- New Navy Lodge in VA Beach, VA
- New NAS Norfolk, VA AMC Air Terminal
- Dos Rios Marine Corps Lodging Near Mexico
- Two New RV/Campgrounds: Fort Wainsright, AK; Wright-Patterson, OH

*Our subscribers travel on less per day . . . the military way!™*    1    *R&R Travel News Report 178 May-June 2001 Volume 31, No. 3*

---

## FREE GIFT with 5-year subscription-

**Military Space-A Air Opportunities Air Route Map** (a $12.95 mail order value)!

## 6 ISSUES PER YEAR

5 Yrs/$59   3 Yrs/$39
2 Yrs/$29   1 Yr/$19

## HOW TO ORDER

**CALL** 703-237-0203 or 1-888-691-0203 and place your credit card order by telephone.

**ORDER** at www.militaryliving.com

**FAX** the subscription form to 703-237-2233.

**MAIL** to P.O. Box 2347
Falls Church, VA 22042-0347

**SEE A SAMPLE ISSUE at www.militaryliving.com**
Click on R&R Travel News.

## Features of the R&R Travel News™

Be "In the Know" Sooner with R&R Travel News!™

Save $$$ on Military Lodging

Reader Trip Reports

Enjoy more Safety & Camaraderie

FLY FREE! Military Space-A Updates & News

Have Fun at Military RV & Camping Areas

Get the Latest News and Updates

# www.militaryliving.com

# CENTRAL ORDER COUPON

P.O. Box 2347, Falls Church, VA 22042-0347
TEL: (703) 237-0203  FAX: (703) 237-2233

**www.militaryliving.c**
**E-mail: militaryliving@aol.c**

| Item # | Publications | ISBN / ISSN | Price | QTY | Exten Amo |
|---|---|---|---|---|---|
| 1 | **R&R Travel News**™. *The worldwide travel newsletter.* 6 issues/year by Standard Business Mail 1 yr/$19.00 - 2 yrs/$29.00 **3 yrs/$39.00 Free Gift - 5 yrs/$59.00 Free Gift** With every **3-Year R&R Subscription or Renewal** you will receive a **FREE GIFT** of Military Living's new United States Military Road Map! (A $8.75 Military Living mail order value!) This special offer ends 28 February 2002. Sorry, no substitution on gift. With every **5-Year R&R Subscription or Renewal** you will receive a **FREE GIFT** of Military Living's new Military Space-A Air Opportunities Air Route Map! (a $13.25 Military Living mail order value!) This special offer ends 28 February 2002. Sorry, no substitution on gift. | 0740-5073 | ❑ new ❑ renewal | | |
| 6 | **Assignment Washington Military Road Atlas.** | 0-914862-91-X | $12.45 | AW | |
| 15 15A | **COLLECTOR'S ITEM! Desert Shield Commemorative Maps.** (Folded) (2 unfolded wall maps in a hard tube) | 0-914862-27-8 0-914862-27-8 | $8.75 $19.30 | MAP DS | |
| 27 | **Military RV, Camping & Outdoor Recreation Around the World Including Golf Courses and Marinas.** | 0-914862-74-X | $16.95 | RVC | |
| 29 | **European U.S. Military Road Atlas, Plus Near East Areas** | 0-914862-73-1 | $24.45 | ERA | |
| 30 | **U.S. Forces Travel Guide to U.S. Military Installations.** | 0-914862-81-2 | $16.45 | TGA | |
| 31 | **Military Space-A Air Opportunities Around the World.** *All New June 2001* | 0-914862-95-2 | $21.45 | SAB | |
| 32 | **Military Space-A Air Basic Training.** | 0-914862-89-8 | $15.95 | BT | |
| 33 | **Military Space-A Air Opportunities Air Route Map** (folded) (2 unfolded wall maps in a hard tube) | 0-914862-88-X | $13.25 $26.50 | MAP SA MAP SA | |
| 34 | **United States Military Road Atlas.** | 0-914862-92-8 | $20.45 | ATL | |
| 35 35A 35B | **U.S. Military Installation Road Map.** (Folded) (1 unfolded laminated wall map in a hard tube) (2 unfolded laminated wall maps in a hard tube) | 0-914862-93-6 0-914862-93-6 0-914862-93-6 | $8.75 $20.25 $35.70 | MAP US | |
| 36 | **Temporary Military Lodging Around the World.** *All New June 2001* | 0-914862-90-1 | $19.95 | TML | |
| | **Virginia Addresses add 4.5% sales tax (Books, Maps, & Atlases only)** | | **TOTAL $** | | |

Mail order prices are for non- APO/FPO addresses within the U.S. APO/FPO addresses must add $4.00 **per order** for insurance and return receipt. Shipments to Canada addresses must add an additional $2.50 **per item ordered** for additional postage, shipping, insurance and processing. We do not ship to overseas/international addresses ot than U.S. Military Post Offices. Sorry, no billing. We're as close as your telephone...by using our Telephone Ordering Service. We honor American Express, MasterCa Visa, and Discover. Call us at **703-237-0203** (Voice Mail after hours); FAX: 703-237-2233 or E-mail: milliving@aol.com and order today! Sorry, no collect calls. Or...fill and mail the order coupon below. Order by internet on our secure web order. Web address– www.militaryliving.com

NAME:________________________________________________

STREET:______________________________________________

CITY/STATE/ZIP:______________________________________

PHONE:__________________________ SIGNATURE:__________________________

Credit Card #__________________________ Card Expiration Date__________________________

Name/Address as it appears on credit card/credit card statement __________________________

The above credit card information is necessary for credit card verification and to obtain approval on your card. It will not be used for any other purpose.

Mail check/money order to Military Living Publications, P.O. Box 2347, Falls Church, VA 22042-0347
Save $$$s by purchasing any of our Books, Maps, and Atlases at your military exchange.
Prices are subject to change. **Please check here if we may ship and bill the difference** ❑

**revised 5/17/**
This form may be dupli

**ALL ORDERS SHIPPED BY 1ST CLASS/PRIORITY MAIL or UPS**